MAJOR FAUNAL REGIONS OF THE WORLD

Nearctic

Palearctic

} Holarctic

Ethiopian

Neotropical

Oriental

Australasian

Oceanic

D0824619

Birds
of the
World:
A CHECKLIST

June 1984

Lazuli Finch
JAMES J. AUDUBON

FROM THE BOOKS OF

Susan Allen

Birds of the World:
A CHECKLIST

James Clements

Facts On File, Inc.
460 Park Avenue South, New York, N.Y. 10016

Birds of the World: A CHECKLIST

Published by Facts On File, Inc.,
460 Park Avenue South, New York, New York, 10016

Library of Congress Cataloging in Publication Data

Clements, James F
  Birds of the world, a checklist.

  Bibliography: p.
  Includes indexes.
  1. Birds.   I. Title.
QL673.C53   1981   598   80-26997
ISBN 0-87196-556-9

Printed in the United States of America

9 8 7 6 5 4 3 2 1

To Christina . . . whose constant inspiration and encouragement was exceeded only by her patience.

Como tu, no hay dos

Contents

Acknowledgments

Since the first edition of *Birds of the World: A Check List* appeared in 1974, I have received numerous suggestions from the ornithological community for improving future editions.

Most of these suggestions were incorporated in the second edition published in 1978.

In this third edition, I have tried to increase the effectiveness and accuracy of the contents even further. I am particularly indebted to Tom Kaiser, a graduate student in ornithology at UCLA for his research assistance, particularly on many of the "unique" specimens described in little-known and difficult to find monographs.

Dr. Hartmut Walter, professor of Geography at UCLA and author of *Eleanora's Falcon* was instrumental in helping me set up the computer numbering system for this edition.

Dr. Charles Collins of California State College at Long Beach, reviewed and made valuable contributions to the taxonomic sequence of the *Apodidae*.

Others I wish to thank for help, encouragement or inspiration are Dr. Ralph Schreiber of the Los Angeles County Museum of Natural History; Dr. John O'Neill, Louisiana State University; Keith Axelson and Herb and Olga Clarke of Los Angeles; Dr. Nathan Gale, Panama; Maurice Rumboll, Argentina; and Frank Todd, director of research at Sea World, San Diego.

My initial inspiration for this checklist came from my association with Arnold Small, my close friend for almost 30 years. My admiration for Arnold's combination of scientific knowledge and field skill continues to grow, and he has offered suggestions for improving the checklist over the years.

Despite all the help I received from scientists, taxonomists and birders, this book is of necessity the product of my own research. Some errors in a work of this scope are almost inevitable. Any errors, omissions or commissions are solely my responsibility.

Hopefully, none of these will affect the usefulness of this checklist.

James F. Clements
1835 Michael Lane
Pacific Palisades, Ca. 90272
July, 1981

Introduction

When I started out 10 years ago to put my life list in some semblance of systematic order, little did I suspect that it would lead to the monumental task of publishing a book of over 500 pages in three editions.

This third edition incorporates a simple, workable computer code that should simplify the transfer of information available to ornithologists, universities, museums, zoological gardens, government agencies and serious amateurs.

Although this computer coding system has taken us on the next step to standardizing a world check list, it has also posed a potential problem with the inclusion of certain birds, and forced me to include some species I felt were not truly "valid" species.

But valid to whom? To the museums, any bird that is (or was) known to science constitutes a valid species if it fits the basic ornithological concept of a species. As set forth by Van Tyne and Berger, a species is a population of similar individuals occupying a definite (and usually continuous) geographical range and breeding among themselves, but normally not breeding with individuals of other species. For a recent discussion of the taxonomic difficulties inherent in modern avian classification, I suggest reading John T. Ratti's article in the November 1980 issue of *American Birds.*

Although there is now no unanimously accepted, regularly appearing compendium of our latest understanding in bird evolution complete with common and scientific names, probably the most widely accepted list is that set forth by Morony, Bock and Farrand of the American Museum of Natural History. While this list satisfies a large segment of the scientific community, it is of little use to the majority of ornithologists and birders due to its lack of common names and ranges.

In the interests of scientific accuracy I have followed the taxonomic sequence in this third edition as set forth by Morony et al. with certain minor exceptions. The basis for the American Museum checklist is the 14-volume *Check-List of the Birds of the World* by James L. Peters. Since the first volume appeared in 1931, incredible strides have been made in ornithology. Recent research in such areas as radioactive DNA hybridization has shed new light on avian relationships, and we find at all taxonomic levels vast numbers of birds involved in complicated clines, superspecies, subgenera and clusters of subspecies.

To give some idea of the vast changes that have occurred since the first volume of Peters was published 50 years ago, the 1978 revision listed 752 species as compared with 853 in the 1931 edition, a change of 101 species. There were in addition 13 new species described since 1930 and 34 birds now considered valid species that Peters originally considered subspecies.

Where I have disagreed with the inclusion or exclusion of a species by Morony, I have stated the authority for this treatment in a special section on pages xxix–xxxvii.

Although I have followed the American Museum specific treatment closely, I have not followed the family treatment in several cases, most notably the *Emberizidae* and *Muscicapidae*. This would have eliminated several family groupings still widely accepted by most taxonomists (Tanagers, Honeycreepers, Babblers, Thrushes) and in the case of the *Muscicapidae* would have created a single family with over 2,000 species.

Of the 9,198 birds included in this edition, Morony and I concur on 9,022. I list 176 that do not appear in the American Museum checklist (see page xxix) and Morony lists 14 that I do not consider valid for the reason or reference cited on page xxxvii.

I have made no effort to describe races or subspecies in this work. Where a recent ruling has combined two formerly separate species, I have included the former species with the survivor as a parenthetical addition. Thus, the merger of Bullock's and Baltimore Orioles into a single species (Northern Oriole) is listed as *Icterus galbula (bullockii)*. This should help those observers using current field guides that still list the two as separate species.

I have tried to indicate under the range the status of birds known from only a single specimen or from such a small series that even if they are scientifically valid, the odds of their being found today outside of a museum is so remote that it is statistically highly improbable. A complete taxonomic list of the 94 species in these two categories appears on pages xxv–xxvii. The 80 species that have become extinct (or presumed so) are listed on page xxiii.

Recent intensive field observations have led to the dramatic rediscovery of the White-winged Guan, Gundlach's Hawk, Kakapo, Takahe, Magenta Petrel and Zapata Rail. The use of mist nets has led to discoveries of new species such as the Neblina Scheech Owl, as well as increasing our knowledge of birds such as *Laterallus xenopterus,* a secretive rail known from a single specimen for over 50 years.

With the relentless destruction of suitable habitat, it is doubtful if most of these "unique" specimens will turn out to be valid species with viable populations in the future.

Wherever possible, I have given the breeding and wintering range of the species within the limited confines that a one-line description will allow. Birds having a very large distribution in certain of the major zoogeographical regions of the world have been so indicated, and the end sheets in both the front and back of the book are color coded to these regions. Their specific coverage is as follows:

Australasian: Australia, Tasmania, New Zealand, New Guinea
Ethiopian: Africa south of the Palearctic region and southern Arabia
Nearctic: North America and most of Mexico
Neotropical: Lowlands of Mexico, Central and South America
Oceanic: Islands of the southwest and central Pacific Ocean
Oriental: India, Sri Lanka, southern China, Malaysia, the Malay archipelago
Palearctic: Europe, North Africa, Asia to the Indus and Himalayas, Atlantic islands

In addition, reference is made to the Holarctic region, which includes the northern Palearctic and Nearctic regions of both the Old and New Worlds. Widespread Amazonia refers to most of the drainage east of the Andes and northern South America. Widespread Southeast Asia does not include India.

Since birds pay no attention to political boundaries, I have tried to use the geographic region that best describes a bird's range. Thus, the arid littoral of Ecuador to Chile (Arica) gives the birder an excellent idea of the range and habitat of the bird. Arica in this case would indicate the southern limit of the bird's range. Tropical, temperate and other introductory adjectives refer to life zones.

Where a particular geographic area is indicated, the location is capitalized. For example, South Africa refers to the country of South Africa, whereas south Africa refers generally to the southern portion of Africa.

In the interest of consistency, I have used the Rand McNally International Atlas for the spelling of names and places.

More specific information on the use of this volume is included on the following page, How To Use This Book.

How To Use This Book

Most experienced ornithologists and taxonomists will need no introduction as to how to use this book.

Some useful hints learned from my research in preparing this volume might prove helpful, however.

The computer coding for each bird relates to order, family and species. The first two digits denote the order, the second two the family, and the last three the species. For example, if you are researching the extinct Cuban Macaw, the code 18 03 141 refers to the 18th order of birds (Psittaciformes), the third family in that order (Psittacidae) and the 141st species in the family (Ara tricolor).

With the use of the common name index in this edition, it should be fairly easy for even the layman to find most birds with little trouble. The common name index refers basically to family names such as thrushes, woodpeckers, flycatchers, tanagers, warblers, etc. Where finer breakdowns are feasible, such as flickers, sapsuckers, piculets, etc., among the woodpeckers, it is a further aid to finding the particular species. This is particularly helpful with some of the larger families that number several hundred birds (ducks, hawks, pheasants, pigeons, parrots, hummingbirds, woodpeckers, ovenbirds, antbirds, tyrant flycatchers, babblers, thrushes, warblers, flycatchers, honeyeaters, tanagers, weavers and finches).

Birds that are still listed as valid species in some field guides but are considered races due to recent study are included in parentheses in the main body of the work following the specific name of the bird. Thus, Stuhlmann's Weaver, now considered a race of wide-ranging African Baglafecht Weaver is recorded as *Ploceus baglafecht (stuhlmanni)*.

The simplest birds to locate are those in monotypic orders, families or genera. To find the Ostrich, for example, go to the common name index and it will refer you to page 3. There in an order all by itself stands the mighty ratite!

Getting a little more complicated, assume you are birding in arid western Australia and you have just identified a Gray Honeyeater. Looking under Honeyeater in the common name index refers you to pages 423-433. There are 173 honeyeaters in this family, of which 106 are called Honeyeaters and the balance Meliphagas,

Myzomelas, Sugarbirds, and so forth. You can look through the 106 honeyeaters until you come to the Gray Honeyeater or you can go to the scientific (generic) index to narrow the selection.

The most probable field guide you will be using in this area is Slater's FIELD GUIDE TO AUSTRALIAN BIRDS, and the Gray Honeyeater is listed as *Lacustroica whitei*. Referring back to the generic index, you will find *Lucustroica* refers you to *Conopophila*, pages 431–432. On these pages there are only four species in the *Conopophila* genus, and *Conopophila whitei* is the first entry.

I have included a cross-reference to almost 600 discontinued genera, so it is highly improbable that you will find a genus listed that will not lead you to the bird. In some instances, such as *Artisornis*, I refer you to two genera, *Orthotomus* and *Bathmocercus* because the bird has variously been placed in either one of those genera by different authorities.

Birds are listed in taxonomic sequence in this volume. Despite the fact that an alphabetical listing might prove easier once you have located the proper genus, it would give a poor, or even erroneous indication of relationships. Birds in large genera (Accipiter, Amazilia, Anas, Nectarinia, Ploceus, Ptilinopus, Turdus, Zosterops) could conceivably be three or four pages away from a bird with extremely close relationships.

In certain cases, you will find a genus with a page reference, and beneath it a genus in parentheses with no page reference. This indicates that I have left the bird in the genus I indicate a page number for, but that the bird is still found occasionally in the other genus.

For example, the Hooded Merganser is listed in Peterson and the ABA checklist as *Lophodytes cucullatus*. Yet some authors include the bird in *Mergus*. Since I have left it in the monotypic genus *Lophodytes*, the bird appears with (Mergus) only as a reference. Looking up Merganser in the common name index would have referred you to page 34, and a quick perusal of the six mergansers would have easily led to the Hooded Merganser.

It is also wise to look through families where hyphenated forms occur. The Rock Jumper and Rock-Jumper are several names apart, as are the Scrub Robin and Scrub-Robin.

Worldwide acceptance and use of the computer coding system will obviously eliminate a great amount of confusion among both common and scientific placement of species. Anyone using the major field guides and references I have outlined on page xv should have no trouble finding any of the 9,198 species of birds covered in this volume.

Major Field Guides and References

Complete publication reference is given in the bibliography on pages 529–533

North America:
  American Birding Association Checklist
  American Ornithologists' Union Checklist of North American Birds
  Peterson: *Field Guide to Western Birds*
  Peterson: *Field Guide to Birds East of the Rockies*
  Peterson: *Field Guide to the Birds of Texas*
Central America:
  Eisenmann: *The Species of Middle American Birds*
  Land: *Birds of Guatemala*
  Peterson and Chalif: *Field Guide to Mexican Birds*
  Ridgely: *Birds of Panama*
  Slud: *Birds of Costa Rica*
West Indies:
  Bond: *Birds of the West Indies*
  Brudenell-Bruce: *Birds of the Bahamas*
  ffrench: *Birds of Trinidad and Tobago*
  Garrido and Montana: *Catálogo de las Aves de Cuba*
South America:
  de Schauensee: *The Species of Birds of South America*
  de Schauensee: *The Birds of Colombia*
  de Schauensee and Phelps: *Birds of Venezuela*
  Harris: *Birds of the Galapagos*
  Haverschmidt: *Birds of Surinam*
  Humphry et al: *Birds of Isla Grande (Tierra del Fuego)*
  Johnson: *Birds of Chile*
  Koepke: *Birds of the Department of Lima, Peru*
  Snyder: *Birds of Guyana*
  Wood: *Birds of the Falkland Islands*

Western Palearctic (Europe, North Africa, Middle East):
  Bannerman: *Handbook of the Birds of Cyprus*
  Benson: *Birds of Lebanon and Jordan*
  Cramp and Simmons: *Birds of the Western Palearctic* (Volumes 1 and 2)
  Etchécopar: *Birds of North Africa*
  Gallagher and Woodcock: *Birds of Oman*
  Hollom: *Checklist of the Birds of Turkey*
  Peterson, Mountfort and Hollom: *Field Guide to the Birds of Britain and Europe*
Sub-Saharan Africa:
  Bannerman: *Birds of West and Equatorial Africa* (2 volumes)
  Benson, Brooke, Dowsett and Irwin: *Birds of Zambia*
  Hall and Moreau: *An Atlas of Speciation in African Passerine Birds*
  Lippens and Wille: *Les Oiseaux du Zaire*
  Mackworth-Praed and Grant: *Handbook of African Birds* (6 volumes)
  McLachlan: *Roberts' Birds of South Africa*
  Prozesky: *Field Guide to the Birds of Southern Africa*
  Serle, Morel and Hartwig: *Field Guide to the Birds of West Africa*
  Urban and Brown: *Checklist of the Birds of Ethiopia*
  Williams: *Field Guide to the Birds of East Africa*
  White: *Revised Checklist of African Non-Passerine Birds*
Indian Ocean Islands:
  Milon, Petter and Randrianasolo: *Faune de Madagascar*
  Penny: *Birds of the Seychelles and Outlying Islands*
  Rand: *Distribution and Habits of Madagascar Birds*
  Staub: *Birds of the Mascarenes and Saint Brandon*
South and East Asia:
  Ali: *Birds of Kerala*
  Ali: *Birds of India and Pakistan* (10 volumes)
  Ali: *Birds of Sikkim*
  Ali: *Birds of the Eastern Himalayas*
  Austin: *The Birds of Korea*
  Delacour: *Birds of Malaysia*
  Dupont: *Philippine Birds*
  Etchécopar and Hüe: *Les Oiseaux de Chine* (non-passereaux)
  Fleming, Fleming and Bangdel: *Birds of Nepal*
  Glenister: *Birds of the Malay Peninsula*
  Gore and Won: *Birds of Korea*
  Henry: *Birds of Ceylon*
  Herklots: *Hong Kong Birds*
  King and Dickenson: *Birds of Southeast Asia*
  Kobayashi: *Birds of Japan*
  Lekagul: *Bird Guide to Thailand*
  Severinghaus and Blackshaw: *New Guide to the Birds of Taiwan*
  Smythies: *Birds of Borneo*
  Vaurie: *Tibet and Its Birds*

Vaurie: *Birds of the Palearctic Fauna* (2 volumes)
Yamashina: *Birds in Japan: A Field Guide*
Australasia:
Belcher: *Birds of Fiji in Color*
Falla, Sibson and Turbott: *New Guide to the Birds of New Zealand*
Macdonald: *Birds of Australia*
Mackay: *Birds of Port Moresby and District*
McGill: *Australian Warblers*
Mercer: *A Field Guide to Fiji Birds*
Officer: *Australian Flycatchers*
Pizzey: *A Field Guide to the Birds of Australia*
Rand and Gilliard: *Handbook of New Guinea Birds*
Slater: *A Field Guide to Australian Birds* (2 volumes)
Oceania:
Alexander: *Birds of the Ocean*
Baker: *Avifauna of Micronesia*
Berger: *Hawaiian Birdlife*
Bruner: *Birds of French Polynesia*
Bryan: *Life in the Marshall Islands*
Dupont: *South Pacific Birds*
Harper and Kinsky: *Southern Albatrosses and Petrels*
Mayr: *Birds of the Southwest Pacific*
Tuck and Heinzel: *Field Guide to Seabirds of Britain and the World*
Specific Families:
Brown and Amadon: *Eagles, Hawks and Falcons* (2 volumes)
Burton: *Owls of the World*
Cooper and Forshaw: *Birds of Paradise and Bower Birds*
Delacour and Amadon: *Curassows and Related Birds*
Delacour: *Pheasants of the World*
Forshaw: *Parrots of the World*
Goodwin: *Crows of the World*
Goodwin: *Pigeons and Doves of the World*
Hancock and Elliot: *Herons of the World*
Johnsgard: *Handbook of Waterfowl Behavior*
Norgaard-Olesen: *Tanagers* (2 volumes)
Ripley: *Rails of the World*
Sparks and Soper: *Penguins*
Todd: *Waterfowl—Ducks, Geese and Swans of the World*
Walkinshaw: *Cranes of the World*

Orders and Families

PART I: NON-PASSERIFORMES

Figure in parentheses indicates number of currently recognized species in each family. Extinct, unique (birds known from a single specimen), extremely small series, doubtful, hypothetical and probable hybrids and races are not included in totals. The number of such species is indicated by a second number in the parentheses. For example, there are 46 valid Tinamous and one unique or doubtful species (*Crypturellus saltuarius*), so the indication for Tinamous is (46-1).

PART II: ORDER 28 PASSERIFORMES (Perching Birds)

Birds that have become extinct (or presumed extinct) since 1600

03	02	002	Dromaius diemenianus	Dwarf Emu
09	03	013	Oceanodroma macrodactyla	Guadalupe Storm Petrel
10	04	014	Phalacrocorax perspicillatus	Spectacled Cormorant
12	02	046	Tadorna cristata	Crested Shelduck
12	02	107	Rhodonessa caryophyllacea	Pink-headed Duck
12	02	127	Camptorhynchus labradorius	Labrador Duck
12	02	143	Mergus australis	Auckland Island Merganser
13	05	007	Polyborus lutosus	Guadalupe Caracara
14	05	139	Ophrysia superciliosa	Indian Mountain Quail
15	07	012	Rallus muelleri	Mueller's Rail
15	07	015	Rallus ecaudatus	Tonga Rail
15	07	018	Rallus wakensis	Wake Island Rail
15	07	022	Nesolimnas dieffenbachii	Dieffenbach's Rail
15	07	023	Cabalus modestus	Chatham Island Rail
15	07	025	Tricholimnas lafresnayanus	New Caledonia Wood Rail
15	07	047	Nesoclopeus peociliptera	Barred-winged Rail
15	07	077	Porzana palmeri	Laysan Rail
15	07	079	Porzana sandwichensis	Hawaiian Rail
15	07	081	Aphanolimnas monasa	Kusaie Rail
15	07	120	Pareudiastes pacificus	Red-billed Rail
15	07	121	Edithornis silvestris	San Cristobal Mountain Rail
15	07	128	Porphyrio albus	White Swamphen
16	08	005	Rhinoptilus bitorquatus	Jerdon's Courser
16	10	031	Prosobonia leucoptera	White-winged Sandpiper
16	16	002	Pinguinus impennis	Great Auk
17	02	001	Raphus cucullatus	Dodo
17	02	002	Raphus solitarius	Reunion Solitaire
17	02	003	Pezophaps solitaria	Rodriguez Solitaire
17	03	029	Columba versicolor	Bonin Island Pigeon

17	03	030	Columba jouyi	Silver-banded Black Pigeon
17	03	108	Ectopistes migratorius	Passenger Pigeon
17	03	169	Gallicolumba norfolciensis	Norfolk Island Dove
17	03	172	Gallicolumba ferruginea	Tanna Ground Dove
17	03	179	Microgoura meeki	Choiseul Crowned Pigeon
17	03	262	Alectroenas nitidissima	Mauritius Blue Pigeon
18	01	046	Charmosyna diadema	New Caledonia Lorikeet
18	03	003	Nestor productus	Norfolk Island Kea
18	03	067	Cyanoramphus zealandicus	Black-fronted Parakeet
18	03	068	Cyanoramphus ulietanus	Society Parakeet
18	03	081	Lophopsittacus mauritanus	Broad-billed Parrot
18	03	082	Necropsittacus rodericanus	Rodriguez Parrot
18	03	083	Mascarinus mascarinus	Mascarene Parrot
18	03	116	Psittacula wardi	Seychelles Parakeet
18	03	119	Psittacula exsul	Newton's Parakeet
18	03	134	Ara autochthones	St. Croix Macaw
18	03	141	Ara tricolor	Cuban Macaw
18	03	172	Conuropsis carolinensis	Carolina Parakeet
20	01	096	Coua delalandei	Delelande's Coua
21	02	101	Sceloglaux albifacies	Laughing Owl
22	05	018	Siphonorhis americanus	Jamaican Pauraque
26	01	076	Halcyon gambieri	Mangareva Kingfisher
26	01	078	Halcyon miyakoensis	Miyako Kingfisher
27	07	176	Campephilus imperialis	Imperial Woodpecker
28	13	004	Xenicus lyalli	Stephen Island Wren
28	35	229	Zoothera terrestris	Kittlitz' Thrush
28	35	285	Turdus ravidus	Grand Cayman Thrush
28	41	076	Acrocephalus familiaris	Laysan Millerbird
28	41	354	Trichocichla rufa	Long-legged Warbler
28	51	025	Dicaeum quadricolor	Four-colored Flowerpecker
28	53	044	Zosterops strenua	Lord Howe White-eye
28	54	140	Moho bishopi	Molokai Oo
28	54	141	Moho apicalis	Oahu Oo
28	54	142	Moho nobilis	Hawaii Oo
28	54	143	Chaetoptila angustipluma	Kioea
28	62	003	Loxops sagittirostris	Greater Amakihi
28	62	006	Hemignathus obscurus	Akialoa
28	62	015	Psittirostra palmeri	Greater Koa Finch
28	62	016	Psittirostra flaviceps	Lesser Koa Finch
28	62	017	Psittirostra kona	Grosbeak Finch
28	62	020	Ciridops anna	Ula-Ai-Hawana
28	62	022	Drepanis pacifica	Mamo
28	62	023	Drepanis funerea	Black Mamo
28	66	085	Cassidix palustris	Slender-billed Grackle
28	67	039	Neospiza concolor	São Thomé Goldfinch
28	67	106	Chaunoproctus ferreorostris	Bonin Islands Grosbeak

28 70 005	Aplonis corvinus	Kusaie Mountain Starling
28 70 006	Aplonis mavornata	Raiatia Starling
28 70 072	Necropsar leguati	Rodriguez Starling
28 70 073	Fregilupus varius	Reunion Starling
28 73 003	Heteralocha acutirostris	Huia (New Zealand Wattlebird)

Birds known from a single specimen (unique species)

05 01 026	Crypturellus saltaurius	Magdalena Tinamou
09 02 035	Pterodroma macgillivrayi	Macgillivray's Petrel
09 02 058	Puffinus heinrothi	Heinroth's Shearwater
14 05 118	Arborophila rufipectus	Boulton's Hill Partridge
15 12 005	Neotis burchellii	Burchell's Bustard
17 03 255	Ptilinopus arcanus	Negros Fruit Dove
18 01 027	Lorius tibialis	Blue-thighed Lory
21 01 012	Phodilus prigoginei	Congo Bay Owl
21 02 006	Otus vandewateri	Sumatra Scops Owl
22 04 004	Aegotheles savesi	New Caledonia Owlet-Nightjar
22 05 061	Caprimulgus ludovicianus	Ethiopian Nightjar
23 03 079	Lophornis melaniae	Dusky Coquette
23 03 082	Lophornis insignibarbis	Bearded Coquette
23 03 099	Chlorostilbon inexpectatus	Berlepsch's Emerald
23 03 103	Chlorostilbon auratus	Cabanis' Emerald
23 03 106	Ptochoptera iolaima	Natterer's Emerald
23 03 111	Thalurania lerchi	Lerch's Woodnymph
23 03 157	Amazilia microrhyncha	Small-billed Azurecrown
23 03 252	Eriocnemis soderstromi	Soderstrom's Puffleg
23 03 329	Acestrura decorata	Decorated Woodstar
23 03 333	Acestrura herterti	Hartert's Woodstar
27 03 057	Pogoniulus makawai	White-chested Tinkerbird
27 03 064	Tricholaema flavibuccale	Tanzanian Barbet
27 05 006	Aulacorhynchus huallagae	Yellow-browed Toucanet
27 07 004	Picumnus fuscus	Rusty-necked Piculet
27 07 025	Picumnus asterias	Blackish Piculet
28 02 037	Xiphorhynchus striatigularis	Stripe-throated Woodcreeper
28 03 050	Leptasthenura xenothorax	White-browed Tit-Spinetail
28 03 155	Xenerpestes singularis	Equatorial Graytail
28 04 162	Pithys castanea	White-masked Antbird
28 04 177	Phlegopsis barringeri	Argus Bare-eye
28 04 197	Grallaria alleni	Moustached Antpitta
28 07 055	Tityra leucura	White-tailed Tityra
28 08 044	Heterocercus luteocephalus	Golden-crowned Manakin
28 09 083	Tyrannus apolites	Heine's Kingbird
28 09 223	Todirostrum senex	Buff-cheeked Tody-Flycatcher
28 09 225	Todirostrum albifacies	White-cheeked Tody-Flycatcher
28 09 230	Todirostrum hypospodium	Berlepsch's Tody-Flycatcher

28	09	241	Idioptilon kaempferi	Kaempfer's Tody-Tyrant
28	09	246	Microcochlearius josephinae	Boat-billed Tody-Tyrant
28	09	282	Phylloscartes roquettei	Minas Gerais Tyrannulet
28	09	309	Serpophaga araguayae	Bananal Tyrannulet
28	17	009	Mirafra candida	Rufous Bushlark
28	35	306	Turdus haplochrous	Unicolored Thrush
28	37	067	Spelaeornis badeigularis	Mishmi Wren-Babbler
28	37	090	Stachyris herberti	Sooty Babbler
28	37	212	Alcippe variegaticeps	Yellow-fronted Fulvetta
28	41	065	Acrocephalus orinus	Large-billed Reed-Warbler
28	41	119	Sylvia ticehursti	Moroccan Warbler
28	41	258	Apalis karamojae	Karamoja Apalis
28	41	444	Sericornis nigroviridis	Black-and-green Sericornis
28	42	110	Newtonia fanovanae	Fanovana Newtonia
28	42	208	Eutrichomyias rowleyi	Rowley's Flycatcher
28	42	243	Monarcha julianae	Kofiau Monarch
28	51	017	Dicaeum proprium	Gray-breasted Flowerpecker
28	52	014	Anthreptes pujoli	Berlioz' Sunbird
28	55	173	Sporophila melanops	Hooded Seedeater
28	57	051	Nemosia rourei	Cherry-throated Tanager
28	57	223	Tangara arnaulti	Arnault's Tanager
28	66	033	Icterus xantholemus	Yellow-throated Oriole
28	67	026	Serinus flavigula	Yellow-throated Seedeater
28	67	071	Acanthis johannis	Warsangli Linnet
28	69	108	Malimbus ballmanni	Ballman's Weaver

Birds known from such a small series that their status is in doubt.

16	10	059	Gallinago imperialis	Bogota Snipe
21	02	111	Strix butleri	Hume's Wood Owl
23	01	032	Schoutedenapus schoutedeni	Congo Swift
23	03	009	Threnetes loehkeni	Bronze-tailed Barbthroat
23	03	087	Popelairia letitiae	Coppery Thorntail
23	03	113	Augasma smaragdinea	Emerald Woodnymph
23	03	114	Neolesbia nehrkorni	Nehrkorn's Sylph
23	03	151	Amazilia cyaneotincta	Blue-spotted Hummingbird
27	07	003	Picumnus fulvescens	Tawny Piculet
28	03	132	Thripophaga cherriei	Orinoco Softtail
28	04	125	Rhopornis ardesiaca	Slender Antbird
28	04	179	Phelgopsis borbae	Pale-face Bare-eye
28	04	183	Formicarius nigricapillus	Black-headed Antthrush
28	04	199	Gralleria chthonia	Tachira Antpitta
28	06	014	Merulaxis stresemanni	Stresemann's Bristlefront
28	06	025	Scytalopus novacapitalis	Brasilia Tapaculo
28	08	015	Pipra vilasbcasi	Golden-crowned Manakin

28	08	016	Pipra obscura	Sick's Manakin
28	09	032	Myiotheretes signatus	Jelski's Bush-Tyrant
28	09	057	Knipolegus subflammulatus	Berlioz' Tyrant
28	09	238	Idioptilon aenigma	Zimmer's Tody-Tyrant
28	21	025	Pycnonotus nieuwenhuisii	Blue-wattled Bulbul
28	41	199	Cisticola restricta	Tana River Cisticola
28	41	334	Macrosphenus kretschmeri	Kretschmer's Longbill
28	42	062	Niltava ruecki	Rueck's Niltava
28	51	001	Melanocharis arfakiana	Obscure Berrypecker
28	57	075	Tachyphonus nattereri	Natterer's Tanager
28	66	017	Cacicus koepckeae	Selva Cacique
28	66	093	Molothrus armenti	Bronze-brown Cowbird
28	68	044	Estrilda thomensis (cinderella)	Neumann's Waxbill
28	77	009	Amblyornis flavifrons	Yellow-fronted Bowerbird

Hypothetical and doubtful species

18	03	180	Pyrrhura hypoxantha	Yellow-sided Conure
23	03	112	Augasma cyaneoberyllina	Berlioz' Woodnymph
28	02	002	Dendrocincla macrorhyncha	Salvadori's Woodcreeper
28	09	239	Idioptilon inornatum	Pelzelni's Tody-Tyrant
28	42	112	Microeca brunneicauda	Brown-tailed Flycatcher
28	57	019	Chlorospingus zeledoni	Volcano Bush-Tanager
28	69	115	Foudia bruanta	Reunion Fody

Probable hybrids

14	05	009	Lophortyx leucoprosopon	Reichenow's Quail
18	03	123	Psittacula intermedia	Intermediate Parakeet
23	03	125	Hylocharis pyropygia	Flame-rumped Sapphire
23	03	246	Heliangelus squamigularis	Olive-throated Sunangel
23	03	247	Heliangelus speciosus	Green-throated Sunangel
23	03	248	Heliangelus rothschildi	Rothschild's Sunangel
23	03	249	Heliangelus luminosus	Glistening Sunangel
23	03	270	Zodalia glyceria	Purple-tailed Comet
23	03	257	Eriocnemis isaacsonii	Isaacson's Puffleg
23	03	275	Metallura purpureicauda	Purple-tailed Thornbill

Probable races or subspecies

10	04	027	Phalacrocorax georgianus	South Georgia Cormorant
14	05	031	Cyrtonyx sallei	Salle's Quail
14	05	184	Rheinartia nigrescens	Malay Crested Argus
15	07	126	Porphyrio madagascariensis	Green-backed Gallinule

15	07	127	Porphyrio poliocephalus	Purple Coot
15	07	129	Porphyrio pulverulentus	Philippine Swamphen
20	01	003	Clamator serratus	Black-crested Cuckoo
20	01	046	Eudynamys cyanocephala	Blue-headed Koel
21	02	090	Ninox spilonota	Cebu Hawk Owl
21	02	091	Ninox spilocephala	Mindanao Hawk Owl
21	02	121	Strix davidi	David's Owl
23	03	168	Amazilia handleyi	Escudo Hummingbird
23	03	174	Eupherusa poliocerca	White-tailed Hummingbird
23	03	245	Heliangelus micrastur	Little Sunangel
26	01	025	Ceyx goodfellowi	Philippine Dwarf Kingfisher
26	01	082	Halcyon hombroni	Hombron's Kingfisher
26	09	003	Phoeniculus granti	Grant's Woodhoopoe
27	01	008	Galbula cyanicollis	Purple-necked Jacamar
27	02	014	Hypnelus bicinctus	Two-banded Puffbird
27	03	029	Megalaima monticola	Mountain Barbet
27	03	082	Trachyphonus usambiro	Black-capped Barbet
27	05	002	Aulacorhynchus caeruleogularis	Blue-throated Toucanet
27	05	023	Selenidera gouldii	Gould's Toucanet
28	02	018	Xiphocolaptes villanovae	Vila Nova Woodcreeper
28	03	029	Cinclodes taczanowskii	Surf Cinclodes
28	03	022	Cinclodes comechingonus	Comechingones Cinclodes
28	03	070	Synallaxis macconnelli	McConnell's Spinetail
28	03	074	Synallaxis maranonica	Marañon Spinetail
28	03	078	Synallaxis albilora	Ochre-breasted Spinetail
28	03	115	Thripophaga heturura	Iquico Canastero
28	03	119	Thripophaga steinbachi	Chestnut Canastero
28	04	023	Thamnophilus cryptoleucus	Castlenau's Antshrike
28	04	204	Grallaria watkinsi	Watkin's Antpitta
28	04	207	Grallaria punensis	Puno Antpitta
28	05	002	Conopophaga cearae	Caatinga Gnateater
28	06	023	Scytalopus vicinior	Nariño Tapaculo
28	07	015	Pipreola lucunda	Orange-breasted Fruiteater
28	07	016	Pipreola pulchra	Masked Fruiteater
28	07	049	Platypsaris homochrous	One-colored Becard
28	07	051	Platypsaris minor	Pink-throated Becard
28	09	257	Myiornis atricapillus	Black-capped Pygmy-Tyrant
28	09	346	Sublegatus arenarum	Scrub Flycatcher
28	09	368	Acrochordopus zeledoni	White-fronted Tyrannulet
28	18	074	Psalidoprocne mangbettorum	Mangbetu Roughwing Swallow
28	20	017	Coracina robusta	Little Cuckoo-Shrike
28	20	057	Campephaga petiti	Pettit's Cuckoo-Shrike
28	20	060	Pericrocotus igneus	Fiery Minivet
28	24	018	Laniarus aethiopicus	Tropical Boubou
28	24	019	Laniarus bicolor	Gabon Boubou
28	24	021	Laniarius erythrogaster	Black-headed Gonolek

28 24 026	Laniarius poensis	Black Mountain Boubou
28 32 006	Campylorhynchus albobrunneus	White-headed Wren
28 33 008	Mimus magnirostris	St. Andrew Mockingbird
28 33 016	Nesomimus parvulus	Galapagos Mockingbird
28 33 017	Nesomimus macdonaldi	Hood Mockingbird
28 33 018	Nesomimus melanotis	Chatham Mockingbird
28 35 304	Turdus hauxwelli	Hauxwell's Thrush
28 35 305	Turdus obsoletus	Pale-vented Thrush
28 41 374	Malurus leuconotus	White-backed Wren
28 41 398	Gerygone hypoxantha	Salvadori's Gerygone
28 41 406	Gerygone cantator	Mangrove Gerygone
28 41 439	Sericornis maculatus	Spotted Sericornis
28 41 440	Sericornis humilis	Brown Sericornis
28 41 454	Calamanthus campestris	Rufous Field Wren
28 42 177	Batis ituriensis	Ituri Puffback
28 42 220	Pomarea iphis	Ua Huka Flycatcher
28 52 010	Anthreptes orientalis	Eastern Violet-backed Sunbird
28 53 061	Zosterops chloronothus	Reunion White-eye
28 55 073	Spizella wortheni	Worthen's Sparrow
28 55 154	Sicalis lebruni	Patagonian Yellow-Finch
28 55 156	Emberizoides duidae	Duida Grass-Finch
28 55 201	Catamenia oreophila	Santa Marta Seedeater
28 57 154	Euphonia elegantissima	Blue-hooded Euphonia
28 57 155	Euphonia cyanocephala	Golden-rumped Euphonia
28 66 019	Cacicus chrysonotus	Bolivian Cacique
28 70 013	Aplonis crassa	Tanimbar Starling
28 70 015	Aplonis insularis	Rennell Starling
28 71 009	Oriolus albiloris	White-lored Oriole
28 77 016	Chlamydera maculata	Western Bowerbird
28 79 077	Corvus unicolor	Banggai Crow

Following is a list of birds that appear in this volume that do not appear in the basic reference work, REFERENCE LIST OF THE BIRDS OF THE WORLD by Morony, Bock and Farand. After each bird's common name I give the reference I used for its inclusion. Since the full title of the reference work and publisher appears in the bibliography I have only given an abbreviated reference here (AOU for American Ornithologists Union, ABA for American Birding Association, etc.). This includes corrections and additions made to the American Museum Checklist including the August 1, 1978 corrigenda and addenda.

12 02 015	Cygnus buccinator	Trumpeter Swan, AOU p. 59
12 02 016	Cygnus bewickii	Bewick's Swan, ABA checklist
12 02 087	Anas superciliosa	Australian Black Duck, Slater p. 230
12 02 096	Anas puna	Puna Teal, deSchauensee p. 42
12 02 133	Melanitta deglandi	White-winged Scoter, AOU p. 92

12	02	147	Oxyura ferruginea	Andean Duck, deSchauensee p. 45
13	05	013	Micrastur gilvicollis	Lined Forest Falcon (Morony omitted in error)
14	04	017	Tympanuchus pallidicinctus	Lesser Prairie Chicken, AOU p. 137
15	02	014	Turnix maculosa	Red-backed Button Quail, Slater p. 263
15	07	132	Fulica cristata	Red-knobbed Coot (Morony omitted in error)
15	12	007	Neotis denhami	Denham's Bustard, Williams p. 74
16	04	002	Haematopus palliatus	American Oystercatcher, AOU p. 164
16	09	047	Charadrius alticola	Puna Plover, deSchauensee p. 87
16	10	044	Coenocorypha pusilla	Chatham Island Snipe, Falla p. 130
17	03	149	Geotrygon chiriquensis	Chiriqui Quail Dove, Ridgely p. 123
17	03	150	Geotrygon albifacies	White-faced Quail Dove, Chalif p. 72
19	01	010	Tauraco persa	Guinea Turaco, Mackworth-Praed & Grant, Ser. 3, Vol. 1, p. 38
19	01	011	Tauraco livingstoni	Livingstone's Turaco, Williams p. 10
19	01	012	Tauraco schalowi	Schalow's Turaco, Williams p. 103
20	01	066	Saurothera vielloti	Puerto Rican Lizard Cuckoo, Bond p. 117
21	02	015	Otus marshalli	Neblina Screech Owl, Auk, Vol. 8, No. 1, Jan. 1981
22	05	027	Caprimulgus anthonyi	Scrub Nightjar, Pers. comm. Dr. John O'Neill
22	05	033	Caprimulgus noctitherus	Puerto Rican Whip-poor-will, Living Bird, Cornell Univ. 1962
23	01	022	Aerodramus sawtelli	Atiu Swiftlet, Pers. comm. Dr. Charles Collins
23	03	250	Heliangelus regalis	Royal Sunangel, Pers. comm. Dr. John O'Neill (new species)
23	03	279	Metallura odomae	Neblina Metaltail, Pers. comm. Dr. John O'Neill (new species)

26 01 051	Halcyon senegaloides	Mangrove Kingfisher (Morony omitted in error)
26 01 082	Halcyon hombroni	Hombron's Kingfisher, Dupont p. 206
26 10 038	Bycanistes brevis	Silvery-cheeked Hornbill (Morony omitted in error)
27 03 029	Megalaima monticola	Mountain Barbet, Smythies p. 325
27 03 056	Pogoniulus leucolaima	Lemon-rumped Tinkerbird, Williams p. 147
27 05 002	Aulacorhynchus caeruleogularis	Blue-throated Toucanet, Ridgely, p. 182
27 05 008	Aulacorhynchus calorhynchus	Yellow-billed Toucanet, deSchauensee p. 207
27 05 017	Pteroglossus frantzii	Fiery-billed Aracari, Ridgely p. 183
27 05 018	Pteroglossus sanguineus	Stripe-billed Aracari, deSchauensee p. 208
27 05 019	Pteroglossus erythropygius	Pale-mandibled Aracari, deSchauensee p. 208
27 05 021	Pteroglossus marie	Brown-mandibled Aracari, deSchauensee p. 210
27 05 034	Ramphastos citreolaemus	Citron-throated Toucan, deSchauensee, p. 212
27 05 035	Ramphastos culminatus	Yellow-ridged Toucan, deSchauensee p. 212
27 05 040	Ramphastos swainsoni	Swainson's Toucan, Ridgely p. 184
27 05 042	Ramphastos aurantiirostris	Orange-billed Toucan, deSchauensee p. 213
27 05 044	Ramphastos cuvieri	Cuvier's Toucan, deSchauensee p. 213
27 04 041	Melanerpes rubrifrons	Red-fronted Woodpecker, deSchauensee p. 223
27 07 061	Campethera taeniolaema	Fine-banded Woodpecker, Williams p. 154
27 07 065	Campethera permista	Green-backed Woodpecker, Williams p. 154
27 07 087	Dendrocopos lugubris	Melancholy Woodpecker, Mackworth-Praed & Grant Ser. 3, Vol. 1, p. 582
27 07 105	Dendrocopos nanus	Indian Pygmy Woodpecker, Ali, Vol. 4, p. 231
27 07 115	Dendrocopos arizonae	Arizona Woodpecker, AOU p. 328

27	07	137	Piculus simplex	Bugaba Woodpecker, Ridgely p. 186
27	07	142	Chrysoptilus melanolaimus	Golden-breasted Woodpecker, deSchauensee p. 218
27	07	148	Colaptes campestroides	Field Flicker, deSchauensee p. 218
27	07	183	Picus viridianus	Streak-breasted Woodpecker, King p. 228
27	07	197	Chrysocolaptes guttacristatus	Crimson-backed Woodpecker, Henry p. 125
28	03	036	Furnarius torridus	Pale-billed Hornero, deSchauensee p. 242
28	03	050	Leptasthenura xenothorax	White-browed Tit-Spinetail, deSchauensee p. 243
28	03	123	Thripophaga cactorum	Cactus Canastero, deSchauensee p. 253
28	03	155	Xenerpestes singularis	Equatorial Graytail, deSchauensee p. 256
28	03	191	Philydor (Simoxenops) striatus	Bolivian Recurvebill, deSchauensee p. 260
28	04	023	Thamnophilus cryptoleucos	Castlenau's Antshrike, deSchauensee p. 271
28	04	228	Grallaricula nana	Slate-crowned Antpitta (Morony omitted in error)
28	04	231	Grallaricula cucullata	Hooded Antpitta (Morony omitted in error)
28	07	014	Pipreola lubomirskii	Black-chested Fruiteater, deSchauensee p. 312
28	07	015	Pipreola jucunda	Orange-breasted Fruiteater, deSchauensee p. 312
28	07	016	Pipreola pulchra	Masked Fruiteater, deSchauensee p. 313
28	07	048	Platypsaris rufus	Crested Becard, deSchauensee p. 320
28	07	049	Platypsaris homochrous	One-colored Becard, Ridgely p. 226
28	07	055	Tityra leucura	White-tailed Tityra, deSchauensee p. 321
28	09	153	Contopus lugubris	Dark Pewee, Ridgely p. 238
28	09	163	Empidonax wrightii	Gray (Wright's) Flycatcher, AOU p. 346; ABA
28	09	264	Hemitriccus cinnamomeipectus	Cinnamon-breasted Tody-Tyrant, Pers. comm. Theodore Parker
28	09	285	Euscarthmus rufomarginatus	Rufous-sided Pygmy-Tyrant (Morony omitted in error)

28	09	368	Acrochordopus zeledoni	White-fronted Tyrannulet, Ridgely p. 256
28	12	019	Pitta reichenowi	Green-breasted Pitta, Serle p. 152
28	12	024	Pitta iris	Black-breasted Pitta, Slater p. 86
28	18	013	Progne cryptoleuca	Cuban Martin, AOU p. 366; ABA
28	18	057	Hirundo neoxena	Welcome Swallow, Slater p. 92
28	20	057	Campephaga petiti	Petit's Cuckoo-Shrike, Mackworth-Praed & Grant, Ser. 3, Vol. 2, p. 400
28	20	060	Pericrocotus igneus	Fiery Minivet, King p. 258
28	21	109	Hypsipetes rufigularis	Zamboanga Bulbul, Dupont p. 284
28	21	117	Hypsipetes castanotus	Chestnut Bulbul, King p. 268
28	24	018	Laniarus aethiopicus	Tropical Boubou, Mackworth-Praed & Grant, Ser. 3, Vol. 2, p. 437
28	24	019	Laniarus bicolor	Gabon Boubou, Mackworth-Praed & Grant, Ser. 3, Vol. 2, p. 439
28	24	021	Laniarus erythrogaster	Black-headed Gonolek, Williams p. 280
28	24	026	Laniarus poensis	Black Mountain Boubou, Williams p. 282
28	24	055	Lanius tephronotus	Tibetan Shrike, King p. 405
28	32	006	Campylorhynchus albobrunneus	White-headed Wren, Ridgely p. 266
28	32	009	Campylorhynchus chiapensis	Giant Wren, Peterson & Chalif p. 171
28	32	030	Thryothorus spadix	Sooty-headed Wren, Ridgely p. 269
28	32	052	Troglodytes brunneicollis	Brown-throated Wren, AOU p. 407; ABA
28	32	053	Troglodytes rufociliatus	Rufous-browed Wren, Peterson & Chalif p. 176
28	32	054	Troglodytes musculus	Tropical House Wren, Peterson & Chalif p. 176
28	32	055	Troglodytes ochraceous	Ochraceous Wren, Ridgely p. 270
28	33	008	Mimus magnirostris	St. Andrew Mockingbird, Bond p. 167
28	33	016	Mimus parvulus	Galapagos Mockingbird, Harris p. 128
28	33	017	Mimus macdonaldi	Hood Mockingbird, Harris p. 128

28 33 018 Mimus melanotis — Chatham Mockingbird, Harris p. 128

28 35 071 Alethe castanea — Fire-crested Alethe, Williams p. 293

28 35 182 Monticola sharpei — Forest Rock-Thrush, Milon et al, p. 207

28 35 192 Monticola gularis — White-throated Rock-Thrush, King p. 344

28 35 241 Catharus frantzii — Ruddy-capped Nightingale-Thrush, (Morony omitted in error)

28 35 268 Turdus hortulorum — Gray-backed Thrush, King p. 347

28 35 305 Turdus obsoletus — Pale-vented Thrush, deSchauensee p. 416

28 35 314 Turdus infuscatus — Black Robin, Peterson & Chalif, p. 184

28 35 316 Turdus assimilis — White-throated Robin, Peterson & Chalif p. 184

28 36 007 Psophodes occidentalis — Chiming Wedgebill, Slater p. 115

28 36 011 Cinclosoma alisteri — Nullarbor Quail-Thrush, Slater p. 109

28 37 035 Pomatorhinus erythrocnemis — Spot-breasted Scimitar-Babbler, King p. 298

28 37 067 Spelaeornis badeigularis — Mishmi Wren-Babbler, Ali, Vol. 6, p. 161

28 37 131 Turdoides leucocephalus — White-headed Babbler, Urban & Brown p. 85

28 37 247 Yuhina humilis — Burmese Yuhina, King p. 328

28 41 006 Polioptila nigriceps — Black-capped Gnatcatcher, Peterson & Chalif p. 190

28 41 383 Amytornis purnelli — Dusky Grasswren, Slater p. 129

28 42 022 Rhinomyias insignis — Luzon Jungle Flycatcher, Dupont p. 330

28 42 023 Rhinomyias goodfellowi — Goodfellow's Jungle Flycatcher, Dupont p. 330

28 42 056 Niltava sumatrana — Rufous-vented Niltava, King p. 389

28 42 057 Niltava (Cyornis) lemprieri — Philippine Hill Niltava, Dupont p. 339

28 42 140 Eopsaltria chrysorrhoa — Northern Yellow Robin, Slater p. 174

28 42 141 Eopsaltria georgiana — White-breasted Robin (Morony omitted in error)

28 42 151 Poecilodryas cerviniventris — Buff-sided Robin, Slater p. 174

28	42	260	Monarcha sericeus	New Hebrides Monarch, Mayr p. 193
28	42	261	Monarcha pileatus	Tufted Monarch, Van Bemmel, p. 67
28	43	006	Aegithalos niveogularis	White-throated Tit, Fleming p. 280
28	45	045	Parus atricristatus	Black-crested Titmouse, AOU p. 390; ABA Checklist
28	47	003	Neositta pileata	Black-capped Sitella, Slater p. 201
28	47	004	Neositta striata	Striated Sitella, Slater p. 201
28	47	005	Neositta leucocephala	White-headed Sitella, Slater p. 201
28	47	006	Neositta leucoptera	White-winged Sitella, Slater p. 202
28	51	049	Dicaeum geelvinkianum	Red-capped Flowerpecker, Rand & Gilliard p. 576
28	52	038	Nectarinia hunteri	Hunter's Sunbird, Williams p. 331
28	53	033	Zosterops meyeni	Philippine White-eye, Dupont p. 399
28	54	065	Meliphaga flavescens	Yellow-tinted Honeyeater, Slater p. 233
28	55	059	Junco caniceps	Gray-headed Junco, AOU p. 611; ABA Checklist
28	55	073	Spizella wortheni	Worthen's Sparrow, Peterson & Chalif p. 255
28	55	124	Incaspiza personata	Rufous-backed Inca-Finch, deSchauensee p. 527
28	55	154	Sicalis lebruni	Patagonian Yellow-Finch, deSchauensee p. 515
28	55	244	Atlapetes gutturalis	Yellow-throated Brush-Finch, Peterson & Chalif p. 245
28	55	260	Atlapetes seebohmi	Bay-crowned Brush-Finch, deSchauensee p. 522
28	55	266	Atlapetes atricapillus	Black-headed Brush-Finch, Ridgely p. 337
28	55	274	Lysurus crassirostris	Sooty-faced Finch, Ridgely p. 338
28	55	300	Caryothraustes poliogaster	Black-faced Grosbeak, Ridgely p. 329
28	57	071	Heterospingus rubrifrons	Sulphur-rumped Tanager, Ridgely p. 325
28	57	075	Tachyphonus nattereri	Natterer's Tanager, deSchauensee p. 486
28	57	105	Ramphocelus icteronotus	Yellow-rumped Tanager, Ridgely p. 320

28	57	130	Anisognathus melanogenys	Black-cheeked Mountain-Tanager, deSchauensee p. 476
28	57	136	Iridosornis reinhardti	Yellow-scarfed Tanager, deSchauensee p. 476
28	57	154	Euphonia elegantissima	Blue-hooded Euphonia, Ridgely p. 314
28	57	155	Euphonia cyanocephala	Golden-rumped Euphonia, Ridgely p. 314
28	57	170	Chlorophonia callophrys	Golden-browed Chlorophonia, Ridgely p. 314
28	57	222	Tangara fucosa	Green-naped Tanager, Ridgely p. 319
28	57	223	Tangara arnaulti	Arnault's Tanager, deSchauensee p. 473
28	58	028	Diglossa plumbea	Slaty Flowerpiercer, Ridgely p. 288
28	65	023	Vireo flavoviridis	Yellow-green Vireo, AOU p. 474; ABA Checklist
28	65	040	Hylophilus olivaceus	Olivaceous Greenlet, deSchauensee p. 427
28	66	025	Icterus chrysocephalus	Moriche Oriole, deSchauensee p. 437
28	66	079	Macroagelaius imthurmi	Golden-tufted Grackle, deSchauensee p. 445
28	66	082	Dives warszewiczi	Scrub Blackbird, deSchauensee p. 434
28	66	093	Molothrus armenti	Bronze-brown Cowbird, deSchauensee p. 429
28	67	012	Serinus ankoberensis	Ankober Serin, pers. comm. Dr. Thomas Howell
28	67	026	Serinus flavigula	Yellow-throated Seedeater, Mackworth-Praed & Grant, Series I, Vol. 2, p. 1076
28	67	027	Serinus dorsostriatus	White-bellied Canary, ibid p. 1063
28	67	075	Leucosticte tephrocotis	Gray-crowned Rosy Finch, AOU p. 564; ABA Checklist
28	67	076	Leucosticte atrata	Black Rosy Finch, AOU p. 566; ABA Checklist
28	67	077	Leucosticte australis	Brown-capped Rosy Finch, AOU p. 566; ABA Checklist
28	68	122	Lonchura nigerrima	Black-breasted Weaver Finch, Mayr p. 301
28	69	118	Foudia omissa	Red Forest Fody, Milon et al p. 247

28 70 064	Spreo shelleyi	Shelley's Starling, Williams p. 392
28 71 014	Oriolus tenuirostris	Slender-billed Oriole, King p. 271
28 76 005	Cracticus cassicus	Black-headed Butcherbird (Morony omitted in error)
28 76 006	Cracticus louisiadensis	Louisiade Butcherbird (Morony omitted in error)
28 76 008	Gymnorhina dorsalis	Western Magpie, Slater p. 280
28 76 009	Gymnorhina hypoleuca	White-backed Magpie, Slater p. 280
28 77 016	Chlamydera guttata	Western Bowerbird, Slater p. 288
28 79 016	Cyanolyca turcosa	Turquoise Jay, deSchauensee p. 398
28 79 019	Cissilopha yucatanica	Yucatan Jay, Peterson & Chalif p. 164
28 79 029	Cyanocorax cyanopogon	White-naped Jay, deSchauensee p. 400
28 79 077	Corvus unicolor	Banggai Crow, Goodwin p. 106

There are several species listed in Morony et al that I have not included in this third edition. Immediately following the scientific name of the bird, I give the reason for this exclusion.

Pelecanus roseus	Pers. comm. Dr. Ralph Schreiber. Also see discussion by Chapin and Amadon in The Ostrich, May 1950.
Tricholimnas conditicius	The actual spelling of this rail is *T. conditicus* (see Ripley p. 68). This unique specimen is probably an immature female of *Rallus sylvestris*.
Gallirallus troglodytes	See Ripley p. 146. This is probably a dimorphic color phase of *Gallirallus australis*.
Pennula millsi	See Ripley p. 236. This rail is probably a dimorphic color phase of the extinct *Porzana sanwichensis*.
Aerodramus salangana	Pers. comm. Dr. Charles Collins (taxonomic revision).
Aerodramus nuditarsus	ibid.
Aerodramus orientalis	ibid.
Galbalcyrhyunchus perusianus	See deSchauensee p. 198 (considered a race of *G. leucotis*).

Sphyrapicus nuchalis

American Ornithologists' Union
taxonomic revision

Sphyrapicus ruber

ibid.

Hypothymis personata

I list as *Hypothymis helenae
(personata)*. Original description in
1907 as *Camiguinia personata* is
synonymous with *Hypothymis
helenae* (see Dupont p. 348).

Monarcha muelleriana

Listed in error. Refers to *Monachella
muelleriana* (pers. comm. Stuart
Keith, American Museum of Natural
History).

Rhipidura clamosa

Listed in error. *R. clamosa* is a race of
R. leucothorax according to Dr.
Jared Diamond (pers. comm. Stuart
Keith).

Psaltriparus melanotis

Now considered a race of *P. minimus*
(Common Bushtit). Taxonomic
revision A.O.U.

PART 1

Non-Passeriformes

Key
+ = slide

	Date	Location

ORDER: STRUTHIONIFORMES
FAMILY: STRUTHIONIDAE (Ostrich)

01 01 001 **Struthio camelus**
+   *Ostrich*   Arid steppes, savanna, semi-desert of Africa

ORDER: RHEIFORMES
FAMILY: RHEIDAE (Rheas)

02 01 001 **Rhea americana**
+   *Greater (Common) Rhea*   Campos of Brazil, Bolivia to Argentina

02 01 002 **Pterocnemia pennata**
+   *Lesser (Darwin's) Rhea*   Puna of Peru, Bolivia to Chile, Argentina
     (endangered)

ORDER: CASUARIIFORMES
FAMILY: CASUARIIDAE (Cassowaries)

03 01 001 **Casuarius casuarius**
    Double-wattled Cassowary   New Guinea; Cape York Peninsula (Australia)

03 01 002 **Casuarius bennetti**
    Dwarf Cassowary   Mountains of New Guinea, New Britain, Japen Islands

03 01 003 **Casuarius unappendiculatus**
    Single-wattled Cassowary   Lowlands of northwest New Guinea, adjacent islands

ORDER: CASUARIIFORMES
FAMILY: DROMAIIDAE (Emus)

03 02 001 **Dromaius novaehollandiae**
    Emu   Widespread Australian mainland

03 02 002 **Dromaius diemenianus**
    Dwarf Emu   Extinct. Inhabited Kangaroo Islands

ORDER: APTERYGIFORMES
FAMILY: APTERYGIDAE (Kiwis)

04 01 001 **Apteryx australis**
    Common (Brown) Kiwi   New Zealand (widespread forested areas)

04 01 002 **Apteryx owenii**
    Little Spotted Kiwi   New Zealand (western districts of South Island)

04 01 003 **Apteryx haasti**
    Great Spotted Kiwi   New Zealand (highland beech forests of South Island)

		Date	Location

ORDER: TINAMIFORMES
FAMILY: TINAMIDAE (Tinamous)

05 01 001	**Tinamus tao**	
	Gray Tinamou	Northern South America to Brazil, Bolivia
05 01 002	**Tinamus solitarius**	
	Solitary Tinamou	Brazil to northeast Argentina
05 01 003	**Tinamus osgoodi**	
	Black Tinamou	Subtropical southwest Colombia (Huila) to southeast Peru
05 01 004	**Tinamus major**	
+eggs	*Great Tinamou*	Southern Mexico to Brazil, Bolivia
05 01 005	**Tinamus guttatus**	
	White-throated Tinamou	Widespread Amazon basin
05 01 006	**Nothocercus bonapertei**	
	Highland Tinamou	Mountains of Costa Rica to Venezuela, Peru
05 01 007	**Nothocercus julius**	
	Tawny-breasted Tinamou	Andes of Venezuela, Colombia, Ecuador to central Peru
05 01 008	**Nothocercus nigrocapillus**	
	Hooded Tinamou	Andes of Peru to Bolivia
05 01 009	**Crypturellus cinereus**	
	Cinereous Tinamou	Widespread Amazon basin
05 01 010	**Crypturellus soui**	
	Little Tinamou	Southern Mexico to Brazil, Bolivia
05 01 011	**Crypturellus ptaritepui**	
	Tepui Tinamou	Venezuela (subtropical mountains of southeast Bolivar)
05 01 012	**Crypturellus obsoletus**	
	Brown Tinamou	Andean slopes of Venezuela to northeast Argentina
05 01 013	**Crypturellus undulatus**	
	Undulated Tinamou	Widespread South America
05 01 014	**Crypturellus brevirostris**	
	Rusty Tinamou	Western Brazil, eastern Peru; Guyana
05 01 015	**Crypturellus bartletti**	
+egg	*Bartlett's Tinamou*	Western Amazonian Brazil, eastern Peru
05 01 016	**Crypturellus variegatus**	
	Variegated Tinamou	Widespread Amazon basin
05 01 017	**Crypturellus atrocapillus**	
	Red-legged Tinamou	Widespread Amazon basin
05 01 018	**Crypturellus noctivagus**	
	Yellow-legged Tinamou	Eastern Brazil (Piaui to Rio Grande do Sul)

		Date	Location
05 01 019	**Crypturellus duidae** *Gray-legged Tinamou*		Venezuela, Colombia (tropical zone)
05 01 020	**Crypturellus strigulosus** *Brazilian Tinamou*		Amazonian Brazil, adjacent Peru, Bolivia
05 01 021	**Crypturellus casiquiare** *Barred Tinamou*		Venezuela (Colombia-Brazil border—endangered)
05 01 022	**Crypturellus cinnamomeus** *Rufescent (Thicket) Tinamou*		Mexico to northwest Venezuela
05 01 023	**Crypturellus idoneus** *Santa Marta Tinamou*		Tropical northern Colombia, adjacent Venezuela
05 01 024	**Crypturellus transfasciatus** *Pale-browed Tinamou*		Western Ecuador to northwest Peru
05 01 025	**Crypturellus boucardi (colombianus)** *Slaty-breasted Tinamou*		Mexico to Costa Rica, Colombia
05 01 026	**Crypturellus saltuarius** *Magdalena Tinamou*		Colombia (Magdalena Valley—known from one specimen)
05 01 027	**Crypturellus kerriae** *Choco Tinamou*		Baudo Mountains of northwest Colombia
05 01 028	**Crypturellus parvirostris** *Small-billed Tinamou*		Amazon basin to northeast Argentina
05 01 029	**Crypturellus tataupa** *Tataupa Tinamou*		Amazon basin to northern Argentina
05 01 030	**Rhynchotus rufescens** *Red-winged Tinamou*		Brazil to Bolivia, Argentina
05 01 031	**Nothoprocta taczanowskii** *Taczanowski's Tinamou*		Andes of Peru (Junin, Cuzco)
05 01 032	**Nothoprocta kalinowskii** *Kalinowski's Tinamou*		Temperate zone of Peru (Libertad and Cuzco)
05 01 033	**Nothoprocta ornata** *Ornate Tinamou*		Andes of Peru to Chile, Argentina
05 01 034	**Nothoprocta perdicaria** *Chilean Tinamou*		Mountains of Atacama to Llanquihue (Chile)
05 01 035	**Nothoprocta cinerascens** *Brushland Tinamou*		Bolivia, Paraguay to western Argentina
05 01 036	**Nothoprocta pentlandii** *Andean Tinamou*		Andes of Ecuador to Chile, Argentina

	Date	Location
05 01 037 **Nothoprocta curvirostris** *Curve-billed Tinamou*		Andes of Ecuador to central Peru
05 01 038 **Nothura maculosa** *Spotted Nothura*		Eastern Brazil to eastern Argentina
05 01 039 **Nothura darwinii** *Darwin's Nothura*		Central Peru to Argentina (Chubut)
05 01 040 **Nothura chacoensis** *Chaco Nothura*		Arid Paraguay, adjacent Argentina
05 01 041 **Nothura minor** *Lesser Nothura*		Eastern and central Brazil
05 01 042 **Nothura boraquira** *White-bellied Nothura*		Northeast Brazil to Paraguay, Bolivia
05 01 043 **Taoniscus nanus** *Dwarf Tinamou*		Eastern Brazil (São Paulo and Paraná)
05 01 044 **Eudromia formosa** *Quebracho Crested-Tinamou*		Chaco of Paraguay, Argentina
05 01 045 **Eudromia elegans** *Elegant Crested-Tinamou*		Pampas of Argentina, adjacent Chile
05 01 046 **Tinamotis pentlandii** *Puna Tinamou*		Puna of Peru to Chile, Argentina
05 01 047 **Tinamotis ingoufi** *Patagonian Tinamou*		Steppes of southern Argentina, Chile

ORDER: SPHENISCIFORMES
FAMILY: SPHENISCIDAE (Penguins)

	Date	Location
06 01 001 **Aptenodytes patagonica** *King Penguin*		Antarctic, subantarctic circumpolar
06 01 002 **Aptenodytes forsteri** *Emperor Penguin*		Antarctic continent, seas to edge of ice pack
05 01 003 **Pygoscelis papua** *Gentoo Penguin*		Antarctic, subantarctic circumpolar
06 01 004 **Pygoscelis adeliae** *Adelie Penguin*		Antarctic seas to edge of ice pack
06 01 005 **Pygoscelis antarctica** *Chinstrap Penguin*		Antarctic seas and adjacent islands
06 01 006 **Eudyptes pachyrhynchus** *Victoria Penguin*		New Zealand (South Island), adjacent subantarctic islands
06 01 007 **Eudyptes robustus** *Snares Island Penguin*		New Zealand (Snares Island and adjacent waters)

		Date	Location

| 06 01 008 | **Eudyptes sciateri** *Erect-crested Penguin* | | Subantarctic New Zealand, Australian waters |

| 06 01 009 | **Eudyptes crestatus** *Rockhopper Penguin* | | Circumpolar temperate subantarctic islands |

| 06 01 010 | **Eudyptes schlegeli** *Royal Penguin* | | Macquarie, Cambell Islands, occasional New Zealand |

| 06 01 011 | **Eudyptes chrysolophus** *Macaroni Penguin* | | Atlantic and Indian ocean subantarctic waters |

| 06 01 012 | **Megadyptes antipodes** *Yellow-eyed Penguin* | | New Zealand (South Island), Auckland, Campbell, Stewart |

| 06 01 013 | **Eudyptula minor** *Little Blue Penguin* | | Australia, Tasmania, New Zealand, Chatham Islands |

| 06 01 014 | **Eudyptula albosignata** *White-flippered Penguin* | | New Zealand (Banks' Peninsula and adjacent waters) |

| 06 01 015 | **Spheniscus demersus** *Cape (Jackass) Penguin* | | Temperate islands and coasts of South Africa |

| 06 01 016 + | **Spheniscus humboldti** *Humboldt Penguin* | | Humboldt Current of Chile, Peru |

| 06 01 017 + | **Spheniscus magellanicus** *Magellanic Penguin* | | Patagonian coasts, Falkland, Staten Islands |

| 06 01 018 | **Spheniscus mendiculus** *Galapagos Penguin* | | Galapagos Islands (endangered) |

ORDER: GAVIIFORMES
FAMILY: GAVIIDAE (Loons)

| 07 01 001 | **Gavia stellata** *Red-throated Loon* *Red-throated Diver (Br.)* | | Holarctic circumpolar |

| 07 01 002 | **Gavia arctica** *Arctic Loon* *Black-throated Diver (Br.)* | | Northern Palearctic |

| 07 01 003 | **Gavia pacifica** *Pacific Loon* | | Northern North America, coastal northeast Siberia |

| 07 01 004 | **Gavia immer** *Common Loon* *Great Northern Diver (Br.)* | | Widespread Nearctic, occasional western Palearctic regions |

| 07 01 005 | **Gavia adamsii** *Yellow-billed Loon* *White-billed Diver (Br.)* | | Holarctic circumpolar |

		Date	Location

ORDER: PODICIPEDIFORMES
FAMILY: PODICIPEDIDAE (Grebes)

08 01 001
+
Tachybaptus ruficollis
Little Grebe
Widespread Palearctic region to New Guinea, Solomons

08 01 002
Tachybaptus novaehollandiae
Australian Dabchick
Indonesia to New Guinea, Australia

08 01 003
Tachybaptus pelzelni
Madagascar Grebe
Widespread throughout Madagascar

08 01 004
Tachybaptus rufolavatus
Alaotra Grebe
Known only from Lake Alaotra, Madagascar

08 01 005
Podilymbus podiceps
Pied-billed Grebe
Widespread Alaska to Argentina; West Indies

08 01 006
Podilymbus gigas
Atitlan Grebe
Restricted to Lake Atitlan, Guatemala (endangered)

08 01 007
+
Rollandia rolland
White-tufted Grebe
Peru, southeast Brazil to Tierra del Fuego; Falklands

08 01 008
Rollandia micropterum
Short-winged Grebe
Andes of Peru, Bolivia (Lake Titicaca and Poopo)

08 01 009
+
Podiceps major
Great Grebe
Tierra del Fuego to Peru, southern Brazil

08 01 010
Podiceps poliocephalus
Hoary-headed Grebe
Australia, Tasmania

08 01 011
Podiceps rufopectus
New Zealand Dabchick
New Zealand (widespread North Island; scarce South Island)

08 01 012
+
Podiceps dominicus
Least Grebe
Extreme southern United States to Argentina; West Indies

08 01 013
Podiceps grisegena
Red-necked Grebe
Widespread Holarctic region

08 01 014
Podiceps cristatus (australis)
Great Crested Grebe
Widespread Palearctic region to Australia

08 01 015
Podiceps auritus
Horned Grebe
Holarctic (western North America and northern Eurasia)

08 01 016
Podiceps nigricollis (caspicus)
Eared Grebe
Widespread Palearctic, Nearctic regions

08 01 017
+
Podiceps occipitalis
Silvery Grebe
Colombia to Argentina, Chile

		Date	Location

08 01 018 **Podiceps taczanowskii**
Puna Grebe
Puna of Peru (Lake Junin—endangered)

08 01 019 **Podiceps gallardoi**
✝ *Hooded Grebe*
Argentina (breeds Lake Escachados, Patagonia) Escarchados

08 01 020 **Aechmophorus occidentalis**
Western Grebe
Alaska to Mexico

ORDER: PROCELLARIIFORMES
FAMILY: DIOMEDEIDAE (Albatrosses)

09 01 001 **Diomedea exulans**
Wandering Albatross
Circumpolar southern oceans, mainly 60° s. to 25° s.

09 01 002 **Diomedea epomophora**
Royal Albatross
Mainly seas adjacent to New Zealand

09 01 003 **Diomedea irrorata**
Waved (Galapagos) Albatross
Galapagos Islands, adjacent Humboldt Current (endangered)

09 01 004 **Diomedea albatrus**
Short-tailed Albatross
North Pacific (Isa Islands—57 pairs in 1978)

09 01 005 **Diomedea nigripes**
Black-footed Albatross
Southern and temperate oceans; breeds Hawaii

09 01 006 **Diomedea immutabilis**
Laysan Albatross
Northern Pacific waters; breeds Hawaii

09 01 007 **Diomedea melanophris**
✝ *Black-browed Albatross*
Circumpolar cold southern oceans

09 01 008 **Diomedea bulleri**
Buller's Albatross
Mainly New Zealand waters, rarely to western South America

09 01 009 **Diomedea cauta**
Shy Albatross
Cold southern oceans, north to 25° south

09 01 010 **Diomedea chlororhynchos**
Yellow-nosed Albatross
South Atlantic and Indian Oceans, east to New Zealand

09 01 011 **Diomedea chrysostoma**
Gray-headed Albatross
High southern latitudes, north to 40° south

09 01 012 **Phoebetria fusca**
Sooty Albatross
South Atlantic and Indian Oceans to about 30° south

09 01 013 **Phoebetria palpebrata**
Light-mantled Albatross
Southern circumpolar seas, mainly 55° to 35° south

		Date	Location

ORDER: PROCELLARIIFORMES
FAMILY: PROCELLARIIDAE (Shearwaters)

09 02 001 ✝	**Macronectes giganteus** *Southern Giant Petrel*	Widespread southern oceans (Antarctica to Tropic of Capricorn)
09 02 002	**Macronectes halli** *Hall's Giant Petrel*	Antarctic circumpolar, breeds north of Antarctic convergence
09 02 003	**Fulmarus glacialis** *Northern Fulmar*	North Atlantic and Pacific, adjacent Arctic seas
09 02 004	**Fulmarus glacialoides** *Southern Fulmar*	Widespread Antarctic circumpolar, southern oceans
09 02 005	**Thalassoica antarctica** *Antarctic Petrel*	Breeds Antarctic continent; disperses cold Antarctic waters
09 02 006 ✝	**Daption capense** *Cape (Pintado) Petrel*	Circumpolar southern oceans, north to Tropic of Capricorn
09 02 007	**Pagodroma nivea** *Snow Petrel*	Restricted to cold Antarctic waters
09 02 008	**Pterodroma macroptera** *Great-winged Petrel*	Southern oceans, mainly between 30° and 50° south
09 02 009	**Pterodroma aterrima** *Reunion Petrel*	Indian Ocean (breeds Mascarene Islands—endangered)
09 02 010	**Pterodroma lessoni** *White-headed Petrel*	Subantarctic, Antarctic seas to edge of ice pack
09 02 011	**Pterodroma hasitata (caribbaea)** *Black-capped Petrel*	West Indies (breeds Hispaniola—endangered)
09 02 012	**Pterodroma cahow** *Bermuda Petrel*	Breeds Bermuda (seriously endangered)
09 02 013	**Pterodroma incerta** *Hooded Petrel*	Cold Indian and Atlantic Oceans (breeds Tristan da Cunha)
09 02 014	**Pterodroma rostrata (becki)** *Tahiti Petrel*	Tropical, subtropical southwest Pacific Ocean south of equator
09 02 015	**Pterodroma alba (wortheni) (oliveri)** *Phoenix Petrel*	Widespread tropical, subtropical Pacific Ocean
09 02 016	**Pterodroma inexpectata** *Scaled (Mottled) Petrel*	New Zealand seas to Aleutians (breeds Stewart, Snares Islands)

		Date	Location
09 02 017	**Pterodroma solandri** *Solander's Petrel*		New Zealand, southeast Australian waters (breeds Lore Howe Island)
09 02 018	**Pterodroma brevirostris** *Kerguelen Petrel*		Circumpolar southern oceans, mainly between 60° and 40° south
09 02 019	**Pterodroma ultima** *Murphy's Petrel*		Central subtropical Pacific Ocean (breeds Austral Islands)
09 02 020	**Pterodroma neglecta (philipii)** *Kermadec Petrel*		Widespread tropical and subtropical Pacific Ocean
09 02 021	**Pterodroma magentae** *Magenta Petrel*		Recently rediscovered on Tubuai Island, southwest Pacific
09 02 022	**Pterodroma arminjoniana (heraldica)** *Herald Petrel*		Circumpolar southern oceans
09 02 023	**Pterodroma mollis** *Soft-plumaged Petrel*		Atlantic and southern Indian Oceans to about 50° south
09 02 024	**Pterodroma baraui** *Barau's Petrel*		Indian Ocean (breeds Reunion Island, disperses eastward)
09 02 025	**Pterodroma phaeopygia** *Dark-rumped Petrel*		Tropical, subtropical Pacific (breeds Hawaii, Galapagos)
09 02 026	**Pterodroma externa (cervicallis)** *White-necked Petrel*		Tropical and subtropical Pacific Ocean
09 02 027	**Pterodroma cooki** *Cook's Petrel*		Colder temperate south Pacific, disperses northward
09 02 028	**Pterodroma leucoptera** *White-winged (Gould's) Petrel*		Tropical and subtropical western Pacific Ocean
09 02 029	**Pterodroma brevipes** *Collared Petrel*		Subtropical and tropical western Pacific Ocean
09 02 030	**Pterodroma hypoleuca** *Bonin Petrel*		Temperate to tropical northwest Pacific Ocean
09 02 031	**Pterodroma nigripennis** *Black-winged Petrel*		Tropical and subtropical Pacific (breeds Kermadec Island)
09 02 032	**Pterodroma axillaris** *Chatham Island Petrel*		Cool south Pacific Ocean (breeds Chatham Island)

	Date	Location
09 02 033 **Pterodroma longirostris** *Stejneger's Petrel*		Southern Pacific Ocean, disperses northward (endangered)
09 02 034 **Pterodroma pycrofti** *Pycroft's Petrel*		Mainly restricted to New Zealand waters
09 02 035 **Pterodroma macgillivrayi** *Macgillivray's Petrel*		Fiji Islands (known from a single specimen)
09 02 036 **Halobaena caerulea** *Blue Petrel*		Circumpolar cold southern oceans north to 40° south
09 02 037 **Pachyptila vittata** *Broad-billed Prion*		Cold southern oceans north to 40° south
09 02 038 **Pachyptila salvini** *Medium-billed Prion*		Southern Indian Ocean (breeds Marion, Crozet Islands)
09 02 039 **Pachyptila desolata** *Dove (Antarctic) Prion*		Subantarctic oceans north to about 35° south
09 02 040 **Pachyptila belcheri** *Slender-billed Prion*		Subantarctic seas (breeds Falklands, Kerguelen Islands)
09 02 041 **Pachyptila turtur** *Fairy Prion*		Subantarctic seas north to about 35° south
09 02 042 **Pachyptila crassirostris** *Fulmar Prion*		Subantarctic Indian Ocean, Australian waters
09 02 043 **Bulweria bulwerii** *Bulwer's Petrel*		Tropical north Atlantic and Pacific (occasional Indian) Oceans
09 02 044 **Bulweria fallax** *Jouanin's Petrel*		Restricted to Arabian Sea and Gulf of Aden
09 02 045 **Procellaria cinerea** *Black-tailed Shearwater*		Southern oceans, rarely north of 30° south
09 02 046 **Procellaria aequinoctialis** *White-chinned Petrel*		Cold southern oceans, from edge of pack ice to 30° south
09 02 047 **Procelliaria parkinsoni** *Black Petrel*		Southern oceans (breeds New Zealand mountain tops)
09 02 048 **Procellaria westlandica** *Westland Petrel*		Breeds New Zealand, disperses into Tasman Sea
09 02 049 **Puffinus leucomelas** *Streaked Shearwater*		Northwest Pacific, disperses to Philippines, Borneo

		Date	Location
09 02 050	**Puffinus diomedea** **(kuhli)** *Cory's Shearwater*		North and south Atlantic Ocean, Mediterranean Sea
09 02 051	**Puffinus creatopus** *Pink-footed Shearwater*		East Pacific Ocean to Baja waters (breeds Juan Fernandez Island)
09 02 052	**Puffinus carneipes** *Flesh-footed Shearwater*		Southern Pacific and Indian Oceans (breeds Australia, New Zealand)
09 02 053	**Puffinus gravis** *Greater Shearwater*		Widespread Atlantic Ocean from Cape Horn to Arctic Circle
09 02 054	**Puffinus pacificus** *Wedge-tailed Shearwater*		Ranges widely over Indian and Pacific Oceans
09 02 055	**Puffinus bulleri** *New Zealand Shearwater*		Widespread southern Pacific Ocean (breeds New Zealand)
09 02 056	**Puffinus griseus** *Sooty Shearwater*		Widespread polar seas to southern oceans
09 02 057	**Puffinus tenuirostris** *Short-tailed Shearwater*		South Pacific Ocean (breeds Australia)
09 02 058	**Puffinus heinrothi** *Heinroth's Shearwater*		New Britain Island (known from a single specimen)
09 02 059	**Puffinus nativitatis** *Christmas Island Shearwater*		Breeds throughout range in tropical Pacific Ocean
09 02 060	**Puffinus puffinus** *Manx Shearwater*		Mediterranean Sea and Atlantic Ocean
09 02 061	**Puffinus gavia** *Fluttering Shearwater*		Mainly confined to Australian and New Zealand waters
09 02 062	**Puffinus huttoni** *Hutton's Petrel*		Mainly confined to New Zealand waters
09 02 063	**Puffinus opisthomelas** *Black-vented Shearwater*		Pacific Coast of North America (British Columbia to Mexico)
09 02 064	**Puffinus auricularis** *Townsend's Shearwater*		Baja and islands off west coast of Mexico
09 02 065	**Puffinus assimilis** **(persicus)** *Little Shearwater*		South Atlantic and Indian Oceans
09 02 066	**Puffinus lherminieri** *Audubon's Shearwater*		Tropical Atlantic, Caribbean, Pacific, Indian Oceans

	Date	Location

ORDER: PROCELLARIIFORMES
FAMILY: HYDROBATIDAE (Storm Petrels)

09 03 001	**Oceanites oceanicus** *Wilson's Storm Petrel*	Widespread oceans of world (breeds Antarctic, subantarctic)
09 03 002	**Oceanites gracilis** *White-vented Storm Petrel*	Humboldt Current of South America (breeds Galapagos Islands)
09 03 003	**Garrodia nereis** *Gray-backed Storm Petrel*	Circumpolar subantarctic waters, ranges north to 35° south
09 03 004	**Pelagodroma marina** *White-faced Storm Petrel*	Widespread tropical and subtropical oceans
09 03 005	**Fregetta grallaria** *White-bellied Storm Petrel*	Widespread southern tropical and subtropical oceans
09 03 006	**Fregetta tropica** **(lineata)** *Black-bellied Storm Petrel*	Breeds subantarctic islands, disperses northward
09 03 007	**Nesofregetta albigularis** **(fuliginosa)** *White-throated Storm Petrel*	Tropical central and western Pacific Ocean
09 03 008	**Hydrobates pelagicus** *British Storm Petrel*	Eastern north and south Atlantic Ocean, Mediterranean Sea
09 03 009	**Halocyptena microsoma** *Least Storm Petrel*	Pacific coast of Baja to Ecuador (breeds San Benito Island)
09 03 010	**Oceanodroma tethys** *Galapagos Storm Petrel*	Peru to California (breeds Galapagos Islands)
09 03 011	**Oceanodroma castro** *Band-rumped Storm Petrel*	Central Pacific and eastern Atlantic Oceans
09 03 012	**Oceanodromo leucorhoa** *Leach's Storm Petrel*	Widespread Atlantic and Pacific Oceans
09 03 013	**Oceanodroma macrodactyla** *Guadalupe Storm Petrel*	Extinct. Inhabited Guadalupe Island off Baja California
09 03 014	**Oceanodroma markhami** *Sooty Storm Petrel*	Humboldt Current of South America (breeding area unknown)
09 03 015	**Oceanodroma matsudairae** *Matsudaira's Storm Petrel*	Subtropical western Pacific Ocean (breeds Volcano Islands)

	Date	Location

09 03 016   **Oceanodroma tristrami**
Tristram's Storm Petrel — Western Pacific Ocean to Bonin Islands (breeds Hawaii)

09 03 017   **Oceanodroma monorhis**
Swinhoe's Storm Petrel — Western Pacific, north Indian Ocean (breeds Pescaror Island)

09 03 018   **Oceanodroma homochroa**
Ashy Storm Petrel — Coastal California, Baja (breeds Farallons, Santa Barbara Islands)

09 03 019   **Oceanodroma hornbyi**
Ringed Storm Petrel — Humboldt Current of Ecuador to Chile (breeds Chilean Andes)

09 03 020   **Oceanodroma furcata**
Fork-tailed Storm Petrel — Northern Pacific and Bering Sea (Kuriles, Aleutians to California)

09 03 021   **Oceanodroma melania**
Black Storm Petrel — Pacific coast of California to Peru (breeds islands off Baja)

ORDER: PROCELLARIIFORMES
FAMILY: PELECANOIDIDAE (Diving Petrels)

09 04 001   **Pelecanoides garnoti**
Peruvian Diving Petrel — Coast of Chile and Peru (Arica to Lobos de Tierra)

09 04 002   **Pelecanoides magellani**
Magellanic Diving Petrel — Islands, channels, fiords of southern Chile and Argentina

09 04 003   **Pelecanoides georgicus**
Georgian Diving Petrel — Breeds South Georgia, Kerguelen, Heard, Auckland Islands

09 04 004   **Pelecanoides urinatrix (exsul)**
Subantarctic Diving Petrel — Widespread southern oceans from 55° to 35° south

ORDER: PELECANIFORMES
FAMILY: PHAETHONTIDAE (Tropicbirds)

10 01 001   **Phaethon aethereus**
Red-billed Tropicbird — Tropical, subtropical Atlantic, Pacific and Indian Oceans

10 01 002   **Phaethon rubricauda**
Red-tailed Tropicbird — Tropical, subtropical Pacific and Indian Oceans (highly pelagic)

10 01 003   **Phaethon lepturus**
White-tailed Tropicbird — Tropical, subtropical Atlantic, Pacific and Indian Oceans

	Date	Location

ORDER: PELECANIFORMES
FAMILY: PELECANIDAE (Pelicans)

10 02 001 +	**Pelecanus onocrotalus** *Eastern White Pelican*	Southern Europe, Asia, Africa
10 02 002	**Pelecanus rufescens** *Pink-backed Pelican*	Madagascar; Africa south of the Sahara; southern Arabia
10 02 003	**Pelecanus phillippensis** *Spot-billed Pelican*	Sri Lanka; India to Malaysia, China, Phillipines, Java
10 02 004	**Pelecanus crispus** *Dalmatian Pelican*	Southeast Europe to southwest Siberia (endangered)
10 02 005	**Pelecanus conspicillatus** *Australian Pelican*	Australia, Tasmania; occasional New Guinea
10 02 006	**Pelecanus erythrorhynchos** *American White Pelican*	Western and central North America to Guatemala
10 02 007	**Pelecanus occidentalis** *Brown Pelican*	Southern United Unites States to northern South America; Galapagos
10 02 008 +	**Pelecanus thagus** *Peruvian Pelican*	Coastal Chile to Peru (possible race *P. occidentalis*)

ORDER: PELECANIFORMES
FAMILY: SULIDAE (Boobies)

10 03 001	**Morus bassanus** *Northern Gannet*	North Atlantic coasts
10 03 002	**Morus capensis** *Cape Gannet*	Islands off South African coasts
10 03 003	**Morus serrator** *Australian Gannet*	Australia, New Zealand, Tasmania
10 03 004 +	**Sula nebouxii** *Blue-footed Booby*	Pacific coast of Mexico to Peru; Galapagos Islands
10 03 005 +	**Sula variegata** *Peruvian Booby*	Humboldt current of Colombia to Chile
10 03 006	**Sula abbotti** *Abbott's Booby*	Restricted to Christmas Island in Indian Ocean (endangered)
10 03 007	**Sula dactylatra** *Masked (Blue-faced) Booby*	Widespread tropical, subtropical oceans

		Date	Location

10 03 008 **Sula sula**
Red-footed Booby
Widespread tropical oceans

10 03 009 **Sula leucogaster**
Brown Booby
Worldwide tropical, subtropical oceans

ORDER: PELECANIFORMES
FAMILY: PHALACROCORACIDAE (Cormorants)

10 04 001 **Phalacrocorax auritus**
Double-crested Cormorant
Widespread North and Central America; West Indies

10 04 002 **Phalacrocorax olivaceus**
✝ *Olivaceous Cormorant*
Southern Texas and Louisiana to Tierra del Fuego; West Indies

10 04 003 **Phalacrocorax sulcirostris**
Little Black Cormorant
Indonesia to Australia, Tasmania, New Zealand, Norfolk Island

10 04 004 **Phalacrocorax carbo**
Great Cormorant
Wide distribution worldwide

10 04 005 **Phalacrocorax lucidus**
White-breasted Cormorant
Coastal and inland Africa south of the Sahara

10 04 006 **Phalacrocorax fuscicollis**
Indian Cormorant
Lagoons and coasts of Sri Lanka, India to Thailand

10 04 007 **Phalacrocorax capensis**
Cape Cormorant
Coastal Africa from Congo River to Cape of Good Hope

10 04 008 **Phalacrocorax nigrogularis**
Socotra Cormorant
Persian gulf, Arabian and Red seas; Socotra Island

10 04 009 **Phalacrocorax neglectus**
Bank Cormorant
Southwest seabord of Africa

10 04 010 **Phalacrocorax capillatus**
Japanese Cormorant
Coastal northeast Asia (breeds Korea, Sakhalin Islands)

10 04 011 **Phalacrocorax penicillatus**
Brandt's Cormorant
Pacific coast of North America (Alaska to Baja California)

10 04 012 **Phalacrocorax aristotelis**
Common Cormorant
Shag (Br.)
Islands and cliffs of western Palearctic region

		Date	Location
10 04 013	**Phalacrocorax pelagicus** *Pelagic Cormorant*		Coastal northern Pacific, south to Japan, China, Mexico
10 04 014	**Phalacrocorax perspicillatus** *Spectacled Cormorant*		Extinct. Inhabited islands in Bering Sea
10 04 015	**Phalacrocorax urile** *Red-faced Cormorant*		Bering Sea, northeast Asia to Aleutian Islands
10 04 016 +	**Phalacrocorax magellanicus** *Rock Cormorant*		Coasts of Chile and Argentina; Falkland Islands
10 04 017	**Phalacrocorax bougainvillii** *Guanay Cormorant*		Pacific coast of Colombia to Chile; occasional Pt. Tombo, Argentina
10 04 018	**Phalacrocorax featherstoni** *Chatham Cormorant*		Restricted to Chatham Islands
10 04 019	**Phalacrocorax varius** *Pied Cormorant*		Coastal Australia and New Zealand (not in Tasmania)
10 04 020	**Phalacrocorax fuscescens** *Black-faced Cormorant*		South coast of Australia, Tasmania, islands of Bass Strait
10 04 021	**Phalacrocorax carunculatus** *Rough-faced Cormorant*		New Zealand, Stewart, Chatham and Bounty Islands
10 04 022	**Phalacrocorax campbelli** *Campbell Island Cormorant*		Campbell and Auckland Islands (off New Zealand)
10 04 023	**Phalacrocorax verrucosus** *Kerguelen Cormorant*		Breeds and disperses around Kerguelen Island
10 04 024 +	**Phalacrocorax gaimardi** *Red-legged Cormorant*		Coast of Peru, Chile; isolated population Pt. Deseado, Argentina
10 04 025	**Phalacrocorax punctatus** *Spotted Cormorant*		New Zealand and Chatham Islands
10 04 026	**Phalacrocorax atriceps** *Blue-eyed Cormorant*		Antarctic and subantarctic Islands
10 04 027	**Phalacrocorax georgianus** *South Georgia Cormorant*		South Georgia Island (probable race *P. atriceps*)
10 04 028 +	**Phalacrocorax albiventer** *King Cormorant*		Islands around South Pole

		Date	Location
10 04 029	**Halietor melanoleucos** *Little Pied Cormorant*		Inland freshwater East Indies to Australia, New Zealand
10 04 030	**Halietor africanus** *Reed Cormorant*		Africa south of the Sahara; Madagascar
10 04 031	**Halietor niger** *Little Cormorant*		Sri Lanka; India, Nepal to Burma, Java, Borneo
10 04 032	**Halietor pygmeus** *Pygmy Cormorant*		Inland lakes and rivers of southeast Europe to central Asia
10 04 033 ✝	**Nannopterum harrisi** *Flightless Cormorant*		Galapagos Islands (endangered)

ORDER: PELECANIFORMES
FAMILY: ANHINGIDAE (Anhingas)

10 05 001 ✝	**Anhinga rufa** *African Darter*	Widespread Africa to India
10 05 002	**Anhinga melanogaster** *Oriental Darter*	Widespread Oriental mainland and islands
10 05 003	**Anhinga novaehollandiae** *Australian Darter*	Australia, New Guinea
10 05 004	**Anhinga anhinga** *American Anhinga*	Southern United States to northern Argentina

ORDER: PELECANIFORMES
FAMILY: FREGATIDAE (Frigatebirds)

10 06 001	**Fregata aquila** *Ascension Frigatebird*	Ascension Island and south tropical Atlantic Ocean
10 06 002	**Fregata andrewsi** *Christmas Frigatebird*	Local to Christmas Island (Indian Ocean) and adjacent seas
10 06 003	**Fregata magnificens** *Magnificent Frigatebird*	Tropical western Atlantic and eastern Pacific Oceans
10 06 004	**Fregata minor** *Great Frigatebird*	Widespread tropical, subtropical seas around the world
10 06 005	**Fregata ariel** *Lesser Frigatebird*	Widespread tropical, subtropical seas around the world

		Date	Location

ORDER: CICONIIFORMES
FAMILY: ARDEIDAE (Herons and Bitterns)

11 01 001   **Botaurus stellaris**
          Great Bittern   Europe, Asia, Africa

11 01 002   **Botaurus poiciloptilus**
          Brown Bittern   Australia, Tasmania, New Zealand

11 01 003   **Botaurus lentiginosus**
          American Bittern   Canada to Panama; West Indies

11 01 004   **Botaurus pinnatus**
          Pinnated Bittern   Mexico to Argentina

11 01 005   **Ixobrychus exilis**
          Least Bittern   Canada to Argentina; West Indies

11 01 006   **Ixobrychus minutus**
          (novaezelandiae)
          Little Bittern   Africa to Asia, New Guinea, Australasia

11 01 007   **Ixobrychus sinensis**
          Yellow Bittern   India to Japan, China, New Guinea

11 01 008   **Ixobrychus involucris**
          Stripe-backed Bittern   Widespread South America

11 01 009   **Ixobrychus eurhythmus**
          Schrenck's Bittern   Siberia to China, Japan, Malaysia

11 01 010   **Ixobrychus**
          cinnamomeus
          Cinnamon Bittern   Northeast and southeast Asia

11 01 011   **Ixobrychus sturmii**
          Dwarf Bittern   Tropical Africa to the Canary Islands

11 01 012   **Ixobrychus flavicollis**
          Black Bittern   Southern Asia to Solomons, Australia

11 01 013   **Zonerodius heliosylus**
          Forest Bittern   New Guinea, Aru Islands

11 01 014   **Tigriornis leucolophus**
          White-crested Bittern   Sierra Leone to Zaire

11 01 015   **Tigrisoma lineatum**
          Rufescent Tiger Heron   Honduras to Argentina

11 01 016   **Tigrisoma fasciatum**
          (salmoni)
          Fasciated Tiger Heron   Costa Rica to Argentina

11 01 017   **Tigrisoma mexicanum**
          Bare-throated Tiger Heron   Mexico to Colombia

11 01 018   **Zebrilus undulatus**
          Zigzag Heron   Widespread Amazon basin

11 01 019   **Gorsachius goisagi**
          Japanese Night Heron   Japan, China, Taiwan, Philippines

		Date	Location
11 01 020	**Gorsachius melanolophus** *Malay Bittern*		Widespread southeast Asia
11 01 021	**Gorsachius magnificus** *White-eared Night Heron*		Southern China; Hainan
11 01 022	**Gorsachius leuconotus** *White-backed Night Heron*		Senegal to the Sudan, Angola, South Africa
11 01 023	**Nycticorax nycticorax** *Black-crowned Night Heron*		Cosmopolitan—almost worldwide distribution
11 02 024 +	**Nycticorax caledonicus** *Rufous (Nankeen) Night Heron*		Indonesia to Australia
11 01 025	**Nycticorax pileatus** *Capped Heron*		Panama to Brazil, Bolivia
11 01 026	**Nycticorax violaceus** *Yellow-crowned Night Heron*		United States to Peru, Brazil; West Indies; Galapagos
11 01 027	**Cochlearius cochlearius** *Boat-billed Heron*		Mexico to Argentina
11 01 028	**Ardeola ralloides** *Squacco Heron*		Africa, Europe, southwest Asia
11 01 029	**Ardeola idae** *Madagascar Heron*		East Africa and Madagascar
11 01 030	**Ardeola grayii** *Indian Pond Heron*		Persian Gulf to India, Malay Peninsula
11 01 031	**Ardeola bacchus** *Chinese Pond Heron*		Japan, China to Malaysia, Borneo
11 01 032	**Ardeola speciosa** *Javanese Pond Heron*		Java, Borneo, Celebes, Lesser Sundas
11 01 033	**Ardeola rufiventris** *Rufous-bellied Heron*		Angola to Uganda, South Africa
11 01 034	**Ardeola ibis** *Cattle Egret*		Almost worldwide distribution
11 01 035 +	**Syrigma sibilatrix** *Whistling Heron*		Venezuela to Argentina
11 01 036	**Butorides virescens** *Green Heron*		Canada to northern South America
11 01 037	**Butorides sundevalli** *Galapagos (Lava) Heron*		Galapagos Islands
11 01 038 +	**Butorides striatus (rogersi)** *Striated Heron*		Wide distribution worldwide

		Date	Location

11 01 039 Hydranassa picata
Pied Heron
New Guinea, Borneo, Celebes to Australia

11 01 040 Hydranassa ardesiaca
Black Heron
Africa; Madagascar

11 01 041 Hydranassa vinaceigula
Brown-throated Heron
Caprivi and southern Transvaal, southern Zambia

11 01 042 Hydranassa caerulea
Little Blue Heron
Eastern United States to Peru, Argentina

11 01 043 Hydranassa tricolor
Louisiana (Tricolored)
Heron
Eastern United States to Brazil; West Indies

11 01 044 Hydranassa rufescens
Reddish Egret
Southern United States to Panama

11 01 045 Egretta sacra
Eastern Reef Egret
Burma to Japan, Australia, New Zealand, Polynesia

11 01 046 Egretta eulophotes
Chinese Egret
China to Philippines, Indonesia (endangered)

11 01 047 Egretta thula
Snowy Egret
United States to Argentina; West Indies, Galapagos
Islands

**11 01 048 Egretta gularis
(schistacea)**
Western Reef Heron
West Africa to Persian Gulf, India, Sri Lanka

11 01 049 Egretta dimorpha
Madagascar Egret
Madagascar and Aldabra Islands

11 01 050 Egretta garzetta
Little Egret
Africa, southern Eurasia to Japan, Australasia

11 01 051 Egretta intermedia
Intermediate Egret
Africa, southern Asia, New Guinea to Australia

11 01 052 Egretta alba
Great Egret
Widespread distribution worldwide

11 01 053 Ardea purpurea
Purple Heron
Widespread Palearctic region, India, Africa; Sri Lanka

11 01 054 Ardea novaehollandiae
White-faced Heron
Australia to Indonesia, New Guinea

11 01 055 Ardea pacifica
White-necked Heron
Australia, New Zealand, New Guinea

11 01 056 Ardea cinerea
Gray Heron
Widespread Palearctic region; Africa

**11 01 057 Ardea herodias
(occidentalis)**
Great Blue Heron
Alaska to northern South America; Galapagos; West
Indies

		Date	Location

| 11 01 058 | **Ardea cocoi** | | |
| ✝ | *Cocoi Heron* | | Widespread South America |

| 11 01 059 | **Ardea melanocephala** | | |
| | *Black-headed Heron* | | Widespread Ethiopian region; Madagascar |

| 11 01 060 | **Ardea humbloti** | | |
| | *Madagascar Heron* | | Confined to Madagascar (endangered) |

| 11 01 061 | **Ardea goliath** | | |
| | *Goliath Heron* | | Africa, Madagascar, Sri Lanka, India |

| 11 01 062 | **Ardea imperialis** | | |
| | *Imperial (White-bellied) Heron* | | India to Burma |

| 11 01 063 | **Ardea sumatrana** | | |
| | *Great-billed Heron* | | Coasts of Malaysia, Indonesia, Australia, New Guinea |

| 11 01 064 | **Agamia agami** | | |
| | *Chestnut-bellied Heron* | | Mexico to Brazil, Bolivia |

ORDER: CICONIIFORMES
FAMILY: BALAENICIPITIDAE (Whale-headed Stork)

| 11 02 001 | **Balaeniceps rex** | | |
| ✝ | *Whale-headed Stork (Shoebill)* | | Sudan, Uganda, Zaire to Zambia |

ORDER: CICONIIFORMES
FAMILY: SCOPIDAE (Hammerhead)

| 11 03 001 | **Scopus umbretta** | | |
| ✝ | *Hammerhead (Hammerkop)* | | Southern and central Africa; Madagascar |

ORDER: CICONIIFORMES
FAMILY: CICONIIDAE (Storks)

| 11 04 001 | **Mycteria americana** | | |
| | *Wood Stork* | | Southern United States to Argentina |

| 11 04 002 | **Mycteria cinerea** | | |
| | *Milky Stork* | | Lowlands of Malaya, Cambodia, Cochinchina, Sumatra, Java |

| 11 04 003 | **Mycteria ibis** | | |
| | *Yellow-billed Stork* | | Africa and Madagascar |

| 11 04 004 | **Mycteria leucocephala** | | |
| | *Painted Stork* | | India to Indochina; Sri Lanka |

		Date	Location
11 04 005	**Anastomus oscitans** *Asian Open-billed Stork*		India to Burma, Cochinchina
11 04 006	**Anastomus lamelligerus** *African Open-billed Stork*		Africa south of the Sahara; Madagascar
11 04 007	**Ciconia nigra** *Black Stork*		Widespread Palearctic regions; Africa
11 04 008	**Ciconia abdimii** *White-bellied Stork*		Africa south of the Sahara
11 04 009	**Ciconia episcopus** **(stormii)** *Woolly-necked Stork*		Africa to Southeast Asia; Sri Lanka
11 04 010 +	**Ciconia maguari** *Maguari Stork*		Widespread South America
11 04 011 +	**Ciconia ciconia** **(boyciana)** *White Stork*		Widespread Palearctic region, tropical Africa
11 04 012	**Ephippiorhynchus** **asiaticus** *Black-necked Stork*		Southern Asia to Indonesia, New Guinea, Australia
11 04 013 +	**Ephippiorhynchus** **senegalensis** *Saddle-billed Stork*		Tropical Africa south of the Sahara
11 04 014 +	**Jabiru mycteria** *Jabiru*		Southern Mexico to Argentina
11 04 015	**Leptoptilos javanicus** *Lesser Adjutant Stork*		Central India to Southeast Asia; Greater Sundas
11 04 016	**Leptoptilos dubius** *Greater Adjutant Stork*		Central India to Southeast Asia
11 04 017 +	**Leptoptilos** **crumeniferus** *Marabou Stork*		Widespread tropical Africa

ORDER: CICONIIFORMES
FAMILY: THRESKIORNITHIDAE (Ibis)

11 05 001 +	**Threskiornis aethiopicus** *Sacred Ibis*		Africa to west Asia, southwest Pacific islands
11 05 002	**Threskiornis** **melanocephalus** *Black-headed Ibis*		Sri Lanka; India to eastern China, Indochina
11 05 003 + (see *Egretta* *alba*)	**Threskiornis molucca** *Australian White Ibis*		Indonesia, New Guinea to Australia

		Date	Location
11 05 004	**Threskiornis spinicollis** *Straw-necked Ibis*		Australia, Tasmania
11 05 005	**Pseudibis papillosa** *White-shouldered Ibis*		Semi-arid regions throughout the Indo-Gangetic Plain
11 05 006	**Pseudibis davisoni** *Oriental Black Ibis*		Widespread southeast Asia
11 05 007	**Thaumatibis gigantea** *Giant Ibis*		Indochina (endemic—endangered)
11 05 008	**Geronticus eremita** *Hermit Ibis*		North and east Africa to Asia Minor (endangered)
11 05 009	**Geronticus calvus** *Bald Ibis*		Mountains of inland regions of South Africa
11 05 010	**Nipponia nippon** *Japanese Crested Ibis*		Sado, Hondo Islands of Japan (nearly extinct)
11 05 011	**Lampribis olivacea** *Olive Ibis*		Forests of west, east Africa
11 05 012	**Lampribis rara** *Spot-breasted Ibis*		Liberia to Cameroon, Zaire
11 05 013	**Hagedashia hagedash** *Hadada Ibis*		Africa south of the Sahara
11 05 014	**Bostrychia carunculata** *Wattled (Carunculated)* *Ibis*		Highlands of Ethiopia and Eritrea
11 05 015 ✝	**Harpiprion caerulescens** *Plumbeous Ibis*		Southern Brazil to Argentina
11 05 016	**Theristicus caudatus** *Buff-necked Ibis*		Panama to Argentina
11 05 017 ✝	**Theristicus melanopis** *Black-faced Ibis*		Arid Peru, Argentina to Tierra del Fuego
11 05 018	**Theristicus branickii** *Andean Ibis*		Andes of Ecuador to extreme northern Chile
11 05 019	**Cercibis oxycera** *Sharp-tailed Ibis*		Northern South America
11 05 020	**Mesembrinibis** **cayennensis** *Green (Cayenne) Ibis*		Costa Rica to Argentina
11 05 021	**Phimosus infuscatus** *Bare-faced Ibis*		Widespread South America
11 05 022	**Eudocimus albus** *American White Ibis*		Southern United States to Peru
11 05 023	**Eudocimus ruber** *Scarlet Ibis*		Venezuela, Colombia, Guianas, Brazil; Trinidad

		Date	Location
11 05 024	**Plegadis falcinellus** *Glossy Ibis*		Almost worldwide distribution
11 05 025	**Plegadis chihi** *White-faced Ibis*		Southern United States discontinuous to Argentina, Chile
11 05 026	**Plegadis ridgwayi** *Puna Ibis*		High Andes of central Peru to northwest Argentina
11 05 027	**Lophotibis cristata** *Madagascar Ibis*		Forests of Madagascar
11 05 028	**Platalea leucorodia** *White Spoonbill*		Palearctic region, tropical Africa
11 05 029	**Platalea minor** *Black-faced Spoonbill*		Manchuria, Korea, eastern China to Indochina
11 05 030	**Platalea alba** *African Spoonbill*		Africa south of the Sahara; Madagascar
11 05 031	**Platalea regia** *Royal Spoonbill*		New Zealand, Australia to New Guinea, Celebes Islands
11 05 032	**Platibis flavipes** *Yellow-billed Spoonbill*		Widespread Australia
11 05 033	**Ajaia ajaja** *Roseate Spoonbill*		Southern United States to Argentina; West Indies

ORDER: CICONIIFORMES
FAMILY: PHOENICOPTERIDAE (Flamingos)

		Date	Location
11 06 001	**Phoenicopterus roseus (antiquorum)** *Eurasian Flamingo*		Palearctic region
11 06 002	**Phoenicopterus ruber** *American (Greater) Flamingo*		Northern South America; West Indies; Galapagos Islands; Africa
11 06 003	**Phoenicopterus chilensis** *Chilean Flamingo*		Southern South America
11 06 004	**Phoeniconaias minor** *Lesser Flamingo*		Africa to India; Madagascar
11 06 005	**Phoenicoparrus andinus** *Andean Flamingo*		Altiplano of Peru, Bolivia, Argentina, Chile
11 06 006	**Phoenicoparrus jamesi** *Puna (James') Flamingo*		Andes of southern Peru, Bolivia, Argentina, Chile

Date   Location

ORDER: ANSERIFORMES
FAMILY: ANHIMIDAE (Screamers)

12 01 001   **Anhima cornuta**
             Horned Screamer   Venezuela to Brazil, Bolivia

12 01 002   **Chauna torquata**
+   *Southern Screamer*   Southern Brazil, Bolivia to Argentina

12 01 003   **Chauna chavaria**
             Northern Screamer   Northwest Venezuela to northern Colombia (Rio
                                        Atrato)

ORDER: ANSERIFORMES
FAMILY: ANATIDAE (Ducks, Geese and Swans)

12 02 001   **Anseranas semipalmata**
             Pied Goose   Australia; sporadic southeast New Guinea

12 02 002   **Dendrocygna guttata**
             Spotted Tree-Duck   Philippines, New Guinea, adjacent islands

12 02 003   **Dendrocygna eytoni**
             Plumed Tree-Duck   Australia; New Zealand?; sporadic to southeast New
                                        Guinea

12 02 004   **Dendrocygna bicolor**
             Fulvous Tree-Duck   Southern United States to Argentina; Asia; Africa

12 02 005   **Dendrocygna arcuata**
             Whistling Tree-Duck   Widespread southwest Pacific to Australia

12 02 006   **Dendrocygna javanica**
             Lesser (Indian) Tree-   Widespread India to Malaysia, Indonesia
             Duck

12 02 007   **Dendrocygna viduata**
+   *White-faced Tree-Duck*   Discontinuous Costa Rica to Brazil; Africa;
                                        Madagascar; Comoros

12 02 008   **Dendrocygna arborea**
             West Indian Tree-Duck   West Indies (endangered)

12 02 009   **Dendrocygna autumnalis**
+   *Black-bellied Tree-Duck* Texas to Argentina

12 02 010   **Cygnus olor**
             Mute Swan   Palearctic; introduced Australia, United States

12 02 011   **Cygnus atratus**
             Black Swan   Australia; Tasmania; introduced to New Zealand

12 02 012   **Cygnus melanocoryphus**
+   *Black-necked Swan*   Southern Brazil to Argentina; Falkland Islands

12 02 013   **Cygnus cygnus**
+   *Whooper Swan*   Widespread Palearctic region

	Date	Location

12 02 014   Cygnus columbianus
Whistling Swan
Holarctic region

12 02 015   Cygnus buccinator
Trumpeter Swan
Alaska, Canada, United States (endangered)

12 02 016   Cygnus bewickii
Bewick's Swan
Northern Palearctic region

12 02 017   Coscoroba coscoroba
Coscoroba Swan
Southern Brazil to Chile, Argentina; Falkland Islands

12 02 018   Anser cygnoides
Chinese Goose
Eastern Palearctic region

**12 02 019   Anser fabalis
(brachyrhynchus)**
Bean Goose
Widespread Palearctic region; India; China

12 02 020   Anser albifrons
White-fronted Goose
Holarctic circumpolar

12 02 021   Anser erythropus
*Lesser White-fronted
Goose*
Northern and eastern Palearctic region

12 02 022   Anser anser
Greylag Goose
Widespread Palearctic region; India; China

12 02 023   Anser indicus
Bar-headed Goose
Central Asia to India, Burma

**12 02 024   Anser caerulescens
(hyperborea)**
Snow Goose
Siberia, Arctic America to Mexico

12 02 025   Anser rossi
Ross' Goose
Canada to southern United States

12 02 026   Anser canagicus
Emperor Goose
Northeast Siberia to coastal western Alaska

12 02 027   Branta sandvicensis
Nene Goose
Endemic to Island of Hawaii (introduced Mauai—
endangered)

12 02 028   Branta canadensis
Canada Goose
Holarctic region (Arctic America to Mexico)

12 02 029   Branta leucopsis
Barnacle Goose
Holarctic circumpolar

**12 02 030   Branta bernicia
(nigricans)**
Brant Goose
Holarctic circumpolar

12 02 031   Branta ruficollis
Red-breasted Goose
Northern and eastern Palearctic region

**12 02 032   Cereopsis
novaehollandiae**
Cape Barren Goose
Bass Strait Islands, adjacent Austrailian mainland
(endangered)

		ODate	Location
12 02 033	**Stictonetta naevosa** *Freckled Duck*		Mainly southern Australia (vagrant to tropics—rare)
12 02 034	**Cyanochen cyanopterus** *Blue-winged Goose*		Highlands of Ethiopia (endangered)
12 02 035	**Chloephaga melanoptera** *Andean Goose*		High Andes of Peru, Bolivia, Chile and Argentina
12 02 036	**Chloephaga picta** *Upland (Magellan) Goose*		Argentina and Chile; Falkland Islands
12 02 037	**Chloephaga hybrida** *Kelp Goose*		Coastal southern Argentina and Chile; Falkland Islands
12 02 038	**Chloephaga poliocephala** *Ashy-headed Goose*		Argentina and Chile; Falkland Islands
12 02 039	**Chloephaga rubidiceps** *Ruddy-headed Goose*		Argentina and Chile; Falkland Islands (endangered)
12 02 040	**Neochen jubatus** *Orinoco Goose*		Orinoco and Amazon River basins south to Argentina
12 02 041	**Alopochen aegyptiacus** *Egyptian Goose*		Africa south of the Sahara and the Nile Valley
12 02 042	**Tadorna ferruginea** *Ruddy Shelduck*		Mediterranean basin to east Asia
12 02 043	**Tadorna cana** *Cape Shelduck*		Southern Africa (Cape Province, Orange Free State, Transvaal)
12 02 044	**Tadorna variegata** *New Zealand Shelduck*		Widespread mountains and foothills of South Island (New Zealand)
12 02 045	**Tadorna tadornoides** *Australian Shelduck*		Southwest and southeast Australia
12 02 046	**Tadorna cristata** *Crested Shelduck*		Extinct. Known from four specimens from Russia, Korea
12 02 047	**Tadorna tadorna** *Common Shelduck*		Widespread Palearctic, Oriental regions
12 02 048	**Tadorna radjah** *Radjah Shelduck*		Australia, New Guinea, Moluccas, adjacent islands
12 02 049	**Tachyeres patachonicus** *Flying Steamer Duck*		Extreme southern tip of South America, Falkland Islands
12 02 050	**Tachyeres pteneres** *Flightless Steamer Duck*		Extreme southern tip of South America (flightless)
12 02 051	**Tachyeres brachypterus** *Falkland Steamer Duck*		Falkland Islands (endemic—flightless)

		Date	Location
12 02 052	**Plectropterus gambensis** *Spur-winged Goose*		Widespread Africa south of the Sahara; Madagascar
12 02 053	**Cairina moschata** *Muscovy Duck*		Widespread southern Mexico to Argentina
12 02 054	**Cairina scutulata** *White-winged Duck*		Widespread southeast Asia (endangered)
12 02 055	**Sarkidiornis melanotos (sylvicola)** *Comb Duck*		Africa to India, Burma, China; South America
12 02 056	**Pteronetta hartlaubii** *Hartlaub's Duck*		West Africa to Zaire, the Sudan
12 02 057	**Nettapus puichellus** *Green Pygmy Goose*		Locally common Australia, New Guinea, Moluccas
12 02 058	**Nettapus coromandelianus** *Cotton Pygmy Goose*		India to southeast Asia, Australia, Philippines
12 02 059	**Nettapus auritus** *African Pygmy Goose*		Africa south of the Sahara; Madagascar
12 02 060	**Callonetta leucophrys** *Ringed Teal*		Southern Brazil to northern Argentina
12 02 061	**Aix sponsa** *Wood Duck*		Widespread and common Canada to Mexico; West Indies
12 02 062	**Aix galericulata** *Mandarin Duck*		Japan, Taiwan, Manchuria, China
12 02 063	**Chenonetta jubata** *Australian Wood Duck*		Widespread and common throughout Australia, Tasmania
12 02 064	**Amazonetta brasiliensis** *Brazilian Duck*		Widespread and common throughout tropical South America
12 02 065	**Hymenolaimus malacorhynchos** *Blue Duck*		Mountain streams of New Zealand
12 02 066	**Merganetta armata** *Torrent Duck*		Andes of Venezuela to Argentina, Chile
12 02 067	**Salvadorina waigiuensis** *Salvadori's Teal*		Mountain streams of New Guinea
12 02 068	**Anas sparsa** *African Black Duck*		Africa south of the Sahara
12 02 069	**Anas penelope** *Eurasian Widgeon*		Widespread Palearctic, Oriental regions

	Date	Location
12 02 070 **Anas americana** *American Wigeon*		Alaska to Central America; West Indies
12 02 071 **Anas sibilatrix** + *Southern (Chiloe) Wigeon*		Southern Brazil to Tierra del Fuego; Falkland Islands
12 02 072 **Anas falcata** + *Falcated Teal*		Eastern Siberia to India, northern Indochina
12 02 073 **Anas strepera** *Gadwall*		Widespread Palearctic, Nearctic regions
12 02 074 **Anas formosa** + *Baikal Teal*		Eastern Palearctic region
12 02 075 **Anas crecca** **(carolinensis)** *Common (Green-winged)* *Teal*		Widespread Europe, Africa, Asia, North America
12 02 076 **Anas flavirostris** *Speckled Teal*		Widespread South America
12 02 077 **Anas capensis** *Cape Wigeon*		Africa north to Ethiopia and eastern Sudan
12 02 078 **Anas gibberifrons** *Gray Teal*		Andamans; Java to Australia, New Zealand
12 02 079 **Anas bernieri** *Madagascar Teal*		Lakes of western Madagascar (endangered)
12 02 080 **Anas castanea** *Chestnut Teal*		Southern Australia and Tasmania
12 02 081 **Anas aucklandica** **(chlorotis)** *Brown Teal*		New Zealand; Auckland, Campbell Islands (rare)
12 02 082 **Anas platyrhynchos** *Mallard*		Alaska to Mexico; North Africa to India, China, Borneo
12 02 083 **Anas rubripes** *American Black Duck*		Canada to southern United States, Bermuda
12 02 084 **Anas melleri** *Meller's Duck*		Widespread eastern Madagascar; Mauritius Island
12 02 085 **Anas undulata** *Yellowbill Duck*		Widespread and abundant Africa south of the Sahara
12 02 086 **Anas poecilorhyncha** *Spotbill Duck*		Eastern Palearctic, Oriental, Australasian regions
12 02 087 **Anas superciliosa** *Australian Black Duck*		Australia, New Guinea, Indonesia, Polynesia, New Zealand
12 02 088 **Anas luzonica** *Philippine Mallard*		Widespread throughout the Philippine Islands

		Date	Location

12 02 089 **Anas specularis**
† *Spectacled Duck* — Mainly forested regions of Argentina and Chile

12 02 090 **Anas specularioides**
† *Crested Duck* — Peru to Chile, Argentina; Falkland Islands

12 02 091 **Anas acuta**
Northern (Common) — Widespread Palearctic, Nearctic, Oriental regions
Pintail

12 02 092 **Anas georgica**
† *Brown Pintail* — Colombia, Ecuador to Chile, Argentina

12 02 093 **Anas bahamensis**
Bahama (White-cheeked) — Widespread South America; West Indies
Pintail

12 02 094 **Anas erythrorhyncha**
Red-billed Duck — Madagascar; east and southern Africa

12 02 095 **Anas versicolor**
† *Silver (Versicolored) Teal* — Southern Brazil to Chile, Argentina; Falkland Islands

12 02 096 **Anas puna**
Puna Teal — Puna of Peru to Chile, Argentina

12 02 097 **Anas punctata**
(hottentota)
Hottentot Teal — Widespread Africa; Madagascar (?)

12 02 098 **Anas querquedula**
Garganey Teal — Widespread Palearctic, Ethiopian and Oriental regions

12 02 099 **Anas discors**
Blue-winged Teal — Alaska to Argentina; West Indies; Galapagos

12 02 100 **Anas cyanoptera**
† (See Silver Teal) *Cinnamon Teal* — Canada to Argentina; Falkland Islands

12 02 101 **Anas platalea**
† *Red Shoveler* — Tierra del Fuego to Peru, southern Brazil; Falkland Islands

12 02 102 **Anas smithi**
Cape Shoveler — Africa (southern Rhodesia south)

12 02 103 **Anas rhynchotis**
Australian Shoveler — Australia, Tasmania, New Zealand

12 02 104 **Anas clypeata**
Northern Shoveler — Holarctic circumpolar, Palearctic region

12 02 105 **Malacorhynchus**
membranaceus
Pink-eared Duck — Nomadic throughout Australia and northern Tasmania

12 02 106 **Marmaronetta**
angustirostris
Marbled Teal — Mediterranean basin to southwest Asia

		Date	Location
12 02 107	**Rhodonessa caryophyllacea** *Pink-headed Duck*		Extinct. Inhabited India to Burma—last recorded 1935
12 02 108	**Netta rufina** *Red-crested Pochard*		Mediterranean basin to central Asia (rare)
12 02 109	**Netta erythrophthalma** *Southern Pochard*		Spottily distributed Africa; northern South America
12 02 110	**Netta peposaca** *Rosy-billed Pochard*		Southeast Brazil to northern Argentina, Chile
12 02 111	**Aythya valisineria** *Canvasback*		Widespread Nearctic region
12 02 112	**Aythya ferina** *Common Pochard*		Widespread Palearctic, Oriental regions
12 02 113	**Aythya americana** *Redhead*		Canada to Mexico; West Indies
12 02 114	**Aythya collaris** *Ring-necked Duck*		Canada to Panama; West Indies
12 02 115	**Aythya australis** *White-eyed Duck*		Australia, New Guinea to Indonesia
12 02 116	**Aythya baeri** *Baer's Pochard*		Eastern Palearctic, Oriental regions (rare)
12 02 117	**Aythya nyroca** *White-eyed Pochard*		Widespread Palearctic region
12 02 118	**Aythya innotata** *Madagascar Pochard*		Northern and eastern Madagascar (endangered)
12 02 119	**Aythya novaeseelandiae** *New Zealand Scaup*		New Zealand, Auckland and Chatham Islands
12 02 120	**Aythya fuligula** *Tufted Duck*		Widespread Palearctic region
12 02 121	**Aythya marila** *Greater Scaup*		Widespread and abundant Holarctic circumpolar
12 02 122	**Aythya affinis** *Lesser Scaup*		Alaska to Ecuador; West Indies
12 02 123	**Somateria mollissima** *Common Eider*		Holarctic circumpolar sea coasts
12 02 124	**Somateria spectabilis** *King Eider*		Arctic circumpolar coastal northern hemisphere
12 02 125	**Somateria fischeri** *Spectacled Eider*		Holarctic circumpolar coasts of Siberia to Alaska
12 02 126	**Polysticta stelleri** *Steller's Eider*		Holarctic circumpolar coasts of eastern Siberia to Alaska

		Date	Location

12 02 127	**Camptorhynchus labradorius**	
	Labrador Duck	Extinct. Inhabited northern Holarctic region
12 02 128	**Histrionicus histrionicus**	
	Harlequin Duck	Holarctic circumpolar
12 02 129	**Clangula hyemalis**	
	Oldsquaw	Holarctic circumpolar
	Long-tailed Duck (Br.)	
12 02 630	**Melanitta nigra**	
	Black Scoter	Holarctic circumpolar
12 02 131	**Melanitta perspicillata**	
	Surf Scoter	Alaska to southern United States, Baja California
12 02 132	**Melanitta fusca**	
	Velvet Scoter	Holarctic circumpolar
12 02 133	**Melanitta deglandi**	
	White-winged Scoter	Alaska to Baja California
12 02 134	**Bucephala albeola**	
	Bufflehead	Widespread and common Alaska to Mexico
12 02 135	**Bucephala islandica**	
	Barrow's Goldeneye	Alaska, Labrador to southern United States
12 02 136	**Bucephala clangula**	
	Common Goldeneye	Widespread Holarctic region
12 02 137	**Lophodytes cucullatus**	
	Hooded Merganser	Discontinuously distributed Alaska to Mexico
12 02 138	**Mergellus albellus**	
	Smew	Widespread northern Palearctic region
12 02 139	**Mergus octosetaceus**	
	Brazilian Merganser	Drainage of Paraguai, Paraná Rivers in Brazil, Paraguay, Argentina
12 02 140	**Mergus serrator**	
	Red-breasted Merganser	Widespread Holarctic region
12 02 141	**Mergus squamatus**	
	Chinese Merganser	Siberia, Manchuria, China (rare)
12 02 142	**Mergus merganser**	
	Common Merganser	Widespread Holarctic region
	Goosander (Br.)	
12 02 143	**Mergus australis**	
	Auckland Island Merganser	Extinct since 1902. Inhabited Auckland Island
12 02 144	**Heteronetta atricapilla**	
	Black-headed Duck	Southeast Brazil to Chile, Argentina
12 02 145	**Oxyura dominica**	
	Masked Duck	Gulf coast of southern Texas to Argentina; West Indies

		Date	Location

12 02 146 **Oxyura jamaicensis**
Ruddy Duck — Canada to Argentina; West Indies

12 02 147 **Oxyura ferruginea**
Andean Duck — Andes of Colombia to Argentina

12 02 148 **Oxyura leucocephala**
White-headed Duck — Mediterranean basin to central Asia

12 02 149 **Oxyura maccoa**
Maccoa Duck — Widespread Ethiopia to South Africa

12 02 150 **Oxyura vittata**
Lake Duck — Southeast Brazil to Argentina, Chile

12 02 151 **Oxyura australis**
Blue-billed Duck — Discontinuously distributed Australia, Tasmania

12 02 152 **Biziura lobata**
+ *Musk Duck* — Southern and western Australia; Tasmania

12 02 153 **Thalassornis leuconotos**
White-backed Duck — South Africa to Ethiopia; Madagascar

ORDER: FALCONIFORMES
FAMILY: CATHARTIDAE (American Vultures)

13 01 001 **Cathartes aura**
+ *Turkey Vulture* — Widespread and abundant Canada to Argentina

13 01 002 **Cathartes burrovianus**
+ *Lesser Yellow-headed Vulture* — Southern Mexico to Argentina

13 01 003 **Cathartes melambrotus**
Greater Yellow-headed Vulture — Northern South America

13 01 004 **Coragyps atratus**
Black Vulture — Extreme southern United States to Argentina

13 01 005 **Sarcoramphus papa**
King Vulture — Southern Mexico to Argentina

13 01 006 **Gymnogyps californianus**
California Condor — Southern coast range of California (on verge of extinction)

13 01 007 **Vultur gryphus**
+ *Andean Condor* — Colombia to Chile, Argentina (endangered)

ORDER: FALCONIFORMES
FAMILY: PANDIONIDAE (Osprey)

13 02 001 **Pandion haliaetus**
Osprey — Cosmopolitan—almost worldwide distribution

	Date	Location

ORDER: FALCONIFORMES
FAMILY: ACCIPITRIDAE (Hawks)

13 03 001   **Aviceda cuculoides**
African Cuckoo Falcon   Africa south of the Sahara

13 03 002   **Aviceda**
madagascariensis
Madagascar Cuckoo   Woodland and scrub of Madagascar
Falcon

13 03 003   **Aviceda jerdoni**
Jerdon's Baza   Sikkim to Laos, Hainan, Philippines, Celebes, Borneo,
                                Sumatra

13 03 004   **Aviceda subscristata**
Crested Baza   Lombok; Moluccas to New Guinea, Solomons,
                                Australia

13 03 005   **Aviceda leuphotes**
Black Baza   Lower Himalayas from Nepal to Szechwan and
                                southern China

13 03 006   **Leptodon cayanensis**
Gray-headed (Cayenne)   Mexico to Argentina; Trinidad
Kite

13 03 007   **Chondrohierax**
uncinatus
Hook-billed Kite   Tropical America from Mexico to Argentina; Tres
                                Marias Islands

13 03 008   **Henicopernis longicauda**
Long-tailed Honey-Buzzard   New Guinea, Arus and adjacent Papuan Islands

13 03 009   **Henicopernis infuscata**
Black Honey-Buzzard   Confined to New Britain Island

13 03 010   **Pernis apivorus**
(ptilorhyncus)
Honey-Buzzard   Europe, Asia, India and Indonesia

13 03 011   **Pernis celebensis**
Barred Honey-Buzzard   Celebes and the Philippines (except Palawan)

13 03 012   **Elanoides forficatus**
Swallow-tailed Kite   Eastern United States to Argentina; West Indies

13 03 013   **Machaerhamphus**
alcinus
Bat Hawk   Africa; Malay peninsula; Sumatra, Borneo, southeast
                                New Guinea

13 03 014   **Gampsonyx swainsonii**
Pearl Kite   Savanna and deciduous woodlands of Nicaragua to
                                Argentina

13 03 015   **Elanus leucurus**
White-tailed Kite   Southern United States to northern Argentina

		Date	Location
13 03 016	**Elanus caeruleus** *Black-shouldered Kite*		Savanna of Africa, southern Asia, East Indies and Arabia
13 03 017	**Elanus notatus** *Australian Black-shouldered Kite*		Savanna and dry forests of Australia
13 03 018	**Elanus scriptus** *Letter-winged Kite*		Dry open country of interior of Australia
13 03 019	**Chelictinia riocourii** *African Swallow-tailed Kite*		Senegal and Gambia to Somalia, Kenya
13 03 020 ✝	**Rostrhamus sociabilis** *Snail (Everglade) Kite*		Lowland freshwater marshes of Florida to Argentina; Cuba
13 03 021	**Rostrhamus hamatus** *Slender-billed Kite*		Surinam and lower Amazon to eastern Peru, Colombia, Panama
13 03 022	**Harpagus bidentatus** *Double-toothed Kite*		Tropical lowlands from Mexico to Bolivia, Brazil; Trinidad
13 03 023 ✝	**Harpagus diodon** *Rufous-thighed Kite*		Forest lowlands of Guyana, Surinam to Paraguay, Argentina
13 03 024 ✝	**Ictinia plumbea** *Plumbeous Kite*		Tropical Mexico to Paraguay, northern Argentina
13 03 025	**Ictinia mississippiensis** *Mississippi Kite*		Southeast United States; migrates to South America
13 03 026	**Lophoictinia isura** *Square-tailed Kite*		Scrub and open country of Australia (not Tasmania)
13 03 027	**Hamirostra melanosternon** *Black-breasted Buzzard Kite*		Northern and interior parts of Australia
13 03 028	**Milvus migrans** *Black (Common) Kite*		Widespread Africa, Palearctic, Oriental, Australasian regions
13 03 029	**Milvus milvus** *Red Kite*		Scandinavia, Russia to Asia Minor, northwest Africa; Canaries
13 03 030	**Haliastur sphenurus** *Whistling Kite*		Australia (except Tasmania); New Caledonia; New Guinea
13 03 031	**Haliastur indus** *Brahminy Kite*		India to China, New Guinea, Solomons, northern Australia

		Date	Location

13 03 032	**Haliaeetus leucogaster** *White-bellied Sea Eagle*	Widespread Oriental region to Australasia
13 03 033	**Haliaeetus sanfordi** *Sanford's Sea Eagle*	Widespread Solomon Islands
13 03 034	**Haliaeetus vocifer** *African Fish Eagle*	Rivers, lakes and seacoasts of Africa
13 03 035	**Haliaeetus vociferoides** *Madagascar Fish Eagle*	Mainly west coast and inland waters of Madagascar
13 03 036	**Haliaeetus leucoryphus** *Pallas' Sea Eagle*	Central Asia to India, Burma, Indochina
13 03 037	**Haliaeetus leucocephalus** *Bald Eagle*	North American continent south to Florida, Baja California
13 03 038	**Haliaeetus albicilla** *White-tailed Eagle*	Coasts and rivers of Palearctic, Oriental regions
13 03 039	**Haliaeetus pelagicus (niger)** *Steller's Sea Eagle*	Seacoasts of northeast Asia, Japan, Korea
13 03 040	**Ichthyophaga nana** *Lesser Fishing Eagle*	Forests of tropical Himalayas to Sumatra, Borneo, Celebes
13 03 041	**Ichthyophaga ichthyaetus** *Grey-headed Fishing Eagle*	Tropical India to Indochina, Borneo, Sumatra, Java, Philippines
13 03 042	**Gypohierax angolensis** *Palm Nut Vulture*	Oil palm forests and savannas of tropical Africa
13 03 043	**Neophron percnopterus** *Egyptian Vulture*	Southern Europe to India; widespread Africa
13 03 044	**Gypaetus barbatus** *Bearded Vulture* *(Lammergeier)*	Mountains of southern Europe to India, Tibet: eastern Africa
13 03 045	**Necrosyrtes monachus** *Hooded Vulture*	Savanna of Eritrea, Sudan to Senegal, Orange River, Natal
13 03 046	**Gyps bengalensis** *Indian White-backed Vulture*	Peninsular India through Burma to Indochina
13 03 047	**Gyps africanus** *African White-backed Vulture*	Open plains and savanna of Africa south of the Sahara
13 03 048	**Gyps indicus** *Long-billed Vulture*	Open country of peninsular India, Burma, Indochina

		Date	Location
13 03 049	**Gyps rueppellii**		
+	*Ruppell's Griffon*		Arid Africa from Eritrea and Sudan to Tanzania, Guinea
13 03 050	**Gyps himalayensis**		
	Himalayan Griffon		Mountains of Afghanistan to Bhutan, Tibet, Sikiang
13 03 051	**Gyps fulvus**		
	Griffon Vulture		Southern Europe to Afghanistan, India; North Africa
13 03 052	**Gyps coprotheres**		
	Cape Vulture		Open plains and mountains of southern Africa
13 03 053	**Torgos tracheliotus**		
	Lappet-faced Vulture		Thornbush, open plains and deserts of Africa
13 03 054	**Sarcogyps calvus**		
	Indian Black Vulture		India, Burma, Thailand, Laos and South Vietnam
13 03 055	**Aegypius monachus**		
	Cinereous Vulture		Mediterranean basin to east Asia
13 03 056	**Trigonoceps occipitalis**		
	White-headed Vulture		Thornbush, deserts of Africa south of the Sahara
13 03 057	**Circaetus gallicus**		
	Short-toed Eagle		Northeast Africa, Eurasia to Mongolia, India, Lesser Sundas
13 03 058	**Circaetus cinereus**		
	Brown Harrier Eagle		Thornbush zone of Africa south of the Sahara
13 03 059	**Circaetus fasciolatus**		
	Southern Banded Snake Eagle		Lowlands of East Africa (Kenya to Natal)
13 03 060	**Circaetus cinerascens**		
	Smaller Banded Snake Eagle		Sierra Leone to Ethiopia, Angola, southwest Africa
13 03 061	**Terathopius ecaudatus**		
+	*Bateleur*		Open savanna and thornbush of Africa south of the Sahara
13 03 062	**Spilornis holospilus**		
	Philippine Serpent Eagle		Open country, river valleys in Philippine Islands
13 03 063	**Spilornis rufipectus**		
	Celebes Serpent Eagle		Grassy savanna of Celebes and Sula Islands
13 03 064	**Spilornis cheela**		
	Crested Serpent Eagle		Tropical India to southeast China, Malaysia, Indonesia, Philippines
13 03 065	**Spilornis klossi**		
	Nicobar Serpent Eagle		Confined to Great Nicobar Island
13 03 066	**Spilornis elgini**		
	Andaman Serpent Eagle		Forests of interior of Andaman Islands

		Date	Location

13 03 067   **Dryotriorchis spectabilis**
Congo Serpent Eagle — Forests of west and central equatorial Africa south to Gabon

13 03 068   **Eutriorchis astur**
Madagascar Serpent Eagle — Lowland humid forests of northeast Madagascar (seriously endangered)

13 03 069   **Polyboroides typus**
African Harrier Hawk — Savanna and forests of Africa south of the Sahara

13 03 070   **Polyboroides radiatus**
Madagascar Harrier Hawk — Wooded districts of Madagascar, from sea level to 5,000 feet

13 03 071   **Geranospiza caerulescens**
Crane Hawk — Tropical lowland Mexico to Bolivia, Paraguay, Argentina

13 03 072   **Circus assimilis**
Spotted Harrier — Australia, Celebes, Timor, Taliabu and Sumba Islands

13 03 073   **Circus aeruginosus**
Marsh Harrier — Widespread Europe, Asia, Africa, Australia, adjacent islands

13 03 074   **Circus ranivorus**
African Marsh Harrier — Uganda and Kenya to Angola, South Africa

13 03 075   **Circus maurus**
Black Harrier — Natal and Cape Province of South Africa

13 03 076   **Circus cyaneus**
Northern Harrier (Marsh Hawk)
Hen Harrier (Br.) — Holarctic region to Oriental mainland; Borneo

13 03 077   **Circus cinereus**
Cinereous Harrier — Colombia, Ecuador to Paraguay, Argentina; Falkland Islands

13 03 078   **Circus macrourus**
Pallid Harrier — Africa; eastern Europe to Siberia, India, Burma

13 03 079   **Circus pygargus**
Montagu's Harrier — Africa; Eurasia to India, China, Andaman Islands

13 03 080   **Circus melanoleucus**
Pied Harrier — Eastern Siberia to Mongolia, Korea, Burma, Borneo, Sula Islands

13 03 081   **Circus buffoni**
Long-winged Harrier — Lowlands of tropical South America; Trinidad

13 03 082   **Melierax metabates**
+   *Dark Chanting Goshawk* — Senegal to Ethiopia; Arabia

13 03 083   **Melierax canorus**
+   *Pale Chanting Goshawk* — Semi-deserts of Somalia to South Africa

		Date	Location

13 03 084 **Melierax gabar**
Gabar Goshawk

Savanna and brachystegia woodland of Senegal to Ethiopia; Arabia

13 03 085 **Megatriorchis doriae**
Doria's Goshawk

Confined to New Guinea

13 03 086 **Erythrotriorchis radiatus**
Red Goshawk

Dry woodland of northern Australia to New South Wales

13 03 087 **Accipiter gentilis**
Northern Goshawk

Holarctic circumpolar mountain forests

13 03 088 **Accipiter henstii**
Henst's Goshawk

Humid forests of Madagascar, from sea level to 6,000 feet

13 03 089 **Accipiter melanoleucus**
Black (Great) Sparrow Hawk

Forested area of Africa south of the Sahara

13 03 090 **Accipiter meyerianus**
Meyers' Goshawk

Moluccas, Solomons, New Britain and adjacent islands

13 03 091 **Accipiter buergersi**
Burger's Sparrow Hawk

Low mountain forests of eastern New Guinea

13 03 092 **Accipiter ovampensis**
Ovampo Sparrow Hawk

Savanna and thornbush veld of Africa south of the Sahara

13 03 093 **Accipiter madagascariensis**
Madagascar Sparrow Hawk

Dry savanna and scrub of Madagascar

13 03 094 **Accipiter gularis**
Japanese Sparrow Hawk

Siberia to China, Burma, Malaya, Indochina, Philippines

13 03 095 **Accipiter virgatus**
Besra Sparrow Hawk

Himalayas to southern China, Philippines, Greater Sundas

13 03 096 **Accipiter nanus**
Celebes Sparrow Hawk

Mountains of Celebes Islands

13 03 097 **Accipiter rhodogaster**
Vinous-breasted Sparrow Hawk

Celebes and adjacent islands (Muna, Buton, Peling, Sula)

13 03 098 **Accipiter erythrauchen**
Moluccan Sparrow Hawk

Confined to the Moluccas Islands

13 03 099 **Accipiter cirrhocephalus**
Collared Sparrow Hawk

Australia, Tasmania, New Guinea to the Moluccas

		Date	Location

13 03 100 **Accipiter brachyurus**
New Britain Sparrow Hawk — Confined to New Britain Island

13 03 101 **Accipiter nisus**
European Sparrow Hawk — Palearctic and Oriental mainland

13 03 102 **Accipiter rufiventris**
Rufous-breasted Sparrow Hawk — Montane forest and woodlands of Ethiopia to South Africa

13 03 103 **Accipiter striatus**
Sharp-shinned Hawk — Widespread North and South America; West Indies

13 03 104 **Accipiter erythropus**
Red-thighed Sparrow Hawk — Forests of Gambia, Cameroon to Zaire, Uganda, Angola

13 03 105 **Accipiter minullus**
African Little Sparrow Hawk — Wooded areas from Ethiopia to South Africa

13 03 106 **Accipiter castanilius**
Chestnut-bellied Sparrow Hawk — Forests of Nigeria and Cameroon to eastern Zaire

13 03 107 **Accipiter tachiro**
African Goshawk — Woodlands and forests of Africa south of the Sahara

13 03 108 **Accipiter trivirgatus**
Crested Goshawk — India south of the Himalayas to China, Philippines, Indonesia, Borneo

13 03 109 **Accipiter griseiceps**
Celebes Crested Goshawk — Celebes and adjacent islands (Muna, Buton, Togian)

13 03 110 **Accipiter trinotatus**
Spot-tailed Accipiter — Celebes and adjacent islands (Muna, Buton)

13 03 111 **Accipiter luteoschistaceus**
Blue and Grey Sparrow Hawk — Mountains of New Britain Island

13 03 112 **Accipiter fasciatus**
Australian Goshawk — Australia, Tasmania, New Guinea to the Lesser Sundas

13 03 113 **Accipiter henicogrammus**
Gray's Goshawk — Islands of Batjan, Halmahera and Morotai (Moluccas)

13 03 114 **Accipiter novaehollandiae**
White Goshawk — Australia, Tasmania, New Guinea to Sumbawa, Ceram, Solomons

13 03 115 **Accipiter griseogularis**
Gray-throated Goshawk — Restricted to the Moluccas Islands

Date   Location

13 03 116   **Accipiter**
            melanochlamys
            Black-mantled Goshawk   Mountain forests of New Guinea

13 03 117   **Accipiter imitator**
            Imitator Sparrow Hawk   Choiseul and Ysabel islands (Solomons)

13 03 118   **Accipiter albogularis**
            Pied Goshawk   Solomon Islands, Santa Cruz Islands, Feni Island

13 03 119   **Accipiter haplochrous**
            New Caledonia Sparrow   Forests of New Caledonia
            Hawk

13 03 120   **Accipiter rufitorques**
            Fiji Goshawk   Widespread Fiji Islands

13 03 121   **Accipiter poliocephalus**
            New Guinea Gray-headed   New Guinea and adjacent islands
            Goshawk

13 03 122   **Accipiter princeps**
            New Britain Gray-headed   New Britain Island (known from 3 specimens)
            Goshawk

13 03 123   **Accipiter soloensis**
            Chinese Goshawk   Central China and Korea to Philippines, Celebes,
                                Sundas, Moluccas

13 03 124   **Accipiter brevipes**
            Levant Sparrow Hawk   Balkans to south Russia, Asia Minor; Egypt

13 03 125   **Accipiter badius**
            Shikra   Transcaucasia to China, Formosa, Indochina: Africa
                       south of Sahara

13 03 126   **Accipiter butleri**
            Nicobar Shikra   Confined to the Nicobar Islands

13 03 127   **Accipiter francesii**
            France's Sparrow Hawk   Woodlands of Madagascar and Comoro Islands

13 03 128   **Accipiter collaris**
            Semicollared Hawk   Subtropical rain forest of Venezuela, Colombia,
                                  Ecuador

13 03 129   **Accipiter superciliosus**
            Tiny Sparrow Hawk   Tropical forests of Nicaragua to northern Argentina

13 03 130   **Accipiter gundlachi**
            Gundlach's Hawk   Lowland forests of Cuba (endangered)

13 03 131   **Accipiter cooperii**
            Cooper's Hawk   Southern Canada to Costa Rica

13 03 132   **Accipiter bicolor**
            (chilensis)
            Bicolored Sparrow Hawk   Southern Mexico to Tierra del Fuego

13 03 133   **Accipiter poliogaster**
            Gray-bellied Goshawk   Lowland forests of South America

	Date	Location

13 03 134 Urotriorchis macrourus
African Long-tailed Hawk   Rain forests of west and central Africa to Ghana

13 03 135 Butastur rufipennis
Grasshopper Buzzard   Tropical Africa south of the Sahara
Eagle

13 03 136 Butastur liventer
Rufous-winged Buzzard   Malay peninsula, Borneo, Java, Celebes, Banggai,
Eagle   Sula Islands

13 03 137 Butastur teesa
White-eyed Buzzard   Northwest India to Assam, Burma, Tenasserim

13 03 138 Butastur indicus
Grey-faced Buzzard Eagle   East Asia, Japan to Malaysia, southwest Pacific
                                islands

**13 03 139 Kaupifalco
monogrammicus**
Lizard Buzzard   Dense savanna and thornbush of Africa south of the
                                Sahara

13 03 140 Leucopternis schistacea
Slate-colored Hawk   Forests of Amazon basin

13 03 141 Leucopternis plumbea
Plumbeous Hawk   Tropical forests of eastern Panama, Colombia,
                                Ecuador, Peru

13 03 142 Leucopternis princeps
Barred Hawk   Subtropical mountain forests of Costa Rica to
                                northern Ecuador

13 03 143 Leucopternis melanops
Black-faced Hawk   Amazonia north of the Amazon River

13 03 144 Leucopternis kuhli
White-browed Hawk   Amazonia south of the Amazon River

13 03 145 Leucopternis lacernulata
White-necked Hawk   Wooded and forested regions of eastern and
                                southern Brazil

**13 03 146 Leucopternis
semiplumbea**
Semiplumbeous Hawk   Humid Honduras and Nicaragua to Panama,
                                Colombia, Ecuador

13 03 147 Leucopternis albicollis
White Hawk   Tropical and subtropical Mexico to Amazonia;
                                Trinidad

**13 03 148 Leucopternis
occidentalis**
Grey-backed Hawk   Tropical and subtropical western Ecuador

13 03 149 Leucopternis polionota
Mantled Hawk   Eastern and southern Brazil, adjacent Paraguay,
                                Argentina

		Date	Location

13 03 150 **Buteogallus anthracinus**
Common Black Hawk

Southwest United States to Peru; West Indies, Cuba

13 03 151 **Buteogallus aequinoctialis**
Rufous Crab Hawk

Lowland swamps from Orinoco delta in Venezuela to Paraná, Brazil

13 03 152 **Buteogallus urubitinga**
Great Black Hawk

Tropical America from Mexico to Argentina; Trinidad; Togago

13 03 153 **Harpyhaliaetus solitarius**
Solitary Eagle

Mountain forests of southern Mexico to Peru

13 03 154 **Harpyhaliaetus coronatus**
Crowned Eagle

Chaco of eastern Bolivia, Paraguay, Brazil to northern Argentina

13 03 155 **Heterospizias meridionalis**
Savannah Hawk

Tropical South America from eastern Panama to Argentina

13 03 156 **Busarellus nigricollis**
✝ *Black-collared Hawk*

Tropical lowlands from southern Mexico to Paraguay, Argentina

13 03 157 **Geranoaetus melanoleucus**
✝ *Black-chested Buzzard-Eagle*

Widespread dry woodlands of South America

13 03 158 **Parabuteo unicinctus**
Bay-winged (Harris') Hawk

Southwest United States to Argentina, Chile

13 03 159 **Buteo nitidus**
Gray Hawk

Tropics and subtropics of southwest United States to Argentina

13 03 160 **Buteo magnirostris**
✝ *Roadside Hawk*

Lower elevations in tropical America from Mexico to Argentina

13 03 161 **Buteo leucorrhous**
✝ *Rufous-thighed Hawk*
White-rumped

Widespread broken forest in subtropical South America

13 03 162 **Buteo ridgwayi**
Ridgway's Hawk

Hispaniola and adjacent islands

13 03 163 **Buteo lineatus**
Red-shouldered Hawk

Mixed deciduous woodlands of southern Canada to central Mexico

13 03 164 **Buteo platypterus**
Broad-winged Hawk

Mixed forests of eastern North America to Brazil, Bolivia, Peru

		Date	Location

13 03 165 **Buteo brachyurus**
(albigula)
Short-tailed Hawk

Widespread southern Florida to Brazil, Argentina, Chile

13 03 166 **Buteo swainsonii**
Swainson's Hawk

Arid regions of western North America; winters to Argentina

13 03 167 **Buteo galapagoensis**
Galapagos Hawk

Galapagos Islands (endangered—population about 130 birds)

13 03 168 **Buteo albicaudatus**
White-tailed Hawk

Tropical, subtropical Texas to Argentina; Curacao; Trinidad; Aruba

13 03 169 **Buteo polyosoma**
Red-backed Hawk

Andes of Colombia to Tierra del Fuego; Falklands; Mas Afuera Island

13 03 170 **Buteo peocilochrous**
Variable (Gurney's) Hawk   Puna of Colombia to Chile, Argentina

13 03 171 **Buteo albonotatus**
Zone-tailed Hawk

Southwest United States to Brazil, Bolivia, Paraguay; Trinidad

13 03 172 **Buteo solitarius**
Hawaiian Hawk

Restricted to the Island of Hawaii (endangered)

13 03 173 **Buteo ventralis**
Rufous-tailed Hawk

Patagonian forests of southern Chile and Argentina

13 03 174 **Buteo jamaicensis**
(harlani)
Red-tailed Hawk

Widespread Alaska to Panama; West Indies

13 03 175 **Buteo buteo (vulpinus)**
Common Buzzard

Widespread Palearctic, Oriental regions

13 03 176 **Buteo oreophilus**
African Mountain Buzzard   Mountain forests of southern Ethiopia to South Africa

13 03 177 **Buteo brachypterus**
Madagascar Buzzard   Woodlands and savanna of Madagascar

13 03 178 **Buteo lagopus**
Rough-legged Hawk   Northern forests and tundra of Holarctic region

13 03 179 **Buteo rufinus**
Long-legged Buzzard

Dry open plains of southeast Europe,North Africa to Afghanistan

13 03 180 **Buteo hemilasius**
Upland Buzzard

Open steppes and mountain slopes of central to southeast Asia

13 03 181 **Buteo regalis**
Ferruginous Hawk   Dry country of southern Canada to northern Mexico

	Date	Location

13 03 182 Buteo auguralis
African Red-tailed Buzzard
Savanna and forests from southern Ethiopia to Sierra Leone, Angola

13 03 183 Buteo rufofuscus
+
Augur Buzzard
Savanna and forests of Ethiopia, Somalia to South Africa

13 03 184 Morphnus guianensis
+
Guiana Crested Eagle
Lowland tropical forests of Honduras to Paraguay, Argentina

13 03 185 Harpia harpyja
Harpy Eagle
Tropical lowlands of southern Mexico to Brazil, Bolivia, Argentina

13 03 186 Harpyopsis novaeguineae
New Guinea Harpy Eagle
Low mountain forests of New Guinea

13 03 187 Pithecophaga jefferyi
Philippine Eagle
Larger islands of Philippines (endangered)

13 03 188 Ictinaetus malayensis
Indian Black Eagle
India to Burma, Malaya, Celebes, Moluccas Islands

13 03 189 Aquila pomarina
Lesser Spotted Eagle
Discontinuously Palearctic; India, Burma, Africa

13 03 190 Aquila clanga
Greater Spotted Eagle
Widespread Palearctic region, Oriental mainland

13 03 191 Aquila rapax (nipalensis)
Tawny (Steppe) Eagle
Widespread Palearctic, Ethiopian regions

13 03 192 Aquila heliaca
Imperial Eagle
Wooded plains of Palearctic region; India, China, Indochina

13 03 193 Aquila wahlbergi
Wahlberg's Eagle
Savanna of Africa south of the Sahara

13 03 194 Aquila gurneyi
Gurney's Eagle
New Guinea, Arus, Japen, western Papuan Islands, Moluccas

13 03 195 Aquila chrysaetos
+
Golden Eagle
Widespread Holarctic regions to North Africa, Himalayas, Mexico

13 03 196 Aquila audax
Wedge-tailed Eagle
Australia, Tasmania; accidental New Guinea

13 03 197 Aquila verreauxi
Verreaux's (Black) Eagle
Mountains, deserts, savanna of Africa south of the Sahara

		Date	Location
13 03 198	**Hieraaetus fasciatus** (spilogaster) *Bonelli's Eagle*		Mediterranean basin to China, Lesser Sundas; Africa south of Sahara
13 03 199	**Hieraaetus pennatus** *Booted Eagle*		Widespread Palearctic, Ethiopian regions; Oriental mainland
13 03 200	**Hieraaetus morphnoides** *Little Eagle*		Forests of New Guinea, Australia (not Tasmania)
13 03 201	**Hieraaetus dubius** (ayresii) *Ayres' Hawk-Eagle*		Woodlands and forests of Africa south of the Sahara
13 03 202	**Hieraaetus kienerii** *Chestnut-bellied Hawk-Eagle*		Forests of Sri Lanka, India to the Philippines, Celebes
13 03 203	**Spizastur melanoleucus** *Black-and-white Hawk-Eagle*		Tropical lowlands of southern Mexico to northern Argentina
13 03 204	**Lophaetus occipitalis** *Long-crested Eagle*		Woodlands of Africa south of the Sahara
13 03 205	**Spizaetus africanus** *Cassin's Hawk-Eagle*		Rain forests of Togo to Cameroon, Gabon, Zaire
13 03 206	**Spizaetus cirrhatus** *Changeable Hawk-Eagle*		Widespread tropical Oriental mainland and islands
13 03 207	**Spizaetus nipalensis** *Mountain Hawk-Eagle*		Japan, China, Formosa, Hainan to India, Sri Lanka
13 03 208	**Spizaetus bartelsi** *Java Hawk-Eagle*		Wooded hills of western Java (rare)
13 03 209	**Spizaetus lanceolatus** *Celebes Hawk-Eagle*		Celebes and adjacent islands (Buton, Muna, Peling, Sulas)
13 03 210	**Spizaetus philippensis** *Philippine Hawk-Eagle*		Philippine Islands, including Palawan (rare)
13 03 211	**Spizaetus alboniger** *Blyth's Hawk-Eagle*		Mountain forests of Malay Peninsula, Sumatra, Borneo
13 03 212	**Spizaetus nanus** *Wallace's Hawk-Eagle*		Lowland forests of Malaya, Sumatra, Borneo
13 03 213	**Spizaetus tyrannus** *Black Hawk-Eagle*		Tropical lowlands of southern Mexico to northern Argentina
13 03 214	**Spizaetus ornatus** *Ornate Hawk-Eagle*		Tropical southern Mexico to northern Argentina; Trinidad; Tobago

		Date	Location

13 03 215	**Stephanoaetus coronatus**		
✝	*Crowned Eagle*		Africa south of the Sahara
13 03 216	**Oroaetus isidori**		
	Isidor's Eagle		Andean forests of Venezuela to Bolivia, northwest Argentina
13 03 217	**Polemaetus bellicosus**		
	Martial Eagle		Savanna and thornbush of Africa south of the Sahara

ORDER: FALCONIFORMES
FAMILY: SAGITTARIIDAE (Secretary Bird)

13 04 001	**Sagittarius serpentarius**		
	Secretary Bird		Open grassy country of Africa south of the Sahara

ORDER: FALCONIFORMES
FAMILY: FALCONIDAE (Falcons)

13 05 001	**Daptrius ater**		
	Yellow-throated Caracara		Widespread Amazon basin
13 05 002	**Daptrius americanus**		
✝	*Red-throated Caracara*		Extreme southern Mexico to southern Brazil, eastern Peru
13 05 003	**Phalcoboenus carunculatus**		
	Carunculated Caracara		Upper treeless Andes of Ecuador, Colombia
13 05 004	**Phalcoboenus megalopterus**		
	Mountain Caracara		Treeless Andes of Peru, Bolivia, Chile, northwest Argentina
13 05 005	**Phalcoboenus albogularis**		
✝	*White-throated Caracara*		Andean slopes of Argentina, Chile to Tierra del Fuego
13 05 006	**Phalcoboenus australis**		
	Striated (Forster's) Caracara		Falkland Islands; casual Tierra del Fuego
13 05 007	**Polyborus lutosus**		
	Guadalupe Caracara		Extinct. Inhabited Guadalupe Island off Baja California
13 05 008	**Polyborus plancus (cheriway)**		
	Crested (Common) Caracara		Southern Florida to Tierra del Fuego; Cuba; Falkland islands

	Date	Location

13 05 009   **Milvago chimango**
+   *Chimango Caracara*   Southern Brazil, Paraguay to Tierra del Fuego; Cape Horn Islands

13 05 010   **Milvago chimachima**
                       Yellow-headed Caracara   Savanna of Panama to Peru, Bolivia, northern Argentina

13 05 011   **Herpetotheres cachinnans**
                       Laughing Falcon   Tropical lowlands from Mexico to Bolivia, Brazil, northern Argentina

13 05 012   **Micrastur ruficollis**
+   *Barred Forest Falcon*   Tropical and subtropical forests of Mexico to northern Argentina

13 05 013   **Micrastur gilvicollis**
                       Lined Forest Falcon   Widespread tropical rainforests of Amazon basin

13 05 014   **Micrastur plumbeus**
                       Plumbeous Forest Falcon   Lowland forests of western Colombia, adjacent Ecuador (rare)

13 05 015   **Micrastur mirandollei**
                       Slaty-backed Forest Falcon   Tropical lowlands of Costa Rica to Peru, Amazonian Brazil (rare)

13 05 016   **Micrastur semitorquatus**
                       Collared Forest Falcon   Forested tropical Mexico to northern Argentina

13 05 017   **Micrastur buckleyi**
                       Buckley's Forest Falcon   Amazonian Ecuador and northeast Peru (known from 10 specimens)

13 05 018   **Spiziapteryx circumcinctus**
+   *Spot-winged Falconet*   Semi-deserts and savanna of western and northern Argentina

13 05 019   **Polihierax semitorquatus**
                       African Pygmy Falcon   Desert and thornbush country of Somalia and Sudan to South Africa

13 05 020   **Polihierax insignis**
                       White-rumped (Fielden's) Falconet   Burma, Tenasserim, Thailand, Cochinchina to South Annam

13 05 021   **Microhierax caerulescens**
                       Red-legged Falconet   Western Himalayas to Burma, Annam, Indochina

13 05 022   **Microhierax fringillarius**
                       Black-legged Falconet   Forests of Tenasserim, Malaya, Sumatra, Borneo, Java, Bali

13 05 023   **Microhierax latifrons**
                       Bornean Falconet   Forests of northwest Borneo (Darvil Bay to Lawas)

	Date	Location

13 05 024 Microhierax erythrogonys
Philippine Falconet
Philippines (Luzon, Mindanao, Mindoro, Bohol, Samar, Cebu, Negros)

13 05 025 Microhierax melanoleucus
Pied Flaconet
Forests of Assam, southeast China and upper Laos

13 05 026 Falco naumanni
Lesser Kestrel
Mediterranean basin to eastern China; Africa

13 05 027 Falco rupicoloides
Greater (White-eyed) Kestrel
Acacia belt of Kenya, Tanzania to South Africa

13 05 028 Falco alopex
Fox Kestrel
Ghana to the Sudan, southern Ethiopia and Kenya

12 05 029 Falco sparverius
American Kestrel
Alaska to Tierra del Fuego; West Indies

13 05 030 Falco tinnunculus
Eurasian (Common) Kestrel
Palearctic, Ethiopian regions; Canary, Cape Verde, Azores

13 05 031 Falco newtoni
Madagascar Kestrel
Madagascar, Aldabra, rarely Comoro Islands (endangered)

13 05 032 Falco punctatus
Mauritius Kestrel
Dense forests of southwest island of Mauritius (almost extinct)

13 05 033 Falco araea
Seychelles Kestrel
Seychelles Islands (Mahe and nearby islands— endangered)

13 05 034 Falco moluccensis
Moluccan Kestrel
Java to Bali, Timor, Celebes and Moluccas

13 05 035 Falco cenchroides
Nankeen (Australian) Kestrel
Australia, New Guinea highlands; migrates to Lesser Sundas, Java

13 05 036 Falco ardosiaceus
Gray Kestrel
Wetter savanna of Africa south of the Sahara

13 05 037 Falco dickinsoni
Dickinson's Kestrel
Low savanna of Tanzania to Angola, Malawi

13 05 038 Falco zoniventris
Madagascar Banded Kestrel
Mainly humid lowland forests of Madagascar

13 05 039 Falco vespertinus
Red-footed Falcon
Widespread Palearctic, Ethiopian regions

13 05 040 Falco chicquera
Red-headed Falcon
Peninsular India; Africa south of the Sahara

	Date	Location

13 05 041   Falco columbarius
   Merlin
Widespread Holarctic regions

13 05 042   Falco berigora
   Brown Falcon
Australia, Tasmania, New Guinea

13 05 043   Falco novaezeelandiae
   New Zealand Falcon
New Zealand (both main and many offshore islands)

13 05 044   Falco subbuteo
   European Hobby
Widespread Palearctic region; migrates to Africa, northern India

13 05 045   Falco cuvieri
   African Hobby
Wetter savanna of Africa south of the Sahara

13 05 046   Falco severus
   Oriental Hobby
Himalayas to Indochina; Sundas, Celebes, Philippines to New Guinea

13 05 047   Falco longipennis
   Little Falcon
Australia; winters New Guinea, New Britain, Moluccas

13 05 048   Falco eleanorae
   Eleanora's Falcon
Canaries; Mediterranean basin islands; Madagascar; Reunion

12 05 049   Falco concolor
   Sooty Falcon
Libyan Desert to Red Sea; occasional Madagascar, Mauritius

13 05 050   Falco rufigularis
+   *Bat Falcon*
Humid tropical lowlands of Mexico to northern Argentina

13 05 051   Falco femoralis
   Aplomado Falcon
Arid southwest United States to Tierra del Fuego; Trinidad

13 05 052   Falco hypoleucos
   Gray Falcon
Arid interior of Australia

13 05 053   Falco subniger
   Black Falcon
Widespread Australia (absent in Tasmania)

13 05 054   Falco biarmicus
   Lanner Falcon
Africa to Arabia, Armenia, Iraq

13 05 055   Falco mexicanus
   Prairie Falcon
Arid interior North America (British Columbia to Mexico)

13 05 056   Falco jugger
   Lagger Falcon
Baluchistan through India to Assam, Burma

13 05 057   Falco cherrug (altaicus)
   Saker Falcon
Widespread Palearctic region

		Date	Location

13 05 058 **Falco rusticolus**
Gyrfalcon

Mountains and tundra of Arctic Europe, Asia, North America

13 05 059 **Falco deiroleucus**
Orange-breasted Falcon

Mountain forests of southern Mexico to Argentina, Paraguay

13 05 060 **Falco fasciinucha**
Taita Falcon

Dry country from southern Ethiopia to the Zambezi River (endangered)

13 05 061 **Falco kreyenborgi**
+ Pallid (Kleinschmidt's) Falcon

Extreme southern Chile, Argentina (endangered)

13 05 062 **Falco peregrinus**
+ Peregrine Falcon

Practially cosmopolitan—wide distribution worldwide

ORDER: GALLIFORMES
FAMILY: MEGAPODIIDAE (Megapodes)

14 01 001 **Megapodius freycinet**
Incubator Bird

Widespread Australasian region to Philippines

14 01 002 **Megapodius laperouse**
Micronesian Incubator Bird

Micronesian Islands

14 01 003 **Megapodius pritchardii**
Nevafou Incubator Bird

Islands of central Polynesia

14 01 004 **Eulipoa wallacei**
Moluccan Scrub Hen

Moluccas and Misol Islands

14 01 005 **Leipoa ocellata**
Mallee Fowl

Endemic to southern Australia

14 01 006 **Alectura lathami**
Brush Turkey

Australia (Cape York Peninsula to Victoria)

14 01 007 **Talegalla cuvieri**
Red-billed Brush Turkey

Lowland forests of northwest New Guinea

14 01 008 **Talegalla fuscirostris**
Black-billed Brush Turkey

Forested lowlands of New Guinea, Aru Islands

14 01 009 **Talegalla jobiensis**
Brown-collared Brush Turkey

Lowland forests of northern New Guinea

14 01 010 **Aepypodius arfakianus**
Wattled Brush Turkey

High mountains of New Guinea, Misol Island

14 01 011 **Aepypodius bruijnii**
Bruijn's Brush Turkey

Waigeu Island (New Guinea—possibly extinct)

14 01 012 **Macrocephalon maleo**
Gray's Brush Turkey

Celebes Islands (endangered)

	Date	Location

ORDER: GALLIFORMES
FAMILY: CRACIDAE (Curassows, Guans, Chachalacas)

14 02 001 **Ortalis vetula**
Plain Chachalaca   Southern tip of Texas to Nicaragua

14 02 002 **Ortalis cinereiceps**
Gray-headed Chachalaca   Honduras to Colombia (west of the Andes)

14 02 003 **Ortalis garrula**
Chestnut-winged   Central America to Colombia
Chachalaca

14 02 004 **Ortalis ruficauda**
Rufous-vented Chachalaca   Colombia, Venezuela; Tobago; Lesser Antilles

14 02 005 **Ortalis erythroptera**
Rufous-headed   Western Ecuador to extreme southwestern Peru
Chachalaca

14 02 006 **Ortalis poliocephala**
(wagleri)
West Mexican Chachalaca   Mexico (southern Sonora to Oaxaca, Chiapas)

14 02 007 **Ortalis canicollis**
Chaco Chachalaca   Chaco of eastern Bolivia to northern Argentina

14 02 008 **Ortalis leucogastra**
White-bellied Chachalaca   Pacific slope of southern Mexico to Nicaragua

14 02 009 **Ortalis motmot**
Variable Chachalaca   Tropical Guianas, Venezuela, Amazonian Brazil

14 02 010 **Penelope argyrotis**
Band-tailed Guan   Highland forests of northern Colombia and Venezuela

14 02 011 **Penelope barbata**
Bearded Guan   Western Andes of Ecuador to Peru

14 02 012 **Penelope montagnii**
Andean Guan   Andes of Venezuela, Colombia to northern Argentina

14 02 013 **Penelope ortoni**
Baudó Guan   Colombia, Ecuador (humid tropics west of Andes)

14 02 014 **Penelope marail**
Marail Guan   Guianas, Venezuela, Brazil north of the Amazon

14 02 015 **Penelope superciliaris**
Rusty-margined Guan   Lowland tropical forest of Brazil to northeast
                                      Argentina

14 02 016 **Penelope dabbenei**
Red-faced Guan   Bolivia to Argentina (slopes of eastern Andes)

14 02 017 **Penelope obscura**
Dusky-legged Guan   Coastal southwest Brazil to northwest Argentina

14 02 018 **Penelope jacquacu**
Spix's Guan   Widespread lower subtropical Amazon basin

	Date	Location
14 02 019 **Penelope albipennis** † *White-winged Guan*		Dry forests of northwest Peru (on verge of extinction)
14 02 020 **Penelope perspicax** *Cauca Guan*		Subtropical western and central Andes of Colombia
14 02 021 **Penelope purpurascens** *Crested Guan*		Mexico to Venezuela, Ecuador
14 02 022 **Penelope jacucaca** *White-browed Guan*		Northeast Brazil (Ceará, Paraiba to Bahia)
14 02 023 **Penelope ochrogaster** *Chestnut-bellied Guan*		Matto Grosso to eastern Brazil (rare)
14 02 024 **Penelope pileata** *White-crested Guan*		Amazonian Brazil (lower Rio Madeira to Tapajos)
14 02 025 **Aburria pipile** (cujubi) *Common Piping Guan*		Widespread tropical forests of Amazon basin; Trinidad
14 02 026 **Aburria jacutinga** *Black-fronted Piping Guan*		Northern South America to northeast Argentina
14 02 027 **Aburria aburri** *Wattled Guan*		Andes of Colombia to Peru (Cuzco)
14 02 028 **Chamaepetes unicolor** *Black Guan*		Cloud forests of Costa Rica and Panama
14 02 029 **Chamaepetes goudotii** *Sickle-winged Guan*		Andes of Colombia, Ecuador and Peru
14 02 030 **Penelopina nigra** *Highland Guan*		Mountain forests of Mexico to Honduras, Nicaragua
14 02 031 **Oreophasis derbianus** *Horned Guan*		Cloud forests of Chiapas and Guatemala (endangered)
14 02 032 **Nothocrax urumutum** *Nocturnal Curassow*		Dense rain forests of western Amazon basin
14 02 033 **Crax tomentosa** *Crestless Curassow*		Guyana, Venezuela to Amazonian Colombia, adjacent Brazil
14 02 034 **Crax salvini** *Salvin's Curassow*		Western Amazon basin
14 02 035 **Crax mitu** *Razor-billed Curassow*		Amazon basin south of the Amazon River
14 02 036 **Crax pauxi** *Helmeted Curassow*		Cloud forests of Venezuela to northeast Colombia
14 02 037 **Crax unicornis** *Southern Helmeted Curassow*		Subtropical eastern Andes of Bolivia

	Date	Location
14 02 038 **Crax rubra** *Great Curassow*		Tropical forests of Mexico to Colombia, Ecuador
14 02 039 **Crax alberti** *Blue-billed Curassow*		Colombia (Santa Marta Mountains to Magdalena Valley)
14 02 040 **Crax daubentoni** *Yellow-knobbed Curassow*		Northern Venezuela, immediately adjacent Colombia
14 02 041 **Crax alector** *Black Curassow*		Tropical forests of northern Amazon basin
14 02 042 **Crax globulosa** *Wattled Curassow*		Tropical forests of western Amazon basin
14 02 043 **Crax fasciolata** *Bare-faced Curassow*		Brazil to northern Argentina
14 02 044 **Crax blumenbachii** *Red-billed Curassow*		Southeast Brazil (nearly extinct)

ORDER: GALLIFORMES
FAMILY: MELEAGRIDIDAE (Turkeys)

14 03 001 **Meleagris gallopavo** *Common Turkey*		United States to southern Mexico
14 03 002 **Agriocharis ocellata** *Ocellated Turkey*		Southern Mexico to Guatemala, Belize

ORDER: GALLIFORMES
FAMILY: TETRAONIDAE (Grouse)

14 04 001 **Dendragapus falcipennis** *Siberian Spruce Grouse*		Coniferous forests of northeast Asia
14 04 002 **Dendragapus canadensis** *Spruce Grouse*		Alaska to United States
14 04 003 **Dendragapus obscurus** *Blue Grouse*		Alaska to southern United States
14 04 004 **Lagopus lagopus (scoticus)** *Willow Ptarmigan*		Widespread Holarctic region
14 04 005 **Lagopus mutus** *Rock Ptarmigan*		Holarctic circumpolar
14 04 006 **Lagopus leucurus** *White-tailed Ptarmigan*		Alaska to the Cascade Mountains
`4 04 007 **Tetrao mlokosiewiczi** *Caucasian Blackcock*		Alpine meadows of Greater and Lesser Caucusus Mountains

		Date	Location
14 04 008	**Tetrao tetrix** *Black Grouse*		Northern Palearctic region
14 04 009	**Tetrao parvirostris** *Black-billed Capercaillie*		Southeast Siberia to northern Manchuria
14 04 010	**Tetrao urogallus** *Capercaillie*		Coniferous forests of northern Palearctic region
14 04 011	**Bonasa umbellus** *Ruffed Grouse*		Forests of Alaska, Canada and United States
14 04 012	**Bonasa sewerzowi** *Severtzov's Hazel Grouse*		Mountains of Tsinghai, Kansu, Sikang, Szechwan
14 04 013	**Bonasa bonasia** *Hazel Grouse*		Widespread Palearctic region
14 04 014	**Centrocercus urophasianus** *Sage Grouse*		Prairies of Canada to southwest United States
14 04 015	**Tympanuchus phasianellus** *Sharp-tailed Grouse*		Prairies of Alaska to New Mexico
14 04 016	**Tympanuchus cupido** *Greater Prairie Chicken*		Prairies of Canada to Texas
14 04 017	**Tympanuchus pallidicinctus** *Lesser Prairie Chicken*		Southwest United States (endangered)

ORDER: GALLIFORMES
FAMILY: PHASIANIDAE (Pheasants)

14 05 001	**Dendrortyx barbatus** *Bearded Wood-Partridge*		Mexico (cloud forests of Vera Cruz, San Luis Potosi—rare)
14 05 002	**Dendrortyx macroura** *Long-tailed Wood-Partridge*		Mexico (Jalisco to Oaxaca)
14 05 003	**Dendrortyx leucophrys** *Highland Wood-Partridge*		Southern Mexico to Costa Rica
14 05 004	**Oreortyx picta** *Mountain Quail*		Highlands of western United States to Baja California
14 05 005	**Callipepla squamata** *Scaled Quail*		Southern United States to Central America
14 05 006	**Lophortyx californica** *California Quail*		Oregon, California and Baja California
14 05 007	**Lophortyx gambelii** *Gambel's Quail*		Southwest United States to northwest Mexico

		Date	Location
14 05 008	**Lophortyx douglasii** *Elegant Quail*		Western Mexico (Sonora to Jalisco, Colima)
14 05 009	**Lophortyx leucoprosopon** *Reichenow's Quail*		Doubtful species (probable hybrid *L. gambelii* x *L. douglasii*
14 05 010	**Philortyx fasciatus** *Banded Quail*		Highlands of south-central Mexico
14 05 011	**Colinus virginianus** *Common Bobwhite*		United States to Guatemala; introduced West Indies
14 05 012	**Colinus nigrogularis** *Yucatán Bobwhite*		Mexico (Yucatán peninsula) to Honduras, Nicaragua
14 05 013	**Colinus leucopogon** *Spot-bellied Bobwhite*		Highlands and Pacific slope of Guatemala to Costa Rica
14 05 014	**Colinus cristatus** *Crested Bobwhite*		Panama to northern Brazil
14 05 015	**Odontophorus gujanensis** *Marbled Wood-Quail*		Costa Rica to Bolivia
14 04 016	**Odontophorus capueira** *Spot-winged Wood-Quail*		Eastern Brazil to northeast Argentina
14 05 017	**Odontophorus erythrops** *Rufous-fronted Wood-Quail*		Honduras to western Colombia and Ecuador
14 05 018	**Odontophorus atrifrons** *Black-fronted Wood-Quail*		Mountain forests of northern Venezuela and Colombia
14 05 019	**Odontophorus melanonotus** *Dark-backed Wood-Quail*		Northwest Ecuador (lower subtropical zone)
14 05 020	**Odontophorus hyperthyrus** *Chestnut Wood-Quail*		Andes of Colombia (subtropical forests)
14 05 021	**Odontophorus speciosus** *Rufous-breasted Wood-Quail*		Ecuador, Peru, Bolivia (forests of tropical zone)
14 05 022	**Odontophorus strophium** *Gorgeted Wood-Quail*		Colombia (known only from eastern Andes at Subia)
14 05 023	**Odontophorus dialeucos** *Taracuna Wood-Quail*		Panama (highlands of Darien, possibly adjacent Colombia)

		Date	Location

14 05 024 **Odontophorus columbianus**
Venezuelan Wood-Quail
Northern Venezuela (Táchira; coastal Carabobo to Miranda)

14 05 025 **Odontophorus leucolaemus**
Black-breasted Wood-Quail
Highlands of Costa Rica and western Panama

14 05 026 **Odontophorus balliviani**
Stripe-faced Wood-Quail
Subtropical Andes of Peru (Cuzco) to Bolivia (Cochabamba)

14 05 027 **Odontophorus stellatus**
Starred Wood-Quail
Western Amazon basin (tropical zone)

14 05 028 **Odontophorus guttatus**
Spotted Wood-Quail
Highlands of southern Mexico to western Panama

14 05 029 **Dactylortyx thoracicus**
Singing Quail
Mexico to El Salvador, Honduras

14 05 030 **Cyrtonyx montezumae**
Montezuma (Harlequin) Quail
Southwest United States to southern Mexico

14 05 031 **Cyrtonyx sallei**
Salle's Quail
Mexico (Guerro—probable race of *C. montezumae*)

14 05 032 **Cyrtonyx ocellatus**
Ocellated Quail
Southern Mexico to Honduras, Nicaragua

14 05 033 **Rhynchortyx cinctus**
Tawny-faced Quail
Caribbean slope of Honduras to northwest Ecuador

14 05 034 **Lerwa lerwa**
Snow Partridge
Himalayas of India, Tibet, western China

14 05 035 **Ammoperdix griseogularis**
See-see Partridge
Southwest Turkey, Iraq to western India

14 05 036 **Ammoperdix heyi**
Sand Partridge
Nile Valley to Sinai peninsula (casual northeast Ethiopia)

14 05 037 **Tetraogallus caucasicus**
Caucasian Snowcock
Rocky heights of Caucasus Mountains

14 05 038 **Tetraogallus caspius**
Caspian Snowcock
Mountains of eastern Turkey to Armenia, Transcaspia

14 05 039 **Tetraogallus tibetanus**
Tibetan Snowcock
Eastern Pamirs to Kansu, Kashmir and Tibetan Himalayas

14 05 040 **Tetraogallus altaicus**
Altai Snowcock
Altai and Sajan Mountains of central Asia

		Date	Location
14 05 041	**Tetraogallus himalayensis** *Himalayan Snowcock*		Himalayas of Afghanistan to Nepal, Tsinghai, Kansu
14 05 042	**Tetraophasis obscurus** *Verreaux's Monal Partridge*		Eastern Tibet to western China
14 05 043	**Tetraophasis szechenyii** *Tibetan Pheasant Grouse*		Mountains of Tibet to western China
14 05 044	**Alectoris graeca** *Rock Partridge*		Alps of France, Italy to Austria, Bulgaria
14 05 045	**Alectoris chukar** *Chukar*		Balkan Peninsula to Pakistan
14 05 046	**Alectoris magna** *Przhevalski's Rock Partridge*		Desolate regions of Tsinghai to Hweiming
14 05 047	**Alectoris philbyi** *Philby's Rock Partridge*		Desolate regions of western Arabia to northern Yemen
14 05 048	**Alectoris barbara** *Barbary Partridge*		Canaries; North Africa to northwest Egypt; Sardinia
14 05 049	**Alectoris rufa** *Red-legged Partridge*		France to Iberian Peninsula, Italy; Corsica
14 05 050	**Alectoris melanocephala** *Arabian Partridge*		Arabia to Aden Protectorate
14 05 051	**Anurophasis monorthonyx** *Snow Mountain Quail*		Snow Mountains of New Guinea
14 05 052	**Francolinus francolinus** *Black Francolin*		Asia Minor to Iraq, Iran, India, Assam
14 05 053	**Francolinus pictus** *Painted Partridge*		Wet grasslands of Indian Subcontinent; Sri Lanka
14 05 054	**Francolinus pintadeanus** *Chinese Francolin*		Widespread southeast Asia
14 05 055	**Francolinus afer** *Red-necked Spurfowl*		Widespread Africa south of the Sahara
14 05 056	**Francolinus swainsonii** *Swainson's Francolin*		Moist bushveld of Rhodesia, Zambia
14 05 057	**Francolinus rufopictus** *Gray-breasted Francolin*		Tanzania, Uganda
14 05 058	**Francolinus leucoscepus** *Yellow-necked Spurfowl*		Somalia, Ethiopia, Kenya, Uganda, Tanzania
14 05 059	**Francolinus erckelii** *Erckel's Francolin*		Eritrea to Egyptian Sudan

		Date	Location
14 05 060	**Francolinus ochropectus** *Tadjoura Francolin*		Confined to juniper forests of Somalia (endangered)
14 05 061	**Francolinus castaneicollis** *Chestnut-naped Francolin*		Ethiopia to Somalia
14 05 062	**Francolinus jacksoni** *Jackson's Francolin*		Mountain forests of Kenya
14 05 063	**Francolinus nobilis** *Handsome Francolin*		Mountain forests of western Uganda, eastern Zaire
14 05 064	**Francolinus camerunensis** *Cameroon Francolin*		Confined to forests of Cameroon Mountain (5000–7000 feet)
14 05 065	**Francolinus swierstrai** *Swierstra's Francolin*		Restricted to central Angola (endangered)
14 05 066	**Francolinus ahantensis** *Ahanta Francolin*		Guinea to Nigeria, Gambia
14 05 067	**Francolinus squamatus** *Scaly Francolin*		Widespread Africa south of the Sahara
14 05 068	**Francolinus griseostriatus** *Gray-striped Francolin*		Restricted to northern Angola (rare and local)
14 05 069	**Francolinus bicalcaratus** *Double-spurred Francolin*		Western Morocco, Senegal to Cameroon
14 05 070	**Francolinus icterorhynchus** *Heuglin's Francolin*		French Equatorial Africa to Zaire, the Sudan
14 05 071	**Francolinus clappertoni** *Clapperton's Francolin*		Nigeria, the Sudan, Uganda, Kenya, Ethiopia
14 05 072	**Francolinus hildebrandti** *Hildebrandt's Francolin*		Zaire to Kenya, Malawi
14 05 073	**Francolinus natalensis** *Natal Francolin*		Scrub country of Zambia to Natal
14 05 074	**Francolinus hartlaubi** *Hartlaub's Francolin*		Angola to Southwest Africa
14 05 075	**Francolinus harwoodi** *Harwood's Francolin*		Southern Ethiopia (known only from Blue Nile gorge)
14 05 076	**Francolinus adspersus** *Red-billed Francolin*		Southern Angola to Zambia, Southwest Africa
14 05 077	**Francolinus capensis** *Cape Francolin*		Riverside scrub of southwestern Cape Province
14 05 078	**Francolinus sephaena (rovuma)** *Crested Francolin*		Widespread Africa south of Sahara

		Date	Location
14 05 079	**Francolinus streptophorus** Ring-necked Francolin		Kenya, Uganda, Tanzania
14 05 080	**Francolinus psilolaemus** Montane Francolin		High mountains of East Africa
14 05 081	**Francolinus shelleyi** Shelley's Francolin		Africa south of the Sahara
14 05 082	**Francolinus africanus** Gray-winged Francolin		Ethiopia to South Africa
14 05 083	**Francolinus levaillantoides** Orange River Francolin		Spottily distributed Zambia to Southwest Africa
14 05 084	**Francolinus levaillantii** Red-winged Francolin		Kenya, Uganda to South Africa
14 05 085	**Francolinus finschi** Finsch's Francolin		*Brachystegia* woodlands of Angola to Gabon (rare)
14 05 086	**Francolinus coqui** Coqui Francolin		Ethiopia to East and central Africa
14 05 087	**Francolinus albogularis** White-throated Francolin		Dense bush of eastern Angola, Zambia
14 05 088	**Francolinus schlegelii** Schlegel's Francolin		Scrub of southwestern Sudan to Zaire
14 05 089	**Francolinus lathami** Forest Francolin		Sierra Leone to Zaire, Uganda, the Sudan
14 05 090	**Francolinus nahani** Nahan's Forest Francolin		Dense forests of Uganda and northeast Zaire
14 05 091	**Francolinus pondicerianus** Gray Francolin		Eastern Iran to India; Sri Lanka
14 05 092	**Francolinus gularis** Swamp Francolin		Restricted to the *terai* of northern India, Nepal
14 05 093	**Perdix perdix** Common (Gray) Partridge		Widespread Palearctic region
14 05 094	**Perdix dauuricae (barbata)** Daurian Partridge		Russia to Manchuria, China, Mongolia
14 05 095	**Perdix hodgsoniae** Tibetan Partridge		Northern India, adjacent Tibet, Szechwan, Kansu
14 05 096	**Rhizothera longirostris** Long-billed Partridge		Malaya, Sumatra, Borneo
14 05 097	**Margaroperdix madagascariensis** Madagascar Partridge		Open fields and plateaus of Madagascar

		Date	Location
14 05 098	**Melanoperdix nigra** *Black Wood Partridge*		Malaya, Sumatra, Borneo
14 05 099	**Coturnix coturnix** *European Quail*		Widespread western Palearctic, Ethiopian regions
14 05 100	**Coturnix japonica** *Japanese Quail*		Widespread eastern Palearctic region
14 05 101	**Coturnix coromandelica** *Black-breasted (Rain)* *Quail*		Sri Lanka; India to Burma, Thailand
14 05 102	**Coturnix delegorguei** *African Harlequin Quail*		Africa south of the Sahara; Madagascar
14 05 103	**Coturnix pectoralis** *Stubble Quail*		Australia, Tasmania (rare)
14 05 104	**Coturnix novaezelandiae** *New Zealand Quail*		New Zealand (presumed extinct since 1870)
14 05 105	**Synoicus ypsilophorus** **(australis)** *Brown Quail*		Malaysia to New Guinea, Australia
14 05 106	**Excalfactoria adansonii** *Blue Quail*		East Africa to Malawi, Rhodesia
14 05 107	**Excalfactoria chinensis** *King Quail*		India to China, Malaysia, Australia
14 05 108	**Perdicula asiatica** *Jungle Bush Quail*		Lowland deciduous jungles of India; Sri Lanka
14 05 109	**Perdicula argoondah** *Rock Bush Quail*		Semi-desert facies of Indian Subcontinent
14 05 110	**Perdicula** **erythrorhyncha** *Painted Bush Quail*		Deciduous biotope of Indian Subcontinent
14 05 111	**Perdicula manipurensis** *Manipur Bush Quail*		Moist deciduous foothills of northern India
14 05 112	**Arborophila torqueola** *Common Hill Partridge*		Dense evergreen forests of Himalayas to Burma
14 05 113	**Arborophila rufogularis** *Rufous-throated Partridge*		Lowlands of India to Indochina
14 05 114	**Arborophila atrogularis** *White-cheeked Partridge*		Lowland evergreen and bamboo forests of India to Burma
14 05 115	**Arborophila crudigularis** *Formosan Hill Partridge*		Mountain forests on island of Formosa
14 05 116	**Arborophila mandellii** *Red-breasted Hill* *Partridge*		Sikkim, Assam, Tibet

	Date	Location
15 05 117 **Arborophila brunneopectus** *Bar-backed Partridge*		India to Indochina, southwest China, Greater Sundas
14 05 118 **Arborophila rufipectus** *Boulton's Hill Partridge*		Hills of western Szechwan (known from one specimen)
14 05 119 **Arborophila gingica** *Collared Hill Partridge*		Mountains of southwest China (Fukien, Kwangtung, Kwangsi)
14 05 120 **Arborophila davidi** *Orange-necked Partridge*		Restricted to Cochinchina (rare)
14 05 021 **Arborophila cambodiana** *Chestnut-headed Partridge*		Lowland forests of Thailand, Cambodia
14 05 122 **Arborophila orientalis** *Sumatra Hill Partridge*		Forests of Sumatra, Java
14 05 123 **Arborophila javanica** *Chestnut-bellied Tree Partridge*		Mountains of western Java
14 05 124 **Arborophila rubrirostris** *Red-billed Tree Partridge*		Mountains of Sumatra
14 05 125 **Arborophila hyperythra** *Red-breasted Tree Partridge*		Borneo (mountains from Kinabalu to upper Kayan)
14 05 126 **Arborophila ardens** *Hainan Hill Partridge*		Restricted to island of Hainan
14 05 127 **Tropicoperdix charltonii** *Scaly-breasted Partridge*		Southwest China; Sumatra; Borneo
14 05 128 **Tropicoperdix chloropus** *Chestnut-breasted Partridge*		Burma, Thailand, Annam; Hong Kong
14 05 129 **Tropicoperdix merlini** *Annam Hill Partridge*		Restricted to hills of Annam (India)
14 05 130 **Caloperdix oculea** *Ferruginous Wood Partridge*		Malaya, Sumatra, Borneo
14 05 131 **Haematortyx sanguiniceps** *Crimson-headed Wood Partridge*		Mountains of Borneo
14 05 132 **Rollulus rouloul** *Crested Wood Partridge*		Widespread Thailand, Malaya, Sumatra, Borneo
14 05 133 **Ptilopachus petrosus** *Stone Partridge*		Senegal to Ethiopia, Kenya
14 05 134 **Bambusicola fytchii** *Bamboo Partridge*		Assam, Burma to China; Taiwan; Hainan

	Date	Location
14 05 135 Bambusicola thoracica *Chinese Bamboo Partridge*		China (Szechwan, Fukien, Kwangsi); Taiwan
14 05 136 Galloperdix spadicea *Red Spurfowl*		Widespread Indian Subcontinent
14 05 137 Galloperdix lunulata *Painted Spurfowl*		Semi-arid steppes of Indian Subcontinent
14 05 138 Galloperdix bicalcarata *Ceylon Spurfowl*		Damp rain forests of southern Sri Lanka
14 05 139 Ophrysia superciliosa *Indian Mountain Quail*		Extinct since about 1868. Inhabited northwest Himalayas
14 05 140 Ithaginis cruentus *Blood Pheasant*		Mountains of Tibet, Nepal, Burma, Yunnan
14 05 141 Tragopan melanocephalus *Western Tragopan*		Deep mountain forests of Garhwal to Kashmir
14 05 142 Tragopan satyra *Satyr Tragopan*		Himalayas of Nepal, Sikkim, Bhutan
14 05 143 Tragopan blythii *Gray-bellied Tragopan*		Himalayas of Bhutan, southeast Tibet, Burma (endangered)
14 05 144 Tragopan temminckii *Temminck's Tragopan*		Mountains of Tibet, Burma, Yunnan to Tonkin
14 05 145 Tragopan caboti *Cabot's Tragopan*		China (mountains of Fukien and Kwangtung)
14 05 146 Pucrasia macrolopha *Koklass Pheasant*		Discontinuous; mountains of Afghanistan, Nepal, Tibet
14 05 147 Lophophorus impejanus *Himalayan Monal Pheasant*		Himalayas of Afghanistan to Bhutan and southern Tibet
14 05 148 Lophophorus sclateri *Sclater's Monal Pheasant*		Himalayas of Assam, Tibet, Burma, Yunnan (endangered)
14 05 149 Lophorhorus lhuysii *Chinese Monal Pheasant*		Mountains of Kokonor and Szechwan (endangered)
14 05 150 Gallus gallus *Red Junglefowl*		Widespread Southeast Asia; Java; Sumatra; Bali
14 05 151 Gallus lafayettei *Ceylon Junglefowl*		Restricted to dense scrub and jungles of Sri Lanka
14 05 152 Gallus sonneratii *Gray Junglefowl*		Bamboo forests of western and southern India
14 05 153 Gallus varius *Green Junglefowl*		Lowlands of Java, Bali and adjacent eastern islands

		Date	Location
14 05 154	**Lophura leucomelana** *Kalij Pheasant*		Western Himalayas to Szechwan, Yunnan, Burma
14 05 155	**Lophura nycthemera** *Silver Pheasant*		Mountains of southern China to Indochina; Hainan
14 05 156	**Lophura imperialis** *Imperial Pheasant*		Restricted to Annam, Laos (rare and endangered)
14 05 157	**Lophura edwardsi** *Edwards' Pheasant*		Dense lowland forests of central Annam (endangered)
14 05 158	**Lophura swinhoei** *Swinhoe's Pheasant*		Dense hill forests of Taiwan (endangered)
14 05 159	**Lophura inornata** *Salvadori's Pheasant*		Restricted to deep mountain forests of Sumatra
14 05 160	**Lophura erythropthalma** *Crestless Fireback*		Lowland jungles of Malaya, Sumatra and Borneo
14 05 161	**Lophura ignita (rufa)** *Crested Fireback*		Lowlands of Malay peninsula, Sumatra, Borneo, Banka
14 05 162	**Lophura diardi** *Siamese Fireback*		Lowlands of southern China, Thailand to Indochina
14 05 163	**Lophura bulweri** *Bulwer's Pheasant*		Submontane forests of interior of Borneo
14 05 164	**Crossoptilon crossoptilon** *Tibetan Eared Pheasant*		Himalayas of eastern Tibet to Sikang, Szechwan, Yunnan
14 05 165	**Crossoptilon mantchuricum** *Brown Eared Pheasant*		Mountains of western China (Shansi and Chihli)
14 05 166	**Crossoptilon auritum** *Blue Eared Pheasant*		China (mountain forests of northwest Kokonor and Kansu)
14 05 167	**Catreus wallichii** *Cheer Pheasant*		Himalayas of Kashmir, Garhwal and Nepal (endangered)
14 05 168	**Syrmaticus ellioti** *Elliot's Pheasant*		Mountains of Chekiang and Fukien (endangered)
14 05 169	**Syrmaticus humiae** *Hume's Pheasant*		Mountains of Assam, India to Thailand
14 05 170	**Syrmaticus mikado** *Mikado Pheasant*		Mountains of central Taiwan (endangered)
14 05 171	**Syrmaticus soemmerringii** *Copper Pheasant*		Coniferous forests of Hondo, Shikoku, and Kyusha (Japan)

		Date	Location
14 05 172	**Syrmaticus reevesii** *Reeve's Pheasant*		Hills of north and central China north of Yangtze river
14 05 173	**Phasianus colchicus** *Ring-necked Pheasant*		Palearctic (introduced North America, Hawaii, New Zealand)
14 05 174	**Phasianus versicolor** *Green Pheasant*		Lowlands of Japanese Islands
14 05 175	**Chrysolophus pictus** *Golden Pheasant*		Mountains of Tsinghai, Kansu to Szechwan, Yunnan, Kwangsi
14 05 176	**Chrysolophus amherstiae** *Lady Amherst's Pheasant*		Mountains of southeast Tibet to southwest China, Burma
14 05 177	**Polyplectron chalcurum** *Bronze-tailed Pheasant*		Mid-mountain forests of Sumatra
14 05 178	**Polyplectron inopinatum** *Rothschild's Pheasant*		Rugged mountain forests of Malay Peninsula
14 05 179	**Polyplectron germaini** *Germain's Peacock Pheasant*		Forests of Cochinchina, southern Annam
14 05 180	**Polyplectron bicalcaratum** *Gray Peacock Pheasant*		Himalayas of India to Indochina; Hainan
14 05 181	**Polyplectron malacense** *Malay Peacock Pheasant*		Peninsular Thailand, Malaya, Sumatra, Borneo
14 05 182	**Polyplectron emphanum** *Palawan Peacock Pheasant*		Damp primary forests of Palawan (endangered)
14 05 183	**Rheinartia ocellata** *Crested Argus*		Malaya, Annam, Laos (forests up to 5,000 feet)
14 05 184	**Rheinartia nigrescens** *Malay Crested Argus*		Malay Peninsula (probably race of *R. ocellata*)
14 05 185	**Argusianus argus** *Great Argus Pheasant*		Peninsular Thailand, Malaya, Sumatra, Borneo
14 05 186	**Pavo cristatus** *Common Peafowl*		Sri Lanka; Indian Subcontinent lowlands
14 05 187	**Pavo muticus** *Green Peafowl*		Bangladesh to Indochina; Java
14 05 188	**Afropavo congensis** *Congo Peacock*		Virgin rain forests of central Zaire (endangered)

		Date	Location

ORDER: GALLIFORMES
FAMILY: NUMIDIDAE (Guineafowl)

14 06 001 **Phasidus niger**
Black Guineafowl

Dense forests of Cameroon to northern Zaire

14 06 002 **Agelastes meleagrides**
White-breasted
Guineafowl

Liberia to Ghana (rare)

14 06 003 **Numida meleagris**
+   **(mitrata)**
Helmeted Guineafowl

Sudan, Ethiopia, Uganda, Kenya to South Africa;
Madagascar

14 06 004 **Guttera plumifera**
Plumed Guineafowl

Forests of Cameroon to northern Zaire

14 06 005 **Guttera edouardi**
Crested Guineafowl

Africa south of the Sahara

14 06 006 **Guttera pucherani**
Kenya Crested Guineafowl

Somalia, Kenya, Tanzania; Zanzibar

14 06 007 **Acryllium vulturinum**
+   _Vulturine Guineafowl_

Somalia, Ethiopia, Kenya, Tanzania

ORDER: GALLIFORMES
FAMILY: OPISTHOCOMIDAE (Hoatzin)

14 07 001 **Opisthocomus hoazin**
+   _Hoatzin_

Widespread Amazon basin

ORDER: GRUIFORMES
FAMILY: MESITORNITHIDAE (Mesites)

15 01 001 **Mesitornis variegata**
White-breasted Mesite

Confined to western part of Madagascar

15 01 002 **Mesitornis unicolor**
Brown Mesite

Confined to forests of eastern Madagascar

15 01 003 **Monias benschi**
Monias (Bensch's Rail)

Coastal forests of southwest Madagascar

ORDER: GRUIFORMES
FAMILY: TURNICIDAE (Hemipodes)

15 02 001 **Turnix sylvatica**
Andalusian Hemipode

Widespread Palearctic, Ethiopian regions

15 02 002 **Turnix worcesteri**
Philippine Button Quail

Philippines (endemic Luzon Island)

	Date	Location
15 02 003	**Turnix nana** *Black-rumped Button Quail*	Kenya to South Africa
15 02 004	**Turnix hottentotta** *Hottentot Button Quail*	Africa south of the Sahara
15 02 005	**Turnix tanki** *Yellow-legged Button Quail*	India to Burma, China, Manchuria, Korea; Andamans, Nicobars
15 02 006	**Turnix suscitator** *Barred Button Quail*	Widespread Oriental mainland and islands
15 02 007	**Turnix nigricollis** *Madagascar Button Quail*	Widespread Madagascar
15 02 008	**Turnix ocellata** *Spotted Button Quail*	Philippines (endemic Luzon Island)
15 02 009	**Turnix melanogaster** *Black-breasted Quail*	Queensland to New South Wales (rare)
15 02 010	**Turnix varia (olivii)** *Painted Button Quail*	Australia, Tasmania
15 02 011	**Turnix castanota** *Chestnut-backed Quail*	Confined to Arnhem Land to Fitzroy River (Australia)
15 02 012	**Turnix pyrrhothorax** *Red-chested Quail*	Confined to eastern half of Australia (rare)
15 02 013	**Turnix velox** *Little Quail*	Widespread Australia
15 02 014	**Turnix maculosa** *Red-backed Button Quail*	Australia, New Guinea, Bismarck Archipelago
15 02 015	**Ortyxelos meiffrenii** *Quail Plover*	Senegal to Kenya, Uganda, the Sudan

ORDER: GRUIFORMES
FAMILY: PEDIONOMIDAE (Collared Hemipode)

15 03 001	**Pedionomus torquatus** *Collared Hemipode*	Southeastern Australia (rare)

ORDER: GRUIFORMES
FAMILY: GRUIDAE (Cranes)

15 04 001	**Grus grus** *Common Crane*	Widespread Palearctic, Oriental mainland
15 04 002	**Grus nigricollis** *Black-necked Crane*	Tibetan plateau of central Asia
15 04 003	**Grus monacha** *Hooded Crane*	Siberia, Manchuria, Japan, Korea (endangered)

	Date	Location

15 04 004	**Grus canadensis** *Sandhill Crane*	Siberia; Alaska to Mexico
15 04 005	**Grus japonensis** *Japanese Crane*	Japan, Korea, China (endangered)
15 04 006	**Grus americana** *Whooping Crane*	Canada to southern United States (seriously endangered)
15 04 007	**Grus vipio** *White-naped Crane*	Siberia to China, Korea, Japan
15 04 008	**Grus antigone** *Sarus Crane*	India to Southeast Asia, the Philippines
15 04 009	**Grus rubicunda** *Australian (Brolga) Crane*	Australia; vagrant to New Guinea
15 04 010	**Grus leucogeranus** *Siberian White Crane*	Spottily distributed Asia (endangered)
15 04 011	**Bugeranus carunculatus** *Wattled Crane*	Ethiopia to South Africa
15 04 012	**Anthropoides virgo** *Demoiselle Crane*	Widespread Palearctic region, Oriental mainland
15 04 013	**Anthropoides paradisea** *Paradise Crane*	Southwest Africa to Malawi, Cape Province
15 04 014	**Balearica pavonina** *Sudan Crowned Crane*	Senegal to Nigeria, Ethiopia
15 04 015	**Balearica regulorum** *South African Crowned Crane*	Marshy areas of Angola, Zambia, Malawi to South Africa

ORDER: GRUIFORMES
FAMILY: ARAMIDAE (Limpkin)

| 15 05 001
 + | **Aramus guarauna**
 Limpkin | Swamps of southern United States to Argentina; West Indies |

ORDER: GRUIFORMES
FAMILY: PSOPHIIDAE (Trumpeters)

15 06 001	**Psophia crepitans** *Gray-winged Trumpeter*	Widespread Amazon basin
15 06 002	**Psophia leucoptera** *Pale-winged Trumpeter*	Widespread Amazon basin
15 06 003	**Psophia viridis** *Dark-winged Trumpeter*	Brazil south of Amazon (Rio Madeira to Pará)

	Date	Location

ORDER: GRUIFORMES
FAMILY: RALLIDAE (Rails)

15 07 001	**Rallus longirostris** *Clapper Rail*	United States to Peru; West Indies
15 07 002	**Rallus elegans** *King Rail*	United States to Mexico
15 07 003	**Rallus limicola** *Virginia Rail*	Canada to Peru, Argentina
15 07 004	**Rallus wetmorei** *Plain-flanked Rail*	Venezuela (coastal mangroves in Aragua)
15 07 005	**Rallus antarcticus** *Austral Rail*	Chile, Argentina (Buenos Aires to Santa Cruz)
15 07 006	**Rallus semiplumbeus** *Bogota Rail*	Colombia (east of Andes in Boyacá and Cundinamarca)
15 07 007	**Rallus aquaticus** *Water Rail*	Widespread Palearctic, Oriental regions
15 07 008	**Rallus caerulescens** *Kaffir Rail*	Africa south of the Sahara
15 07 009	**Rallus madagascariensis** *Madagascar Rail*	Highland forests of Madagascar
15 07 010	**Rallus pectoralis** *Lewin Water Rail*	Australia to New Guinea
15 07 011	**Rallus mirificus** *Brown-banded Rail*	Philippines (endemic Luzon Island)
15 07 012	**Rallus muelleri** *Mueller's Rail*	New Zealand (Auckland Island? Probable race *R. pectoralis*)
15 07 013	**Rallus striatus** *Slaty-breasted Rail*	Widespread Oriental mainland and islands
15 07 014	**Rallus philippensis** *Banded Rail*	Australasia, Oceanic region to Philippines
15 07 015	**Rallus ecaudatus** *Tonga Rail*	Extinct. Inhabited Tonga Islands (Nuafou, Keppel, Uea)
15 07 016	**Rallus torquatus** *Barred Rail*	Philippines to New Guinea, Celebes Islands
15 07 017	**Rallus owstoni** *Guam Rail*	Confined to Guam Island (Marianas)
15 07 018	**Rallus wakensis** *Wake Island Rail*	Extinct since about 1944. Inhabited Wake Island
15 07 019	**Rallus sanguinolentus** *Plumbeous Rail*	Peru of Argentina, Chile, southern Brazil

		Date	Location

15 09 020	**Rallus nigricans** *Blackish Rail*		Widespread South America to northeast Argentina
15 07 021	**Rallus maculatus** *Spotted Rail*		Mexico to Argentina; West Indies
15 07 022	**Nesolimnas dieffenbachii** *Dieffenbach's Rail*		Extinct. Inhabited Chatham Island, possibly Pitt Island
15 07 023	**Cabalus modestus** *Chatham Island Rail*		Extinct. Inhabited Chatham, Mangare and Pitt Islands
15 07 024	**Atlantisia rogersi** *Atlantis Rail*		Inaccessible Island, Tristan da Cunha (flightless)
15 07 025	**Tricholimnas lafresnayanus** *New Caledonia Wood Rail*		New Caledonia (probably extinct—flightless)
15 07 026	**Tricholimnas sylvestris** *Lord Howe Wood Rail*		Lord Howe Island (endangered—flightless)
15 07 027	**Dryolimnas cuvieri** *White-throated Rail*		Madagascar, Aldabra islands (flightless)
15 07 028	**Rougetius rougetii** *Rouget's Rail*		Confined to highlands of Ethiopia
15 07 029	**Amaurolimnas concolor** *Uniform Crake*		Southern Mexico to Bolivia
15 07 030	**Rallina fasciata** *Malay Banded Crake*		Oriental mainland and islands to Australia
15 07 031	**Rallina eurizonoides** *Philippine Banded Crake*		Widespread Oriental mainland and islands
15 07 032	**Rallina canningi** *Andaman Banded Crake*		Confined to Andaman Islands
15 07 033	**Rallina tricolor** *Red-necked Rail*		Australia to New Guinea, Bismarck Archipelago
15 07 034	**Rallicula rubra** *Chestnut Rail*		High mountain forests of western half of New Guinea
15 07 035	**Rallicula mayri** *Mayr's Chestnut Rail*		Cyclops Mountains of New Guinea
15 07 036	**Rallicula leucospila** *White-striped Chestnut Rail*		Vogelkop and Wandammen Mountains of New Guinea
15 07 037	**Rallicula forbesi** *Forbes' Chestnut Rail*		Mountain forests of east and central New Guinea
15 07 038	**Cyanolimnas cerverai** *Zapata Rail*		Southwest Cuba (confined to Zapata Swamp—endangered)

		Date	Location
15 07 039	**Aramides mangle** *Little Wood Rail*		Brazil (coastal mangroves of Maranhão to Rio de Janeiro)
15 07 040	**Aramides cajanea** *Gray-necked Wood Rail*		Southern Mexico to Argentina (mainly east of Andes)
15 07 041	**Aramides wolfi** *Brown Wood Rail*		Tropical Pacific Colombia to northwest Ecuador
15 07 042	**Aramides ypecaha** *Giant Wood Rail*		Southern Brazil to Argentina (saw grass swamps)
15 07 043	**Aramides axillaris** *Rufous-necked Wood Rail*		Tropical Mexico to Colombia, Venezuela, Surinam
15 07 044	**Aramides calopterus** *Red-winged Wood Rail*		Forest streams of eastern Ecuador, Peru, adjacent Brazil
15 07 045 +	**Aramides saracura** *Slaty-breasted Wood Rail*		Southeast Brazil (Minas Gerais) to northeast Argentina
15 07 046	**Aramidopsis plateni** *Platen's Rail*		Confined to Celebes Islands (endangered—flightless)
15 07 047	**Nesoclopeus poeciloptera** *Barred-wing Rail*		Fiji Islands (Vita Levu and Ovalau—possibly extinct)
15 07 048	**Nesoclopeus woodfordi** *Woodford's Rail*		Confined to Solomon Islands (flightless)
15 07 049	**Gymnocrex rosenbergii** *Schlegel's Rail*		Confined to the Celebes Islands
15 07 050	**Gymnocrex plumbeiventris** *Bare-eyed Rail*		New Guinea, northern Moluccas and adjacent islands
15 07 051	**Gallirallus australis** *Weka*		New Zealand and adjacent islands (endangered—flightless)
15 07 052	**Habropteryx insignis** *Sclater's Rail*		Confined to New Britain Island (flightless)
15 07 053	**Habroptila wallacii** *Wallace's Rail*		Moluccas (confined to Halmahera Island—flightless)
15 07 054	**Megacrex inepta** *New Guinea Flightless Rail*		Mangroves of northern and southern New Guinea (flightless)
15 07 055	**Eulabeornis castaneoventris** *Aru Chestnut Rail*		Confined to Aru Islands and north coast of Australia

		Date	Location
15 07 056	**Himantornis haematopus** *Nkulengu Rail*		Liberia to Zaire
15 07 057	**Canirallus oculeus** *Gray-throated Rail*		Forest streams of Liberia to western Uganda
15 07 058	**Canirallus kioloides** *Madagascar Gray-throated Rail*		Humid rain forests of eastern Madagascar
15 07 059	**Crecopsis egregia** *African Crake*		Africa south of the Sahara
15 07 060	**Crex crex** *Corncrake*		Widespread Europe, Africa, Asia to Australia
15 07 061	**Anurolimnas castaneiceps** *Chestnut-headed Crake*		Tropical forests of southeast Colombia to eastern Peru
15 07 062	**Limnocorax flavirostra** *Black Crake*		Africa south of the Sahara
15 07 063	**Porzana parva** *Little Crake*		Widespread Palearctic, Ethiopian regions
15 07 064	**Porzana pusilla** *Baillon's Crake*		Widespread Palearctic, Ethiopian, Australasian regions
15 07 065	**Porzana porzana** *Spotted Crake*		Eurasia to India, northwest China
15 07 066	**Porzana marginalis** *Striped Crake*		Spottily distributed Africa; Aldabra Island (rare)
15 07 067	**Porzana fluminea** *Australian Spotted Crake*		Southern Australia; Tasmania
15 07 068	**Porzana carolina** *Sora Rail*		Canada to Peru; West Indies
15 07 069	**Porzana spiloptera** *Dot-winged Crake*		Uruguay (Canelones) to northern Argentina (San Juan)
15 07 070	**Porzana flaviventer** *Yellow-breasted Crake*		Mexico to Argentina; West Indies
15 07 071	**Porzana albicollis** *Ash-throated Crake*		Widespread South America; Trinidad
15 07 072	**Porzana fusca** *Ruddy-breasted Crake*		Widespread Oriental mainland and islands
15 07 073	**Porzana paykullii** *Band-bellied Crake*		Eastern Asia; Greater Sundas; Philippines
15 07 074	**Porzana olivieri** *Olivier's Rail*		Savanna of western Madagascar (rare)

		Date	Location
15 07 075	**Porzana bicolor** *Black-tailed Crake*		Himalayas of Nepal to Laos
15 07 076	**Porzana tabuensis** *Spotless Crake*		Philippine Islands to Polynesia; Australia
15 07 077	**Porzana palmeri** *Laysan Rail*		Extinct since 1944. Inhabited Laysan Island
15 07 078	**Porzana cinerea** *White-browed Crake*		Malaysia to Indonesia, the Philippines, Australia
15 07 079	**Porzana sandwichensis** *Hawaiian Rail*		Extinct. Inhabited main island of Hawaii
15 07 080	**Nesophylax ater** *Henderson Island Rail*		Restricted to Henderson Island, Paumotu group (endangered)
15 07 081	**Aphanolinmas monasa** *Kusaie Rail*		Restricted to Kusaie Island, Micronesia (probably extinct)
15 07 082	**Laterallus jamaicensis** *Black Rail*		United States to Argentina, Chile; winters West Indies
15 07 083	**Laterallus xenopterus** *Rufous-faced Crake*		Campos of Paraguay, adjacent Brazil (rare and local)
15 07 084	**Laterallus spilonotus** *Galapagos Rail*		Restricted to Galapagos Islands
15 07 085	**Laterallus exilis** *Gray-breasted Crake*		Honduras to Amazonian Brazil, eastern Peru
15 07 086	**Laterallus albigularis** *White-throated Rail*		Costa Rica to Ecuador
15 07 087	**Laterallus melanophaius** *Rufous-sided Crake*		Widespread South America (mainly east of Andes)
15 07 088	**Laterallus ruber** *Red Rail*		Mexico to Nicaragua (tropical zone)
15 07 089	**Laterallus levraudi** *Rusty-flanked Crake*		Venezuela (subtropical zone north of Orinoco)
15 07 090	**Laterallus viridis** *Russet-crowned Crake*		Amazon basin (widespread tropical zone)
15 07 091	**Laterallus fasciatus** *Black-banded Crake*		Western Amazonian Brazil; adjacent Colombia to Peru
15 07 092	**Laterallus leucopyrrhus** *Red-and-white Crake*		Coastal southeast Brazil to northeast Argentina
15 07 093	**Micropygia schomburgkii** *Ocellated Crake*		Guyana to eastern Colombia, southern Brazil

	Date	Location
15 07 094 **Coturnicops exquisitus** *Button Crake*		Siberia to Japan, northern China
15 07 095 **Coturnicops noveboracensis** *Yellow Rail*		Canada, western United States to Mexico
15 07 096 **Coturnicops notatus** *Speckled Crake*		Spottily distributed South America (rare)
15 07 097 **Neocrex erythrops** *Paint-billed Crake*		Widespread South America; Galapagos Islands
15 07 098 **Sarothrura pulchra** *White-spotted Pygmy Crake*		Sudan, Kenya, Zaire to South Africa
15 07 099 **Sarothrura elegans** *Buff-spotted Crake*		Kenya to Somalia, Cameroon
15 07 100 **Sarothrura rufa** *Red-chested Crake*		Africa south of the Sahara
15 07 101 **Sarothrura lugens (lynesi) (lineata)** *Chestnut-headed Crake*		Grassy marshes of Cameroon to Angola, Tanzania
15 07 102 **Sarothrura boehmi** *Streaky-breasted Crake*		Senegal to Kenya, Rhodesia
15 07 103 **Sarothrura affinis** *Striped Crake*		Kenya, the Sudan to South Africa
15 07 104 **Sarothrura insularis** *Madagascar Crake*		Forests of eastern Madagascar
15 07 105 **Sarothrura ayresi** *White-winged Crake*		Ethiopia to South Africa
15 07 106 **Sarothrura watersi** *Water's Crake*		Highlands of extreme northern Madagascar (rare)
15 07 107 **Porphyriops melanops** *Spot-flanked Gallinule*		Widespread South America
15 07 108 **Tribonyx ventralis** *Black-tailed Native-Hen*		Widespread Australia
15 07 109 **Tribonyx mortierii** *Tasmanian Native-Hen*		Restricted to the Island of Tasmania (flightless)
15 07 110 **Amaurornis akool** *Brown Crake*		India to southern China, Burma, Hong Kong
15 07 111 **Amaurornis olivacea** *Bush-Hen*		Australia, Solomons, New Guinea, Moluccas, the Philippines
15 07 112 **Amaurornis isabellina** *Celebes Moorhen*		Celebes Islands
15 07 113 **Amaurornis phoenicurus** *White-breasted Waterhen*		Widespread Oriental mainland and islands

		Date	Location

15 07 114 **Gallicrex cinerea**
Watercock
Widespread Oriental mainland and islands

15 07 115 **Gallinula tenebrosa**
+ *Dusky Moorhen*
Indonesia to New Guinea, Australia

15 07 116 **Gallinula chloropus**
Common Gallinule
Cosmopolitan except for Australasian region

15 07 117 **Gallinula angulata**
Lesser Moorhen
Africa south of the Sahara

15 07 118 **Porphyriornis nesiotis**
South Atlantic Moorhen
Confined to Tristan Island (South Atlantic Ocean—seriously endangered)

15 07 119 **Porphyriornis comeri**
Gough Island Moorhen
Confined to Gough island (South Atlantic Ocean—flightless)

15 07 120 **Pareudiastes pacificus**
Red-billed Rail
Tahiti and adjacent islands (probably extinct—flightless)

15 07 121 **Edithornis silvestris**
San Cristobal Mountain Rail
Known from one specimen, San Cristobal, Solomons (flightless)

15 07 122 **Porphyrula alleni**
Allen's Gallinule
Africa south of the Sahara; Madagascar

15 07 123 **Porphyrula martinica**
+ *Purple Gallinule*
Southern United States to Argentina; West Indies

15 07 124 **Porphyrula flavirostris**
Azure Gallinule
Widespread rice fields and marshes of South America

15 07 125 **Porphyrio porphyrio (poliocephalus)**
+ *Purple Swamphen*
Widespread Africa, Eurasia to Australia

15 07 126 **Porphyrio madagascariensis**
Green-backed Gallinule
Nile delta; Madagascar (possible race *P. porphyrio*)

15 07 127 **Porphyrio poliocephalus**
Purple Coot
Widespread Southeast Asia (probable race *P. porphyrio*)

15 07 128 **Porphyrio albus**
White Swamphen
Extinct since 1834. Inhabited Lord Howe Island

15 07 129 **Porphyrio pulverulentus**
Philippine Swamphen
Widespread Philippines (probable race *P. porphyrio*)

15 07 130 **Notornis mantelli**
Takahe
Southern mountains of New Zealand (endangered—flightless)

15 07 131 **Fulica atra**
Common Coot
Palearctic, Oriental, Australasian regions

		Date	Location
15 07 132	**Fulica cristata** *Red-knobbed Coot*		Ethiopia to South Africa; Madagascar
15 07 133	**Fulica americana** **(ardesiaca)** *American Coot*		Canada to Argentina, Chile; West Indies
15 07 134 +	**Fulica armillata** *Red-gartered Coot*		Southeast Brazil to Chile, Argentina (Tierra del Fuego)
15 07 135	**Fulica caribaea** *Caribbean Coot*		West Indies; Trinidad; coast of Venezuela
15 07 136 +	**Fulica leucoptera** *White-winged Coot*		Extreme southeast Brazil to Bolivia, Tierra del Fuego
15 07 137 +	**Fulica rufifrons** *Red-fronted Coot*		Southeast Brazil to Chile, Argentina (Tierra del Fuego)
15 07 138	**Fulica gigantea** *Giant Coot*		Andes of southern Peru to northern Chile, Argentina
15 07 139	**Fulica cornuta** *Horned Coot*		Puna of Bolivia to northern Chile (endangered)

ORDER: GRUIFORMES
FAMILY: HELIORNITHIDAE (Sun Grebes)

15 08 001	**Podica senegalensis** *African Finfoot*		East, central and southern Africa
15 08 002	**Heliopais personata** *Masked (Asian) Finfoot*		Pakistan to Malaya, Indochina; Sumatra
15 08 003	**Heliornis fulica** *Sungrebe*		Southern Mexico to Argentina

ORDER: GRUIFORMES
FAMILY: RHYNOCHETIDAE (Kagu)

15 09 001	**Rhynochetos jubatus** *Kagu*		Restricted to New Caledonia (on the verge of extinction—flightless)

ORDER: GRUIFORMES
FAMILY: EURYPYGIDAE (Sun Bittern)

15 10 001 +	**Eurypgya helias** *Sun Bittern*		Southern Mexico to southern Peru

Date   Location

ORDER: GRUIFORMES
FAMILY: CARIAMIDAE (Seriemas)

15 11 001   **Cariama cristata**
             Red-legged Seriema   Central Brazil to northern Argentina

15 11 002   **Chunga burmeisteri**
             Black-legged Seriema   Paraguay, adjacent northern Argentina

ORDER: GRUIFORMES
FAMILY: OTIDIDAE (Bustards)

15 12 001   **Tetrax tetrax**
             Little Bustard   Southern Palearctic region

15 12 002   **Otis tarda**
             Giant Bustard   Discontinuously distributed Palearctic region

15 12 003   **Neotis cafra**
             Stanley Bustard   Africa south of the Sahara

15 12 004   **Neotis ludwigii**
             Ludwig's Bustard   South Africa (Southwest Africa to Cape Province)

15 12 005   **Neotis burchellii**
             Burchell's Bustard   Jebel Dul, south of Sennaar (known from one
                                           specimen)

15 12 006   **Neotis nuba**
             Nubian Bustard   River Niger to Lake Chad, the Sudan

15 12 007   **Neotis denhami**
  +   *Denham's Bustard*   Ethiopia to South Africa

15 12 008   **Neotis heuglinii**
             Heuglin's Bustard   Somalia, Ethiopia, Kenya

15 12 009   **Choriotis arabs**
  +   *Arabian Bustard*   North Africa to Asia Minor

15 12 010   **Choriotis kori**
             Kori Bustard   Ethiopia to South Africa

15 12 011   **Choriotis nigriceps**
             Great Indian Bustard   Semi-deserts of India (endangered)

15 12 012   **Choriotis australis**
             Australian Bustard   Australia, New Guinea

15 12 013   **Chlamydotis undulata**
             Houbara Bustard   North Africa to India; the Canary Islands

15 12 014   **Lophotis savilei**
             Savile's Bustard   Senegal to Nigeria

15 12 015   **Lophotis ruficrista**
             Buff-crested Bustard   Ethiopia to South Africa

		Date	Location
15 12 016	**Afrotis atra** *Black Bustard*		South Africa (Southwest Africa to Cape Province)
15 12 017	**Eupodotis vigorsii** *Black-throated Bustard*		Southwest Africa to Cape Province
15 12 018	**Eupodotis ruppellii** *Rüppell's Bustard*		Angola to Southwest Africa
15 12 019	**Eupodotis humilis** *Little Brown Bustard*		Restricted to Somalia
15 12 020	**Eupodotis senegalensis** *White-bellied Bustard*		Senegal to Sudan, Ethiopia, Kenya, Tanzania
15 12 021	**Eupodotis caerulescens** *Blue Bustard*		Confined to extreme southern tip of Africa (rare)
15 12 022	**Eupodotis bengalensis** *Bengal Florican*		Northern India to Cochinchina
15 12 023	**Lissotis melanogaster** *Black-bellied Bustard*		Africa south of the Sahara
15 12 024	**Lissotis hartlaubii** *Hartlaub's Bustard*		Ethiopia, Kenya, Uganda, Tanzania
15 12 025	**Sypheotides indica** *Lesser Florican*		Widespread Indian Subcontinent

ORDER: CHARADRIIFORMES
FAMILY: JACANIDAE (Jacanas)

16 01 001	**Microparra capensis** *Lesser Jacana*	East and central Africa
16 01 002	**Actophilornis africana** *African Jacana*	Africa south of the Sahara
16 01 003	**Actophilornis albinucha** *Madagascar Jacana*	Small lakes and rivers of Madagascar (rare in east)
16 01 004	**Irediparra gallinacea** *Comb-crested Jacana*	Southeast Asia to Australia
16 01 005	**Hydrophasianus chirurgus** *Pheasant-tailed Jacana*	Widespread Oriental mainland and islands
16 01 006	**Metopidius indicus** *Bronze-winged Jacana*	India to Indochina; Celebes; Sumatra; Java
16 01 007	**Jacana spinosa** *Northern Jacana*	Texas to Panama
16 01 008	**Jacana jacana** *Wattled Jacana*	Eastern Panama to Argentina

	Date	Location

ORDER: CHARADRIIFORMES
FAMILY: ROSTRATULIDAE (Painted Snipe)

16 02 001 **Rostratula benghalensis**
† *Painted Snipe*   Africa to Asia, Australia

16 02 002 **Nycticryphes semicollaris**
South American Painted Snipe   Southeast Brazil to Argentina, Chile

ORDER: CHARADRIIFORMES
FAMILY: DROMADIDAE (Crab Plover)

16 03 001 **Dromas ardeola**
Crab Plover   Shores and islands of Indian Ocean

ORDER: CHARADRIIFORMES
FAMILY: HAEMATOPODIDAE (Oystercatchers)

16 04 001 **Haematopus ostralegus**
Common Oystercatcher   Ethiopian, Palearctic, Oriental, Australasian regions

16 04 002 **Haematopus palliatus**
† *American Oystercatcher*   United States to Argentina

16 04 003 **Haematopus bachmani**
Black Oystercatcher   Aleutian Islands to Baja California

16 04 004 **Haematopus moquini**
African Black Oystercatcher   Gabon coast to Natal; eastern Canary Islands

16 04 005 **Haematopus unicolor**
New Zealand Oystercatcher   New Zealand (North, South and Stewart Islands)

16 04 006 **Haematopus leucopodus**
† *Magellanic Oystercatcher*   Coasts of Chile, Argentina

16 04 007 **Haematopus ater**
† *Blackish Oystercatcher*   Peru to Tierra del Fuego

16 04 008 **Haematopus fuliginosus**
Sooty Oystercatcher   Coastal Australia and Tasmania

ORDER: CHARADRIIFORMES
FAMILY: IBIDORHYNCHIDAE (Ibisbill)

16 05 001 **Ibidorhyncha struthersii**
Ibisbill   Himalayas of Turkestan to Tibet, Assam, Burma

	Date	Location

ORDER: CHARADRIIFORMES
FAMILY: RECURVIROSTRIDAE (Avocets and Stilts)

16 06 001 **Himantopus himantopus**
Common Stilt   Widespread Palearctic, Ethiopian, Oriental regions

16 06 002 **Himantopus melanurus**
Southern Stilt   Widespread South America

16 06 003 **Himantopus mexicanus**
+   *Black-necked Stilt*   Widespread United States to northern South America

16 06 004 **Himantopus ceylonensis**
Ceylon Stilt   Widespread Sri Lanka

16 06 005 **Himantopus**
leucocephalus
Pied Stilt   East Indies to Australia, New Zealand

16 06 006 **Himantopus knudseni**
Hawaiian Stilt   Widespread Hawaiian islands

16 06 007 **Himantopus**
novaezelandiae
Black Stilt   Widespread New Zealand (rare on South Island)

16 06 008 **Himantopus meridionalis**
Black-winged Stilt   Widespread South Africa

16 06 009 **Cladorhynchus**
leucocephalus
Banded Stilt   Southern Australia

16 06 010 **Recurvirostra avosetta**
Pied Avocet   Palearctic, Ethiopian, Oriental regions

16 06 011 **Recurvirostra americana**
American Avocet   Canada to Guatemala

16 06 012 **Recurvirostra**
novaehollandiae
Red-necked Avocet   Widespread Australia; rare Tasmania, New Zealand

16 06 013 **Recurvirostra andina**
Andean Avocet   Southern Peru to western Argentina, Chile

ORDER: CHARADRIIFORMES
FAMILY: BURHINIDAE (Stone Curlews)

16 07 001 **Burhinus oedicnemus**
Stone Curlew   Palearctic, Ethiopian, Oriental regions

16 07 002 **Burhinus senegalensis**
Senegal Thick-knee   Senegal to Kenya, Uganda, Ethiopia

16 07 003 **Burhinus vermiculatus**
+   *Water Dikkop*   Kenya, Uganda, Tanzania to South Africa

Date   Rsu1Location

16 07 004 **Burhinus capensis**
+   *Spotted Thick-knee*   Senegal to the Sudan, South Africa; southwest Arabia

16 07 005 **Burhinus bistriatus**
           Double-striped Thick-knee   Mexico to northern Brazil; Hispaniola

16 07 006 **Burhinus superciliaris**
+   *Peruvian Thick-knee*   Ecuador to northern Chile

16 07 007 **Burhinus magnirostris**
+   *Australian Stone Curlew*   Widespread southern Australia

16 07 008 **Esacus recurvirostris**
           Great Stone Curlew   India; Sri Lanka

16 07 009 **Esacus magnirostris**
           Beach Curlew   Malaya, Philippines to New Guinea, Australia

ORDER: CHARADRIIFORMES
FAMILY: GLAREOLIDAE (Pratincoles)

16 08 001 **Pluvianus aegyptius**
           Egyptian Plover   Rivers and lakes of tropical Africa

16 08 002 **Rhinoptilus africanus**
+   *Two-banded Courser*   Kenya, Tanzania to South Africa

16 08 003 **Rhinoptilus cinctus**
+   *Heuglin's Courser*   Sudan, Ethiopia to Rhodesia

16 08 004 **Rhinoptilus chalcopterus**
           Violet-tipped Courser   Africa south of the Sahara

16 08 005 **Rhinoptilus bitorquatus**
           Jerdon's Courser   Probably extinct. Last reported from India in 1900

16 08 006 **Cursorius cursor**
           Cream-colored Courser   Cape Verde and Canaries; North Africa to India

16 08 007 **Cursorius
coromandelicus**
           Indian Courser   Open fields of Indian subcontinent; Sri Lanka

16 08 008 **Cursorius temminckii
(rufus)**
           Temminck's Courser   Gambia to Ethiopia, South Africa

16 08 009 **Stiltia isabella**
           Australian Pratincole   Australia, New Guinea, Borneo

16 08 010 **Glareola pratincola**
+   *Collared Pratincole*   Palearctic, Ethiopian, Oriental, Australasian regions

16 08 011 **Glareola maldivarum**
           Eastern Practincole   Asia to Australia

16 08 012 **Glareola nordmanni**
           Black-winged Pratincole   Southern Europe, Africa, Asia Minor

		Date	Location
16 08 013	**Glareola ocularis** *Madagascar Pratincole*		Madagascar; adjacent East Africa
16 08 014	**Glareola nuchalis** *White-collared Pratincole*		East Africa to Rhodesia
16 08 015	**Glareola cinerea** *Gray Pratincole*		West Africa (river banks of Mali to Zaire)
16 08 016	**Glareola lactea** *Milky (Little) Pratincole*		Sri Lanka; India to Indochina

ORDER: CHARADRIIFORMES
FAMILY: CHARADRIIDAE (Plovers)

		Location
16 09 001	**Vanellus vanellus** *Northern (Common)* *Lapwing*	Widespread Palearctic region
16 09 002	**Vanellus crassirostris** *Long-toed Lapwing*	Southern Sudan to Rhodesia
16 09 003	**Vanellus armatus** *Blacksmith Plover*	Kenya to South Africa
16 09 004	**Vanellus spinosus** *Spur-winged Lapwing*	Northeast Africa to Southeast Asia
16 09 005	**Vanellus duvaucelii** *River Lapwing*	River bars of India to Southeast Asia; Hainan
16 09 006	**Vanellus tectus** *Blackhead Plover*	Senegal to Ethiopia, Somalia, Kenya
16 09 007	**Vanellus malabaricus** *Yellow-wattled Lapwing*	Sri Lanka; Nepal, India
16 09 008	**Vanellus albiceps** *White-headed Plover*	Uganda, Tanzania to Rhodesia
16 09 009	**Vanellus lugubris** *Senegal Plover*	Africa south of the Sahara
16 09 010	**Vanellus melanopterus** *Black-winged Plover*	Highlands of Ethiopia to South Africa
16 09 011	**Vanellus coronatus** *Crowned Lapwing*	Southern Africa
16 09 012	**Vanellus senegallus** *Wattled Plover*	East and central Africa
16 09 013	**Vanellus melanocephalus** *Spot-breasted Plover*	Restricted to highlands of Ethiopia
16 09 014	**Vanellus superciliosus** *Brown-chested Wattled Plover*	Kenya, Tanzania, Uganda, Zaire

	Date	Location

16 09 015 **Vanellus gregarius**
Sociable Plover
Widespread Ethiopian, Palearctic regions

16 09 016 **Vanellus leucurus**
White-tailed Plover
East Africa to India

16 09 017 **Vanellus cayanus**
Pied Plover
Colombia to Paraguay

16 09 018 **Vanellus chilensis**
+ *Southern Lapwing*
Widespread South America

16 09 019 **Vanellus resplendens**
Andean Lapwing
Andes of South America

16 09 020 **Vanellus cinereus**
Grey-headed Lapwing
Siberia to India, Southeast Asia

16 09 021 **Vanellus indicus**
Red-wattled Lapwing
Transcaspia to Southeast Asia; Sumatra

16 09 022 **Vanellus macropterus**
Javanese Wattled Lapwing
Sumatra, Java, Timor Islands

16 09 023 **Vanellus tricolor**
Banded Plover
Widespread Australia, Tasmania

16 09 024 **Vanellus miles
(novaehollandiae)**
Masked Plover
Australia, New Zealand, New Guinea

16 09 025 **Pluvialis apricaria**
Eurasian Golden Plover
Widespread Palearctic region

16 09 026 **Pluvialis dominica**
+ *American Golden Plover*
Wide distribution worldwide

16 09 027 **Pluvialis squatarola**
*Black-bellied (Gray)
Plover*
Wide distribution worldwide

16 09 028 **Charadrius obscurus**
Red-breasted Dotterel
New Zealand (spottily distributed)

16 09 029 **Charadrius hiaticula**
Ringed Plover
Widespread Palearctic, Ethiopian regions

16 09 030 **Charadrius
semipalmatus**
Semipalmated Plover
Alaska to Argentina; Galapagos; West Indies

16 09 031 **Charadrius placidus**
Long-billed Plover
Widespread northeast Asia to Southeast Asia

16 09 032 **Charadrius dubius**
Little Ringed Plover
Widespread Ethiopian, Palearctic, Oriental regions;
New Guinea

16 09 033 **Charadrius wilsonia**
Wilson's Plover
United States to Peru, Brazil; West Indies

16 09 034 **Charadrius vociferus**
Killdeer
Southern Canada to northern Chile; West Indies

	Date	Location
16 09 035 **Charadrius melodus** *Piping Plover*		Canada, United States
16 09 036 **Charadrius thoracicus** *Black-banded Sandplover*		Confined to east and south coasts of Madagascar
16 09 037 **Charadrius pecuarius** *Kittlitz's Plover*		Africa south of the Sahara
16 09 038 **Charadrius sanctaehelenae** *St. Helena Plover*		St. Helena Island (Gulf of Guinea)
16 09 039 **Charadrius tricollaris** *Three-banded Plover*		Africa south of the Sahara; Madagascar
16 09 040 **Charadrius alexandrinus** *Snowy (Kentish) Plover*		Cosmopolitan—almost worldwide distribution
16 09 041 **Charadrius marginatus** *White-fronted Sandplover*		East, central Africa; Madagascar
16 09 042 **Charadrius occidentalis** *Chilean Plover*		Arid littoral of Peru and Chile
16 09 043 **Charadrius ruficapillus** *Red-capped Dotterel*		Coastal Australia
16 09 044 **Charadrius peronii** *Malaysian Plover*		Malaya, Indochina, Sundas, Celebes, Philippines
16 09 045 **Charadrius venustus (pallidus)** *Chestnut-banded Sandplover*		Kenya, Tanzania to coastal Southwest Africa
16 09 046 **Charadrius collaris** *Collared Plover*		Southern Mexico to Argentina
16 09 047 **Charadrius alticola** *Puna Plover*		Andes of Peru to Argentina, Chile
16 09 048 **Charadrius bicinctus** *Double-banded Dotterel*		Australia, Tasmania; New Zealand
16 09 049 **Charadrius falklandicus** *Two-banded Plover*		Southern Brazil to Tierra del Fuego
16 09 050 **Charadrius mongolus** *Mongolian Plover*		Widespread Ethiopian, Palearctic, Oriental, Australasian regions
16 09 051 **Charadrius leschenaultii** *Greater Sandplover*		Widespread Ethiopian, Palearctic, Oriental, Australasian regions
16 09 052 **Charadrius asiaticus** *Caspian Plover*		Africa to Eurasia
16 09 053 **Charadrius veredus** *Oriental Plover*		Mongolia to Australia

Date	Location

16 09 054 **Charadrius modestus**
+ *Rufous-chested Dotterel*
Southern Brazil to Tierra del Fuego; Falklands

16 09 055 **Charadrius montanus**
Mountain Plover
Canada to Mexico

16 09 056 **Charadrius melanops**
Black-fronted Dotterel
Australia, New Zealand; rare Tasmania

16 09 057 **Charadrius cinctus**
Red-kneed Dotterel
Australia, occasional to New Guinea

16 09 058 **Charadrius rubricollis**
Australian Plover
Southern Australia, Tasmania

16 09 059 **Thinornis novaeseelandiae**
Shore Plover
Confined to Southeast Island in Chathams (endangered)

16 09 060 **Anarhynchus frontalis**
Wrybill Plover
New Zealand (mainly North Island coasts)

16 09 061 **Phegornis mitchellii**
Diademed Plover
High Andes of southern Peru to Argentina, Chile

16 09 062 **Peltohyas australis**
Inland Dotterel
Australia (semi-arid interior)

16 09 063 **Eudromias morinellus**
Common Dotterel
Discontinuously distributed Holarctic region

16 09 064 **Eudromias ruficollis**
+ *Tawny-throated Dotterel*
Northern Peru to Tierra del Fuego

16 09 065 **Pluvianellus socialis**
+ *Magellanic Plover*
Tierra del Fuego area of Chile, Argentina

ORDER: CHARADRIIFORMES
FAMILY: SCOLOPACIDAE (Sandpipers)

16 10 001 **Limosa limosa**
Black-tailed Godwit
Palearctic, Ethiopian, Oriental, Australasian regions

16 10 002 **Limosa haemastica**
+ *Hudsonian Godwit*
Alaska to Tierra del Fuego

16 10 003 **Limosa lapponica**
Bar-tailed Godwit
Palearctic, Ethiopian, Oriental, Australasian regions; Alaska

16 10 004 **Limosa fedoa**
Marbled Godwit
Canada to Chile

16 10 005 **Numenius minutus**
Little Curlew
Northeast Asia to Australia

	Date	Location
16 10 006 **Numenius borealis** *Eskimo Curlew*		Nearly extinct. Holarctic, winters south to Argentina
16 10 007 **Numenius phaeopus** *Whimbrel*		Holarctic: wanders worldwide
16 10 008 **Numenius tahitiensis** *Bristle-thighed Curlew*		Holarctic
16 10 009 **Numenius tenuirostris** *Slender-billed Curlew*		Northern Palearctic Region
16 10 010 **Numenius arquata** *Eurasian Curlew*		Palearctic, Oriental regions
16 10 011 **Numenius madagascariensis** *Eastern Curlew*		Northeast Asia to Australasian region
16 10 012 **Numenius americanus** *Long-billed Curlew*		Canada to Guatemala
16 10 013 **Bartramia longicauda** *Upland Sandpiper*		Alaska to Argentina, Chile; West Indies
16 10 014 **Tringa erythropus** *Spotted Redshank*		Widespread Palearctic, Ethiopian, Oriental regions
16 10 015 **Tringa totanus** *Common Redshank*		Widespread Palearctic, Ethiopian, Oriental regions
16 10 016 **Tringa stagnatilis** *Marsh Sandpiper*		Palearctic, Ethiopian, Oriental, Australasian regions
16 10 017 **Tringa nebularia** *Common Greenshank*		Palearctic, Ethiopian, Oriental, Australasian regions
16 10 018 **Tringa guttifer** *Spotted Greenshank*		Eastern Palearctic region and Southeast Asia
16 10 019 **Tringa melanoleuca** *Greater Yellowlegs*		Alaska to Argentina, Chile
16 10 020 **Tringa flavipes** *Lesser Yellowlegs*		Alaska to Argentina, Chile
16 10 021 **Tringa ochropus** *Green Sandpiper*		Palearctic, Ethiopian, Oriental regions
16 10 022 **Tringa solitaria** *Solitary Sandpiper*		Alaska to Argentina; West Indies; Galapagos
16 10 023 **Tringa glareola** *Wood Sandpiper*		Palearctic, Ethiopian, Oriental, Australasian regions
16 10 024 **Catoptrophorus semipalmatus** *Willet*		Southern Canada to northern Chile; Galapagos; West Indies
16 10 025 **Xenus cinereus** *Terek Sandpiper*		Palearctic, Ethiopian, Oriental, Australasian regions

		Date	Location
16 10 026	**Actitis hypoleucos** *Common Sandpiper*		Widespread Palearctic, Oriental, Australasian regions
16 10 027	**Actitis macularia** *Spotted Sandpiper*		Alaska to Tierra del Fuego; Galapagos; West Indies
16 10 028	**Heteroscelus brevipes** *Polynesian Tattler*		Siberia to Australia
16 10 029	**Heteroscelus incanus** *Wandering Tattler*		North America, South America, Australasia
16 10 030	**Prosobonia cancellata** *Sharp-billed Sandpiper*		Tuamotu Islands, French Polynesia (endangered)
16 10 031	**Prosobonia leucoptera** *White-winged Sandpiper*		Extinct. Known from a single specimen from Tahiti
16 10 032	**Arenaria interpres** *Ruddy Turnstone*		Almost worldwide distribution
16 10 033	**Arenaria melanocephala** *Black Turnstone*		Alaska to Baja, California
16 10 034	**Phalaropus tricolor** *Wilson's Phalarope*		Canada to Argentina; Galapagos Islands
16 10 035	**Phalaropus lobatus** *Northern Phalarope*		Circumboreal
16 10 036	**Phalaropus fulicarius** *Red Phalarope*		Arctic circumpolar
16 10 037	**Scolopax rusticola** *Eurasian Woodcock*		Palearctic, Oriental regions
16 10 038	**Scolopax mira** *Amani Woodcock*		Restricted to northern Ryukyus (Japan)
16 10 039	**Scolopax saturata** *Javanese Woodcock*		Mountains of Sumatra, Java, New Guinea
16 10 040	**Scolopax celebensis** *Celebes Woodcock*		Celebes Islands
16 10 041	**Scolopax rochussenii** *Obi Woodcock*		Restricted to Obi Island (Moluccas)
16 10 042	**Scolopax minor** *American Woodcock*		Canada, United States
16 10 043	**Coenocorypha aucklandica** *Subantarctic Snipe*		Auckland, Snares, Antipodes Islands (endangered)
16 10 044	**Coenocorypha pusilla** *Chatham Island Snipe*		Chatham Island (off New Zealand)
16 10 045	**Gallinago solitaria** *Solitary Snipe*		Eastern Palearctic, Oriental regions
16 10 046	**Gallinago hardwickii** *Latham's Snipe*		Japan to Australasia

		Date	Location
16 10 047	**Gallinago nemoricola** *Wood Snipe*		Sri Lanka; India to the Himalayas
16 10 048	**Gallipago stenura** *Pintail Snipe*		Eastern Palearctic, Oriental mainland and islands
16 10 049	**Gallinago megala** *Swinhoe's Snipe*		Central Asia to Australasia
16 10 050	**Gallinago nigripennis** *African Snipe*		Ethiopia to South Africa
16 10 051	**Gallinago macrodactyla** *Madagascar Snipe*		Humid areas of eastern Madagascar
16 10 052	**Gallinago media** *Great Snipe*		Widespread Palearctic, Ethiopian regions; India
16 10 053	**Gallinago gallinago** *Common Snipe*		Wide distribution worldwide
16 10 054	**Gallinago paraguaiae** *Puna Snipe*		Andes of South America
16 10 055	**Gallinago nobilis** *Noble Snipe*		Venezuela, Colombia, Ecuador
16 10 056	**Gallinago undulata** *Giant Snipe*		Northern South America south to Paraguay
16 10 057	**Gallinago stricklandii** *Cordilleran Snipe*		Andes of southern South America
16 10 058	**Gallinago jamesoni** *Andean Snipe*		Andes of northern South America
16 10 059	**Gallinago imperialis** *Bogota Snipe*		Colombia (known from two specimens)
16 10 060	**Lymnocrpytes minimus** *Eurasian Jacksnipe*		Palearctic, Ethiopian, Oriental regions
16 10 061	**Limnodromus griseus** *Short-billed Dowitcher*		Alaska to Brazil, Peru; West Indies
16 10 062	**Limnodromus scolopaceus** *Long-billed Dowitcher*		Siberia; North America; South America
16 10 063	**Limnodromus semipalmatus** *Asiatic Dowitcher*		Widespread Asia
16 10 064	**Aphriza virgata** *Surfbird*		Alaska to Tierra del Fuego; Galapagos
16 10 065	**Calidris canutus** *Red Knot*		Almost worldwide distribution
16 10 066	**Calidris tenuirostris** *Great Knot*		East Asia to India, Australasia
16 10 067	**Calidris alba** *Sanderling*		Almost worldwide distribution

		Date	Location

16 10 068 **Calidris pusilla**
Semiplamated Sandpiper
Arctic North America to Chile

16 10 069 **Calidris mauri**
Western Sandpiper
Siberia; Alaska to Peru

16 10 070 **Calidris ruficollis**
Rufous-necked Sandpiper
Palearctic, Ethiopian, Australasian regions

16 10 071 **Calidris minuta**
Little Stint
Africa, Europe, Asia, Madagascar

16 10 072 **Calidris temminckii**
Temminck's Stint
Ethiopian, Palearctic, Australasian regions

16 10 073 **Calidris subminuta**
Long-toed Stint
Siberia to Australia

16 10 074 **Calidris minutilla**
Least Sandpiper
Alaska to Chile; West Indies; Galapagos

16 10 075 **Calidris fuscicollis**
White-rumped Sandpiper
Alaska to Argentina, Chile; West Indies

16 10 076 **Calidris bairdii**
Baird's Sandpiper
North America, South America, Europe, Africa

16 10 077 **Calidris melanotos**
Pectoral Sandpiper
North and South America; eastern Palearctic to Australasia

16 10 078 **Calidris acuminata**
Sharp-tailed Sandpiper
Alaska to California; Siberia to Australasia

16 10 079 **Calidris maritima**
Purple Sandpiper
Widespread Palearctic, Holarctic regions

16 10 080 **Calidris ptilocnemis**
Rock Sandpiper
Siberia; Alaska south to Oregon coast

16 10 081 **Calidris alpina**
Dunlin
Holarctic; Palearctic, Ethiopian, Oriental regions

16 10 082 **Calidris ferruginea (testacea)**
Curlew Sandpiper
Wide distribution worldwide (casual North America)

16 10 083 **Eurynorhynchus pygmeus**
Spoonbill Sandpiper
Northeast Asia to Malaysia, India

16 10 084 **Limicola falcinellus**
Broad-billed Sandpiper
Palearctic, Oriental, Australasian region

16 10 085 **Micropalama himantopus**
Stilt Sandpiper
Arctic North America to South America

16 10 086 **Tryngites subruficollis**
Buff-breasted Sandpiper
North and South America; accidental Asia

16 10 087 **Philomachus pugnax**
+ *Ruff*
Wide distribution worldwide except South America

	Date	Location

ORDER: CHARADRIIFORMES
FAMILY: THINOCORIDAE (Seedsnipes)

16 11 001 **Attagis gayi**
Rufous-bellied Seedsnipe   Andes of Ecuador to western Argentina, Chile

16 11 002 **Attagis malouinus**
White-bellied Seedsnipe   Southern Argentina, Chile; Falkland, Staten Islands

16 11 003 **Thinocorus orbignyianus**
+   *Gray-breasted Seedsnipe*   High Andes of Peru to western Argentina, Chile

16 11 004 **Thinocorus rumicivorus**
+   *Least Seedsnipe*   Ecuador to Tierra del Fuego

ORDER: CHARADRIIFORMES
FAMILY: CHIONIDIDAE (Sheathbills)

16 12 001 **Chionis alba**
+   *Snowy Sheathbill*   Antarctic Peninsula to southern Argentina, Chile;
                                        Falklands

16 12 002 **Chionis minor**
Black-faced Sheathbill   Antarctica: breeds Marion, Prince Edward, Kerguelen,
                                   Heard Islands

ORDER: CHARADRIIFORMES
FAMILY: STERCORARIIDAE (Skuas)

16 13 001 **Catharacta skua**
Great Skua   Widespread oceans of the world

16 13 002 **Catharacta maccormicki**
+   *South Polar Skua*   Widespread southern oceans; wanders widely

16 13 003 **Stercorarius pomarinus**
Pomarine Jaeger   Arctic circumpolar; wanders widely September to
                           April to 50° south

16 03 004 **Stercorarius parasiticus**
Parasitic Jaeger   Widespread oceans of the world to 60° south

16 13 005 **Stercorarius**
longicaudus
Long-tailed Jaeger   Breeds Arctic circumpolar; winters south of equator

ORDER: CHARADRIIFORMES
FAMILY: LARIDAE (Gulls and Terns)

16 14 001 **Gabianus pacificus**
Pacific Gull   South Australian and Tasmanian coasts

16 14 002 **Leucophaeus scoresbii**
+   *Dolphin Gull*   Southern Chile, Argentina; Falkland Islands

	Date	Location

16 14 003 **Pagophila alba**
+   **(eburnea)**
           Ivory Gull
Arctic circumpolar (mainly ice pack association)

16 14 004 **Larus fuliginosus**
           Lava Gull
Restricted to Galapagos Islands

16 14 005 **Larus modestus**
+   *Gray Gull*
Pacific coast of Ecuador to Chile; breeds inland deserts

16 14 006 **Larus heermanni**
           Heerman's Gull
Mainly coast of California and Baja California

16 14 007 **Larus leucopthalmus**
           White-eyed Gull
Gulf of Suez through Red Sea, Gulf of Aden, Somalia

16 14 008 **Larus hemprichii**
+   *Sooty (Aden) Gull*
Coastal East Africa to Persian Gulf

16 14 009 **Larus belcheri**
+   *Band-tailed Gull*
Coasts of southern South America

16 14 010 **Larus crassirostris**
           Black-tailed Gull
Pacific coast of East Asia; breeds coastal Japan and China

16 14 011 **Larus audouinii**
           Audouin's Gull
Spottily distributed Mediterranean Islands (endangered)

16 14 012 **Larus delawarensis**
           Ring-billed Gull
Widespread Canada to Gulf of Mexico; West Indies

16 14 013 **Larus kamtschatschensis**
           Kamchatka Gull
Coasts of northeast Asia

16 14 014 **Larus canus**
           Mew (Common) Gull
Holarctic circumpolar

16 14 015 **Larus argentatus**
           Herring Gull
Widespread circumpolar northern hemisphere

16 14 016 **Larus cachinnans**
           Yellow-legged Gull
Mediterranean basin

16 14 017 **Larus thayeri**
           Thayer's Gull
Arctic North America south to New Jersey, Baja California

16 14 018 **Larus fuscus**
           Lesser Black-backed Gull
Widespread coastal Africa and Eurasia

16 14 019 **Larus californicus**
           California Gull
Pacific coast of British Columbia to southern Mexico

16 14 020 **Larus occidentalis**
           Western Gull
Pacific coast of British Columbia to Baja California

16 14 021 **Larus dominicanus**
+   *Kelp Gull*
Circumpolar southern oceans

		<u>Date</u>	<u>Location</u>
16 14 022	**Larus schistisagus** *Slaty-backed Gull*		Pacific coast of northeast Asia, coastal China
16 14 023	**Larus marinus** *Greater Black-backed Gull*		Mainly Atlantic sector of Holarctic region
16 14 024	**Larus glaucescens** *Glaucous-winged Gull*		Breeds Siberia, Aleutians; winters to Japan, Baja California
16 14 025	**Larus hyperboreus** *Glaucous Gull*		Arctic circumpolar, disperses southward in winter
16 14 026	**Larus glaucoides** *Iceland Gull*		Breeds Arctic; winters south to British Isles, New York
16 14 027	**Larus ichthyaetus** *Great Black-headed Gull*		Russia to Mediterranean; southeast Asia
16 14 028 +	**Larus atricilla** *Laughing Gull*		Eastern Canada to northern South America; West Indies
16 14 029 +	**Larus brunnicephalus** *Brown-headed Gull*		Central Asia to Sri Lanka, India, Indochina
16 14 030 +	**Larus cirrocephalus** *Gray-headed Gull*		Widespread coastal Africa; coastal southeast South America
16 14 031	**Larus serranus** *Andean Gull*		Andes of Ecuador to Argentina, Chile
16 14 032	**Larus pipixcan** *Franklin's Gull*		Canada to Chile; Galapagos Islands
16 14 033	**Larus novaehollandiae** *Silver Gull*		South Africa to Australia, New Zealand waters
16 14 034	**Larus melanocephalus** *Mediterranean Gull*		Mediterranean coasts
16 14 035	**Larus relictus** *Relict Gull*		Kazahkstan (small colony on Lake Alakul— endangered)
16 14 036	**Larus bulleri** *Black-billed Gull*		New Zealand (widespread South Island rivers and lakes)
16 14 037 +	**Larus maculipennis** *Brown-hooded Gull*		Coastal Brazil, Uruguay, Argentina, Chile; Falkland Islands
16 14 038	**Larus ridibundus** *Black-headed Gull*		Widespread Palearctic, Oriental regions; New Guinea
16 14 039	**Larus genei** *Slender-billed Gull*		Mediterranean; Black Sea to Persian Gulf

		Date	Location
16 14 040	**Larus philadelphia** *Bonaparte's Gull*		Widespread North America south to Gulf of Panama
16 14 041	**Larus minutus** *Little Gull*		Northern Palearctic region
16 14 042	**Larus saundersi** *Saunder's Gull*		Northeast Asia, eastern China to Taiwan, Hainan
16 14 043	**Rhodostethia rosea** *Ross' Gull*		Northern Holarctic waters, rarely south of Arctic Circle
16 14 044	**Rissa tridactyla** *Black-legged Kittiwake*		Circumpolar northern oceans
16 14 045	**Rissa brevirostris** *Red-legged Kittiwake*		Holarctic waters, breeds Aleutians, Bering Sea
16 14 046 +	**Creagrus furcatus** *Swallow-tailed Gull*		Breeds Galapagos Islands; wanders to west coast of South America
16 14 047	**Xema sabini** *Sabine's Gull*		Holarctic circumpolar; winters to Peru, West Africa
16 14 048	**Cihldonias hybrida** **(leucopareia)** *Whiskered Tern*		Widespread swamps and lagoons of Eastern hemisphere
16 14 049	**Cihldonias leucoptera** *White-winged Black Tern*		Palearctic, Ethiopian, Oriental, Australasian regions
16 14 050	**Cihldonias nigra** *Black Tern*		Inland Europe and North America, southward in winter
16 14 051 +	**Phaetusa simplex** *Large-billed Tern*		Tropical South America east of the Andes
16 14 052	**Gelochelidon nilotica** *Gull-billed Tern*		Wide distribution worldwide
16 14 053	**Hydroprogne caspia** **(tschegrava)** *Caspian Tern*		Wide distribution worldwide
16 14 054	**Sterna aurantia** *River Tern*		Islands and lakes of Sri Lanka, India to Burma, Malay Peninsula
16 14 055 +	**Sterna hirundinacea** *South American Tern*		Both coasts of South America, south to Tropic of Capricorn
16 14 056	**Sterna hirundo** *Common Tern*		Wide distribution worldwide
16 14 057	**Sterna paradisaea** *Arctic Tern*		Breeds Arctic circumpolar; winters to Antarctic seas

		Date	Location
16 14 058	**Sterna vittata** *Antarctic Tern*		Circumpolar southern oceans and Antarctic seas
16 14 059	**Sterna virgata** *Kerguelen Tern*		Breeds Marion, Crozet, Kerguelen, Heard Islands
16 14 060	**Sterna forsteri** *Forster's Tern*		Canada to Guatemala, occasionally Panama
16 14 061	**Sterna trudeaui** *Trudeau's Tern*		Coastal southern South America, south of Tropic of Capricorn
16 14 062	**Sterna dougallii** *Roseate Tern*		Wide distribution worldwide
16 14 063	**Sterna striata** *White-fronted Tern*		Breeds New Zealand waters; disperses to Australia, Tasmania
16 14 064	**Sterna repressa** *White-cheeked Tern*		Red Sea, Persian Gulf to west coast of India
16 14 065	**Sterna sumatrana** *Black-naped Tern*		Tropical islands in Indian and west Pacific Ocean
16 14 066	**Sterna melanogaster** **(acuticauda)** *Black-bellied Tern*		Sri Lanka; India to Southeast Asia
16 14 067	**Sterna aleutica** *Aleutian Tern*		Breeds coastal Alaska, eastern Siberia; accidental Japan
16 14 068	**Sterna lunata** *Spectacled Tern*		Tropical Pacific Ocean, most abundant in central Pacific
16 14 069	**Sterna anaethetus** *Bridled Tern*		Widespread islands in tropical, subtropical oceans
16 14 070	**Sterna fuscata** *Sooty Tern*		Widespread tropical, subtropical oceans; highly pelagic
16 14 071	**Sterna nereis** *Nereis Tern*		Australia, Tasmania, New Zealand to New Caledonia
16 14 072	**Sterna albistriata** *Black-fronted Tern*		New Zealand (breeds South Island; wanders to Stewart, North Island)
16 14 073	**Sterna superciliaris** *Yellow-billed Tern*		Breeds river sandbanks from Orinoco to Rio la Plata
16 14 074	**Sterna balaenarum** *Damara Tern*		Confined to west coast of southern Africa
16 14 075	**Sterna lorata** *Peruvian Tern*		Endemic to Humboldt Current of Ecuador to Chile

		Date	Location
16 14 076	**Sterna albifrons** *Little (Least) Tern*		Widespread tropical to temperate parts of world
16 14 077	**Sterna saundersi** *Saunders' Tern*		Red Sea, Persian Gulf, islands in Indian Ocean
16 14 078	**Sterna bergii** *Great Crested Tern*		Indian Ocean, Persian Gulf to Australia, South Africa
16 14 079	**Sterna bengalensis** *Lesser Crested Tern*		Red Sea, coastal east Africa, Indian Ocean to Australia
16 14 080	**Sterna maxima** *Royal Tern*		United States to Argentina; West Indies; Africa; Galapagos
16 14 081	**Sterna zimmermanni** *Chinese Crested Tern*		Coast of China (Fukien to Shantung); Borneo?
16 14 082 +	**Sterna eurygnatha** *Cayenne Tern*		East coast of Colombia to Argentina; Lesser Antilles
16 14 083	**Sterna elegans** *Elegant Tern*		Breeds Baja; disperses from California to Chile
16 14 084	**Sterna sandvicensis** *Sandwich Tern*		Atlantic coasts of both Americas, Europe, Africa
16 14 085 +	**Larosterna inca** *Inca Tern*		West coast of South America from Ecuador to Chile
16 14 086	**Procelsterna cerulea (albivitta)** *Blue-gray Noddy*		Central and southern Pacific Ocean
16 14 087	**Anous stolidus** *Common (Brown) Noddy*		Circumequatorial tropical oceans
16 14 088	**Anous tenuirostris** *Lesser (Black) Noddy*		Breeds islands in Indian Ocean to western Australia
16 14 089 +	**Anous minutus** *White-capped Noddy*		Tropical Atlantic and Pacific Oceans
16 14 090	**Gygis alba** *White (Fairy) Tern*		Circumequatorial tropical oceans

ORDER: CHARADRIIFORMES
FAMILY: RYNCHOPIDAE (Skimmers)

16 15 001	**Rynchops niger (nigra)** *Black Skimmer*		United States to Argentina, Chile
16 15 002	**Rynchops flavirostris** *African Skimmer*		Rivers, lakes, coasts throughout tropical Africa
16 15 003	**Rynchops albicollis** *Indian Skimmer*		Rivers, lakes of India to southeast China, Burma, Indochina

		Date	Location

ORDER: CHARADRIIFORMES
FAMILY: ALCIDAE (Auks, Murres and Puffins)

16 16 001	**Alle alle** *Dovekie* *Little Auk (Br.)*	North Atlantic and adjacent Arctic seas
16 16 002	**Pinguinus impennis** *Great Auk*	Extinct. Last pair slaughtered in 1844 off Iceland
16 16 003	**Alca torda** *Razorbill*	North Atlantic and adjacent Arctic seas
16 16 004	**Uria lomvia** *Thick-billed Murre*	Cold oceans of northern hemisphere
16 16 005	**Uria aalge** *Common Murre* *Guillemot (Br.)*	Holarctic circumpolar
16 16 006	**Cepphus grylle** *Black Guillemot*	North Atlantic and adjacent Arctic seas
16 16 007	**Cepphus columba** *Pigeon Guillemot*	North Pacific and Bering Sea; winters to Japan, California
16 16 008	**Cepphus carbo** *Spectacled Guillemot*	Sea of Okhutsk, Sea of Japan to Bering Sea
16 16 009	**Brachyramphus marmoratus** *Marbled Murrelet*	Northern Pacific (south to Japan and California)
16 16 010	**Brachyramphus brevirostris** *Kittlitz's Murrelet*	Northern Pacific and Bering Sea to Alaska; winters to Japan
16 16 011	**Brachyramphus hypoleucus** *Xantus' Murrelet*	Coasts of California and Baja; breeds Channel Islands
16 16 012	**Brachyramphus craveri** *Craveri's Murrelet*	Coasts of California and Mexico; breeds Gulf of California
16 16 013	**Synthliboramphus antiquus** *Ancient Murrelet*	Northern Pacific Ocean and Bering Sea; winters to Japan and Baja
16 16 014	**Snythliboramphus wumizusume** *Japanese Murrelet*	Restricted to Japanese waters (endangered)
16 16 015	**Ptychoramphus aleuticus** *Cassin's Auklet*	Aleutian Islands to Baja California

		Date	Location
16 16 016	**Cyclorrhynchus psittacula** *Parakeet Auklet*		Northern Pacific and Bering Sea; winters to Japan, California
16 16 017	**Aethia cristatella** *Crested Auklet*		Northern Pacific and Bering Sea, adjacent Arctic waters
16 16 018	**Aethia pusilla** *Least Auklet*		Northern Pacific, Bering Sea; winters to Japan, Aleutians
16 16 019	**Aethia pygmaea** *Whiskered Auklet*		Northern Pacific, Bering Sea, Kuriles, Aleutians
16 16 020	**Cerorhinca monocerata** *Rhinoceros Auklet*		Northern Pacific; winters to Japan, Baja California
16 16 021	**Fratercula arctica** *Common (Atlantic) Puffin*		Both sides of north Atlantic, adjacent Arctic seas
16 16 022	**Fratercula corniculata** *Horned Puffin*		Northern Pacific and Bering Sea, Alaska; winters to California
16 16 023	**Lunda cirrhata** *Tufted Puffin*		Northern Pacific and Bering Sea to Kuriles, California

ORDER: COLUMBIFORMES
FAMILY: PTEROCLIDAE (Sandgrouse)

17 01 001	**Syrrhaptes tibetanus** *Tibetan Sandgrouse*		Inhospitable wastes of central Asia to Sikkim Himalayas
17 01 002	**Syrrhaptes paradoxus** *Pallas' Sandgrouse*		Steppes of China, Russia, Mongolia, Manchuria
17 01 003	**Pterocles alchata** *Pin-tailed Sandgrouse*		Arid Mediterranean basin to India
17 01 004	**Pterocles namaqua** *Namaqua Sandgrouse*		South Africa (drier parts of Angola to the Cape)
17 01 005	**Pterocles exustus** *Chestnut-bellied Sandgrouse*		Barren plains of Africa to India
17 01 006	**Pterocles senegallus** *Spotted Sandgrouse*		Deserts of northwest Africa to Pakistan
17 01 007	**Pterocles orientalis** *Black-bellied Sandgrouse*		Arid Mediterranean basin to India
17 01 008	**Pterocles coronatus** *Crowned Sandgrouse*		Bare Sahara deserts to Pakistan

		Date	Location
17 01 009	**Pterocles gutturalis** *Yellow-throated Sandgrouse*		Ethiopia to South Africa
17 01 010	**Pterocles burchelli** *Burchell's Sandgrouse*		South Africa
17 01 011	**Pterocles personatus** *Madagascar (Masked) Sandgrouse*		Dry areas of west and southwest Madagascar
17 01 012 +	**Pterocles decoratus** *Black-faced Sandgrouse*		Ethiopia, Somalia to Tanzania
17 01 013	**Pterocles lichtensteinii** *Lichtenstein's Sandgrouse*		Arid North Africa to India
17 01 014	**Pterocles bicinctus** *Double-banded Sandgrouse*		Southern Africa
17 01 015	**Pterocles indicus** *Painted Sandgrouse*		Punjab and Ganges River south to Mysore and Madras
17 01 016	**Pterocles quadricinctus** *Four-banded Sandgrouse*		Lake Chad to Ethiopia, Kenya, Uganda

ORDER: COLUMBIFORMES
FAMILY: RAPHIDAE (Dodos and Solitaires)

17 02 001	**Raphus cucullatus** *Dodo*	Extinct since 1680. Inhabited Mauritius, Mascarene Islands
17 02 002	**Raphus solitarius** *Reunion Solitaire*	Extinct since 1750. Inhabited Reunion, Mascarene Islands
17 02 003	**Pezophaps solitaria** *Rodriguez Solitaire*	Extinct since 1800. Inhabited Rodriguez, Mascarene Islands

ORDER: COLUMBIFORMES
FAMILY: COLUMBIDAE (Pigeons and Doves)

17 03 001	**Columba livia** *Rock Dove*	Palearctic. Domesticated and distributed worldwide
17 03 002	**Columba rupestris** *Eastern Rock Pigeon*	Central, east Asia to China, Korea, the Himalayas
17 03 003	**Columba leuconota** *Snow Pigeon*	Himalayas of Afghanistan to Tibet, Burma

		Date	Location
17 03 004	**Columba guinea** *Speckled Pigeon*		Africa south of the Sahara
17 03 005	**Columba albitorques** *White-collared Pigeon*		Highlands of central and eastern Ethiopia; Eritrea
17 03 006	**Columba oenas** *Stock Dove*		Western Palearctic region
17 03 007	**Columba eversmanni** *Yellow-eyed Stock Dove*		Aral Sea to northern Afghanistan, northern India
17 03 008	**Columba oliviae** *Somali Stock Dove*		Coastal deserts of Somalia
17 03 009	**Columba palumbus** *Wood Pigeon*		Western Palearctic regions; Azores; northern India
17 03 010	**Columba trocaz** *Trocaz Pigeon*		Restricted to Madeira (Canary Islands)
17 03 011	**Columba bollii** *Boll's Pigeon*		High altitude laurel forests of Canary Islands
17 03 012	**Columba unicincta** *African Wood Pigeon*		Equatorial rain forests of Africa
17 03 013	**Columba junoniae** *Laurel Pigeon*		Laurel forests of La Palma, Gomera Islands (Canaries)
17 03 014	**Columba arquatrix** *Olive Pigeon*		Ethiopia to South Africa, Angola
17 03 015	**Columba sjostedti** *Cameroon Olive Pigeon*		Highland forests of Cameroon
17 03 016	**Columba thomensis** *São Thomé Olive Pigeon*		Confined to São Thomé Island (Gulf of Guinea)
17 03 017	**Columba pollenii** *Comoro Olive Pigeon*		High evergreen forests of the Comoro Islands
17 03 018	**Columba hodgsonii** *Speckled Wood Pigeon*		Himalayas of Kashmir to western China, Burma
17 03 019	**Columba albinucha** *White-naped Pigeon*		Forests of eastern Zaire and western Uganda
17 03 020	**Columba pulchricollis** *Ashy Wood Pigeon*		Mountain forests of Nepal, Sikkim, Tibet to Burma
17 03 021	**Columba elphinstonii** *Nilgiri Wood Pigeon*		Forests of southwest India
17 03 022	**Columba torringtoni** *Ceylon Wood Pigeon*		Evergreen and deciduous forests of Sri Lanka
17 03 023	**Columba punicea** *Purple Wood Pigeon*		Eastern India, western China to Indochina; Hainan
17 03 024	**Columba argentina** *Silver Pigeon*		Sumatra, Borneo, North Natunas, Rhio Archipelago

		Date	Location
17 03 025	**Columba palumboides** *Andaman Wood Pigeon*		Forests of Andaman and Nicobar Islands
17 03 026	**Columba janthina** *Black Wood Pigeon*		Dense evergreen forests of Ryukyu, Bonin, Volcano Islands
17 03 027	**Columba vitiensis** *White-throated Pigeon*		Philippines to New Guinea, Fiji, Samoa
17 03 028	**Columba leucomela** *White-headed Pigeon*		Coastal forests of eastern Australia
17 03 029	**Columba versicolor** *Bonin Wood Pigeon*		Extinct since 1889. Inhabited Bonin Islands
17 03 030	**Columba jouyi** *Silver-banded Black Pigeon*		Okinawa, Ryukyu, Borodino Islands (probably extinct)
17 03 031	**Columba pallidiceps** *Yellow-legged Pigeon*		Forests of Bismarck Archipelago and Solomon Islands
17 03 032	**Columba leucocephala** *White-crowned Pigeon*		Florida; offshore islands West Indies to Panama
17 03 033	**Columba squamosa** *Red-necked Pigeon*		West Indies (widespread Greater and Lesser Antilles)
17 03 034	**Columba speciosa** *Scaled Pigeon*		Tropical southeast Mexico to Bolivia, Brazil
17 03 035	**Columba picazuro** *Picazuro Pigeon*		Open country of northeast Brazil to northeast Argentina
17 03 036	**Columba corensis** *Bare-eyed Pigeon*		Arid coasts of Colombia, Venezuela and adjacent islands
17 03 037	**Columba maculosa** *Spotted Pigeon*		Arid temperate Bolivia, southern Peru to northern Argentina
17 03 038	**Columba fasciata** *Band-tailed Pigeon*		Highlands of southwest Canada to northern Argentina
17 03 039	**Columba araucana** *Chilean Pigeon*		Andean lowlands of Chile, Argentina (endangered)
17 03 040	**Columba caribaea** *Ring-tailed Pigeon*		Inland wooded areas of Jamaica
17 03 041	**Columba cayennensis** *Rufous Pigeon*		Southeast Mexico to Peru, Paraguay, Brazil
17 03 042	**Columba flavirostris** *Red-billed Pigeon*		Southern Texas to Nicaragua, Costa Rica; Tres Marias Islands

		Date	Location

17 03 043   **Columba oenops**
Salvin's Pigeon   Subtropical woodlands Upper Marañon Valley (Peru)

17 03 044   **Columba inornata**
Plain Pigeon   Cuba, Isle of Pines, Hispaniola, Jamaica, Puerto Rico (endangered)

17 03 045   **Columba plumbea**
Plumbeous Pigeon   Tropical eastern Colombia to Bolivia, Guianas, Brazil

17 03 046   **Columba subvinacea**
Ruddy Pigeon   Costa Rica to Peru, Bolivia, all of Brazil

17 03 047   **Columba nigrirostris**
Short-billed Pigeon   Lowland rain forest of southeast Mexico to eastern Panama

17 03 048   **Columba goodsoni**
Dusky Pigeon   Tropical western Colombia to western Ecuador

17 03 049   **Columba delegorguei**
Delegorgue's Pigeon   Highlands of Kenya, Sudan to South Africa

17 03 050   **Columba iriditorques**
Bronze-naped Pigeon   Sierra Leone to Angola, Zaire

17 03 051   **Columba malherbii**
São Thomé Bronze-naped Pigeon   São Thomé, Principe, Annobon Islands (Gulf of Guinea)

17 03 052   **Columba mayeri**
Pink Pigeon   Mauritius Island (on the verge of extinction)

17 03 053   **Streptopelia turtur**
Turtle Dove   Europe, North Africa to India

17 03 054   **Streptopelia lugens**
Dusky Turtle Dove   Eastern Zaire to Ethiopia, Rhodesia; Yemen

17 03 055   **Streptopelia hypopyrrha**
Adamawa Turtle Dove   Highlands of Cameroon and Nigeria

17 03 056   **Streptopelia orientalis**
Rufous Turtle Dove   India, Himalayas, central Asia to Indochina

17 03 057   **Streptopelia bitorquata**
Javanese Turtle Dove   Java, Lesser Sundas, Philippines, Sulu Archipelago

17 03 058   **Streptopelia decaocto**
Collared Dove   Europe, North Africa to Burma, China, Korea

17 03 059   **Streptopelia risoria**
Ringed Turtle Dove   Domesticated. Wide distribution worldwide

17 03 060   **Streptopelia roseogrisea**
African Turtle Dove   North Africa to western Arabia

17 03 061   **Streptopelia reichenowi**
White-winged Turtle Dove   *Borassus* palm areas of southern Ethiopia (endangered)

		Date	Location
17 03 062	**Streptopelia decipiens** *African Mourning Dove*		Africa south of the Sahara
17 03 063	**Streptopelia semitorquata** *Red-eyed Dove*		Africa south of the Sahara
17 03 064	**Streptopelia capicola** *Ring-necked Dove*		Ethiopia to Angola, South Africa
17 03 065	**Streptopelia vinacea** *Vinaceous Dove*		Dry savanna from Senegal to Eritrea
17 03 066	**Streptopelia tranquebarica** *Red Turtle Dove*		Widespread Oriental mainland; Philippines; Andamans
17 03 067	**Streptopelia picturata** *Madagascar Turtle Dove*		Madagascar, Comoro, Seychelles and Aldabra Islands
17 03 068	**Streptopelia chinensis** *Spotted Dove*		Pakistan to southeast China
17 03 069	**Streptopelia senegalensis** *Laughing Dove*		Widespread Africa to India
17 03 070	**Aplopelia larvata (simplex)** *Lemon Dove*		Ethiopia to Cameroon, Angola, South Africa
17 03 071	**Macropygia unchall (tusalia)** *Barred Cuckoo Dove*		Himalayas to Assam, Malaya, Sumatra, Java, Hainan
17 03 072	**Macropygia amboinensis** *Pink-breasted Cuckoo Dove*		New Guinea, Celebes, Sulas, Moluccas Islands
17 03 073	**Macropygia phasianella** *Slender-billed Cuckoo Dove*		Eastern Australia to the Greater Sundas, Philippines
17 03 074	**Macropygia magna** *Large Cuckoo Dove*		Southern Celebes and Tanimbar Islands
17 03 075	**Macropygia rufipennis** *Andaman Cuckoo Dove*		Secondary growth on Andaman and Nicobar Islands
17 03 076	**Macropygia nigrirostris** *Black-billed Cuckoo Dove*		New Guinea, Bismarck and D'Entrecasteaux Archipelago
17 03 077	**Macropygia mackinlayi** *Mackinlay's Cuckoo Dove*		New Hebrides, Solomons, New Britain, adjacent islands
17 03 078	**Macropygia ruficeps** *Little Cuckoo Dove*		Burma to Indochina; Lesser and Greater Sundas

		Date	Location

17 03 079 **Reinwardtoena reinwardtsi**
Great Cuckoo Dove
Mountain forests of New Guinea to the Solomons

17 03 080 **Reinwardtoena browni**
Brown's Cuckoo Dove
Forests of New Britain and Duke of York Island

17 03 081 **Reinwardtoena crassirostris**
Crested Long-tailed Pigeon
Hill forests of the Solomon Islands

17 03 082 **Turacoena manadensis**
White-faced Pigeon
Celebes, Buton, Peling and Sula Islands

17 03 083 **Turacoena modesta**
Timor Black Pigeon
Woodlands of Timor Island (Lesser Sundas)

17 03 084 **Turtur chalcospilos**
Green-spotted Wood Dove
Ethiopia, Somalia to South Africa

17 03 085 **Turtur abyssinicus**
Black-billed Wood Dove
Drier tropical Africa from Senegal to Eritrea

17 03 086 **Turtur afer**
Blue-spotted Wood Dove
Africa south of the Sahara (except Cape District)

17 03 087 **Turtur tympanistria**
+ *Tambourine Dove*
Riparian woods of Sierra Leone to Ethiopia

17 03 088 **Turtur brehmeri**
Blue-headed Wood Dove
Forests of Sierra Leone to northern Zaire

17 03 089 **Oena capensis**
+ *Namaqua Dove*
Africa south of the Sahara; Arabia; Madagascar

17 03 090 **Chalcophaps indica**
Emerald Dove
Widespread Oriental mainland and islands to Australia

17 03 091 **Chalcophaps stephani**
Brown-backed Emerald Dove
Celebes, New Guinea and Solomon Islands

17 03 092 **Henicophaps albifrons**
Black Bronzewing
New Guinea and adjacent islands

17 03 093 **Henicophaps foersteri**
New Britain Bronzewing
Restricted to New Britain Island

17 03 094 **Phaps chalcoptera**
Common Bronzewing
Dry open scrubland of Australia and Tasmania

17 03 095 **Phaps elegans**
Brush Bronzewing
Coastal heathlands of southeast and southwest Australia; Tasmania

17 03 096 **Phaps histrionica**
Flock Pigeon
Grasslands and semi-deserts of interior of Australia

17 03 097 **Ocyphaps lophotes**
+ *Crested Pigeon*
Widespread Australia

	Date	Location

17 03 098 Petrophassa plumifera
White-bellied Plumed Pigeon
Central and interior of tropical northern Australia

17 03 099 Petrophassa ferruginea
Red Plumed Pigeon
Dry areas of northern and western Australia

17 03 100 Petrophassa scripta
Squatter Pigeon
Queensland to New South Wales (Australia)

17 03 101 Petrophassa smithii
Partridge Pigeon
Kimberley Division and Northern Territory of Australia

17 03 102 Petrophassa rufipennis
Chestnut-quilled Rock Pigeon
Confined to Arnhem Land, northern Australia

17 03 103 Petrophassa albipennis
White-quilled Rock Pigeon
Confined to Kimberley area of northern Australia

17 03 104 Geopelia cuneata
Diamond Dove
Widespread savannas of Australia

17 03 105 Geopelia striata
(placida)
Zebra Dove
Widespread Southeast Asia to Australia

17 03 106 Geopelia humeralis
+
Bar-shouldered Dove
Northern and eastern Australia; New Guinea lowlands

17 03 107 Leucosarcia
melanoleuca
Wonga Pigeon
Rain forests of Queensland to Victoria (Australia)

17 03 108 Ectopistes migratorius
Passenger Pigeon
Extinct since 1914. Ranged from Canada to United States

17 03 109 Zenaida macroura
Mourning Dove
Southern Canada to Panama; West Indies

17 03 110 Zenaida auriculata
+
Eared Dove
Widespread South America; Trinidad, Tobago

17 03 111 Zenaida aurita
Zenaida Dove
Widespread West Indies; coastal Yucatán Peninsula

17 03 112 Zenaida galapagoensis
Galapagos Dove
Endemic to Galapagos Islands

17 03 113 Zenaida asiatica
White-winged Dove
Southwest United States to northern Chile

17 03 114 Columbina passerina
Common Ground Dove
Southern United States to central Ecuador, Brazil

17 03 115 Columbina minuta
Plain-breasted Ground Dove
Southern Mexico to northern Paraguay, Brazil

17 03 116 Columbina buckleyi
Buckley's Ground Dove
Arid tropical northwest Peru, adjacent Ecuacor

		Date	Location
17 03 117	**Columbina talpacoti** *Ruddy Ground Dove*		Widespread northern Mexico to northern Argentina
17 03 118	**Columbina picui** *Picui Ground Dove*		Northeast Brazil to southern Peru, central Argentina
17 03 119	**Columbina cruziana** *Gold-billed Ground Dove*		Arid coast of Ecuador, Peru, northern Chile
17 03 120	**Columbina cyanopis** *Blue-eyed Ground Dove*		Interior of Brazil (Matto Grosso)
17 03 121	**Claravis pretiosa** *Blue Ground Dove*		Southern Mexico to northern Argentina
17 03 122	**Claravis godefrida** *Purple-barred Ground Dove*		Wooded country of southeast Brazil, adjacent Paraguay
17 03 123	**Claravis mondetoura** *Maroon-chested Ground Dove*		Mountains of Mexico to Peru, Bolivia
17 03 124	**Metriopelia ceciliae** *Bare-faced Ground Dove*		Arid temperate puna zone of Peru, Bolivia, northern Chile
17 03 125	**Metriopelia morenoi** *Bare-eyed Ground Dove*		Temperate and puna zones of northwest Argentina
17 03 126	**Metriopelia melanoptera** *Black-winged Ground Dove*		Andes of Colombia to Argentina, Chile
17 03 127	**Metriopelia aymara** *Bronze-winged Ground Dove*		Puna zone of southern Peru to northern Chile, Argentina
17 03 128	**Scardafella inca** *Inca Dove*		Southern United States to Nicaragua, Costa Rica
17 03 129	**Scardafella squammata** *Scaly Dove*		Arid tropical zone of Venezuela, Colombia to southeast Brazil
17 03 130	**Uropelia campestris** *Long-tailed Ground Dove*		Campos of Brazil to eastern Bolivia
17 03 131	**Leptotila verreauxi** *White-tipped Dove*		Semi-arid country from Texas to Argentina
17 03 132	**Leptotila megalura** *White-faced Dove*		Subtropical Bolivia, Argentina (Jujuy, Salta, Tucuman)
17 03 133	**Leptotila rufaxilla** *Gray-fronted Dove*		Humid forests of eastern Colombia to Paraguay, all Brazil
17 03 134	**Leptotila plumbeiceps (battyi)** *Gray-headed Dove*		Tropical southern Mexico to western Colombia

		Date	Location

17 03 135	**Leptotila pallida** *Pallid Dove*		Tropical Pacific coast of western Colombia and Ecuador
17 03 136	**Leptotila wellsi** *Grenada Dove*		Lowlands of Grenada Island (West Indies)
17 03 137	**Leptotila jamaicensis** *White-bellied Dove*		Jamaica, Grand Cayman, St. Andrews, Cozumel, Holbox Islands
17 03 138	**Leptotila cassini** *Cassin's Dove*		Humid lowland forests southeast Mexico to western Colombia
17 03 139	**Leptotila ochraceiventris** *Ochre-bellied Dove*		Tropical, subtropical southwest Ecuador to Peru
17 03 140	**Leptotila conoveri** *Tolima Dove*		Subtropical central Andes of Colombia
17 03 041	**Geotrygon lawrencii** *Lawrence's Quail Dove*		Humid mountain forests of southeast Mexico to Panama
17 03 142	**Geotrygon costaricensis** *Costa Rican Quail Dove*		Subtropical rain forest of Costa Rica to Panama
17 03 143	**Geotrygon goldmani** *Goldman's Quail Dove*		Subtropical northwest Colombia, adjacent Panama
17 03 144	**Geotrygon saphirina** *Sapphire Quail Dove*		Tropical Colombia west of Andes to Peru
17 03 145	**Geotrygon caniceps** *Gray-headed Quail Dove*		Mountain forests of Dominica; rare in Cuba
17 03 146	**Geotrygon versicolor** *Crested Quail Dove*		Forests of the Island of Jamaica
17 03 147	**Geotrygon veraguensis** *Veragua Quail Dove*		Subtropical forests of Colombia to Peru, Bolivia
17 03 148	**Geotrygon linearis** *Lined Quail Dove*		Humid mountain forests of eastern Colombia, Venezuela
17 03 149	**Geotrygon chiriquensis** *Chiriqui Quail Dove*		Humid mountain forests Costa Rica to western Panama
17 03 150	**Geotrygon albifacies** *White-faced Quail Dove*		Humid mountain forests southern Mexico to Nicaragua
17 03 151	**Geotrygon frenata** **(erythropareia)** *White-throated Quail Dove*		Subtropical forests of Columbia to Peru, Bolivia
17 03 152	**Geotrygon chrysia** *Key West Quail Dove*		Semi-arid lowlands of Cuba, Bahamas, Hispaniola

		Date	Location

17 03 153 **Geotrygon mystacea**
Bridled Quail Dove — Dry woodlands of Virgin Islands and Lesser Antilles

17 03 154 **Geotrygon violacea**
Violaceous Quail Dove — Nicaragua to Argentina (east of Andes)

17 03 155 **Geotrygon montana (martinica)**
Ruddy Quail Dove — Tropical southern Mexico to northern Argentina; Lesser Antilles

17 03 156 **Starnoenas cyanocephala**
Blue-headed Quail Dove — Lowland forests of Cuba; extinct on Isle of Pines

17 03 157 **Caloenas nicobarica**
Nicobar Pigeon — Andamans, Nicobars, Sundas, Philippines to Solomons

17 03 158 **Gallicolumba luzonica**
Luzon Bleeding-heart Pigeon — Forests of Luzon and Polillo Islands (Philippines)

17 03 159 **Gallicolumba criniger**
Bartlett's Bleeding-heart Pigeon — Forests of Mindanao, Leyte, Samar, Basilan (Philippines)

17 03 160 **Gallicolumba platenae**
Mindoro Bleeding-heart Pigeon — Forests of Island of Mindoro (Philippines)

17 03 161 **Gallicolumba keayi**
Negros Bleeding-heart Pigeon — Forests of Island of Negros (Philippines)

17 03 162 **Gallicolumba menagei**
Tawi-Tawi Bleeding-heart Pigeon — Forests of Tawi-Tawi Island (Philippines)

17 03 163 **Gallicolumba rufigula**
Golden-heart Pigeon — New Guinea, Arus and western Papuan Islands

17 03 164 **Gallicolumba tristigmata**
Celebes Quail Dove — Primeval forests of Celebes Islands

17 03 165 **Gallicolumba jobiensis**
White-breasted Ground Dove — New Guinea, Bismarck Archipelago and Solomon Islands

17 03 166 **Gallicolumba kubaryi**
Truk Island Ground Dove — Truk and Ponapé Islands (Eastern Carolines)

17 03 167 **Gallicolumba erythroptera**
White-collared Ground Dove — Forests of Society and Taumotu Islands

17 03 168 **Gallicolumba xanthonura**
White-throated Ground Dove — Forests of Yap and Marianas Islands

		Date	Location

17 03 169 **Gallicolumba norfolciensis**
Norfolk Island Dove   Extinct. Inhabited Norfolk Island

17 03 170 **Gallicolumba stairi**
Friendly Ground Dove   Fiji, Tonga and Samoan Islands

17 03 171 **Gallicolumba sanctaecrucis**
Santa Cruz Ground Dove   Tinakula and Utupua (Santa Cruz Islands); New Hebrides

17 03 172 **Gallicolumba ferruginea**
Tanna Ground Dove   Extinct. Known from one specimen from Tanna Island

17 03 173 **Gailicolumba salamonis**
Thick-billed Ground Dove   Woodlands of Ramos and San Cristobal Islands (Solomons)

17 03 174 **Gallicolumba rubescens**
Marquesas Ground Dove   Fatuhuku and Hatutu Islands (Marquesas—endangered)

17 03 175 **Gallicolumba beccarii**
Gray-breasted Ground Dove   Mountain forests of New Guinea, Admiralty, Rennell, Solomons

17 03 176 **Gallicolumba canifrons**
Palau Ground Dove   Woodlands of Palau Islands (endangered)

17 03 177 **Gallicolumba hoedtii**
Wetar Island Ground Dove   Confined to Wetar Island (Lesser Sundas)

17 03 178 **Trugon terrestris**
Thick-billed Ground Pigeon   Lowland forests of New Guinea and Salawati Island

17 03 179 **Microgoura meeki**
Choiseul Crowned Pigeon   Extinct. Last seen 1904 Choiseul (Solomon Islands)

17 03 180 **Otidiphaps nobilis**
Pheasant Pigeon   New Guinea, Batanta, Waigeu, Arus, Ferguson Island

17 03 181 **Goura cristata**
Blue Crowned Pigeon   Northwestern New Guinea and western Papuan Islands

17 03 182 **Goura scheepmakeri**
Maroon-breasted Crowned Pigeon   Forests of southeastern New Guinea

17 03 183 **Goura victoria**
Victoria Crowned Pigeon   Northern New Guinea, Japen and Biak Islands (endangered)

17 03 184 **Didunculus strigirostris**
Tooth-billed Pigeon   Upolu and Savaii Islands (Samoa—endangered)

17 03 185 **Phapitreron leucotis**
Lesser Brown Fruit Dove   Woodlands of Philippine Islands

17 03 186 **Phapitreron amethystina**
Greater Brown Fruit Dove   Deep forests of Philippine Islands

		Date	Location
17 03 187	**Treron fulvicollis** *Cinnamon-headed Green Pigeon*		Malay Peninsula, Sumatra, Borneo
17 03 188	**Treron olax** *Little Green Pigeon*		Malay Peninsula, Sumatra, Java, Borneo
17 03 189	**Treron vernans** *Pink-necked Green Pigeon*		Southeast Asia; Sumatra and Java to Philippines, Celebes
17 03 190	**Treron bicincta** *Orange-breasted Green Pigeon*		India, Indo-Malayan region; Hainan; Java; Celebes
17 03 191	**Treron pompadora** *Pompadour Green Pigeon*		Sri Lanka; India to Indochina; Philippines; Sulu Archipelago
17 03 192	**Treron curvirostra** *Thick-billed Green Pigeon*		Widespread Oriental mainland and islands
17 03 193	**Treron griseicauda** *Gray-faced Green Pigeon*		Sumatra, Java, Bali to the Celebes, Sanghir Islands
17 03 194	**Treron teysmanni** *Sumba Island Green Pigeon*		Confined to Sumba Island (Lesser Sundas)
17 03 195	**Treron floris** *Flores Green Pigeon*		Confined to the Lesser Sunda Islands
17 03 196	**Treron psittacea** *Timor Green Pigeon*		Confined to Timor and Samau Islands (Lesser Sundas)
17 03 197	**Treron capellei** *Large Green Pigeon*		Malay peninsula, Java, Sumatra and Borneo
17 03 198	**Treron phoenicoptera** *Yellow-legged Green Pigeon*		Sri Lanka; India to Annam, Laos, Cochinchina
17 03 199	**Treron waalia** *Yellow-bellied Green Pigeon*		Dry savanna and thorn scrub of Senegal to Eritrea
17 03 200	**Treron australis** *Madagascar Green Pigeon*		Madagascar and Moheli Islands; adjacent East Africa
17 03 201	**Treron calva (delalandii)** *African Green Pigeon*		Forested Africa south of the Sahara
17 03 202	**Treron pembaensis** *Pemba Island Green Pigeon*		Confined to Pemba Island (off East African coast)
17 03 203	**Treron sanctithomae** *São Thomé Green Pigeon*		São Thomé and Rollas Islet in Gulf of Guinea

		Date	Location
17 03 204	**Treron apicauda** *Pin-tailed Green Pigeon*		Himalayan foothills from India to Laos
17 03 205	**Treron oxyura** *Yellow-bellied Pintail Pigeon*		Mountains of Sumatra and western Java
17 03 206	**Treron seimundi** *White-bellied Pintail Pigeon*		Mountain ranges and foothills of Malay Peninsula
17 03 207	**Treron sphenura** **(korthalsi)** *Wedge-tailed Green Pigeon*		India to Indochina; Sumatra, Java, Lombok
17 03 208	**Treron sieboldii** *White-bellied Green Pigeon*		Japan, Korea, southern China to Annam
17 03 209	**Treron formosae** *Formosan Green Pigeon*		Formosa; Ryukyus; Batan, Calayan, Camiguin Islands (Philippines)
17 03 210	**Ptilinopus cinctus** *Black-backed Fruit Dove*		Indonesian islands from Timor, Wetar, Flores to Damar, Babar
17 03 211	**Ptilinopus alligator** *Black-banded Pigeon*		Headwaters of South Alligator River (Northern Territory of Australia)
17 03 212	**Ptilinopus dohertyi** *Red-naped Fruit Dove*		Confined to forests of Sumba Island (Indonesia)
17 03 213	**Ptilinopus porphyrea** *Pink-necked Fruit Dove*		Forests of Sumatra, Java and Bali
17 03 214	**Ptilinopus marchei** *Marche's Fruit Dove*		Mountain forests of Luzon and Polillo Islands (Philippines)
17 03 215	**Ptilinopus merrilli** *Merrill's Fruit Dove*		Mountain forests of Luzon and Polillo Islands (Philippines)
17 03 216	**Ptilinopus occipitalis** *Yellow-breasted Fruit Dove*		Lowland primeval forests of Philippines (except Luzon)
17 03 217	**Ptilinopus fischeri** *Fischer's Fruit Dove*		Mountain forests of Celebes Islands
17 03 218	**Ptilinopus jambu** *Jambu Fruit Dove*		Malay Peninsula, Rhio Archipelago, Sumatra, Borneo
17 03 219	**Ptilinopus subgularis** *Dark-chinned Fruit Dove*		Lowland primeval forests of Celebes and adjacent islands

		Date	Location

17 03 220 **Ptilinopus leclancheri**
Black-chinned Fruit Dove Forests of Philippine Islands

17 03 221 **Ptilonopus formosus**
Scarlet-breasted Fruit Dove Hill forests of northern Moluccas (Ternate, Batjan, Obi)

17 03 222 **Ptilinopus magnificus**
Wompoo Pigeon New Guinea and adjacent islands and eastern Australia

17 03 223 **Ptilinopus perlatus**
Pink-spotted Fruit Dove New Guinea, western Papuan Islands, Arus

17 03 224 **Ptilinopus ornatus**
Ornate Fruit Dove Lowland and hill forests of New Guinea

17 03 225 **Ptilinopus tannensis**
Silver-shouldered Fruit Dove New Hebrides and Banks Island

17 03 226 **Ptilinopus aurantiifrons**
Orange-fronted Fruit Dove New Guinea, Arus, western Papuan Islands

17 03 227 **Ptilinopus wallacii**
Wallace's Fruit Dove Lowland forests of New Guinea, adjacent southwest islands

17 03 228 **Ptilinopus superbus**
Superb Fruit Dove Celebes to Moluccas, New Guinea, northeast Australia

17 03 229 **Ptilinopus perousii**
Many-colored Fruit Dove Samoan, Fiji and Tonga Islands

17 03 230 **Ptilinopus porphyraceus (ponapensis)**
Purple-capped Fruit Dove Fiji, Tonga, Samoa and Caroline Islands

17 03 231 **Ptilinopus pelewensis**
Palau Fruit Dove Woods and thickets of Palau Islands

17 03 232 **Ptilinopus rarotongensis**
Rarotongan Fruit Dove Confined to Raratonga Island (Hervey group)

17 03 233 **Ptilinopus roseicapilla**
Marianas Fruit Dove Saipan, Tinian, Rota, Guam Islands (Marianas)

17 03 234 **Ptilinopus regina (ewingi)**
Pink-capped Fruit Dove Eastern Lesser Sunda Islands; northeastern Australia

17 03 235 **Ptilinopus richardsii**
Silver-capped Fruit Dove Ugi, Santa Anna, Rennell Islands (Solomons)

17 03 236 **Ptilinopus purpuratus (chrysogaster) (coralensis)**
Tahitian Fruit Dove Society Islands and Lau Archipelago

		Date	Location
17 03 237	**Ptilinopus greyii** *Grey's Fruit Dove*		Santa Cruz, New Hebrides, Loyalty, New Caledonia Islands
17 03 238	**Ptilinopus huttoni** *Rapa Island Fruit Dove*		Confined to Rapa Island (Austral group)
17 03 239	**Ptilinopus dupetithouarsii** *White-capped Fruit Dove*		Woodlands of Marquesas Islands
17 03 240	**Ptilinopus mercierii** *Red-moustached Fruit Dove*		Nukuhiva and Hivaoa Islands (Marquesas)
17 03 241	**Ptilinopus insularis** *Henderson Island Fruit Dove*		Confined to Henderson Island (Pitcairn group)
17 03 242	**Ptilinopus coronulatus** *Lilac-capped Fruit Dove*		Lowland forests of New Guinea and adjacent islands
17 03 243	**Ptilinopus pulchellus** *Crimson-capped Fruit Dove*		New Guinea and western Papuan Islands
17 03 244	**Ptilinopus monacha** *Blue-capped Fruit Dove*		Halmahera, Ternate, Batjan Islands (northern Moluccas)
17 03 245	**Ptilinopus rivoli** *White-bibbed Fruit Dove*		Moluccas to New Guinea, Bismarck Archipelago
17 03 246	**Ptilinopus solomonensis** *Yellow-bibbed Fruit Dove*		Solomons, Bismarck Archipelago, islands in Geelvink Bay
17 03 247	**Ptilinopus viridis** **(geelvinkiana)** **(pectoralis)** *Red-bibbed Fruit Dove*		Southern Moluccas to New Guinea, Solomon Islands
17 03 248	**Ptilinopus eugeniae** *White-headed Fruit Dove*		San Cristobal and Ugi Islands (Solomons)
17 03 249	**Ptilinopus iozonus** *Orange-bellied Fruit Dove*		Lowland forests of New Guinea and adjacent islands
17 03 250	**Ptilinopus insolitus** *Knob-billed Fruit Dove*		New Ireland, New Britain, Duke of York, St. Mathias Islands
17 03 251	**Ptilinopus hyogastra** *Gray-headed Fruit Dove*		Halmahera and Batjan Islands (northern Moluccas)
17 03 252	**Ptilinopus granulifrons** *Carunculated Fruit Dove*		Forests of Obi Island (central Moluccas)
17 03 253	**Ptilinopus melanospila** *Black-naped Fruit Dove*		Philippines to Celebes, Togian, Lesser Sundas

		Date	Location
17 03 254	**Ptilinopus naina** *Dwarf Fruit Dove*		Southeast New Guinea; Waigeu, Salawati, Misol Islands
17 02 255	**Ptilinopus arcanus** *Negros Fruit Dove*		Philippines (known from one specimen from Negros Island)
17 03 256	**Ptilinopus victor** *Orange Dove*		Forests of Fiji Islands
17 03 257	**Ptilinopus luteovirens** *Golden Dove*		Woodlands of Fiji Islands
17 02 258	**Ptilinopus layardi** *Yellow-headed Dove*		Kandavu and Ono Islands (Fiji Islands)
17 03 259	**Drepanoptila holosericea** *Cloven-feathered Dove*		Forests of New Caledonia and Isle of Pines (endangered)
17 03 260	**Alectroenas madagascariensis** *Madagascar Blue Pigeon*		Restricted to evergreen forests of Madagascar
17 03 261	**Alectroenas sganzini** *Comoro Blue Pigeon*		Evergreen forests of Comoro and Aldabra Islands
17 03 262	**Alectroenas nitidissima** *Mauritius Blue Pigeon*		Extinct. Inhabited riverside forest canopy of Mauritius Island
17 03 263	**Alectroenas pulcherrima** *Seychelles Blue Pigeon*		Evergreen forests of Seychelles Islands
17 03 264	**Ducula poliocephala** *Pink-beilied Imperial Pigeon*		Occurs on most of the Philippine Islands
17 03 265	**Ducula forsteni** *Celebes Imperial Pigeon*		Dense primeval mountain forests of Celebes Islands
17 03 266	**Ducula mindorensis** *Mindoro Imperial Pigeon*		Highlands of Mindoro Island (Philippines—endangered)
17 03 267	**Ducula radiata** *Gray-headed Imperial Pigeon*		Mountain forests of Celebes Islands
17 03 268	**Ducula carola** *Spotted Imperial Pigeon*		Luzon, Mindoro, Negros, Mindanao Islands (Philippines)
17 03 269	**Ducula aenea (aneothorax)** *Green Imperial Pigeon*		Widespread Oriental mainland and islands

		Date	Location

17 03 270 **Ducula perspicillata**
White-eyed Imperial Pigeon
Forests of Moluccan Islands

17 03 271 **Ducula concinna**
Blue-tailed Imperial Pigeon
Islands east of Celebes to Arus (off New Guinea)

17 03 272 **Ducula pacifica**
Pacific Pigeon
Widespread Pacific islands from New Guinea to Samoa

17 03 273 **Ducula oceanica**
Micronesian Pigeon
Woodlands of Caroline, Palau, Marshall Islands

17 03 274 **Ducula aurorae**
Society Islands Pigeon
Society Islands of Makatea, Aurora (extinct on Tahiti)

17 03 275 **Ducula galeata**
Marquesas Pigeon
Nearing extinction (50 birds on Nukuhiva Island in 1952)

17 03 276 **Ducula rubricera**
Red-knobbed Pigeon
Lowlands of Bismarck Archipelago and Solomon Islands

17 03 277 **Ducula myristicivora**
Black-knobbed Pigeon
Western Papuan Islands and islands in Geelvink Bay

17 03 278 **Ducula rufigaster**
Rufous-bellied Imperial Pigeon
New Guinea, Japen, adjacent western Papuan Islands

17 03 279 **Ducula basilica**
Moluccan Fruit Pigeon
Forests of northern and central Moluccan Islands

17 03 280 **Ducula finschii**
Finsch's Imperial Pigeon
Confined to forests of Bismarck Archipelago

17 03 281 **Ducula chalconota**
Mountain Fruit Pigeon
High forests of mountains of New Guinea

17 03 282 **Ducula pistrinaria**
Island Imperial Pigeon
Solomon Islands to Bismarck Archipelago, Admiralty Islands

17 03 283 **Ducula rosacea**
Pink-headed Imperial Pigeon
Lesser Sundas; islands in Flores Sea; occasional Celebes

17 03 284 **Ducula whartoni**
Christmas Island Imperial Pigeon
Inland plateau of Christmas Island (Indian ocean)

17 03 285 **Ducula pickeringii**
Gray Imperial Pigeon
Islands off northeast Borneo, Sulu Archipelago, Talaut Islands

17 03 286 **Ducula latrans**
Peale's Pigeon
Vanua Levu, Viti Levu, Ovalau, Kandavu, Matuku (Fijis)

	Date	Location

17 03 287 **Ducula brenchleyi**
Chestnut-bellied Pigeon — Primarily mountain forests of Solomon Islands

17 03 288 **Ducula bakeri**
Baker's Pigeon — Mountain forests of New Hebrides and Banks Islands

17 03 289 **Ducula goliath**
New Caledonian Pigeon — Mountain forests of New Caledonia, Isle of Pines (endangered)

17 03 290 **Ducula pinon**
Pinon Imperial Pigeon — Lowlands of New Guinea, adjacent islands and archipelagoes

17 03 291 **Ducula melanochroa**
Black Imperial Pigeon — Forests of Bismarck Archipelago

17 03 292 **Ducula mullerii**
Muller's Imperial Pigeon — Riverine lowlands of New Guinea and Aru Islands

17 03 293 **Ducula zoeae**
Zoe Imperial Pigeon — Lowland forests of New Guinea and adjacent islands

17 03 294 **Ducula badia**
Mountain Imperial Pigeon — India to Southeast Asia; Hainan; Greater Sundas

17 03 295 **Ducula lacernulata**
Dark-backed Imperial Pigeon — Wooded mountains of Java, Bali, Lombok, Flores Islands

17 03 296 **Ducula cineracea**
Timor Imperial Pigeon — Mountain forests of Timor and Wetar Islands (Lesser Sundas)

17 03 297 **Ducula bicolor (melanura)**
Pied Imperial Pigeon — Andamans, Nicobars to Philippines, New Guinea, Moluccas

17 03 298 **Ducula luctuosa**
Celebes Pied Imperial Pigeon — Celebes, Sula, Peling and Banggai Islands

17 03 299 **Ducula spilorrhoa**
Nutmeg (Torres Strait) Pigeon — Coastal northern Australia to New Guinea

17 03 300 **Lopholaimus antarcticus**
Topknot Pigeon — Coastal Queensland to Victoria (Australia)

17 03 301 **Hemiphaga novaeseelandiae**
New Zealand Pigeon — Forests of New Zealand and adjacent islands

17 03 302 **Cryptophaps poecilorrhoa**
Celebes Dusky Pigeon — Primeval mountain forests of Celebes Islands

17 03 303 **Gymnophaps albertisii**
Bare-eyed Mountain Pigeon — Moluccas, Solomons, New Guinea, Bismarck Archipelago

	Date	Location

17 03 304 Gymnophaps mada
Long-tailed Mountain Pigeon

Mountain forests of Buru and Ceram Islands (Moluccas)

17 03 305 Gymnophaps solomonensis
Pale Mountain Pigeon

Hill forests of Solomon Islands

ORDER: PSITTACIFORMES
FAMILY: LORIIDAE (Lories and Lorikeets)

18 01 001 Chalcopsitta atra
Black Lory

Western New Guinea, adjacent islands

18 01 002 Chalcopsitta duivenbodei
Duyvenbode's Lory

Lowlands of northern New Guinea

18 01 003 Chalcopsitta sintillata
Yellow-streaked Lory

Southern New Guinea and Aru Islands

18 01 004 Chalcopsitta cardinalis
Cardinal Lory

Solomon Islands and adjacent islands

18 01 005 Eos cyanogenia
Black-winged Lory

Islands in Geelvink Bay (New Guinea)

18 01 006 Eos squamata
Violet-necked Lory

Moluccas to western Papuan Islands

18 01 007 Eos reticulata
Blue-streakd Lory

Tanimbar Island (Indonesia)

18 01 008 Eos histrio
Red and Blue Lory

Sangir Islands (Indonesia)

18 01 009 Eos bornea
Red Lory

Moluccas Islands (Indonesia)

18 01 010 Eos semilarvata
Blue-eared Lory

Mountains of Ceram Island (Indonesia)

18 01 011 Pseudeos fuscata
Dusky Lory

New Guinea, Salawati and Japen Islands

18 01 012 Trichoglossus ornatus
Ornate Lory

Celebes and adjacent larger offshore islands

18 01 013 Trichoglossus haematodus
Rainbow Lory

Widespread Australia, Indonesia, New Guinea, Solomons

18 01 014 Trichoglossus rubiginosus
Ponape Lory

Ponapé Island (Caroline Islands)

		Date	Location
18 01 015	**Trichoglossus johnstoniae** *Johnstone's Lorikeet*		Philippine Islands (mountains of Mindanao)
18 01 016	**Trichoglossus flavovirdis** *Yellow and Green Lorikeet*		Celebes and Sula Islands (Indonesia)
18 01 017	**Trichoglossus chlorolepidotus** *Scaly-breasted Lorikeet*		Cape York Peninsula to Sydney (Australia)
18 01 018	**Trichoglossus euteles** *Perfect Lorikeet*		Lesser Sunda Islands (Indonesia)
18 01 019	**Trichoglossus versicolor** *Varied Lorikeet*		Lowlands of tropical northern Australia
18 01 020	**Trichoglossus iris** *Iris Lory*		Timor and Wetar Islands (Lesser Sundas)
18 01 021	**Trichoglossus goldiei** *Goldie's Lorikeet*		Mountains of New Guinea
18 01 022	**Lorius hypoinochrous** *Purple-bellied Lory*		New Guinea, Papuan islands to Bismarck Archipelago
18 01 023	**Lorius lory** *Black-capped Lory*		New Guinea and adjacent islands
18 01 024	**Lorius albidinuchus** *White-naped Lory*		New Ireland Island (rare)
18 01 025	**Lorius chlorocercus** *Yellow-bibbed Lory*		Eastern Solomon Islands (not on Bougainville)
18 01 026	**Lorius domicellus** *Purple-naped Lory*		Ceram and Amboina Islands (Indonesia)
18 01 027	**Lorius tibialis** *Blue-thighed Lory*		Moluccas Islands (unique—probable aberrant *L. domicellus*)
18 01 028	**Lorius garrulus** *Chattering Lory*		Moluccas Islands
18 01 029	**Phigys solitarius** *Collared Lory*		Fiji Islands
18 01 030	**Vini australis** *Blue-crowned Lory*		Samoa, Tonga to Lau Archipelago
18 01 031	**Vini kuhlii** *Kuhl's Lory*		Austral Islands (Rimitara, Tubuai)
18 01 032	**Vini stepheni** *Stephen's Lory*		Henderson Island (Pitcairn group)
18 01 033	**Vini peruviana** *Tahitian Lory*		Society, Tuamotu, Cook Islands (endangered)
18 01 034	**Vini ultramarina** *Ultramarine Lory*		Marquesas Islands (verge of extinction)

	Date	Location
18 01 035 **Glossopsitta concinna** *Musk Lorikeet*		Queensland to Victoria; Tasmania; Kangaroo Island
18 01 036 **Glossopsitta pusilla** *Little Lorikeet*		Eastern Australia, Tasmania
18 01 037 **Glossopsitta porphyrocephala** *Purple-crowned Lorikeet*		Southern Australia (excluding Tasmania)
18 01 038 **Charmosyna palmarum** *Palm Lorikeet*		New Hebrides, Duff, Santa Cruz, Banks Islands
18 01 039 **Charmosyna rubrigularis** *Red-chinned Lorikeet*		New Britain, New Ireland, Karkar Island
18 01 040 **Charmosyna meeki** *Meek's Lorikeet*		Mountains of the Solomon Islands
18 01 041 **Charmosyna toxopei** *Blue-fronted Lorikeet*		Buru Island (Indonesia—known from 7 specimens)
18 01 042 **Charmosyna multistriata** *Striated Lorikeet*		Western New Guinea (Snow Mountains to Fly River)
18 01 043 **Charmosyna wilhelminae** *Wilhelmina's Lorikeet*		Highlands of New Guinea
18 01 044 **Charmosyna rubronotata** *Red-spotted Lorikeet*		Salawati, Biak, northwest New Guinea
18 01 045 **Charmosyna placentis** *Red-flanked Lorikeet*		Moluccas to New Guinea, Bismarck Archipelago
18 01 046 **Charmosyna diadema** *New Caledonian Lorikeet*		Extinct since 1860. Inhabited New Caledonia Island
18 01 047 **Charmosyna amabilis** *Red-throated Lorikeet*		Fiji Islands (Viti Levu, Ovalau, Taveuni)
18 01 048 **Charmosyna margarethae** *Dutchess Lorkeet*		Solomon Islands (mainly mountain forests)
18 01 049 **Charmosyna pulchella** *Fairy Lorikeet*		Mid-mountain forests of New Guinea
18 01 050 **Charmosyna josefinae** *Josefine's Lory*		Mountains of New Guinea (Vogelkop to Sepic)
18 01 051 **Charmosyna papou** *Papuan Lory*		Mountains of New Guinea (Vogelkop to Papua)
18 01 052 **Oreopsittacus arfaki** *Whiskered Lorikeet*		Mountains of New Guinea (Vogelkop to Papua)
18 01 053 **Neopsittacus musschenbroekii** *Musschenbroek's Lorikeet*		Mountains of New Guinea (Vogelkop to Papua)
18 01 054 **Neopsittacus pullicauda** *Emerald Lorikeet*		New Guinea (Snow Mountains to southern Papua)

		Date	Location

ORDER: PSITTACIFORMES
FAMILY: CACATUIDAE (Cockatoos)

18 02 001	**Prosciger atterimus** *Palm Cockatoo*	Queensland; New Guinea; Aru Islands
18 02 002	**Calyptorhynchus funereus (baudinii)** *Black Cockatoo*	Southeast and southwest Australia
18 02 003	**Calyptorhynchus magnificus** *Red-tailed Cockatoo*	Widespread Australia
18 02 004	**Calyptorhynchus lathami** *Glossy Cockatoo*	Queensland to Victoria; Kangaroo Island
18 02 005	**Callocephalon fimbriatum** *Gang-gang Cockatoo*	Extreme southeast Australia
18 02 006 +	**Eolophus roseicapillus** *Galah*	Widespread interior of Australia
18 02 007	**Cacatua leadbeateri** *Major Mitchell's Cockatoo*	Interior of Australia
18 02 008	**Cacatua sulphurea** *Lesser Sulphur-crested Cockatoo*	Celebes, Sundas, adjacent Indonesian islands
18 02 009 +	**Cacatua galerita** *Sulphur-crested Cockatoo*	New Guinea, Indonesia to Australia
18 02 010	**Cacatua ophthalmica** *Blue-eyed Cockatoo*	New Britain and New Ireland Islands
18 02 011	**Cacatua moluccensis** *Salmon-crested Cockatoo*	Southern Moluccas Islands
18 02 012	**Cacatua alba** *White Cockatoo*	Northern and central Moluccas
18 02 013	**Cacatua haematuropygia** *Red-vented Cockatoo*	Philippine Islands and Palawan
18 02 014	**Cacatua goffini** *Goffin's Cockatoo*	Tanimbar Islands (Indonesia)
18 02 015	**Cacatua sanguinea** *Little Corella*	Australia, southern New Guinea
18 02 016	**Cacatua tenuirostris** *Long-billed Corella*	Southeast and southwest Australia
18 02 017	**Cacatua ducorps** *Ducorp's Cockatoo*	Eastern Solomons (Bougainville to Malaita)
18 02 018	**Nymphicus hollandicus** *Cockatiel*	Widespread Australia (mainly interior)

		Date	Location

ORDER: PSITTACIFORMES
FAMILY: PSITTACIDAE (Parrots)

18 03 001	**Nestor nobabilis** *Kea*	New Zealand (mountains of South Island)
18 03 002	**Nestor meridionalis** *Kaka*	New Zealand and some offshore islands
18 03 003	**Nestor productus** *Norfolk Island Kea*	Extinct since 1851. Inhabited Norfolk Island
18 03 004	**Micropsitta pusio** *Buff-faced Pygmy Parrot*	New Guinea to Bismarck Archipelago
18 03 005	**Micropsitta keiensis** *Yellow-capped Pygmy Parrot*	New Guinea and adjacent western Papuan Islands
18 03 006	**Micropsitta geelvinkiana** *Geelvink Pygmy Parrot*	Numfor and Biak Islands (New Guinea)
18 03 007	**Micropsitta meeki** *Meek's Pygmy Parrot*	Admiralties (St. Matthias and Squally Islands)
18 03 008	**Micropsitta finschii** *Finsch's Pygmy Parrot*	Solomon Islands and Bismarck Archipelago
18 03 009	**Micropsitta bruijnii** *Red-breasted Pygmy Parrot*	Moluccas, Solomons, New Guinea, Bismarck Archipelago
18 03 010	**Opopsitta gulielmiterti** *Orange-breasted Fig Parrot*	New Guinea, Salawati, Aru Islands
18 03 011	**Opopsitta diophthalma** *Double-eyed Fig Parrot*	Coastal northeast Australia to New Guinea
18 03 012	**Psittaculirostris desmarestii** *Desmarest's Fig Parrot*	New Guinea and western Papuan Islands
18 03 013	**Psittaculirostris edwardsii** *Edward's Fig Parrot*	Lowland forests of northeast New Guinea
18 03 014	**Psittaculirostris salvadorii** *Salvadori's Fig Parrot*	Northern coast of West Irian (New Guinea)
18 03 015	**Bolbopsittacus lunulatus** *Guaiabero*	Widespread throughout the Philippine Islands
18 03 016	**Psittinus cyanurus** *Blue-rumped Parrot*	Malaya, Sumatra, Borneo
18 03 017	**Psittacella brehmii** *Brehm's Parrot*	Mountains of New Guinea
18 03 018	**Psittacella picta** *Painted Parrot*	High mountain forests of New Guinea

Date	Location

18 03 019 **Psittacella modesta**
Modest Parrot
Mountains of western New Guinea

18 03 020 **Psittacella madaraszi**
Madarasz's Parrot
Mountains of eastern New Guinea

18 03 021 **Geoffroyus geoffroyi**
Red-cheeked Parrot
Widespread Indonesia, New Guinea to Australia

18 03 022 **Geoffroyus simplex**
Blue-collared Parrot
Mountain forests of New Guinea

18 03 023 **Geoffroyus heteroclitus**
Singing Parrot
Bismarck Archipelago and Solomon Islands

18 03 024 **Prioniturus discurus**
*Blue-crowned Racket-
tailed Parrot*
Philippine Islands (also Jolo Island)

18 03 025 **Prioniturus luconensis**
Green Racket-tailed Parrot
Philippines (Luzon and Marinduque Islands)

18 03 026 **Prioniturus montanus**
*Mountain Racket-tailed
Parrot*
Philippine Islands and Sulu Archipelago

18 03 027 **Prioniturus mada**
Buru Racket-tailed Parrot
Mountains of Buru Island (Moluccas)

18 03 028 **Prioniturus platurus**
*Golden-mantled Racket-
tailed Parrot*
Celebes and adjacent islands

18 03 029 **Prioniturus flavicans**
*Red-spotted Racket-tailed
Parrot*
Celebes, Peleng, Togian Islands

18 03 030 **Tanygnathus
megalorynchos**
Great-billed Parrot
New Guinea, Celebes, Lesser Sundas, Moluccas

18 03 031 **Tanygnathus lucionensis**
Blue-naped Parrot
Philippines and adjacent islands

18 03 032 **Tanygnathus
sumatranus**
Müller's Parrot
Philippines, Celebes and Sulu Archipelago

18 03 033 **Tanygnathus heterurus**
Rufous-tailed Parrot
Celebes Islands (unique—probable aberrant *T. sumatranus*)

18 03 034 **Tanygnathus gramineus**
Black-lored Parrot
Mountains of Buru Island (Moluccas)

18 03 035 **Eclectus roratus**
Eclectus Parrot
Australia, New Guinea, Solomon Islands

18 03 036 **Psittrichas fulgidus**
Pesquet's Parrot
Mountain forests of New Guinea

18 03 037 **Prosopeia tabuensis**
Red Shining Parrot
Fiji Islands

	Date	Location
18 03 038 **Prosopeia personata** *Masked Shining Parrot*		Fiji Islands (Viti Levu only—endangered)
18 03 039 **Alisterus scapularis** *Australian King Parrot*		Coastal eastern Australia (Queensland to Victoria)
18 03 040 **Alisterus chloropterus** *Green-winged King Parrot*		New Guinea (east of the Weyland Mountains)
18 03 041 **Alisterus amboinensis** *Amboina King Parrot*		Sulas, Moluccas to New Guinea
18 03 042 **Aprosmictus erythropterus** *Red-winged Parrot*		Eucalyptus forests of Australia, New Guinea
18 03 043 **Aprosmictus jonquillaceus** *Timor Red-winged Parrot*		Timor and Wetar Islands (Lesser Sundas)
18 03 044 **Polytelis swainsonii** *Superb Parrot*		Victoria, New South Wales (Australia)
18 03 045 **Polytelis anthopeplus** *Regent Parrot*		Southwest, eastern South Australia
18 03 046 **Polytelis alexandrae** *Princess Parrot*		Interior of west and central Australia
18 03 047 **Purpureicephalus spurius** *Red-capped Parrot*		Southwestern Australia
18 03 048 **Barnardius barnardi** *Mallee Ringneck Parrot*		Interior of eastern Australia
18 03 049 **Barnardius zonarius** *Port Lincoln Parrot*		Central and western Australia
18 03 050 **Platycercus caledonicus** *Green Rosella*		Tasmania and islands of Bass Strait
18 03 051 **Platycercus elegans** *Crimson Rosella*		Queensland to Victoria; Tasmania
18 03 052 **Platycercus flaveolus** *Yellow Rosella*		South Australia, New South Wales, Victoria
18 03 053 **Platycercus adelaidae** *Adelaide Rosella*		South Australia (Flinders Range to Fleurieu Peninsula)
18 03 054 **Platycercus eximius** *Eastern Rosella*		Queensland to Victoria; Tasmania
18 03 055 **Platycercus adscitus** *Pale-headed Rosella*		Queensland, New South Wales
18 03 056 **Platycercus venustus** *Northern Rosella*		Northern Territory, Western Australia
18 03 057 **Platycercus icterotis** *Western Rosella*		Southwestern Australia

	Date	Location
18 03 058	**Psephotus haematonotus** *Red-rumped Parrot*	Interior of southeast Australia
18 03 059	**Psephotus varius** *Mulga Parrot*	Interior of southern Australia
18 03 060	**Psephotus haematogaster** *Blue-Bonnet*	Interior of southeast, southern Australia
18 03 061	**Psephotus chrysopterygius** *Golden-shouldered Parrot*	Queensland (seriously endangered)
18 03 062	**Psephotus pulcherrimus** *Paradise Parrot*	Queensland, New South Wales (possibly extinct)
18 03 063	**Cyanoramphus unicolor** *Antipodes Green Parakeet*	Antipodes Island (endangered)
18 03 064	**Cyanoramphus novaezelandiae** *Red-fronted Parakeet*	New Zealand, Norfolk, New Caledonia Islands
18 03 065	**Cyanoramphus auriceps** *Yellow-fronted Parakeet*	New Zealand and outlying islands (endangered)
18 03 066	**Cyanoramphus malherbi** *Orange-fronted Parakeet*	South Island, New Zealand (rare—endangered)
18 03 067	**Cyanoramphus zealandicus** *Black-fronted Parakeet*	Extinct since 1844. Inhabited Tahiti, Society Islands
18 03 068	**Cyanoramphus ulietanus** *Society Parakeet*	Extinct since 1773. Inhabited Raiatea, Society Islands
18 03 069	**Eunymphicus cornutus** *Horned Parakeet*	New Caledonia, Ouvea island (Loyalty islands—endangered)
18 03 070	**Neophema bourkii** *Bourke's Parrot*	Interior of south and central Australia
18 03 071	**Neophema chrysostoma** *Blue-winged Parrot*	Queensland to Victoria; Tasmania
18 03 072	**Neophema elegans** *Elegant Parrot*	Southwest and southeast Australia
18 03 073	**Neophema petrophila** *Rock Parrot*	Coastal southern Australia, adjacent islands
18 03 074	**Neophema chrysogaster** *Orange-bellied Parrot*	Southeast Australia, Tasmania (endangered)
18 03 075	**Neophema pulchella** *Turquoise Parrot*	Queensland to Victoria (endangered)
18 03 076	**Neophema splendida** *Scarlet-chested Parrot*	Interior of southern Australia (endangered)

		Date	Location
18 03 077	**Lathamus discolor** *Swift Parrot*		Southeast Australia, Tasmania
18 03 078	**Melopsittacus undulatus** *Budgerigar*		Interior of Australia
18 03 079	**Pezoporus wallicus** *Ground Parrot*		Coastal Australia, Tasmania (endangered)
18 03 080	**Geopsittacus occidentalis** *Night Parrot*		Interior of Australia (possibly extinct)
18 03 081	**Lophopsittacus mauritanus** *Broad-billed Parrot*		Extinct since 1638. Inhabited Mauritius, Mascarene Islands
18 03 082	**Necropsittacus rodericanus** *Rodriguez Parrot*		Extinct since 1731. Inhabited Rodriguez, Mascarene Islands
18 03 083	**Mascarinus mascarinus** *Mascarene Parrot*		Extinct since 1834. Inhabited Reunion and possibly Mauritius Islands
18 03 084	**Coracopsis vasa** *Vasa Parrot*		Madagascar, Comoro Islands
18 03 085	**Coracopsis nigra** *Black Parrot*		Madagascar, Comoro, Praslin Island (Seychelles)
18 03 086	**Psittacus erithacus** *Gray Parrot*		Gulf of Guinea islands to Kenya, Tanzania
18 03 087	**Poicephalus robustus** *Cape Parrot*		West, central and south Africa
18 03 088	**Poicephalus gulielmi** *Jardine's Parrot*		Ghana to Zaire, Kenya, Tanzania
18 03 089	**Poicephalus cryptoxanthus** *Brown-headed Parrot*		Kenya to Rhodesia
18 03 090	**Poicephalus crassus** *Niam-Niam Parrot*		Cameroon to Zaire, the Sudan
18 03 091	**Poicephalus senegalus** *Senegal Parrot*		Central-western Africa (Senegal to Zaire)
18 03 092	**Poicephalus rufiventris** *Red-bellied Parrot*		Dry thornbush of Ethiopia and Somalia
18 03 093	**Poicephalus meyeri** *Meyer's Parrot*		Ethiopian region to South Africa
18 03 094	**Poicephalus rueppellii** *Rüppell's Parrot*		Coastal southern Angola to Southwest Africa
18 03 095	**Poicephalus flavifrons** *Yellow-faced Parrot*		Highland *hagenia* forests of Ethiopia

		Date	Location

18 03 096 **Agapornis cana**
           Gray-headed Lovebird   Madagascar; introduced adjacent islands

18 03 097 **Agapornis pullaria**
           Red-faced Lovebird   Lowlands of Senegal to Tanzania

18 03 098 **Agapornis taranta**
           Black-winged Lovebird   Juniper forests of Ethiopia and Eritrea

18 03 099 **Agapornis swinderniana**
           Black-collared Lovebird   Lowland evergreen forests of Senegal to Uganda

18 03 100 **Agapornis roseicollis**
           Peach-faced Lovebird   Dry country of southwestern Africa

18 03 101 **Agapornis fischeri**
           Fischer's Lovebird   Inland plateau of Kenya, Uganda, Tanzania

18 03 102 **Agapornis personata**
           Masked Lovebird   Inland plateau of Kenya, Uganda, Tanzania

18 03 103 **Agapornis lilianae**
           Nyasa Lovebird   Tanzania, Zambia to Rhodesia

18 03 104 **Agapornis nigrigenis**
           Black-cheeked Lovebird   Southwestern Zambia to northwestern Rhodesia

18 03 105 **Loriculus vernalis**
           Vernal Hanging Parrot   India to Malaya, Indochina

18 03 106 **Loriculus beryllinus**
           Ceylon Hanging Parrot   Lowlands and hills of Sri Lanka

18 03 107 **Loriculus philippensis**
           Philippine Hanging Parrot Philippine Islands and Sulu Archipelago

18 03 108 **Loriculus galgulus**
           *Blue-crowned Hanging   Malay Peninsula, Sumatra, Borneo
           Parrot*

18 03 109 **Loriculus stigmatus**
           Celebes Hanging Parrot   Celebes, Togian, Butung, Muna Islands

18 03 110 **Loriculus amabilis**
           Moluccan Hanging Parrot   Great Sangi, Sula, Peling, Banggai Islands
                                       (Moluccas)

18 03 111 **Loriculus exilis**
           Green Hanging Parrot   Northern and southeastern Celebes Islands

18 03 112 **Loriculus flosculus**
           Wallace's Hanging Parrot Flores Island (Lesser Sundas—almost unknown)

18 03 113 **Loriculus pusillus**
           *Yellow-throated Hanging   Islands of Java and Bali (Indonesia)
           Parrot*

18 03 114 **Loriculus aurantifrons**
           *Orange-fronted Hanging   New Guinea, Misol Island to Bismarck Archipelago
           Parrot*

18 03 115 **Psittacula eupatria**
           Alexandrine Parakeet   Sri Lanka; India to Indochina; Andamans

		Date	Location
18 03 116	**Psittacula wardi** *Seychelles Parakeet*	Extinct since 1900. Inhabited Mahe, Silhouette (Seychelles)	
18 03 117	**Psittacula krameri** *Rose-ringed Parakeet*	North Africa to India, Burma; Sri Lanka	
18 03 118	**Psittacula echo** *Mauritius Parakeet*	Mauritius Island (Indian Ocean—endangered)	
18 03 119	**Psittacula exsul** *Newton's Parakeet*	Extinct since 1875. Inhabited Rodriguez, Mascarene Islands	
18 03 120	**Psittacula himalayana (finschii)** *Slaty-headed Parakeet*	Himalayas of Kashmir to Indochina	
18 03 121	**Psittacula cyanocephala** *Plum-headed Parakeet*	Sri Lanka; India north to the Himalayas	
18 03 122	**Psittacula roseata** *Blossom-headed Parakeet*	Lower Himalayas to Thailand, South Vietnam	
18 03 123	**Psittacula intermedia** *Intermediate Parakeet*	India (possible hybrid—known from seven skins)	
18 03 124	**Psittacula columboides** *Malabar Parakeet*	Hills forests of the Malabar coast of India	
18 03 125	**Psittacula calthorpae** *Emerald-collared Parakeet*	Restricted to the hills of Sri Lanka	
18 03 126	**Psittacula derbiana** *Derbyan Parakeet*	Szechwan, Yunnan and southeast Tibet	
18 03 127	**Psittacula alexandri** *Moustached Parakeet*	India to Southeast Asia; Greater Sundas; Hainan	
18 03 128	**Psittacula caniceps** *Blyth's Parakeet*	Restricted to the Nicobar Islands	
18 03 129	**Psittacula longicauda** *Long-tailed Parakeet*	Malaya, Sumatra, Borneo; Andamans; Nicobars	
18 03 130	**Anodorhynchus hyacinthinus** *Hyacinth Macaw*	Tropical eastern Brazil (rare)	
18 03 031	**Anodorhynchus glaucus** *Glaucous Macaw*	Paraguay, Uruguay, adjacent Brazil (rare)	
18 03 132	**Anodorhynchus leari** *Lear's Macaw*	Eastern Brazil (Pernambuco, Bahia—endangered)	
18 03 133	**Cyanopsitta spixii** *Spix's Macaw*	Eastern Brazil (Piaui—very rare)	
18 03 134	**Ara autocthones** *St. Croix Macaw*	Known from a sub-fossil tibiotarsus found on St. Croix Island, West Indies	

		Date	Location
18 03 135 +	**Ara araraura** *Blue and Yellow Macaw*		Eastern Panama to Paraguay, Brazil
18 03 136	**Ara caninde** *Caninde Macaw*		Paraguay and Bolivia (known from five specimens)
18 03 137	**Ara militaris** *Military Macaw*		Mexico to northwest Argentina
18 03 138	**Ara ambigua** *Buffon's Macaw*		Nicaragua to western Colombia and Ecuador
18 03 139 +	**Ara macao** *Scarlet Macaw*		Southern Mexico to Bolivia (Santa Cruz), Brazil
18 03 140	**Ara chloroptera** *Green-winged Macaw*		Eastern Panama to northern Argentina, Brazil
18 03 141	**Ara tricolor** *Cuban Macaw*		Extinct since 1864. Inhabited Cuba
18 03 142	**Ara rubrogenys** *Red-fronted Macaw*		Bolivia (Cochabamba—almost unknown)
18 03 143	**Ara severa** *Chestnut-fronted Macaw*		Eastern Panama to Bolivia, southern Brazil
18 03 144	**Ara auricollis** *Golden-collared Macaw*		Bolivia, Paraguay, adjacent Brazil, Argentina
18 03 145	**Ara manilata** *Red-bellied Macaw*		Northern South America through Amazonian Brazil
18 03 146	**Ara maracana** *Blue-winged Macaw*		Amazonian Brazil, Paraguay, northeast Argentina
18 03 147	**Ara couloni** *Blue-headed Macaw*		Eastern Peru (probably adjacent Brazil)
18 03 148	**Ara nobilis** *Red-shouldered Macaw*		Guianas, eastern Venezuela to southern Brazil
18 03 149 +	**Aratinga acuticaudata** *Blue-crowned Conure*		Colombia and Venezuela to northern Argentina
18 03 150	**Aratinga guarouba** *Golden Conure*		Northeast Brazil (Pará to Maranhão—endangered)
18 03 151	**Aratinga holochlora** *Green Conure*		Northwest Mexico to Nicaragua; Socorro Island
18 03 152	**Aratinga finschi** *Finsch's Conure*		Caribbean Costa Rica to western Panama
18 03 153	**Aratinga wagleri** *Scarlet-fronted Conure*		Venezuela, Colombia to southern Peru
18 03 154	**Aratinga mitrata** *Mitred Conure*		Central Peru to western Argentina (Cordoba)
18 03 155	**Aratinga erythrogenys** *Red-masked Conure*		Arid western Ecuador to western Peru

		Date	Location
18 03 156	**Aratinga leucophthalmus** *White-eyed Conure*		Guianas, Venezuela to Brazil, Argentina
18 03 157	**Aratinga chloroptera** *Hispaniolian Conure*		Confined to the Island of Hispaniola
18 03 158	**Aratinga euops** *Cuban Conure*		Confined to heavily forested regions of Cuba
18 03 159	**Aratinga auricapilla** *Golden-capped Conure*		Eastern Brazil (Bahia to Rio Grando do Sul)
18 03 160	**Aratinga jandaya** *Jandaya Conure*		Northeast Brazil (Goiás and adjacent areas)
18 03 161	**Aratinga solstitialis** *Sun Conure*		Guianas, southeast Venezuela, Amazonian Brazil
18 03 162	**Aratinga weddellii** *Dusky-headed Conure*		Southeast Colombia to Bolivia, adjacent Brazil
18 03 163	**Aratinga nana (astec)** *Olive-throated (Aztec) Conure*		Jamaica; southeast Mexico to western Panama
18 03 164	**Aratinga canicularis** *Orange-fronted Conure*		Mexico (Sinaloa) to western Costa Rica
18 03 165	**Aratinga pertinax** *Brown-throated Conure*		Panama through northern Amazonian Brazil
18 03 166	**Aratinga cactorum** *Cactus Conure*		Inland *caatinga* of eastern Brazil
18 03 167	**Aratinga aurea** *Peach-fronted Conure*		Widespread Brazil south to northern Argentina
18 03 168	**Nandayus nenday** *Nanday (Black-hooded) Conure*		Northern Argentina, adjacent Bolivia, Brazil
18 03 169	**Leptosittaca branickii** *Golden-plumed Conure*		Temperate Andes of Colombia, Ecuador, Peru
18 03 170	**Ognorhynchus icterotis** *Yellow-eared Conure*		Andes of Colombia to northern Ecuador
18 03 171	**Rhynchopsitta pachyrhyncha (terrisi)** *Thick-billed Parrot*		Mountains of northern Mexico (endangered)
18 03 172	**Conuropsis carolinensis** *Carolina Parakeet*		Extinct since 1914. Inhabited southeast United States
18 03 173	**Cyanoliseus patagonus** *Patagonian Conure*		Central Chile and western Argentina
18 03 174	**Pyrrhura cruentata** *Blue-throated Conure*		Eastern Brazil (Bahia to São Paulo)
18 03 175	**Pyrrhura devillei** *Black-winged Conure*		Eastern Bolivia, Paraguay, southwest Matto Grosso

		Date	Location
18 03 176 +	**Pyrrhura frontalis** *Maroon-bellied Conure* Reddish		Southeast Brazil (Bahia) to northern Argentina
18 03 177	**Pyrrhura perlata** *Pearly Conure*		Eastern Brazil (Pará, Maranhão)
18 03 178	**Pyrrhura rhodogaster** *Crimson-bellied Conure*		Northern Brazil (south of the Amazon)
18 03 179	**Pyrrhura molinae** *Green-cheeked Conure*		Southern Matto Grosso to northwest Argentina
18 03 180	**Pyrrhura hypoxantha** *Yellow-sided Conure*		Brazilian Matto Grosso (probable aberrant *P. molinae*)
18 03 181	**Pyrrhura leucotis** *White-eared Conure*		Venezuela and eastern Brazil (discontinuously distributed)
18 03 182	**Pyrrhura picta** *Painted Conure*		Guianas, Venezuela to Bolivia, Amazonian Brazil
18 03 183	**Pyrrhura viridicata** *Santa Marta Conure*		Subtropical Santa Marta mountains of Colombia
18 03 184	**Pyrrhura egregia** *Fiery-shouldered Conure*		Southeast Venezuela; adjacent Guyana, Brazil
18 03 185	**Pyrrhura melanura (berlepschi)** *Maroon-tailed Conure*		Southern Venezuela to northeast Peru, western Brazil
18 03 186	**Pyrrhura rupicola** *Black-capped Conure*		Subtropical eastern Peru, Bolivia, adjacent Brazil
18 03 187	**Pyrrhura albipectus** *White-necked Conure*		Subtropical forests of southeast Ecuador
18 03 188	**Pyrrhura calliptera** *Flame-winged Conure*		Eastern Andes of Colombia (Boyacá, Cundinamarca)
18 03 189	**Pyrrhura hoematotis** *Red-eared Conure*		Coastal subtropical Venezuela
18 03 190	**Pyrrhura rhodocephala** *Rose-headed Conure*		Subtropical mountains of western Venezuela
18 03 191	**Pyrrhura hoffmanni** *Hoffman's Conure*		Southern Costa Rica and western Panama
18 03 192	**Enicognathus ferrugineus** *Austral Conure*		*Nothofagus* forests of southern Chile and Argentina
18 03 193	**Enicognathus leptorhynchus** *Slender-billed Conure*		Chile (coastal Aconcagua to Aysén)
18 03 194 + (incl. nest)	**Myiopsitta monachus** *Monk Parakeet*		Central Bolivia to Argentina, southern Brazil

	Date	Location
18 03 195 **Bolborhynchus aymara** *Sierra Parakeet*		Eastern Andes of Bolivia to Argentina, Chile
18 03 196 **Bolborhynchus aurifrons** *Mountain Parakeet*		Peru and Bolivia to Argentina, Chile
18 03 197 **Bolborhynchus lineola** *Barred Parakeet*		Southern Mexico to Colombia, central Peru
18 03 198 **Bolborhynchus orbygnesius** *Andean Parakeet*		Puna of Peru and northern Bolivia
18 03 199 **Bolborhynchus ferrugineifrons** *Rufous-fronted Parakeet*		Central Andes of Colombia (Tolima, Cauca)
18 03 200 **Forpus cyanopygius** *Mexican Parrotlet*		Arid tropical western Mexico; Tres Marias Islands
18 03 201 **Forpus passerinus** *Green-rumped Parrotlet*		Venezuela, Guianas, Amazonian Brazil; Trinidad
18 03 202 **Forpus xanthopterygius** *Blue-winged Parrotlet*		Northern Colombia to northeast Argentina, Brazil
18 03 203 **Forpus conspicillatus** *Spectacled Parrotlet*		Eastern Panama to Colombia, western Venezuela
18 03 204 **Forpus sclateri** *Sclater's Parrotlet*		Guianas, Venezuela to northern Boliva, Brazil
18 03 205 **Forpus coelestis** *Pacific Parrotlet*		Arid Pacific slope of Ecuador to Peru
18 03 206 **Forpus xanthops** *Yellow-faced Parrotlet*		Northern Peru (found only in Marañon Valley)
18 02 207 **Brotogeris tirica** *Plain Parakeet*		Eastern Brazil (Bahia to Rio Grande do Sul)
18 03 208 **Brotogeris versicolurus** *Canary-winged Parakeet*		Northern South America to northern Argentina, Brazil
18 03 209 **Brotgeris pyrrhopterus** *Gray-cheeked Parakeet*		Western Ecuador to extreme northwest Peru
18 03 210 **Brotogeris jugularis** *Orange-chinned Parakeet*		Southwest Mexico to northern Colombia, Venezuela
18 03 211 **Brotogeris cyanoptera** *Cobalt-winged Parakeet*		Widespread tropical western Amazon basin
18 03 212 **Brotogeris chrysopterus** *Golden-winged Parakeet*		Guianas, eastern Venezuela, Amazonian Brazil
18 03 213 **Brotogeris sanctithomae** *Tui Parakeet*		Tropical forests of Amazon basin
18 03 214 **Nannopsittaca panychlora** *Tepui Parrotlet*		Humid subtropical mountain forests of Venezuela

		Date	Location
18 03 215	**Touit batavica** *Seven-colored Parrotlet*		Surinam, Guyana, Venezuela; Trinidad; Tobago
18 03 216	**Touit huetii** *Scarlet-shouldered Parrotlet*		Northern South America to Peru, Brazil (Pará)
18 03 217	**Touit dilectissima (costaricensis)** *Red-winged Parrotlet*		Southern Costa Rica to northwest Ecuador
18 03 218	**Touit purpurata** *Sapphire-rumped Parrotlet*		Guianas, Venezuela, adjacent Brazil, Colombia
18 03 219	**Touit melanonota** *Brown-backed Parrotlet*		Coastal southeast Brazil (Bähia to São Paulo)
18 03 220	**Touit stictoptera** *Spot-winged Parrotlet*		Subtropical Andes of Colombia and Ecuador
18 03 221	**Touit surda** *Golden-tailed Parrotlet*		Coastal eastern Brazil (Pernambuco to São Paulo)
18 03 222	**Pionites melanocephala** *Black-headed Caique*		Tropical savanna of northern Amazon basin
18 03 223	**Pionites leucogaster** *White-bellied Caique*		Tropical forests of southern Amazon basin
18 03 224	**Pionopsitta pileata** *Pileated Parrot*		Southeast Brazil (Bahia) to northeast Argentina
18 03 225	**Pionopsitta haematotis** *Brown-hooded Parrot*		Southern Caribbean Mexico to northwest Colombia
18 03 226	**Pionopsitta pulchra** *Rose-faced Parrot*		Tropical Colombia, Ecuador (west of the Andes)
18 03 227	**Pionopsitta barrabandi** *Barraband's Parrot*		Tropical forests of western Amazon basin
18 03 228	**Pionopsitta pyrilia** *Saffron-headed Parrot*		Northeast Venezuela, adjacent Colombia, Panama
18 03 229	**Pionopsitta caica** *Caica Parrot*		Eastern Venezuela, Guianas, adjacent Brazil
18 03 230	**Gypopsitta vulturina** *Vulturine Parrot*		Tropical northeast Brazil (south of Amazon)
18 03 231	**Hapalopsittaca amazonina** *Rusty-faced Parrot*		Andes of western Venezuela, Colombia, Ecuador
18 03 232	**Hapalopsittaca melanotis** *Black-winged Parrot*		Temperate forests of central Peru and Bolivia
18 03 233 +	**Graydidascalus brachyurus** *Short-tailed Parrot*		Tropical forests of lower Amazon basin

		Date	Location
18 03 234	**Pionus menstruus** *Blue-headed Parrot*		Costa Rica to northern Bolivia, central Brazil
18 03 235	**Pionus sordidus** *Red-billed Parrot*		Venezuela, western Colombia to northern Bolivia
18 03 236 +	**Pionus maximiliani** *Scaly-headed Parrot*		Southeast Brazil (Ceará) to northern Argentina
18 03 237	**Pionus tumultuosus** *Plum-crowned Parrot*		Mountains of eastern Peru to Bolivia (Cochabamba)
18 03 238	**Pionus seniloides** *White-headed Parrot*		Mountains of Venezuela through western Ecuador
18 03 239	**Pionus senilis** *White-capped Parrot*		Rain forests of southeast Mexico to western Panama
18 03 240	**Pionus chalcopterus** *Bronze-winged Parrot*		Andes of western Venezuela to northwest Peru
18 03 241	**Pionus fuscus** *Dusky Parrot*		Savanna and forests of northeast Amazon basin
18 03 242	**Amazona collaria** *Yellow-billed Amazon*		Mid-level, wet limestone forests of Jamaica
18 03 243	**Amazona leucocephala** *Cuban Amazon*		Bahamas, Cuba and adjacent islands
18 03 244	**Amazona ventralis** *Hispaniolian Amazon*		Hispaniola and adjacent offshore islands
18 03 245	**Amazona albifrons** *White-fronted Amazon*		Dry western Mexico (Nayarit) to Costa Rica
18 03 246	**Amazona xantholora** *Yellow-lored Amazon*		Yucatán Peninsula to Belize; Cozumel Island
18 03 247	**Amazona agilis** *Black-billed Amazon*		Mid-level, wet limestone forests of Jamaica
18 03 248	**Amazona vittata** *Puerto Rican Amazon*		Puerto Rico (almost extinct—population about 20 birds in 1980)
18 03 249	**Amazona tucumana** *Alder (Tucuman) Amazon*		Alder forests of southeast Bolivia, northwest Argentina
18 03 250	**Amazona pretrei** *Red-spectacled Amazon*		Southeast Brazil (São Paulo) to northeast Argentina
18 03 251	**Amazona viridigenalis** *Green-cheeked Amazon*		Northeast Mexico (Nuevo León to Veracruz)
18 03 252	**Amazona finschi** *Lilac-crowned Amazon*		Western Mexico (Sonora to Oaxaca)
18 03 253	**Amazona autumnalis** *Red-lored Amazon*		Eastern Mexico to Ecuador, northwest Brazil
18 03 254	**Amazona brasiliensis** *Red-tailed Amazon*		Southeast Brazil (São Paulo to Rio Grande do Sul)

		Date	Location
18 03 255	**Amazona dufresniana** *Blue-cheeked Amazon*		Guianas, Venezuela, east-central Brazil
18 03 256	**Amazona festiva** *Festive Amazon*		Widespread riverine forests of Amazon basin
18 03 257	**Amazona xanthops** *Yellow-faced Amazon*		*Cerrado* plateau of eastern and central Brazil
18 03 258	**Amazona barbadensis** *Yellow-shouldered* *Amazon*		Arid coastal Venezuela, adjacent offshore islands
18 03 259	**Amazona aestiva** *Blue-fronted Amazon*		Lower Amazon basin to northern Argentina
18 03 260	**Amazona ochrocephala** *Yellow-crowned Amazon*		Central Mexico to Peru, upper Amazon basin
18 03 261	**Amazona amazonica** *Orange-winged Amazon*		Widespread Amazonia; Trinidad; Tobago
18 03 262	**Amazona mercenaria** *Scaly-naped Amazon*		Mountains of Venezuela to northwest Bolivia
18 03 263	**Amazona farinosa** *Mealy Amazon*		Tropical southeast Mexico through Amazon basin
18 03 264	**Amazona vinacea** *Vinaceous Amazon*		Southeast Brazil (Bahia) to northeast Argentina
18 03 265	**Amazona versicolor** *St. Lucia Amazon*		St. Lucia Island (West Indies—endangered)
18 03 266	**Amazona arausiaca** *Red-necked Amazon*		Island of Dominica (West Indies—endangered)
18 03 267	**Amazona guildingii** *St. Vincent Amazon*		St. Vincent Island (West Indies—endangered)
18 03 268	**Amazona imperialis** *Imperial Amazon*		Island of Dominica (West Indies—endangered)
18 03 269	**Deroptyus accipitrinus** *Hawk-headed Parrot*		Widespread northern Amazonia
18 03 270	**Triclaria malachitacea** *Purple-bellied Parrot*		Southeast Brazil (Bahia to Rio Grande do Sul)
18 03 271	**Strigops habroptilus** *Kakapo*		New Zealand (flightless—on verge of extinction)

ORDER: MUSOPHAGIFORMES
FAMILY: MUSOPHAGIDAE (Turacos)

19 01 001	**Corythaeola cristata** *Great Blue Turaco*		West, central and east Africa
19 01 002	**Crinifer piscator** **(africanus)** *Gray Plantain-Eater*		Senegal to the lower Congo River

		Date	Location

19 01 003　Crinifer zonurus
Eastern Gray Plantain-Eater　　　Ethiopia to Tanzania

19 01 004　Corythaixoides concolor
Common Go-away Bird　　　Tanzania to South Africa

19 01 005　Corythaixoides personata
Bare-faced Go-away Bird　　　Ethiopia to Rhodesia

19 01 006　Corythaixoides leucogaster
†　　*White-bellied Go-away Bird*　　　East and central Africa

19 01 007　Musophaga violacea
Violet Turaco　　　Gambia to Nigeria, Cameroon

19 01 008　Musophaga rossae
Ross' Turaco　　　West, central and east Africa

19 01 009　Tauraco corythaix
Knysna Turaco　　　Central and southern Africa

19 01 010　Tauraco persa
Guinea Turaco　　　Western Africa (Senegal to Angola, Zaire)

19 01 011　Tauraco livingstonii
Livingstone's Turaco　　　East and southern Africa

19 01 012　Tauraco schalowi
Schalow's Turaco　　　Kenya to Rhodesia, Malawi

19 01 013　Tauraco schuetii
Black-billed Turaco　　　Zaire, Uganda, Kenya

19 01 014　Tauraco fischeri
Fischer's Turaco　　　Kenya, Tanzania; Zanzibar

19 01 015　Tauraco erythrolophus
†　　*Red-crested Turaco*　　　Angola, Zaire (woodlands and savanna)

19 01 016　Tauraco bannermani
Bannerman's Turaco　　　Cloud forests of Cameroon Mountains

19 01 017　Tauraco macrorhynchus
Black-tip Crested Turaco　　　Sierra Leone to lower Congo River

19 01 018　Tauraco hartlaubi
Hartlaub's Turaco　　　Highland forests of Kenya and northern Tanzania

19 01 019　Tauraco leucotis
White-cheeked Turaco　　　Highlands of Ethiopia

19 01 020　Tauraco ruspolii
Prince Ruspoli's Turaco　　　Lake Abaya, southwest Ethiopia (endangered)

19 01 021　Tauraco leucolophus
White-crested Turaco　　　Cameroons to Sudan, Uganda, Kenya

		Date	Location
19 01 022	**Tauraco porphyreolophus** *Violet-crested Turaco*		East, southern Africa
19 01 023	**Tauraco johnstoni** *Ruwenzori Turaco*		Ruwenzori Mountains and eastern Zaire border

ORDER: CUCULIFORMES
FAMILY: CUCULIDAE (Cuckoos)

20 01 001	**Clamator glandarius** *Great Spotted Cuckoo*		Africa, southern Europe, Asia Minor
20 01 002	**Clamator coromandus** *Chestnut-winged Cuckoo*		Widespread Oriental region mainland and islands
20 01 003	**Clamator serratus** *Black-crested Cuckoo*		Africa (possibly conspecific with *C. jacobinus*)
20 01 004	**Clamator jacobinus** *Pied (Black-and-white) Cuckoo*		Africa south of the Sahara to southeast Asia
20 01 005	**Clamator levaillanti (cafer)** *Levaillant's Cuckoo*		Africa south of the Sahara
20 01 006	**Pachycoccyx audeberti** *Thick-billed Cuckoo*		East, central, west Africa; Madagascar
20 01 007	**Cuculus crassirostris** *Celebes Cuckoo*		Celebes Islands
20 01 008	**Cuculus sparverioides (bocki)** *Large Hawk Cuckoo*		Widespread southeast Asia to India
20 01 009	**Cuculus varius** *Common Hawk Cuckoo*		Sri Lanka; India to Burma
20 01 010	**Cuculus vagans (nanus)** *Moustached Hawk Cuckoo*		Malaya, Thailand, Java, Borneo
20 01 011	**Cuculus fugax** *Hodgson's Hawk Cuckoo*		Widespread southeast Asia to India; Japan
20 01 012	**Cuculus solitarius** *Red-chested Cuckoo*		Africa south of the Sahara
20 01 013	**Cuculus cafer (clamosus)** *Black Cuckoo*		Widespread Africa south of the Sahara
20 01 014	**Cuculus micropterus** *Indian Cuckoo*		Widespread southeast Asia to India

		<u>Date</u>	<u>Location</u>
20 01 015	**Cuculus canorus** *Common Cuckoo*		Africa, Eurasia to southeast Asia
20 01 016	**Cuculus saturatus** *Oriental Cuckoo*		India to southeast Asia; Australasia
20 01 017	**Cuculus poliocephalus** *Little Cuckoo*		Widespread Oriental mainland and islands; Africa
20 01 018	**Cuculus pallidus** *Pallid Cuckoo*		Moluccas, New Guinea, Australia, Tasmania
20 01 019	**Cercococcyx mechowi** *Dusky Long-tailed Cuckoo*		Guinea and Sierra Leone to Angola, Zaire
20 01 020	**Cercococcyx olivinus** *Olive Long-tailed Cuckoo*		Ghana to Zaire, Angola
20 01 021	**Cercococcyx montanus** *Barred Long-tailed Cuckoo*		Zaire, Uganda to Zambia
20 01 022	**Cacomantis sonneratii** *Banded Bay Cuckoo*		India to Indochina; Greater Sundas; Philippines
20 01 023	**Cacomantis merulinus** *Plaintive Cuckoo*		India to Indochina; Philippines; Greater Sundas; Celebes
20 01 024	**Cacomantis variolosus** *Brush Cuckoo*		Australia to New Guinea, Malaysia, Solomons
20 01 025	**Cacomantis castaneiventris** *Chestnut-breasted Cuckoo*		New Guinea; Queensland (northeast Australia)
20 01 026	**Cacomantis heinrichi** *Heinrich's Cuckoo*		Moluccas Islands
20 01 027	**Cacomantis pyrrhophanus** *Fan-tailed Cuckoo*		Australia to Arus, New Guinea; New Caledonia
20 01 028	**Rhamphomantis megarhynchus** *Long-billed Cuckoo*		New Guinea and adjacent islands
20 01 029	**Chrysococcyx osculans** *Black-eared Cuckoo*		Australia to New Guinea, Arus, Moluccas
20 01 030	**Chrysococcyx cupreus** *Emerald Cuckoo*		Africa south of the Sahara
20 01 031	**Chrysococcyx flavigularis** *Yellow-throated Green Cuckoo*		Sierra Leone to western Uganda
20 01 032	**Chrysococcyx klaas** *Klaas' Cuckoo*		Africa south of the Sahara; Arabia
29 01 033	**Chrysococcyx caprius** *Didric Cuckoo*		Africa south of the Sahara

		Date	Location
20 01 034	**Chalcites maculatus** *Asian Emerald Cuckoo*		Himalayas to southeast Asia; Andamans, Sumatra, Nicobars
20 01 035	**Chalcites xanthorhynchus** *Violet Cuckoo*		Widespread Oriental region mainland and islands
20 01 036	**Chalcites basalis** *Horsfield's Bronze Cuckoo*		Australia, Tasmania to New Guinea, Greater Sundas
20 01 037	**Chalcites lucidus** *Shining Bronze Cuckoo*		Australia; New Guinea and islands of Papuan region
20 01 038	**Chalcites malayanus (minutillus)** *Little Bronze Cuckoo*		Australia to New Guinea, Malaysia, Sundas, Philippines
20 01 039	**Chalcites crassirostris** *Island Cuckoo*		Moluccas Islands
20 01 040	**Chalcites meyeri** *Meyers' Bronze Cuckoo*		Mountains of New Guinea
20 01 041	**Chalcites ruficollis** *Reddish-throated Bronze Cuckoo*		High mountains of New Guinea
20 01 042	**Caliechthrus leucolophus** *White-crowned Koel*		New Guinea and Salawati Island
20 01 043	**Surniculus lugubris** *Drongo Cuckoo*		Widespread Oriental region mainland and islands
20 01 044	**Microdynamis parva** *Black-capped Cuckoo*		New Guinea (lowlands up to 5,000 feet—rare)
20 01 045	**Eudynamys scolopacea (cyanocephala)** *Common Koel*		India to southeast Asia, Australasia
20 01 046	**Eudynamys cyanocephala** *Blue-headed Koel*		Eastern Australia (probable race of *E. scolopacea*)
20 01 047	**Urodynamis taitensis** *Long-tailed Cuckoo*		Breeds New Zealand; winters Polynesia, Micronesia to New Guinea
20 01 048	**Scythrops novaehollandiae** *Channel-billed Cuckoo*		Australia to New Guinea, Indonesia, Bismarck Archipelago
20 01 049	**Coccyzus pumilus** *Dwarf Cuckoo*		Tropical northern Colombia and Venezuela
20 01 050	**Coccyzus cinereus** *Ash-colored Cuckoo*		Uruguay, Paraguay, Bolivia, northern Argentina

		Date	Location
20 01 051	**Coccyzus erythropthalmus** *Black-billed Cuckoo*		Canada to Argentina
20 01 052	**Coccyzus americanus** *Yellow-billed Cuckoo*		Canada to Argentina; West Indies
20 01 053	**Coccyzus euleri** *Pearly-breasted Cuckoo*		Widespread South America south to northeast Argentina
20 01 054	**Coccyzus minor** *Mangrove Cuckoo*		Southern Florida to northern Brazil; West Indies
20 01 055	**Coccyzus melacoryphus** *Dark-billed Cuckoo*		South America; Galapagos Islands
20 01 056	**Coccyzus lansbergi** *Gray-capped Cuckoo*		Venezuela, Colombia to western Peru
20 01 057	**Hyetornis pluvialis** *Chestnut-bellied Cuckoo*		Hills and mountains of Jamaica
20 01 058	**Hyetornis rufigularis** *Bay-breasted Cuckoo*		Hispaniola and Gonâve Islands
20 01 059	**Piaya cayana** *Squirrel Cuckoo*		Mexico to northeast Argentina
20 01 060	**Piaya melanogaster** *Black-bellied Cuckoo*		Northern South America and western Amazon basin
20 01 061	**Piaya minuta** *Little Cuckoo*		Eastern Panama (Darien) through Amazon basin
20 01 062	**Saurothera merlini** *Great Lizard Cuckoo*		Bahamas, Cuba, Isle of Pines
20 01 063	**Saurothera vetula** *Jamaican Lizard Cuckoo*		Semi-arid woodlands of Jamaica
20 01 064	**Saurothera longirostris** *Hispaniolan Lizard Cuckoo*		Confined to woodlands and thickets of Hispaniola
20 01 065	**Saurothera vielloti** *Puerto Rican Lizard Cuckoo*		Semi-arid woodlands of Puerto Rico
20 01 066	**Ceuthmochares aereus** *Green Coucal (Yellowbill)*		Fernando Po to Uganda, Tanzania, Ethiopia
20 01 067	**Rhopodytes diardi** *Black-bellied Malcoha*		Malaya, Sumatra, Borneo
20 01 068	**Rhopodytes sumatranus** *Chestnut-bellied Malcoha*		Sumatra, Borneo, Malaya, peninsular Thailand
20 01 069	**Rhopodytes tristis** *Green-billed Malcoha*		Himalayas to Indochina; Hainan; Sumatra
20 01 070	**Rhopodytes viridirostris** *Blue-faced Malcoha*		India; Sri Lanka

		Date	Location

20 01 071   **Taccocua leschenaultii**
Southern Sirkeer   Sri Lanka; India to Assam

20 01 072   **Rhinortha chlorophaea**
Raffle's Malcoha   Malaya, peninsular Thailand, Sumatra, Java, Borneo

20 01 073   **Zanclostomus javanicus**
Red-billed Malcoha   Malaya, peninsular Thailand, Sumatra, Java, Borneo

20 01 074   **Rhamphococcyx calyorhynchus**
Celebes Malcoha   Celebes Islands

20 01 075   **Rhamphococcyx curvirostris**
Chestnut-breasted Malcoha   Widespread southeast Asia

20 01 076   **Phaenicophaeus pyrrhocephalus**
Red-faced Malcoha   Endemic to Sri Lanka (nearing extinction)

20 01 077   **Dasylophus superciliosus**
Rough-crested Cuckoo   Philippine Islands

20 01 078   **Lepidogrammus cumingi**
Scale-feathered Cuckoo   Philippines (restricted to Luzon Island)

20 01 079   **Crotophaga major**
Greater Ani   Eastern Panama (Darien) to northeast Argentina

20 01 080   **Crotophaga ani**
Smooth-billed Ani   Southern United States to Argentina; West Indies

20 01 081   **Crotophaga sulcirostris**
Groove-billed Ani   Southern Texas to northern Argentina

20 01 082   **Guira guira**
Guira Cuckoo   Southern Amazonian Brazil to Bolivia, Argentina

20 01 083   **Tapera naevia**
Striped Cuckoo   Southern Mexico to northern Argentina

20 01 084   **Morococcyx erythropygus**
Lesser Ground Cuckoo   Arid lowlands of western Mexico to Costa Rica

20 01 085   **Dromococcyx phasianellus**
Pheasant Cuckoo   Southern Mexico to northeast Argentina

20 01 086   **Dromococcyx pavoninus**
Pavonine Cuckoo   Widespread tropical South America

20 01 087   **Geococcyx californianus**
Greater Roadrunner   Southern United States to southern Mexico

20 01 088   **Geococcyx velox**
Lesser Roadrunner   Southern Mexico to Nicaragua

		Date	Location

20 01 089 Neomorphus geoffroyi
Rufous-vented Ground Cuckoo — Nicaragua to southern Brazil

20 01 090 Neomorphus squamiger
Scaled Ground Cuckoo — Central Amazonian Brazil

20 01 091 Neomorphus radiolosus
Banded Ground Cuckoo — Tropical southwest Colombia to northwest Ecuador

20 01 092 Neomorphus rufipennis
Rufous-winged Ground Cuckoo — Guianas, Venezuela, northern Brazil

20 01 093 Neomorphus pucheranii
Red-billed Ground Cuckoo — Northeast Peru, adjacent western Brazil

20 01 094 Carpococcyx radiceus
Malay Ground Cuckoo — Sumatra and Borneo

20 01 095 Carpococcyx renauldi
Coral-billed Ground Cuckoo — Burma to Indochina

20 01 096 Coua delalandei
Delelande's Coua — Extinct since about 1930. Inhabited eastern Madagascar

20 01 097 Coua gigas
Giant Coua — Savanna of western and southern Madagascar

20 01 098 Coua coquereli
Coquerel's Coua — Dense forests of western Madagascar

20 01 099 Coua serriana
Red-breasted Coua — Highland forests of northeast Madagascar

20 01 100 Coua reynaudii
Red-fronted Coua — Coastal highland forests of Madagascar

20 01 101 Coua cursor
Running Coua — Semi-arid lowland forests of southern Madagascar

20 01 102 Coua ruficeps
Red-capped Coua — Dry regions of western Madagascar

20 01 103 Coua cristata
Crested Coua — Dense humid forests of Madagascar

20 01 104 Coua verreauxi
Verreaux's Coua — Semi-arid woodlands of Madagascar

20 01 105 Coua caerulea
Blue Coua — Confined to forests of eastern Madagascar

20 01 106 Centropus milo
Buff-headed Coucal — Solomon Islands

20 01 107 Centropus goliath
Goliath Cuckoo — Northern Moluccas Islands

20 01 108 Centropus violaceus
Violaceous Cuckoo — New Ireland and New Britain Islands

		Date	Location
20 01 109	**Centropus menbeki** *New Guinea Coucal*		New Guinea, Aru and west Papuan Islands
20 01 110	**Centropus ateralbus** *Pied Coucal*		New Ireland and New Britain Islands
20 01 111	**Centropus chalybeus** *Biak Island Coucal*		Biak and Numfor Islands (New Guinea)
20 01 112	**Centropus phasianius** *Pheasant Coucal*		Australia, New Guinea and adjacent Papuan Islands
20 01 113	**Centropus spilopterus** *Kai Island Coucal*		Kai Islands (southwest Pacific)
20 01 114	**Centropus bernsteini** *Bernstein's Coucal*		New Guinea (lowlands up to 1,500 feet)
20 01 115	**Centropus chlororhynchus** *Green-billed Coucal*		Forests of wet zone of Sri Lanka
20 01 116	**Centropus rectunguis** *Short-toed Coucal*		Malaya (uncommon); Sumatra, Borneo
20 01 117	**Centropus steerii** *Steere's Coucal*		Philippines (endemic Mindoro Island)
20 01 118	**Centropus sinensis** **(andamanensis)** *Greater Coucal*		Widespread Oriental region mainland and islands
20 01 119	**Centropus nigrorufus** *Sunda Coucal*		Sumatra and Java
20 01 120	**Centropus viridis** *Philippine Coucal*		Widespread Philippine Islands
20 01 121	**Centropus toulou** *Black Coucal*		Africa to India
20 01 122	**Centropus bengalensis** *Lesser Coucal*		Southeast Asia; Philippines, Sundas, Moluccas
20 01 123	**Centropus grillii** *Black-bellied Coucal*		Africa south of the Sahara
20 01 124	**Centropus epomidis** *Rufous-bellied Coucal*		Gold Coast to southern Nigeria
20 01 125	**Centropus leucogaster** *Black-throated Coucal*		Cameroon to Zaire
20 01 126	**Centropus anselli** *Gabon Coucal*		Cameroon to Angola, Zaire
20 01 127	**Centropus monachus** **(cupreicaudus)** *Blue-headed Coucal*		Ghana to Kenya, Uganda, Ethiopia and South Africa
20 01 128	**Centropus senegalensis** *Senegal Coucal*		Senegal to Ethiopia, Egypt, south to Rhodesia

		Date	Location

20 01 129 **Centropus superciliosus**
          White-browed Coucal
          Savanna of east and central Africa

20 01 130 **Centropus melanops**
          Black-faced Coucal
          Philippines (Basilan, Bohol, Leyte, Samar, Mindanao)

20 01 131 **Centropus celebensis**
          Celebes Coucal
          Confined to central Celebes Islands

20 01 132 **Centropus unirufus**
          Rufous Coucal
          Philippine Islands (Luzon and Polillo)

ORDER: STRIGIFORMES
FAMILY: TYTONIDAE (Barn Owls)

21 01 001 **Tyto soumagnei**
          Madagascar Owl
          Forests of eastern Madagascar (endangered)

21 01 002 **Tyto alba**
          Barn Owl
          Cosmopolitan; nearly worldwide distribution

21 01 003 **Tyto rosenbergii**
          Celebes Barn Owl
          Rain forests of Celebes Islands

21 01 004 **Tyto nigrobrunnea**
          Sula Barn Owl
          Known only from the Sula Islands

21 01 005 **Tyto inexpectata**
          Minahassa Barn Owl
          Confined to northern peninsula of Celebes Island

21 01 006 **Tyto novaehollandiae**
          Masked Owl
          Open forests of Australia, extreme southeast New Guinea

21 01 007 **Tyto aurantia**
          New Britain Barn Owl
          Confined to New Britain Island

21 01 008 **Tyto tenebricosa**
          Sooty Owl
          Dense rain forests of eastern Australia, New Guinea

21 01 009 **Tyto capensis**
          African Grass Owl
          Widespread Africa south of the Sahara

21 01 010 **Tyto longimembris**
          Common Grass Owl
          India to southeast Asia, Philippines, Australia

21 01 011 **Phodilus badius**
          Bay Owl
          Nepal to Indochina, Greater Sundas; Sri Lanka

21 01 012 **Phodilus prigoginei**
          Congo Bay Owl
          Eastern Zaire (known from one specimen from Lake Tanganyika)

	Date	Location

ORDER: STRIGIFORMES
FAMILY: STRIGIDAE (Owls)

21 02 001	**Otus sagittatus** *White-fronted Scops Owl*	Tropical forests of Malay Peninsula, Indochina
21 02 002	**Otus rufescens** *Reddish Scops Owl*	Lowland primary forests of Malaya, Greater Sundas
21 02 003	**Otus icterorhynchus** *Sandy Scops Owl*	Tropical rain forests of Ghana to eastern Zaire
21 02 004	**Otus ireneae** *Sokoke Scops Owl*	Sokoke Forest of the Kenya coast (endangered)
21 02 005	**Otus spilocephalus** *Mountain Scops Owl*	Dense jungles of Nepal to Indochina, Greater Sundas
21 02 006	**Otus vandewateri** *Sumatra Scops Owl*	Mountains of Sumatra (known from one specimen)
21 02 007	**Otus balli** *Andaman Scops Owl*	Confined to the Andaman Islands
21 02 008	**Otus alfredi** *Flores Scops Owl*	Mountains of Flores Island (Lesser Sundas)
21 02 009	**Otus brucei (sunia)** *Oriental Scops Owl*	Woodlands of Palearctic, Oriental regions
21 02 010	**Otus scops** *Common Scops Owl*	Widespread Palearctic, Oriental regions
21 02 011	**Otus umbra** *Mentaur Scops Owl*	Islands off Java (Simalur and Engano)
21 02 012	**Otus senegalensis** *African Scops Owl*	Widespread Ethiopian region
21 02 013	**Otus flammeolus** *Flammulated Owl*	Woodlands of British Columbia to Mexico, Guatemala
21 02 014	**Otus brookii** *Rajah Scops Owl*	Subtropical forests of Java, Sumatra, Borneo
21 02 015	**Otus rutilus** *Madagascar Scops Owl*	Widespread woodlands of Madagascar
21 02 016	**Otus manadensis** *Celebes Scops Owl*	Forests of Celebes Islands
21 02 017	**Otus beccarii** *Moluccan Scops Owl*	Forests of Moluccas Islands
21 02 018	**Otus silvicolus** *Lesser Sunda Scops Owl*	Coastal forests of Flores, Sumbawa (Lesser Sundas)
21 02 019	**Otus whiteheadi** *Luzon Scops Owl*	Philippines (confined to Luzon Island)

		Date	Location

21 02 020	**Otus insularis** *Seychelles Scops Owl*		Pemba, Comoros and Seychelles Islands
21 02 021	**Otus bakkamoena** *Collared Scops Owl*		Light woodlands of Oriental mainland and islands
21 02 022	**Otus asio (kennicotti)** *Common Screech Owl*		North America woodlands from Alaska to Mexico
21 02 023	**Otus trichopsis** *Whiskered Owl*		Dry montane forests of Arizona to Nicaragua, Honduras
21 02 024	**Otus barbarus** *Bearded Screech Owl*		High montane forests of northern Guatemala, Chiapas
21 02 025	**Otus marshalli** *Cloud-forest Screech Owl*		Peru (cloud forests of Cordillera Vilcabamba, Dept.. of Cuzco)
21 02 026	**Otus guatemalae** *Vermiculated Screech Owl*		Mexico through western South America to Bolivia
21 02 027	**Otus roboratus** *Roborate Screech Owl*		Scrub steppes of western Peru
21 02 028	**Otus cooperi** *Pacific Screech Owl*		Pacific scrub, mangroves of Mexico to Costa Rica
21 02 029	**Otus choliba** *Tropical Screech Owl*		Savanna of Costa Rica to northern Argentina
21 02 030	**Otus atricapillus** *Black-capped Screech Owl*		Deciduous forests of southeast Brazil to northeast Argentina
21 02 031	**Otus ingens** *Rufescent Screech Owl*		Andes of Colombia to central Bolivia
21 02 032	**Otus watsonii** *Tawny-bellied Screech Owl*		Tropical rainforests of Amazon basin
21 02 033	**Otus nudipes** *Puerto Rican Screech Owl*		Submontane woodlands of Puerto Rico (endangered)
21 02 034	**Otus clarkii** *Bare-shanked Screech Owl*		Montane forests of Costa Rica to eastern Panama
21 02 035	**Otus albogularis** *White-throated Screech Owl*		Temperate Andean forests of Venezuela to Bolivia
21 02 036	**Otus minimus** *Bolivian Screech Owl*		Highlands of Bolivia (probable race of *O. ingens*)
21 02 037	**Otus leucotis** *White-faced Scops Owl*		Thornscrub of Africa south of the Sahara

		Date	Location

21 02 038	**Otus hartlaubi** *São Thomé Scops Owl*	Highlands of São Thomé island (Gulf of Guinea)
21 02 039	**Pyrroglaux podargina** *Palau Scops Owl*	Confined to Palau Island (endangered)
21 02 040	**Mimizuku gurneyi** *Giant Scops Owl*	Forests of Mindanao, Marinduque Islands (endangered)
21 02 041	**Jubula lettii** *Maned Owl*	Tropical forests of Liberia to Cameroon, Zaire
21 02 042	**Lophostrix cristata** *Crested Owl*	Tropical forests of southern Mexico to Bolivia, Brazil
21 02 043	**Bubo virginianus** *Great Horned Owl*	Widespread woodlands of North and South America
21 02 044	**Bubo bubo** *Northern Eagle Owl*	Widespread Palearctic region to India and southern China
21 02 045	**Bubo capensis** *Cape Eagle Owl*	Montane forests of Ethiopia to South Africa
21 02 046	**Bubo africanus** *Spotted Eagle Owl*	Savanna of Africa south of the Sahara; southern Arabia
21 02 047	**Bubo poensis** *Fraser's Eagle Owl*	Equatorial rain forests of Ghana to Zaire
21 02 048	**Bubo nipalensis** *Forest Eagle Owl*	Heavy rain forests of India to southeast Asia
21 02 049	**Bubo sumatrana** *Malay Eagle Owl*	Rain forests of Malaya, Java, Sumatra, Borneo
21 02 050	**Bubo shelleyi** *Shelley's Eagle Owl*	Equatorial rain forests of Liberia to Zaire
21 02 051	**Bubo lacteus** *Milky Eagle Owl*	Riverine forests of Africa south of the Sahara
21 02 052	**Bubo coromandus** *Dusky Eagle Owl*	Riverine forests of India to Indochina
21 02 053	**Bubo leucostictus** *Akun Eagle Owl*	Equatorial rain forests of Sierra Leone to Zaire
21 02 054	**Bubo philippensis** *Philippine Eagle Owl*	Tropical rain forests of Philippine Islands
21 02 055	**Ketupa blakistoni** *Blakiston's Fish Owl*	Eastern Siberia to Manchuria, Japan, Korea
21 02 056	**Ketupa zeylonensis** *Brown Fish Owl*	Widespread Indian Subcontinent
21 02 057	**Ketupa flavipes** *Tawny Fish Owl*	Forest streams of India to Indochina; Formosa

		Date	Location
21 02 058	**Ketupa ketupa** *Malay Fish Owl*		Burma to Malaya; Greater Sundas; Bali
21 02 059	**Scotopelia peli** *Pel's Fishing Owl*		Sparsely distributed Africa south of the Sahara
21 02 060	**Scotopelia ussheri** *Rufous Fishing Owl*		Rain forests of Sierra Leone to Ghana
21 02 061	**Scotopelia bouvieri** *Vermiculated Fishing Owl*		Riverine forest strips of Liberia to Zaire
21 02 062	**Pulsatrix perspicillata** *Spectacled Owl*		Rain forests of southern Mexico to northeast Argentina
21 02 063	**Pulsatrix koeniswaldiana** *White-chinned Owl*		Tropical southeast Brazil to northeast Argentina
21 02 064	**Pulsatrix melanota** *Rusty-barred Owl*		Tropical southeast Colombia to northern Bolivia
21 02 065	**Nyctea scandiaca** *Snowy Owl*		Arctic circumpolar
21 02 066	**Surnia ulula** *Northern Hawk Owl*		Boreal forests of northern hemisphere
21 02 067	**Glaucidium passerinum** *Eurasian Pygmy Owl*		Mixed forests of northern Palearctic region
21 02 068	**Glaucidium gnoma** *Northern Pygmy Owl*		Woodlands of southern Alaska to Guatemala
21 02 069	**Glaucidium siju** *Cuban Pygmy Owl*		Confined to Cuba and the Isle of Pines
21 02 070 +	**Glaucidium minutissimum** *Least Pygmy Owl*		Tropical southern Mexico to Paraguay, Brazil
21 02 071 +	**Glaucidium jardinii** *Andean Pygmy Owl*		Mountains of Costa Rica to Bolivia
21 02 072 +	**Glaucidium brasilianum (nanum)** *Ferruginous Pygmy Owl*		Woodlands of southeast Arizona to Tierra del Fuego
21 02 073 +	**Glaucidium perlatum** *Pearl-spotted Owlet*		Savanna of Africa south of the Sahara
21 02 074 +	**Glaucidium tephronotum** *Red-chested Owlet*		Dense equatorial forests of Ghana to Zaire
21 02 075	**Glaucidium capense** *Barred Owlet*		Acacia bush zone of southern Africa
21 02 076	**Glaucidium brodiei** *Collared Pygmy Owl*		Himalayas to western China, Malaya, Sumatra, Borneo
21 02 077	**Glaucidium radiatum** *Barred Jungle Owlet*		Deciduous forests of Indian Subcontinent; Sri Lanka

		Date	Location
21 02 078	**Glaucidium cuculoides** *Cuckoo Owlet*		Himalayas to China, Indochina; Java; Bali
21 02 079	**Glaucidium sjostedti** **(castanonotum)** *Chestnut-backed Owlet*		Tropical forests of Gabon, Cameroon to Zaire
21 02 080	**Xenoglaux loweryi** *Long-whiskered Owlet*		Subtropical cloud forest of Puru in Amazonas and San Martin
21 02 081	**Micrathene whitneyi** *Elf Owl*		Southwestern United States to southern Mexico
21 02 082	**Uroglaux dimorpha** *Papuan Hawk Owl*		Lowland forests of New Guinea and Japen Island
21 02 083	**Ninox rufa** *Rufous Owl*		New Guinea, Arus, coastal northern Australia
21 02 084	**Ninox strenua** *Powerful Owl*		Forested gullies of Queensland to Victoria
21 02 085	**Ninox connivens** *Barking Owl*		Savanna of Australia, New Guinea, Moluccas
21 02 086	**Ninox novaeseelandiae** *Boobook Owl*		Australia; New Zealand; New Guinea; Flores Island
21 02 087	**Ninox scutulata** *Oriental Hawk Owl*		Forests and scrub of Oriental mainland and islands
21 02 088	**Ninox affinis** *Andaman Hawk Owl*		Confined to Andaman and Nicobar Islands
21 02 089	**Ninox superciliaris** *Madagascar Hawk Owl*		Wooded areas of western Madagascar
21 02 090	**Ninox philippensis** *Philippine Hawk Owl*		Forests throughout the Philippine Islands
21 02 091	**Ninox spilonota** *Cebu Hawk Owl*		Cebu, Sibuyan, Tablas Islands (probable race *N. philippensis*)
21 02 092	**Ninox spilocephala** *Mindanao Hawk Owl*		Basilan and Mindanao Islands (probable race *N. philippensis*)
21 02 093	**Ninox perversa** *Ochre-bellied Hawk Owl*		Deep virgin forests of Celebes Islands
21 02 094	**Ninox squamipila** *Moluccan Hawk Owl*		Northern Moluccas, Tanimbar, Christmas Islands
21 02 095	**Ninox theomacha** *Sooty-backed Hawk Owl*		Lowland forests of New Guinea and adjacent islands
21 02 096	**Ninox punctulata** *Speckled Hawk Owl*		Open forests of Celebes Islands
21 02 097	**Ninox meeki** *Admiralty Islands Hawk Owl*		Confined to forests of the Admiralty Islands

		Date	Location
21 02 098	**Ninox solomonis** *New Ireland Hawk Owl*		Confined to New Britain and New Ireland Islands
21 02 099	**Ninox odiosa** *New Britain Hawk Owl*		Confined to New Britain Island
21 02 100	**Ninox jacquinoti** *Solomon Islands Hawk Owl*		Confined to the Solomon Islands
21 02 101	**Gymnoglaux lawrencii** *Bare-legged Owl*		Dense forests in limestone country of Cuba
21 02 102	**Sceloglaux albifacies** *Laughing Owl*		New Zealand (last seen 1914—probably extinct)
21 02 103	**Athene noctua** *Little Owl*		Widespread Palearctic region
21 02 104	**Athene brama** *Spotted Little Owl*		India to Burma, Indochina
21 02 105	**Athene blewitti** *Forest Little Owl*		Montane deciduous forest of northern India
21 02 106	**Speotyto cunicularia** *Burrowing Owl*		Southern Canada to Argentina (terrestial)
21 02 107	**Ciccaba virgata** *Mottled Owl*		Tropical forests of Mexico to northeast Argentina
21 02 108	**Ciccaba nigrolineata** *Black-and-white Owl*		Forest borders of Mexico to northwest Peru
21 02 109	**Ciccaba huhula** *Black-banded Owl*		Rain forests, coffee plantations of Amazonia
21 02 110	**Ciccaba albitarsus** *Rufous-banded Owl*		Temperate Andes of Venezuela to northern Bolivia
21 02 111	**Ciccaba woodfordii** *African Wood Owl*		Forests and woodlands of Africa south of the Sahara
21 02 112	**Strix butleri** *Hume's Wood Owl*		Arabia, Sinai peninsula (known from 3 specimens)
21 02 113	**Strix seloputo** *Spotted Wood Owl*		Lowlands of Malaya, Indochina, Java, Palawan
21 02 114	**Strix ocellata** *Mottled Wood Owl*		Lowlands of India to western Burma
21 02 115	**Strix leptogrammica** *Brown Wood Owl*		Temperate forests of Oriental mainland and islands
21 02 116	**Strix aluco** *Tawny Owl*		Woodlands and forests of Palearctic region
21 02 117	**Strix occidentalis** *Spotted Owl*		Coniferous forests of British Columbia to central Mexico

		Date	Location

21 02 118 **Strix varia**
Barred Owl
Mixed forests of Canada to Guatemala, Honduras

21 02 119 **Strix hylophila**
Rusty-barred Owl
Southeast Brazil (Minas Gerais) to northeast Argentina

21 02 120 **Strix rufipes**
Rufous-legged Owl
Northern Argentina to Tierra del Fuego; rare Falklands

21 02 121 **Strix uralensis**
Ural Owl
Coniferous forests of northern Palearctic region

21 02 122 **Strix davidi**
David's Owl
Mountains of western China (probable race of *S. uralensis*)

21 02 123 **Strix nebulosa**
Great Gray Owl
Boreal forests of northern hemisphere

21 02 124 **Rhinoptynx clamator**
Striped Owl
Southern Mexico to northern Argentina, Brazil

21 02 125 **Asio otus**
Long-eared Owl
Widespread Holarctic, Palearctic regions

21 02 126 **Asio stygius**
Stygian Owl
Forests of Mexico to northern Argentina

21 02 127 **Asio abyssinicus**
Abyssinian Long-eared Owl
Spottily distributed mountains of east and central Africa

21 02 128 **Asio madagascariensis**
Madagascar Long-eared Owl
Humid forests of eastern Madagascar

21 02 129 **Asio flammeus**
+ *Short-eared Owl*
Cosmopolitan; almost worldwide distribution

21 02 130 **Asio capensis (helvola)**
African Marsh Owl
Marsh and grassy areas of Africa; Madagascar

21 02 131 **Pseudoscops grammicus**
Jamaican Owl
Woodlands and open country of Jamaica

21 02 132 **Nesasio solomonensis**
Fearful Owl
Bougainville, Santa Isabel, Choiseul Islands (Solomons)

21 02 133 **Aegolius funereus**
Tengmalm's (Boreal) Owl
Northern coniferous forests of Holarctic region

21 02 134 **Aegolius acadicus**
+ *Saw-whet Owl*
Woodlands of Canada to southern Mexico

21 02 135 **Aegolius ridgwayi**
Unspotted Saw-whet Owl
Southern Mexico to southern Costa Rica

	Date	Location

21 02 136 **Aegolius harrisii**
†   *Buff-fronted Owl*   Northwest South America; northeast Argentina (discontinuous distribution)

ORDER: CAPRIMULGIFORMES
FAMILY: STEATORNITHIDAE (Oilbird)

22 01 001 **Steatornis caripensis**
†   *Oilbird*   Northern South America to northwest Bolivia; Trinidad

ORDER: CAPRIMULGIFORMES
FAMILY: PODARGIDAE (Frogmouths)

22 02 001 **Podargus strigoides (plumiferus)**
    Tawny Frogmouth   Widespread Australia, Tasmania

22 02 002 **Podargus papuensis**
    Paupan Frogmouth   Queensland; New Guinea, west Papuan Islands

22 02 003 **Podargus ocellatus**
    Marbled Frogmouth   New Guinea, Arus, Solomons, Cape York Peninsula

22 02 004 **Batrachostomus auritus**
    Large Frogmouth   Malaya, peninsular Thailand, Sumatra, Borneo

22 02 005 **Batrachostomus harterti**
    Dulit Frogmouth   Submontane Borneo (known from 7 specimens)

22 02 006 **Batrachostomus septimus**
    Philippine Frogmouth   Found throughout the Philippine Islands

22 02 007 **Batrachostomus stellatus**
    Gould's Frogmouth   Malay peninsula, Sumatra, Borneo

22 02 008 **Batrachostomus moniliger**
    Ceylon Frogmouth   Restricted to Sri Lanka and India

22 02 009 **Batrachostomus hodgsoni**
    Hodgson's Frogmouth   Bangladesh to Burma, Thailand

22 02 010 **Batrachostomus poliolophus**
    Pale-headed Frogmouth   Bangladesh, Sikkim to Burma, Thailand

22 02 011 **Batrachostomus mixtus**
    Sharpe's Frogmouth   Submontane Borneo, Sumatra

		Date	Location
22 02 012	**Batrachostomus javensis** *Javan Frogmouth*		Sumatra, Java, Borneo, Palawan, Indochina
22 02 013	**Batrachostomus affinis** *Blyth's Frogmouth*		Malay peninsula, Sumatra, Java

ORDER: CAPRIMULGIFORMES
FAMILY: NYCTIBIIDAE (Potoos)

22 03 001	**Nyctibius grandis** *Great Potoo*	Tropical Guatemala south through Amazon basin
22 03 002	**Nyctibius aethereus** *Long-tailed Potoo*	Tropical northern South America to Paraguay
22 03 003	**Nyctibius griseus (jamaicensis)** *Common Potoo*	Southern Mexico to Argentina; Jamaica; Hispaniola
22 03 004	**Nyctibius leucopterus** *White-winged Potoo*	Widespread tropical Amazon basin
22 03 005	**Nyctibius bracteatus** *Rufous Potoo*	Tropical Colombia to Peru east of Andes

ORDER: CAPRIMULGIFORMES
FAMILY: AEGOTHELIDAE (Owlet-Nightjars)

22 04 001	**Aegotheles crinifrons** *Moluccan Owlet-Nightjar*	Halmahera and Batjan Islands (Moluccas)
22 04 002	**Aegotheles insignis** *Large Owlet-Nightjar*	Mountains of New Guinea
22 04 003	**Aegotheles cristatus** *Australian Owlet-Nightjar*	Australia, Tasmania, southern New Guinea
22 04 004	**Aegotheles savesi** *New Caledonian Owlet-Nightjar*	New Caledonia (known from a single specimen)
22 04 005	**Aegotheles bennettii** *Barred Owlet-Nightjar*	New Guinea and adjacent islands
22 04 006	**Aegotheles wallacii** *Wallace's Owlet-Nightjar*	New Guinea and Aru Islands
22 04 007	**Aegotheles albertisii** *Mountain Owlet-Nightjar*	High mountain forests of New Guinea
22 04 008	**Aegotheles archboldi** *Archbold's Owlet-Nightjar*	Snow and Weyland mountains of New Guinea

		Date	Location

ORDER: CAPRIMULGIFORMES
FAMILY: CAPRIMULGIDAE (Nightjars)

22 05 001	**Lurocalis semitorquatus**	
	Semicollared Nighthawk	Central America to northern Argentina
22 05 002	**Chordeiles pusillus**	
	Least Nighthawk	Campos, savannas of tropical Amazon basin
22 05 003	**Chordeiles rupestris**	
+	*Sand-colored Nighthawk*	Sandbars, river banks of tropical Amazon basin
22 05 004	**Chordeiles acutipennis**	
	Lesser Nighthawk	Open country of western United States to Paraguay
22 05 005	**Chordeiles minor**	
	Common Nighthawk	Northern Canada to Argentina; West Indies
22 05 006	**Nyctiprogne leucopyga**	
	Band-tailed Nighthawk	Savannas of tropical Amazon basin
22 05 007	**Podager nacunda**	
+	*Nacunda Nighthawk*	Tropical South America to northern Argentina
22 05 008	**Eurostopodus guttatus**	
	Spotted Nightjar	Australia, Arus, New Guinea and New Ireland
22 05 009	**Eurostopodus mystacalis (albogularis)**	
	White-throated Nightjar	Australia, New Guinea, Solomons
22 05 010	**Eurostopodus diabolicus**	
	Celebes Nightjar	Celebes Islands
22 05 011	**Eurostopodus papuensis**	
	Papuan Nightjar	New Guinea and Salawati Island
22 05 012	**Eurostopodus archboldi**	
	Archbold's Nightjar	Mountains of New Guinea
22 05 013	**Eurostopodus temminckii**	
	Malaysian Eared Nightjar	Malaya, Sumatra, Borneo, Banka Islands
22 05 014	**Eurostopodus macrotis**	
	Great Eared Nightjar	India to southeast Asia; Philippines; Celebes
22 05 015	**Veles binotatus**	
	Brown Nightjar	Ghana to Cameroon, Zaire
22 05 016	**Nyctidromus albicollis**	
	Common Pauraque	Southern United States to northeast Argentina
22 05 017	**Phalaenoptilus nuttallii**	
	Common Poor-will	Southern British Columbia to central Mexico
22 05 018	**Siphonorhis americanus**	
	Jamaican Pauraque	Extinct since 1859. Inhabited Jamaica
22 05 019	**Siphonorhis brewsteri**	
	Least Pauraque	Semi-arid lowlands of Hispaniola, Gonâve Islands
22 05 020	**Otophanes mcleodii**	
	Eared Poorwill	Western Mexico (Sonora to Guerrero—rare)

		Date	Location
22 05 021	**Otophanes yucatanicus** *Yucatán Poorwill*		Yucatán Peninsula, Belize, Petén of Guatemala
22 05 022	**Nyctiphrynus ocellatus** *Ocellated Poorwill*		Tropical forests of Colombia to northern Argentina
22 05 023	**Caprimulgus carolinensis** *Chuck-will's-widow*		United States: winters to Colombia, West Indies
22 05 024	**Caprimulgus rufus** *Rufous Nightjar*		Tropical woodlands of Central America to Argentina
22 05 025	**Caprimulgus cubanensis** *Antillean Nightjar*		Cuba, Isle of Pines, Hispaniola
22 05 026	**Caprimulgus sericocaudatus** *Silky-tailed Nightjar*		Eastern Peru (Yarinacocha) to Argentina (Misiones)
22 05 027	**Caprimulgus anthonyi** *Scrub Nightjar*		Arid scrub of Marañon Valley of southeast Ecuador to northwest Peru
22 05 028	**Caprimulgus salvini** *Tawny-collared Nightjar*		Lowlands of eastern Mexico to Nicaragua
22 05 029	**Caprimulgus badius** *Yucatán Nightjar*		Yucatán Peninsula to northern Nicaragua
22 05 030	**Caprimulgus ridgwayi** *Buff-collared Nightjar*		Western Mexico to Guatemala, Honduras
22 05 031	**Caprimulgus vociferus** *Whip-poor-will*		Canada to Costa Rica; Cuba
22 05 032	**Caprimulgus saturatus** *Sooty Nightjar*		Mountains of Costa Rica and western Panama
22 05 033	**Caprimulgus noctitherus** *Puerto Rican Whip-poor-will*		Arid lowlands of southwest Puerto Rico
22 05 034	**Caprimulgus longirostris** *Band-winged Nightjar*		Venezuela through western South America to Argentina, Chile
22 05 035	**Caprimulgus cayennensis** *White-tailed Nightjar*		Campos, savannas of Costa Rica to Colombia, Guianas
22 05 036	**Caprimulgus candicans** *White-winged Nightjar*		Southern Brazil (Matto Grosso, São Paulo), Paraguay
22 05 037	**Caprimulgus maculicaudus** *Spot-tailed Nightjar*		Tropical southwest Mexico to Peru, Bolivia
22 05 038	**Caprimulgus parvulus** *Little Nightjar*		Widespread tropical woodlands of South America

		Date	Location
22 05 039	**Caprimulgus maculosus** *Cayenne Nightjar*		Dry open country of French Guiana
22 05 040	**Caprimulgus nigrescens** *Blackish Nightjar*		Sandy savannas of tropical Amazon basin
22 05 041	**Caprimulgus whiteleyi** *Roraiman Nightjar*		Venezuela (Bolivar on Cerros Roraima and Ptari-Tepui)
22 05 042	**Caprimulgus hirundinaceus** *Pygmy Nightjar*		Eastern Brazil (Ceará, Piaui, Bahia)
22 05 043	**Caprimulgus ruficollis** *Red-necked Nightjar*		Iberian Peninsula; Morocco to Tunisia
22 05 044	**Caprimulgus indicus** *Gray (Jungle) Nightjar*		Siberia to Oriental mainland and islands
22 05 045	**Caprimulgus europaeus** *European Nightjar*		Palearctic, Oriental regions; winters South Africa
22 05 046	**Caprimulgus aegyptius** *Egyptian Nightjar*		Algerian Sahara to Aral Sea, Baluchistan Desert
22 05 047	**Caprimulgus mahrattensis** *Sykes' Nightjar*		Desert edges of India, Afghanistan, Iran
22 05 048	**Caprimulgus centralasicus** *Vaurie's Nightjar*		Desert edges of western Sinkiang
22 05 049	**Caprimulgus nubicus** *Nubian Nightjar*		Northeast Africa to Palestine, Arabia
22 05 050	**Caprimulgus eximius** *Golden Nightjar*		Sandy deserts of southern Sahara and Sudan
22 05 051	**Caprimulgus madagascariensis** *Madagascar Nightjar*		Widespread wooded areas of Madagascar
22 05 052	**Caprimulgus macrurus** *Large-tailed Nightjar*		Widespread Oriental region; New Guinea to Australia
22 05 053	**Caprimulgus pectoralis (fraenatus)** *Dusky Nightjar*		Ethiopia to South Africa
22 05 054	**Caprimulgus rufigena** *Rufous-cheeked Nightjar*		Dry areas of extreme southern Africa
22 05 055	**Caprimulgus donaldsoni** *Donaldson-Smith's Nightjar*		Ethiopia to East Africa
22 05 056	**Caprimulgus poliocephalus** *Abyssinian Nightjar*		Ethiopia, Tanzania, Kenya

		Date	Location
22 05 057	**Caprimulgus asiaticus** *Indian Nightjar*		Sri Lanka; Iran, India to Indochina
22 05 058	**Caprimulgus natalensis** *Natal Nightjar*		Africa south of the Sahara
22 05 059	**Caprimulgus inornatus** *Plain Nightjar*		Desert edges of western Africa to Arabia
22 05 060	**Caprimulgus stellatus** *Star-spotted Nightjar*		Ethiopia to Somalia (rare)
22 05 061	**Caprimulgus ludovicianus** *Ethiopian Nightjar*		Southwest Ethiopia—known from a single specimen
22 05 062	**Caprimulgus monticolus** *Franklin's Nightjar*		India to southeast China
22 05 063	**Caprimulgus affinis** *Savanna Nightjar*		Widespread Oriental mainland and islands
22 05 064	**Caprimulgus tristigma** *Freckled Nightjar*		Africa south of the Sahara
22 05 065	**Caprimulgus concretus** *Bonaparte's Nightjar*		Sumatra, Borneo, Billiton Island
22 05 066	**Caprimulgus pulchellus** *Salvadori's Nightjar*		Confined to the Island of Sumatra
22 05 067	**Caprimulgus enarratus** *Collared Nightjar*		Dense forests of eastern Madagascar
22 05 068	**Caprimulgus batesi** *Bates' Nightjar*		Cameroon to Zaire
22 05 069	**Scotornis fossii** *Gabon Nightjar*		Africa south of the Sahara
22 05 070	**Scotornis climacurus** *Long-tailed Nightjar*		Senegal to Tanzania
22 05 071	**Macrodipteryx longipennis** *Standard-wing Nightjar*		Sudan, Kenya, Uganda, Ethiopia
22 05 072	**Semeiophorus vexillarius** *Pennant-winged Nightjar*		Sudan to southern Africa
22 05 073	**Hydropsalis climacocerca** *Ladder-tailed Nightjar*		Sandbars of tropical western Amazon basin
22 05 074	**Hydropsalis brasiliana** *Scissor-tailed Nightjar*		Eastern Peru, Amazonian Brazil to central Argentina
22 05 075	**Uropsalis segmentata** *Swallow-tailed Nightjar*		Temperate, páramo zone of Colombia to Bolivia
22 05 076	**Uropsalis lyra** *Lyre-tailed Nightjar*		Andes of Venezuela, Colombia, Ecuador, Peru

		Date	Location

22 05 077   **Macropsalis creagra**
        Long-trained Nightjar   Southeast Brazil (Espirito Santo to Rio Grande do Sul)

22 05 078   **Eleothreptus anomalus**
        Sickle-winged Nightjar   Swamps of southeast Brazil to northeast Argentina

ORDER: APODIFORMES
FAMILY: APODIDAE (Swifts)

23 01 001   **Cypseloides fumigatus**
        Sooty Swift   Southeast Brazil to northwest Argentina

23 01 002   **Cypseloides major**
        Rothschild's Swift   Northwestern Argentina (possible race *C. fumigatus*)

23 01 003   **Cypseloides senex**
        Great Dusky Swift   Central and southern Brazil to northeast Argentina

23 01 004   **Cypseloides cherriei**
        Spot-fronted Swift   Subtropical Costa Rica to Colombia, Venezuela

23 01 005   **Cypseloides cryptus**
        White-chinned Swift   Honduras to Guyana, Colombia, Ecuador, Peru

23 01 006   **Cypseloides lemosi**
        White-chested Swift   Colombia (upper Cauca Valley)

23 01 007   **Cypseloides niger**
        Black Swift   Alaska to Central America; West Indies

23 01 008   **Cypseloides phelpsi**
        Tepui Swift   Southeast Venezuela, northwest Guyana, adjacent Brazil (Roraima)

23 01 009   **Cypseloides rutilus**
        Chestnut-collared Swift   Tropical, subtropical Mexico to Bolivia

23 01 010   **Streptoprocne zonaris**
        White-collared Swift   Tropical to temperate Mexico to Argentina

23 01 011   **Streptoprocne biscutata**
        Biscutate Swift   Eastern Brazil (Piaui to Rio Grande do Sul)

23 01 012   **Streptoprocne semicollaris**
        White-naped Swift   Mountains of western and central Mexico

23 01 013   **Hydrocharis gigas**
        Giant Swiftlet   Malay Peninsula; Sumatra; Java

23 01 014   **Aerodramus spodiopygius**
        White-rumped Swiftlet   Australia to Fiji, New Guinea, adjacent islands

23 01 015   **Aerodramus francicus**
        Mascarene Swiftlet   Mauritius and Reunion Islands

		Date	Location
23 01 016	**Aerodramus elaphrus** *Seychelles Swiftlet*		Confined to Seychelles Islands
23 01 017	**Aerodramus unicolor** *Indian Swiftlet*		Sri Lanka; Indian Subcontinent
23 01 018	**Aerodramus vanikorensis** *Mossy-nest Swiftlet*		Celebes, Solomons, New Caledonia, New Guinea
23 01 019	**Aerodramus inquieta** *Carolines Swiftlet*		Micronesia (Caroline and Marianna Islands)
23 01 020	**Aerodramus hirundinaceus** *Mountain Swiftlet*		New Guinea and Japen Island
23 01 021	**Aerodramus leucophaeus (ocista)** *Polynesian Swiftlet*		Marquesas, Society Islands
23 01 022	**Aerodramus sawtelli** *Atiu Swiftlet*		Cook Islands (Polynesia)
23 01 023	**Aerodramus brevirostris** *Himalayan Swiftlet*		Himalayas to China, Assam, Indochina
23 01 024	**Aerodramus whiteheadi** *Whitehead's Swiftlet*		Philippine Islands, New Guinea
23 01 025	**Aerodramus papuensis** *Three-toed Swiftlet*		Western New Guinea (from sea level to 1800 meters)
23 01 026	**Aerodramus fuciphaga** *Edible-nest (Thunberg's) Swiftlet*		Widespread Southeast Asia
23 01 027	**Aerodramus maxima** *Black-nest (Lowe's) Swiftlet*		Widespread Oriental mainland and islands
23 01 028	**Aerodramus marginata** *Philippine Swiftlet*		Philippine Islands (Luzon to Palawan)
23 01 029	**Collocalia esculenta** *Glossy Swiftlet*		Malaysia, Philippines, islands of southwest Pacific
23 01 030	**Collocalia troglodytes** *Pygmy Swiftlet*		Philippines (Luzon to Mindanao and Palawan)
23 01 031	**Schoutedenapus myoptilus** *Scarce Swift*		Ethiopia to Malawi, Zaire (endangered)
23 01 032	**Schoutedenapus schoutedeni** *Congo Swift*		Eastern Zaire (known from two specimens from Mt. Nyombe)

		Date	Location
23 01 033	**Mearnsia picina** *Philippine Spinetail*		Philippines (Cebu, Leyte, Mindanao and Negros Islands)
23 01 034	**Mearnsia novaeguineae** *New Guinea Spinetail*		Lowlands of New Guinea
23 01 035	**Zoonavena grandidieri** *Madagascar Spinetail*		Lowlands of Madagascar
23 01 036	**Zoonavena thomensis** *São Thomé Spinetail*		São Thomé and Principe Islands (Gulf of Guinea)
23 01 037	**Zoonavena sylvatica** *White-rumped Spinetail*		India to Bangladesh, Nepal, Sikkim
23 01 038	**Telacanthura ussheri** *Mottle-throated Needletail*		East Africa to Zimbabwe
23 01 039	**Telacanthura melanopygia** *Chapin's Spinetail*		Cameroon and northeast Zaire
23 01 040	**Raphidura leucopygialis** *Silver-rumped Swift*		Malaya, Borneo, Java
23 01 041	**Raphidura sabini** *Sabine's Spinetail*		Sierra Leone to Zaire, Uganda
23 01 042	**Neafrapus cassini** *Cassin's Spinetail*		Nigeria to Zaire
23 01 043	**Neafrapus boehmi** *Boehm's Spinetail*		Kenya, Tanzania to Angola, Rhodesia
23 01 044	**Hirundapus caudacutus** *White-throated Needletail*		Eastern Palearctic; winters to Australia and Tasmania
23 01 045	**Hirundapus cochinchinensis** *White-vented Needletail*		Widespread Southeast Asia
23 01 046	**Hirundapus giganteus** *Brown Needletail*		Widespread Oriental region mainland and islands
23 01 047	**Hirundapus celebensis** *Purple Needletail*		Confined to the Celebes Islands
23 01 048	**Chaetura spinicauda** *Band-rumped Swift*		Tropical Costa Rica to Colombia, northern Amazonian Brazil
23 01 049	**Chaetura martinica** *Lesser Antillean Swift*		Guadeloupe, Dominica, Martinique, St. Lucia Islands
23 01 050	**Chaetura cinereiventris** *Gray-rumped Swift*		Tropical, subtropical Nicaragua to Argentina
23 01 051	**Chaetura pelagica** *Chimney Swift*		Southern Canada to Peru, Brazil

		Date	Location
23 01 052	**Chaetura vauxi** *Vaux's Swift*		Alaska to Venezuela, Colombia
23 01 053	**Chaetura chapmani** *Chapman's Swift*		Lowland forests northeast South America to Amazon basin; Trinidad
23 01 054	**Chaetura andrei** *Ashy-tailed Swift*		Campos of Surinam, Venezuela to northern Argentina
23 01 055	**Chaetura brachyura** *Short-tailed Swift*		Tropical South America to Amazonian Brazil, Peru
23 01 056	**Aeronautes saxatalis** *White-throated Swift*		Southern Canada to Guatemala, El Salvador
23 01 057	**Aeronautes montivagus** *White-tipped (Mountain) Swift*		Mountains of Venezuela to Peru, Bolivia
23 01 058	**Aeronautes andecolus** *Andean Swift*		Andes of Peru to Chile, Argentina
23 01 059	**Tachornis phoenicobia** *Antillean Palm Swift*		Cuba, Isle of Pines, Jamaica and Hispaniola
23 01 060	**Tachornis furcata** *Pygmy Swift*		Tropical northeast Colombia and Venezuela (endangered)
23 01 061	**Tachornis squamata** *Fork-tailed Palm Swift*		*Mauritia* palm zone of northeast South America and Amazon basin
23 01 062	**Panyptila sanctihieronymi** *Greater Swallow-tailed (Geronimo) Swift*		Mexico to Nicaragua, Honduras
23 01 063	**Panyptila cayennensis** *Lesser Swallow-tailed Swift*		Southern Mexico to Peru, Brazil
23 01 064	**Cypsiurus batasiensis** *Asian Palm Swift*		India to Indochina, Philippines, Greater and Lesser Sundas
23 01 065 +	**Cypsiurus parvus** *African Palm Swift*		Widespread Africa south of the Sahara
23 01 066	**Apus melba** *Alpine Swift*		Mediterranean basin to southern Africa, east to India
23 01 067	**Apus aequatorialis (reichenowi)** *Mottled Swift*		Ethiopia to South Africa
23 01 068	**Apus alexandri** *Alexander's Swift*		Africa south of the Sahara

	Date	Location
23 01 069 Apus barbatus (sladeniae) *African Swiftlet*		Africa south of the Sahara and ajdacent islands
23 01 070 Apus pallidus *Pallid Swift*		Mediterranean basin east to India
23 01 071 Apus berliozi *Socotra (Watson's) Swift*		Socotra Island (Indian Ocean) and coastal Kenya
23 01 072 Apus bradfieldi *Bradfield's Swift*		Mountains of southwest Africa
23 01 073 Apus niansae *Nyanza Swift*		Eritrea, Ethiopia to Kenya, Tanzania
23 01 074 Apus apus *Common Swift*		Palearctic region; winters to South Africa
23 01 075 Apus acuticaudus *Dark-backed Swift*		Mountains of Nepal to Assam
23 01 076 Apus pacificus *Fork-tailed Swift*		Eastern Palearctic; winters to Australasian region
23 01 077 Apus affinis *House Swift*		Africa to Oriental mainland and islands
23 01 078 Apus horus *Horus Swift*		Sudan and Ethiopia to South Africa
23 01 079 Apus caffer *White-rumped Swift*		Africa south of the Sahara; Iberian Peninsula
23 01 080 Apus batesi *Bates' Swift*		Cameroon to Zaire

ORDER: APODIFORMES
FAMILY: HEMIPROCNIDAE (Treeswifts)

23 02 001 Hemiprocne coronata *Crested Treeswift*		India, southwest China to Indochina
23 02 002 Hemiprocne longipennis *Gray-rumped Treeswift*		India to Malaya, Sumatra, Borneo, Java, Celebes
23 02 003 Hemiprocne mystacea *Moustached Swift*		Moluccas to New Guinea, Solomons, Bismarck Archipelago
23 02 004 Hemiprocne comata *White-whiskered Treeswift*		Malay peninsula, Sumatra, Borneo, Philippines

Date   Location

ORDER: APODIFORMES
FAMILY: TROCHILIDAE (Hummingbirds)

23 03 001 **Doryfera johannae**
+   *Blue-fronted Lancebill*   Highlands of western South America to southeast Peru

23 03 002 **Doryfera ludovicae**
           Green-fronted Lancebill   Mountains of Costa Rica to northwest Bolivia

23 03 003 **Androdon aequatorialis**
+   *Tooth-billed Hummingbird*   Eastern Panama to Pacific Colombia and Ecuador

23 03 004 **Ramphodon naevius**
           Saw-billed Hermit   Southeast Brazil (Minas Gerais to Rio Grande do Sul)

23 03 005 **Glaucis dohrnii**
           Hook-billed Hermit   Southeast Brazil (Espirito Santo, adjacent Bahia)

23 03 006 **Glaucis aenea**
           Bronzy Hermit   Tropical Nicaragua to Pacific Colombia and Ecuador

23 03 007 **Glaucis hirsuta**
+   *Rufous-breasted Hermit*   Central Panama to Brazil, northern Bolivia

23 03 008 **Threnetes niger**
           Sooty Barbthroat   Forests of French Guiana

23 03 009 **Threnetes loehkeni**
           Bronze-tailed Barbthroat   Northeast Brazil (Amapá—known from 6 specimens)

23 03 010 **Threnetes cristinae**
           Christine's Barbthroat   Brazil (new species described 1975)

23 03 011 **Threnetes grzimeki**
           Grzimek's Barbthroat   Brazil (new species described 1973)

23 03 012 **Threnetes leucurus**
+   *Pale-tailed Barbthroat*   Northern South America to Peru, northern Bolivia

23 03 013 **Threnetes ruckeri**
           Band-tailed Barbthroat   Tropical Guatemala to northern Venezuela, northwest Ecuador

23 03 014 **Phaethornis yaruqui**
           White-whiskered Hermit   Tropical Pacific Colombia, northwest Ecuador

23 03 015 **Phaethornis guy**
           Green Hermit   Tropical, subtropical Costa Rica to Ecuador, Peru

23 03 016 **Phaethornis syrmatophorus**
           Tawny-bellied Hermit   Tropical, subtropical, Colombia, Ecuador, northern Peru

23 03 017 **Phaethornis superciliosus**
           Long-tailed Hermit   Tropical Mexico to Amazonian Brazil, Bolivia

	Date	Location
23 03 018 **Phaethornis malaris** *Great-billed Hermit*		Tropical French Guiana and adjacent Brazil (Amapá)
23 03 019 **Phaethornis margarettae** *Margaret's Hermit*		Southeast Brazil (Espírito Santo)
23 03 020 **Phaethornis eurynome** *Scale-throated Hermit*		Southeast Brazil to northeast Argentina
23 03 021 **Phaethornis nigrirostris** *Black-billed Hermit*		Southeast Brazil (Espírito Santo)
23 03 022 **Phaethornis hispidus** *White-bearded Hermit*		Tropical Venezuela to Bolivia, western Brazil
23 03 023 **Phaethornis anthophilus** *Pale-bellied Hermit*		Tropical eastern Panama, northern Colombia and Venezuela
23 03 024 **Phaethornis bourcieri** *Straight-billed Hermit*		Tropical northern South America to Peru, Amazonian Brazil
23 03 025 **Phaethornis philippii** *Needle-billed Hermit*		Eastern Peru, western Brazil south of the Amazon
23 03 026 **Phaethornis koepckeae** *Koepke's Hermit*		Upper tropical hill forests of Peru in Amazonas, Huanuco
23 03 027 **Phaethornis squalidus (rupurumi)** *Dusky-throated Hermit*		Venezuela, Colombia, Guyana, Amazonian Brazil
23 03 028 **Phaethornis augusti** *Sooty-capped Hermit*		Upper tropical Guyana, Venezuela, Colombia
23 03 029 **Phaethornis pretrei** *Planalto Hermit*		Central Brazil to eastern Bolivia, northern Argentina
23 03 030 **Phaethornis subochraceus** *Buff-bellied Hermit*		Eastern Bolivia, western Matto Grosso of Brazil
23 03 031 **Phaethornis nattereri** *Cinnamon-throated Hermit*		Spottily distributed Brazil to eastern Bolivia
23 03 032 **Phaethornis maranhaoensis** *Maranhão Hermit*		Known only from Brazil (Imperatriz, Maranhão)
23 03 033 **Phaethornis gounellei** *Broad-tipped Hermit*		Eastern Brazil (Piaui, Ceará, Bahia)
23 03 034 **Phaethornis ruber** *Reddish Hermit*		Tropical northern South America to Bolivia, Brazil
23 03 035 **Phaethornis stuarti** *White-browed Hermit*		Tropical southeast Peru, northern Bolivia

	Date	Location

23 03 036 **Phaethornis griseogularis (porcullae)**
Gray-chinned Hermit — Northern South America to Peru, Bolivia

23 03 037 **Phaethornis longuemareus (adolphi)**
✝
Little Hermit — Tropical Mexico to eastern Peru, Amazon basin

23 03 038 **Phaethornis idaliae**
Minute Hermit — Southeast Brazil (Espirito Santo, Rio de Janeiro)

23 03 039 **Eutoxeres aquila**
✝
White-tipped Sicklebill — Tropical Costa Rica to northeast Peru

23 03 040 **Eutoxeres condamini**
✝
Buff-tailed Sicklebill — Tropical southeast Colombia to southeast Peru

23 03 041 **Phaeochroa cuvierii**
Scaly-breasted Hummingbird — Open woodlands of Guatemala to northern Colombia

23 03 042 **Campylopterus curvipennis**
Wedge-tailed Sabrewing — Tropical eastern Mexico to Guatemala

23 03 043 **Campylopterus largipennis**
Gray-breasted Sabrewing — Tropical northern South America to Bolivia, Brazil

23 03 044 **Campylopterus rufus**
Rufous Sabrewing — Highlands of southern Mexico (Chiapas), Guatemala, El Salvador

23 03 045 **Campylopterus hyperythrus**
Rufous-breasted Sabrewing — Subtropical southeast Venezuela, adjacent Brazil

23 03 046 **Campylopterus duidae**
Buff-breasted Sabrewing — Subtropical southeast Venezuela, adjacent Brazil

23 03 047 **Campylopterus hemileucurus**
Violet Sabrewing — Highlands of southern Mexico to western Panama

23 03 048 **Campylopterus ensipennis**
White-tailed Sabrewing — Tropical, subtropical Venezuela; Trinidad; Tobago

23 03 049 **Campylopterus falcatus**
Lazuline Sabrewing — Subtropical to temperate Venezuela, Colombia, Ecuador

23 03 050 **Campylopterus phainopeplus**
Santa Marta Sabrewing — Confined to Santa Marta Mountains of Colombia

	Date	Location
23 03 051 **Campylopterus villaviscensio** *Napo Sabrewing*		Eastern Ecuador (headwaters of Rio Napo)
23 03 052 **Eupetomena macroura** *Swallow-tailed Hummingbird*		Savannas of northern South America to Paraguay
23 03 053 **Florisuga mellivora** *White-necked Jacobin*		Tropical Southern Mexico to Peru, Amazonian Brazil
23 03 054 **Melanotrochilus fuscus** *Black Jacobin*		*Capoeira* zone of coastal eastern Brazil
23 03 055 **Colibri delphinae** *Brown Violetear*		Tropical, subtropical Guatemala to Brazil, Bolivia
23 03 056 **Colibri thalassinus** *Green Violetear*		Open mountain slopes of southern Mexico to Bolivia
23 03 057 **Colibri coruscans** *Sparkling Violetear*		Open mountain slopes of Venezuela to northwest Argentina
23 03 058 **Colibri serrirostris** *White-vented Violetear*		Savanna of Bolivia, northwest Argentina, southern Brazil
23 03 059 **Anthracothorax viridigula** *Green-throated Mango*		Tropical savanna of Venezuela, Guianas, northern Brazil
23 03 060 **Anthracothorax prevostii** *Green-breasted Mango*		Tropical Mexico to western Colombia, Ecuador, Peru
23 03 061 **Anthracothorax nigricollis** *Black-throated Mango*		Tropical Panama, Colombia east of Andes to Argentina
23 03 062 **Anthracothorax veraguensis** *Veraguan Mango*		Pacific slope of western Panama (Chiriqui, Veraguas)
23 03 063 **Anthracothorax dominicus** *Dominican Mango*		Widespread Hispaniola
23 03 064 **Anthracothorax viridis** *Green Mango*		Highlands of Puerto Rico
23 03 065 **Anthracothorax mango** *Jamaican Mango*		Semiarid woodlands of Jamaica
23 03 066 **Avocettula recurvirostris** *Fiery-tailed Awlbill*		Tropical northern South America to Brazil, Ecuador
23 03 067 **Eulampis jugularis** *Purple-throated Carib*		Mountain forests of Lesser Antilles

		Date	Location
23 03 068	**Sericotes holosericeus** *Green-throated Carib*		Lowland forests of Lesser Antilles
23 03 069	**Chrysolampis mosquitus** *Ruby-topaz Hummingbird*		Tropical northern South America to Amazonian Brazil
23 03 070	**Orthorhyncus cristatus** *Antillean Crested* *Hummingbird*		Widespread Lesser Antilles
23 03 071	**Klais guimeti** *Violet-headed* *Hummingbird*		Highlands of Nicaragua, Honduras to Bolivia
23 03 072	**Abeillia abeillei** *Emerald-chinned* *Hummingbird*		Mountains of southeast Mexico to Nicaragua
23 03 073	**Stephanoxis lalandi** *Black-breasted* *Plovercrest*		Savanna of southeast Brazil to northeast Argentina
23 03 074	**Lophornis ornata** *Tufted Coquette*		Tropical Guianas, Venezuela, adjacent Brazil; Trinidad
23 03 075	**Lophornis gouldii** *Dot-eared Coquette*		Savannas of northeast Brazil to southeast Bolivia
23 03 076	**Lophornis magnifica** *Frilled Coquette*		Forest and scrub of east and central Brazil
23 03 077	**Lophornis delattrei** *Rufous-crested Coquette*		Tropical, subtropical southwest Mexico to Bolivia
23 03 078	**Lophornis stictolopha** *Spangled Coquette*		Andes of Venezuela, Ecuador, Colombia, Peru
23 03 079	**Lophornis melaniae** *Dusky Coquette*		Colombia (known from a single specimen)
23 03 080	**Lophornis chalybea** *Festive Coquette*		Northern South America to Bolivia, Amazonian Brazil
23 02 081	**Lophornis pavonina** *Peacock Coquette*		Forests of Venezuela, Guyana
23 03 082	**Lophornis insignibarbis** *Bearded Coquette*		Colombia (known from a single specimen)
23 03 083	**Paphosia helenae** *Black-crested Coquette*		Caribbean slope of southern Mexico to Costa Rica
23 03 084	**Paphosia adorabilis** *Adorable Coquette*		Central and southwest Costa Rica to southwest Panama
23 03 085	**Popelairia popelairii** *Wire-crested Thorntail*		Tropical, subtropical eastern Colombia to Peru
23 03 086	**Popelairia langsdorffi** *Black-bellied Thorntail*		Tropical northern South America to Brazil, Peru

	Date	Location
23 03 087 **Popelairia letitiae** *Coppery Thorntail*		Bolivia (known from two male specimens)
23 03 088 **Popelairia conversii** *Green Thorntail*		Tropical Costa Rica to Pacific Colombia and Ecuador
23 03 089 **Discosura longicauda** *Racket-tailed Coquette*		Tropical Venezuela, Guianas, northeast Brazil
23 03 090 **Chlorestes notatus** *Blue-chinned Sapphire*		Tropical northern South America to Peru, Brazil
23 03 091 **Chlorostilbon mellisugus** *Blue-tailed Emerald*		Tropical to temperate Costa Rica to Bolivia, Brazil
23 03 092 **Chlorostilbon aureoventris** *Glittering-bellied Emerald*		Savannas of eastern Brazil to Bolivia, northern Argentina
23 03 093 **Chlorostilbon canivetii (assimilis)** *Fork-tailed Emerald*		Tropical Mexico to Caribbean coast of South America
23 03 094 **Chlorostilbon ricordii** *Cuban Emerald*		Northern Bahamas; Cuba; Isle of Pines
23 03 095 **Chlorostilbon swainsonii** *Hispaniolian Emerald*		Mountain slopes of Hispaniola
23 03 096 **Chlorostilbon maugaeus** *Puerto Rican Emerald*		Forests, hills, coffee plantations of Puerto Rico
23 03 097 **Chlorostilbon gibsoni** *Red-billed Emerald*		Tropical, subtropical northern Colombia, Venezuela
23 03 098 **Chlorostilbon russatus** *Coppery Emerald*		Highlands of northern Colombia, adjacent Venezuela
23 03 099 **Chlorostilbon inexpectatus** *Berlepsch's Emerald*		Colombia (unique—probable variant *C. poortmanni*)
23 03 100 **Chloristilbon stenura** *Narrow-tailed Emerald*		Tropical to temperate Venezuela, eastern Colombia
23 03 101 **Chlorostilbon alice** *Green-tailed Emerald*		Subtropical Venezuela (mountains north of Orinocco)
23 03 102 **Chlorostilbon poortmanni (euchloris)** *Short-tailed Emerald*		Tropical, subtropical Colombia, northwest Venezuela
23 03 103 **Chlorostilbon auratus** *Cabanis' Emerald*		Peru (unique—probable aberrant *C. poortmanni*)
23 03 104 **Cynanthus sordidus** *Dusky Hummingbird*		Mexico (Jalisco to Guerrero, Hidalgo, Puebla)
23 03 105 **Cynanthus latirostris** *Broad-billed Hummingbird*		Arid southwest United States to southern Mexico

		Date	Location
23 03 106	**Ptochoptera iolaima** *Natterer's Emerald*		Brazil (Ypanema: unique—probably an artifact)
23 03 107	**Cyanophaia bicolor** *Blue-headed Hummingbird*		Lesser Antilles (Dominica and Martinique)
23 03 108	**Thalurania furcata** **(ridgwayi)** *Common Woodnymph*		Widespread tropical Mexico to northern Argentina
23 03 109	**Thalurania watertonii** *Long-tailed Woodnymph*		Forests of coastal Brazil (Pará to Bahia)
23 03 110	**Thalurania glaucopis** *Violet-capped Woodnymph*		Southeast Brazil (Bahia) to northeast Argentina
23 03 111	**Thalurania lerchi** *Lerch's Woodnymph*		Colombia (unique—probable hybrid)
23 03 112	**Augasma** **cyaneoberyllina** *Berlioz's Woodnymph*		Brazil (doubtful species—status uncertain)
23 03 113	**Augasma smaragdinea** *Emerald Woodnymph*		Southeast Brazil (known from six old specimens)
23 03 114	**Neolesbia nehrkorni** *Nehrkorn's Sylph*		Colombia (known from two specimens—probable hybrid)
23 03 115	**Panterpe insignis** *Fiery-throated Hummingbird*		Mountains of Costa Rica and western Panama
23 03 116	**Damophila julie** **(panamensis)** *Violet-bellied Hummingbird*		Tropical Costa Rica to western Ecuador
23 03 117	**Lepidopyga** **coeruleogularis** *Sapphire-throated Hummingbird*		Tropical Costa Rica to extreme northwest Colombia
23 03 118	**Lepidopyga lilliae** *Sapphire-bellied Hummingbird*		Colombia (mangroves of mouth of Magdalena River)
23 03 119	**Lepidopyga goudoti** *Shining-green Hummingbird*		Tropical northwest Venezuela, Colombia
23 03 120	**Hylocharis xantusii** *Xantus' Hummingbird*		Confined to southern half of Baja California
23 03 121	**Hylocharis leucotis** *White-eared Hummingbird*		Highlands of southern Arizona to Honduras, Nicaragua
23 03 122	**Hylocharis eliciae** *Blue-throated Goldentail*		Lowlands of eastern Mexico to eastern Panama

		Date	Location

23 03 123	**Hylocharis sapphirina** *Rufous-throated Sapphire*		Tropical northern South America to northern Argentina
23 03 124	**Hylocharis cyanus** *White-chinned Sapphire*		Tropical northern South America to Bolivia, Brazil
23 03 125	**Hylocharis pyropygia** *Flame-rumped Sapphire*		Brazil (probable hybrid—known from 5 specimens)
23 03 126	**Hylocharis chrysura** *Gilded Hummingbird*		Brazil (Minas Gerais) to Bolivia, northern Argentina
23 03 127	**Hylocharis grayi** *Blue-headed Sapphire*		Tropical eastern Panama to northwest Ecuador
23 03 128	**Chrysuronia oenone** *Golden-tailed Sapphire*		Tropical Venezuela east of Andes to Bolivia
23 03 129	**Goldmania violiceps** *Violet-capped Hummingbird*		Subtropical eastern Panama to Colombia (endangered)
23 03 130	**Goethalsia bella** *Rufous-cheeked Hummingbird*		Eastern Panama to Colombia (Chocó—endangered)
23 03 131	**Trochilus polytmus** *Streamertail*		Semiarid lowlands to mountains of Jamaica
23 03 132	**Leucochloris albicollis** *White-throated Hummingbird*		Brazil (Minas Gerais) to northeast Argentina
23 03 133	**Polytmus guainumbi** *White-tailed Goldenthroat*		Savannas and grasslands of tropical South America
23 03 134	**Polytmus milleri** *Tepui Goldenthroat*		Subtropical mountains of southern Venezuela
23 03 135	**Polytmus theresiae** *Green-tailed Goldenthroat*		Savannas of northern South America to Amazonian Brazil
23 03 136	**Leucippus fallax** *Buffy Hummingbird*		Arid Caribbean littoral of Colombia, Venezuela
23 03 137	**Leucippus baeri** *Tumbes Hummingbird*		Arid littoral of Peru (Tumbes, Piura)
23 03 138	**Leucippus taczanowskii** *Spot-throated Hummingbird*		Arid coastal Peru (Piura to Ancash)
23 03 139	**Leucippus chlorocercus** *Olive-spotted Hummingbird*		Dry scrub of Ecuador, adjacent Peru, Brazil
23 03 140	**Taphrospilus hypostictus** *Many-spotted Hummingbird*		Dry scrub of eastern Ecuador to northwest Argentina

	Date	Location
23 03 141	**Amazilia chionogaster**	
	White-bellied Hummingbird	Northern Peru to western Argentina, Matto Grosso
23 03 142 +	**Amazilia viridicauda** *Green-and-white Hummingbird*	Peru (southern Huanuco to southern Puno)
23 03 143	**Amazilia candida** *White-bellied Emerald*	Lowlands, foothills of southeast Mexico to Costa Rica
23 03 144	**Amazilia chionopectus** *White-chested Emerald*	Tropical Guianas, northeast Venezuela; Trinidad
23 03 145	**Amazilia versicolor (hollandi)** *Versicolored Emerald*	Tropical northern South America to northeast Argentina
23 03 146	**Amazilia luciae** *Honduras Emerald*	Confined to Honduras (endangered)
23 03 147	**Amazilia fimbriata** *Glittering-throated Emerald*	Tropical South America east of Andes to northern Bolivia
23 03 148	**Amazilia distans** *Tachira Emerald*	Tropical Venezuela (known only from Táchira)
23 03 149	**Amazilia lactea** *Sapphire-spangled Emerald*	Tropical Venezuela, Peru, Bolivia, eastern Brazil
23 03 150	**Amazilia amabilis (decora)** *Blue-chested Hummingbird*	Tropical Nicaragua to Pacific Colombia and Ecuador
23 03 151	**Amazilia cyaneotincta** *Blue-spotted Hummingbird*	Colombia (Bogotá—known from two specimens)
23 03 152	**Amazilia rosenbergi** *Purple-chested Hummingbird*	Pacific coast of Colombia and northwest Ecuador
23 03 153	**Amazilia boucardi** *Mangrove Hummingbird*	Pacific mangrove swamps of Costa Rica
23 03 154	**Amazilia franciae** *Andean Emerald*	Subtropical Andes of Colombia to northern Peru
23 03 155	**Amazilia leucogaster** *Plain-bellied Emerald*	Tropical Venezuela, Guianas, eastern Brazil
23 03 156	**Amazilia cyanocephala** *Red-billed Azurecrown*	Mountains of southeast Mexico to Nicaragua
23 03 157	**Amazilia microrhyncha** *Small-billed Azurecrown*	Honduras (known from a single specimen)
23 03 158	**Amazilia cyanifrons** *Indigo-capped Hummingbird*	Tropical, subtropical forests of Colombia

	Date	Location

23 03 159 Amazilia beryllina
Berylline Hummingbird   Northwest Mexico to Guatemala, Honduras

23 03 160 Amazilia cyanura
Blue-tailed Hummingbird   Pacific slope of southern Mexico (Chiapas) to Costa Rica

23 03 161 Amazilia saucerrottei
Blue-vented Hummingbird   Semiarid Nicaragua, Costa Rica to Venezuela, Colombia

23 03 162 Amazilia tobaci
Copper-rumped   Tropical, subtropical Venezuela; Trinidad; Tobago
Hummingbird

23 03 163 Amazilia viridigaster
Green-bellied   Colombia, Venezuela, Guyana, adjacent Brazil
Hummingbird

23 03 164 Amazilia edward
Snowy-breasted   Southwestern Costa Rica and adjacent western
Hummingbird   Panama

23 03 165 Amazilia rutila
Cinnamon Hummingbird   Mexico to Costa Rica; Tres Marias Islands

23 03 166 Amazilia yucatanensis
Buff-bellied Hummingbird   Southern Texas to Guatemala, Belize

23 03 167 Amazilia tzacatl
Rufous-tailed Hummingbird Tropical eastern Mexico to Colombia, Ecuador

23 03 168 Amazilia handleyi
Escudo Hummingbird   Panama (Isla Escudo de Veragua—probable race of
                             A. tzacatl)

23 03 169 Amazilia castaneiventris
Chestnut-bellied   Subtropical Colombia (Boyacá—endangered)
Hummingbird

23 03 170 Amazilia amazilia
Amazilia Hummingbird   Arid southern Ecuador, Peru

23 03 171 Amazilia viridifrons
Green-fronted   Southern Mexico (Guerrero to Chiapas)
Hummingbird

23 03 172 Amazilia violiceps
(verticalis)
Violet-crowned   Southern Arizona to southern Mexico
Hummingbird

23 03 173 Eupherusa eximia
Stripe-tailed Hummingbird Humid rain forests of southern Mexico to Panama

23 03 174 Eupherusa poliocerca
White-tailed Hummingbird   Southwest Mexico (probable race of *E. eximia*)

23 03 175 Eupherusa cyanopyrys
Oaxaca Hummingbird   Mountainous Pacific slope of Oaxaca (Mexico)

Date   Location

23 03 176	**Eupherusa nigriventris** *Black-bellied Hummingbird*	Highlands of Costa Rica and western Panama
23 03 177	**Elvira chionura** *White-tailed Emerald*	Highlands of southwest Costa Rica, western Panama
23 03 178	**Elvira cupreiceps** *Coppery-headed Emerald*	Costa Rica (Caribbean slope of central highlands)
23 03 179	**Microchera albocoronata** *Snowcap*	Caribbean slope of Nicaragua to western Panama
23 03 180	**Chalybura buffonii** *White-vented Plumeleteer*	Central Panama to Venezuela, Colombia, Ecuador
23 03 181	**Chalybura urochrysia (melanorrhoa)** *Bronze-tailed Plumeleteer*	Tropical Nicaragua to Pacific Colombia, Ecuador
23 03 182	**Aphantochroa cirrochloris** *Sombre Hummingbird*	Forest and scrub of east and central Brazil
23 03 183	**Lampornis clemenciae** *Blue-throated Hummingbird*	Mountains of southwest United States to southern Mexico
23 03 184	**Lampornis amethystinus** *Amethyst-throated Hummingbird*	Mountains of tropical Mexico to Honduras
23 03 185	**Lampornis viridipallens** *Green-throated Mountain Gem*	Mountains of southern Mexico (Chiapas) to Honduras
23 03 186	**Lampornis hemileucus** *White-bellied Mountain Gem*	Caribbean slope of Costa Rica, western Panama
23 03 187	**Lampornis castaneoventris (calolaema)** *White-throated Mountain Gem*	Highlands of western Panama (Chiriqui)
23 03 188	**Lampornis cinereicauda** *Gray-tailed Mountain Gem*	Mountains of Costa Rica and western Panama
23 03 189	**Lamprolaima rhami** *Garnet-throated Hummingbird*	Mountains of southern Mexico to Honduras
23 03 190	**Adelomyia melanogenys** *Speckled Hummingbird*	Subtropical western South American to northwest Argentina
23 03 191	**Anthocephala floriceps** *Blossomcrown*	Subtropical Colombia (Santa Marta Mountains)

	Date	Location

23 03 192 **Urosticte benjamini**
Whitetip

Subtropical Colombia, Ecuador, northeast Peru

23 03 193 **Phlogophilus hemileucurus**
Ecuadorian Piedtail

Tropical Ecuador (headwaters of Rio Napo)

23 03 194 **Phlogophilus harterti**
Peruvian Piedtail

Tropical southeast Peru (endangered)

23 03 195 **Clytolaema rubricauda**
+ *Brazilian Ruby*

Southeast Brazil (Goias to Rio Grande do Sul)

23 03 196 **Polyplancta aurescens**
Gould's Jewelfront

Tropical forest and scrub of Amazon basin

23 03 197 **Heliodoxa rubinoides**
Fawn-breasted Brilliant

Subtropical Andes of Colombia, Ecuador, northeast Peru

23 03 198 **Heliodoxa leadbeateri**
Violet-fronted Brilliant

Tropical western South America (Venezuela to Bolivia)

23 03 199 **Heliodoxa jacula**
+ *Green-crowned Brilliant*

Highlands of Costa Rica to Colombia, western Ecuador

23 03 200 **Heliodoxa xanthogonys**
Velvet-crowned Brilliant

Subtropical Guyana, Venezuela, adjacent Brazil

23 03 201 **Heliodoxa schreibersii**
+ *Black-throated Brilliant*

Tropical eastern Ecuador, adjacent Peru, Bolivia

23 03 202 **Heliodoxa gularis**
Pink-throated Brilliant

Tropical northeast Ecuador, Peru, adjacent Colombia

23 03 203 **Heliodoxa branickii**
+ *Rufous-webbed Brilliant*

Forest edges of southeast Peru, northern Bolivia

23 03 204 **Heliodoxa imperatrix**
Empress Brilliant

Subtropical western Colombia to northwest Ecuador

23 03 205 **Eugenes fulgens**
Rivoli's Hummingbird

Mountains of southwest United States to western Panama

23 03 206 **Hylonympha macrocerca**
Scissor-tailed Hummingbird

Venezuela (mountains of Paria Peninsula—endangered)

23 03 207 **Sternoclyta cyanopectus**
Violet-chested Hummingbird

Lower subtropical Andes of Venezuela

23 03 208 **Topaza pella**
Crimson Topaz

Tropical Guianas, Venezuela, adjacent Brazil, Ecuador

	Date	Location

23 03 209   **Topaza pyra**
Fiery Topaz

Tropical Venezuela east of Andes to Peru

23 03 210   **Oreotrochilus melanogaster**
Black-breasted Hillstar

Temperate Andes of Peru (Junin and Lima)

23 03 211   **Oreotrochilus estella**
＋   *Andean Hillstar*

Rocky Andean slopes of Ecuador to Argentina, Chile

23 03 212   **Oreotrochilus leucopleurus**
White-sided Hillstar

Andes of Bolivia, Argentina, Chile

23 03 213   **Oreotrochilus adela**
Wedge-tailed Hillstar

Temperate Andes of southern Bolivia

23 03 214   **Urochroa bougueri**
White-tailed Hillstar

Highlands of Colombia, Ecuador

23 03 215   **Patagona gigas**
Giant Hummingbird

Arid temperate Ecuador to Chile, Argentina

23 03 216   **Aglaeactis cupripennis**
Shining Sunbeam

Temperate Andes of Colombia, Ecuador, Peru

23 03 217   **Aglaeactis aliciae**
Purple-backed Sunbeam

Temperate Andes of Peru (Libertad and Ancash)

23 03 218   **Aglaeactis castelnaudii**
White-tufted Sunbeam

Temperate Andes of Peru (Huánuco, Junin, Cuzco)

23 03 219   **Aglaeactis pamela**
Black-hooded Sunbeam

Temperate Bolivia (La Paz, Cochabamba)

23 03 220   **Lafresnaya lafresnayi**
Mountain Velvetbreast

Andes of Venezuela, Colombia, Ecuador, Peru, Bolivia

23 03 221   **Pterophanes cyanopterus**
Great Sapphirewing

Temperate Andes of Colombia to central Bolivia

23 03 222   **Coeligena coeligena**
＋   *Bronzy Inca*

Subtropical Andes of Venezuela, Colombia to Bolivia

23 03 223   **Coeligena wilsoni**
Brown Inca

Subtropical western Colombia, western Ecuador

23 03 224   **Coeligena prunellei**
Black Inca

Temperate eastern Andes of Colombia

23 03 225   **Coeligena torquata**
＋   *Collared Inca*

Andes of Venezuela, Colombia, Ecuador, Peru, Bolivia

23 03 226   **Coeligena phalerata**
White-tailed Starfrontlet

Colombia (tropical to temperate Santa Marta Mountains)

23 03 227   **Coeligena bonapartei**
Golden-bellied Startfrontlet

Andes of Venezuela, Colombia

		Date	Location

23 03 228	**Coeligena orina**	
	Dusky Starfrontlet	Temperate western Andes of Colombia
23 03 229	**Coeligena helianthea**	
	Blue-throated Starfrontlet	Andes of extreme western Venezuela, Colombia
23 03 230	**Coeligena lutetiae**	
	Buff-winged Starfrontlet	Temperate central Andes of Colombia, Ecuador
23 03 231	**Coeligena violifer**	
	Violet-throated Starfrontlet	Subtropical Andes of Peru to Bolivia
23 03 232	**Coeligena iris**	
	Rainbow Starfrontlet	Andes of southern Ecuador to southeast Peru
23 03 233 +	**Ensifera ensifera**	
	Sword-billed Hummingbird	Andes of Venezuela to northern Bolivia
23 03 234 +	**Sephanoides sephaniodes**	
	Green-backed Firecrown	Western Argentina, Chile; Juan Fernandez Islands
23 03 235	**Sephanoides fernandensis**	
	Juan Fernandez Firecrown	Confined to Juan Fernandez Islands (off Chile)
23 03 236	**Boissonneaua flavescens**	
	Buff-tailed Coronet	Andes of northwest Venezuela, Colombia, Ecuador
23 03 237 +	**Boissonneaua matthewsii**	
	Chestnut-breasted Coronet	Subtropical Andes of Colombia, Ecuador, Peru
23 03 238	**Boissonneaua jardini**	
	Velvet-purple Coronet	Pacific Colombia to northwest Ecuador
23 03 239	**Heliangelus mavors**	
	Orange-throated Sunangel	Andes of northwest Venezuela to eastern Colombia
23 03 240	**Heliangelus spencei**	
	Merida Sunangel	Subtropical, temperate Andes of Venezuela (Mérida)
23 03 241 +	**Heliangelus amethysticollis (clarisse)**	
	Amethyst-throated Sunangel	Andes of Venezuela, Colombia, Ecuador, Peru, Bolivia
23 03 242	**Heliangelus strophianus**	
	Gorgeted Sunangel	Subtropical southwest Colombia to northwest Ecuador
23 03 243	**Heliangelus exortis (micraster)**	
	Tourmaline Sunangel	Andes of Colombia, Ecuador to northern Peru
23 03 244	**Heliangelus viola**	
	Purple-throated Sunangel	Subtropical, temperate western Ecuador, northern Peru

	Date	Location
23 03 245 **Heliangelus micrastur** *Little Sunangel*		Andes of Ecuador and Peru (probable race *H. exortis*)
23 03 246 **Heliangelus squamigularis** *Olive-throated Sunangel*		Probable hybrid *Heliangelus* sp. x *Eriocnemis* sp.
23 03 247 **Heliangelus speciosus** *Green-throated Sunangel*		Probable hybrid *Heliangelus* sp. x *Eriocnemis* sp.
23 03 248 **Heliangelus rothschildi** *Rothschild's Sunangel*		Probable hybrid *Heliangelus* sp. x *Eriocnemis* sp.
23 03 249 **Heliangelus luminosus** *Glistening Sunangel*		Probable hybrid *Rhamphomicron microrhynchum* x *Heliangelus* sp.
23 03 250 **Heliangelus regalis** *Royal Sunangel*		Northern Peru in Cajamarca (discovered 1979)
23 03 251 **Eriocnemis nigrivestis** *Black-breasted Puffleg*		Temperate northern Ecuador (Quito)
23 03 252 **Eriocnemis soderstromi** *Soderstrom's Puffleg*		Ecuador (unique—probable aberrant *E. godini*)
23 03 253 **Eriocnemis vestitus** *Glowing Puffleg*		Temperate, páramo zone of Venezuela, Colombia, Ecuador
23 03 254 **Eriocnemis godini** *Turquoise-throated Puffleg*		Temperate Colombia (Bogotá), northwest Ecuador
23 03 255 **Eriocnemis cupreoventris** *Coppery-bellied Puffleg*		Subtropical, temperate Andes of Venezuela, Colombia
23 03 256 **Eriocnemis luciani** *Sapphire-vented Puffleg*		Subtropical western Andes of Colombia, Ecuador, Peru
23 03 257 **Eriocnemis isaacsonii** *Isaacson's Puffleg*		Colombia (known from 3 specimens—probable hybrid)
23 03 258 **Eriocnemis mosquera** *Golden-breasted Puffleg*		Temperate Andes of Colombia to northern Ecuador
23 03 259 **Eriocnemis glaucopoides** *Blue-capped Puffleg*		Temperate Andes of Bolivia, northwest Argentina
23 03 260 **Eriocnemis mirabilis** *Colorful Puffleg*		Subtropical western Andes of Colombia (Cauca)
23 03 261 **Eriocnemis alinae** *Emerald-bellied Puffleg*		Eastern Andes of Colombia, Ecuador, Peru

		Date	Location

23 03 262 **Eriocnemis derbyi**
Black-thighed Puffleg   Central Andes of Colombia to northern Ecuador

23 03 263 **Haplophaedia aureliae**
Greenish Puffleg   Highlands of eastern Panama, Colombia to Bolivia

23 03 264 **Haplophaedia lugens**
Hoary Puffleg   Andes of Colombia (Nariño), northwest Ecuador

23 03 265 **Ocreatus underwoodii**
Booted Racquet-tail   Andes of Venezuela to Bolivia

23 03 266 **Lesbia victoriae**
Black-tailed Trainbearer   Andes of Colombia, Ecuador, Peru

23 03 267 **Lesbia nuna**
Green-tailed Trainbearer   Andes of northwest Venezuela to Bolivia

23 03 268 **Sappho sparganura**
Red-tailed Comet   Temperate Andes of Bolivia, western Argentina, Chile

23 03 269 **Polyonymus caroli**
Bronze-tailed Comet   Pacific slope of Andes of Peru

23 03 270 **Zodalia glyceria**
Purple-tailed Comet   Colombia (Popoyán—probable hybrid)

23 03 271 **Ramphomicron
microrhynchum**
Purple-backed Thornbill   Andes of northwest Venezuela to southern Peru

23 03 272 **Ramphomicron dorsale**
Black-backed Thornbill   Santa Marta mountains of Colombia

23 03 273 **Metallura phoebe**
Black Metaltail   Andes of Peru to northern Bolivia

23 03 274 **Metallura theresiae**
Coppery Metaltail   Temperate zone of northern Peru

23 03 275 **Metallura purpureicauda**
Purple-tailed Thornbill   Colombia (probable hybrid)

23 03 276 **Metallura aeneocauda
(malagae)**
Scaled Metaltail   Subtropical, temperate Andes of Peru, Bolivia

23 03 277 **Metallura baroni**
Violet-throated Metaltail   Arid temperate Andes of southwest Ecuador
                                       (Cuenca)

23 03 278 **Metallura eupogon**
Fire-throated Metaltail   Temperate Andes of central Peru (Huánuco, Junin)

23 03 279 **Metallura odomae**
Neblina Metaltail   Temperate forests of Peru in Department of Piura

23 03 280 **Metallura williami**
Viridian Metaltail   Temperatue, páramo Andes of Colombia, Ecuador

23 03 281 **Metallura tyrianthina**
Tyrian Metaltail   Subtropical to páramo Andes of Venezuela to Bolivia

	Date	Location

23 03 282 Metallura iracunda
Perija Metaltail
Perija mountains of Venezuela and Colombia

23 03 283 Chalcostigma ruficeps
Rufous-capped Thornbill
Temperate Andes of Ecuador to Peru, Bolivia

23 03 284 Chalcostigma olivaceum
Olivaceous Thornbill
Temperate, páramo of central Peru to northern Bolivia

23 03 285 Chalcostigma stanleyi
Blue-mantled Thornbill
High Andes of Ecuador, Peru, northern Bolivia

23 03 286 Chalcostigma heteropogon
Bronze-tailed Thornbill
Temperate, páramo zone of Colombia, Venezuela

23 03 287 Chalcostigma herrani
Rainbow-bearded Thornbill
Temperate zone of Colombia to northern Ecuador

23 03 288 Oxypogon guerinii
Bearded Helmetcrest
Páramo zone of northwest Venezuela, Colombia

23 03 289 Opisthoprora euryptera
Mountain Avocetbill
Temperate central Andes of Colombia, northeast Ecuador

23 03 290 Taphrolesbia griseiventris
Gray-bellied Comet
Temperate zone of northwest Peru

23 03 291 Aglaiocercus kingi
+ **(emmae)**
Long-tailed Sylph
Mountains of Venezuela to Bolivia

23 03 292 Aglaiocercus coelestis
Violet-tailed Sylph
Mountains of Colombia to southwest Ecuador

23 03 293 Oreonympha nobilis
+ *Bearded Mountaineer*
Arid temperate Andes of Peru (Huancavelica, Cuzco)

23 03 294 Augastes scutatus
Hyacinth Visorbearer
Southeast Brazilian plateau (Minas Gerais, Bahia)

23 03 295 Augastes lumachellus
Hooded Visorbearer
Cerrado of eastern Brazil (Bahia—possibly extinct)

23 03 296 Schistes geoffroyi
Wedge-billed Hummingbird
Western South America (Venezuela to Bolivia)

23 03 297 Heliothryx barroti
+ *Purple-crowned Fairy*
Tropical southern Mexico to Pacific Colombia, Ecuador

23 03 298 Heliothryx aurita
Black-eared Fairy
Tropical northern South America to Peru, Amazonian Brazil

23 03 299 Heliactin cornuta
Horned Sungem
Caatinga of Surinam to central Brazil, adjacent Bolivia

		Date	Location
23 03 300	**Loddigesia mirabilis** *Marvelous Spatuletail*		Andes of Peru (endangered)
23 03 301	**Heliomaster constantii** *Plain-capped Starthroat*		Arid lowlands of Mexico (Sonora) to Costa Rica
23 03 302	**Heliomaster longirostris** *Long-billed Starthroat*		Southern Mexico to Brazil, Bolivia; Trinidad
23 03 303	**Heliomaster squamosus** *Stripe-breasted Starthroat*		Coastal eastern Brazil (Pernambuco to São Paulo)
23 03 304	**Heliomaster furcifer** *Blue-tufted Starthroat*		Tropical Colombia to Amazonian Brazil, central Argentina
23 03 305	**Rhodopis vesper** *Oasis Hummingbird*		Arid western Peru to northern Chile
23 03 306	**Thaumastura cora** *Peruvian Sheartail*		Arid coastal Peru (Libertad to Arequipa)
23 03 307	**Philodice evelynae** *Bahama Woodstar*		Scrubby woodlands of Bahamas (endangered)
23 03 308	**Philodice bryantae** *Costa Rican Woodstar*		Highlands of Costa Rica and western Panama
23 03 309	**Philodice mitchellii** *Purple-throated Woodstar*		Tropical western Andes of Colombia to Ecuador
23 03 310	**Doricha enicura** *Slender Sheartail*		Highlands of southern Mexico (Chiapas) to Honduras
23 03 311	**Doricha eliza** *Mexican Sheartail*		Southern Mexico (Vera Cruz and Yucatán Peninsula)
23 03 312	**Tilmatura dupontii** *Sparkling-tailed Hummingbird*		Highlands of southern Mexico to Nicaragua
23 03 313	**Microstilbon burmeisteri** *Slender-tailed Woodstar*		Highlands of eastern Bolivia to northwest Argentina
23 03 314	**Calothorax lucifer** *Lucifer Hummingbird*		Mountains of southern Texas to southern Mexico
23 03 315	**Calothorax pulcher** *Beautiful Hummingbird*		Southern Mexico (Guerrero to Chiapas)
23 03 316	**Archilochus colubris** *Ruby-throated Hummingbird*		Canada to Panama; West Indies
23 03 317	**Archilochus alexandri** *Black-chinned Hummingbird*		Canada to Mexico (west of the Rockies)
23 03 318	**Calliphlox amethystina** *Amethyst Woodstar*		Widespread tropical South America to northeast Argentina

		Date	Location

23 03 319	**Mellisuga minima**	
	Vervain Hummingbird	Jamaica, Hispaniola and adjacent islands
23 03 320	**Calypte anna**	
	Anna's Hummingbird	California, Arizona, Baja; winters to Sonora
23 03 321	**Calypte costae**	
	Costa's Hummingbird	Southwest United States to northern Mexico
23 03 322	**Calypte helenae**	
	Bee Hummingbird	Confined to Cuba, Isle of Pines (endangered)
23 03 323	**Stellula calliope**	
	Calliope Hummingbird	Highlands of Canada to Mexico
23 03 324	**Atthis heloisa**	
	Bumblebee Hummingbird	Mountains of Mexico (Sinaloa to Vera Cruz)
23 03 325	**Atthis ellioti**	
	Wine-throated Hummingbird	Mountains of southern Mexico (Chiapas) to Honduras
23 03 326 +	**Myrtis fanny**	
	Purple-collared Woodstar	Tropical to temperate southern Ecuador to Peru
23 03 327 †	**Eulidia yarrellii**	
	Chilean Woodstar	Arid northern Chile (rare and local)
23 03 328 +	**Myrmia micrura**	
	Short-tailed Woodstar	Tropical arid western Ecuador to Peru (Libertad)
23 03 329	**Acestrura mulsant**	
	White-bellied Woodstar	Andes of Colombia to northern Bolivia
23 03 330	**Acestrura decorata**	
	Decorated Woodstar	Bogota? (known from a single specimen—probably a hybrid)
23 03 331	**Acestrura bombus**	
	Little Woodstar	Tropical, subtropical Ecuador to Peru
23 03 332	**Acestrura heliodor**	
	Gorgeted Woodstar	Subtropical eastern Panama, Venezuela, Colombia, Ecuador
23 03 333	**Acestrura berlepschi**	
	Esmeraldas Woodstar	Tropical zone of western Ecuador
23 03 334	**Acestrura harterti**	
	Hartert's Woodstar	Colombia (Ibagué—unique; probably a hybrid)
23 03 335	**Chaetocercus jourdanii**	
	Rufous-shafted Woodstar	Tropical, subtropical Venezuela, Colombia; Trinidad
23 03 336	**Selasphorus platycercus**	
	Broad-tailed Hummingbird	Mountains of southwest United States to Guatemala
23 03 337	**Selasphorus rufus**	
	Rufous Hummingbird	Alaska to southern Mexico
23 03 338	**Selasphorus sasin**	
	Allen's Hummingbird	Oregon to northwest Mexico

		Date	Location

23 03 339	**Selasphorus flammula**	
	Volcano Hummingbird	High mountains of Costa Rica; adjacent Panama
23 03 340	**Selasphorus torridus**	
	Heliotrope-throated Hummingbird	High mountains of Costa Rica, western Panama
23 03 341	**Selasphorus simoni**	
	Cerise-throated Hummingbird	Highlands of Costa Rica
23 03 342	**Selasphorus ardens**	
	Glow-throated Hummingbird	Panama (highlands of eastern Chiriqui)
23 03 343	**Selasphorus scintilla**	
	Scintillant Hummingbird	Highlands of Costa Rica, western Panama

ORDER: COLIIFORMES
FAMILY: COLIIDAE (Colies)

24 01 001	**Colius striatus**	
	Speckled Mousebird	Africa south of the Sahara
24 01 002	**Colius castanotus**	
	Red-backed Mousebird	Congo River mouth and Angola
24 01 003	**Colius colius**	
	White-backed Mousebird	Thick scrub and forest borders of South Africa
24 01 004	**Colius leucocephalus**	
	White-headed Mousebird	Somalia, Kenya, Tanzania, Ethiopia
24 01 005	**Colius indicus**	
	Red-faced Mousebird	Tanzania to Rhodesia
24 01 006	**Colius macrourus**	
	Blue-naped Mousebird	Senegal to the Sudan, Ethiopia, East Africa

ORDER: TROGONIFORMES
FAMILY: TROGONIDAE (Trogons)

25 01 001	**Pharomachrus mocinno**	
	Resplendent Quetzal	Cloud forests of Mexico to western Panama (endangered)
25 01 002	**Pharomachrus antisianus**	
	Crested Quetzal	Subtropical Andes of Venezuela, Colombia to Bolivia
25 01 003	**Pharomachrus fulgidus**	
	White-tipped Quetzal	Subtropical Venezuela; Santa Marta Mountains of Colombia
25 01 004	**Pharomachrus auriceps**	
	Golden-headed Quetzal	Mountains of eastern Panama to Bolivia

Date   Location

25 01 005 Pharomachrus pavoninus
Pavonine Quetzal — Tropical South America to Bolivia, western Brazil

25 01 006 Euptilotis neoxenus
Eared Trogon — Mountain forests of western Mexico (rare)

25 01 007 Priotelus temnurus
Cuban Trogon — Forests of Cuba, Isle of Pines

25 01 008 Temnotrogon roseigaster
Hispaniolian Trogon — Mountain forests of Hispaniola

25 01 009 Trogon massena
Slaty-tailed Trogon — Humid lowland forests of southern Mexico to Ecuador

25 01 010 Trogon clathratus
Lattice-tailed Trogon — Carribean coast of Costa Rica to western Panama

25 01 011 Trogon melanurus
Black-tailed Trogon — Central Panama to Bolivia and Amazonian Brazil

25 01 012 Trogon comptus
Blue-tailed Trogon — Colombia (lower Cauca, upper Altrato Valleys)

25 01 013 Trogon viridis (chionurus) (bairdii)
White-tailed Trogon — Southwest Costa Rica to Brazil, Bolivia

25 01 014 Trogon citreolus
Citreoline Trogon — Coastal lowlands and foothills of Mexico to Costa Rica

25 01 015 Trogon mexicanus
Mexican Trogon — Highlands of Mexico to Honduras

25 01 016 Trogon elegans
Elegant Trogon — Southern Arizona to Costa Rica

25 01 017 Trogon collaris
Collared Trogon — Eastern Mexico to Ecuador, Amazonian Brazil

25 01 018 Trogon aurantiiventris
Orange-bellied Trogon — Highlands of Costa Rica, western Panama

25 01 019 Trogon personatus
Masked Trogon — Highlands of Guyana, Venezuela, Colombia to Bolivia

25 01 020 Trogon rufus
† *Black-throated Trogon* — Tropical Honduras to eastern Brazil, northeast Argentina

25 01 021 Trogon surrucura
† *Surucua Trogon* — Forests of eastern Brazil (Bahia) to northeast Argentina

25 01 022 Trogon curucui
Blue-crowned Trogon — Tropical Colombia to western Brazil, northern Argentina

25 01 023 Trogon violaceus
Violaceous Trogon — Tropical southern Mexico to Brazil, Peru, Bolivia

		Date	Location

25 01 024 Apaloderma narina
Narina Trogon — Ethiopia, east and central Africa

25 01 025 Apaloderma aequatoriale
Bare-cheeked Trogon — Cameroon to Zaire

25 01 026 Heterotrogon vittatus
Bar-tailed Trogon — East Africa to Rhodesia, Malawi

25 01 027 Harpactes reinwardtii
Blue-billed Trogon — Confined to Islands of Sumatra and Java

25 01 028 Harpactes fasciatus
Indian Trogon — Forests of Sri Lanka, peninsular India

25 01 029 Harpactes kasumba
Red-naped Trogon — Malaya, Sumatra, Borneo

25 01 030 Harpactes diardii
Diard's Trogon — Malaya, Sumatra, Borneo

25 01 031 Harpactes ardens
Philippine Trogon — Widespread throughout the Philippine Islands

25 01 032 Harpactes whiteheadi
Whitehead's Trogon — Confined to mountains of Borneo

25 01 033 Harpactes orrhophaeus
Cinnamon-rumped Trogon — Malaya (rare), Sumatra, Borneo

25 01 034 Harpactes duvaucelii
Scarlet-rumped Trogon — Malaya, Sumatra, Borneo

25 01 035 Harpactes oreskios
Orange-breasted Trogon — Widespread Southeast Asia

25 01 036 Harpactes erythrocephalus
Red-headed Trogon — Nepal to Sikiang, Thailand; Hainan; Sumatra

25 01 037 Harpactes wardi
Ward's Trogon — Bhutan, Assam to Burma, Tonkin

ORDER: CORACIIFORMES
FAMILY: ALCEDINIDAE (Kingfishers)

26 01 001 Ceryle lugubris
Crested Kingfisher — Kashmir to Burma, China; Japan; Hainan

26 01 002 Ceryle maxima
+ Giant Kingfisher — Widespread Africa south of the Sahara

26 01 003 Ceryle torquata
+ Ringed Kingfisher — Mexico to Tierra del Fuego; Lesser Antilles; Trinidad

26 01 004 Ceryle alcyon
Belted Kingfisher — Alaska to Panama; West Indies

		Date	Location

26 01 005 Ceryle rudis
Pied Kingfisher
Widespread Africa to southeast Asia

26 01 006 Chloroceryle amazona
+ *Amazon Kingfisher*
Southern Mexico to Argentina (east of Andes)

26 01 007 Chloroceryle americana
+ *Green Kingfisher*
Southern Texas to northern Argentina, Chile

26 01 008 Chloroceryle inda
Green-and-rufous Kingfisher
Nicaragua to Peru, Brazil, Bolivia

26 01 009 Chloroceryle aenea
+ *American Pygmy Kingfisher*
Southern Mexico to Peru, Brazil, Bolivia

26 01 010 Alcedo hercules
Blyth's Kingfisher
Himalayas of Sikkim to Burma, Indochina

26 01 011 Alcedo atthis
Common (River) Kingfisher
Palearctic, Oriental regions to New Guinea, Solomons

26 01 012 Alcedo semitorquata
Half-collared Kingfisher
Ethiopia to South Africa (uncommon and local)

26 01 013 Alcedo meninting
Blue-eared Kingfisher
Widespread Oriental mainland and islands

26 01 014 Alcedo quadribrachys
Shining Blue Kingfisher
Forests of West Africa to Kenya, Tanzania, Zambia

26 01 015 Alcedo euryzona
Blue-banded Kingfisher
Malay Peninsula, Java, Sumatra, Borneo

26 01 016 Alcedo coerulescens
Small Blue Kingfisher
Java, Bali, Lombok, Sumbawa Islands

26 01 017 Alcedo cristata
Malachite Kingfisher
Widespread and common East and central Africa

26 01 018 Alcedo leucogaster
White-bellied Kingfisher
West and central Africa

26 01 019 Myioceyx lecontei
African Dwarf Kingfisher
Sierra Leone to western Uganda

26 01 020 Ispidina picta
+ *African Pygmy Kingfisher*
Africa south of the Sahara

26 01 021 Ispidina madagascariensis
Madagascar Pygmy Kingfisher
Forests of eastern Madagascar

26 01 022 Ceyx cyanopectus
Dwarf River Kingfisher
Widespread throughout the Philippine Islands

26 01 023 Ceyx argentatus
Silvery Kingfisher
Widespread throughout the Philippine Islands

	Date	Location
26 01 024 **Ceyx lepidus** *Dwarf Forest Kingfisher*		New Guinea, Philippines, Solomons, Moluccas
26 01 025 **Ceyx goodfellowi** *Philippine Dwarf Kingfisher*		Philippine Islands (possible race of *C. lepidus*)
26 01 026 **Ceyx azureus** *Azure Kingfisher*		Moluccas to New Guinea and Australia
26 01 027 **Ceyx websteri** *Bismarck Kingfisher*		New Britain, New Hanover, New Ireland, Rook Islands
26 01 028 **Ceyx pusillus** *Little Kingfisher*		Australia, New Guinea, Solomons, Moluccas
26 01 029 **Ceyx erithacus** *Black-backed Kingfisher*		India to southeast Asia, the Philippines
26 01 030 **Ceyx rufidorsum** *Rufous-backed Kingfisher*		Forests of Malay peninsula, Sundas, Philippines
26 01 031 **Ceyx melanurus** *Philippine Forest Kingfisher*		Widespread throughout the Philippine Islands
26 01 032 **Ceyx fallax** *Celebes Forest Kingfisher*		Celebes, Sangir Islands
26 01 033 **Pelargopsis amauroptera** *Brown-winged Kingfisher*		Bangladesh, Assam to Malaya
26 01 034 **Pelargopsis capensis** *Stork-billed Kingfisher*		Widespread Oriental mainland and islands
26 01 035 **Pelargopsis melanorhyncha** *Black-billed Kingfisher*		Celebes and Sula Islands
26 01 036 **Lacedo pulchella** *Banded Kingfisher*		Widespread forests of southeast Asia
26 01 037 **Dacelo novaeguineae (gigas)** *Kookaburra*		Australia, Tasmania, Kangaroo Islands
26 01 038 **Dacelo leachii** *Blue-winged Kookaburra*		Australia; southeast New Guinea
26 01 039 **Dacelo tyro** *Aru Giant Kingfisher*		New Guinea, Aru Islands
26 01 040 **Dacelo gaudichaud** *Rufous-bellied Giant Kingfisher*		New Guinea and adjacent islands
26 01 041 **Clytoceyx rex** *Shovel-billed Kingfisher*		New Guinea (Arfak Mountains to southeast lowlands)
26 01 042 **Melidora macrorrhina** *Hook-billed Kingfisher*		New Guinea and adjacent islands

		Date	Location
26 01 043	**Cittura cyanotis** *Blue-eared Kingfisher*		Celebes and Sangir Islands
26 01 044	**Halcyon coromanda** *Ruddy Kingfisher*		Widespread Oriental mainland and islands
26 01 045	**Halcyon badia** *Chocolate-backed Kingfisher*		West Africa to western Uganda
26 01 046	**Halcyon smyrnensis** *White-breasted Kingfisher*		Asia Minor to southeast Asia; Philippines; Andamans
26 01 047	**Halcyon pileata** *Black-capped Kingfisher*		Widespread Oriental mainland and islands; China
26 01 048	**Halcyon cyanoventris** *Java Kingfisher*		Java and Bali
26 01 049	**Halcyon leucocephala** *Gray-headed Kingfisher*		Ethiopia to east and central Africa
26 01 050	**Halcyon senegalensis** *Woodland Kingfisher*		Senegal to Ethiopia and South Africa
26 01 051	**Halcyon senegaloides** *Mangrove Kingfisher*		Coast of Kenya to South Africa
26 01 052	**Halcyon malimbica** *Blue-breasted Kingfisher*		Senegal to Uganda, Tanzania
26 01 053 +	**Halcyon albiventris** *Brown-hooded Kingfisher*		East and central Africa
26 01 054 +	**Halcyon chelicuti** *Striped Kingfisher*		Africa south of the Sahara
26 01 055	**Halcyon nigrocyanea** *Blue-black Kingfisher*		New Guinea and western Papuan Islands
26 01 056	**Halcyon winchelli** *Winchell's Kingfisher*		Widespread throughout the Philippine Islands
26 01 057	**Halcyon diops** *Moluccan Kingfisher*		Restricted to the northern Moluccas Islands
26 01 058	**Halcyon lazuli** *Lazuli Kingfisher*		Restricted to the southern Moluccas Islands
26 01 059	**Halcyon macleayii** *Australian Forest Kingfisher*		Northern Australia; eastern New Guinea
26 01 060	**Halcyon albonotata** *New Britain Kingfisher*		Restricted to New Britain Island
26 01 061	**Halcyon leucopygia** *Ultramarine Kingfisher*		Restricted to the Solomon Islands
26 01 062	**Halcyon farquhari** *Chestnut-bellied Kingfisher*		Restricted to the New Hebrides Islands
26 01 063	**Halcyon pyrrhopygia** *Red-backed Kingfisher*		Savannas of interior of Australia

		Date	Location

26 01 064	**Halcyon torotoro** *Yellow-billed Kingfisher*		Northeast Queensland, New Guinea, Arus
26 01 065	**Halcyon megarhyncha** *Mountain Yellow-billed Kingfisher*		Mountains of New Guinea
26 01 066	**Halcyon australasia** *Lesser Sundas Kingfisher*		Restricted to the Lesser Sunda Islands
26 01 067	**Halcyon sancta** *Sacred Kingfisher*		Sumatra to New Guinea; Australia; New Zealand
26 01 068	**Halcyon cinnamomina** *Micronesian Kingfisher*		Restricted to the islands of Micronesia
26 01 069	**Halcyon funebris** *Halmahera Kingfisher*		Restricted to Halmahera Island (Moluccas)
26 01 070	**Halcyon chloris** *White-collared Kingfisher*		Ethiopia to Australasia, islands of southwest Pacific
26 01 071	**Halcyon saurophaga** *White-headed Kingfisher*		New Guinea and Bismarck Archipelago
26 01 072	**Halcyon recurvirostris** *Flat-billed Kingfisher*		Upolu and Savaii Islands (Samoa—endangered)
26 01 073	**Halcyon venerata** *Venerated Kingfisher*		Confined to Tahiti, Moorea (Society Islands)
26 01 074	**Halcyon tuta** *Borabora Kingfisher*		Restricted to Borabora (Society Islands)
26 01 075	**Halcyon ruficollaris** *Cook Island Kingfisher*		Cook Island (wooded mangroves of north end of Mangia Island)
26 01 076	**Halcyon gambieri** *Mangareva Kingfisher*		Extinct since 1841. Inhabited Tuamotu Archipelago
26 01 077	**Halcyon godeffroyi** *Marquesas Kingfisher*		Restricted to the Marquesas Islands (endangered)
26 01 078	**Halcyon miyakoensis** *Miyako Kingfisher*		Extinct. Known from one specimen from Ryukyu Islands collected 1887
26 01 079	**Halcyon bougainvillei** *Moustached Kingfisher*		Restricted to the Solomon Islands
26 01 080	**Halcyon concreta** *Rufous-collared Kingfisher*		Malaya, Sumatra, Borneo, Banka, Billiton Islands
26 01 081	**Halcyon lindsayi** *Spotted Wood Kingfisher*		Restricted to Luzon and Negros Islands (Philippines)
26 01 082	**Halcyon hombroni** *Hombron's Kingfisher*		Philippines (Mindanao—probable race *H. lindsayi*)

		Date	Location
26 01 083	**Halcyon fulgida** *Blue-and-white Kingfisher*		Lombok, Sumbawa and Flores Islands (Lesser Sundas)
26 01 084	**Halcyon monacha** *Celebes Lowland Kingfisher*		Lowlands of Celebes Islands
26 01 085	**Halcyon princeps** *Celebes Mountain Kingfisher*		Mountains of Celebes Islands
26 01 086	**Tanysiptera hydrocharis** *Aru Paradise Kingfisher*		New Guinea and Aru Islands
26 01 087	**Tanysiptera galatea** *Common Paradise Kingfisher*		Moluccas Islands to New Guinea
26 01 088	**Tanysiptera riedelii** *Biak Paradise Kingfisher*		Confined to Biak Island (off New Guinea)
26 01 089	**Tanysiptera carolinae** *Numfor Paradise Kingfisher*		Confined to Numfor Island (off New Guinea)
26 01 090	**Tanysiptera ellioti** *Kofiau Paradise Kingfisher*		Confined to Kofiau Island (off New Guinea)
26 01 091	**Taysiptera nympha** *Pink-breasted Paradise Kingfisher*		New Guinea (spottily distributed—rare)
26 01 092	**Tanysiptera danae** *Brown-backed Paradise Kingfisher*		Lowlands of southeast New Guinea
26 01 093	**Tanysiptera sylvia** *White-tailed Kingfisher*		Austalia, New Guinea, Bismarck Archipelago

ORDER: CORACIIFORMES
FAMILY: TODIDAE (Todies)

26 02 001	**Todus multicolor** *Cuban Tody*		Forests and woodlands of Cuba and Isle of Pines
26 02 002	**Todus angustirostris** *Narrow-billed Tody*		Dense mountain jungles of Hispaniola
26 02 003	**Todus todus** *Jamaican Tody*		Wooded hills and mountains of Jamaica
26 02 004	**Todus mexicanus** *Puerto Rican Tody*		Semiarid coasts to humid mountains of Puerto Rico

Date   Location

26 02 005   **Todus subulatus**
            Broad-billed Tody   Semiarid regions of Hispaniola and Gonâve Island

ORDER: CORACIIFORMES
FAMILY: MOMOTIDAE (Motmots)

26 03 001   **Hylomanes momotula**
+   *Tody Motmot*   Tropical southern Mexico to Colombia

26 03 002   **Aspatha gularis**
            Blue-throated Motmot   Highlands of southern Mexico (Chiapas) to
                                         Honduras

26 03 003   **Electron platyrhynchum**
+   *Broad-billed Motmot*   Tropical Honduras to Brazil, Peru, Bolivia

26 03 004   **Electron carinatum**
            Keel-billed Motmot   Caribbean slope of southern Mexico to Costa Rica

26 03 005   **Eumomota superciliosa**
            Turquoise-browed Motmot   Semiarid southern Mexico to Costa Rica

26 03 006   **Baryphthengus
            ruficapillus**
            Rufous-capped Motmot   Eastern Brazil (Bahia) to Paraguay, northeast
                                         Argentina

26 03 007   **Baryphthengus martii**
+   *Rufous Motmot*   Tropical Nicaragua to western and Amazonian South
                                         America

26 03 008   **Momotus mexicanus**
            Russet-crowned Motmot   Arid northern Mexico (Sonora) to Guatemala

26 03 009   **Momotus momota**
            Blue-crowned Motmot   Tropical Mexico to Argentina

ORDER: CORACIIFORMES
FAMILY: MEROPIDAE (Bee-eaters)

26 04 001   **Nyctyornis amictus**
            Red-bearded Bee-eater   Malaya, Sumatra, Borneo, Banka Islands

26 04 002   **Nyctyornis athertoni**
            Blue-bearded Bee-eater   India to southern China, Indochina; Hainan

26 04 003   **Meropogon forsteni**
            Celebes Bee-eater   Celebes Islands

26 04 004   **Merops gularis**
            Black Bee-eater   Sierra Leone to Ghana, Angola, Uganda

26 04 005   **Merops muelleri**
            Blue-headed Bee-eater   Cameroon to Uganda, Kenya, Zaire

	Date	Location

26 04 006 +	**Merops bulocki** *Red-throated Bee-eater*	Open country of Senegal to Ethiopia, the Sudan
26 04 007 +	**Merops bullockoides** *White-fronted Bee-eater*	Semiarid river beds of southern Africa
26 04 008	**Merops pusillus** *Little Bee-eater*	Senegal to Ethiopia, South Africa
25 04 009	**Merops variegatus** *Blue-breasted Bee-eater*	Cameroon to Angola, Uganda, Tanzania
26 04 010 +	**Merops oreobates** *Cinnamon-chested Bee-eater*	Forests of east and central Africa
26 04 011	**Merops hirundineus** *Swallow-tailed Bee-eater*	Africa south of the Sahara
26 04 012	**Merops breweri** *Black-headed Bee-eater*	Moist forests of Nigeria to Zaire
26 04 013 +	**Merops revoilii** *Somali Bee-eater*	Arid Ethiopia, Somalia, Kenya
26 04 014	**Merops albicollis** *White-throated Bee-eater*	Dry belt of Africa south of the Sahara
26 04 015	**Merops orientalis** *Green Bee-eater*	North Africa to India, Indochina; Sri Lanka
26 04 016	**Merops boehmi** *Boehm's Bee-eater*	Zaire, Tanzania to Rhodesia, Malawi
26 04 017	**Merops viridis** *Blue-throated Bee-eater*	Widespread southeast Asia
26 04 018	**Merops superciliosus** **(persicus)** *Blue-cheeked Bee-eater*	Ethiopia to South Africa, northwest India; Madagascar
26 04 019	**Merops philippinus** *Blue-tailed Bee-eater*	Widespread Oriental mainland and islands to New Guinea
26 04 020	**Merops ornatus** *Rainbow Bee-eater*	Australia to New Guinea; Sundas; Solomons
26 04 021	**Merops apiaster** *European Bee-eater*	Southern Europe to South Africa, Afghanistan, India
26 04 022	**Merops leschenaulti** *Chestnut-headed Bee-eater*	India to Indochina; Andamans; Java; Sumatra
26 04 023	**Merops malimbicus** *Rosy Bee-eater*	Open country of Ghana to Nigeria, Gabon, Zaire
26 04 024 +	**Merops nubicus** **(nubicoides)** *Carmine Bee-eater*	Widespread Africa south of the Sahara

	Date	Location

ORDER: CORACIIFORMES
FAMILY: CORACIIDAE (Rollers)

26 05 001	**Coracias garrulus**	
	Eurasian Roller	Widespread Palearctic and Ethiopian regions
26 05 002	**Coracias abyssinica**	
	Abyssinian Roller	East and central Africa to Arabia
26 05 003	**Coracias caudata**	
	Lilac-breasted Roller	Thornveld savannas of Ethiopia to South Africa
26 05 004	**Coracias spatulata**	
	Racket-tailed Roller	Savannas of Angola, Zaire to Rhodesia, Tanzania
26 05 005	**Coracias naevia**	
	Rufous-crowned Roller	Savanna thornveld of Africa south of the Sahara
26 05 006	**Coracias benghalensis**	
	Indian (Burmese) Roller	Persian Gulf to Indochina
26 05 007	**Coracias temminckii**	
	Celebes Roller	Celebes Islands
26 05 008	**Coracias cyanogaster**	
	Blue-bellied Roller	Senegal and Gambia to the Sudan
26 05 009	**Eurystomus glaucurus**	
	Broad-billed Roller	Senegal to Ethiopia; Madagascar; winters to South Africa
26 05 010	**Eurystomus gularis**	
	Blue-throated Roller	West Africa to western Uganda
26 05 011	**Eurystomus orientalis (pacificus)**	
	Dollar Bird	Widespread Oriental and Australasian regions

ORDER: CORACIIFORMES
FAMILY: BRACHYPTERACIIDAE (Ground Rollers)

26 06 001	**Brachypteracias leptosomus**	
	Short-legged Ground Roller	Humid forests of Madagascar—rare
26 06 002	**Brachypteracias squamigera**	
	Scaled Ground Roller	Humid forests of Madagascar—rare and local
26 06 003	**Atelornis pittoides**	
	Pitta-like Ground Roller	Forests of eastern and northern Madagascar
26 06 004	**Atelornis crossleyi**	
	Crossley's Ground Roller	Forests of central, northern and eastern Madagascar
26 06 005	**Uratelornis chimaera**	
	Long-tailed Ground Roller	Lowlands of southwest Madagascar—endangered

Date   Location

ORDER: CORACIIFORMES
FAMILY: LEPTOSOMATIDAE (Cuckoo Roller)

26 07 001   **Leptosomus discolor**
            Cuckoo Roller   Widespread wooded regions of Madagascar

ORDER: CORACIIFORMES
FAMILY: UPUPIDAE (Hoopoes)

26 08 001   **Upupa epops (africana)**
+   _Common Hoopoe_   Southern Europe to South Africa and southern Asia

ORDER: CORACIIFORMES
FAMILY: PHOENICULIDAE (Woodhoopoes)

26 09 001   **Phoeniculus purpureus**
            Green Woodhoopoe   Forested rivers of Africa south of the Sahara

26 09 002   **Phoeniculus damarensis**
            Violet Woodhoopoe   Arid thornbush of Ethiopia to Southwest Africa

26 09 003   **Phoeniculus granti**
            Grant's Woodhoopoe   Southwest Kenya (possible race _P. damarensis_)

26 09 004   **Phoeniculus bollei**
            White-headed   Montane forests of Ghana to Kenya, Uganda
            Woodhoopoe

26 09 005   **Phoeniculus**
            castaneiceps
            Forest Woodhoopoe   Forests of Ghana to northern Zaire, Uganda

26 09 006   **Phoeniculus aterrimus**
            Black Woodhoopoe   Senegal to Uganda, southwest Ethiopia

26 09 007   **Rhinopomastus minor**
            Abyssinian Scimitar-bill Ethiopia to East Africa

26 09 008   **Rhinopomastus**
            cyanomelas
            Common Scimitar-bill   Angola, Uganda, Kenya to South Africa

ORDER: CORACIIFORMES
FAMILY: BUCEROTIDAE (Hornbills)

26 10 001   **Tockus birostris**
            Indian Gray Hornbill   Drier parts of Indian Subcontinent

26 10 002   **Tockus fasciatus**
            African Pied Hornbill   Cameroon to Angola, Uganda, Zaire, southwest
                                      Sudan

		Date	Location
26 10 003	**Tockus semifasciatus** *Allied Hornbill*		Senegal and Gambia to Ghana
26 10 004	**Tockus alboterminatus** *Crowned Hornbill*		Light forests of Ethiopia to South Africa
26 10 005	**Tockus bradfieldi** *Bradfield's Hornbill*		*Baikiaea* woodlands of Kalahari Desert of South Africa
26 10 006	**Tockus pallidirostris** *Pale-billed Hornbill*		Dry bush of Angola to Zaire, Zambia and Tanzania
26 10 007	**Tockus nasutus** *African Gray Hornbill*		Dry acacia, savanna of Africa south of the Sahara
26 10 008	**Tockus hemprichii** *Hemprich's Hornbill*		Eritrea, Ethiopia and Somalia
26 10 009	**Tockus monteiri** *Monteiro's Hornbill*		Angola to Southwest Africa
26 10 010	**Tockus griseus (gingalensis)** *Malabar Gray Hornbill*		Moist diciduous forests of southern India; Sri Lanka
26 10 011	**Tockus hartlaubi** *Dwarf Black Hornbill*		Guinea, Liberia to Zaire, Uganda
26 10 012	**Tockus camurus** *Red-billed Dwarf Hornbill*		Swampy forests of Liberia to Uganda
26 10 013 +	**Tockus erythrohynchus** *Red-billed Hornbill*		Savannas of Africa south of the Sahara
26 10 014	**Tockus flavirostris** *Yellow-billed Hornbill*		Savanna and thornveld of Ethiopia to South Africa
26 10 015	**Tockus deckeni (jacksoni)** *Von der Decken's Hornbill*		Ethiopia to Kenya, Tanzania, Uganda
26 10 016	**Berenicornis comatus** *White-crowned Hornbill*		Malaya, Sumatra, Borneo, Indochina
26 10 017	**Berenicornis albocristatus** *White-crested Hornbill*		Forests of Sierra Leone to Zaire, Uganda
26 10 018	**Ptilolaemus tickelli** *Brown Hornbill*		Evergreen forests of Assam, southwest China to Indochina
26 10 019	**Anorrhinus galeritus** *Bushy-crested Hornbill*		Malay Peninsula, Sumatra, Borneo
26 10 020	**Penelopides panini** *Tarictic Hornbill*		Widespread throughout Philippine Islands
26 10 021	**Penelopides exarhatus** *Celebes Hornbill*		Restricted to the Celebes Islands

	Date	Location

26 10 022 Aceros nipalensis
Rufous-cheeked Hornbill   Nepal to southwest China, Thailand, Indochina

26 10 023 Aceros corrugatus
Wrinkled Hornbill   Oriental mainland and islands

26 10 024 Aceros leucocephalus
Writhe-billed Hornbill   Widespread Southeast Asia

26 10 025 Aceros cassidix
Buton Hornbill   Restricted to the Celebes Islands

26 10 026 Aceros undulatus
Wreathed Hornbill   East India to Indochina; Andamans; Greater Sundas

26 10 027 Aceros plicatus
Papuan Hornbill   Burma, Malaya to New Guinea, Bismarck Archipelago

26 10 028 Aceros everetti
Sumba Hornbill   Restricted to Sumba Island (Lesser Sundas)

26 10 029 Aceros narcondami
Narcondam Hornbill   Confined to Narcondam Island (Andamans—endangered)

26 10 030 Anthracoceros malayanus
Malaysian Black Hornbill   Oriental mainland and islands

26 10 031 Anthracoceros malabaricus
Pied Hornbill   India to southern China, Indochina; Greater Sundas

26 10 032 Anthracoceros coronatus
Malabar Pied Hornbill   Open mixed forests of western Indian Subcontinent; Sri Lanka

26 10 033 Anthracoceros montani
Sulu Hornbill   Jolu, Sulu and Tawi Tawi Islands (Philippines)

26 10 034 Anthracoceros marchei
Palawan Hornbill   Balabac, Basuanga, Calamianes, Palawan Islands

26 10 035 Bycanistes bucinator
Trumpeter Hornbill   Forests of Angola to Kenya

26 10 036 Bycanistes cylindricus
Brown-cheeked Hornbill   High forests of western Africa

26 10 037 Bycanistes subcylindricus
Black-and-white Casqued Hornbill   Wet lowlands of Ghana to Angola, Kenya, Tanzania

26 10 038 Bycanistes brevis
Silvery-cheeked Hornbill   Coastal montane forests of Ethiopia to Rhodesia

26 10 039 Ceratogymna atrata
Black-casqued Hornbill   Liberia to Angola, Uganda; Fernando Po

		Date	Location
26 10 040	**Ceratogymna elata** *Yellow-casqued Hornbill*		Senegal to western Cameroon
26 10 041	**Buceros rhinoceros** *Rhinoceros Hornbill*		Malaya, Sumatra, Borneo, Java
26 10 042	**Buceros bicornis** *Great Indian Hornbill*		India to Sikiang, Malaya, Sumatra (endangered)
26 10 043	**Buceros hydrocorax** *Rufous Hornbill*		Widespread throughout the Philippine Islands
26 10 044	**Rhinoplax vigil** *Helmeted Hornbill*		Malaya, Sumatra, Borneo
26 10 045 †	**Bucorvus abyssinicus** *Abyssinian Ground Hornbill*		Gambia to Somalia, Ethiopia (terrestial)
26 10 046 †	**Bucorvus leadbeateri** *African Ground Hornbill*		Southern half of Africa (terrestial)

ORDER: PICIFORMES
FAMILY: GALBULIDAE (Jacamars)

27 01 001	**Galbalcyrhynchus leucotis (purusianus)** *Chestnut Jacamar*		Widespread tropical Amazon basin
27 01 002	**Brachygalba albogularis** *White-throated Jacamar*		Borders of Peru and Brazil (Rios Purús and Javari)
27 01 003	**Brachygalba lugubris** *Brown Jacamar*		Tropical Guianas, Venezuela, Amazon basin
27 01 004	**Brachygalba goeringi** *Pale-headed Jacamar*		Tropical northwest Venezuela, northeast Colombia
27 01 005 +	**Brachygalba salmoni** *Dusky-backed Jacamar*		Tropical eastern Panama (Darien), northwest Colombia
27 01 006	**Jacamaralcyon tridactyla** *Three-toed Jacamar*		Southeast Brazil (Minas Gerais to Paraná)
27 01 007	**Galbula albirostris** *Yellow-billed Jacamar*		Northern South America to Peru, Amazonian Brazil
27 01 008	**Galbula cyanicollis** *Purple-necked Jacamar*		Brazil south of Amazon (probable race of *G. albirostris*)
27 01 009	**Galbula galbula** *Green-tailed Jacamar*		Guianas, Venezuela, Colombia, northern Brazil
27 01 010	**Galbula ruficauda** *Rufous-tailed Jacamar*		Lowlands of southern Mexico to northeast Argentina

		Date	Location
27 01 011	**Galbula tombacea** *White-chinned Jacamar*		Colombia to Peru, western Amazonian Brazil
27 01 012	**Galbula cyanescens** *Blue-fronted Jacamar*		Eastern Peru, western Brazil (east to Rio Purús)
27 01 013	**Galbula pastazae** *Coppery-chested Jacamar*		Upper tropical, subtropical eastern Ecuador, adjacent Brazil
27 01 014	**Galbula leucogastra** *Bronzy Jacamar*		Northern South America through the Amazon basin
27 01 015	**Galbula dea** *Paradise Jacamar*		Northern South America through Amazonian Brazil, Bolivia
27 01 016	**Jacamerops aurea** *Great Jacamar*		Tropical Costa Rica to Bolivia, Amazonian Brazil

ORDER: PICIFORMES
FAMILY: BUCCONIDAE (Puffbirds)

27 02 001	**Notharchus macrorhynchos** *White-necked Puffbird*		Southern Mexico to northeast Argentina
27 02 002	**Notharchus pectoralis** *Black-breasted Puffbird*		Central Panama, Colombia to northwest Ecuador
27 02 003	**Notharchus ordii** *Brown-banded Puffbird*		Venezuela (Amazonas), adjacent northern Brazil
27 02 004	**Notharchus tectus** *Pied Puffbird*		Costa Rica to Peru, northeast Brazil
27 02 005	**Bucco macrodactylus** *Chestnut-capped Puffbird*		Venezuela to Bolivia, west Amazonian Brazil
27 02 006	**Bucco tamatia** *Spotted Puffbird*		Guianas, Venezuela to Peru, Amazonian Brazil
27 02 007	**Bucco noanamae** *Sooty-capped Puffbird*		Colombia (Gulf of Urabá to Rio San Juan)
27 02 008	**Bucco capensis** *Collared Puffbird*		Guianas to Peru, Amazonian Brazil
27 02 009	**Nystalus radiatus** *Barred Puffbird*		Central Panama to Pacific Colombia, Ecuador
27 02 010	**Nystalus chacuru** *White-eared Puffbird*		Campos of Brazil to eastern Peru, Argentina (Misiones)
27 02 011	**Nystalus striolatus** *Striolated Puffbird*		Eastern Ecuador to northern Bolivia, Brazil

		Date	Location
27 02 012 +	**Nystalus maculatus** *Spot-backed Puffbird*		Southeast Brazil to northern Argentina
27 02 013	**Hypnelus ruficollis** *Russet-throated Puffbird*		Woodlands and arid coasts of Venezuela, Colombia
27 02 014	**Hypnelus bicinctus** *Two-banded Puffbird*		Colombia (Catatumbo region—probable race of *H. ruficollis*)
27 02 015	**Malacoptila striata** *Crescent-chested Puffbird*		Eastern Brazil (Maranhão, Bahia to Santa Catarina)
27 02 016 +	**Malacoptila fusca** *White-chested Puffbird*		Northern South America to Peru, Amazonian Brazil
27 02 017 +	**Malacoptila semicincta** *Semicollared Puffbird*		Southeast Peru, southwest Brazil, northern Bolivia
27 02 018	**Malacoptila fulvogularis** *Black-streaked Puffbird*		Savanna of eastern Colombia to northern Bolivia
27 02 019	**Malacoptila rufa** *Rufous-necked Puffbird*		Northeast Peru, adjacent Amazonian Brazil
27 02 020 +	**Malacoptila panamensis** *White-whiskered Puffbird*		Southern Mexico to Colombia, western Ecuador
27 02 021	**Malacoptila mystacalis** *Moustached Puffbird*		Upper tropical, subtropical Venezuela, Colombia
27 02 022	**Micromonacha lanceolata** *Lanceolated Monklet*		Costa Rica to eastern Peru, west Amazonian Brazil
27 02 023	**Nonnula rubecula** *Rusty-breasted Nunlet*		Surinam, Venezuela to Brazil, northeast Argentina
27 02 024	**Nonnula sclateri** *Fulvous-chinned Nunlet*		Southeast Peru (Loreto), adjacent southwest Brazil
27 02 025	**Nonnula brunnea** *Brown Nunlet*		Eastern Andes of Colombia, Ecuador, Peru
27 02 026 +	**Nonnula frontalis** *Gray-cheeked Nunlet*		Central Panama to Colombia (possible race of *N. ruficapilla*)
27 02 027	**Nonnula ruficapilla** *Rufous-capped Nunlet*		Colombia to eastern Peru, west Amazonian Brazil
27 02 028	**Nonnula amaurocephala** *Chestnut-headed Nunlet*		Western Amazonian Brazil (lower Rio Solimões)
27 02 029	**Hapaloptila castanea** *White-faced Nunbird*		Subtropical Pacific Colombia to northeast Peru
27 02 030	**Monasa atra** *Black Nunbird*		Guianas, Venezuela south of Orinoco, northern Brazil
27 02 031 +	**Monasa nigrifrons** *Black-fronted Nunbird*		Eastern Colombia to northern Bolivia, Amazonian Brazil

	Date	Location

27 02 032 **Monasa morphoeus**
White-fronted Nunbird
Nicaragua to northern Bolivia, Brazil (Amazonas)

27 02 033 **Monasa flavirostris**
Yellow-billed Nunbird
Eastern Colombia to Peru, west Amazonian Brazil

27 02 034 **Chelidoptera tenebrosa**
Swallow-wing
South America east of the Andes to Bolivia, Brazil

ORDER: PICIFORMES
FAMILY: CAPITONIDAE (Barbets)

27 03 001 **Capito aurovirens**
Scarlet-crowned Barbet
Colombia to eastern Peru, west Amazonian Brazil

27 03 002 **Capito maculicoronatus**
Spot-crowned Barbet
Central Panama to northern Colombia

27 03 003 **Capito squamatus**
Orange-fronted Barbet
Southwest Colombia (Nariño), western Ecuador

27 03 004 **Capito hypoleucus**
White-mantled Barbet
Central Colombia (Cauca, Magdalena Valleys)

27 03 005 **Capito dayi**
Black-girdled Barbet
Brazil south of Amazon to Matto Grosso, Pará

27 03 006 **Capito quinticolor**
Five-colored Barbet
Pacific Colombia (Rio San Juan to Nariño)

27 03 007 **Capito niger**
Black-spotted Barbet
Northern South America to Bolivia, Amazonian Brazil

27 03 008 **Eubucco richardsoni**
Lemon-throated Barbet
Eastern Colombia to Peru, west Amazonian Brazil

27 03 009 **Eubucco bourcierii**
Red-headed Barbet
Highlands of Costa Rica to Colombia, Ecuador, Peru

27 03 010 **Eubucco tucinkae**
Scarlet-hooded Barbet
Southeast Peru (Puno, southeast Loreto)

27 03 011 **Eubucco versicolor**
Versicolored Barbet
Tropical, subtropical Peru, northern Bolivia

27 03 012 **Semnornis frantzii**
Prong-billed Barbet
Highlands of Costa Rica, western Panama

27 03 013 **Semnornis ramphastinus**
Toucan Barbet
Upper tropical, subtropical western Colombia,
Ecuador

27 03 014 **Psilopogon pyrolophus**
Fire-tufted Barbet
Forests of Malaya, Sumatra

27 03 015 **Megalaima virens**
Great Barbet
Kashmir to Burma, southern China, Indochina

27 03 016 **Megalaima lagrandieri**
Red-vented Barbet
South Vietnam, Laos, Cochinchina

		Date	Location

27 03 017   **Megalaima zeylanica**
                Green Barbet
Sri Lanka; *terai* of Nepal and India

27 03 018   **Megalaima lineata**
                Lineated Barbet
Nepal to Malaya, Indochina, Java, Bali

27 03 019   **Megalaima viridis**
                Small Green Barbet
Evergreen and moist-deciduous biotope of India

27 03 020   **Megalaima faiostricta**
                Green-eared Barbet
Southern China to Indochina

27 03 021   **Megalaima corvina**
                Brown-throated Barbet
Restricted to the Island of Java

27 03 022   **Megalaima chrysopogon**
                Gold-whiskered Barbet
Malaya, peninsular Thailand, Sumatra, Borneo

27 03 023   **Megalaima rafflesii**
                Red-crowned Barbet
Malaya, peninsular Thailand, Sumatra, Borneo

27 03 024   **Megalaima mystacophanos**
                Red-throated (Gaudy) Barbet
Malaya, peninsular Thailand, Sumatra, Borneo

27 03 025   **Megalaima javensis**
                Black-banded Barbet
Restricted to the Island of Java

27 03 026   **Megalaima flavifrons**
                Yellow-fronted Barbet
Lowland forests of Sri Lanka (endemic)

27 03 027   **Megalaima franklinii**
                Golden-throated Barbet
India to Yunnan, Malaya, Indochina

27 03 028   **Megalaima oorti**
                Black-browed Barbet
Southern China to Indochina; Hainan; Taiwan; Sumatra

27 03 029   **Megalaima monticola**
                Mountain Barbet
Mountains of Borneo (possible race *M. oorti*)

27 03 030   **Megalaima asiatica**
                Blue-throated Barbet
India, Nepal to Sikiang, Indochina

27 03 031   **Megalaima incognita**
                Moustached Barbet
Tenasserim, Thailand, Indochina (endemic)

27 03 032   **Megalaima henricii**
                Yellow-crowned Barbet
Malaya, Sumatra, Borneo

27 03 033   **Megalaima armillaris**
                Blue-crowned Barbet
Restricted to the Islands of Java and Bali

27 03 034   **Megalaima pulcherrima**
                Golden-naped Barbet
Restricted to the mountains of Borneo

27 03 035   **Megalaima australis**
                Blue-eared Barbet
East India to Indochina; Greater Sundas

27 03 036   **Megalaima eximia**
                Black-throated Barbet
Restricted to the mountains of Borneo

		Date	Location

27 03 037 **Megalaima rubricapilla**
Crimson-throated Barbet — Evergreen biotope of India; Sri Lanka

27 03 038 **Megalaima haemacephala**
Coppersmith Barbet — India to Indochina; Java, Sumatra, Philippines

27 03 039 **Calorhamphus fuliginosus**
Brown Barbet — Malaya, peninsular Thailand, Sumatra, Borneo

27 03 040 **Gymnobucco calvus**
Naked-faced Barbet — Highlands of Guinea to Zaire, northern Angola

27 03 041 **Gymnobucco peli**
Bristle-nosed Barbet — Ghana to Cameroon and lower Congo River

27 03 042 **Gymnobucco sladeni**
Sladen's Barbet — Known only from western and eastern Zaire

27 03 043 **Gymnobucco bonapartei**
✝ *Gray-throated Barbet* — West Africa to Kenya, Uganda

27 03 044 **Buccanodon leucotis**
White-eared Barbet — Evergreen forests of Kenya, Tanzania to South Africa

27 03 045 **Buccanodon olivaceum**
Green Barbet — Coastal forests of Kenya, Tanzania to Malawi

27 03 046 **Buccanodon anchietae**
Yellow-headed Barbet — Open woodlands of Angola to Zaire, Zambia

27 03 047 **Buccanodon whytii**
Whyte's Barbet — *Brachystegia* woodlands of Tanzania to Rhodesia

27 03 048 **Pogoniulus duchaillui**
Yellow-spotted Barbet — Heavy forests of Liberia to Kenya, Uganda

27 03 049 **Pogoniulus scolopaceus**
Speckled Tinkerbird — Lowland forests of Guinea to Kenya, Uganda, Angola

27 03 050 **Pogoniulus leucomystax**
Moustached Green Tinkerbird — Mountain forests of central Kenya to Malawi

27 03 051 **Pogoniulus simplex**
Green Tinkerbird — Coastal forests of Kenya, Tanzania to Malawi

27 03 052 **Pogoniulus coryphaeus**
Western Green Tinkerbird — Wooded mountains of Cameroon, Nigeria to Uganda

27 03 053 **Pogoniulus pusillus**
Red-fronted Tinkerbird — Acacia belt of Eritrea, Somalia to Uganda, Tanzania

27 03 054 **Pogoniulus chrysoconus**
Yellow-fronted Tinkerbird — Africa south of the Sahara

27 03 055 **Pogoniulus bilineatus**
✝ *Golden-rumped Tinkerbird* — Forests of Uganda, Kenya to South Africa

27 03 056 **Pogoniulus leucolaima**
Lemon-rumped Tinkerbird — Senegal to Angola, Tanzania; Fernando Po

		Date	Location
27 03 057	**Pogoniulus makawai** *White-chested Tinkerbird*		Zambia (known from a single specimen)
27 03 058	**Pogoniulus subsulphureus** *Yellow-throated Tinkerbird*		Heavy forests of Guinea to Uganda; Fernando Po
27 03 059	**Pogoniulus atroflavus** *Red-rumped Tinkerbird*		Forests of Senegal to Cabinda, Zaire
27 03 060	**Tricholaema lacrymosum** *Spot-flanked Barbet*		Savanna of Kenya, Uganda, Tanzania
27 03 061	**Tricholaema leucomelan** *Pied Barbet*		Ethiopia to South Africa
27 03 062	**Tricholaema diadematum** *Red-fronted Barbet*		Acacia woodlands of southern Sudan to Tanzania, Malawi
27 03 063	**Tricholaema melanocephalum** *Brown-throated Barbet*		Semiarid Ethiopia to Kenya, Tanzania
27 03 064	**Tricholaema flavibuccale** *Tanzanian Barbet*		Tanzania (known from a single specimen)
27 03 065	**Tricholaema hirsutum** (flavipunctatum) *Hairy-breasted Barbet*		Forests of west Africa to Uganda
27 03 066	**Lybius undatus** *Banded Barbet*		Confined to Ethiopian plateau (rare)
27 03 067	**Lybius vieilloti** *Vieillot's Barbet*		Dry savanna of Senegal to Ethiopia
27 03 068	**Lybius torquatus** *Black-collared Barbet*		Savanna of Zaire, Kenya to South Africa
27 03 069	**Lybius guifsobalito** *Black-billed Barbet*		Eritrea, Ethiopia, southern Sudan, western Uganda
27 03 070	**Lybius rubrifacies** *Red-faced Barbet*		Savanna of southwest Uganda and northwest Tanzania
27 03 071	**Lybius chaplini** *Chaplin's Barbet*		Known only from Zambia (rare)
27 03 072	**Lybius leucocephalus** (senex) *White-headed Barbet*		Savanna of southern Sudan to Tanzania, Angola, Zambia
27 03 073	**Lybius minor** (macclouni) *Black-backed Barbet*		Southern Zaire to Angola, Zambia, Rhodesia

		Date	Location

27 03 074 **Lybius melanopterus**
Brown-breasted Barbet
Ethiopia to Mozambique; Zanzibar

27 03 075 **Lybius bidentatus**
Double-toothed Barbet
Senegal to Ethiopia, Uganda, Kenya, Tanzania

27 03 076 **Lybius dubius**
Bearded Barbet
Semiarid Senegal to Nigeria, Cameroon

27 03 077 **Lybius rolleti**
Black-breasted Barbet
Wild fig belt of southern Sudan to western Uganda

27 03 078 **Trachyphonus purpuratus**
Yellow-billed Barbet
Sierra Leone to Uganda, Kenya, Angola

27 03 079 **Trachyphonus vaillantii**
Levaillant's Barbet
Dry woodland of Angola, Tanzania to South Africa

27 03 080 **Trachyphonus erythrocephalus**
Red-and-yellow Barbet
Semiarid Somalia, Ethiopia to Kenya, Tanzania

27 03 081 **Trachyphonus darnaudii**
D'Arnaud's Barbet
Sudan, Ethiopia to Kenya, Tanzania

27 03 082 **Trachyphonus usambiro**
Black-capped Barbet
Kenya and Tanzania (possible race of *T. darnaudii*)

27 03 083 **Trachyphonus margaritatus**
Yellow-breasted Barbet
Semiarid Nigeria to Red Sea environs

ORDER: PICIFORMES
FAMILY: INDICATORIDAE (Honeyguides)

27 04 001 **Prodotiscus insignis**
Cassin's Honeyguide
Africa south of the Sahara

27 04 002 **Prodotiscus zambesiae**
Green-backed Honeyguide
Angola to Rhodesia (possible race *P. insignis*)

27 04 003 **Prodotiscus regulus**
Wahlberg's Honeyguide
Africa south of the Sahara

27 04 004 **Melignomon zenkeri**
Zenker's Honeyguide
Forests of southern Cameroon, northern Zaire (rare)

27 04 005 **Indicator maculatus**
Spotted Honeyguide
Gambia, Cameroon to Uganda, Ethiopia

27 04 006 **Indicator variegatus**
Scaly-throated Honeyguide
Ethiopia, the Sudan to South Africa

27 04 007 **Indicator indicator**
Black-throated Honeyguide
Africa south of the Sahara

	Date	Location

| 27 04 008 | **Indicator minor** | | |
| | *Lesser Honeyguide* | | Africa south of the Sahara |

| 27 04 009 | **Indicator conirostris** | | |
| | *Thick-billed Honeyguide* | | Southern Nigeria, Cameroon to Kenya |

27 04 010	**Indicator exilis**		
✝	**(narokensis)**		
	Least Honeyguide		Ghana to the Sudan, Uganda, Tanzania; Fernando Po

| 27 04 011 | **Indicator willcocksi** | | |
| | *Willcock's Honeyguide* | | Guinea to Cameroon, Zaire |

| 27 04 012 | **Indicator meliphilus** | | |
| | *Eastern Least Honeyguide* | | Uganda, Kenya to Botswanna, eastern Angola |

| 27 04 013 | **Indicator pumilio** | | |
| | *Dwarf Honeyguide* | | Highlands of Lake Kivu to Lake Tanganyika |

| 27 04 014 | **Indicator xanthonotus** | | |
| | *Yellow-rumped Honeyguide* | | Himalayas of Kashmir, Nepal, Sikkim, Assam, Burma |

| 27 04 015 | **Indicator archipelagicus** | | |
| | *Malaysian Honeyguide* | | Malaya, peninsular Thailand, Sumatra, Borneo |

| 27 04 016 | **Melichneutes robustus** | | |
| | *Lyre-tailed Honeyguide* | | Nigeria to Angola, Zaire, western Uganda |

ORDER: PICIFORMES
FAMILY: RAMPHASTIDAE (Toucans)

| 27 05 001 | **Aulacorhynchus prasinus** | | |
| | *Emerald Toucanet* | | Highlands of southern Mexico to Nicaragua |

| 27 05 002 | **Aulacorhynchus caeruleogularis** | | |
| | *Blue-throated Toucanet* | | Highlands of Costa Rica, Panama (possible race *A. prasinus*) |

| 27 05 003 | **Aulacorhynchus sulcatus** | | |
| | *Groove-billed Toucanet* | | Subtropical coastal mountains of Venezuela |

| 27 05 004 | **Aulacorhynchus derbianus** | | |
| ✝ | *Chestnut-tipped Toucanet* | | Guyana, Venezuela to northwest Bolivia |

| 27 05 005 | **Aulacorhynchus haematopygus** | | |
| | *Crimson-rumped Toucanet* | | Highlands of Venezuela, Colombia to western Ecuador |

| 27 05 006 | **Aulacorhynchus huallagae** | | |
| | *Yellow-browed Toucanet* | | Andes of Peru (Libertad—known from one specimen) |

		Date	Location

27 05 007
✝ **Aulacorhynchus coeruleicinctis**
Blue-banded Toucanet — Andes of central Peru, northern Bolivia

27 05 008 Aulacorhynchus calorhynchus
Yellow-billed Toucanet — Northwest Venezuela to Santa Marta Mountains of Colombia

27 05 009 Pteroglossus viridis
Green Araçari — Guianas, southeast Venezuela, northeast Brazil

27 05 010 Pteroglossus inscriptus
Lettered Araçari — Southeast Colombia to northern Bolivia, southwest Brazil

27 05 011 Pteroglossus bitorquatus
Red-necked Araçari — Tropical Brazil south of the Amazon

27 05 012 Pteroglossus flavirostris
Ivory-billed Araçari — Venezuela, Colombia to northeast Peru, northwest Brazil

27 05 013 Pteroglossus aracari
Black-necked Araçari — Tropical eastern Venezuela, Guianas, eastern Brazil

27 05 014 Pteroglossus castanotis
Chestnut-eared Araçari — Tropical Colombia to northeast Argentina

27 05 015 Ptergolossus pluricinctus
Many-banded Araçari — Tropical forests of western Amazon basin

27 05 016 Pteroglossus torquatus
Collared Araçari — Southern Mexico to northern Colombia and Venezuela

27 05 017 Pteroglossus frantzii
Fiery-billed Araçari — Pacific slope of Costa Rica to Panama

27 05 018 Pteroglossus sanguineus
Stripe-billed Araçari — Pacific Colombia, northwest Ecuador

27 05 019 Pteroglossus erythropygius
Pale-mandibled Araçari — Tropical western Ecuador (Esmeraldas to Chanchan)

27 05 020
✝ **Pteroglossus beauharnaesii**
Curl-crested Araçari — Amazonian Peru, western Brazil, adjacent Bolivia

27 05 021 Pteroglossus marie
✝ *Brown-mandibled Araçari* — Amazonian Peru, western Brazil, northern Bolivia

27 05 022 Selenidera maculirostris
Spot-billed Toucanet — Tropical Brazil south of Amazon to northeast Argentina

27 05 023 Selenidera gouldii
Gould's Toucanet — Brazil (Ceará to Pará—probable race of *S. maculirostris*)

	Date	Location

27 05 024 **Selenidera reinwardtii**
+   *Golden-collared Toucanet*   Andes of eastern Colombia to Peru, western Brazil

27 05 025 **Selenidera nattereri**
    Tawny-tufted Toucanet   Guianas to southeast Colombia, adjacent Brazil

27 05 026 **Selenidera culik**
    Guianan Toucanet   Tropical Guianas, Venezuela, adjacent Brazil

27 05 027 **Selenidera spectabilis**
    Yellow-eared Toucanet   Tropical Honduras to northwest Colombia

27 05 028 **Baillonius bailloni**
    Saffron Toucanet   Southeast Brazil (Espirito Santo to Santa Catarina)

27 05 029 **Andigena hypoglauca**
    Gray-breasted Mountain   Andes of Colombia to central Peru (Junin)
    Toucan

27 05 030 **Andigena laminirostris**
    Plate-billed Mountain   Andes of Colombia (western Nariño), western
    Toucan   Ecuador

27 05 031 **Andigena cucullata**
    Hooded Mountain Toucan   Andes of eastern Peru to northern Bolivia

27 05 032 **Andigena nigrirostris**
    Black-billed Mountain   Northwest Venezuela, Colombia to northeast Ecuador
    Toucan

27 05 033 **Ramphastos vitellinus**
    Channel-billed Toucan   Tropical Guianas, Venezuela, Brazil

27 05 034 **Ramphastos citreolaemus**
    Citron-throated Toucan   Northern Colombia to northwest Venezuela

27 05 035 **Ramphastos culminatus**
    Yellow-ridged Toucan   Tropical Colombia to Bolivia, west Amazonian Brazil

27 05 036 **Ramphastos discolorus**
+   *Red-breasted Toucan*   Southeast Brazil (Goiás), to Paraguay, northern
     Argentina

27 05 037 **Ramphastos brevis**
    Choco Toucan   Pacific slope of Colombia, northwest Ecuador

27 05 038 **Ramphastos sulfuratus**
+   *Keel-billed Toucan*   Southern Mexico to northern Colombia, Venezuela

27 05 039 **Ramphastos toco**
+   *Toco Toucan*   Guianas to northern Brazil, Bolivia, Argentina

27 05 040 **Ramphastos swainsonii**
    Chestnut-mandibled   Honduras to Colombia, western Ecuador
    Toucan

27 05 041 **Ramphastos ambiguus**
    Black-mandibled Toucan   Eastern Panama to Venezuela, Colombia, Peru

27 05 042 **Ramphastos aurantiirostris**
    Orange-billed Toucan   Tropical forests of Guianas, eastern Venezuela

		Date	Location

27 05 043 **Ramphastos tucanus**
Red-billed Toucan — Guianas, Venezuela, Colombia, Amazonian Brazil

27 05 044 **Ramphastos cuvieri**
Cuvier's Toucan — Widespread tropical Amazon basin

ORDER: PICIFORMES
FAMILY: JYNGIDAE (Wrynecks)

27 06 001 **Jynx torquilla**
Eurasian Wryneck — Widespread Palearctic, Oriental mainland; Hainan; Taiwan

27 06 002 **Jynx ruficollis**
Red-breasted Wryneck — Africa south of the Sahara

ORDER: PICIFORMES
FAMILY: PICIDAE (Woodpeckers)

27 07 001 **Picumnus cinnamomeus**
Chestnut Piculet — Caribbean lowlands of northwest Venezuela to Colombia

27 07 002 **Picumnus rufiventris**
† *Rufous-breasted Piculet* — Tropical Colombia, Ecuador to Bolivia, southwest Brazil

27 07 003 **Picumnus fulvescens**
Tawny Piculet — Brazil (Pernambuco, Alagoas—known from 5 specimens)

27 07 004 **Picumnus fuscus**
Rusty-necked Piculet — Brazil (Matto Grosso—known from a single specimen)

27 07 005 **Picumnus castelnau**
Plain-breasted Piculet — Tropical eastern Ecuador, eastern Peru

27 07 006 **Picumnus spilogaster**
White-bellied Piculet — Tropical French Guiana to Venezuela, northeast Brazil

27 07 007 **Picumnus minutissimus**
Arrowhead Piculet — Tropical Guianas, eastern Brazil to northern Bolivia

27 07 008 **Picumnus squamulatus**
Scaled Piculet — Northern Colombia, Venezuela (Santa Marta to Meta)

27 07 009 **Picumnus limae**
Ochraceous Piculet — Northeast Brazil (Ceará to Alagoas)

27 07 010 **Picumnus olivaceus**
Olivaceous Piculet — Guatemala to Venezuela, Colombia, western Ecuador

		Date	Location
27 07 011	**Picumnus granadensis** *Grayish Piculet*		Colombia (Cauca, Dagua, Patia valleys)
27 07 012	**Picumnus nebulosus** *Mottled Piculet*		Southeast Brazil (Paraná) to northeast Argentina
27 07 013	**Picumnus nigropunctatus** *Black-dotted Piculet*		Venezuela (forests of the Orinoco Delta)
27 07 014	**Picumnus exilis** *Golden-spangled Piculet*		Tropical Venezuela, Guianas, Brazil
27 07 015	**Picumnus borbae** *Bar-breasted Piculet*		Tropical eastern Peru, Brazil south of the Amazon
27 07 016	**Picumnus aurifrons** *Gold-fronted Piculet*		Widespread tropical western Amazon basin
27 07 017	**Picumnus temminckii** *Ochre-collared Piculet*		Southeast Brazil, Paraguay, northeast Argentina
27 07 018	**Picumnus cirratus** *White-barred Piculet*		Northern South America to northern Argentina
27 07 019	**Picumnus dorbygnianus** *Ocellated Piculet*		Peru (Junin, Cuzco) to northwest Argentina
27 07 020	**Picumnus sclateri** *Ecuadorean Piculet*		Arid scrub of western Ecuador, northwest Peru
27 07 021	**Picumnus subtilis** *White-breasted Piculet*		Tropical foothills of southeast Peru (Cuzco)
27 07 022	**Picumnus steindachneri** *Speckle-chested Piculet*		Peru ~~(Huallaga River drainage)~~
27 07 023	**Picumnus varzeae** *Varzea Piculet*		Northeast Brazil (lower Rio Jamundá)
27 07 024	**Picumnus pygmaeus** *Spotted Piculet*		*Caatinga* of eastern Brazil (Maranhão to Bahia)
27 07 025	**Picumnus asterias** *Blackish Piculet*		Brazil (unique—probable aberrant *P. pygmaeus*)
27 07 026	**Picumnus pumilus** *Orinoco Piculet*		Savanna of Colombia (Vichada), northwest Brazil
27 07 027	**Picumnus innominatus** *Speckled Piculet*		Himalayas of India to Indochina, Sumatra, Borneo
27 07 028	**Verreauxia africana** *African Piculet*		Cameroon, Gabon to Zaire
27 07 029	**Sasia ochracea** *White-browed Piculet*		Himalayas of Garhwal, Nepal to Sikiang, Thailand
27 07 030	**Sasia abnormis** *Rufous Piculet*		Bamboo forests of Malaya, Sumatra, Borneo, Thailand

		Date	Location
27 07 031	**Nesoctites micromegas** *Antillean Piculet*		Hispaniola and Gonave Islands
27 07 032	**Leuconerpes candidus** *White Woodpecker*		Campos of Surinam, Brazil to northern Argentina
27 07 033	**Asyndesmus lewis** *Lewis' Woodpecker*		Southwest Canada, western United States; winters to Baja, California, Sonora
27 07 034	**Melanerpes herminieri** *Guadeloupe Woodpecker*		Wooded hills of Guadeloupe Island (Lesser Antilles)
27 07 035	**Melanerpes portoricensis** *Puerto Rican Woodpecker*		Woodlands of Puerto Rico and Vieques Island
27 07 036	**Melanerpes erythrocephalus** *Red-headed Woodpecker*		Southern Canada to southern United States
27 07 037	**Melanerpes formicivorus** *Acorn Woodpecker*		Pine-oak zone of western United States to Colombia
27 07 038	**Melanerpes cruentatus** *Yellow-tufted Woodpecker*		Tropical South America to northern Bolivia, Brazil
27 07 039	**Melanerpes flavifrons** *Yellow-fronted Woodpecker*		Southeast Brazil (Goiás) to northeast Argentina
27 07 040	**Melanerpes chrysauchen** *Golden-naped Woodpecker*		Forests of southwest Costa Rica to northern Colombia
27 07 041	**Melanerpes rubrifrons** *Red-fronted Woodpecker*		Tropical Venezuela, Guianas, northern Brazil
27 07 042	**Melanerpes superciliaris** *Bahama Woodpecker*		Bahama, Cuba, Isle of Pines, Grand Cayman (endangered)
27 07 043	**Melanerpes radiolatus** *Jamaican Woodpecker*		Lowlands to mountain rain forests of Jamaica
27 07 044	**Melanerpes striatus** *Hispaniolian Woodpecker*		Lowlands to mountain forests of Hispaniola
27 07 045	**Melanerpes rubricapillus** *Red-crowned Woodpecker*		Costa Rica to Venezuela, Surinam, Colombia
27 07 046	**Melanerpes hoffmannii** *Hoffmann's Woodpecker*		Southern Honduras to Costa Rica
27 07 047	**Centurus pucherani** *Black-cheeked Woodpecker*		Tropical southeast Mexico to western Ecuador
27 07 048	**Centurus cactorum** *White-fronted Woodpecker*		Southeast Peru, Bolivia, Brazil to Argentina

		Date	Location

27 07 049	**Centurus chrysogenys** *Golden-cheeked* *Woodpecker*	Western Mexico (Sinaloa to Oaxaca)
27 07 050	**Centurus hypopolius** *Gray-breasted* *Woodpecker*	Restricted to southwestern Mexico
27 07 051	**Centurus uropygialis** *Gila Woodpecker*	Arid lowlands of southwest United States to central Mexico
27 07 052	**Centurus pygmaeus** *Yucatán Woodpecker*	Yucatán Peninsula and Cozumel Island (Mexico)
27 07 053	**Centurus aurifrons** *Golden-fronted* *Woodpecker*	Southwest Oklahoma, Texas to Costa Rica
27 07 054	**Centurus carolinus** *Red-bellied Woodpecker*	Restricted to eastern United States
27 07 055	**Sphyrapicus varius** **(nuchalis) (ruber)** *Common Sapsucker*	North America; winters to Panama; West Indies
27 07 056	**Sphyrapicus thyroideus** *Williamson's Sapsucker*	British Columbia, western United States; winters to northern Mexico
27 07 057	**Xiphidiopicus percussus** *Cuban Green Woodpecker*	Woodlands of Cuba, Isle of Pines
27 07 058	**Campethera nubica** **(scriptoricauda)** *Nubian Woodpecker*	Zaire to Ethiopia, Kenya, Uganda, Tanzania, Mozambique
27 07 059	**Campethera bennettii** *Bennett's Woodpecker*	Angola to Tanzania, eastern South Africa
27 07 060	**Campethera abingoni** *Golden-tailed Woodpecker*	Senegal, Gambia to southwest Sudan, Angola
27 07 061	**Campethera** **taeniolaema** *Fine-banded Woodpecker*	Highlands of eastern Zaire to Kenya, Uganda, Tanzania
27 07 062	**Campethera notata** *Knysna Woodpecker*	Coastal bush of Cape Province to Natal
27 07 063	**Campethera cailliautii** *Little Spotted Woodpecker*	Uganda to Angola, Rhodesia, Zambia, Mozambique
27 07 064	**Campethera maculosa** *Golden-backed* *Woodpecker*	Forests of Portugese Guinea to Ghana

		Date	Location
27 07 065	**Campethera permista** *Green-backed Woodpecker*		Ghana to the Sudan, Uganda, Angola, Zaire
27 07 066	**Campethera tullbergi** *Tullberg's Woodpecker*		Highlands of Cameroon Mountain; Fernando Po
27 07 067	**Campethera nivosa** *Buff-spotted Woodpecker*		Senegal to Angola, Zaire, Uganda
27 07 068	**Campethera caroli** *Brown-eared Woodpecker*		Sierra Leone to Angola, Zaire, southern Sudan
27 07 069	**Campethera punctuligera** *Fine-spotted Woodpecker*		Senegal to southern Sudan, Zaire, Cameroon
27 07 070	**Geocolaptes olivaceus** *Ground Woodpecker*		Dry hilly country of South Africa (terrestial)
27 07 071	**Dendropicos elachus** *Little Gray Woodpecker*		Desert edges of Senegal to western Sudan
27 07 072	**Dendropicos abyssinicus** *Abyssinian Woodpecker*		Restricted to highlands of Ethiopia
27 07 073	**Dendropicos poecilolaemus** *Uganda Spotted Woodpecker*		Upland savanna of Nigeria to western Kenya
27 07 074	**Dendropicos fuscescens** *Cardinal Woodpecker*		Africa south of the Sahara
27 07 075	**Dendropicos gabonensis** *Gabon Woodpecker*		Lowland forests of Nigera, Cameroon to Zaire
27 07 076	**Dendropicos stierlingi** *Stierling's Woodpecker*		Mozambique and Malawi (rare)
27 07 077	**Mesopicos xantholophus** *Yellow-crested Woodpecker*		Cameroon to northern Angola, Kenya, Uganda
27 07 078	**Mesopicos pyrrhogaster** *Fire-bellied Woodpecker*		Forests of Guinea to southern Uganda
27 07 079	**Mesopicos elliotii (johnstoni)** *Elliot's Woodpecker*		Gabon to Cameroon, Angola, Uganda; Fernando Po
27 07 080	**Mesopicos goertae** *Gray Woodpecker*		Senegal to southern Sudan, Uganda, Angola
27 07 081	**Mesopicos griseocephalus** *Olive Woodpecker*		Evergreen forests of Uganda, Zaire to South Africa
27 07 082	**Thripias namaquus** *Bearded Woodpecker*		Angola, Uganda to South Africa

	Date	Location
27 07 083 **Dendrocopos temminckii** *Celebes Pygmy Woodpecker*		Restricted to Celebes Islands
27 07 084 **Dendrocopos moluccensis** *Brown-capped Woodpecker*		India to Malaya; Greater and Lesser Sundas
27 07 085 **Dendrocopos maculatus** *Philippine Pygmy Woodpecker*		Widespread throughout Philippine Islands
27 07 086 **Dendrocopos obsoletus** *Brown-backed Woodpecker*		Savanna of Senegal to Ethiopia, Uganda
27 07 087 **Dendrocopos lugubris** *Melancholy Woodpecker*		Open woodlands of Guinea to Ghana
27 07 088 **Dendrocopos kizuki** *Japanese Pygmy Woodpecker*		Japanese Islands; Manchuria to Hopeh; Korea
27 07 089 **Dendrocopos canicapillus (hardwickii)** *Gray-headed Pygmy Woodpecker*		Manchuria to Malaya, Indochina, Sumatra, Borneo; Hainan
27 07 090 **Dendrocopos minor** *Lesser Spotted Woodpecker*		Widespread mixed forests of Palearctic region
27 07 091 **Dendrocopos macei (analis)** *Fulvous-breasted Woodpecker*		India to Indochina; Andamans, Sumatra, Java, Bali
27 07 092 **Dendrocopos atratus** *Stripe-breasted Woodpecker*		Assam to southwest China, Indochina
27 07 093 **Dendrocopos auriceps** *Brown-fronted Woodpecker*		Mixed forests of northeast Afghanistan to central Nepal
27 07 094 **Dendrocopos mahrattensis** *Yellow-crowned Woodpecker*		Sri Lanka; India to Indochina
27 07 095 **Dendrocopos dorae** *Arabian Woodpecker*		Acacia belt of Arabia to Aden Protectorate; Yemen
27 07 096 **Dendrocopos hyperythrus** *Rufous-bellied Woodpecker*		Himalayas of Kashmir to Assam, Sikiang, Indochina

		Date	Location

27 07 097 **Dendrocopos cathparius**
Crimson-breasted Woodpecker
Himalayas of Nepal to Szechwan, northwest Indochina

27 07 098 **Dendrocopos darjellensis**
Darjeeling Woodpecker
Himalayas of Nepal to Szechwan, Burma

27 07 099 **Dendrocopos leucotos**
White-backed Woodpecker
Open deciduous forests of Palearctic region

27 07 100 **Dendrocopos medius**
Middle Spotted Woodpecker
Continental Europe to Asia Minor, Caucasus, Iran

27 07 101 **Dendrocopos himalayensis**
Himalayan Pied Woodpecker
Himalayas of Afghanistan to Nepal

27 07 102 **Dendrocopos assimilis**
Sind Woodpecker
Lowlands of Pakistan, India, Baluchistan, Iran

27 07 103 **Dendrocopos syriacus**
Syrian Woodpecker
Deciduous forests of central Europe to Baluchistan

27 07 104 **Dendrocopos leucopterus**
White-winged Woodpecker
Asia Minor (Transcaspia to Sinkiang)

27 07 105 **Dendrocopos nanus**
Indian Pygmy Woodpecker
Widespread Oriental mainland and islands

27 07 106 **Dendrocopos major**
Great Spotted Woodpecker
Mixed forests of Palearctic, Oriental mainland

27 07 107 **Dendrocopos mixtus**
Checkered Woodpecker
Eastern Brazil (Goiás) to Argentina (Chubut)

27 07 108 **Dendrocopos lignarius**
Striped Woodpecker
Highlands of Bolivia to Argentina, Chile

27 07 109 **Dendrocopos scalaris**
Ladder-backed Woodpecker
Arid southwest United States to southern Mexico

27 07 110 **Dendrocopos nuttallii**
Nuttall's Woodpecker
California to northwest Baja California

27 07 111 **Dendrocopos borealis**
Red-cockaded Woodpecker
Restricted to southeast United States

27 07 112 **Dendrocopos stricklandi**
Brown-barred Woodpecker
High mountains of south-central Mexico

27 07 113 **Dendrocopos villosus**
Hairy Woodpecker
Widespread Alaska to Panama; Bahamas Islands

		Date	Location
27 07 114	**Dendrocopos albolarvatus** *White-headed Woodpecker*		Highlands of British Columbia to California, Nevada
27 07 115	**Dendrocopos arizonae** *Arizona Woodpecker*		Mountains of southeast Arizona and western Mexico
27 07 116	**Dendrocopos pubescens** *Downy Woodpecker*		Alaska to southern United States
27 07 117	**Picoides tridactylus** *Northern Three-toed Woodpecker*		Circumpolar boreal forests of Holarctic region
27 07 118	**Picoides arcticus** *Black-backed Woodpecker*		Boreal forests of Alaska, Canada, United States
27 07 119	**Venilornis callonotus** *Scarlet-backed Woodpecker*		Arid southwest Colombia to northwest Peru
27 07 120	**Venilornis dignus** *Yellow-vented Woodpecker*		Mountains of Venezuela, Colombia, Ecuador, Peru
27 07 021	**Venilornis nigriceps** *Bar-bellied Woodpecker*		Andes of Colombia to northern Bolivia
27 07 122	**Venilornis fumigatus** *Smoky-brown Woodpecker*		Subtropical eastern Mexico to northwest Argentina
27 07 123	**Venilornis passerinus** *Little Woodpecker*		Tropical South America to northeast Argentina
27 07 124	**Venilornis frontalis** *Dot-fronted Woodpecker*		Central and eastern Bolivia to northwest Argentina
27 07 125	**Venilornis spilogaster** *White-spotted Woodpecker*		Southeast Brazil (Minas Gerais) to northwest Argentina
27 07 126	**Venilornis sanguineus** *Blood-colored Woodpecker*		Mangroves, swamps of the Guianas
27 07 127	**Venilornis maculifrons** *Yellow-eared Woodpecker*		Eastern Brazil (Minas Gerais, Espirito Santo, Rio de Janeiro)
27 07 128	**Venilornis affinis** *Red-stained Woodpecker*		Northern South America to Bolivia, Amazonian Brazil
27 07 129	**Vernilornis cassini** *Golden-collared Woodpecker*		Tropical Guianas, Venezuela, Colombia, adjacent Brazil

		Date	Location
27 07 130	**Venilornis kirkii** *Red-rumped Woodpecker*		Tropical Costa Rica to northern South America; Trinidad; Tobago
27 07 131	**Piculus leucolaemus** *White-throated Woodpecker*		Colombia to Peru, Bolivia, west Amazonian Brazil
27 07 132	**Piculus flavigula** *Yellow-throated Woodpecker*		Tropical South America to eastern Peru, Brazil
27 07 133	**Piculus chrysochloros** *Golden-green Woodpecker*		Tropical eastern Panama to northern Argentina
27 07 134	**Piculus aurulentus** *White-browed Woodpecker*		Southeast Brazil (Minas Gerais) to northeast Argentina
27 07 135	**Piculus rubiginosus (aeruginosus)** *Golden-olive Woodpecker*		Subtropical Mexico to northwest Argentina
27 07 136	**Piculus auricularis** *Gray-crowned Woodpecker*		Mexico (Pacific slope of Sonora to Guerrero)
27 07 137	**Piculus simplex** *Bugaba Woodpecker*		Honduras, Nicaragua, Costa Rica, western Panama
27 07 138	**Piculus rivolii** *Crimson-mantled Woodpecker*		Andes of Venezuela, Colombia to northern Bolivia
27 07 139	**Chrysoptilus atricollis** *Black-necked Woodpecker*		Tropical, subtropical cactus zone of western Peru
27 07 140	**Chrysoptilus punctigula** *Spot-breasted Woodpecker*		Tropical Panama to Peru, Bolivia, Brazil
27 07 141	**Chrysoptilus melanochloros** *Green-barred Woodpecker*		Eastern Brazil (Maranhão) to north-central Argentina
27 07 142	**Chrysoptilus melanolaimus** *Golden-breasted Woodpecker*		Eastern Bolivia to central Argentina
27 07 143	**Colaptes auratus (cafer) (chrysoides)** *Common Flicker*		Alaska to Mexico; West Indies
27 07 144	**Colaptes fernandinae** *Fernandina's Flicker*		Lowland palm groves of Cuba (rare and local)
27 07 145	**Colaptes pitius** *Chilean Flicker*		Chile (Coquimbo to Magallenes), adjacent Argentina

		Date	Location

27 07 146 **Colaptes rupicola**
           Andean Flicker   Andes of Peru, Bolivia, northern Chile, Argentina

27 07 147 **Colaptes campestris**
           Campo Flicker   Savanna of Surinam to Brazil, Bolivia, Argentina

27 07 148 **Colaptes campestroides**
           Field Flicker   Savanna of southeast Brazil to Argentina (Rio Negro)

27 07 149 **Celeus loricatus**
           Cinnamon Woodpecker   Tropical Nicaragua to Colombia, northwest Ecuador

27 07 150 **Celeus undatus**
           Waved Woodpecker   Tropical eastern Venezuela, Guianas, adjacent Brazil

27 07 151 **Celeus grammicus**
           Scale-breasted Woodpecker Tropical South America to Bolivia, Amazonian Brazil

27 07 152 **Celeus castaneus**
           Chestnut-colored Woodpecker Tropical southeast Mexico to northwest Panama

27 07 153 **Celeus elegans**
           Chestnut (Elegant) Woodpecker Northern South America to Bolivia, Brazil

27 07 154 **Celeus lugubris**
           Pale-crested Woodpecker Southeast Brazil to northwest Argentina, Bolivia

27 07 155 **Celeus flavescens**
           Blond-crested Woodpecker Amazonian Brazil to eastern Bolivia, northeast Argentina

27 07 156 **Celeus flavus**
           Cream-colored Woodpecker Tropical South America to Brazil, northern Bolivia

27 07 157 **Celeus spectabilis**
           Rufous-headed Woodpecker Tropical eastern Ecuador to Peru, northeast Bolivia

27 07 158 **Celeus torquatus**
           Ringed Woodpecker   Tropical South America to Brazil, northern Bolivia

27 07 159 **Micropternus brachyurus**
           Rufous Woodpecker   India to Indochina; Greater Sundas; Hainan

27 07 160 **Dryocopus galeatus**
           Helmeted Woodpecker   Southeast Brazil (São Paulo) to northeast Argentina

27 07 161 **Dryocopus schulzi (major)**
           Black-bodied Woodpecker Woodlands and scrub of Paraguay to central Argentina

27 07 162 **Dryocopus lineatus**
           Lineated Woodpecker   Tropical southern Mexico to northern Argentina

		Date	Location
27 07 163	**Dryocopus pileatus** *Pileated Woodpecker*		Forests of southern Canada to southern United States
27 07 164	**Dryocopus javensis** *White-bellied Woodpecker*		Widespread Oriental region mainland and islands
27 07 165	**Dryocopus martius** *Black Woodpecker*		Coniferous and beech forests of Palearctic region
27 07 166	**Phloeoceastes guatemalensis** *Pale-billed Woodpecker*		Northern Mexico to western Panama
27 07 167	**Phloeoceastes melanoleucos** *Crimson-crested Woodpecker*		Panama to Argentina (mainly east of the Andes)
27 07 168	**Phloeoceastes gayaquilensis** *Guayaquil Woodpecker*		Tropical southwest Colombia to northwest Peru
27 07 169	**Phloeoceastes pollens** *Powerful Woodpecker*		Mountains of Venezuela, Colombia, Ecuador, Peru
27 07 170	**Phloeoceastes haematogaster** *Crimson-bellied Woodpecker*		Panama, western Colombia to eastern Peru
27 07 171	**Phloeoceastes robustus** *Robust Woodpecker*		Eastern Brazil (Bahia) to northeast Argentina
27 07 172	**Phloeoceastes rubricollis** *Red-necked Woodpecker*		Guianas to eastern Colombia, northern Bolivia
27 07 173	**Phloeoceastes leucopogon** *Cream-backed Woodpecker*		Paraguay to Uruguay; adjacent Brazil and Argentina
27 07 174	**Campephilus magellanicus** *Magellanic Woodpecker*		Forests of southern Argentina, Chile
27 07 175	**Campephilus principalis** *Ivory-billed Woodpecker*		Extinct United States. May survive in extreme eastern Cuba
27 07 176	**Campephilus imperialis** *Imperial Woodpecker*		Sierra Madre of northwest Mexico (possibly extinct)
27 07 177	**Picus miniaceus** *Banded Woodpecker*		Malay Peninsula, Java, Sumatra, Borneo
27 07 178	**Picus puniceus** *Crimson-winged Woodpecker*		Malay Peninsula, Java, Sumatra, Borneo

	Date	Location

27 07 179   Picus chlorolophus
Lesser Yellownape   Himalayas of India to Indochina; Sumatra; Hainan

27 07 180   Picus mentalis
Checker-throated   Malay Peninsula; Java, Sumatra, Borneo
Woodpecker

27 07 181   Picus flavinucha
Greater Yellownape   Himalayas to southern China, Malaya; Sumatra;
                             Hainan

27 07 182   Picus vittatus
Laced Woodpecker   Pakistan to Indochina; Sumatra; Java

27 07 183   Picus viridanus
Streak-breasted   Burma to the Malay Peninsula
Woodpecker

27 07 184   Picus xanthopygaeus
(myrmecophoneus)
Streak-throated   Widespread India to Southeast Asia
Woodpecker

27 07 185   Picus squamatus
Scaly-bellied Woodpecker   Conifererous forests of Iran, Afghanistan to Sikkim

27 07 186   Picus awokera
Japanese Woodpecker   Japanese Islands (Hondo to Tanegashima and
                             Yakushima)

27 07 187   Picus canus
Gray-headed Woodpecker   Widespread Palearctic, Oriental mainland and islands

27 07 188   Picus erythropygius
Black-headed   Burma, Thailand to Indochina, Cochinchina
Woodpecker

27 07 189   Picus rabieri
Red-collared Woodpecker   Southwest China to Annam, Tonkin, Laos

27 07 190   Picus viridis
Green Woodpecker   Open deciduous woodlands of Palearctic region

27 07 191   Picus vaillantii
Algerian Woodpecker   Morocco, Algeria, Tunisia

27 07 192   Dinopium rafflesii
Olive-backed Woodpecker   Malay Peninsula, Sumatra, Borneo, Banka

27 07 193   Dinopium shorii
Himalayan Goldenback   Himalayas of Garhwal to northern Burma

27 07 194   Dinopium javanense
Common Goldenback   India to Indochina; Greater Sundas; Philippine Islands

27 07 195   Dinopium benghalense
Lesser Goldenback   Sri Lanka; India to Assam, western Burma

27 07 196   Chrysocolaptes validus
Orange-backed   Malay Peninsula, Java, Sumatra, Borneo
Woodpecker

		Date	Location

27 07 197 **Chrysocolaptes guttacristatus**
Crimson-backed Woodpecker
Widespread wet zone and mountains of Sri Lanka

27 07 198 **Chrysocolaptes lucidus**
Greater Goldenback
Widespread Oriental region mainland and islands

27 07 199 **Chrysocolaptes festivus**
Black-backed Woodpecker
Light forests of peninsular India; Sri Lanka

27 07 200 **Gecinulus grantia**
Pale-headed Woodpecker
Bamboo zone of Nepal to southwest China, Indochina

27 07 201 **Gecinulus viridis**
Bamboo Woodpecker
Bamboo zone of Malaya, Tenasserim, Burma

27 07 202 **Sapheopipo noguchii**
Noguchi's Woodpecker
Confined to Okinawa Island (endangered—20 pairs 1973)

27 07 203 **Blythipicus rubiginosus**
Maroon Woodpecker
Malay Peninsula, Sumatra, Borneo

27 07 204 **Blythipicus pyrrhotis**
Red-eared (Bay) Woodpecker
Nepal to southern China, Malaya, Indochina; Hainan

27 07 205 **Meiglyptes tristis**
Buff-rumped Woodpecker
Malay Peninsula, Java, Sumatra, Borneo

27 07 206 **Meiglyptes jugalaris**
Black-and-buff Woodpecker
Open forests of Burma, Tenasserim, Thailand, Indochina

27 07 207 **Meiglyptes tukki**
Buff-necked Woodpecker
Malay Peninsula, Sumatra, Borneo

27 07 208 **Hemicircus concretus**
Gray-and-buff Woodpecker
Malay Peninsula, Java, Sumatra, Borneo

27 07 209 **Hemicircus canente**
Heart-spotted Woodpecker
Bamboo forests of Oriental region mainland

27 07 210 **Mulleripicus fulvus**
Celebes Woodpecker
Restricted to the Celebes Islands

27 07 211 **Mulleripicus funebris**
Sooty Woodpecker
Widespread throughout the Philippine Islands

27 07 212 **Mulleripicus pulverulentus**
Great Slaty Woodpecker
Widespread Oriental mainland and islands

PART II

Order: Passeriformes

Perching Birds

	Date	Location

ORDER: PASSERIFORMES
FAMILY: EURYLAIMIDAE (Broadbills)

28 01 001 **Smithornis capensis**
African Broadbill
Dense forests of Sierra Leone to Tanzania, South Africa

28 01 002 **Smithornis rufolateralis**
Red-sided Broadbill
Dense forests of Liberia to Cameroon, Zaire

28 01 003 **Smithornis sharpei**
Gray-headed Broadbill
Fernando Po, Cameroon, northeast Zaire

28 01 004 **Pseudocalyptomena graueri**
Grauer's Broadbill
Zaire (known only from Costermansville District)

28 01 005 **Corydon sumatranus**
Dusky Broadbill
Malaya, Indochina, Sumatra, Borneo

28 01 006 **Cymbirhynchus macrorhynchus**
Black-and-red Broadbill
Burma to Malay Peninsula, Indochina, Sumatra, Borneo

28 01 007 **Eurylaimus javanicus**
Banded Broadbill
Southern Burma to Malay Peninsula, Indochina, Greater Sundas

28 01 008 **Eurylaimus ochromalus**
Black-and-yellow Broadbill
Malay Peninsula, Borneo, Sumatra

28 01 009 **Eurylaimus steerii**
Wattled Broadbill
Philippines (Mindanao, Bohol, Leyte, Samar)

28 01 010 **Serilophus lunatus**
Silver-breasted Broadbill
Nepal to Yunnan, Indochina; Hainan

28 01 011 **Psarisomus dalhousiae**
Long-tailed Broadbill
Himalayas of Nepal to Indochina; Sumatra; Borneo

28 01 012 **Calyptomena viridis**
Lesser Green Broadbill
Malay Peninsula; Sumatra; Borneo

28 01 013 **Calyptomena hosei**
Magnificent Green Broadbill
Borneo (spottily distributed submontane forests)

28 01 014 **Calyptomena whiteheadi**
Whitehead's Broadbill
Borneo (tropical montane forests)

FAMILY: DENDROCOLAPTIDAE (Woodcreepers)

28 02 001 **Dendrocincla tyrannina**
Tyrannine Woodcreeper
Central Andes of Venezuela, Colombia to Peru

28 02 002 **Dendrocincla macrorhyncha**
Salvadori's Woodcreeper
Northeast Ecuador (probable aberrant *D. tyranninia*)

	Date	Location

28 02 003 Dendrocincia fuliginosa
Plain-brown Woodcreeper

Tropical Honduras to northeast Argentina

28 02 004 Dendrocincla anabatina
Tawny-winged Woodcreeper

Rain forests of eastern Mexico to western Panama

28 02 005 Dendrocincla merula
White-chinned Woodcreeper

Northern South America to Brazil, northern Bolivia

28 02 006 Dendrocincia homochroa
Ruddy Woodcreeper

Southern Mexico to northern Colombia and Venezuela

28 02 007 Deconychura longicauda
✝ *Long-tailed Woodcreeper*

Southeast Honduras to Bolivia, Amazonian Brazil (Matto Grosso)

28 02 008 Deconychura stictolaema
Spot-throated Woodcreeper

Tropical Venezuela to Ecuador, Peru, Amazonian Brazil

28 02 009 Sittasomus griseicapillus
✝ *Olivaceous Woodcreeper*

Tropical, subtropical Mexico to northern Argentina

28 02 010 Glyphorhynchus spirurus
✝ *Wedge-billed Woodcreeper*

Southern Mexico to northern Bolivia, eastern Brazil

28 02 011 Drymornis bridgesii
Scimitar-billed Woodcreeper

Uruguay, Paraguay to central Argentina

28 02 012 Nasica longirostris
Long-billed Woodcreeper

Tropical northern South America to Brazil, Bolivia

28 02 013 Dendrexetastes rufigula
Cinnamon-throated Woodcreeper

Northern South America to southwest Brazil, Bolivia

28 02 014 Hylexetastes perrotii
Red-billed Woodcreeper

Northeast South America to Amazonian Brazil

28 02 015 Hylexetastes stresemanni
Bar-bellied Woodcreeper

Forests of eastern Peru, western Brazil

28 02 016 Xiphocolaptes promeropirhynchus
✝ *Strong-billed Woodcreeper*

Highlands of Mexico to Bolivia, Amazonian Brazil

28 02 017 Xiphocolaptes albicollis
White-throated Woodcreeper

Eastern Brazil (Bahia) to northeast Argentina

		Date	Location
28 02 018	**Xiphocolaptes villanovae** *Vila Nova Woodcreeper*		Brazil (Bahia—probable race of *X. albicollis*)
28 02 019	**Xiphocolaptes falcirostris** *Moustached Woodcreeper*		Eastern Brazil (Maranhão to Bahia)
28 02 020	**Xiphocolaptes franciscanus** *Snethlage's Woodcreeper*		Eastern Brazil (known only from Minas Gerais)
28 02 021	**Xiphocolaptes major** *Great Rufous Woodcreeper*		Brazil (Matto Grosso) to northern Argentina
28 02 022	**Dendrocolaptes certhia** *Barred Woodcreeper*		Tropical southern Mexico to Bolivia, Amazonian Brazil
28 02 023	**Dendrocolaptes concolor** *Concolor Woodcreeper*		Central Brazil south of the Amazon
28 02 024	**Dendrocolaptes hoffmannsi** *Hoffman's Woodcreeper*		Central Brazil south of the Amazon
28 02 025 †	**Dendrocolaptes picumnus** *Black-banded Woodcreeper*		Highlands of southern Mexico (Chiapas) to northwest Argentina
28 02 026	**Dendrocolaptes platyrostris** *Planalto Woodcreeper*		Eastern Brazil (Piaui) to northern Argentina (Chaco)
28 02 027	**Xiphorhynchus picus** *Straight-billed Woodcreeper*		Central Panama to Amazonian Brazil, Bolivia
28 02 028	**Xiphorhynchus necopinus** *Zimmer's Woodcreeper*		Brazil (middle and lower Amazon River)
28 02 029	**Xiphorhynchus obsoletus** *Striped Woodcreeper*		Northern South America to Peru, Amazonian Brazil
28 02 030	**Xiphorhynchus ocellatus** *Ocellated Woodcreeper*		Northern South America to Bolivia, Amazonian Brazil
28 02 031	**Xiphorhynchus spixii** *Spix's Woodcreeper*		Northern South America to Bolivia, Amazonian Brazil
28 02 032	**Xiphorhynchus elegans** *Elegant Woodcreeper*		Eastern Peru, northern Bolivia, Amazonian Brazil
28 02 033	**Xiphorhynchus pardalotus** *Chestnut-rumped Woodcreeper*		Guianas, Venezuela, east Amazonian Brazil

		Date	Location

28 02 034 **Xiphorhynchus guttatus**
Buff-throated Woodcreeper — Humid Guatemala to northern Bolivia, southeast Brazil

28 02 035 **Xiphorhynchus eytoni**
Dusky-billed Woodcreeper — Amazonian Brazil (possible race of *X. guttatus*)

28 02 036 **Xiphorhynchus flavigaster**
Ivory-billed Woodcreeper — Tropical northern Mexico to northwest Costa Rica

28 02 037 **Xiphorhynchus striatigularis**
Stripe-throated Woodcreeper — Northeast Mexico (Tamaulipas—known from one specimen)

28 02 038 **Xiphorhynchus lachrymosus**
Black-striped Woodcreeper — Eastern Nicaragua to Colombia, northwest Ecuador

28 02 039 **Xiphorhynchus erythropygius**
Spotted Woodcreeper — Southern Mexico to Colombia, western Ecuador

28 02 040 **Xiphorhynchus triangularis**
Olive-backed Woodcreeper — Lower Andes of Venezuela to northern Bolivia

28 02 041 **Lepidocolaptes leucogaster**
White-striped Woodcreeper — Western and central Mexico

28 02 042 **Lepidocolaptes souleyetii**
Streak-headed Woodcreeper — Southern Mexico to northwest Peru, northern Brazil

28 02 043 **Lepidocolaptes anguistirostris**
Narrow-billed Woodcreeper — Eastern Brazil (Ceará) to northern Argentina, Bolivia

28 02 044 **Lepidocolaptes affinis**
†
Spot-crowned Woodcreeper — Highlands of eastern Mexico to Venezuela, Bolivia

28 02 045 **Lepidocolaptes squamatus**
Scaled Woodcreeper — Eastern Brazil (Piauí) to Argentina (Misiones)

28 02 046 **Lepidocolaptes fuscus**
Lesser Woodcreeper — Eastern Brazil (Ceará) to Argentina (Misiones)

28 02 047 **Lepidocolaptes albolineatus**
Lineated Woodcreeper — Northern South America to Bolivia, Amazonian Brazil

		Date	Location

28 02 048
+
Campylorhamphus pucherani
Greater Scythebill
Andes of Colombia, Ecuador, Peru

28 02 049
+
Campylorhamphus trochilirostris
Red-billed Scythebill
Eastern Panama to Argentina, Brazil (Paraná)

28 02 050
Campylorhamphus falcularius
Black-billed Scythebill
Southeast Brazil (Espirito Santo) to Argentina (Misiones)

28 02 051
Campylorhamphus pusillus
Brown-billed Scythebill
Highlands of Costa Rica to Guyana, northern Peru

28 02 052
Campylorhamphus procurvoides
Curve-billed Scythebill
Guianas, Venezuela, Colombia, Amazonian Brazil

FAMILY: FURNARIIDAE (Ovenbirds)

28 03 001
Geositta poeciloptera
Campo Miner
Campos of eastern Brazil

28 03 002
+
Geositta cunicularia
Common Miner
High plateau of southern Peru to Tierra del Fuego

28 03 003
Geositta maritima
Grayish Miner
Mainly arid littoral of Peru and Chile

28 03 004
Geositta peruviana
Coastal Miner
Arid coastal Peru (Tumbes to Ica)

28 03 005
Geositta punensis
Puna Miner
Andes of southern Peru to Argentina, Chile (Atacama)

28 03 006
Geositta saxicolina
Dark-winged Miner
Andes of Peru (Lima, Junin to Huancavelica)

28 03 007
Geositta isabellina
Creamy-rumped Miner
Mountains of Chile (Atacama to Talca), adjacent Argentina

28 03 008
Geositta antarctica
Short-billed Miner
Southern Chile, Argentina (wanders to Mendoza)

28 03 009
Geositta rufipennis
Rufous-banded Miner
Andes of Bolivia, Argentina and Chile

28 03 010
Geositta crassirostris
Thick-billed Miner
Western slope of Peruvian Andes (Lima, Ayacucho)

28 03 011
Geositta excelsior
Stout-billed Miner
Páramo of Colombia, Ecuador and Peru

		Date	Location
28 03 012	**Geositta tenuirostris** *Slender-billed Miner*		Andes of Peru to northwest Argentina (Catamarca)
28 03 013	**Upucerthia certhioides** *Chaco Earthcreeper*		Chaco of Paraguay, Argentina (Jujuy to Mendoza)
28 03 014	**Upucerthia ruficauda** *Straight-billed Earthcreeper*		Andes of southwest Peru, Bolivia, Argentina, Chile
28 03 015	**Upucerthia andaecola** *Rock Earthcreeper*		Andes of Bolivia, northwest Argentina, adjacent Chile
28 03 016	**Upucerthia albigula** *White-throated Earthcreeper*		Arid Andes of southwest Peru, northern Chile
28 03 017	**Upucerthia serrana** *Striated Earthcreeper*		Temperate western Andes of Peru
28 03 018	**Upucerthia dumetaria** *Scale-throated Earthcreeper*		Semiarid southern Peru to Tierra del Fuego
28 03 019	**Upucerthia validirostris** *Buff-breasted Earthcreeper*		Andes of western Argentina (Salta to Mendoza)
28 03 020	**Upucerthia jelskii** *Plain-breasted Earthcreeper*		Andes of Peru (Ancash) to northern Chile
28 03 021 +	**Cinclodes fuscus** *Bar-winged Cinclodes*		Andes of Venezuela, Colombia to Tierra del Fuego
? 28 03 022	**Cinclodes comechingonus** *Comechingones Cinclodes*		Argentina (Comechingonus—possible race *C. fuscus*)
28 03 023	**Cinclodes pabsti** *Long-tailed Cinclodes*		Plateau region of southeast Brazil (Rio Grande do Sul)
28 03 024	**Cinclodes atacamensis** *White-winged Cinclodes*		Andes of Peru to Chile, Argentina (Cordoba)
28 03 025	**Cinclodes palliatus** *White-bellied Cinclodes*		Andes of Peru (San Martin, Junin, Lima, Huancavelica)
28 03 026	**Cinclodes outstaleti** *Gray-flanked Cinclodes*		Southern Chile, Argentina (Mendoza to Cape Horn)
28 03 027 +	**Cinclodes patagonicus** *Dark-bellied Cinclodes*		Southern Chile, Argentina (Mendoza to Tierra del Fuego)
28 03 028	**Cinclodes nigrofumosus** *Seaside Cinclodes*		Rocky coast of Peru (Lima) to Chile (Valdivia)

		Date	Location

28 03 029 Cinclodes taczanowskii
Surf Cinclodes — Rocky coasts of Peru (possible race *C. nigrofumosus*)

28 03 030 Cinclodes antarcticus
Blackish Cinclodes — Tierra del Fuego; Staten, Falkland Islands

28 03 031 Chilia melanura
Crag Chilia — Mountains of Chile (Aconcagua to Colchagua)

28 03 032 Furnarius minor
Lesser Hornero — Amazonian Brazil, adjacent Colombia, Peru

28 03 033 Furnarius figulus
Wing-banded Hornero — Open scrub of Amazonian Brazil

28 03 034 Furnarius tricolor
Tricolored Hornero — Western Amazonian Brazil, adjacent Peru and Bolivia

28 03 035 Furnarius leucopus
Pale-legged Hornero — Northern South America to Brazil, northern Bolivia

28 03 036 Furnarius torridus
Pale-billed Hornero — Northeast Amazonian Peru, adjacent Brazil

28 03 037 Furnarius rufus
Rufous Hornero — Eastern Brazil (Goiás) to central Argentina

28 03 038 Furnarius cristatus
Crested Hornero — Paraguayan chaco; western Argentina

28 03 039 Sylviothorhynchus desmursii
Des Murs' Wiretail — Argentina (Nequen to Santa Cruz); adjacent Chile

28 03 040 Aphrastura spinicauda
Thorn-tailed Rayadito — Argentina (Nequen to Tierra del Fuego, adjacent Chile)

28 03 041 Aphrastura masafuerae
Mas Afuera Rayadito — Mas Afuera Island (off Chile—endangered)

28 03 042 Leptasthenura fuliginiceps
Brown-capped Tit-Spinetail — Andes of Bolivia to Argentina (Cordoba)

28 03 043 Leptasthenura yanacensis
Tawny Tit-Spinetail — Andes of Peru (Ancash) to Bolivia

28 03 044 Leptasthenura platensis
Tufted Tit-Spinetail — Extreme southeast Brazil to Argentina (Chubut)

28 03 045 Leptasthenura aegithaloides
Plain-mantled Tit-Spinetail — Arid southern Peru to central Argentina, Chile

28 03 046 Leptasthenura setaria
Araucaria Tit-Spinetail — Southeast Brazil (Paraná) to northeast Argentina)

28 03 047 Leptasthenura striata
Streaked Tit-Spinetail — Arid southwest Peru, northern Chile

		Date	Location
28 03 048	**Leptasthenura striolata** *Striolated Tit-Spinetail*		Southeast Brazil (Paraná, Rio Grande do Sul)
28 03 049	**Leptasthenura pileata** *Rusty-crowned Tit-Spinetail*		Andes of Peru (Cajamarca to Huancavelica)
28 03 050 +	**Leptasthenura xenothorax** *White-browed Tit-Spinetail*		Peru (unique—probable race of *L. pileata*)
38 03 051 +	**Leptasthenura andicola** *Andean Tit-Spinetail*		Andes of Venezuela, Colombia to northeast Bolivia
28 03 052 +	**Schizoeaca fuliginosa** *White-chinned Thistletail*		Highlands of Venezuela, Colombia to Peru
28 03 053	**Schizoeaca moreirae** *Itatiaia Spinetail*		Southeast Brazil (Minas Gerais, Espirito Santo)
28 03 054	**Synallaxis phryganophila** *Chotoy Spinetail*		Southeast Brazil (Bahia) to Bolivia, Argentina
28 03 055	**Synallaxis ruficapilla** *Rufous-capped Spinetail*		Eastern Brazil (Pernambuco to northeast Argentina)
28 03 056	**Synallaxis superciliosa** *Buff-browed Spinetail*		Subtropical eastern Bolivia to northwest Argentina
28 03 057	**Synallaxis poliophrys** *Gray-browed Spinetail*		Known only from French Guiana
28 03 058	**Synallaxis frontalis** *Sooty-fronted Spinetail*		Eastern Brazil to Bolivia, Argentina (Buenos Aires)
28 03 059 +	**Synallaxis azarae** *Azara's Spinetail*		Andes of northwest Venezuela to Bolivia
28 03 060	**Synallaxis elegantior** *Elegant Spinetail*		Subtropical eastern Andes of Colombia and western Venezuela
28 03 061	**Synallaxis albigularis** *Dark-breasted Spinetail*		Tropical eastern Colombia, Peru, western Brazil
28 03 062	**Synallaxis albescens** *Pale-breasted Spinetail*		Costa Rica to central Argentina (east of Andes)
28 03 063	**Synallaxis spixi** *Chicli Spinetail*		Brazil (Minas Gerais) to Argentina (Buenos Aires)
28 03 064	**Synallaxis hypospodia** *Cinereous-breasted Spinetail*		Brazil (Ceará) to eastern Bolivia and Peru
28 03 065	**Synallaxis infuscata** *Pernambuco Spinetail*		Southeast Brazil to northeast Argentina (Misiones)
28 03 066 +	**Synallaxis brachyura** *Slaty Spinetail*		Honduras to western Ecuador, eastern Brazil (Goiás)

		Date	Location
28 03 067	**Synallaxis courseni** *Apurimac Spinetail*		Andes of south-central Peru (Ahancay)
28 03 068	**Synallaxis moesta** *Dusky Spinetail*		Eastern Colombia, Ecuador to northeast Peru
28 03 069 +	**Synallaxis cabanisi** *Cabanis' Spinetail*		Tropical Surinam to northern Bolivia
28 03 070	**Synallaxis macconnelli** *McConnell's Spinetail*		Venezuela (Bolivar—possible race *S. cabanisi*)
28 03 071	**Synallaxis subpudica** *Silvery-throated Spinetail*		Subtropical, temperate eastern Andes of Colombia
28 03 072	**Synallaxis tithys** *Blackish-headed Spinetail*		Arid tropical southwest Ecuador, northwest Peru
28 03 073	**Synallaxis cinerascens** *Gray-bellied Spinetail*		Southeast Brazil to northeast Argentina, Paraguay
28 03 074	**Synallaxis maranonica** *Marañon Spinetail*		Peru (upper Marañon drainage—possible race *S. gujanensis*)
28 03 075	**Synallaxis propinqua** *White-bellied Spinetail*		French Guiana, Amazonian Brazil to Peru, Bolivia
28 03 076	**Synallaxis hellmayri** *Red-shouldered Spinetail*		Eastern Brazil (Piaui and Bahia)
28 03 077	**Synallaxis gujanensis** *Plain-crowned Spinetail*		Widespread tropical Amazon basin
28 03 078	**Synallaxis albilora** *Ochre-breasted Spinetail*		Matto Grosso, adjacent Paraguay (possible race *S. gujanensis*)
28 03 079 +	**Synallaxis rutilans** *Ruddy Spinetail*		Guianas, Venezuela to northern Bolivia, Brazil
28 03 080	**Synallaxis cherriei** *Chestnut-throated Spinetail*		Tropical eastern Ecuador, Peru, Brazil (Matto Grosso)
28 03 081 +	**Synallaxis unirufa** *Rufous Spinetail*		Andes of northwest Venezuela to Peru (Junin)
28 03 082	**Synallaxis castanea** *Chestnut Spinetail*		Coastal mountains of Venezuela (Aragua, Miranda, Distrito Federal)
28 03 083	**Synallaxis fuscorufa** *Rusty-headed Spinetail*		Santa Marta Mountains of Colombia
28 03 084	**Synallaxis zimmeri** *Russet-bellied Spinetail*		Temperate Andes of Peru (Ancash)
28 03 085	**Synallaxis erythrothorax** *Rufous-breasted Spinetail*		Gulf lowlands of Mexico to Honduras
28 03 086	**Synallaxis cinnamomea** *Stripe-breasted Spinetail*		Highlands of Venezuela, Colombia; Trinidad; Tobago

	Date	Location
28 03 087 **Synallaxis stictothorax** *Necklaced Spinetail*		Arid tropical southwest Ecuador, western Peru
28 03 088 **Synallaxis candei** *White-whiskered Spinetail*		Northwest Venezuela to central Colombia
28 03 089 **Synallaxis kollari** *Hoary-throated Spinetail*		Campos of northern Brazil (Roraima)
28 03 090 **Synallaxis scutata** *Ochre-cheeked Spinetail*		Cerrado of eastern Brazil to Argentina (Catamarca)
28 03 091 **Synallaxis gularis** *White-browed Spinetail*		Andes of Venezuela, Colombia to Peru (Junin)
28 03 092 **Certhiaxis erythrops** *Red-faced Spinetail*		Humid mountain forests of Costa Rica to Ecuador
28 03 093 **Certhiaxis demissa** *Tepui Spinetail*		Mountains of Venezuela, Guyana, adjacent Brazil
28 03 094 **Certhiaxis antisiensis** *Line-cheeked Spinetail*		Andes of western Ecuador to Peru (Lima)
28 03 095 **Certhiaxis pallida** *Pallid Spinetail*		Southeast Brazil (Minas Gerais to São Paulo)
28 03 096 **Certhiaxis curtata (furcata)** *Ash-browed Spinetail*		Andes of Colombia to Peru (Cuzco)
28 03 097 **Certhiaxis obsoleta** *Olive Spinetail*		Southeast Brazil (São Paulo) to northeast Argentina
28 03 098 **Certhiaxis hellmayri** *Streak-capped Spinetail*		Bromelias of Santa Marta Mountains of Colombia
28 03 099 **Certhiaxis subscristata** *Crested Spinetail*		Venezuela north of the Orinoco, adjacent Colombia
28 03 100 **Certhiaxis pyrrhophia** *Stripe-crowned Spinetail*		Paraguay, adjacent Bolivia, Brazil, Uruguay, Argentina
28 03 101 **Certhiaxis marcapatae** *Marcapata Spinetail*		Andes of Peru (Marcapata, Cuzco)
28 03 102 **Certhiaxis albiceps** *Light-crowned Spinetail*		Andes of southern Peru, Bolivia (La Paz, Cochabamba)
28 03 103 **Certhiaxis semicinerea** *Gray-headed Spinetail*		Eastern Brazil (Ceará, Bahia, southeast Goiás)
28 03 104 **Certhiaxis albicapilla** *Creamy-chested Spinetail*		Temperate Andes of Peru (Junin to Cuzco)
28 03 105 **Certhiaxis vulpina** *Rusty-backed Spinetail*		Tropical Panama to Brazil, eastern Peru and Bolivia
28 03 106 **Certhiaxis muelleri** *Scaled Spinetail*		Brazil (lower Amazon river)

		Date	Location
28 03 107	**Certhiaxis gutturata** *Speckled Spinetail*		Tropical South America to Brazil, northern Bolivia
28 03 108	**Certhiaxis sulphurifera** *Sulphur-bearded Spinetail*		Extreme southeast Brazil to Argentina (Rio Negro)
28 03 109	**Certhiaxis cinnamomea** *Yellow-throated Spinetail*		Widespread tropical South America to northern Argentina
28 03 110	**Certhiaxis mustelina** *Red-and-white Spinetail*		Amazonian Brazil, northeast Peru
28 03 111 +	**Thripophaga pyrrholeuca** *Lesser Canastero*		Argentina (Rio Negro); winters to southern Bolivia
28 03 112	**Thripophaga baeri** *Short-billed Canastero*		Extreme southeast Brazil to Argentina (Rio Negro)
28 03 113	**Thripophaga pudibunda** *Canyon Canastero*		Andes of western Peru and Bolivia
28 03 114	**Thripophaga ottonis** *Rusty-fronted Canastero*		Temperate Andes of southeast Peru
28 03 115	**Thripophaga heterura** *Iquico Canastero*		Bolivia (probable race *A. pudibunda*)
28 03 116	**Thripophaga modesta** *Cordilleran Canastero*		Semiarid Andes of Peru to central Argentina and Chile
28 03 117 +	**Thripophaga dorbignyi** *Creamy-breasted Canastero*		Arid Andes of Peru to Argentina and Chile
28 03 118	**Thripophaga berlepschi** *Berlepsch's Canastero*		Andes of Bolivia (La Paz, Illampu)
28 03 119	**Thripophaga steinbachi** *Chestnut Canastero*		Andes of western Argentina (possible race of *A. dorbignyi*)
28 03 120	**Thripophaga humicola** *Dusky-tailed Canastero*		Semiarid Argentina (Mendoza) and adjacent Chile
28 03 121 +	**Thripophaga patagonica** *Patagonian Canastero*		Semiarid southern Argentina (Mendoza to Chubut)
28 03 122	**Thripophaga humilis** *Streak-throated Canastero*		Arid temperate Andes of Peru to Bolivia (La Paz)
28 03 123	**Thripophaga cactorum** *Cactus Canastero*		Arid Pacific slope and western Andes of Peru
28 03 124	**Thripophaga anthoides** *Austral Canastero*		Andes of Peru to Tierra del Fuego; Staten Island
28 03 125	**Thripophaga wyatti** *Streak-backed Canastero*		Andes of western Venezuela to Peru

		Date	Location

28 03 126	**Thripophaga punensis** *Puno Canastero*	Andes of southern Peru, adjacent Bolivia
28 03 127	**Thripophaga sclateri** *Cordoba Canastero*	Argentina (mountains of Cordoba—endangered)
28 03 128	**Thripophaga urubambensis** *Line-fronted Canastero*	Humid temperate Andes of Peru and Bolivia
28 03 129	**Thripophaga virgata** *Junin Canastero*	Andes of Peru (Lima, Junin, Cuzco)
28 03 130	**Thripophaga maculicauda** *Scribble-tailed Canastero*	Andes of southern Peru, Bolivia and northwest Argentina
28 03 131	**Thripophaga flammulata** *Many-striped Canastero*	Andes of Colombia, Ecuador and Peru
28 03 132	**Thripophaga cherriei** *Orinoco Softtail*	Venezuela (upper Orinoco—known from two specimens)
28 03 133	**Thripophaga macroura** *Striated Softtail*	Southeast Brazil (Bahia and Espirito Santo)
28 03 134 +	**Thripophaga hudsoni** *Hudson's Canastero*	Uruguay, Argentina (Buenos Aires to Chubut)
28 03 135	**Thripophaga hypochondriacus** *Great Spinetail*	Upper arid Marañon Valley of northern Peru
28 03 136	**Phacellodomus rufifrons** *Rufous-fronted Thornbird*	Widespread campos of tropical South America
28 03 137	**Phacellodomus sibilatrix** *Little Thornbird*	Central Paraguay to Argentina (Cordoba, Buenos Aires)
28 03 138	**Phacellodomus striaticeps** *Streak-fronted Thornbird*	Highlands of southeast Peru to northwest Argentina
28 03 139	**Phacellodomus erythrophthalmus** *Red-eyed Thornbird*	Coastal Brazil (Bahia to Rio Grande do Sul)
28 03 142 +	**Phacellodomus striaticollis** *Freckle-breasted Thornbird*	Southeast Brazil (Paraná) to Bolivia, Argentina
28 03 143	**Phacellodomus dorsalis** *Chestnut-backed Thornbird*	Arid northern Peru (Cajamarca)
28 03 144	**Phacellodomus ruber** *Greater Thornbird*	Southeast Brazil (Bahia) to Bolivia, Argentina

		Date	Location

28 03 145	**Phacellodomus fusciceps** *Plain Softtail*	Tropical western Amazon basin
28 03 144	**Phacellodomus berlepschi** *Russet-mantled Softtail*	Eastern Andes of Peru (Amazonas)
28 03 145	**Phacellodomus dendrocolaptoides** *Canebrake Groundcreeper*	Southeast Brazil (Paraná) to northeast Argentina (Misiones)
28 03 146	**Spartonoica maluroides** *Bay-capped Wren-Spinetail*	Extreme southeast Brazil to Argentina (Rio Negro)
28 03 147 +	**Phleocryptes melanops** *Wren-like Rushbird*	Cattail marshes of Peru, Brazil to Tierra del Fuego
28 03 148 + (nest)	**Limnornis curvirostris** *Curve-billed Reedhaunter*	Southeast Brazil, Uruguay to northeast Argentina
28 03 149	**Limnornis rectirostris** *Straight-billed Reedhaunter*	Extreme southeast Brazil to Argentina (Entre Rios)
28 03 150	**Anumbius annumbi** *Firewood-gatherer*	Eastern Brazil (Goiás) to Argentina (Chubut)
28 03 151	**Coryphistera alaudina** *Lark-like Bushrunner*	Paraguay, adjacent Brazil, Bolivia, Argentina
28 03 152 +	**Eremobius phoenicurus** *Band-tailed Earthcreeper*	Argentina (Nequén to Santa Cruz)
28 03 153	**Siptornis striaticollis** *Spectacled Prickletail*	Andes of Colombia and Ecuador
28 03 154	**Metopothrix aurantiacus** *Orange-fronted Plushcrown*	Tropical western Amazon basin (Colombia to Bolivia)
28 03 155	**Xenerpestes singularis** *Equatorial Graytail*	Andes of eastern Ecuador (known from one specimen)
28 03 156	**Xenerpestes minlosi** *Double-banded Graytail*	Tropical eastern Panama, Colombia
28 03 157	**Margarornis adustus** *Roraiman Barbtail*	Guyana, southern Venezuela, adjacent Brazil
28 03 158	**Margarornis guttuligera** *Rusty-winged Barbtail*	Andes of extreme northwest Venezuela to Peru
28 03 159	**Margarornis brunnescens** *Spotted Barbtail*	Highlands of Costa Rica to Bolivia (Cochabamba)

	Date	Location

28 03 160 Margarornis tatei
White-throated Barbtail   Coastal mountains of Venezuela

28 03 161 Margarornis rubiginosus
Ruddy Treerunner   Mountains of Costa Rica and western Panama

28 03 162 Margarornis stellatus
Fulvous-dotted Treerunner   Western Andes of Colombia, northwest Ecuador

28 03 163 Margarornis bellulus
Beautiful Treerunner   Mountains of eastern Panama (Darien)

28 03 164 Margarornis squamiger
Pearled Treerunner   Highlands of northwest Venezuela to Colombia

28 03 165 Lochmias nematura
+   *Sharp-tailed Streamcreeper*   Spottily distributed Panama to northeast Argentina

28 03 166 Pseudoseisura cristata
Rufous-breasted Cacholote   *Cerrado* of eastern Brazil to Bolivia, Paraguay

28 03 167 Pseudoseisura lophotes
Brown Cacholote   Extreme southeast Brazil to Bolivia, Argentina

28 03 168 Pseudoseisura gutturalis
+ (and not)   *White-throated Cacholote*   Widespread arid stony country of Argentina

28 03 169 Pseudocolaptes lawrencii
Buffy Tuftedcheek   Mountains of Costa Rica to western Colombia, Ecuador

28 03 170 Pseudocolaptes boissonneautii
+   *Streaked Tuftedcheek*   Andes of northwest Venezuela to Bolivia

28 03 171 Berlepschia rikeri
Point-tailed Palmcreeper   *Mauritia* palms of Guyana, Amazonian Brazil, Venezuela

28 03 172 Phylidor strigilatus
Chestnut-winged Hookbill   Tropical western Amazon basin

28 03 173 Philydor subulatus
+   *Striped Woodhaunter*   Tropical Nicaragua to Peru, west Amazonian Brazil

28 03 174 Philydor guttulatus
Guttulated Foliage-gleaner   Mountains of Venezuela

28 03 175 Philydor subalaris
Lineated Foliage-gleaner   Mountains of Costa Rica to southeast Peru

28 03 176 Philydor rufosuperciliatus
+   *Buff-browed Foliage-gleaner*   Andes of Peru to northeast Argentina, southeast Brazil

		Date	Location
28 03 177 +	**Philydor striaticollis** *Montane Foliage-gleaner*		Andes of Venezuela, Colombia to northern Bolivia
28 03 178	**Philydor amaurotis** *White-browed Foliage-gleaner*		Southeast Brazil (Rio de Janeiro) to northeast Argentina
28 03 179	**Philydor variegaticeps** *Scaly-throated Foliage-gleaner*		Mountains of southern Mexico to Colombia, Ecuador
28 03 180	**Philydor ruficaudatus** *Rufous-tailed Foliage-gleaner*		Widespread tropical forests of Amazon basin
28 03 181	**Philydor erythrocercus** *Rufous-rumped Foliage-gleaner*		Tropical western Panama to Bolivia, Amazonian Brazil
28 03 182	**Philydor erythropterus** *Chestnut-winged Foliage-gleaner*		Widespread tropical forests of Amazon basin
28 03 183	**Philydor lichtensteini** *Ochre-breasted Foliage-gleaner*		Eastern Brazil (Goiás) to northeast Argentina
28 03 184	**Philydor erythronotus** *Santander Foliage-gleaner*		Colombia (probable race *P. erythrocercus*)
28 03 185	**Philydor atricapillus** *Black-capped Foliage-gleaner*		Eastern Brazil (Bahia) to northeast Argentina (Misiones)
28 03 186	**Philydor rufus** *Buff-fronted Foliage-gleaner*		Mountains of Costa Rica to northeast Argentina
28 03 187	**Philydor pyrrhodes** *Cinnamon-rumped Foliage-gleaner*		Widespread tropical northern South America
28 03 188	**Philydor dimidiatus** *Russet-mantled Foliage-gleaner*		Brazil (Goiás, Minas Gerais) to Paraguay
28 03 189	**Philydor fuscus** *White-collared Foliage-gleaner*		Southeast Brazil (Minas Gerais to Santa Catarina)
28 03 190 +	**Philydor ucayalae** *Peruvian Recurvebill*		Eastern Peru (Madre de Dios, Ucayali Rivers)
28 03 191	**Philydor striatus** *Bolivian Recurvebill*		Tropical northern Bolivia (La Paz and Cochabamba)

	Date	Location

28 03 192 Philydor leucophrys
Pale-browed Treehunter — Coastal Brazil (Bahia to Santa Catarina)

28 03 193 Thripadectes ignobilis
Uniform Treehunter — Western Andes of Colombia, western Ecuador

28 03 194 Thripadectes rufobrunneus
Streak-breasted Treehunter — Highlands of Costa Rica and western Panama

28 03 195 Thripadectes melanorhynchus
Black-billed Treehunter — Eastern Andes of Colombia to Peru

28 03 196 Thripadectes holostictus
+ *Striped Treehunter* — Andes of Venezuela to northern Bolivia

28 03 197 Thripadectes virgaticeps
Streak-capped Treehunter — Humid Andean forests of Venezuela to Ecuador

28 03 198 Thripadectes scrutator
Buff-throated Treehunter — Temperate Andes of southeast Peru (Cuzco, Junin)

28 03 199 Thripadectes flammulatus
Flammulated Treehunter — Andes of Venezuela to western Ecuador

28 03 200 Automolus ruficollis
Rufous-necked Foliage-gleaner — Humid forests of southwest Ecuador, northern Peru

28 03 201 Automolus ochrolaemus
+ *Buff-throated Foliage-gleaner* — Southern Mexico to northern Bolivia, Amazonian Brazil

28 03 202 Automolus infuscatus
Olive-backed Foliage-gleaner — Widespread tropical forests of Amazon basin

28 03 203 Automolus dorsalis
+ *Crested Foliage-gleaner* — Tropical southeast Colombia to Peru (Puno)

28 03 204 Automolus leucophthalmus
White-eyed Foliage-gleaner — Brazil (Paraiba) to northeast Argentina (Misiones)

28 03 205 Automolus melanopezus
+ *Brown-rumped Foliage-gleaner* — Tropical forests of western Amazon basin

28 03 206 Automolus albigularis (roraimae)
White-throated Foliage-gleaner — Mountains of southern Venezuela, adjacent Brazil

28 03 207 Automolus rubiginosus
+ *Ruddy Foliage-gleaner* — Highlands of southern Mexico to Bolivia

		Date	Location
28 03 208	**Automolus rufipileatus** *Chestnut-crowned Foliage-gleaner*		Northern South America to Brazil, northern Bolivia
28 03 209	**Automolus rectirostris** *Chestnut-capped Foliage-gleaner*		Brazil (Bahia to Paraná, Matto Grosso)
28 03 210	**Automolus erythrocephalus** *Henna-hooded Foliage-gleaner*		Tropical forests of southwest Ecuador, northwest Peru
28 03 211	**Sclerurus mexicanus** *Tawny-throated Leafscraper*		Southern Mexico to northern Bolivia, southern Brazil
28 03 212	**Sclerurus rufigularis** *Short-billed Leafscraper*		Guianas to Colombia, Bolivia, Amazonian Brazil
28 03 213	**Sclerurus albigularis** *Gray-throated Leafscraper*		Humid forests of Costa Rica to Bolivia; Trinidad
28 03 214	**Sclerurus caudacutus** *Black-tailed Leafscraper*		Guianas to Colombia, Bolivia, southern Brazil
28 03 215	**Sclerurus scansor** *Rufous-breasted Leafscraper*		Brazil (Ceará) to northeast Argentina (Misiones)
28 03 216	**Sclerurus guatemalensis** *Scaly-throated Leafscraper*		Tropical Mexico to Pacific Colombia, Ecuador
28 03 217	**Xenops contaminatus** *Sharp-billed Treehunter*		Brazil (Espirito Santo) to northeast Argentina (Misiones)
28 03 218	**Xenops milleri** *Rufous-tailed Xenops*		Widespread tropical forests of Amazon basin
28 03 219	**Xenops tenuirostris** *Slender-billed Xenops*		Widespread swampy forests of Amazon basin
28 03 220	**Xenops minutus** *Plain Xenops*		Southern Mexico to northeast Argentina, Brazil
28 03 221	**Xenops rutilans** *Streaked Xenops*		Highlands of Costa Rica to Argentina; Trinidad
28 03 222	**Megaxenops parnaguae** *Great Xenops*		Eastern Brazil (Ceará, Piaui, Bahia)
28 03 223	**Pygarrhichas albogularis** *White-throated Treehunter*		Argentina (Nequen to Tierra del Fuego); Chile

		Date	Location

FAMILY: FORMICARIIDAE (Antbirds)

28 04 001 **Cymbilaimus lineatus**
✝   *Fasciated Antshrike*   Nicaragua to Bolivia, Brazil (east of Andes)

28 04 002 **Hypoedaleus guttatus**
         Spot-backed Antshrike   Eastern Brazil (Goiás, Bahia) to Argentina
                                        (Misiones)

28 04 003 **Batara cinerea**
         Giant Antshrike   Coastal southeast Brazil to northern Argentina

28 04 004 **Mackenziaena severa**
         Tufted Antshrike   Southeast Brazil (Minas Gerais) to northeast
                                        Argentina

28 04 005 **Mackenziaena leachii**
         Large-tailed Anshrike   Southeast Brazil (Minas Gerais) to northeast
                                        Argentina

28 04 006 **Frederickena viridis**
         Black-throated Antshrike   Tropical Guianas, Venezuela, northern Brazil

28 04 007 **Frederickena unduligera**
         Undulated Antshrike   Topical forests of western Amazon basin

28 04 008 **Taraba major**
         Great Antshrike   Tropical southern Mexico to northern Argentina

28 04 009 **Sakesphorus
         canadensis**
         Black-crested Antshrike   Widespread tropical Amazon basin

28 04 010 **Sakesphorus cristatus**
         Silvery-cheeked Antshrike   Campos of eastern Brazil (Piaui, Ceará, Bahia)

28 04 011 **Sakesphorus bernardi**
✝   *Collared Antshrike*   Arid tropical western Ecuador to northern Peru

28 04 012 **Sakesphorus
         melanonotus**
         Black-backed Antshrike   Semiarid northwest Venezuela to northeast Colombia

28 04 013 **Sakesphorus
         melanothorax**
         Band-tailed Antshrike   Surinam, French Guiana, adjacent Brazil (Rio
                                        Tapajos)

28 04 014 **Sakesphorus luctuosus**
         Glossy Antshrike   Riparian thickets of Amazonian Brazil

28 04 015 **Biatas nigropectus**
         White-bearded Antshrike   Southeast Brazil to northeast Argentina (Misiones)

28 04 016 **Thamnophilus doliatus**
         Barred Antshrike   Tropical Mexico to northern Argentina, Brazil

28 04 017 **Thamnophilus
         multistriatus**
         Bar-crested Antshrike   Upper tropical and subtropical Colombia

		Date	Location
28 04 018	**Thamnophilus palliatus** *Lined Antshrike*		Widespread forests and thickets of Amazon basin
28 04 019	**Thamnophilus bridgesi** *Black-hooded Antshrike*		Costa Rica and Pacific western Panama
28 04 020	**Thamnophilus nigriceps** *Black Antshrike*		Eastern Panama, Caribbean lowlands of Colombia
28 04 021	**Thammophilus praecox** *Cocha Antshrike*		Eastern Ecuador (upper Rio Napo)
28 04 022	**Thamnophilus nigrocinereus** *Blackish-gray Antshrike*		Widespread forests of western Amazon basin
28 04 023	**Thamnophilus cryptoleucus** *Castlenau's Antshrike*		Western Amazon basin (possible race *T. nigrocinereus*)
28 04 024	**Thamnophilus aethiops** *White-shouldered Antshrike*		Widespread tropical forests of Amazon basin
28 04 025	**Thamnophilus unicolor** *Uniform Antshrike*		Andes of Colombia to northeast Peru
28 04 026	**Thamnophilus schistaceus** *Black-capped Antshrike*		Eastern Columbia to northern Bolivia, adjacent Brazil
28 04 027	**Thamnophilus murinus** *Mouse-colored Antshrike*		Forest undergrowth, savanna of Amazon basin
28 04 028	**Thamnophilus aroyae** *Upland Antshrike*		Upper tropical southeast Peru, northwest Bolivia
28 04 029	**Thamnophilus punctatus** *Slaty Antshrike*		Guatemala to Bolivia, Brazil (east of Andes)
28 04 030	**Thamnophilus amazonicus** *Amazonian Antshrike*		Guianas to Venezuela, Bolivia, Amazonian Brazil
28 04 031	**Thamnophilus insignis** *Streak-backed Antshrike*		Mountain forests of southern Venezuela
28 04 032	**Thamnophilus caerulescens** *Variable Antshrike*		Eastern Peru, Brazil to northern Argentina
28 04 033	**Thamnophilus ruficapillus** *Rufous-capped Antshrike*		Subtropical Peru, Brazil to northern Argentina
28 04 034	**Thamnophilus torquatus** *Rufous-winged Antshrike*		Eastern Brazil (Pará to Minas Gerais, Matto Grosso)
28 04 035	**Pygiptila stellaris** *Spot-winged Antshrike*		Widespread forest treetops of Amazon basin

	Date	Location

28 04 036 **Megastictus**
margaritatus
Pearly Antshrike   Forests of tropical western Amazon basin

28 04 037 **Neoctantes niger**
Black Bushbird   Tropical western Amazon basin

28 04 038 **Clytoctantes alixi**
Recurve-billed Bushbird   Tropical northwest Venezuela to Colombia (Cauca)

28 04 039 **Xenornis setifrons**
Speckle-breasted   Eastern Panama, western Colombia (Chocó)
Antshrike

28 04 040 **Thamnistes anabatinus**
Russet Antshrike   Humid forests of southeast Mexico to Bolivia

28 04 041 **Dysithamnus**
stictothorax
Spot-breasted Antvireo   Eastern Brazil (Bahia to Santa Catarina)

28 04 042 **Dysithamnus mentalis**
+   *Plain Antvireo*   Southern Mexico to northeast Argentina, Brazil

28 04 043 **Dysithamnus striaticeps**
Streak-crowned Antvireo   Nicaragua to Caribbean Costa Rica (adjacent
Panama?)

28 04 044 **Dysithamnus puncticeps**
Spot-crowned Antvireo   Tropical eastern Panama to Pacific Colombia,
Ecuador

28 04 045 **Dysithamnus**
xanthopterus
Rufous-backed Antvireo   Southeast Brazil (Espirito Santo to Paraná)

28 04 046 **Thamnomanes**
ardesiacus
Dusky-throated Antshrike   Widespread tropical forests Amazon basin

28 04 047 **Thamnomanes**
saturninus
Saturnine Antshrike   Tropical western Amazonian Brazil, northeast Peru

28 04 048 **Thamnomanes**
occidentalis
Western Antshrike   Andes of Colombia (Cauca), eastern Ecuador

28 04 049 **Thamnomanes**
plumbeus
Plumbeous Antshrike   Subtropical forests of Amazon basin

28 04 050 **Thamnomanes caesius**
Cinereous Antshrike   Tropical South America to southern Brazil, Peru

28 04 051 **Thamnomanes**
+   **schistogynus**
Bluish-slate Antshrike   Eastern Peru to northern Bolivia, southwest Brazil

28 04 052 **Myrmotherula brachyura**
+   *Pygmy Antwren*   Tropical eastern Panama to Amazonian Brazil, Bolivia

		Date	Location
28 04 053	**Myrmotherula obscura** *Short-billed Antwren*		Tropical Colombia to Peru, west Amazonian Brazil
28 04 054	**Myrmotherula sclateri** *Sclater's Antwren*		Southeast Peru (Balta), adjacent Amazonian Brazil
28 04 055	**Myrmotherula klagesi** *Klages' Antwren*		Lower Amazonian Brazil (Rio Tapajos)
28 04 056	**Myrmotherula surinamensis** *Streaked Antwren*		Panama to Guianas, eastern Peru, Amazonian Brazil
28 04 057	**Myrmotherula ambigua** *Yellow-throated Antwren*		Southeast Colombia, adjacent Venezuela and Brazil
28 04 058	**Myrmotherula cherriei** *Cherrie's Antwren*		Southern Venezuela, adjacent Brazil and Colombia
28 04 059	**Myrmotherula guttata** *Rufous-bellied Antwren*		Savanna of Guianas, Venezuela, northern Brazil
28 04 060	**Myrmotherula longicauda** *Stripe-chested Antwren*		Colombia to northern Bolivia (east of Andes)
28 04 061	**Myrmotherula hauxwelli** *Plain-throated Antwren*		Eastern Colombia to northern Bolivia, Amazonian Brazil
28 04 062	**Myrmotherula gularis** *Star-throated Antwren*		Southeast Brazil (Minas Gerias to Rio Grande do Sul)
28 04 063	**Myrmotherula gutturalis** *Brown-bellied Antwren*		Guianas, Venezuela, northeast Brazil north of Amazon
28 04 064	**Myrmotherula fulviventris** *Fulvous-bellied Antwren*		Tropical forests of Honduras to western Ecuador
28 04 065	**Myrmotherula leucophthalma** *White-eyed Antwren*		Tropical Amazonian Brazil, adjacent Ecuador to Bolivia
28 04 066	**Myrmotherula haematonota** *Stipple-throated Antwren*		Widespread tropical western Amazon basin
28 04 067	**Myrmotherula ornata** *Ornate Antwren*		Western Amazonian Brazil, adjacent Colombia to Bolivia
28 04 068	**Myrmotherula erythrura** *Rufous-tailed Antwren*		Amazonian Brazil, adjacent Colombia to Bolivia
28 04 069	**Myrmotherula erythronotos** *Black-hooded Antwren*		Southeast Brazil (Espirito Santo to Rio de Janeiro)

		Date	Location

28 04 070	**Myrmotherula axillaris** *White-flanked Antwren*	Tropical Honduras to northern Bolivia, Brazil
28 04 071	**Myrmotherula schisticolor** *Slaty Antwren*	Mountains of Mexico (Chiapas) to southeast Peru
28 04 072	**Myrmotherula longipennis** *Long-winged Antwren*	Northern South America to Peru, Brazil
28 04 073	**Myrmotherula sunensis** *Rio Suno Antwren*	Tropical southeast Colombia to Peru (Junin)
28 04 074	**Myrmotherula minor** *Salvadori's Antwren*	Northeast Peru to southeast Brazil
28 04 075	**Myrmotherula iheringi** *Ihering's Antwren*	Brazil (west Amazon basin and Matto Grosso); adjacent Peru
28 04 076	**Myrmotherula grisea** *Ashy Antwren*	Bolivia (La Paz—known from seven specimens)
28 04 077	**Myrmotherula unicolor** *Unicolored Antwren*	Southeast Brazil (Espirito Santo to Rio Grande do Sul)
28 04 078	**Myrmotherula behni** *Plain-winged Antwren*	Guianas to Colombia, adjacent Brazil
28 04 079	**Myrmotherula urosticta** *Band-tailed Antwren*	Brazil (Bahia, Minas Gerais, Espirito Santo)
28 04 080 +	**Myrmotherula menetriesii** *Gray Antwren*	Tropical northern South America to Brazil, Bolivia
28 04 081	**Myrmotherula assimillis** *Leaden Antwren*	West Amazonian Brazil, adjacent Peru, Bolivia
28 04 082	**Dichrozona cincta** *Banded Antbird*	Venezuela, Colombia to Bolivia, Amazonian Brazil
28 04 083	**Myrmorchilus strigilatus** *Stripe-backed Antbird*	Coastal eastern Brazil to northwest Argentina
28 04 084	**Herpsilochmus pileatus** *Black-capped Antwren*	Eastern Brazil to Peru, northwest Argentina
28 04 085	**Herpsilochmus sticturus** *Spot-tailed Antwren*	Tropical Amazon basin north of the Amazon
28 04 086	**Herpsilochmus stictocephalus** *Todd's Antwren*	Forest treetops of Venezuela to French Guiana
28 04 087	**Herpsilochmus dorsimaculatus** *Spot-backed Antwren*	Tropical northwest Brazil, adjacent Venezuela, Colombia

	Data	Location
28 04 088	**Herpsilochmus roraimae** *Roraiman Antwren*	Guyana, southern Venezuela, adjacent Brazil
28 04 089	**Herpsilochmus pectoralis** *Pectoral Antwren*	Dry *caatinga* of Brazil (coastal Maranhão, Bahia)
28 04 090	**Herpsilochmus longirostris** *Large-billed Antwren*	Brazilian plateau (Piaui to Matto Grosso)
28 04 091	**Herpsilochmus axillaris** *Yellow-breasted Antwren*	Colombia to eastern Ecuador, eastern Peru
28 04 092	**Herpsilochmus rufimarginatus** *Rufous-winged Antwren*	Panama to northeast Argentina, Amazonian Brazil
28 04 093	**Microrhopias quixensis** *Dot-winged Antwren*	Tropical southern Mexico to Bolivia, Amazonian Brazil
28 04 094	**Formicivora iheringi** *Narrow-billed Antwren*	Eastern Brazil (interior of Bahia)
28 04 095	**Formicivora grisea** *Black-breasted Antwren*	Guianas to Colombia, Amazonian Brazil
28 04 096	**Formicivora serrana** *Serra Antwren*	Brazil (*serras* of Minas Gerais to Rio de Janeiro)
28 04 097	**Formicivora melanogaster** *Black-bellied Antwren*	*Cerrado* of eastern Brazil; eastern Bolivia
28 04 098	**Formicivora rufa** *Rusty-backed Antwren*	Savannas and campos of Amazon basin
28 04 099	**Drymophila ferruginea** *Ferruginous Antbird*	Southeast Brazil (Bahia) to Argentina (Misiones)
28 04 100	**Drymophila genei** *Rufous-tailed Antbird*	Brazil (Minas Gerais, Espirito Santo, Rio de Janeiro)
28 04 101	**Drymophila ochropyga** *Ochre-rumped Antbird*	Southeast Brazil (Minas Gerais to São Paulo)
28 04 102	**Drymophila devillei** *Striated Antbird*	Southeast Peru to northern Bolivia, Amazonian Brazil
28 04 103	**Drymophila caudata** *Long-tailed Antbird*	Mountains of Venezuela to northern Bolivia
28 04 104	**Drymophila malura** *Dusky-tailed Antbird*	Brazil (Espirito Santo) to Argentina (Misiones)
28 04 105	**Drymophila squamata** *Scaled Antbird*	Humid coastal forests of Brazil (Bahia to São Paulo)
28 04 106	**Terenura maculata** *Streak-capped Antwren*	Brazil (Minas Gerais) to Argentina (Misiones)
28 04 107	**Terenura callinota** *Rufous-rumped Antwren*	Mountains of Panama to Guyana, Peru (Junin)

	Date	Location

28 04 108 Terenura humeralis
Chestnut-shouldered Antwren
Tropical west Amazonian Brazil, adjacent Ecuador, Peru

28 04 109 Terenura sharpei
Yellow-rumped Antwren
Subtropical Peru (Puno) to Bolivia (Cochabamba)

28 04 110 Terenura spodioptila
Ash-winged Antwren
Guyana to Colombia, adjacent Brazil

28 04 111 Cercomacra cinerascens
Gray Antbird
Widespread tropical Amazon basin

28 04 112 Cercomacra brasilliana
Rio de Janeiro Antbird
Brazil (Minas Gerais, Rio de Janeiro, Espirito Santo)

28 04 113 Cercomacra tyrannina
Dusky Antbird
Southern Mexico to central Peru, western Brazil

28 04 114 Cercomacra nigrescens
Blackish Antbird
Tropical northern South America to Brazil, Bolivia

28 04 115 Cercomacra ferdinandi
Bananal Antbird
Brazil (western Goiás—known only from Ilha do Bananal)

28 04 116 Cercomacra serva
Black Antbird
Southeast Colombia to northern Bolivia, adjacent Brazil

28 04 117 Cercomacra nigricans
Jet Antbird
Panama to southeast Peru, northern Brazil (Roraima)

28 04 118 Cercomacra carbonaria
Rio Branco Antbird
Brazil (known only from Rio Branco, Roraima)

28 04 119 Cercomacra melanaria
Matto Grosso Antbird
Tropical northern Bolivia, Brazilian Matto Grosso

28 04 120 Sipia berlepschi
Stub-tailed Antbird
Tropical Pacific Colombia to northwest Ecuador

28 04 121 Sipia rosenbergi
Esmeraldas Antbird
Tropical Pacific Colombia to northwest Ecuador

28 04 122 Pyriglena leuconota
White-backed Fire-eye
Southeast Colombia to Bolivia, Amazonian Brazil

28 04 123 Pyriglena atra
Fringe-backed Fire-eye
Eastern Brazil (coastal Bahia)

28 04 124 Pyriglena leucoptera
White-shouldered Fire-eye
Southeast Brazil (Bahia) to Argentina (Misiones)

28 04 125 Rhopornis ardesiaca
Slender Antbird
Eastern Brazil (Bahia—known from three specimens)

28 04 126 Myrmoborus leucophrys
White-browed Antbird
Tropical South America to Bolivia, Amazonian Brazil

28 04 127 Myrmoborus lugubris
Ash-breasted Antbird
Southeast Colombia to Peru, Amazonian Brazil

	Date	Location

28 04 128 **Myrmoborus**
✝ **myotherinus**
    Black-faced Antbird   Eastern Colombia to Bolivia, west Amazonian Brazil

28 04 129 **Myrmoborus melanurus**
    Black-tailed Antbird   Tropical eastern Peru (Ucayali River drainage)

28 04 130 **Hypocnemis cantator**
    Warbling Antbird   Tropical South America to Bolivia, Amazonian Brazil

28 04 131 **Hypocnemis hypoxantha**
    Yellow-browed Antbird   Tropical forests of western Amazon basin

28 04 132 **Hypocnemoides**
    melanopogon
    Black-chinned Antbird   Tropical South America to Peru, Amazonian Brazil

28 04 133 **Hypocnemoides**
    maculicauda
    Band-tailed Antbird   Riparian thickets of western Amazon basin

28 04 134 **Myrmochanes**
    hemileucus
    Black-and-white Antbird   Tropical western Amazon basin

28 04 135 **Gymnocichla nudiceps**
✝   *Bare-crowned Antbird*   Tropical Guatemala to northern Colombia

28 04 136 **Sclateria naevia**
✝   *Silvered Antbird*   Widespread tropical Amazon basin; Trinidad

28 04 137 **Percnostola rufifrons**
    Black-headed Antbird   Guianas to Venezuela, adjacent Brazil

28 04 138 **Percnostola macrolopha**
✝   *White-lined Antbird*   Peru (Madre de Dios and Cuzco)

28 04 139 **Percnostola schistacea**
    Slate-colored Antbird   West Amazonian Brazil, adjacent Colombia, Peru

28 04 140 **Percnostola leucostigma**
✝   *Spot-winged Antbird*   Widespread tropical, subtropical Amazon basin

28 04 141 **Percnostola caurensis**
    Caura Antbird   Venezuela south of the Orinoco; adjacent Brazil

28 04 142 **Percnostola lophotes**
    Rufous-crested Antbird   Tropical eastern Peru (Loreto and Puno)

28 04 143 **Myrmeciza exsul**
✝   *Chestnut-backed Antbird*   Tropical Nicaragua to Pacific Colombia, Ecuador

28 04 144 **Myrmeciza longipes**
    White-bellied Antbird   Tropical Panama to Guyana; adjacent Brazil

28 04 145 **Myrmeciza ferruginea**
    Ferruginous-backed
    Antbird   Tropical Guianas, west Amazonia Brazil

28 04 146 **Myrmeciza ruficauda**
    Scalloped Antbird   Coastal Brazil (Paraiba to Santa Catarina)

		Date	Location

28 04 147	**Myrmeciza loricata** *White-bibbed Antbird*	Southeast Brazil (Bahia to São Paulo)
28 04 148	**Myrmeciza squamosa** *Squamate Antbird*	Southeast Brazil (Rio de Janeiro southwards)
28 04 149	**Myrmeciza laemosticta** *Dull-mantled Antbird*	Costa Rica to Ecuador, Venezuela
28 04 150	**Myrmeciza pelzeini** *Gray-bellied Antbird*	Tropical southeast Venezuela, adjacent Colombia
28 04 151	**Myrmeciza hemimelaena** *Chestnut-tailed Antbird*	Tropical Amazonian Brazil, adjacent Colombia to Bolivia
28 04 152	**Myrmeciza hyperythra** *Plumbeous Antbird*	Southeast Colombia to Bolivia, west Amazonian Brazil
28 04 153	**Myrmeciza goeldii** *Goeld's Antbird*	Brazil (upper Rio Purus); southeast Peru (Balta)
28 04 154	**Myrmeciza melanoceps** *White-shouldered Antbird*	Colombia to Peru; west Amazonian Brazil
28 04 155	**Myrmeciza fortis** *Sooty Antbird*	Tropical eastern Colombia to Peru, west Amazonian Brazil
28 04 156	**Myrmeciza immaculata** *Immaculate Antbird*	Highlands of Costa Rica to Ecuador, Venezuela
28 04 157	**Myrmeciza griseiceps** *Gray-headed Antbird*	Subtropical southwest Ecuador, northwest Peru
28 04 158	**Myrmeciza atrothorax** *Black-throated Antbird*	Tropical South America to Bolivia, Amazonian Brazil
28 04 159	**Myrmeciza stictothorax** *Spot-breasted Antbird*	Brazil (west bank of Rio Tapajos)
28 04 160	**Myrmeciza disjuncta** *Yapacana Antbird*	Tropical forests of Venezuela (central Amazonas)
28 04 161	**Pithys albifrons** *White-plumed Antbird*	Widespread tropical Amazon basin
28 04 162	**Pithys castanea** *White-masked Antbird*	Peru (lower Rio Pastaza, Loreto—unique)
28 04 163	**Gymnopithys rufigula** *Rufous-throated Antbird*	Tropical Guianas, Venezuela, Amazonian Brazil
28 04 164	**Gymnopithys salvini** *White-throated Antbird*	Tropical Amazonian Brazil, adjacent Peru, Bolivia
28 04 165	**Gymnopithys lunulata** *Lunulated Antbird*	Tropical southeast Ecuador to Peru (Rio Ucayali)
28 04 166	**Gymnopithys leucaspis** **(bicolor)** *Bicolored Antbird*	Tropical Honduras to northern Peru, Amazonian Brazil

	Date	Location

28 04 167 **Rhegmatorhina gymnops**
Bare-eyed Antbird
Brazil south of Amazon (Rios Tapajós and Xingú)

28 04 168 **Rhegmatorhina berlepschi**
Harlequin Antbird
Brazil (west bank of Rio Tapajós)

28 04 169 **Rhegmatorhina cristata**
Chestnut-crested Antbird
Brazil, Colombia (known only from Rio Vaupés)

28 04 170 **Rhegmatorhina hoffmannsi**
White-breasted Antbird
Southwest Brazil (east bank Rio Madeira)

28 04 171 **Rhegmatorhina**
+ **melanosticta**
Hairy-crested Antbird
Tropical southeast Colombia to Bolivia, Brazil

28 04 172 **Hylophylax naevioides**
+ *Spotted Antbird*
Tropical Nicaragua to Pacific Colombia, Ecuador

28 04 173 **Hylophylax naevia**
Spot-backed Antbird
Tropical South America to Bolivia, Amazonian Brazil

28 04 174 **Hylophylax punctulata**
Dot-backed Antbird
Tropical Amazonian Brazil, adjacent Peru, Venezuela

28 04 175 **Hylophylax poecilonota**
+ *Scale-backed Antbird*
Tropical South America to southeast Peru, Brazil

28 04 176 **Phlegopsis**
+ **nigromaculata**
Black-spotted Bare-eye
Amazonian Brazil, adjacent Colombia to Bolivia

28 04 177 **Phlegopsis barringeri**
Argus Bare-eye
Colombia (southeast Nariño—known from one specimen)

28 04 178 **Phlegopsis erythroptera**
Reddish-winged Bare-eye
Tropical forest undergrowth of Amazon basin

28 04 179 **Phlegopsis borbae**
Pale-faced Bare-eye
Brazil (Rio Tapajós—known from two specimens)

28 04 180 **Phaenostictus**
+ **mcleannani**
Ocellated Antbird
Tropical Nicaragua to northwest Ecuador

28 04 181 **Formicarius colma**
Rufous-capped Antthrush
Guianas, Venezuela, west Amazonian Brazil

28 04 182 **Formicarius analis**
+ *Black-faced Antthrush*
Southern Mexico to Brazil, Bolivia, Trinidad

28 04 183 **Formicarius rufifrons**
Rufous-fronted Antthrush
Eastern Peru (Madre de Dios—known from 2 specimens)

28 04 184 **Formicarius nigricapillus**
Black-headed Antthrush
Costa Rica to Pacific Colombia, western Ecuador

28 04 185 **Formicarius rufipectus**
Rufous-breasted Antthrush
Highland forests of Costa Rica to eastern Peru

		Date	Location
28 04 186	**Chamaeza campanisona** *Short-tailed Antthrush*		Northern South America to Brazil, northeast Argentina
28 04 187	**Chamaeza nobillis** *Striated Antthrush*		Amazonian Brazil, adjacent Colombia to Peru
28 04 188	**Chamaeza ruficauda** *Rufous-tailed Antthrush*		Mountains of Venezuela, Colombia; southeast Brazil
28 04 189	**Chamaeza mollissima** *Barred Antthrush*		Andes of Colombia to northern Bolivia (La Paz)
28 04 190 +	**Myrmornis torquata** *Wing-banded Antbird*		Tropical Nicaraqua to Ecuador, Amazonian Brazil
28 04 191	**Pittasoma michleri** *Black-crowned Antpitta*		Tropical Costa Rica to northwest Colombia (Chocó)
28 04 192	**Pittasoma rufopileatum** *Rufous-crowned Antpitta*		Pacific slopes of Colombia, northwest Ecuador
28 04 193 +	**Grallaria squamigera** *Undulated Antpitta*		Andes of northwest Venezuela to northern Bolivia
28 04 194	**Grallaria gigantea** *Giant Antpitta*		Central Andes of Colombia, east and west Ecuador
28 04 195	**Grallaria excelsa** *Great Antpitta*		Subtropical forests of northwest Venezuela
28 04 196	**Grallaria varia** *Variegated Antpitta*		Guianas, Venezuela to northeast Argentina, Brazil
28 04 197	**Grallaria alleni** *Moustached Antipitta*		Subtropical central Andes of Colombia (known from one specimen)
28 04 198	**Grallaria guatimalensis** *Scaled Antpitta*		Mountains of central Mexico to Peru; Trinidad
28 04 199	**Grallaria chthonia** *Táchira Antpitta*		Venezuela (Táchira—known from 3 speciments)
28 04 200	**Grallaria haplonota** *Plain-backed Antpitta*		Highlands of Venezuela, Colombia, western Ecuador
20 04 201	**Grallaria dignissima** *Ochre-striped Antpitta*		Tropical southeast Colombia, eastern Ecuador
28 04 202	**Grallaria eludens** *Elusive Antpitta*		Peru (known only from Rio Curanja, Balta)
28 04 203	**Grallaria ruficapilla** *Chestnut-crowned Antpitta*		Highlands of Venezuela to northwest Peru
28 04 204	**Grallaria watkinsi** *Watkin's Antpitta*		Southwest Ecuador, northwest Peru (probable race *G. ruficapilla*)
28 04 205	**Grallaria bangsi** *Santa Marta Antpitta*		Subtropical Santa Marta Mountains of Colombia

		Data	Location
28 04 206 +	**Grallaria andicola** *Stripe-headed Antpitta*		Temperate Andes of Peru, northwest Bolivia
28 04 207	**Grallaria punensis** *Puno Antipitta*		Southeast Peru (Puno—probable race *G. andicola*).
28 04 208	**Grallaria rufocinerea** *Bicolored Antpitta*		Andes of Colombia (Antioquia and Caldas)
28 04 209	**Grallaria nuchalis** *Chestnut-naped Antpitta*		Highland forests of Colombia and Ecuador
28 04 210	**Grallaria albigula** *White-throated Antpitta*		Andes of southern Peru to northwest Argentina
28 04 211	**Grallaria erythroleuca** *Red-and-white Antpitta*		Temperate Andes of southeast Peru (Cuzco)
28 04 212 +	**Grallaria hypoleuca (capitalis) (prezewalskii)** *White-bellied Antpitta*		Subtropical Andes of Colombia to northern Peru
28 04 213	**Grallaria griseonucha** *Gray-naped Antpitta*		Andes of Venezuela (Mérida and Táchira)
28 04 214 +	**Grallaria rufula** *Rufous Antpitta*		Andes of northwest Venezuela to northern Bolivia
28 04 215	**Grallaria erythrotis** *Rufous-faced Antpitta*		Subtropical northern Bolivia (La Paz, Cochabamba)
28 04 216 +	**Grallaria quitensis** *Tawny Antpitta*		Andean forests of Colombia to northern Peru
28 04 217	**Grallaria milleri** *Brown-banded Antpitta*		Temperate central Andes of Colombia (Caldas)
28 04 218	**Hylopezus perspicillatus** *Streak-chested Antpitta*		Tropical Nicaragua to Colombia, western Ecuador
28 04 219	**Hylopezus macularius** *Spotted Antpitta*		Tropical northern South America to Brazil, Bolivia
28 04 220 +	**Hylopezus fulviventris** *Fulvous-bellied Antpitta*		Tropical Nicaragua to Pacific Colombia, Ecuador
28 04 221	**Hylopezus berlepschi** *Amazonian Antpitta*		Tropical Amazonian Brazil, adjacent Peru, Bolivia
28 04 222	**Hylopezus ochroleucus** *Speckle-breasted Antpitta*		Eastern Brazil (Ceará) to Argentina (Misiones)
28 04 223	**Myrmothera campanisona** *Thrush-like Antpitta*		Tropical South America to Amazonian Brazil, Peru
28 04 224	**Myrmothera simplex** *Brown-breasted Antpitta*		Mountains of southern Venezuela, adjacent Brazil
28 04 225 +	**Grallaricula flavirostris** *Ochre-breasted Antpitta*		Highlands of Costa Rica to northern Bolivia

	Date	Location

28 04 226 Grallaricula ferrugineipectus
Rusty-breasted Antpitta   Subtropical mountains of Venezuela to Peru

28 04 227 Grallaricula loricata
Scallop-breasted Antpitta   Subtropical coastal mountains of Venezuela

28 04 228 Grallaricula nana
Slate-crowned Antpitta   Mountains of Venezuela, Colombia, Ecuador

28 04 229 Grallaricula peruviana
Peruvian Antpitta   Subtropical western Andes of Peru (Piura)

28 04 230 Grallaricula lineifrons
Crescent-faced Antpitta   Temperate Andes of northeast Ecuador, Colombia

28 04 231 Grallaricula cucullata
Hooded Antpitta   Subtropical Andes of Colombia, Venezuela (Táchira)

FAMILY: CONOPOPHAGIDAE (Gnateaters)

28 05 001 Conopophaga lineata (cearae)
Rufous Gnateater   *Caatinga* of eastern Brazil to Argentina (Misiones)

28 05 002 Conopophaga cearae
Caatinga Gnateater   Northeast Brazil (Ceará to Bahia—possible race *C. lineata*)

28 05 003 Conopophaga aurita
Chestnut-belted Gnateater   Tropical South America to west Amazonian Brazil, Peru

28 05 004 Conopophaga roberti
Hooded Gnateater   *Capoeira* of eastern Brazil (Pará to Ceará)

28 05 005 Conopophaga peruviana
Ash-throated Gnateater   Southwest Amazonian Brazil, adjacent Peru, Ecuador

28 05 006 Conopophaga ardesiaca
Slaty Gnateater   Andes of southeast Peru, Bolivia

28 05 007 Conopophaga castaneiceps
Chestnut-crowned Gnateater   Andes of Colombia, Ecuador, northern Peru

28 05 008 Conopophaga melanops
Black-cheeked Gnateater   Eastern Brazil (Paraiba to São Paulo)

28 05 009 Conopophaga melanogaster
Black-bellied Gnateater   Southwest Amazonian Brazil, adjacent Bolivia (Beni)

28 05 010 Corythopis delalandi
Southern Antpipit   Eastern Brazil (Maranhão) to northeast Argentina

28 05 011 Corythopis torquata
+   *Ringed Antpipit*   Tropical South America to Amazonian Brazil, Bolivia

Date   Location

FAMILY: RHINOCRYPTIDAE (Tapaculos)

28 06 001	**Pteroptochos castaneus** *Chestnut-throated Huet-huet*	Forests of Chile (Colchagua to Rio Bio-Bio)
28 06 002	**Pteroptochos tarnii** *Black-throated Huet-huet*	Dense beech forests of southern Chile, Argentina
28 06 003	**Pteroptochos megapodius** *Moustached Turca*	Northern coastal mountains of Chile
28 06 004	**Scelorchilus albicollis** *White-throated Tapaculo*	Semiarid Chile (Atacama to Curicó)
28 06 005	**Scelorchilus rubecula** *Chucao Tapaculo*	Dense beech forests of southern Chile, Argentina
28 06 006	**Rhinocrypta lanceolata** *Crested Gallito*	Bolivia (Santa Cruz), Paraguay, western Argentina
28 06 007	**Teledromas fuscus** *Sandy Gallito*	Western Argentina (Salta, Tucumán, Rio Negro)
28 06 008	**Liosceles thoracicus** *Rusty-belted Tapaculo*	Southeast Colombia to Peru, western Brazil
28 06 009	**Melanopareia torquata** *Collared Crescentchest*	Open *cerrado* of eastern Brazil, northeast Bolivia
28 06 010	**Melanopareia maximilliani** *Olive-crowned Crescentchest*	Subtropical Bolivia, Paraguay, northern Argentina
28 06 011	**Melanopareia maranonica** *Marañon Crescentchest*	Peru (arid upper Marañon Valley)
28 06 012	**Melanopareia elegans** *Elegant Crescentchest*	Tropical western Ecuador, northwest Peru
28 06 013	**Psilorhamphus guttatus** *Spotted Bamboowren*	Southeast Brazil (Minas Gerais) to Argentina (Misiones)
28 06 014	**Merulaxis stresemanni** *Stresemann's Bristlefront*	Eastern Brazil (Bahia—known from two speciments)
28 06 015	**Merulaxis ater** *Slaty Bristlefront*	Southeast Brazil (southern Bahia to Paraná)
28 06 016	**Eugralla paradoxa** *Ochre-flanked Tapaculo*	Chile (Maule to Chiloé) to Argentina (Rio Negro)
28 06 017	**Myornis senillis** *Ash-colored Tapaculo*	Temperate central and eastern Andes of Colombia
28 06 018	**Scytalopus unicolor** *Unicolored Tapaculo*	Mossy Andean forests of Venezuela to Bolivia

	Date	Location

28 06 019 Scytalopus speluncae
Mouse-colored Tapaculo — Southeast Brazil (Minas Gerais) to Argentina (Misiones)

28 06 020 Scytalopus macropus
+ Large-footed Tapaculo — Andean mountain torrents of Peru

28 06 021 Scytalopus femoralis
Rufous-vented Tapaculo — Mossy Andean forests of Colombia to western Ecuador

28 06 022 Scytalopus panamensis
Pale-throated Tapaculo — Mossy mountain forests of eastern Panama to Ecuador

28 06 023 Scytalopus vicinior
Nariño Tapaculo — Eastern Panama to western Ecuador (possible race S. panamensis)

28 06 024 Scytalopus latebricola
Brown-rumped Tapaculo — Mountains of Venezuela, Colombia, Ecuador

28 06 025 Scytalopus novacapitalis
Brasilia Tapaculo — Eastern Brazil (Goiás—known from three specimens)

28 06 026 Scytalopus indigoticus
White-breasted Tapaculo — Southeast Brazil (Bahia to Rio Grande do Sul)

28 06 027 Scytalopus magellanicus
Andean Tapaculo — Andes of Venezuela to Tierra del Fuego; Falklands

28 06 028 Scytalopus argentifrons
Silvery-fronted Tapaculo — Mountains of Costa Rica and western Panama

28 06 029 Scytalopus supercillaris
White-browed Tapaculo — Highlands of Bolivia (Chuquisaca), northwest Argentina

28 06 030 Acropternis orthonyx
Ocellated Tapaculo — Andes of Venezuela, Colombia, Ecuador

FAMILY: COTINGIDAE (Cotingas)

28 07 001 Phoenicircus carnifex
Guianan Red Cotinga — Tropical Guianas, Venezuela, northern Amazonian Brazil

28 07 002 Phoenicircus nigricollis
Black-necked Red Cotinga — Tropical South America to Brazil, northeast Peru

28 07 003 Laniisoma elegans
Shrike-like Cotinga — Northwest Venezuela to Bolivia, southeast Brazil

28 07 004 Phibalura flavirostris
+ Swallow-tailed Cotinga — Southeast Brazil to northeast Argentina; northwest Bolivia

		Date	Location

28 07 005 **Tijuca atra**
Black-and-gold Cotinga   Southeast Brazil (Espirito Santo to São Paulo)

28 07 006 **Carpornis cucullatus**
Hooded Berryeater   Southeast Brazil (Espirito Santo to Rio Grande do Sul)

28 07 007 **Carpornis melanocephalus**
Black-headed Berryeater   Southeast Brazil (Bahia to São Paulo)

28 07 008 **Ampelion rubrocristatus**
+
Red-crested Cotinga   Andes of western Venezuela to northwest Bolivia

28 07 009 **Ampelion rufaxilla**
Chestnut-crested Cotinga   Subtropical Andes of Colombia to northwest Bolivia

28 07 010 **Ampelion stresemanni**
+
White-cheeked Cotinga   Peru (west slope of Andes in Ancash and Lima)

28 07 011 **Ampelion sclateri**
Bay-vented Cotinga   Peru (eastern Andes of Huanuco and Junin)

28 07 012 **Pipreola riefferii**
Green-and-black Fruiteater   Mountains of Venezuela to Peru

28 07 013 **Pipreola intermedia**
+
Band-tailed Fruiteater   Subtropical eastern Andes of Peru, northwest Bolivia

28 07 014 **Pipreola lubomirskii**
Black-chested Fruiteater   Subtropical Andes of Colombia to northern Peru

28 07 015 **Pipreola jucunda**
Orange-breasted Fruiteater   Pacific slope of Colombia and Ecuador (possible race *P. aureopectus*)

28 07 016 **Pipreola pulchra**
+
Masked Fruiteater   Subtropical eastern Andes of Peru (possible race *P. Aureopectus*)

28 07 017 **Pipreola aureopectus**
Golden-breasted Fruiteater   Mountains of northwest Venezuela, western Colombia

28 07 018 **Pipreola frontalis**
Scarlet-breasted Fruiteater   Eastern Andes of Ecuador to northwest Bolivia

28 07 019 **Pipreola formosa**
Handsome Fruiteater   Mountains of northern Venezuela

28 07 020 **Pipreola chlorolepidota**
Fiery-throated Fruiteater   Uplands of eastern Ecuador and central Peru

28 07 021 **Pipreola whitelyi**
Red-banded Fruiteater   Mountains of Venezuela (Bolivar), adjacent Guyana

28 07 022 **Pipreola arcuata**
+
Barred Fruiteater   Andes of northwest Venezuela to northwest Bolivia

28 07 023 **Ampeliodes tschudii**
Scaled Fruiteater   Andes of northwest Venezuela to Peru (Junin)

	Date	Location

28 07 024 Iodopleura pipra
Buff-throated Purpletuft — Guyana; southeast Brazil (Minas Gerais to São Paulo)

28 07 025 Iodopleura fusca
Dusky Purpletuft — Tropical Guianas, Venezuela (southern Bolivar)

28 07 026 Iodopleura isabellae
White-browed Purpletuft — Widespread tropical Amazon basin

28 07 027 Calyptura cristata
Kinglet Calyptura — Southeast Brazil (Espirito Santo, Rio de Janeiro)

28 07 028 Lipaugus fuscocinereus
Dusky Piha — Andes of Colombia, eastern Ecuador

28 07 029 Lipaugus vociferans
Screaming Piha — Northern South America to Brazil, northern Bolivia

28 07 030 Lipaugus lanioides
Cinnamon-vented Piha — Southeast Brazil (Minas Gerais to Santa Catarina)

28 07 031 Lipaugus streptophorus
Rose-collared Piha — Mountains of Guyana, Venezuela, adjacent Brazil

28 07 032 Lipaugus subalaris
Gray-tailed Piha — Mountains of eastern Ecuador to Peru (Junin)

28 07 033 Lipaugus cryptolophus
Olivaceous Piha — Andean forests of Colombia to Peru (Huánuco)

28 07 034 Lipaugus unirufus
Rufous Piha — Gulf lowlands of southern Mexico to western Ecuador

28 07 035 Chirocylla uropygialis
Scimitar-winged Piha — Andes of northern Bolivia (La Paz and Cochabamba)

28 07 036 Pachyramphus viridis
Green-backed Becard — South America to northern Argentina, southern Brazil

28 07 037 Pachyramphus versicolor
Barred Becard — Mountains of Costa Rica to Bolivia (Cochabamba)

28 07 038 Pachyramphus surinamus
Glossy-backed Becard — Tropical Surinam, French Guiana, northeast Brazil

28 07 039 Pachyramphus spodiurus
Slaty Becard — Tropical northwest Ecuador to northwest Peru

28 07 040 Pachyramphus rufus
Cinereous Becard — Tropical Panama to northeast Peru, Amazonian Brazil

28 07 041 Pachyramphus castaneus
Chestnut-crowned Becard — Venezuela to northeast Argentina, adjacent Brazil

28 07 042 Pachyramphus cinnamomeus
Cinnamon Becard — Tropical southern Mexico to northwest Ecuador

	Date	Location

28 07 043 Pachyramphus polychopterus
White-winged Becard

Guatemala to northwest Bolivia, Uruguay, northern Argentina

28 07 044 Pachyramphus marginatus
Black-capped Becard

Northern South America to Brazil, eastern Bolivia

28 07 045 Pachyramphus albogriseus
Black-and-white Becard

Nicaragua to Pacific Colombia, Ecuador, Peru

28 07 046 Pachyramphus major
Gray-collared Becard

Tropical southern Mexico to eastern Nicaragua

28 07 047 Platypsaris niger
Jamaican Becard

Wooded hills of Jamaica

28 07 048 Platypsaris rufus
Crested Becard

Southeast Peru, southern Brazil to central Argentina

28 07 049 Platypsaris homochrous
One-colored Becard

Eastern Panama to northwest Peru (possible race *P. aglaiae*)

28 07 050 Platypsaris aglaiae
Rose-throated Becard

Southern Arizona, Texas to northern Costa Rica

28 07 051 Platypsaris minor
Pink-throated Becard

South America to Amazonian Brazil (possible race *P. aglaiae*)

28 07 052 Tityra cayana
Black-tailed Tityra

Tropical South America to Bolivia, northeast Argentina

28 07 053 Tityra semifasciata
Masked Tityra

Tropical Mexico to Amazonian Brazil, Bolivia

28 07 054 Titrya inquisitor
Black-crowned Tityra

Southern Mexico to northeast Argentina, Brazil

28 07 055 Tityra leucura
White-tailed Tityra

Brazil (upper Rio Madeira—unique, doubtful species)

28 07 056 Porphyrolaema porphyrolaema
Purple-throated Cotinga

Southern Colombia to eastern Peru, western Brazil

28 07 057 Cotinga amabilis
Lovely Cotinga

Caribbean slope of southern Costa Rica to Panama

28 07 058 Cotinga ridgwayi
Turquoise Cotinga

Pacific slope of southwest Costa Rica to Panama

28 07 059 Cotinga nattererii
Blue Cotinga

Tropical central Panama to northwest Ecuador

28 07 060 Cotinga maynana
Plum-throated Cotinga

Southeast Colombia to Bolivia, western Brazil

	Date	Location
28 07 061 **Cotinga cayana** *Spangled Cotinga*		Tropical South America to Brazil, northern Bolivia
28 07 062 **Cotinga cotinga** *Purple-breasted Cotinga*		Tropical Guianas, Venezuela, northern Brazil
28 07 063 **Cotinga maculata** *Banded Cotinga*		Coastal mountain forests of southeast Brazil
28 07 064 **Xipholena punicea** *Pompadour Cotinga*		Northern South America to Ecuador, Amazonian Brazil
28 07 065 **Xipholena lamellipennis** *White-tailed Cotinga*		Northeast Brazil south of the Amazon
28 07 066 **Xipholena atropurpurea** *White-winged Cotinga*		Coastal Brazil (Paraiba to Rio de Janeiro)
28 07 067 **Carpodectes nitidus** *Snowy Cotinga*		Caribbean slope of Honduras to western Panama
28 07 068 **Caropdectes antoniae** *Yellow-billed Cotinga*		Pacific slope of southwest Costa Rica and Panama
28 07 069 **Carpodectes hopkei** *White Cotinga*		Pacific coast of Colombia, northwest Ecuador
28 07 070 **Conioptilon mcilhennyi** *Black-faced Cotinga*		Tropical southeast Peru (Loreto, Madre de Diós)
28 07 071 **Gymnoderus foetidus** *Bare-necked Fruitcrow*		Tropical South America to Amazonian Brazil, Bolivia
28 07 072 **Haematoderus militaris** *Crimson Fruitcrow*		Tropical Guianas, lower Amazon region of Brazil
28 07 073 **Querula purpurata** *Purple-throated Fruitcrow*		Tropical Costa Rica to Amazonian Brazil, Bolivia
28 07 074 **Pyroderus scutatus** *Red-ruffed Fruitcrow*		Widespread forests of northern South America to Argentina
28 07 075 **Cephalopterus glabricollis** *Bare-necked Umbrellabird*		Highlands of Costa Rica and western Panama
28 07 076 **Cephalopterus ornatus** *Amazonian (Ornate) Umbrellabird*		South America to Amazonian Brazil, northern Bolivia
28 07 077 **Cephalopterus penduliger** *Long-wattled Umbrellabird*		Pacific slope of Colombia (Cauca) to western Ecuador
28 07 078 **Perissocephalus tricolor** *Capuchinbird*		Tropical Guinanas, Venezuela, northern Amazonian Brazil

		Date	Location

28 07 079 **Procnias tricarunculata**
Three-wattled Bellbird
Highlands of Nicaragua, Costa Rica, Panama

28 07 080 **Procnias alba**
White Bellbird
Guianas, southeast Venezuela, adjacent Brazil

28 07 081 **Procnias averano**
Bearded Bellbird
Forests of Guyana, Venezuela, adjacent Brazil,
Colombia

28 07 082 **Procnias nudicollis**
Bare-throated Bellbird
Southeast Brazil (Bahia) to northeast Argentina

28 07 083 **Rupicola rupicola**
Guianan Cock-of-the-Rock
Tropical northern Amazon basin (endangered)

28 07 084 **Rupicola peruviana**
Andean Cock-of-the-Rock
Andes of Venezuela to Bolivia (La Paz,
Cochabamba)

FAMILY: PIPRIDAE (Manakins)

28 08 001 **Pipra aureola**
Crimson-hooded Manakin
Guianas, Venezuela, east Amazonian Brazil

28 08 002 **Pipra fasciicauda**
+ *Band-tailed Manakin*
Tropical eastern Peru, Brazil to northeast Argentina

28 08 003 **Pipra erythrocephala**
+ *Golden-headed Manakin*
Eastern Panama to northern Brazil, northeast Peru

28 08 004 **Pipra rubrocapilla**
Red-headed Manakin
Tropical northeast Peru, Brazil, northern Bolivia

28 08 005 **Pipra mentalis**
Red-capped Manakin
Tropical southeast Mexico to northwest Ecuador

28 08 006 **Pipra chloromeros**
Round-tailed Manakin
Highlands of northeast Peru to northern Bolivia

28 08 007 **Pipra cornuta**
Scarlet-horned Manakin
Mountains of southern Venezuela, Guyana, adjacent
Brazil

28 08 008 **Pipra pipra**
+ *White-crowned Manakin*
Highlands of Costa Rica to Peru, Brazil

28 08 009 **Pipra isidorei**
Blue-rumped Manakin
Tropical eastern Colombia (Meta) to Peru
(Huánuco)

28 08 010 **Pipra caeruleocapilla**
+ *Cerulean-capped Manakin*
Foothills and Andes of central and eastern Peru

28 08 011 **Pipra coronata**
(exquisita)
Blue-crowned Manakin
Costa Rica to western Brazil, northern Bolivia

		Date	Location
28 08 012	**Pipra serena** *White-fronted Manakin*		Tropical South America north of the Amazon
28 08 013	**Pipra iris** *Opal-crowned Manakin*		Tropical east Amazonian Brazil
28 08 014	**Pipra nattereri** *Snow-capped Manakin*		Central Amazonian Brazil (Rio Madeira to Rio Xingú)
28 08 015	**Pipra vilasboasi** *Golden-crowned Manakin*		Brazil (Rio Tapajós—known from three specimens)
28 08 016	**Pipra obscura** *Sick's Manakin*		Brazil (Rio Tapajós—known from two speciments)
28 08 017	**Teleonema filicauda** *Wire-tailed Manakin*		Venezuela to northeast Peru, western Brazil
28 08 018	**Antilophia galeata** *Helmeted Manakin*		*Capoeira* of central Brazil to northeast Paraguay
28 08 019	**Chiroxiphia linearis** *Long-tailed Manakin*		Pacific slope of southern Mexico to Costa Rica
28 08 020	**Chiroxiphia pareola** *Blue-backed Manakin*		South America to southeast Brazil, northern Bolivia
28 08 021	**Chiroxiphia lanceolata** *Lance-tailed Manakin*		Costa Rica to northern Colombia and Venezuela
28 08 022	**Chiroxiphia caudata** *Swallow-tailed Manakin*		Southeast Brazil (Bahia) to northeast Argentina
28 08 023	**Masius chrysopterus** *Golden-winged Manakin*		Andes of northwest Venezuela to northeast Peru
28 08 024	**Illicura militaris** *Pin-tailed Manakin*		Forest treetops, *capoeira* of southeast Brazil
28 08 025	**Corapipo gutturails** *White-throated Manakin*		Guianas, southern Venezuela, adjacent Brazil
28 08 026 ✝	**Corapipo leucorrhoa (altera)** *White-ruffed Manakin*		Southeast Honduras to Venezuela, Colombia
28 08 027	**Manacus manacus** *White-bearded Manakin*		South America to northeast Argentina, southern Brazil
28 08 028	**Manacus cerritus** *Almirante Manakin*		Caribbean slope of extreme western Panama
28 08 029	**Manacus candei** *White-collared Manakin*		Caribbean slope of southern Mexico to Costa Rica (Panama?)
28 08 030	**Manacus aurantiacus** *Orange-collared Manakin*		Pacific slope of Costa Rica to western Panama
28 08 031 ✝	**Manacus vitellinus** *Golden-collared Manakin*		Western Panama, adjacent Costa Rica to Colombia

		Date	Location

28 08 032 **Machaeropterus**
+ **pyrocephalus**
Fiery-capped Manakin — Venezuela to northwest Bolivia, Brazil

28 08 033 **Machaeropterus regulus**
Striped Manakin — Tropical Venezuela to northeast Peru, Brazil

28 08 034 **Allocotopterus**
deliciousus
Club-winged Manakin — Pacific slope of Colombia to northwest Ecuador

28 08 035 **Xenopipo atronitens**
Black Manakin — Savanna, *cerrado* of northern Amazon basin

28 08 036 **Chloropipo unicolor**
+ *Jet Manakin* — Highlands of Peru (Cajamarca, San Martin, Junin)

28 08 037 **Chloropipo uniformis**
Olive Manakin — Mountains of Venezuela, adjacent Brazil, Guyana

28 08 038 **Chloropipo holochlora**
+ *Green Manakin* — Eastern Panama, Colombia to eastern Peru

28 08 039 **Chloropipo flavicapilla**
Yellow-headed Manakin — Central and western Andes of Colombia

28 08 040 **Neopipo cinnamomea**
Cinnamon Manakin — South America to Amazonian Brazil, southeast Peru

28 08 041 **Heterocercus linteatus**
Flame-crowned Manakin — Tropical Peru, southern Amazonian Brazil

28 08 042 **Heterocercus flavivertex**
Yellow-crowned Manakin — Southern Venezuela, adjacent Brazil, Colombia

28 08 043 **Heterocercus**
aurantiivertex
Orange-crowned Manakin — Tropical eastern Ecuador to northeast Peru

28 08 044 **Heterocercus**
luteocephalus
Golden-crested Manakin — South America (locality unknown—unique)

28 08 045 **Neopelma aurifrons**
Wied's Manakin — Eastern Brazil (Bahia to São Paulo)

28 08 046 **Neopelma**
sulphureiventer
Sulphur-bellied Manakin — Eastern Peru, northern Bolivia, adjacent Brazil

28 08 047 **Neopelma**
chrysocephalum
Saffron-crested Manakin — Guianas, Venezuela, Colombia, adjacent Brazil

28 08 048 **Neopelma pallescens**
Pale-bellied Manakin — Campos and *cerrado* of eastern Brazil

28 08 049 **Tyranneutes virescens**
Tiny Manakin — Tropical South America north of the Amazon

		Date	Location
28 08 050	**Tyranneutes stolzmanni** *Dwarf Manakin*		Southern Venezuela to Bolivia, Brazilian Matto Grosso
28 08 051	**Piprites pileatus** *Black-capped Manakin*		Coastal southeast Brazil to Argentina (Misiones)
28 08 052	**Piprites chloris** *Wing-barred Manakin*		South America to northeast Argentina, southern Brazil
28 08 053	**Piprites griseiceps** *Gray-headed Manakin*		Caribbean slope of Nicaragua and Costa Rica
28 08 054	**Sapayoa aenigma** *Broad-billed Manakin*		Tropical eastern Panama to northwest Ecuador
28 08 055 +	**Schiffornis major** *Greater Manakin*		Southern Venezuela to Bolivia, Amazonian Brazil
28 08 056	**Schiffornis virescens** *Greenish Manakin*		Southeast Brazil (Bahia) to Argentina (Misiones)
28 08 057 +	**Schiffornis turdinus** *Thrush-like Manakin*		Southern Mexico to northern Bolivia, Brazil

FAMILY: TYRANNIDAE (Tyrant Flycatchers)

28 09 001 +	**Agriornis livida** *Great Shrike-Tyrant*		Coast and mountains of southern Argentina, Chile
28 09 002 +	**Agriornis microptera** *Gray-bellied Shrike-Tyrant*		Southeast Peru to southern Argentina, Chile
28 09 003 +	**Agriornis montana** *Black-billed Shrike-Tyrant*		Andes of southeast Colombia to Argentina, Chile
28 09 004	**Agriornis albicauda** *White-tailed Shrike-Tyrant*		Temperate Andes of Ecuador to northwest Argentina
28 09 005	**Neoxolmis rufiventris** *Chocolate-vented Tyrant*		Argentina, Chile; winters north to Uruguay
28 09 006	**Xolmis cinerea** *Gray Monjita*		Surinam, Brazil, Bolivia to northern Argentina
28 09 007	**Xolmis velata** *White-rumped Monjita*		Campos of eastern Brazil, Paraguay, Bolivia
28 09 008	**Xolmis dominicana** *Black-and-white Monjita*		Southeast Brazil (Paraná) to northern Argentina
28 09 009	**Xolmis coronata** *Black-crowned Monjita*		Southern Argentina; winters to Bolivia, Brazil
28 09 010	**Xolmis irupero** *White Monjita*		Eastern Brazil (Ceará) to central Argentina, Bolivia
28 09 011 +	**Xolmis murina** *Mouse-brown Monjita*		Southern Argentina; winters to Paraguay, Bolivia

	Date	Location

28 09 012 Xolmis rubetra
Rusty-backed Monjita — Western Argentina (Chubut, Santa Fe, Mendoza, Tucumán)

28 09 013 Xolmis rufipennis
Rufous-webbed Tyrant — Subtropical, tropical Andes of Peru and Bolivia

28 09 014 Pyrope pyrope
Fire-eyed Diucon — Andes of Chile and Argentina to Tierra del Fuego

28 09 015 Muscisaxicola rufivertex
Rufous-naped Ground-Tyrant — Andes of Peru to Chile, Argentina

28 09 016 Muscisaxicola albilora
White-browed Ground-Tyrant — Andes of Chile, Argentina; winters north to Ecuador

28 09 017 Muscisaxicola juninensis
Puna Ground-Tyrant — Andes of Peru to northern Chile, Argentina

28 09 018 Muscisaxicola flavinucha
Ochre-naped Ground-Tyrant — Andes of Chile, Argentina; winters north to Peru

28 09 019 Muscisaxicola capistrata
Cinnamon-bellied Ground-Tyrant — Andes of southern Peru to Tierra del Fuego

28 09 020 Muscisaxicola frontalis
Black-fronted Ground-Tyrant — Chile, Argentina; winters north to central Peru

28 09 021 Muscisaxicola albifrons
White-fronted Ground-Tyrant — Andes of Peru, Bolivia to northern Chile

28 09 022 Muscisaxicola alpina
Plain-capped Ground-Tyrant — Andes of Colombia to western Argentina, Chile

28 09 023 Muscisaxicola macloviana
Dark-faced Ground-Tyrant — Southern Argentina, Chile; winters to Peru

28 09 024 Muscisaxicola maculirostris
Spot-billed Ground-Tyrant — Temperate Andes of Colombia to Argentina, Chile

28 09 025 Muscisaxicola fluviatilis
Little Ground-Tyrant — Southwest Amazonian Brazil, adjacent Peru, Bolivia

28 09 026 Muscigralla brevicauda
Short-tailed Ground-Tyrant — Coastal southwest Ecuador to northern Chile

28 09 027 Lessonia rufa (oreas)
Rufous-backed Negrito — Temperate southern Peru to Tierra del Feugo

28 09 028 Myiotheretes pernix
Santa Marta Bush-Tyrant — Temperate Santa Marta Mountains of Colombia

	Date	Location
28 09 029 **Myiotheretes striaticollis** *Streak-throated Bush-Tyrant*		Andes of northwest Venezuela to northwest Argentina
28 09 030 **Myiotheretes fumigatus** ⊹ *Smoky Bush-Tyrant*		Andes of northwest Venezuela to Peru (Junin)
28 09 031 **Myiotheretes fuscorufus** ⊹ *Rufous-bellied Bush-Tyrant*		Temperate southeast Peru, northern Bolivia
28 09 032 **Myiotheretes signatus** *Jelski's Bush-Tyrant*		Andes of Peru (Junin—known from two specimens)
28 09 033 **Myiotheretes erythropygius** *Red-rumped Bush-Tyrant*		Mountains of northern Colombia to northwest Bolivia
28 09 034 **Ochthoeca oenanthoides** *d'Orbigny's Chat-Tyrant*		Andes of Peru to northwest Argentina, Chile
28 09 035 **Ochthoeca fumicolor** ⊹ *Brown-backed Chat-Tyrant*		Andes of northwest Venezuela to northern Bolivia
28 09 036 **Ochthoeca leucophrys** ⊹ *White-browed Chat-Tyrant*		Temperate Andes of Peru, Chile, Argentina (La Rioja)
28 09 037 **Ochthoeca piurae** *Piura Chat-Tyrant*		Andes of northwest Peru (Piura to Ancash)
28 09 038 **Ochthoeca rufipectoralis** ⊹ *Rufous-breasted Chat-Tyrant*		Andes of northwest Venezuela to northwest Bolivia
28 09 039 **Ochthoeca frontalis** ⊹ *Crowned Chat-Tyrant*		Temperate Andes of Colombia to northwest Bolivia
28 09 040 **Ochthoeca cinnamomeiventris** ⊹ *Slaty-backed Chat-Tyrant*		Andes of Venezuela to northern Bolivia
28 09 041 **Ochthoeca pulchella** ⊹ *Golden-browed Chat-Tyrant*		Andes of southern Ecuador to northwest Bolivia
28 09 042 **Ochthoeca diadema** *Yellow-bellied Chat-Tyrant*		Andes of western Venezuela to Peru (Junin)
28 09 043 **Sayornis phoebe** *Eastern Pheobe*		Eastern North America; winters to eastern Mexico
28 09 044 **Sayornis nigricans (latirostris)** *Black Phoebe*		Southwest United States to northwest Argentina
28 09 045 **Sayornis saya** *Say's Phoebe*		Western North America (Alaska to Mexico)
28 09 046 **Colonia colonus** *Long-tailed Tyrant*		Tropical southern Honduras to northeast Argentina

		Date	Location
28 09 047	**Gubernetes yetapa** *Streamer-tailed Tyrant*		Southern Brazil, Bolivia to central Argentina
28 09 048	**Alectrurus tricolor** *Cock-tailed Tyrant*		Southern Brazil, Bolivia to northern Argentina
28 09 049	**Yetapa risoria** *Strange-tailed Tyrant*		Southern Brazil to central Argentina (San Luis)
28 09 050	**Knipolegus lophotes** *Crested Black-Tyrant*		Southern Brazil (Minas Gerais, Goiás) to Uruguay
28 09 051	**Knipolegus nigerrimus** *Velvety Black-Tyrant*		Southeast Brazil (Minas Gerais to São Paulo)
28 09 052	**Knipolegus aterrimus** *White-winged Black-Tyrant*		Subtropical northern Peru to Argentina (Chubut)
28 09 053	**Knipolegus orenocensis** *Riverside Tyrant*		Tropical Venezuela, western Brazil to northeast Peru
28 09 054	**Knipolegus poecilurus** *Rufous-tailed Tyrant*		Venezuela to northern Bolivia, Brazil (Roraima)
28 09 055	**Knipolegus cyanirostris** *Blue-billed Black-Tyrant*		Southeast Brazil (Minas Gerais) to eastern Argentina
28 09 056	**Knipolegus cabanisi** *Plumbeous Tyrant*		Southeast Peru to northwest Argentina (Cajamarca)
28 09 057	**Knipolegus subflammulatus** *Berlioz's Tyrant*		Bolivia (probable immature *K. cabanisi*—known from four specimens)
28 09 058	**Phaeotriccus poecilocercus** *Amazonian Black-Tyrant*		Amazonian Brazil, adjacent Peru, Venezuela, Guyana
28 09 059	**Phaeotriccus hudsoni** *Hudson's Black-Tyrant*		Central Argentina; winters to Bolivia, Matto Grasso
28 09 060	**Entotriccus striaticeps** *Cinereous Tyrant*		Northwest Argentina to Bolivia, Brazil (Matto Grasso)
28 09 061	**Hymenops perspicillata** *Spectacled Tyrant*		Southern Brazil, Bolivia to Chile, Argentina
28 09 062	**Muscipipra vetula** *Shear-tailed Gray-Tyrant*		Southeast Brazil to northeast Argentina, Paraguay
28 09 063	**Fluvicola pica (albiventris)** *Pied Water-Tyrant*		Widespread tropical South America
28 09 064	**Fluvicola nengeta** *Masked Water-Tyrant*		Arid tropical southwest Ecuador to Peru, eastern Brazil

		Date	Location
28 09 065	**Arundinicola leucocephala** *White-headed Marsh-Tyrant*		South America (east of Andes) to northern Argentina
28 09 066	**Pyrocephalus rubinus** *Vermilion Flycatcher*		Arid southwest United States to Argentina; Galapagos Islands
28 09 067	**Ochthornis littoralis** *Drab Water-Tyrant*		Tropical South America to western Bolivia, Brazil
28 09 068	**Tumbezia salvini** *Tumbes Tyrant*		Arid littoral of northwest Peru (Tumbes to Libertad)
28 09 069	**Satrapa icterophrys** *Yellow-browed Tyrant*		Brazil to Argentina; winters north to Venezuela
28 09 070	**Machetornis rixosus** *Cattle Tyrant*		Tropical Venezuela to eastern Brazil, central Argentina
28 09 071	**Sirystes sibilator** *Sirystes*		Panama to northeast Argentina, eastern Brazil
28 09 072	**Muscivora forficata** *Scissor-tailed Flycatcher*		South-central United States; winters to Panama
28 09 073	**Muscivora tyrannus** *Fork-tailed Flycatcher*		Southern Mexico to central Argentina (Rio Negro)
28 09 074	**Tyrannus tyrannus** *Eastern Kingbird*		Central Canada to Gulf of Mexico; winters to northern Argentina
28 09 075	**Tyrannus cubensis** *Giant Kingbird*		Cuba, Isle of Pines, Caicos, Great Inagua, Isla Mujeres
28 09 076	**Tyrannus melancholicus** *Tropical Kingbird*		Southwest United States to central Argentina
28 09 077	**Tyrannus couchii** *Couch's Kingbird*		Extreme southern Texas to southern Mexico (Veracruz)
28 09 078	**Tyrannus dominicensis** *Gray Kingbird*		Southern Florida, West Indies; winters to northern South America
28 09 079	**Tyrannus caudifasciatus** *Loggerhead Kingbird*		West Indies (widespread Greater Antilles)
28 09 080	**Tyrannus verticalis** *Western Kingbird*		Southwest Canada to northwest Mexico; winters to Nicaragua
28 09 081	**Tyrannus niveigularis** *Snowy-throated Kingbird*		Tropical Pacific Colombia, Ecuador to northwest Peru
28 09 082	**Tyrannus albogularis** *White-throated Kingbird*		Widespread tropical Amazon basin, the Guianas

	Date	Location
28 09 083 **Tyrannus apolites** Heine's Kingbird		Brazil (Rio de Janeiro—probable hybrid)
28 09 084 **Tyrannus vociferans** Cassin's Kingbird		Western United States to central Mexico; winters in Guatemala
28 09 085 **Tyrannus crassirostris** Thick-billed Kingbird		Western Mexico to Guatemala; casual Arizona, New Mexico
28 09 086 **Tyrannopsis sulphurea** Sulphury Flycatcher		Tropical Guianas to Peru, Amazon basin
28 09 087 **Tyrannopsis luteiventris** Dusky-chested Flycatcher		South America to eastern Peru, west Amazonian Brazil
28 09 088 **Empidonomus varius** Variegated Flycatcher		Northern South America to central Argentina (La Pampa)
28 09 089 **Empidonomus aurantioatrocristatus** Crowned Slaty Flycatcher		Widespread tropical Amazon basin to central Argentina
28 09 090 **Legatus leucophaius** Piratic Flycatcher		Tropical southern Mexico to northern Argentina
28 09 091 **Conopias trivirgata** Three-striped Flycatcher		Venezuela to northeast Argentina, Amazonian Brazil
28 09 092 **Conopias cinchoneti** Lemon-browed Flycatcher		Andes of northwest Venezuela to Peru (Cuzco)
28 09 093 **Conopias parva** White-ringed Flycatcher		Costa Rica to Pacific Colombia, northern Brazil
28 09 094 **Megarhynchus pitangua** Boat-billed Flycatcher		Mexico to Argentina (mainly east of the Andes)
28 09 095 **Myiodynastes luteiventris** Sulphur-bellied Flycatcher		Southeast Arizona to Costa Rica; winters to Bolivia
28 09 096 **Myiodynastes maculatus** Streaked Flycatcher		Tropical Mexico to Brazil, Argentina (La Pampa)
28 09 097 **Myiodynastes bairdi** Baird's Flycatcher		Arid coastal Ecuador to northwest Peru
28 09 098 **Myiodynastes chrysocephalus** Golden-crowned Flycatcher		Mountains of eastern Panama to southern Peru
28 09 099 **Myiodynastes hemichrysus** Golden-bellied Flycatcher		Highlands of Costa Rica and western Panama

	Date	Location
28 09 100 **Myiozetetes cayanensis** *Rusty-margined Flycatcher*		Panama to southeast Brazil, eastern Bolivia
28 09 101 **Myiozetetes granadensis** *Gray-capped Flycatcher*		Nicaragua to northern Bolivia, western Brazil
28 09 102 **Myiozetetes similis** *Social Flycatcher*		Tropical Mexico to Brazil, northeast Argentina
28 09 103 **Myiozetetes inornatus** *White-bearded Flycatcher*		Tropical savanna, llanos of Venezuela
28 09 104 **Pitangus sulphuratus** *Great Kiskadee*		Tropical southeast Texas to central Argentina
28 09 105 **Pitangus lictor** *Lesser Kiskadee*		Tropical Panama to northern Bolivia, southern Brazil
28 09 106 **Myiarchus semirufus** *Rufous Flycatcher*		Arid coastal Peru (Tumbes to northern Lima)
28 09 107 **Myiarchus validus** *Rufous-tailed Flycatcher*		Wooded hills and mountains of Jamaica
28 09 108 **Myiarchus ferox** *Short-crested Flycatcher*		Tropical Costa Rica to northwest Argentina; Tobago
28 09 109 **Myiarchus venezuelensis** *Venezuela Flycatcher*		Tropical northwest Venezuela to Colombia; Tobago
28 09 110 **Myiarchus panamensis** *Panama Flycatcher*		Southwest Costa Rica to northern Venezuela
28 09 111 **Myiarchus apicalis** *Apical Flycatcher*		Arid scrub of Colombia (west of eastern Andes)
28 09 112 **Myiarchus cephalotes** *Pale-edged Flycatcher*		Highlands of eastern Venezuela to northern Bolivia
28 09 113 **Myiarchus phaeocephalus** *Sooty-crowned Flycatcher*		Arid western Ecuador to northwest Peru (Piura)
28 09 114 **Myiarchus tyrannulus** *Wied's Crested Flycatcher*		Southwest United States to northern Argentina
28 09 115 **Myiarchus nuttingi** *Nutting's Flycatcher*		Semiarid western Mexico to northwest Costa Rica
28 09 116 **Myiarchus oberi** *Lesser Antillean Flycatcher*		Widespread throughout the Lesser Antilles
28 09 117 **Myiarchus nugator** *Grenada Flycatcher*		Lesser Antilles (St. Vincent, Grenadines and Grenada)
28 09 118 **Myiarchus yucatanensis** *Yucatán Flycatcher*		Mexico (Yucatán Peninsula and Cozumel Island)
28 09 119 **Myiarchus stolidus** *Stolid Flycatcher*		Widespread West Indies

	Date	Location
27 09 120	**Myiarchus antillarum** Antillean Flycatcher	Puerto Rico, Viques, Culebra, St. Thomas, St. John
28 09 121	**Myiarchus sagrae** Cuban Flycatcher	Bahamas, Cuba, Isle of Pines, Grand Cayman Island
28 09 122	**Myiarchus swainsoni** Swainson's Flycatcher	Tropical South America to northeast Argentina
28 09 123	**Myiarchus crinitus** Great Crested Flycatcher	Southeast Canada to Gulf states; winters to Colombia
28 09 124	**Myiarchus cinerascens** Ash-throated Flycatcher	Semiarid western United States to Costa Rica
28 09 125	**Myiarchus tuberculifer** Olivaceous Flycatcher	Southwest United States to Brazil, Argentina; Jamaica; Trinidad
28 09 126	**Myiarchus barbirostris** Jamaican Flycatcher	Widespread Island of Jamaica
28 09 127	**Myiarchus magnirostris** Galapagos Tyrant Flycatcher	Restricted to the Galapagos Islands
28 09 128	**Attila spadiceus** Bright-rumped Attila	Southern Mexico to Brazil, northern Bolivia
28 09 129	**Attila bolivianus** Dull-capped Attila	Eastern Peru, northern Bolivia, southwest Brazil
28 09 130	**Attila rufus** Gray-hooded Attila	Mountains of southeast Brazil (Bahia to Santa Catarina)
28 09 131	**Attila citriniventris** Citron-bellied Attila	Venezuela, Ecuador, adjacent Peru, northwest Brazil
28 09 132	**Attila cinnamomeus** Cinnamon Attila	South America to northern Bolivia, Amazonian Brazil
28 09 133	**Attila torridus** Ochraceous Attila	Tropical western Ecuador (Esmeraldas to Peruvian border)
28 09 134	**Pseudattila phoenicurus** Rufous-tailed Attila	Tropical Venezuela to Brazil, northeast Argentina
28 09 135	**Rhytipterna simplex** Grayish Mourner	Tropical South America to Brazil, Bolivia
28 09 136	**Rhytipterna immunda** Pale-bellied Mourner	Tropical French Guiana to Colombia, adjacent Brazil
28 09 137	**Rhytipterna holerythra** Rufous Mourner	Tropical Guatemala to northwest Ecuador
28 09 138	**Casiornis rufa** Rufous Casiornis	Campos of eastern Brazil to northern Argentina
28 09 139	**Casiornis fusca** Ash-throated Casiornis	Caatinga, scrub of eastern and central Brazil

	Date	Location

28 09 140	**Laniocera hypopyrrha**	
+	*Cinereous Mourner*	Northern South America to Brazil, northern Bolivia
28 09 141	**Laniocera rufescens**	
	Speckled Mourner	Southeast Mexico to northwest Ecuador
28 09 142	**Nesotriccus ridgwayi**	
	Cocos Island Flycatcher	Cocos Island (off Costa Rica—endangered)
28 09 143	**Deltarhynchus flammulatus**	
	Flammulated Flycatcher	Semiarid coastal Mexico (Sinaloa to Chiapas)
28 09 144	**Nuttallornis borealis**	
	Olive-sided Flycatcher	Widespread temperate North America; winters to Peru
28 09 145	**Contopus virens**	
	Eastern Wood Pewee	Eastern North America; winters to Peru, western Brazil
28 09 146	**Contopus sordidulus (richardsonii)**	
	Western Wood Pewee	Western North America; winters to Bolivia
28 09 147	**Contopus latirostris**	
	Lesser Antillean Pewee	Mountain forests of Puerto Rico and Lesser Antilles
28 09 148	**Contopus caribaeus**	
	Greater Antillean Pewee	Forests of Bahamas and Greater Antilles
28 09 149	**Contopus cinereus**	
	Tropical Pewee	Southern Mexico to northern Argentina
28 09 150	**Contopus albogularis**	
	White-throated Pewee	Tropical French Guiana, Surinam, northeast Brazil
28 09 151	**Contopus nigrescens**	
	Blackish Pewee	Mountains of eastern Ecuador, northeast Peru, Guyana
28 09 152	**Contopus pertinax**	
	Coues' Flycatcher	Highlands of southwest United States to Nicaragua
28 09 153	**Contopus lugubris**	
	Dark Pewee	Highlands of Costa Rica and western Panama
28 09 154	**Contopus fumigatus**	
+	*Smoke-colored Pewee*	Highlands of South America to northwest Argentina
28 09 155	**Contopus ochraceus**	
	Ochraceous Pewee	Mountains of Costa Rica and western Panama (rare)
28 09 156	**Empidonax flaviventris**	
	Yellow-bellied Flycatcher	Eastern Canada and United States; winters to Panama
28 09 157	**Empidonax virescens**	
	Acadian Flycatcher	Eastern North America; winters to Ecuador
28 09 158	**Empidonax minimus**	
	Least Flycatcher	Northeast North America; winters to Panama

		Date	Location
28 09 159	**Empidonax trailii** *Willow (Traill's)* *Flycatcher*		North America; winters to Argentina
28 09 160	**Empidonax alnorum** *Alder Flycatcher*		Canada, northern United States; winters to Panama
28 09 161	**Empidonax hammondii** *Hammond's Flycatcher*		Western North America; winters to Nicaragua
28 09 162	**Empidonax oberholseri** *Dusky Flycatcher*		Western North America; winters to southern Mexico
28 09 163	**Empidonax wrightii** *Gray (Wright's)* *Flycatcher*		Western United States; winters to central Mexico
28 09 164	**Empidonax affinis** *Pine Flycatcher*		Oak-pine forests of Mexico; winters to Guatemala
28 09 165	**Empidonax difficilis** *Western Flycatcher*		Widespread Alaska to Honduras
28 09 166	**Empidonax flavescens** *Yellowish Flycatcher*		Highlands of southern Mexico to western Panama
28 09 167	**Empidonax euleri** **(lawrencei)** *Euler's Flycatcher*		Widespread South America; West Indies
28 09 168	**Empidonax lawrencei** *Lawrence's Flycatcher*		Widespread northern South America; Grenada
27 09 169	**Empironax griseipectus** *Gray-breasted Flycatcher*		Arid tropical southwest Ecuador to northwest Peru
28 09 170	**Empidonax albigularis** *White-throated Flycatcher*		Highlands of Mexico to Panama
28 09 171	**Empidonax atriceps** *Black-capped Flycatcher*		Mountains of Costa Rica and western Panama
27 09 172	**Empidonax fulvifrons** *Buff-breasted Flycatcher*		Highlands of southwest United States to Honduras
27 09 173	**Cnemotriccus fuscatus** *Fuscous Flycatcher*		Tropical South America to northeast Argentina, Brazil
28 09 174	**Mitrephanes** **phaeocercus** *Tufted Flycatcher*		Highlands of Mexico to Bolivia
28 09 175	**Xenotriccus callizonus** *Belted Flycatcher*		Highlands of southeast Mexico (Chiapas), Guatemala
28 09 176	**Aechmolophus** **mexicanus** *Pileated Flycatcher*		Highlands of Mexico (Michoacan to Oaxaca)
28 09 177	**Terenotriccus erythrurus** *Ruddy-tailed Flycatcher*		Southeast Mexico to Amazonian Brazil, northern Bolivia

	Date	Location
28 09 178 **Aphanotriccus capitalis** *Tawny-chested Flycatcher*		Nicaragua and Caribbean slope of Costa Rica
28 09 179 **Aphanotriccus audax** *Black-billed Flycatcher*		Tropical eastern Panama and northwest Colombia
28 09 180 **Myiobius villosus** ✝ *Tawny-breasted Flycatcher*		Mountains of eastern Panama to northwest Bolivia
28 09 181 **Myiobius barbatus** *Whiskered Flycatcher*		Northern South America to Peru, Brazil
28 09 182 **Myiobius sulphureipygius** ✝ *Sulphur-rumped Flycatcher*		Southern Mexico to western Ecuador
27 09 183 **Myiobius atricaudus** *Black-tailed Flycatcher*		Costa Rica to Brazil, Peru (Junin)
28 09 184 **Myiotriccus ornatus** ✝ *Ornate Flycatcher*		Tropical, subtropical Andes of Colombia to Peru
28 09 185 **Pyrrhomyias cinnamomea** ✝ *Cinnamon Flycatcher*		Mountains of Venezuela to northwest Argentina
28 09 186 **Myiophobus flavicans** ✝ *Flavescent Flycatcher*		Mountains of Venezuela to eastern Peru (Junin)
28 09 187 **Myiophobus phoenicomitra** *Orange-crested Flycatcher*		Tropical western Colombia, northern Ecuador
28 09 188 **Myiophobus cryptoxanthus** *Olive-chested Flycatcher*		Tropical eastern Ecuador, northeast Peru
28 09 189 **Myiophobus inornatus** *Unadorned Flycatcher*		Eastern Andes of southeast Peru, northwest Bolivia
28 09 190 **Myiophobus pulcher** *Handsome Flycatcher*		Subtropical Andes of Colombia to Peru (Puno)
28 09 191 **Myiophobus lintoni** *Orange-banded Flycatcher*		Andes of southern Ecuador (Azuay, Loja)
28 09 192 **Myiophobus ochraceiventris** ✝ *Ochraceous-breasted Flycatcher*		Mountains of central Peru to Bolivia (La Paz)
28 09 193 **Myiophobus roraimae** *Roraiman Flycatcher*		Mountains of Guyana, Venezuela, Colombia to Peru
28 09 194 **Myiophobus fasciatus** *Bran-colored Flycatcher*		Widespread Costa Rica to Argentina, Brazil
28 09 195 **Hirundinea ferruginea** *Cliff Flycatcher*		Tropical South America to northern Argentina, Brazil

	Date	Location
28 09 196 **Onychorhynchus coronatus** *Amazonian Royal Flycatcher*		Widespread tropical Amazon basin
28 09 197 **Onychorhynchus mexicanus** *Northern Royal Flycatcher*		Gulf lowlands of Mexico to northern Colombia
28 09 198 **Platyrinchus platyrhynchos** *White-crested Spadebill*		Tropical South America to northern Bolivia, Brazil
28 09 199 **Playtrinchus leucoryphus** *Russet-winged Spadebill*		Southeast Brazil (Espirito Santo) to Paraguay
28 09 200 **Platyrinchus mystaceus** *White-throated Spadebill*		Southern Mexico to northeast Argentina, Brazil
28 09 201 **Platyrinchus coronatus** *Golden-crowned Spadebill*		Tropical Nicaragua to Peru, Amazonian Brazil
28 09 202 **Playtyrinchus saturatus** *Cinnamon-breasted Spadebill*		Tropical South America to Peru, Amazonian Brazil
28 09 203 **Platyrinchus flavigularis** *Yellow-throated Spadebill*		Tropical northwest Venezuela to eastern Peru
28 09 204 **Cnipodectes subbrunneus** *Brownish Flycatcher*		Tropical Panama to eastern Peru, western Brazil
28 09 205 **Tolmomyias sulphurescens** *Yellow-olive Flycatcher*		Southern Mexico to northern Argentina, Brazil
28 09 206 **Tolmomyias assimilis** *Yellow-margined Flycatcher*		Costa Rica to northwest Bolivia, Amazonian Brazil
28 09 207 **Tolmomyias poliocephalus** *Gray-crowned Flycatcher*		Tropical South America to northern Bolivia, Brazil
28 09 208 **Tolmomyias flaviventris** *Yellow-breasted Flycatcher*		Tropical South America to northern Bolivia, Brazil
28 09 209 **Rhynchocyclus olivaceus** *Olivaceous Flatbill*		Tropical Panama to northern Bolivia, southeast Brazil
28 09 210 **Rhynchocyclus brevirostris** *Eye-ringed Flatbill*		Tropical southern Mexico to northwest Ecuador
28 09 211 **Rhynchocyclus fulvipectus** *Fulvous-breasted Flatbill*		Tropical subtropical Colombia to northern Bolivia

		Date	Location
28 09 212	**Ramphotrigon ruficauda** *Rufous-tailed Flatbill*		Tropical Amazon basin and the Guianas
28 09 213 +	**Ramphotrigon fuscicauda** *Dusky-tailed Flatbill*		Tropical northeast Ecuador to Bolivia (rare)
27 09 214	**Ramphotrigon megacephala** *Large-headed Flatbill*		Tropical Venezuela to northeast Argentina, Brazil
28 09 215	**Todirostrum nigriceps** *Black-headed Tody-Flycatcher*		Tropical Costa Rica to western Ecuador, Venezuela
28 09 216	**Todirostrum chrysocrotaphum** *Yellow-browed Tody-Flycatcher*		Tropical South America to Bolivia, Amazonian Brazil
28 09 217	**Todirostrum pictum** *Painted Tody-Flycatcher*		Guianas and northern Brazil
28 09 218	**Todirostrum calopterum** *Golden-winged Tody-Flycatcher*		Tropical southeast Colombia to eastern Peru
28 09 219 +	**Todirostrum poliocephalum** *Gray-headed Tody-Flycatcher*		Southeast Brazil (Minas Gerais to Santa Catarina)
28 09 220 +	**Todirostrum cinereum** *Common Tody-Flycatcher*		Southern Mexico to Bolivia, throughout Brazil
28 09 221	**Todirostrum maculatum** *Spotted Tody-Flycatcher*		Tropical South America to Bolivia, Amazonian Brazil
28 09 222	**Todirostrum fumifrons** *Smoke-fronted Tody-Flycatcher*		Tropical Surinam to eastern Brazil (Bahia)
28 09 223	**Todirostrum senex** *Buff-cheeked Tody-Flycatcher*		Brazil (Rio Madeira—known from one specimen)
28 09 224	**Todirostrum capitale** *Black-and-white Tody-Flycatcher*		Tropical southeast Colombia to northeast Peru
28 09 225	**Todirostrum albifacies** *White-cheeked Tody-Flycatcher*		Southeast Peru (Rio Colorado—known from one specimen)
28 09 226	**Todirostrum russatum** *Ruddy Tody-Flycatcher*		Subtropical Venezuela (Bolivar), adjacent Brazil
28 09 227	**Todirostrum plumbeiceps** *Ochre-faced Tody-Flycatcher*		Southeast Peru, southern Brazil to northern Argentina

		Date	Location
28 09 228	**Todirostrum latirostre** *Rusty-fronted Tody-Flycatcher*		Tropical southeast Colombia to Brazil, Paraguay
28 09 229	**Todirostrum sylvia** *Slate-headed Tody-Flycatcher*		Tropical southern Mexico to Amazonian Brazil
28 09 230	**Todirostrum hypospodium** *Berlepsch's Tody-Flycatcher*		Colombia (unique—probably aberrant *T. sylvia*)
28 09 231	**Ceratotriccus furcatus** *Fork-tailed Pygmy-Tyrant*		Southeast Brazil (Espirito Santa to São Paulo)
28 09 232	**Oncostoma cinereigulare** *Northern Bentbill*		Tropical southern Mexico to western Panama
28 09 233	**Oncostoma olivaceum** *Southern Bentbill*		Tropical central Panama to northern Colombia (Chocó)
28 09 234	**Idioptilon nidipendulum** *Hangnest Tody-Tyrant*		Southeast Brazil (Bahia to São Paulo)
28 09 235 ✛	**Idioptilon rufigulare** *Buff-throated Tody-Tyrant*		Eastern Andes of Peru, northern Bolivia (rare)
28 09 236	**Idioptilon striaticolle** *Stripe-necked Tody-Tyrant*		Tropical Amazonian Brazil, adjacent Colombia to Bolivia
28 09 237	**Idioptilon spodiops** *Yungas Tody-Tyrant*		Uplands of northern Bolivia (La Paz, Cochabamba)
28 09 238	**Idioptilon aenigma** *Zimmer's Tody-Tyrant*		Brazil (Rio Tapajós—known from two specimens)
28 09 239	**Idioptilon inornatum** *Pelzelni's Tody-Tyrant*		Brazil (Rio Icaná—probably aberrant *I. margaritaceiventer*)
28 09 240	**Idioptilon mirandae** *Buff-breasted Tody-Tyrant*		*Caatinga* of eastern Brazil (Ceará to Santa Catarina)
28 09 241	**Idioptilon kaempferi** *Kaempfer's Tody-Tyrant*		Southeast Brazil (Santa Catarina—known from one specimen)
28 09 242 ✛	**Idioptilon margaritaceiventer** *Pearly-vented Tody-Tyrant*		Arid littoral of Venezuela to northern Argentina
28 09 243	**Idioptilon granadense** *Black-throated Tody-Tyrant*		Subtropical, temperate mountains of Venezuela to Peru
28 09 244	**Idioptilon zosterops** *White-eyed Tody-Tyrant*		Tropical South America to Brazil, northern Bolivia

		Date	Location
28 09 245	**Idioptilon orbitatum** *Eye-ringed Tody-Tyrant*		Southeast Brazil (Minas Gerais to São Paulo)
28 09 246	**Microcochlearius josephinae** *Boat-billed Tody-Tyrant*		Guyana (Rio Amapá—known from a single specimen)
28 09 247	**Snethlagea minor** *Snethlage's Tody-Tyrant*		Tropical Amazonian Brazil, adjacent Surinam
28 09 248	**Poecilotriccus ruficeps** *Rufous-crowned Tody-Tyrant*		Subtropical Andes of Venezuela to northern Peru
28 09 249	**Taeniotriccus andrei** *Black-chested Tody-Tyrant*		Tropical Venezuela, adjacent Brazil (Rio Tapajós)
28 09 250 +	**Lophotriccus pileatus** *Scale-crested Pygmy-Tyrant*		Mountains of Costa Rica to Peru, southwest Brazil
28 09 251	**Lophotriccus vitiosus** *Double-banded Pygmy-Tyrant*		Guianas to eastern Peru, Amazonian Brazil
28 09 252	**Lophotriccus eulophotes** *Long-crested Pygmy-Tyrant*		Southwest Brazil (Rio Purus); southeast Peru (rare)
28 09 253	**Colopteryx galeatus** *Helmeted Pygmy-Tyrant*		Tropical Guianas to Colombia, Amazonian Brazil
28 09 254	**Atalotriccus pilaris** *Pale-eyed Pygmy-Tyrant*		Tropical Pacific Panama to Guyana
28 09 255	**Myiornis auricularis** *Eared Pygmy-Tyrant*		Central Peru to Paraguay, eastern Brazil
28 09 256	**Myiornis ecaudatus** *Short-tailed Pygmy-Tyrant*		Northern South America east of Andes, Amazonian Brazil
28 09 257	**Myiornis atricapillus** *Black-capped Pygmy-Tyrant*		Costa Rica to western Ecuador (possible race *M. ecaudatus*)
28 09 258	**Pseudotriccus pelzelni** *Bronze-olive Pygmy-Tyrant*		Mountains of eastern Panama to Peru (Puno)
28 09 259	**Pseudotriccus simplex** *Hazel-fronted Pygmy-Tyrant*		Subtropical Andes of southeast Peru, northwest Bolivia
28 09 260 +	**Pseudotriccus ruficeps** *Rufous-headed Pygmy-Tyrant*		Andes of Colombia to northwest Bolivia

		Date	Location
28 09 261	**Hemitriccus diops** *Drab-breasted Pygmy-Tyrant*		Southeast Brazil (Bahia) to Argentina (Misiones)
28 09 262	**Hemitriccus obsoletus** *Brown-breasted Pygmy-Tyrant*		Coastal mountains of southeast Brazil
28 09 263	**Hemitriccus flammulatus** *Flammulated Pygmy-Tyrant*		Southeast Peru, northern Bolivia, adjacent Matto Grosso
28 09 264	**Hemitriccus cinnamomeipectus** *Cinnamon-breasted Tody-Tyrant*		Northern Peru (Cajamarca, Amazonas, San Martin), adjacent Ecuador?
28 09 265	**Pogonotriccus eximius** *Southern Bristle-Tyrant*		Southeast Brazil (Minas Gerais) to Argentina (Misiones)
28 09 266	**Pogonotriccus ophthalmicus** *Marbled-faced Bristle-Tyrant*		Subtropical mountains of Venezuela to Bolivia
28 09 267	**Pogonotriccus gualaquizae** *Ecuadorian Bristle-Tyrant*		Subtropical Andes of eastern Ecuador to Peru
28 09 268	**Pogonotriccus poecilotis** *Variegated Bristle-Tyrant*		Subtropical mountains of Venezuela to northern Peru
28 09 269	**Pogonotriccus orbitalis** *Spectacled Bristle-Tyrant*		Subtropical Andes of Ecuador to northern Bolivia
28 09 270	**Pogonotriccus venezuelanus** *Venezuelan Bristle-Tyrant*		Lower subtropical mountains of Venezuela
28 09 271	**Pogonotriccus flaviventris** *Yellow-bellied Bristle-Tyrant*		Upper tropical mountains of Venezuela
28 09 272	**Leptotriccus sylviolus** *Bay-ringed Tyrannulet*		Southeast Brazil (Espirito Santo) to Argentina (Misiones)
28 09 273	**Phylloscartes flavovirens** *Yellow-green Tyrannulet*		Confined to Panama (Canal Zone eastward)
28 09 274	**Phylloscartes virescens** *Olive-green Tyrannulet*		Tropical Guianas and Surinam
28 09 275	**Phylloscartes ventralis** *Mottle-cheeked Tyrannulet*		Mountains of Peru to eastern Brazil, northern Argentina

	Date	Location

28 09 276	**Phylloscartes chapmani**	
	Chapman's Tyrannulet	Subtropical mountains of Venezuela (Bolivar and Amazonas)
28 09 277	**Phylloscartes nigrifrons**	
	Black-fronted Tyrannulet	Mountains of Venezuela (Bolivar and Amazonas)
28 09 278	**Phylloscartes oustaleti**	
	Oustalet's Tyrannulet	Southeast Brazil (Espirito Santo to Santa Catarina)
28 09 279	**Phylloscartes difficilis**	
	Serra do Mar Tyrannulet	Coastal mountains of southeast Brazil
28 09 280	**Phylloscartes paulistus**	
	São Paulo Tyrannulet	Southeast Brazil (Espirito Santo) to eastern Paraguay
28 09 281	**Phylloscartes superciliaris**	
	Rufous-browed Tyrannulet	Mountains of Costa Rica to Colombia, Venezuela
28 09 282	**Phylloscartes roquettei**	
	Minas Gerais Tyrannulet	Brazil (Minas Gerais—known from a single specimen)
28 09 283	**Capsiempis flaveola**	
	Yellow Tyrannulet	Nicaragua to northeast Argentina, southeast Brazil
28 09 284 +	**Euscarthmus meloryphus**	
	Tawny-crowned Pygmy-Tyrant	Tropical South America to northern Argentina, Brazil
28 09 285	**Euscarthmus rufomarginatus**	
	Rufous-sided Pygmy-Tyrant	Savanna, *cerrado* of Surinam, eastern Brazil
28 09 286	**Pseudocolopteryx dinellianus**	
	Dinelli's Doradito	Subtropical northeast Argentina, adjacent Bolivia, Paraguay
28 09 287	**Pseudocolopteryx sclateri**	
	Crested Doradito	Tropical Guyana, eastern Brazil to northern Argentina
28 09 288	**Pseudocolopteryx acutipennis**	
	Subtropical Doradito	Subtropical Andes of Colombia to northwest Argentina
28 09 289	**Pseudocolopteryx flaviventris**	
	Warbling Doradito	Southeast Brazil to Argentina (Chubut), Chile
28 09 290	**Polystictus pectoralis**	
	Bearded Tachuri	Tropical South America to northern Argentina
28 09 291	**Polystictus superciliaris**	
	Gray-backed Tachuri	Campos of eastern Brazil (Minas Gerais, Bahia)

		Date	Location
28 09 292	**Culicivora caudacuta** *Sharp-tailed Tyrant*		Southeast Brazil (São Paulo) to northern Argentina
28 09 293 +	**Tachuris rubrigastra** *Many-colored Rush-Tyrant*		Marshes of Peru, southern Brazil to central Argentina
28 09 294 +	**Anairetes parulus** *Tufted Tit-Tyrant*		Andes of Colombia to Tierra del Fuego
28 09 295	**Anairetes fernandezianus** *Juan Fernandez Tit-Tyrant*		Endemic to Más A Tierra Island (off Chile)
28 09 296	**Anairetes flavirostris** *Yellow-billed Tit-Tyrant*		Andes of Peru to Bolivia, Argentina, Chile
28 09 297	**Anairetes reguloides** **(nigrocristatus)** *Pied-crested Tit-Tyrant*		Foothills of southwest Peru, northern Chile
28 09 298	**Anairetes alpinus** *Ash-breasted Tit-Tyrant*		Andes of Peru (Ancash) to northern Bolivia (La Paz)
28 09 299	**Uromyias agilis** *Agile Tit-Tyrant*		Andes of Venezuela, Colombia, Ecuador
28 09 300	**Uromyias agraphia** *Unstreaked Tit-Tyrant*		Eastern Andes of Peru (Huanaco to Cuzco—rare)
28 09 301	**Stigmatura napensis** *Lesser Wagtail-Tyrant*		Tropical Amazonian Brazil, adjacent Peru, Ecuador
28 09 302	**Stigmatura budytoides** *Greater Wagtail-Tyrant*		Northeast Brazil to central Argentina (Rio Negro)
28 09 303	**Serpophaga hypoleuca** *River Tyrannulet*		Tropical Venezuela, Amazonian Brazil, adjacent Peru
28 09 304	**Serpophaga cinerea** *Torrent Tyrannulet*		Rocky mountain streams of Costa Rica to Bolivia
28 09 305	**Serpophaga subcristata** *White-crested Tyrannulet*		Eastern Brazil to northern Bolivia, central Argentina
28 09 306	**Serpophaga munda** *White-bellied Tyrannulet*		Southern Brazil, Bolivia to central Argentina
28 09 307	**Serpophaga griseiceps** *Gray-crowned Tyrannulet*		Highlands of Bolivia (Cochabamba—rare)
28 09 308 +	**Serpophaga nigricans** *Sooty Tyrannulet*		Southeast Brazil, Bolivia to Argentina (Rio Negro)
28 09 309	**Serpophaga araguayae** *Bananal Tyrannulet*		Brazil (Rio Araguia—known from a single specimen)
28 09 310	**Inezia subflava** *Pale-tipped Tyrannulet*		Tropical Colombia to the Guianas, Amazonian Brazil
28 09 311	**Inezia tenuirostris** *Slender-billed Tyrannulet*		Arid northwest Venezuela to northern Colombia

	Date	Location

28 09 312 **Inezia inornata**
+   *Plain Tyrannulet*

Scrub of Bolivia, southern Brazil to northwest Argentina

28 09 313 **Mecocerculus leucophrys**
           White-throated Tyrannulet

Mountains of Venezuela to northwest Argentina

28 09 314 **Mecocerculus poecilocercus**
           White-tailed Tyrannulet

Andes of Colombia to Peru (Junin, Cuzco)

28 09 315 **Mecocerculus hellmayri**
           Buff-banded Tyrannulet

Andes of southeast Peru, Bolivia, northwest Argentina

28 09 316 **Mecocerculus calopterus**
           Rufous-winged Tyrannulet

Subtropical Andes of western Ecuador to northern Peru

28 09 317 **Mecocerculus minor**
           Sulphur-bellied Tyrannulet

Mountains of Venezuela, Colombia to central Peru

28 09 318 **Mecocerculus stictopterus**
           White-banded Tyrannulet

Andes of Venezuela to northwest Bolivia

28 09 319 **Colorhamphus parvirostris**
           Patagonian Tyrant

Chile, Argentina, (Nequen, Valdivia to Tierra del Fuego)

28 09 320 **Xenopsaris albinucha**
           White-naped Xenopsaris

Tropical Venezuela to northern Argentina

28 09 321 **Elaenia flavogaster**
           Yellow-bellied Elaenia

Southern Mexico to northern Argentina; Trinidad; Tobago

28 09 322 **Elaenia martinica**
           Caribbean Elaenia

West Indies, extralimital Caribbean Islands

28 09 323 **Elaenia spectabilis**
           Large Elaenia

Widespread tropical South America to northern Argentina

28 09 324 **Elaenia albiceps**
+   *White-crested Elaenia*

Andes of Colombia to Tierra del Fuego

28 09 325 **Elaenia parvirostris**
           Small-billed Elaenia

Widespread woodlands, forest edges of South America

28 09 326 **Elaenia mesoleuca**
           Olivaceous Elaenia

Southeast Brazil to northern Argentina (Santa Fe)

28 09 327 **Elaenia strepera**
           Slaty Elaenia

Bolivia to northwest Argentina; winters to Colombia

		Date	Location
28 09 328	**Elaenia gigas** *Mottle-backed (Giant)* *Elaenia*		Tropical eastern Colombia to Bolivia
28 09 329	**Elaenia pelzelni** *Brownish Elaenia*		Tropical Amazonian Brazil, adjacent Peru
28 09 330	**Elaenia cristata** *Plain-crested Elaenia*		Widespread tropical savanna, *cerrado* of Amazon basin
28 09 331	**Elaenia chiriquensis** *Lesser Elaenia*		Costa Rica to Bolivia, Paraguay, southeast Brazil
28 09 332	**Elaenia ruficeps** *Rufous-crowned Elaenia*		Lowlands of Guianas to Colombia, adjacent Brazil
28 09 333	**Elaenia frantzii** *Mountain Elaenia*		Highlands of Guatemala to Colombia, northwest Venezuela
28 09 334	**Elaenia obscura** *Highland Elaenia*		Andes of Peru to southeast Brazil, northern Argentina
28 09 335	**Elaenia dayi** *Great Elaenia*		Subtropical mountains of Venezuela (Bolivar, Amazonas)
28 09 336	**Elaenia pallatangae** *Sierran Elaenia*		Mountains of Guyana, Venezuela to northern Bolivia
28 09 337	**Elaenia fallax** *Greater Antillean Elaenia*		Highlands of Hispaniola and Jamaica
28 09 338	**Myiopagis gaimardii** *Forest Elaenia*		Tropical Panama to Bolivia, southeast Brazil; Trinidad
28 09 339	**Myiopagis caniceps** *Gray Elaenia*		Tropical Panama to northern Argentina
28 09 340	**Myiopagis subplacens** *Pacific Elaenia*		Arid tropical western Ecuador to northwest Peru
28 09 341	**Myiopagis flavivertex** *Yellow-crowned Elaenia*		Tropical South America to Amazonian Brazil, Peru
28 09 342	**Myiopagis viridicata** *Greenish Elaenia*		Tropical southern Mexico to northern Argentina
28 09 343	**Myiopagis cotta** *Jamaican Elaenia*		Widespread mountains and lowlands of Jamaica
28 09 344	**Suiriri suiriri** *Suiriri Flycatcher*		Campos of Brazil to Bolivia, Argentina
28 09 345	**Sublegatus modestus** *Short-billed Flycatcher*		Southeast Brazil to Argentina (La Pampa)
28 09 346	**Sublegatus arenarum** *Scrub Flycatcher*		Costa Rica to Amazonian Brazil (possible race *S. modestus*)

		Date	Location

28 09 347 **Phaeomyias murina**
Mouse-colored Tyrannulet   Tropical Panama to Brazil, northwest Argentina; Trinidad

28 09 348 **Phaeomyias leucospodia**
Gray-and-white Tyrannulet   Arid littoral of southwest Ecuador, northwest Peru

28 09 349 **Camptostoma imberbe**
Northern Beardless Flycatcher   Southwest United States to Costa Rica

28 09 350 **Camptostoma obsoletum**
Southern Beardless Flycatcher   Costa Rica to northern Argentina, Brazil

28 09 351 **Xanthomyias virescens**
Greenish Tyrannulet   Venezuela to Brazil, northeast Argentina

28 09 352 **Xanthomyias reiseri**
Reiser's Tyrannulet   Eastern Brazil (Piauí) to northeast Paraguay

28 09 353 **Xanthomyias sclateri**
Sclater's Tyrannulet   Subtropical southeast Peru to northwest Argentina

28 09 354 **Phyllomyias fasciatus**
Planalto Tyrannulet   Eastern Brazil (Ceará) to northeast Argentina

28 09 355 **Phyllomyias griseiceps**
Sooty-headed Tyrannulet   Tropical eastern Panama to Amazonian Brazil

28 09 356 **Tyranniscus nigrocapillus**
†
Black-capped Tyrannulet   Andes of northwest Venezuela to Peru (Junin)

28 09 357 **Tyranniscus uropygialis**
Tawny-rumped Tyrannulet   Andes of northwest Venezuela to Bolivia

28 09 358 **Tyranniscus cinereiceps**
†
Ashy-headed Tyrannulet   Subtropical Andes of Colombia to Peru (Cuzco)

28 09 359 **Tyranniscus australis**
Olrog's Tyrannulet   Northwest Argentina in Jujuy (Yuto)

28 09 360 **Tyranniscus vilissimus**
Paltry Tyrannulet   Mountains of southern Mexico to Colombia, Venezuela

28 09 361 **Tyranniscus bolivianus**
Bolivian Tyrannulet   Andes of southeast Peru to northern Bolivia

28 09 362 **Tyranniscus cinereicapillus**
Red-billed Tyrannulet   Tropical northeast Ecuador, Peru (Ayacucho, Junin)

28 09 363 **Tyranniscus gracilipes**
Slender-footed Tyrannulet   Northern South America to Bolivia, Brazil

28 09 364 **Tyranniscus viridiflavus**
Golden-faced Tyrannulet   Northern Venezuela to Peru (Huánuco, Junin)

		Date	Location

28 09 365 Oreotriccus plumbeiceps
Plumbeous-crowned Tyrannulet
Subtropical Andes of Colombia to Peru (Cuzco)

28 09 366 Oreotriccus griseocapillus
Gray-capped Tyrannulet
Southeast Brazil (Minas Gerais to Santa Catarina)

28 09 367 Tyrannulus elatus
Yellow-crowned Tyrannulet
Tropical Panama to Bolivia, Amazonian Brazil

28 09 368 Acrochordopus zeledoni
White-fronted Tyrannulet
Highlands of Costa Rica to Peru (possible race *A. burmeisteri*)

28 09 369 Acrochordopus burmeisteri
Rough-legged Tyrannulet
Highlands of Venezuela to northern Argentina

28 09 370 Ornithion inerme
White-lored Tyrannulet
Tropical South America to Amazonian Brazil, adjacent Peru

28 09 371 Ornithion semiflavum
Yellow-bellied Tyrannulet
Tropical southern Mexico to Colombia, Venezuela

28 09 372 Ornithion brunneicapillum
Brown-capped Tyrannulet
Caribbean slope of Costa Rica and Panama

28 09 373 Leptopogon superciliaris
Slaty-capped Flycatcher
Mountains of Costa Rica to northern Bolivia

28 09 374 Leptopogon amaurocephalus
Sepia-capped Flycatcher
Southern Mexico to northern Argentina, Brazil

28 09 375 Leptopogon rufipectus
Rufous-breasted Flycatcher
Subtropical Andes of Venezuela to Ecuador

28 09 376 Leptopogon taczanowskii
Inca Flycatcher
Subtropical central Andes of Peru (Amazonas to Cuzco)

28 09 377 Mionectes striaticollis
Streak-necked Flycatcher
Subtropical Andes of Colombia to northern Bolivia

28 09 378 Mionectes olivaceus
Olive-striped Flycatcher
Costa Rica to Peru (Puno)

28 09 379 Pipromorpha oleaginea
Ochre-bellied Flycatcher
Tropical southern Mexico to Bolivia, Brazil; Trinidad

28 09 380 Pipromorpha macconnelli
McConnell's Flycatcher
Northern South America to Bolivia, Amazonian Brazil

	Date	Location

28 09 381   **Pipromorpha rufiventris**
              Gray-hooded Flycatcher   Southeast Brazil (Espirito Santo to Rio Grande do Sul)

FAMILY: OXYRUNCIDAE (Sharpbill)

28 10 001   **Oxyruncus cristatus**
              Sharpbill   Discontinuously distributed Costa Rica to Paraguay, Brazil

FAMILY: PHYTOTOMIDAE (Plantcutters)

28 11 001   **Phytotoma rutila**
              White-tipped Plantcutter   Highlands of Bolivia, Paraguay, Uruguay, Argentina

28 11 002   **Phytotoma rara**
+   *Rufous-tailed Plantcutter*   Central Chile, Argentina (Nequen to Rio Negro)

28 11 003   **Phytotoma raimondii**
              Peruvian Plantcutter   Coastal northwest Peru (Tumbes to Lima)

FAMILY: PITTIDAE (Pittas)

28 12 001   **Pitta phayrei**
              Eared Pitta   Forests of southwest China to Indochina

28 12 002   **Pitta nipalensis**
              Blue-naped Pitta   Lowlands of Nepal to Yunnan, Indochina; Tonkin

28 12 003   **Pitta soror**
              Blue-rumped Pitta   Southeast China to Indochina; Hainan

28 12 004   **Pitta oatesi**
              Rusty-naped Pitta   Southwest China to Indochina

28 12 005   **Pitta schneideri**
              Schneider's Pitta   Mountains of northern Sumatra (rare)

28 12 006   **Pitta caerulea**
              Giant Pitta   Malay Peninsula, Sumatra, Borneo

28 12 007   **Pitta kochi**
              Koch's Pitta   Philippines (endemic northern Luzon Island—endangered)

28 12 008   **Pitta erythrogaster (mackloti)**
              Blue-breasted Pitta   Java to Philippines, Celebes, New Guinea, Cape York Peninsula of Australia

28 12 009   **Pitta arcuata**
              Blue-banded Pitta   Primary submontane forests of Borneo

		Date	Location
28 12 010	**Pitta granatina** *Garnet Pitta*		Lowlands of Malay Peninsula, Borneo, Sumatra
28 12 011	**Pitta cyanea** *Blue Pitta*		Lowland forests of southeast India to Indochina
28 12 012	**Pitta ellioti** *Bar-bellied Pitta*		Confined to lowland forests of Indochina
28 12 013	**Pitta guajana** *Banded Pitta*		Malay Peninsula, Java, Sumatra, Borneo
28 12 014	**Pitta gurneyi** *Gurney's Pitta*		Lowland forests of Tenasserim to peninsular Thailand
28 12 015	**Pitta baudi** *Blue-headed Pitta*		Primary lowland forests of Borneo
28 12 016	**Pitta sordida** *Hooded Pitta*		Widespread Oriental region mainland and islands
28 12 017	**Pitta brachyura** **(megarhynca)** **(nympha)** *Fairy Pitta*		Widespread Oriental region mainland and islands
28 12 018	**Pitta angolensis** *African Pitta*		West Africa to Angola, Tanzania
28 12 019	**Pitta reichenowi** *Green-breasted Pitta*		Dense forests of Cameroon to Uganda
28 12 020	**Pitta superba** *Superb Pitta*		Admiralty Islands (known only from Manus Island)
28 12 021	**Pitta maxima** *Halmahera Pitta*		Restricted to Halmahera Island (Moluccas)
28 12 022	**Pitta steerei** *Steere's Pitta*		Philippines (Mindanao, Bohol, Leyte, Samar)
28 12 023	**Pitta moluccensis** *Blue-winged Pitta*		Widespread Southeast Asia
28 12 024	**Pitta iris** *Black-breasted Pitta*		Australia (Northern Territory westward)
28 12 025	**Pitta versicolor** *Buff-breasted Pitta*		Cape York Peninsula to New South Wales; New Guinea
28 12 026	**Pitta anerythura** *Black-faced Pitta*		Solomon Islands (Ysabel, Bougainville, Choiseul)

FAMILY: ACANTHISITTIDAE (New Zealand Wrens)

28 13 001	**Acanthisitta chloris** *Rifleman*		Throughout New Zealand, adjacent offshore islands

		Date	Location

28 13 002   **Xenicus longipes**
            Bush Wren   New Zealand (remote forests of North Island—endangered)

28 13 003   **Xenicus gilviventris**
            South Island Rock Wren   New Zealand (subalpine scrub of South Island)

28 13 004   **Xenicus lyalli**
            Stephen Island Wren   Extinct. Extirpated by cats on Stephen Island, New Zealand about 1894

FAMILY: PHILEPITTIDAE (False Sunbirds)

28 14 001   **Philepitta castanea**
            Velvety Asity   Highland forests of eastern Madagascar

28 14 002   **Philepitta schlegeli**
            Schlegel's Asity   Dense forests of western Madagascar

28 14 003   **Neodrepanis coruscans**
            Wattled Asity   Highland forests of eastern Madagascar

28 14 004   **Neodrepanis hypoxantha**
            Small-billed Asity   Madagascar (on verge of extinction—recently rediscovered)

FAMILY: MENURIDAE (Lyrebirds)

28 15 001   **Menura superba (novaehollandiae)**
            Superb Lyrebird   Coastal southeast Queensland to Victoria

28 15 002   **Menura alberti**
            Albert's Lyrebird   Mountain forests of Queensland to New South Wales

FAMILY: ATRICHORNITHIDAE (Scrub-birds)

28 16 001   **Atrichornis clamosus**
            Noisy Scrub-bird   Southwestern Australia (Two People Bay—endangered)

28 16 002   **Atrichornis rufescens**
            Rufous Scrub-bird   Queensland to New South Wales (endangered)

	Date	Location

FAMILY: ALAUDIDAE (Larks)

28 17 001	**Mirafra javanica** *Singing Bushlark*	Africa; Southern Asia to Australia
28 17 002	**Mirafra hova** *Madagascar Bushlark*	Widespread Madagascar
28 17 003	**Mirafra cordofanica** *Kordofan Bushlark*	Senegal to the Central African Republic
28 17 004	**Mirafra williamsi** *William's Bushlark*	Lava deserts of northern Kenya
28 17 005	**Mirafra cheniana** *Latakoo Bushlark*	Grassy uplands of Zambia, Rhodesia to Cape Province
28 17 006	**Mirafra albicauda** *White-tailed Bushlark*	Central African Republic to Tanzania
28 17 007	**Mirafra passerina** *Monontonous Bushlark*	Lowland thornveld and savanna of South Africa
28 17 008	**Mirafra pulpa** *Friedman's Lark*	East Arica—rare and local
28 17 009	**Mirafra candida** *Rufous Bushlark*	Kenya (Guaso Niyro River—known from a single specimen)
28 17 010	**Mirafra hypermetra** *Red-winged Bushlark*	Somalia, Ethiopia to Tanzania
28 17 011	**Mirafra somalica** *Somali Long-billed Lark*	Confined to dry acacia of northeast Somalia
28 17 012	**Mirafra africana** *Rufous-naped Bushlark*	Widespread Africa south of the Sahara
28 17 013	**Mirafra chuana** *Short-clawed Lark*	Zambia to Cape Province
28 17 014	**Mirafra angolensis** *Angolan Lark*	Highlands of southern Zaire, adjacent Angola, Zambia
28 17 015	**Mirafra rufocinnamomea** *Flappet Lark*	Widespread Africa south of the Sahara
28 17 016	**Mirafra apiata (damarensis)** *Clapper Lark*	Open rocky bush country of extreme southern Africa
28 17 017	**Mirafra africanoides** *Fawn-colored Bushlark*	Dry bush country of eastern and southern Africa
28 17 018	**Mirafra collaris** *Collared Lark*	Dry acacia of Ethiopia and Somalia
28 17 019	**Mirafra assamica** *Rufous-winged Bushlark*	Dry country of Sri Lanka; India to Indochina

		Date	Location

28 17 020	**Mirafra rufa** *Rusty Bushlark*	Somalia to Kenya, Niger
28 17 021	**Mirafra gilletti** *Gillett's Lark*	Ethiopia to Somalia
28 17 022	**Mirafra degodiensis** *Sidamo Lark*	Ethiopia (arboreal savanna of southern Ethiopia)
28 17 023	**Mirafra poecilosterna** *Pink-breasted Lark*	Somalia to Tanzania
28 17 024	**Mirafra sabota** *Sabota Lark*	Bush country of Rhodesia to South Africa (aboreal)
28 17 025	**Mirafra erythroptera** *Red-winged Bushlark*	Stony open plains and plateaus of India
28 17 026	**Mirafra nigricans** *Dusky Bushlark*	Angola, Tanzania to South Africa
28 17 027	**Heteromirafra ruddi** *Rudd's Lark*	Confined to South Africa
28 17 028	**Heteromirafra sidamoensis** *Sidamo Bushlark*	Ethiopia (described 1975 from Sidamo Plateau)
28 17 029	**Certhilauda curvirostris** *Long-billed Lark*	Arid Angola to South Africa
28 17 030	**Certhilauda albescens** *Karoo Lark*	Deserts of coastal and inland tip of South Africa
28 17 031	**Certhilauda albofasciata** *Spike-heeled Lark*	Arid bush and deserts of Angola to South Africa
28 17 032	**Eremopterix australis** *Black-eared Finch-Lark*	Grassy plains of Southwest Africa to Cape Province
28 17 033	**Eremopterix leucotis** *Chestnut-backed Sparrow-Lark*	Arid Africa south of the Sahara
28 17 034	**Eremopterix signata** *Chestnut-headed Sparrow-Lark*	Arid Somalia, Ethiopia, Kenya, the Sudan
28 17 035	**Eremopterix verticalis** *Gray-backed Sparrow-Lark*	Dry regions of Angola to South Africa
28 17 036	**Eremopterix nigriceps** *White-fronted Sparrow-Lark*	Deserts of Spanish Sahara to the Nile Valley
28 17 037	**Eremopterix grisea** *Ashy-crowned Finch-Lark*	Indo-Gangetic plain to *terai* of Nepal; Sri Lanka
28 17 038	**Eremopterix leucopareia** *Fischer's Sparrow-Lark*	Grassy plains of Kenya, Tanzania, Malawi

		Date	Location
28 17 039	**Ammomanes cincturus** *Bar-tailed Lark*		Deserts of southern Palearctic region
28 17 040	**Ammomanes phoenicurus** *Rufous-tailed Finch-Lark*		Deserts of Iran to India
28 17 041	**Ammomanes deserti** *Desert Lark*		Deserts of southern Palearctic region
28 17 042	**Ammomanes dunni** *Dunn's Lark*		Semiarid Sahara Desert east of the Sudan, Arabia
28 17 043	**Ammomanes grayi** *Gray's Lark*		Confined to Namib Desert of Southwest Africa
28 17 044	**Ammomanes burrus** *Ferruginous Lark*		Lowlands of Southwest Africa to Cape Province
28 17 045	**Alaemon alaudipes** *Bifasciated Lark*		Deserts of Cape Verde Archipelago to western India
28 17 046	**Alaemon hamertoni** *Lesser Hoopoe-Lark*		Confined to arid regions of Somalia
28 17 047	**Rhamphocorys clotbey** *Clotbey Lark*		Stony deserts of North Africa to northern Arabia
28 17 048	**Melanocorypha calandra** *Calandra Lark*		Arid Mediterranean basin to Afghanistan, Turkestan
28 17 049	**Melanocorypha bimaculata** *Bimaculated Lark*		India to central Asia; winters to South Africa
28 17 050	**Melanocorypha maxima** *Long-billed Calandra Lark*		High plateau of Kashmir to Tibet, western China
28 17 051	**Melanocorypha mongolica** *Mongolian Lark*		High steppes of Siberia to Mongolia, Manchuria
28 17 052	**Melanocorypha leucoptera** *White-winged Lark*		Arid steppes of Palearctic region
28 17 053	**Melanocorypha yeltoniensis** *Black Lark*		Grassy, saline steppes of Palearctic region
28 17 054	**Calandrella cinerea (brachydactila)** *Short-toed Lark*		Widespread Palearctic, Ethiopian, Oriental mainland
28 17 055	**Calandrella blanfordi** *Blanford's Lark*		Eritrea to Somalia (possible race *C. cinerea*)
28 17 056	**Calandrella acutirostris** *Hume's Lark*		Semi-deserts of Iran to eastern Tibet
28 17 057	**Calandrella raytal** *Indian Sandlark*		Sandy river beds of Iran to Burma

	Date	Location
28 17 058 **Calandrella rufescens** *Lesser Short-toed Lark*		Arid regions of Europe, North Africa to India
28 17 059 **Calandrella cheleensis** *Mongolian Lark*		Arid northeast Mongolia, Gobi Desert to northeast China
28 17 060 **Calandrella razae** *Raza Island Lark*		Confined to Raza Island (Cape Verde Islands—endangered)
28 17 061 **Calandrella conirostris** *Pink-billed Lark*		Semiarid bush country of South Africa
28 17 062 **Calandrella starki** *Stark's Lark*		Dry, grassy country of Southwest Africa
28 17 063 **Calandrella sclateri** *Sclater's Lark*		Dry bush country of Southwest Africa to Cape Province
28 17 064 **Calandrella fringillaris** *Botha's Lark*		Confined to semiarid bush of South Africa
28 17 065 **Calandrella obbiensis** *Obbia Lark*		Confined to semiarid regions of Somalia
28 17 066 **Calandrella personata** *Masked Lark*		Confined to highlands of eastern Ethiopia
28 17 067 **Chersophilus duponti** *Dupont's Lark*		Arid Algeria to Egypt; occasionally Mediterranean Europe
28 17 068 **Pseudalaemon fremantlii** *Short-tailed Lark*		Confined to Ethiopia and Somalia
28 17 069 **Galerida cristata** *Crested Lark*		Semi-deserts of Palearctic region, Indian Subcontinent
28 17 070 **Galerida theklae** *Thekla Lark*		Semi-deserts of southern Palearctic region
28 17 071 **Galerida malabarica** *Short-crested Lark*		Arid North Africa to coastal western India
28 17 072 **Galerida deva** *Syke's Crested Lark*		Mainly confined to semiarid central plateau of India
28 17 073 **Galerida modesta (bucolica)** *Sun Lark*		Southern Sudan to northern Uganda, Zaire
28 17 074 **Galerida magnirostris** *Thick-billed Lark*		Confined to Cape Province of South Africa
28 17 075 **Lullula arborea** *Wood Lark*		Dry grasslands of western Palearctic region
28 17 076 **Alauda arvensis** *Common Skylark*		Widespread Palearctic region; introduced Australasia, Vancouver

	Date	Location

28 17 077 **Alauda gulgula**
Oriental Skylark
Widespread Oriental region mainland and islands

28 17 078 **Eremophila alpestris**
Horned Lark
Widespread Palearctic, Nearctic regions; winters to Colombia

28 17 079 **Eremophila bilopha**
Temminck's Lark
Deserts of North Africa to western Iraq

FAMILY: HIRUNDINIDAE (Swallows)

28 18 001 **Pseudochelidon eurystomina**
African River Martin
West Africa (Gabon, lower Congo and Ubangi Rivers)

28 18 002 **Pseudochelidon sirintarae**
White-eyed River Martin
Known only from central Thailand

28 18 003 **Tachycineta bicolor**
Tree Swallow
Alaska to United States; winters to Colombia, Guyana, West Indies

28 18 004 **Tachycineta albilinea**
Mangrove Swallow
Coastal tropical Mexico to coastal northwest Peru

28 18 005 **Tachycineta albiventer**
+
White-winged Swallow
Tropical South America to Argentina; Trinidad

28 18 006 **Tachycineta leucorrhoa**
White-rumped Swallow
Brazil (Minas Gerais) to northern Argentina

28 18 007 **Tachycineta leucopyga**
Chilean Swallow
Southern Brazil to Chile (Atacama), Tierra del Fuego

28 18 008 **Tachycineta thalassina**
Violet-green Swallow
Western North America; winters to Honduras, Panama

28 18 009 **Callichelidon cyaneoviridis**
Bahama Swallow
Pine forests of Bahamas; winters to Cuba; vagrant to Florida

28 18 010 **Kalochelidon euchrysea**
Golden Swallow
High mountains of Hispaniola and Jamaica

28 18 011 **Progne tapera**
+
Brown-chested Martin
Panama to Brazil, central Argentina

28 18 012 **Progne subis**
Purple Martin
Canada to Mexico; winters to West Indies, Colombia, Brazil

28 18 013 **Progne cryptoleuca**
Cuban Martin
Cuba and Isle of Pines (casual southern Florida)

		Date	Location

28 18 014 Progne dominicensis
Snowy-bellied Martin
West Indies (except Cuba and Isle of Pines; Tobago

28 18 015 Progne chalybea
Gray-breasted Martin
Southern Texas to Argentina; Trinidad

28 18 016 Progne modesta
Southern Martin
Panama to Argentina (Chubut); Galapagos Islands

28 18 017 Notiochelidon murina
Brown-bellied Swallow
Mountains of Venezuela to Bolivia (La Paz)

28 18 018 Notiochelidon cyanoleuca
Blue-and-white Swallow
Highlands of Costa Rica to Tierra del Fuego

28 18 019 Notiochelidon flavipes
Pale-footed Swallow
Central Andes of Colombia, Peru (Junin)

28 18 020 Notiochelidon pileata
Black-capped Swallow
Highlands of southern Mexico (Chipas) to El Salvador

28 18 021 Atticora fasciata
White-banded Swallow
Tropical South America to Bolivia, Amazonian Brazil

28 18 022 Atticora melanoleuca
Black-collared Swallow
Northern South America to southeast Colombia, Brazil

28 18 023 Neochelidon tibialis
White-thighed Swallow
Tropical Panama to Amazonian Brazil, northern Argentina

28 18 024 Alopochelidon fucata
Tawny-headed Swallow
Venezuela to southern Brazil, central Argentina

28 18 025 Stelgidopteryx ruficollis
Rough-winged Swallow
Southern Canada to central Argentina; Trinidad

28 18 026 Cheramoeca leucosternum
White-backed Swallow
Dry interior of Australia

28 18 027 Pseudhirundo griseopyga (andrewi)
Gray-rumped Swallow
Central Sudan and Ethiopia to South Africa

28 18 028 Riparia paludicola
Plain Martin
Africa to India, Indochina; Taiwan; Phillippines

28 18 029 Riparia congica
Congo Martin
Middle and lower Congo River and lower Ubangi

28 18 030 Riparia riparia
Bank Swallow (Sand Martin)
Almost worldwide distribution tin temperate regions

28 18 031 Riparia cincta
Banded Martin
Widespread Africa south of the Sahara

		Date	Location
28 18 032	**Phedina borbonica** *Mascarene Martin*		Madagascar; Reunion; Mauritius; Pemba Islands
28 18 033	**Phedina brazzae** *Brazza's Martin*		Rivers of south-central Zaire (rare)
28 18 034	**Ptyonoprogne rupestris** *Crag Martin*		Southern Europe to central Asia, north Africa
28 18 035	**Ptyonogrogne obsoleta** *Pale Crag Martin*		Widespread North Africa to India
28 18 036	**Ptyonoprogne fuligula** *African Rock Martin*		Widespread Africa south of the Sahara
28 18 037	**Ptyonoprogne concolor** *Dusky Crag Martin*		India, southwest China to Indochina
28 18 038	**Hirundo rustica** *Barn Swallow*		Cosmopolitan; almost worldwide distribution
28 18 039	**Hirundo lucida** *Red-chested Swallow*		Senegal to Ethiopia
28 18 040	**Hirundo angolensis** *Angola Swallow*		Kenya, Uganda to Rhodesia
28 18 041	**Hirundo tahitica** *Pacific Swallow*		Southern India to islands of Polynesia
28 18 042	**Hirundo albigularis** *White-throated Swallow*		South Africa; wanders to Angola, Zambia
28 18 043	**Hirundo aethiopica** *Ethiopian Swallow*		Widespread Ethiopian region
28 18 044	**Hirundo smithii** *Wire-tailed Swallow*		Tropical Africa to India, Indochina
28 18 045	**Hirundo atrocaerulea** *Blue Swallow*		South Africa; wanders to Uganda, Malawi
28 18 046	**Hirundo nigrita** *White-throated Blue Swallow*		Sierra Leone to southern Zaire
28 18 047	**Hirundo leucosoma** *Pied-winged Swallow*		Senegal to Nigeria
28 18 048	**Hirundo megaensis** *White-tailed Swallow*		Endemic to highlands of southern Ethiopia
28 18 049	**Hirundo nigrorufa** *Black-and-rufous Swallow*		Angola, southern Zaire and Zambia
28 18 050	**Hirundo dimidiata** *Pearl-breasted Swallow*		Widespread open woodlands of southern half of Africa
28 18 051	**Hirundo cucullata** *Greater Striped Swallow*		South Africa; wanders to Zaire and Zambia

		Date	Location
28 18 052 +	**Hirundo abyssinica** *Lesser Striped Swallow*		Widespread Africa south of the Sahara
28 18 053	**Hirundo semirufa** *Rufous-chested Swallow*		Widespread Africa south of the Sahara
28 18 054	**Hirundo senegalensis** *African Mosque Swallow*		Africa south of the Sahara
28 18 055 +	**Hirundo daurica** *Red-rumped Swallow*		Southern Palearctic, Ethiopian regions; India; Sri Lanka
28 18 056	**Hirundo striolata** *Striated Swallow*		India to Southeast Asia
28 18 057	**Hirundo neoxena** *Welcome Swallow*		Widespread Australia, Tasmania
28 18 058	**Petrochelidon rufigula** *Angolan Cliff Swallow*		Angola, southwest Zaire and Zambia
28 18 059	**Petrochelidon preussi** *Preuss's Cliff Swallow*		Mali to Ghana, Zaire
28 18 060	**Petrochelidon andecola** *Andean Swallow*		Puna of Peru to northern Chile, eastern Bolivia
28 18 061	**Petrochelidon nigricans** *Tree Martin*		Australia, New Guinea, Greater and Lesser Sundas
28 18 062	**Petrochelidon spilodera** *African Cliff Swallow*		South Africa; wanders to Zaire, Namibia
28 18 063	**Petrochelidon pyrrhonota** *Cliff Swallow*		Alaska, Canada to southern Mexico; winters to Argentina
28 18 064	**Petrochelidon fulva** *Cave Swallow*		Texas to northwest Peru; West Indies
28 18 065	**Petrochelidon fluvicola** *Indian Cliff Swallow*		Afghanistan to Sikkim, India
28 18 066	**Petrochelidon ariel** *Fairy Martin*		Widespread Australia, Tasmania
28 18 067	**Petrochelidon fuliginosa** *Dusky Cliff Swallow*		Western and southern Cameroon and Gabon
28 18 068	**Delichon urbica** *Common House Martin*		Widespread Palearctic, Ethiopian, Oriental mainland
28 18 069	**Delichon dasypus** *Asian House Martin*		East Asia, Japan to Malaysia
28 18 070	**Delichon nipalensis** *Nepal House Martin*		Himalayas of India to Burma, Indochina
28 18 071	**Psalidoprocne fuliginosa** *Cameroun Roughwing Swallow*		Known only from Cameroon Mountain; Fernando Po

		Date	Location

28 18 072 **Psalidoprocne albiceps**
White-headed Roughwing Swallow — Sudan, Kenya, Uganda to Rhodesia

28 18 073 **Psalidoprocne pristoptera**
Blue Roughwing Swallow — High plateau of Ethiopia and Eritrea

28 18 074 **Psalidoprocne mangbettorum**
Mangbetu Roughwing Swallow — Savanna of eastern Zaire (possible race *P. pristoptera*)

28 18 075 **Psalidoprocne oleaginea**
Ethiopian Roughwing Swallow — Southwestern slopes of Ethiopian Plateau

28 18 076 **Psalidoprocne antinorii**
Brown Roughwing Swallow — Highland evergreen forests of Ethiopia

28 18 077 **Psalidoprocne petiti**
Petit's Roughwing Swallow — Cameroons to Gabon, lower Congo River

28 18 078 **Psalidoprocne holomelaena**
Black Roughwing Swallow — Highlands of Kenya to South Africa

28 18 079 **Psalidoprocne orientalis**
Eastern Roughwing Swallow — Highlands of Ethiopia to Rhodesia

28 18 080 **Psalidoprocne chalybea**
Shari Roughwing Swallow — Cameroon to eastern Zaire

28 18 081 **Psalidoprocne obscura**
Fanti Roughwing Swallow — Sierra Leone to Nigeria

28 18 082 **Psalidoprocne nitens**
Square-tailed Roughwing Swallow — Sierra Leone to Zaire

FAMILY: MOTACILLIDAE (Wagtails and Pipits)

28 19 001 **Dendronanthus indicus**
Forest Wagtail — Widespread Oriental region mainland and islands

28 19 002 **Motacilla flava**
Yellow Wagtail — Widespread Palearctic, Oriental region to Australia; Alaska

28 19 003 **Motacilla citreola**
Yellow-hooded Wagtail — Russian and China; winters to India and Burma

28 19 004 **Motacilla cinerea (caspica)**
Gray Wagtail — Widespread Palearctic, Oriental region to New Guinea

		Date	Location
28 19 005	**Motacilla alba** *White (Pied) Wagtail*		Widespread Palearctic and Oriental regions; Alaska
28 19 006	**Motacilla grandis** *Japanese Wagtail*		Japanese Islands; wanders to coastal China, Korea, Taiwan
28 19 007	**Motacilla madaraspatensis** *Large Pied Wagtail*		Sandy river banks of Kashmir, Nepal, Sikkim, India
28 19 008	**Motacilla aguimp** *African Pied Wagtail*		Widespread Africa south of the Sahara
28 18 009	**Motacilla clara** *Mountain Wagtail*		Rocky streams and waterfalls of Africa south of the Sahara
28 19 010	**Motacilla capensis** *Cape Wagtail*		Swamps of Kenya, Uganda, Tanzania to South Africa
28 19 011	**Motacilla flaviventris** *Madagascar Wagtail*		Highlands of Madagascar
28 19 012	**Tmetothylacus tenellus** *Golden Pipit*		Dry scrub of Ethiopia, Somalia, Sudan to Tanzania
28 19 013	**Macronyx capensis** *Cape Longclaw*		Dry grassy plains of Rhodesia to South Africa
28 19 014	**Macronyx croceus** *Yellow-throated Longclaw*		Widespread wet grasslands of Africa south of the Sahara
28 19 015	**Macronyx fullebornii** *Fulleborn's Longclaw*		Highland downs of Angola, Tanzania, Rhodesia, Zambia
28 19 016	**Macronyx sharpei** *Sharpe's Longclaw*		Grassy highland plains of Kenya
28 19 017	**Macronyx flavicollis** *Ethiopian Longclaw*		Endemic to high mountain plateau of Ethiopia
28 10 018	**Macronyx aurantiigula** *Pangani Longclaw*		Open thornbush of Kenya to northeast Tanzania
28 19 019	**Macronyx ameliae** *Rosy-breasted Longclaw*		Open grasslands of Kenya to Tanzania, Mozambique
28 19 020	**Macronyx grimwoodi** *Grimwood's Longclaw*		Marshy grasslands of eastern Angola to Zambia
28 19 021	**Anthus novaeseelandiae (richardii) (australis)** *Richard's Pipit*		Widespread Palearctic, Oriental, Australasian regions
28 19 022	**Anthus godlewskii** *Blyth's Pipit*		Sri Lanka; India to Mongolia; Andaman Islands
28 10 023	**Anthus campestris** *Tawny Pipit*		Barren rocky areas of Palearctic region

		Date	Location
28 19 024	**Anthus similis** *Long-billed Pipit*		Widespread Africa to India
28 19 025	**Anthus vaalensis** *Sandy Pipit*		Sandy lowlands of Ethiopia to South Africa
28 19 026	**Anthus leucophrys** *Plain-backed Pipit*		Widespread grassy plains of Africa south of the Sahara
28 19 027	**Anthus pallidiventris** *Long-legged Pipit*		Forest clearings of coastal Gabon to Angola
28 19 028	**Anthus pratensis** *Meadow Pipit*		Tundra and grasslands of western Palearctic region
28 19 029	**Anthus trivialis** *Tree Pipit*		Widespread Palearctic region; migrant to India and Africa
28 19 030	**Anthus hodgsoni** *Indian Tree Pipit*		Widespread Oriental region mainland and islands
28 19 031	**Anthus roseatus** *Rosy Pipit*		India to Tibet, Burma; Hainan
28 19 032	**Anthus cervinus** *Red-throated Pipit*		Widespread Palearctic, Oriental regions; occasional North America
28 19 033	**Anthus gustavi** *Petchora Pipit*		Siberia to southeast Asia; Borneo; Philippines; Taiwan
28 19 034	**Anthus spinoletta** *Water Pipit*		Widespread marshy areas of Holarctic region
28 19 035	**Anthus nilghiriensis** *Nilgiri Pipit*		Upland grasslands of extreme southern India (Kerala)
28 19 036	**Anthus sylvanus** *Upland Pipit*		Grassy Himalayan hillsides of Afghanistan to Yunnan
28 19 037	**Anthus berthelotii** *Berthelot's Pipit*		Confined to Madeira and Porto Santo Islands (Canaries)
28 19 038	**Anthus lineiventris** *Striped Pipit*		Rocky hillsides of Kenya, Tanzania, Angola to South Africa
28 19 039	**Anthus brachyurus** *Short-tailed Pipit*		Highland grasslands of Angola, Zaire, Uganda to Zambia
28 19 040	**Anthus caffer** *Little Tawny Pipit*		Dry thornbush of Kenya to South Africa
28 19 041	**Anthus sokokensis** *Sokoke Pipit*		Scrub forest of coastal Kenya to Tanzania (rare)

		Date	Location

28 19 042	**Anthus melindae**		
	Malindi Pipit		Confined to coastal district of Kenya (rare and local)
28 19 043	**Anthus chloris**		
	Yellow-breasted Pipit		Open grasslands of eastern half of South Africa
28 19 044	**Anthus crenatus**		
	Rock Pipit		Mountain slopes of southeastern South Africa
28 19 045	**Anthus gutturalis**		
	New Guinea Pipit		Alpine grasslands of New Guinea
28 19 046	**Anthus spragueii**		
	Sprague's Pipit		Great plains of North America; winters to southern Mexico
28 19 047	**Anthus furcatus**		
	Short-billed Pipit		Puna of Peru to Argentina, extreme southeast Brazil
28 19 048	**Anthus lutescens**		
	Yellowish Pipit		Pacific Panama to northern Argentina, Chile
28 19 049	**Anthus chacoensis**		
	Chaco Pipit		Paraguay, adjacent Argentina (Formosa, Chaco)
28 19 050	**Anthus correndera**		
	Correndera Pipit		Highlands of Peru, southeast Brazil to Tierra del Fuego
28 19 051	**Anthus antarcticus**		
	South Georgia Pipit		Restricted to Island of South Georgia
28 19 052	**Anthus natterei**		
	Ochre-breasted Pipit		Southeast Brazil to Paraguay, northeast Argentina
28 19 053	**Anthus hellmayri**		
	Hellmayr's Pipit		Highlands of southern Peru to Argentina, eastern Brazil
28 19 054	**Anthus bogotensis**		
	Páramo Pipit		Páramo of Venezuela to western Argentina

FAMILY: CAMPEPHAGIDAE (Cuckoo-Shrikes)

28 20 001	**Pteropodocys maxima**		
	Ground Cuckoo-Shrike		Drier parts of interior of Australia
28 20 002	**Coracina novaehollandiae**		
	Black-faced Cuckoo-Shrike		India to southeast Asia to Australia
28 20 003	**Coracina fortis**		
	Buru Cuckoo-Shrike		Buru Island (southern Moluccas)
28 20 004	**Coracina atriceps**		
	Seram Cuckoo-Shrike		Northern and southern Moluccas Islands

	Date	Location
28 20 005 **Coracina pollens** *Kai Cuckoo-Shrike*		Kai and Tanimbar Islands (Moluccas)
28 20 006 **Coracina schistacea** *Sula Cuckoo-Shrike*		Sula Island (between Celebes and Moluccas)
28 20 007 **Coracina caledonica** *Melanesian Graybird*		New Caledonia to the Solomon Islands
28 20 008 **Coracina caeruleogrisea** *Stout-billed Graybird*		New Guinea; Arus; Japen Island
28 20 009 **Coracina temminckii** *Celebes Graybird*		Celebes Islands
28 20 010 **Coracina larvata** *Black-faced Graybird*		Sumatra; Java; Borneo
28 20 011 **Coracina striata** *Bar-bellied Graybird*		Malay Peninsula; Andamans; Sumatra; Java; Philippines
28 20 012 **Coracina bicolor** *Muna Graybird*		Muna Island (Celebes)
28 20 013 **Coracina lineata** *Lineated Graybird*		Australia to New Guinea, Solomons, Bismarck Archipelago
28 20 014 **Coracina boyeri** *Rufous-underwing Graybird*		New Guinea; Misol and Japen Islands
28 20 015 **Coracina leucopygia** *Muna Cuckoo-Shrike*		Muna Island (Celebes)
28 20 016 **Coracina papuensis** *Papuan Graybird*		Queensland; New Guinea; Moluccas; Solomons
28 20 017 **Coracina robusta** *Little Cuckoo-Shrike*		Eastern Australia (possible race C. *papuensis*)
28 20 018 **Coracina longicauda** *Black-hooded Graybird*		Dense mountain forests of eastern and central New Guinea
28 20 019 **Coracina parvula** *Halmahera Graybird*		Halmahera Island (Moluccas)
28 20 020 **Coracina abbotti** *Luzon Graybird*		High mountains of the Celebes Islands
28 20 021 **Coracina analis** *New Caledonian Graybird*		New Caledonia and Loyalty Islands
28 20 022 **Coracina caesia** *Gray Cuckoo-Shrike*		Sudan, Ethiopia to South Africa
28 20 023 **Coracina pectoralis** *White-breasted Cuckoo-Shrike*		*Brachystegia* woodlands of Africa

		Date	Location
28 20 024	**Coracina graueri** *Grauer's Cuckoo-Shrike*		Highlands adjacent to Lake Tanganyika (endangered)
28 20 025	**Coracina cinerea** *Madagascar Cuckoo-Shrike*		Woodlands and mangroves of Madagascar
28 20 026	**Coracina azurea** *Blue Cuckoo-Shrike*		Forests of Sierra Leone to the Congo River
28 20 027	**Coracina typica** *Mauritius Cuckoo-Shrike*		Mauritius Island (Indian Ocean—endangered)
28 20 028	**Coracina newtoni** *Reunion Cuckoo-Shrike*		Reunion Island (Indian Ocean-endangered)
28 20 029	**Coracina coerulescens** *Luzon Graybird*		Philippines (endemic Luzon Island)
28 20 030	**Coracina dohertyi** *Sumba Graybird*		Sumba Island (Lesser Sundas)
28 20 031	**Coracina tenuirostris** *Cicadabird*		Australia to New Guinea, Celebes, Solomons
28 20 032	**Coracina morio** *Muller's Graybird*		Philippines and Celebes to New Guinea
28 20 033	**Coracina schisticeps** *Gray's Graybird*		New Guinea; Misol Island; d'Entrecasteaux Archipelago
28 20 034	**Coracina melaena** *Black Graybird*		New Guinea and adjacent islands
28 20 035	**Coracina montana** *Black-bellied Graybird*		Mountains of New Guinea
28 20 036	**Coracina holopolia** *Black-bellied Cuckoo-Shrike*		Solomon Islands
28 20 037	**Coracina mcgregori** *Sharp-tailed Graybird*		Philippines (endemic Mindanao Island)
28 20 038	**Coracina ostenta** **(panayensis)** *White-winged Graybird*		Philippines (endemic Guimaras, Negros, Panay Islands)
28 20 039	**Coracina polioptera** *Indochinese Cuckoo-Shrike*		Indochina, Burma, Thailand
28 20 040	**Coracina melaschista** *Black-winged Cuckoo-Shrike*		Himalayas of India to China, Indochina; Hainan; Taiwan
28 20 041	**Coracina fimbriata** *Lesser Cuckoo-Shrike*		Peninsular Thailand, Malaya; Greater Sundas

		Date	Location
28 20 042	**Coracina melanoptera** *Black-headed Cuckoo-Shrike*		Sri Lanka; India to southern China, Assam, Burma
28 20 043	**Campochaera sloetii** *Orange Cuckoo-Shrike*		New Guinea (Idenburg River to Astrolabe Mountains)
28 20 044	**Chlamydochaera jefferyi** *Black-breasted Triller*		Borneo (spottily distributed mountains Kinabalu to Dulit)
28 20 045	**Lalage melanoleuca** *Black-and-white Triller*		Philippine Islands; New Guinea
28 20 046	**Lalage nigra** *Pied Triller*		Malaya; Nicobars; Greater Sundas; Celebes; Philippines
28 20 047	**Lalage sueurii** *White-winged Triller*		Java; Lesser Sundas; Philippines; Celebes to Australia
28 20 048	**Lalage aurea** *Moluccan Triller*		Northern Moluccas Islands
28 20 049	**Lalage atrovirens** *Black-browed Triller*		Western New Guinea and adjacent islands
28 20 050	**Lalage leucomela** *Varied Triller*		Northern Australia to New Guinea, Bismarck Archipelago
28 20 051	**Lalage maculosa** *Polynesian Triller*		Common throughout Fiji Islands and Samoa
28 20 052	**Lalage sharpei** *Samoan Triller*		Highland forests of Upolu, Savaii Islands (Samoa)
28 20 053	**Lalage leucopyga** *Long-tailed Triller*		New Caledonia, Norfolk to New Hebrides and San Cristobal
28 20 054	**Campephaga phoenicea (sulphurata)** *Red-shouldered Cuckoo-Shrike*		Africa south of the Sahara
28 20 055	**Campephaga quiscalina** *Purple-throated Cuckoo-Shrike*		Widespread tropical forests of Africa
28 20 056	**Campephaga lobata** *Wattled Cuckoo-Shrike*		Gold Coast of Africa (known from 5 specimens)
28 20 057	**Campephaga petiti** *Petit's Cuckoo-Shrike*		Gabon to Angola, western Kenya (possible race *C. phoenicea*)
28 20 058	**Pericrocotus roseus** *Rosy Minivet*		Afghanistan, India to southern China, Indochina

		Date	Location
28 20 059	**Pericrocotus divaricatus** (tegimae) *Ashy Minivet*		Widespread Oriental mainland and islands
28 20 060	**Pericrocotus igneus** *Fiery Minivet*		Malaya; Sumatra; Borneo; Palawan (possible race *P. cinnamomeus*)
28 20 061	**Pericrocotus cinnamomeus** *Small Minivet*		India to Indochina; Andamans; Java; Bali; Lombok; Flores
28 20 062	**Pericrocotus lansbergei** *Sumbawa Minivet*		Sumbawa and Flores Islands (Lesser Sundas)
28 20 063	**Pericrocotus erythropygius** *White-bellied Minivet*		Dry scrub of India to Burma
28 20 064	**Pericrocotus solaris** (montanus) *Mountain Minivet*		Nepal to Indochina; Sumatra; Borneo; Hainan; Taiwan
28 20 065	**Pericrocotus ethologus** *Long-tailed Minivet*		Oak, pine forests of India, Afghanistan to Indochina
28 20 066	**Pericrocotus brevirostris** *Short-billed Minivet*		Himalayas of Nepal to western China, Indochina
28 20 067	**Pericrocotus miniatus** *Sunda Minivet*		Highlands of Sumatra and Java
28 20 068	**Pericrocotus flammeus** *Scarlet Minivet*		Widespread Oriental mainland and islands
28 20 069	**Hemipus picatus** *Pied Wood-Shrike*		India to Indochina; Sumatra; Borneo
28 20 070	**Hemipus hirundinaceus** *Black-winged Flycatcher-Shrike*		Malay Peninsula; Java; Sumatra; Borneo
28 20 071	**Tephrodornis gularis** (virgatus) *Large Wood-Shrike*		India to Indochina; Greater Sundas; Hainan
28 20 072	**Tephrodornis pondicerianus** *Common Wood-Shrike*		Sri Lanka; India, Nepal to Indochina

FAMILY: PYCNONOTIDAE (Bulbuls)

28 21 001	**Spizixos canifrons** *Crested Finchbill*		Assam to southwest China, Burma, Laos, Tonkin
28 21 002	**Spizixos semitorques** *Collared Finchbill*		Mountains of Southern China to Tonkin; Taiwan

		Date	Location
28 21 003	**Pycnonotus zeylanicus** *Straw-headed Bulbul*		Widespread Malay Peninsula; Java; Sumatra; Borneo
28 21 004	**Pycnonotus striatus** *Striated Bulbul*		Oak-rhododendron forests of Nepal to southern China
28 21 005	**Pycnonotus leucogrammicus** *Streaked Bulbul*		Mountain forests of Burma, Thailand, Laos, Tonkin
28 21 006	**Pycnonotus tympanistrigus** *Olive-crowned Bulbul*		Highlands of western Sumatra
28 21 007	**Pycnonotus melanoleucos** *Black-and-white Bulbul*		Malay Peninsula; Sumatra; Borneo
28 21 008	**Pycnonotus priocephalus** *Gray-headed Bulbul*		Dense evergreen swampy jungles of southwest India
28 21 009	**Pycnonotus atriceps** *Black-headed Bulbul*		Widespread Oriental mainland and islands
28 21 010	**Pycononotus melanicterus (dispar)** *Black-crested Bulbul*		Sri Lanka; India to Indochina; Greater Sundas
28 21 011	**Pycnonotus squamatus** *Scaly-breasted Bulbul*		Submontane forests of Malay Peninsula; Sumatra; Borneo
28 21 012	**Pycnonotus cyaniventris** *Gray-bellied Bulbul*		Forests of Malay Peninsula; Sumatra; Borneo
28 21 013	**Pycnonotus jocosus** *Red-whiskered Bulbul*		Widespread Oriental mainland and islands; introduced United States
28 21 014	**Pycnonotus xanthorrhous** *Brown-breasted Bulbul*		Scrub of southern China to Indochina
28 21 015	**Pycnonotus sinensis** *Light-vented Bulbul*		Southern China to Indochina; Hainan; Taiwan
28 21 016	**Pycnonotus taivanus** *Formosan Bulbul*		Confined to Island of Taiwan
28 21 017	**Pycnonotus leucogenys** *White-cheeked Bulbul*		Arabia to India, Nepal, Sikkim, Assam
28 21 018	**Pycnonotus cafer** *Red-vented Bulbul*		Sri Lanka; India to Burma, Indochina; Java
28 21 019	**Pycnonotus aurigaster** *Sooty-headed Bulbul*		Southern China to Indochina; Java
28 21 020	**Pycnonotus xanthopygos (tricolor)** *Black-capped Bulbul*		Common and widespread Africa south of the Sahara

		Date	Location
28 21 021	**Pycnonotus nigricans** *Black-fronted Bulbul*		Dry regions of Angola, Namibia to Cape Province
28 21 022	**Pycnonotus capensis** *Cape Bulbul*		Southwestern and southern Cape Province
28 21 023	**Pycnonotus barbatus (dodsoni)** *White-vented Bulbul*		Arid Ethiopia, Somalia to Tanzania
28 21 024	**Pycnonotus eutilotus** *Puff-backed Bulbul*		Malay Peninsula; Sumatra; Borneo
28 21 025	**Pycnonotus nieuwenhuisii** *Blue-wattled Bulbul*		Forests of Sumatra; Borneo (known from 2 specimens)
28 21 026	**Pycnonotus urostictus** *Yellow-wattled Bulbul*		Widespread throughout the Philippine Islands
28 21 027	**Pycnonotus bimaculatus** *Orange-spotted Bulbul*		Java; Sumatra; Bali
28 21 028	**Pycnonotus finlaysoni** *Stripe-throated Bulbul*		Southwest China to Malaya, Indochina
28 21 029	**Pycnonotus xantholaemus** *Yellow-throated Bulbul*		Sparsely distributed thorn scrub of southern India
28 21 030	**Pycnonotus penicillatus** *Yellow-eared Bulbul*		Common in highlands of Sri Lanka
28 21 031	**Pycnonotus flavescens** *Flavescent Bulbul*		Assam, southwest China to Indochina; Borneo
28 21 032	**Pycnonotus goiavier** *Yellow-vented Bulbul*		Malay Peninsula, Indochina; Greater Sundas; Philippines
28 21 033	**Pycnonotus luteolus** *White-browed Bulbul*		Open arid scrub of peninsular India; Sri Lanka
28 21 034	**Pycnonotus plumosus** *Olive-winged Bulbul*		Malay peninsula; Java; Sumatra; Borneo; Palawan
28 21 035	**Pycnonotus blanfordi** *Streak-eared Bulbul*		Widespread lowlands of Southeast Asia
28 21 036	**Pycnonotus simplex** *Cream-vented Bulbul*		Malay Peninsula; Java; Sumatra; Borneo
28 21 037	**Pycnonotus brunneus** *Red-eyed Bulbul*		Malay Peninsula; Sumatra; Borneo
28 21 038	**Pycnonotus erythropthalmos** *Spectacled Bulbul*		Malay Peninsula; Sumatra; Borneo
28 21 039	**Pycnonotus masukuensis** *Shelley's Greenbul*		Riverine forests of Kenya to Botswanna

		Date	Location
28 21 040	**Pycnonotus montanus** *Cameroon Mountain Greenbul*		Highlands of Cameroon Mountain (very rare)
28 21 041	**Pycnonotus virens** *Little Greenbul*		Gambia to Angola, Tanzania, Mozambique
28 21 042	**Pycnonotus hallae** *Hall's Greenbul*		Dry scrub of East Africa
28 21 043	**Pycnonotus gracilis** *Gray Greenbul*		Equatorial forests of Sierra Leone to Angola, Kenya, Zaire
28 21 044	**Pycnonotus ansorgei** *Ansorge's Greenbul*		Equatorial forests of Sierra Leone to Zaire
28 21 045	**Pycnonotus curvirostris** *Cameroon Sombre Greenbul*		Equatorial forests of Sierra Leone to Zaire
28 21 046	**Pycnonotus importunus (insularis)** *Sombre Greenbul*		Kenya, Tanzania to South Africa
28 21 047	**Pycnonotus latirostris** *Yellow-whiskered Greenbul*		Southern Sudan, eastern Zaire, adjacent East Africa
28 21 048	**Pycnonotus gracilirostris** *Slender-billed Greenbul*		Widespread Senegal to Zaire, Tanzania
28 21 049	**Pycnonotus tephrolaemus** *Olive-breasted Mountain Greenbul*		Montane forests of Nigeria to Zaire, Kenya
28 21 050	**Pycnonotus milanjensis** *Stripe-cheeked Greenbul*		Submontane scrub of Kenya to Mozambique, Rhodesia
28 21 051	**Calyptocichia serina** *Serene Greenbul*		Secondary forests of Sierra Leone to eastern Zaire
28 21 052	**Baeopogon indicator** *Honeyguide Greenbul*		Sierra Leone to the Sudan, Uganda, eastern Zaire
28 21 053	**Baepogon clamans** *Sjöstedt's Greenbul*		Primary forests of Cameroon and northern Zaire
28 21 054	**Ixonotus guttatus** *Spotted Greenbul*		Ghana, Liberia to Gabon, Zaire, Uganda
28 21 055	**Chlorocichia falkensteini** *Yellow-necked Bulbul*		Forest edges of Cameroon to Angola
28 21 056	**Chlorocichla simplex** *Simple Greenbul*		Senegal to Angola, southwestern Zaire
28 21 057	**Chlorocichla flavicollis** *Yellow-throated Greenbul*		Senegal to Kenya, Tanzania, Zambia, Angola

		Date	Location
28 21 058	**Chlorocichla flaviventris** *Yellow-bellied Greenbul*		Dense scrub of Tanzania to Namibia, South Africa
28 21 059	**Chlorocichla laetissima** *Joyful Greenbul*		Northeast Zaire to the Sudan and western Kenya
28 21 060	**Chlorocichla prigoginei** *Congo Greenbul*		Known only from highlands of Zaire
28 21 061	**Thescelocichla leucopleura** *White-tailed Greenbul*		Swampy areas of Senegal to Zaire, Uganda
28 21 062	**Phyllastrephus scandens** *African Leaf Love*		Senegal to the Sudan, Uganda, Tanzania
28 21 063	**Phyllastrephus terrestris** *Terrestial Bulbul*		Arid scrub of Angola, Rhodesia to South Africa
28 21 064	**Phyllastrephus strepitans** *Northern Brownbul*		Arid scrub of Sudan, Ethiopia to Tanzania
28 21 065	**Phyllastrephus cerviniventris** *Gray Olive Greenbul*		Kenya to Zaire, Zambia, Mozambique
28 21 066	**Phyllastrephus fulviventris** *Pale Olive Greenbul*		Savanna forests of the Congo basin
28 21 067	**Phyllastrephus poensis** *Cameroon Olive Greenbul*		Montane forests of Fernando Po, Nigeria, Cameroon
28 21 068	**Phyllastrephus hypochloris** *Toro Olive Greenbul*		Equatorial forests of Zaire to the Sudan, Uganda
28 21 069	**Phyllastrephus baumanni** *Baumann's Greenbul*		Sierra Leone to southern Zaire
28 21 070	**Phyllastrephus poliocephalus** *Yellow-bellied Greenbul*		Montane rain forests of Cameroon, Obudu Plateau
28 21 071	**Phyllastrephus flavostriatus (alfredi)** *Yellow-streaked Greenbul*		Evergreen forests of Kenya, Tanzania to South Africa
28 21 072	**Phyllastrephus debilis** *Slender Greenbul*		Forests and woodlands of Kenya to Zambia, Mozambique
28 21 073	**Phyllastrephus lorenzi** *Sassi's Olive Greenbul*		Eastern Zaire (Welle, Beni, Irumu areas—rare)
28 21 074	**Phyllastrephus albigularis** *White-throated Greenbul*		Sierra Leone to Cameroon, Gabon, Sudan, Uganda

		Date	Location
28 21 075 +	**Phyllastrephus fischeri** *Fischer's Greenbul*		Highland forests of Somalia to Rhodesia
28 21 076	**Phyllastrephus orostruthus** *Dappled Mountain Greenbul*		High montane forests of Tanzania and Mozambique (endangered)
28 21 077	**Phyllastrephus icterinus** *Icterine Greenbul*		Primary forests of Sierra Leone to central Zaire
28 21 078	**Phyllastrephus xavieri** *Xavier's Greenbul*		Primary forests of Cameroon to Zaire
28 21 079	**Phyllastrephus madagascariensis** *Common Tetraka*		Forests of Madagascar
28 21 080	**Phyllastrephus zosterops** *Short-billed Tetraka*		Forests of Madagascar
28 21 081	**Phyllastrephus apperti** *Appert's Tetraka*		Subdesert of southwest Madagascar (Ankazaobo)
28 21 082	**Phyllastrephus tenebrosus** *Dusky Tetraka*		Forests of eastern Madagascar
28 21 083	**Phyllastrephus xanthophrys** *Yellow-browed Tetraka*		Highland forests of eastern Madagascar (rare)
28 21 084	**Phyllastrephus cinereiceps** *Gray-crowned Tetraka*		Highland forests of eastern Madagascar
28 21 085 +	**Bleda syndactyla** *Common Bristlebill*		Southern Sudan to northeast Zaire, Uganda, Kenya
28 21 086	**Bleda eximia** *Green-tailed Bristlebill*		Forests of Sierra Leone to southern Sudan, Uganda
28 21 087	**Bleda canicapilla** *Gray-headed Bristlebill*		Forests of Gambia to southern Nigeria
28 21 088	**Nicator chloris** *Common Nicator*		Widespread tropical forests of Africa south of Sahara
28 21 089	**Nicator gularis** *Eastern Nicator*		Forests of Kenya, Tanzania to South Africa
28 21 090	**Nicator vireo** *Yellow-throated Nicator*		Forests of Cameroon to northern Angola, Uganda
28 21 091	**Criniger barbatus** *Bearded Bulbul*		Primary forests of Sierra Leone to eastern Zaire
28 21 092	**Criniger calurus** *Red-tailed Greenbul*		Sierra Leone to southern Sudan, Kenya, Uganda

		Date	Location

28 21 093 Criniger ndussumensis
White-bearded Greenbul Primary forest of eastern Zaire (Bori)

28 21 094 Criniger olivaceus
*Yellow-throated Olive
Greenbul* Senegal to southern Nigeria, northern Zaire

28 21 095 Criniger finschii
Finsch's Bulbul Malay Peninsula; Sumatra; Borneo

**28 21 096 Criniger flaveolus
(gulgaris)**
White-throated Bulbul Himalayas of India, Yunnan to Burma

28 21 097 Criniger pallidus
Puff-throated Bulbul Southern China to Indochina; Hainan

28 21 098 Criniger ochraceus
Ochraceous Bulbul Malay Peninsula, Indochina; Sumatra; Borneo

28 21 099 Criniger bres
Gray-cheeked Bulbul Malay Peninsula; Java; Sumatra; Borneo; Palawan

28 21 100 Criniger phaeocephalus
Yellow-bellied Bulbul Malay Peninsula; Sumatra; Borneo

28 21 101 Setornis criniger
Hook-billed Bulbul Primary lowland forests of Borneo and Banka Island

28 21 102 Hypsipetes viridescens
Olive (Viridescent) Bulbul Assam to Burma, Thailand

28 21 103 Hypsipetes propinquus
Gray-eyed Bulbul Southern China to Thailand, Indochina

28 21 104 Hypsipetes charlottae
Buff-vented Bulbul Malay Peninsula; Sumatra; Borneo; Palawan

**28 21 105 Hypsipetes
palawanensis**
Golden-eyed Bulbul Confined to Palawan Island (Philippine Sea)

28 21 106 Hypsipetes criniger
Hairy-backed Bulbul Malay Peninsula; Sumatra; Borneo

28 21 107 Hypsipetes philippinus
Philippine Bulbul Widespread throughout the Philippine Islands

28 21 108 Hypsipetes siquijorensis
Mottled-breasted Bulbul Philippines (Siquijor, Rombion and Tablas Islands)

28 21 109 Hypsipetes rufigularis
Zamboanga Bulbul Philippines (Basilan and Mindanao Islands)

28 21 110 Hypsipetes everetti
Plain-throated Bulbul Widespread Philippine Islands and Sulu Archipelago

28 21 111 Hypsipetes affinis
Golden Bulbul Sulas and Moluccas Islands

28 21 112 Hypsipetes indicus
Yellow-browed Bulbul Evergreen biotope of west coast of peninsular India

		Date	Location
28 21 113	**Hypsipetes mcclellandii** *Mountain Bulbul*		Southern China to Indochina; Hainan
28 21 114	**Hypsipetes malaccensis** *Streaked Bulbul*		Malay Peninsula; Sumatra; Borneo
28 21 115	**Hypsipetes virescens** *Rufous-bellied Bulbul*		Himalayas of Nepal to Yunnan, Malaya, Indochina
28 21 116	**Hypsipetes flavala** *Ashy Bulbul*		Himalayas of Garhwal to Indochina; Sumatra; Borneo
28 21 117	**Hypsipetes castanotus** *Chestnut Bulbul*		Southeast China to Tonkin; Hainan
28 21 118	**Hypsipetes amaurotis** *Chestnut-eared Bulbul*		Philippines (Bataan Peninsula, Calayan, Fuga, Camiguin Islands)
28 21 119	**Hypsipetes crassirostris** *Thick-billed Bulbul*		Confined to Aldabra Island (Seychelles)
28 21 120	**Hypsipetes borbonicus** *Olivaceous Bulbul*		Confined to Mauritius and Reunion Islands (endangered)
28 21 121	**Hypsipetes madagascariensis** *Black Bulbul*		Madagascar; Seychelles; India to Indochina; Hainan; Taiwan
28 21 122	**Hypsipetes nicobariensis** *Nicobar Bulbul*		Confined to the Nicobar Islands (Indian ocean)
28 21 123	**Hypsipetes thompsoni** *White-headed Bulbul*		Burma to northeast Thailand
28 21 124	**Neolestes torquatus** *Black-collared Bulbul*		Open country of Angola and eastern Zaire
28 21 125	**Tylas eduardi** *Kinkimavo*		Forests of Madagascar

FAMILY: IRENIDAE (Leafbirds)

28 22 001	**Aegithina tiphia** *Common Iora*		India to Indochina; Java; Sumatra; Borneo
28 22 002	**Aegithina nigrolutea** *Marshall's Iora*		Lowlands of Pakistan and northwest India
28 22 003	**Aegithina viridissima** *Green Iora*		Malay Peninsula; Sumatra; Borneo
28 22 004	**Aegithina lafresnayei** *Great Iora*		Southwest China to Malaya, Indochina

		Date	Location
28 22 005	**Chloropsis flavipennis** *Yellow-quilled Leafbird*		Philippines (Cebu, Leyte, Mindanao Islands)
28 22 006	**Chloropsis palawanensis** *Palawan Leafbird*		Philippines (Balabac, Palawan, Calamianes Islands)
28 22 007	**Chloropsis sonnerati** *Greater Green Leafbird*		Malay Peninsula; Sumatra; Java; Borneo
28 22 008	**Chloropsis cyanopogon** *Lesser Green Leafbird*		Malay Peninsula; Sumatra; Borneo
28 22 009	**Chloropsis cochinchinensis** *Blue-winged Leafbird*		India to Indochina; Java; Sumatra; Borneo
28 22 010	**Chloropsis aurifrons** *Golden-fronted Leafbird*		Sri Lanka; India to Indochina; Sumatra
28 22 011	**Chloropsis hardwickii** *Orange-bellied Leafbird*		Himalayas of Garhwal to Sikiang, Malaya, Indochina
28 22 012	**Chloropsis venustra** *Blue-masked Leafbird*		Confined to Island of Sumatra
28 22 013	**Irena puella** *Fairy Bluebird*		India to Indochina; Greater Sundas; Palawan; Andamans
28 22 014	**Irena cyanogaster** *Philippine Fairy Bluebird*		Widespread throughout the Philippine Islands

FAMILY: PRIONOPIDAE (Helmet-Shrikes)

28 23 001	**Eurocephalus rueppelli** *Rueppell's Shrike*	White Nile Valley of the Sudan
28 23 002	**Eurocephalus anguitimens** *White-crowned Shrike*	Widespread Ethiopian region
28 23 003	**Prionops plumata (cristata)** *Straight-crested Helmet-Shrike*	Widespread thornbush country of Ethiopian region
28 23 004	**Prionops poliolopha** *Gray-crested Helmet-Shrike*	Kenya to the Tabora District of Tanzania
28 23 005	**Prionops caniceps** *Red-billed Helmet-Shrike*	Mountains of eastern Zaire, Ruwenzori and Kivu area (rare)
28 23 007	**Prionops retzii** *Retz's Helmet-Shrike*	Kenya to Angola, South Africa
28 23 008	**Prionops gabela** *Angola Helmet-Shrike*	Known only from western Angola (rare)

	Date	Location

28 23 009 **Prionops scopifrons**
Chestnut-fronted Helmet-Shrike — Kenya, Tanzania to Mozambique

FAMILY: LANIIDAE (Shrikes)

28 24 001 **Lanioturdus torquatus**
Chat Shrike — Thornbush of southern Angola and Namibia

28 24 002 **Nilaus afer (nigritemporalis)**
Brubru Shrike — Widespread Africa south of the Sahara

28 24 003 **Dryoscopus pringlii**
Pringle's Puffback — Lowland thornbush of Ethiopia, Somalia, Kenya

28 24 004 **Dryoscopus gambensis**
Gambian Puffback — Widespread lowlands of Ethiopian region

28 24 005 **Dryoscopus cubia**
Black-backed Puffback — Open woodlands of Kenya to South Africa

28 24 006 **Dryoscopus senegalensis (affinis)**
Zanzibar Puffback — Lowlands of Nigeria to Kenya; Zanzibar; Mafia Island

28 24 007 **Dryoscopus angolensis**
Pink-footed Puffback — Northern Angola to Zaire, Tanzania

28 24 008 **Dryoscopus sabini**
Sabine's Puffback — Forests of Sierra Leone to Nigeria

28 24 009 **Tchagra minuta**
Blackcap Bush-Shrike — Widespread Ethiopian region

28 24 010 **Tchagra senegala**
Black-headed Bush-Shrike — Widespread Africa south of the Sahara

28 24 011 **Tchagra tchagra**
Tchagra Bush-Shrike — Thornveld of southern tip of Africa

28 24 012 **Tchagra australis**
Brown-headed Bush-Shrike — Widespread Kenya to South Africa

28 24 013 **Tchagra jamesi**
Three-streaked Bush-Shrike — Dense thorn scrub of Ethiopia, Somalia and Kenya

28 24 014 **Tchagra cruenta**
Rosy-patched Bush-Shrike — Widespread Ethiopian region

28 24 015 **Laniarius ruficeps**
Red-naped Bush-Shrike — Lowland scrub of Ethiopia, Somalia and Kenya

28 24 016 **Laniarius luhderi**
Luhder's Bush-Shrike — Cameroon, Angola to western Tanzania

28 24 017 **Laniarius ferrugineus**
Southern Boubou — Widespread Ethiopia to South Africa

	Date	Location
28 24 018 **Laniarius aethiopicus**		
Tropical Boubou		Africa south of the Sahara (possible race *L. ferrugineus*)
28 24 019 **Lanarius bicolor**		
Gabon Boubou		Gabon to Angola (possible race *L. ferrugineus*)
28 24 020 **Laniarius barbarus**		
Barbary Shrike (Gonolek)		Senegal to Uganda, Zaire
28 24 021 **Laniarius erythrogaster**		
Black-headed Gonolek		Cameroon to Ethiopia, Tanzania (possible race *L. barbarus*)
28 24 022 **Laniarius mufumbiri**		
Mufumbiri Gonolek		Forests adjacent to Lake Edward and Lake Victoria
28 24 023 **Laniarius atrococcineus**		
Crimson-breasted Boubou		Thornveld of southern Angola to South Africa
28 24 024 **Laniarius atroflavus**		
Yellow-breasted Boubou		Restricted to Cameroon highlands and Obudu Plateau
28 24 025 **Laniarius fulleborni**		
Fulleborn's Boubou		Highland evergreen forests of Tanzania, Zambia, Malawi
28 24 026 **Laniarius poensis**		
Black Mountain Boubou		Highlands of Cameroon to Ruwenzoris (possible race *L. fulleborni*)
28 24 027 **Laniarius funebris**		
Slate-colored Boubou		Dry scrub of Sudan, Ethiopia, Somalia to Tanzania
28 24 028 **Laniarius leucorhynchus**		
Sooty Boubou		Sierra Leone to the Sudan, Uganda, Zaire
28 24 029 **Telophorus bocagei**		
Gray-green Bush-Shrike		Cameroon to northern Angola, Kenya, Uganda
28 24 030 **Telophorus sulfureopectus**		
Sulphur-breasted Bush-Shrike		Widespread lowlands of Ethiopian region
28 24 031 **Telophorus olivaceus**		
Olive Bush-Shrike		Evergreen forests of South Africa
28 24 032 **Telophorus nigrifrons**		
Black-fronted Bush-Shrike		Kenya to eastern Angola, Rhodesia, Mozambique
28 24 033 **Telophorus multicolor**		
Many-colored Bush-Shrike		Cameroon, Gabon to Uganda, northern Angola
28 24 034 **Telophorus kupeensis**		
Kupe Bush-Shrike		Restricted to Kupe Mountain forests (Cameroon)
28 24 035 **Telophorus zeylonus**		
Bokmakierie		Open bush of Angola, Zambia to South Africa
28 24 036 **Telophorus viridis**		
Perrin's Bush-Shrike		Gallery forests of Loango coast to Angola

		Date	Location

28 24 037   **Telophorus quadricolor**
Four-colored Bush-Shrike   Dense coastal bush of Kenya to South Africa

28 24 038   **Telophorus dohertyi**
Doherty's Bush-Shrike   Mountain highlands of western Kenya, Uganda to eastern Zaire

28 24 039   **Malaconotus cruentus**
Rosy-patched Shrike   Widespread Ethiopian region

28 24 040   **Malaconotus lagdeni**
Lagden's Bush-Shrike   Mountain forests of Ghana to Ruwenzori and Kivu Mountains

28 24 041   **Malaconotus gladiator**
Cameroon Mountain Bush-Shrike   Restricted to Cameroon Mountain and adjacent highlands

28 24 042   **Malaconotus blanchoti (hypopyrrhus)**
Gray-headed Bush-Shrike   Widespread Ethiopian region

28 24 043   **Malaconotus alius**
Uluguru Bush-Shrike   Known only from Uluguru Mountains of eastern Tanzania (rare)

28 24 044   **Corvinella corvina**
Yellow-billed Shrike   Woodlands of Senegal to the Sudan and Kenya

28 24 045   **Corvinella melanoleuca**
Magpie Shrike   Southern Angola to Kenya, Tanzania, Mozambique

28 24 046   **Lanius tigrinus**
Tiger Shrike   Widespread east Asia, Oriental mainland and islands

28 24 047   **Lanius souzae**
Souza's Shrike   Angola to Zaire, Tanzania, Zambia, Mozambique

28 24 048   **Lanius bucephalus**
Bull-headed Shrike   Northeast Asia to eastern China; Taiwan; Korea

28 24 049   **Lanius cristatus**
Brown Shrike   Widespread Oriental mainland and islands; winters Africa

28 24 050   **Lanius collurio**
Red-backed Shrike   Widespread Palearctic region; winters to South Africa

28 24 051   **Lanius collurioides**
Burmese Shrike   Assam to southern China; Burma, Indochina

28 24 052   **Lanius gubernator**
Emin's Shrike   Cameroon to the Sudan, Zaire

28 24 053   **Lanius vittatus**
Bay-backed Shrike   Transcaspia to India, Afghanistan, Baluchistan

28 24 054   **Lanius schach**
Long-tailed Shrike   Transcaspia to Southeast Asia; winters to New Guinea

28 24 055   **Lanius tephronotus**
Tibetan Shrike   Kashmir to Tibet, southern China, Thailand

		Date	Location
28 24 056	**Lanius validirostris** *Strong-billed Shrike*		Philippines (Luzon, Mindanao, Mindoro Islands)
28 24 057	**Lanius mackinnoni** *Mackinnon's Shrike*		Open woodlands surrounding the Congo Forest basin
28 24 058	**Lanius minor** *Lesser Gray Shrike*		Southern Palearctic region; winters to South Africa
28 24 059	**Lanius ludovicianus** *Loggerhead Shrike*		Southern Canada to southern Mexico
28 24 060	**Lanius excubitor** **(elegans)** *Northern Shrike*		Widespread Palearctic, Holarctic, Oriental, Ethiopian regions
28 24 061	**Lanius excubitorius** *Gray-backed Fiscal*		Ethiopia, Kenya, Uganda, Tanzania
28 24 062	**Lanius sphenocercus** *Chinese Gray Shrike*		Eastern Palearctic mainland
28 24 063	**Lanius cabanisi** *Long-tailed Fiscal*		Open scrub of Somalia to Kenya, Tanzania
28 24 064	**Lanius dorsalis** *Taita Fiscal*		Desert bush of Ethiopia to Kenya, Tanzania
28 24 065	**Lanius somalicus** *Somali Fiscal*		Dry thornbush of Ethiopia, Somalia, Kenya
28 24 066	**Lanius collaris** **(marwitzi)** *Common Fiscal*		Widespread Africa south of the Sahara
28 24 067	**Lanius newtoni** *Newton's Fiscal*		Confined to São Thomé Island (Gulf of Guinea)
28 24 068	**Lanius senator** *Woodchat Shrike*		Southern Europe to India; winters North Africa
28 24 069	**Lanius nubicus** *Masked Shrike*		Southeast Europe to Asia Minor; North Africa
28 24 070	**Pityriasis gymnocephala** *Bald-headed Wood-Shrike*		Confined to lowland forests of Borneo (rare)

FAMILY: VANGIDAE (Vanga Shrikes)

		Date	Location
28 25 001	**Calicalicus** **madagascariensis** *Red-tailed Vanga*		Coastal forests of Madagascar
28 25 002	**Schetba rufa** *Rufous Vanga*		Forests of Madagascar
28 25 003	**Vanga curvirostris** *Hook-billed Vanga*		Widespread Madagascar

		Date	Location

28 25 004	**Xenopirostris xenopirostris** *LaFresnaye's Vanga*		Lowland forests of southern Madagascar
28 25 005	**Xenopirostris damii** *Van Dam's Vanga*		Forests of northwest Madagascar (Ankarafantsika—rare)
28 25 006	**Xenopirostris polleni** *Pollen's Vanga*		Forests of eastern Madagascar (Ambohimahasoa—rare)
28 25 007	**Falculea palliata** *Sickle-billed Vanga*		Chiefly *baobab* regions of Madagascar
28 25 008	**Leptopterus viridis** *White-headed Vanga*		Forests of Madagascar
28 25 009	**Leptopterus chabert** *Chabert Vanga*		Widespread Madagascar
28 25 010	**Leptopterus madagascarinus** *Blue Vanga*		Dry forests of eastern Madagascar; Moheli (?)
28 25 011	**Oriolia bernieri** *Bernier's Vanga*		Woodlands of eastern Madagascar (rare)
28 25 012	**Euryceros prevostii** *Helmetbird*		Dense forests of northeast Madagascar

FAMILY: HYPOSITTIDAE (Coral-billed Nuthatch)

| 28 26 001 | **Hyposdta corallirostris**
Coral-billed Nuthatch | | Forests and plateaus of eastern Madagascar |

FAMILY: PTILOGONATIDAE (Silky-Flycatchers)

28 27 001	**Ptilogonys cinereus** *Gray Silky-Flycatcher*		Oak-pine forests of northern Mexico to Guatemala
28 27 002	**Ptilogonys caudatus** *Long-tailed Silky-Flycatcher*		Mountains of Costa Rica and western Panama
28 27 003	**Phainopepla nitens** *Phainopepla*		Arid southwest United States to southern Mexican Plateau
28 27 004	**Phainoptila melanoxantha** *Black-and-yellow Silky-Flycatcher*		Mountains of Costa Rica and western Panama

	Date	Location

FAMILY: BOMBYCILLIDAE (Waxwings)

28 28 001 **Bombycilla garrulus**
Bohemian Waxwing   Holarctic circumpolar regions
Waxwing (Br.)

28 28 002 **Bombycilla japonica**
Japanese Waxwing   Japan, Manchuria, Sakhalin

28 28 003 **Bombycilla cedrorum**
Cedar Waxwing   North America; winters to Panama, rarely West Indies

FAMILY: Hypocoliidae (Hypocolius)

28 29 001 **Hypocolius ampelinus**
Gray Hypocolius   Semi-deserts of North Africa to Iran, Afghanistan,
                            India

FAMILY: DULIDAE (Palm Chat)

28 30 001 **Dulus dominicus**
Palm Chat   Hispaniola, Gonâve and Saona Islands (West Indies)

FAMILY: CINCLIDAE (Dippers)

28 31 001 **Cinclus cinclus**
White-bellied Dipper   Mountain streams of Palearctic region

28 31 002 **Cinclus pallasii**
Brown Dipper   Himalayas of Kashmir to China, Korea, Japan,
                            Indochina

28 31 003 **Cinclus mexicanus**
American Dipper   Western mountain streams of Aleutians to Panama

28 31 004 **Cinclus leucocephalus**
White-capped Dipper   Mountain streams of Venezuela to northern Bolivia

28 31 005 **Cinclus schulzi**
Rufous-throated Dipper   Mountains of northwestern Argentina south to
                            Catamarca

FAMILY: TROGLODYTIDAE (Wrens)

28 32 001 **Campylorhynchus
jocosus**
Boucard's Wren   Arid pine forests of southern Mexican plateau

		Date	Location

28 32 002 **Campylorhynchus gularis**
Spotted Wren
Mountains and foothills of northern and central Mexico

28 32 003 **Campylorhynchus yucatanicus**
Yucatán Wren
Restricted to arid northern Yucatán Peninsula

28 32 004 **Campylorhynchus brunneicapillus**
Cactus Wren
Arid southwest United States to central and northeast Mexico

28 32 005 **Campylorhynchus griseus**
Bicolored Wren
Tropical Colombia to Guyana, adjacent Brazil

28 32 006 **Campylorhynchus albobrunneus**
+
White-headed Wren
Pacific Colombia, adjacent Panama (possible race *C. turdinus*)

28 32 007 **Campylorhynchus rufinucha**
Rufous-naped Wren
Arid lowlands of southwest Mexico to northwest Costa Rica

28 32 008 **Campylorhynchus turdinus**
Thrush-like Wren
Tropical Colombia to eastern Bolivia, Amazonian Brazil

28 32 009 **Campylorhynchus chiapensis**
Giant Wren
Humid lowlands of Pacific coast of Chiapas (Mexico)

28 32 010 **Campylorhynchus nuchalis**
Stripe-backed Wren
Tropical northern Venezuela, Colombia

28 32 011 **Campylorhynchus fasciatus**
+
Fasciated Wren
Arid littoral of southwest Ecuador, northern Peru

28 32 012 **Campylorhynchus zonatus**
Band-backed Wren
Gulf slope of Mexico to northwest Ecuador

28 32 013 **Campylorhynchus megalopterus**
Gray-barred Wren
Conifer forests of southern Mexican Plateau

28 32 014 **Odontorchilus cinereus**
Tooth-billed Wren
Amazonian Brazil (Rio Xingú to Tapajós)

28 32 015 **Odontorchilus branickii**
Gray-mantled Wren
Mainly highlands of Colombia to Peru

	Date	Location

28 32 016 **Salpinctes obsoletus**
Rock Wren
Southwest Canada, western United States to Costa Rica

28 32 017 **Catherpes mexicanus**
Canyon Wren
Southwest Canada, western United States to southern Mexico

28 32 018 **Hylorchilus sumichrasti**
Slender-billed Wren
Southeast Mexico (Veracruz, Oaxaca, Chiapas—rare)

28 32 019 **Cinnycerthia unirufa**
Rufous Wren
Mountain forests of Venezuela to Ecuador

28 32 020 **Cinnycerthia peruana**
Sepia-brown Wren
Andes of Colombia to northern Bolivia

28 32 021 **Cistothorus platensis**
Sedge (Short-billed Marsh) Wren
Southern Canada to Tierra del Fuego; Falkland Islands

28 32 022 **Cistothorus meridae**
Páramo Wren
Páramo grasslands of northwest Venezuela

28 32 023 **Cistothorus apolinari**
Apolinar's Marsh Wren
Eastern Andes of Colombia (Páramo de Sumapaz)

28 32 024 **Telmatodytes palustris**
Long-billed Marsh Wren
Southern Canada, United States; winters to Mexico

28 32 025 **Thryomanes bewickii**
Bewick's Wren
Southwestern, central Canada to southern Mexico

28 32 026 **Thryomanes sissonii**
Socorro Wren
Socorro Island (off western Mexico—endangered)

28 32 027 **Ferminia cerverai**
Zapata Wren
Cuba (dense shrubbery of Zapata Swamp)

28 32 028 **Thryothorus atrogularis**
Black-throated Wren
Caribbean slope of Nicargua to western Panama

28 32 029 **Thryothorus fasciatoventris**
Black-bellied Wren
Tropical Costa Rica to northwest Colombia

28 32 030 **Thryothorus spadix**
Sooty-headed Wren
Highlands of eastern Panama to western Colombia

28 32 031 **Thryothuros euophrys**
Plain-tailed Wren
Andes of southwest Colombia to southeast Peru

28 32 032 **Thryothorus genibarbis**
Moustached Wren
Capoeira, cerrado of Venezuela to Peru, Brazil

28 32 033 **Thryothorus coraya**
Coraya Wren
Northern South America to Peru, Amazonian Brazil

28 32 034 **Thryothorus felix**
Happy Wren
Pacific slope of Mexico (Sonora to Oaxaca)

		Date	Location

28 32 035 **Thryothorus maculipectus**
Spot-breasted Wren
Discontinuously distributed southeast Mexico to northwest Peru

28 32 036 **Thryothorus rutilus**
Rufous-breasted Wren
Southwest Costa Rica to Venezuela; Trinidad; Tobago

28 32 037 **Thryothorus nigricapillus (semibadius)**
Black-capped (Bay) Wren
Lowlands of Nicaragua to western Ecuador

28 32 038 **Thryothorus thoracicus**
Stripe-breasted Wren
Tropical Nicaragua to northwest Ecuador

28 32 039 **Thryothorus pleurostictus**
Banded Wren
Pacific slope of southwest Mexico to northwest Costa Rica

28 32 040 **Thryothorus ludovicianus (albinucha)**
Carolina Wren
Southeastern Canada to Nicaragua

28 32 041 **Thryothorus rufalbus**
Rufous-and-white Wren
Pacific slope of Chiapas to Colombia, Venezuela

28 32 042 **Thryothorus nicefori**
Niceforo's Wren
Andes of Colombia (Santander)

28 32 043 **Thryothorus sinaloa**
Bar-vented (Sinaloa) Wren
Pacific slope of Mexico (Sonora to Guerrero)

28 32 044 **Thryothorus modestus**
Plain Wren
Pacific slope of Chiapas to central Panama

28 32 045 **Thryothorus leucotis**
Buff-breasted Wren
Tropical Panama to Peru (Junin), southeast Brazil

28 32 046 **Thryothorus superciliaris**
Superciliated Wren
Arid littoral of southwest Ecuador to Peru (Ancash)

28 32 047 **Thryothorus guarayanus**
Fawn-breasted Wren
Northern Bolivia to western Matto Grosso of Brazil

28 32 048 **Thryothorus longirostris**
Long-billed Wren
Caatinga of interior of eastern Brazil

28 32 049 **Thryothorus griseus**
Gray (Amazon) Wren
Tropical western Brazil (southwest Amazonas)

28 32 050 **Troglodytes troglodytes**
Northern (Winter) Wren
Wren (Br)
Widespread Holarctic region

28 32 051 **Troglodytes aedon (tanneri)**
Northern House Wren
Southern Canada to Isthmus of Tehuantepec

		Date	Location

28 32 052 Troglodytes brunneicollis
Brown-throated Wren — Mountains of southeast Arizona to Oaxaca (Mexico)

28 32 053 Troglodytes rufociliatus
Rufous-browed Wren — Mountains of Chiapas (Mexico) to Honduras

28 32 054 Troglodytes musculus (beani)
Tropical House Wren — Gulf slope of Mexico to Tierra del Fuego; Falkland Islands

28 32 055 Troglodytes ochraceous
Ochraceous Wren — Highlands of Costa Rica and western Panama

28 32 056 Troglodytes solstitialis
✝
Mountain Wren — Mountains of Venezuela to northwest Argentina

28 32 057 Troglodytes rufulus
Tepui Wren — Mountains of Venezuela, adjacent Brazil (Roraima)

28 32 058 Thryorchilus browni
Timberline Wren — Mountain peaks of Costa Rica and western Panama

28 32 059 Uropsila leucogastra
White-bellied Wren — Gulf lowlands of Mexico to Guatemala, Honduras

28 32 060 Henicorhina leucosticta
White-breasted Wood-Wren — Tropical southern Mexico to Amazon basin

28 32 061 Henicorhina leucophrys
✝
Gray-breasted Wood-Wren — Highlands of southern Mexico to Bolivia, Amazonian Brazil

28 32 062 Henicorhina leucoptera
Bar-winged Wood-Wren — Cordillera del Condor on Peru-Ecuador border

28 32 063 Microcerculus marginatus (philomela)
✝
Nightingale Wren — Humid forests of Chiapas (Mexico) to Amazonia

28 32 064 Microcerculus ustulatus
Flutist Wren — Mountains of Guyana, Venezuela, adjacent Brazil

28 32 065 Microcerculus bambla
Wing-banded Wren — Guianas, Venezuela, adjacent Brazil, Ecuador, Peru

28 32 066 Cyphorhinus thoracicus
Chestnut-breasted Wren — Andes of Colombia to Peru (Puno)

28 32 067 Cyphorhinus arada (phaeocephalus)
✝
Musician Wren — Honduras to Bolivia, west Amazonian Brazil

Date   Location

FAMILY: MIMIDAE (Mockingbirds and Thrashers)

28 33 001 **Dumetella carolinensis**
           Gray (Northern) Catbird   Eastern Canada to Gulf states; winters to West
                                           Indies, Panama

28 33 002 **Melanoptila glabrirostris**
           Black Catbird   Coastal Yucatan to northwest Honduras, adjacent
                                           islands

28 33 003 **Melanotis caerulescens**
           Blue Mockingbird   Mexico (southern Sonora to Isthmus of
                                           Tehuantepec)

28 33 004 **Melanotis hypoleucus**
           Blue-and-white   Highlands of Chiapas (Mexico) to Honduras
           Mockingbird

28 33 005 **Mimus polyglottos**
           Northern Mockingbird   Southern Canada to Isthmus of Tehuantepec; West
                                           Indies

28 33 006 **Minus gilvus**
           Tropical Mockingbird   Southern Mexico to southeast Brazil; Lesser Antilles

28 33 007 **Mimus gundlachii**
           Bahama Mockingbird   Bahamas; Jamaica; cays off northern Cuba

28 33 008 **Mimus magnirostris**
           St. Andrew Mockingbird   Caribbean (St. Andrew Island—possible race *M.
                                           gilvus*)

28 33 009 **Mimus thenca**
           Chilean Mockingbird   Coastal Chile (Atacama to Valdivia)

28 33 010 **Mimus longicaudatus**
           Long-tailed Mockingbird   Arid littoral of southwest Ecuador to Peru
                                           (Arequipia)

28 33 011 **Mimus saturninus**
           Chalk-browed Mockingbird   Eastern Brazil to eastern Bolivia, northern Argentina

28 33 012 **Mimus patagonicus**
           Patagonian Mockingbird   Argentina, Chile (Aysén to Tierra del Fuego)

28 33 013 **Mimus triurus**
           White-banded Mockingbird   Southern Brazil to central Argentina; rarely Chile

28 33 014 **Mimus dorsalis**
           Brown-backed   Andes of Bolivia to northwest Argentina (Jujuy)
           Mockingbird

28 33 015 **Nesomimus trifasciatus**
           Charles Mockingbird   Galapagos Islands (*Nesomimus* genus forms a
                                           possible superspecies)

28 33 016 **Nesomimus parvulus**
           Galapagos Mockingbird   Galapagos Islands (endemic Champion, Gardner-
                                           near Floreana Islands)

28 33 017 **Nesomimus macdonaldi**
           macdonaldi   Galapagos Islands (endemic Hood Island)
           Hood Mockingbird

	Date	Location

28 33 018 Nesomimus melanotis
Chatham Mockingbird

Galapagos Islands (endemic San Cristobal Island)

28 33 019 Mimodes graysoni
Socorro Thrasher

Socorro Island (off western Mexico—endangered)

28 33 020 Oreoscoptes montanus
Sage Thrasher

Arid British Columbia to central Mexico
(Guanajuato), Baja California

28 33 021 Toxostoma rufum
Brown Thrasher

Southern Canada to Gulf states (east of Rocky
Mountains)

28 33 022 Toxostoma longirostre
Long-billed Thrasher

Arid southern Texas to southern Mexico

28 33 023 Toxostoma guttatum
Cozumel Thrasher

Confined to Cozumel Island (off Yucatán Peninsula)

28 33 024 Toxostoma cinereum
Gray Thrasher

Desert scrub of Baja California to about 31° south

28 33 025 Toxostoma bendirei
Bendire's Thrasher

Arid southwest United States to northern Mexico
(Sinaloa)

28 33 026 Toxostoma ocellatum
Ocellated Thrasher

Oak-pine highlands of south-central Mexico

28 33 027 Toxostoma curvirostre
Curve-billed Thrasher

Arid southwest United States to southern Mexico
(Oaxaca)

28 33 028 Toxostoma lecontei
LeConte's Thrasher

Arid southwest United States to central Baja
California, Sonora

28 33 029 Toxostoma redivivum
California Thrasher

Chaparrel belt of northern California to northwest
Baja California

28 33 030 Toxostoma dorsale
Crissal Thrasher

Arid southwest United States to central Mexican
Plateau

28 33 031 Cinclocerthia ruficauda
Brown Trembler

Rain forests of West Indies (endangered)

**28 33 032 Ramphocinclus
brachyurus**
White-breasted Thrasher

Martinique and St. Lucia Islands (endangered)

28 33 033 Donacobius atricapillus
*Black-capped
Mockingthrush*

Tropical eastern Panama (Darien) to northern
Argentina

28 33 034 Margarops fuscatus
Pearly-eyed Thrasher

Mainly uplands of Bahamas to Puerto Rico and
Lesser Antilles

28 33 035 Margarops fuscus
Scaly-breasted Thrasher

Semiarid woodlands of Lesser Antilles Islands

	Date	Location

FAMILY: PRUNELLIDAE: (Accentors)

28 34 001   **Prunella collaris**
Alpine Accentor   Discontinuous high elevations of Palearctic region

28 34 002   **Prunella himalayana**
Altai Accentor   Lake Baikal to Pakistan, Nepal, Sikkim

28 34 003   **Prunella rubeculoides**
Robin Accentor   Himalayas of Pakistan to Inner Mongolia

28 34 004   **Prunella strophiata**
Rufous-breasted Accentor   Himalayas of Afghanistan to Shensi, northeast Burma

28 34 005   **Prunella montanella**
Siberian Accentor   Mountains of Siberia, Manchuria, China, Korea

28 34 006   **Prunella fulvescens**
Brown Accentor   Desert biotype of Afghanistan, Kashmir, Nepal to Yunnan

28 34 007   **Prunella ocularis**
Radde's Accentor   Armenia, Iran to Turkey

28 34 008   **Prunella atrogularis**
Black-throated Accentor   Ural Mountains to Afghanistan, Kashmir, Garhwal, Nepal

28 34 009   **Prunella koslowi**
Kozlov's Accentor   Mountains of Mongolia

28 34 010   **Prunella modularis**
Dunnock (Hedge Sparrow)   Widespread Palearctic region

28 34 011   **Prunella rubida**
Japanese Accentor   Common montane resident on major Japanese Islands

28 34 012   **Prunella immaculata**
Maroon-backed Accentor   Nepal, Sikkim to Szechwan, northeast Burma

FAMILY: TURDIDAE (Thrushes)

28 35 001   **Brachypteryx stellata**
Gould's Shortwing   Himalayas of Nepal to southwest China, Burma, Tonkin

28 35 002   **Brachypteryx hyperythra**
Rusty-breasted Shortwing   Dense bamboo jungles of Sikkim, Bhutan

28 35 003   **Brachypteryx major**
White-bellied Shortwing   Evergreen biotope of southwest India

28 35 004   **Brachypteryx calligyna**
Celebes Shortwing   Confined to the Celebes Islands

28 35 005   **Brachypteryx leucophrys**
Lesser Shortwing   Himalayas of Nepal to Malaya, Indochina; Sumatra; Java

		Date	Location
28 35 006	**Brachypteryx montana** (cruralis) *White-browed Shortwing*		Widespread Oriental region mainland and islands
28 35 007	**Erythropygia coryphaeus** *Karoo Scrub-Robin*		Arid sandy Namibia to Cape Province
28 35 008	**Erythropygia leucophrys** (zambesiana) *White-winged Scrub-Robin*		Semiarid scrub of Kenya to South Africa
28 35 009	**Erythropygia hartlaubi** *Brown-backed Scrub-Robin*		Cameroon to Uganda, Tanzania, northern Angola
28 35 010	**Erythropygia galactotes** *Rufous Bush-Robin*		Europe to Asia Minor, North Africa
28 35 011	**Erythropygia paena** *Kalahari Scrub-Robin*		Thorn scrub of southern Angola to Cape Province
28 35 012	**Erythropygia leucosticta** *Western Bearded Scrub-Robin*		Sierra Leone to northeast Zaire, northern Angola
28 35 013	**Erythropygia quadrivirgata** *Eastern Bearded Scrub-Robin*		Scrub of Somalia to Mozambique, Natal
28 35 014	**Erythropygia barbata** *Bearded Scrub-Robin*		Scrub of Angola to Botswanna, southwest Tanzania
28 35 015	**Erythropygia signata** *Brown Scrub-Robin*		Forests of Natal and eastern Cape Province
28 35 016	**Namibornis herero** *Herero Chat*		Rocky bush country of western Namibia
28 35 017	**Cercotrichas podobe** *Black Scrub-Robin*		Arid bush of Senegal to Somalia, western Arabia
28 35 018	**Pinarornis plumosus** *Boulder Chat*		Rocky hillsides of Rhodesia and Mozambique
28 35 019	**Chaetops frenatus** *Rock Jumper*		Rocky mountains of Natal to Cape Province
28 35 020	**Drymodes brunneopygia** *Southern Scrub-Robin*		Discontinuous distribution western, southern Australia
28 35 021	**Drymodes superciliaris** *Northern Scrub-Robin*		Cape York Peninsula; New Guinea; Arus
28 35 022 †	**Pogonocichla stellata** *White-starred Bush-Robin*		Forests of Kenya to South Africa
28 35 023	**Pogonocichla swynnertoni** *Swynnerton's Robin*		High forests of eastern Rhodesia (rare and local)

		Date	Location

28 35 024 **Erithacus gabela**
Gabela Akalat
Mountain rain forests of southern Angola (Gabela District)

28 35 025 **Erithacus cyornithopsis**
Whiskered Akalat
Sierra Leone to eastern Zaire, Uganda

28 35 026 **Erithacus aequatorialis**
✝ *Equatorial Akalat*
Dense forests of eastern Zaire to western Kenya

28 35 027 **Erithacus erythrothorax**
✝ *Forest Robin*
Swampy forests of eastern Zaire to western Uganda, the Sudan

28 35 028 **Erithacus sharpei**
Sharpe's Akalat
Bamboo zone of southern Tanzania to Zambia

28 35 029 **Erithacus gunningi**
Gunning's Akalat
Coastal evergreen forests of Kenya to Mozambique (rare)

28 35 030 **Erithacus rubecula**
European Robin
Widespread western Palearctic region

28 35 031 **Erithacus akahige**
Japanese Robin
East Asia; Japan; Ryukyu Islands; Taiwan

28 35 032 **Erithacus komadori**
Ryukyu Robin
Confined to the Ryukyu Islands (Japanese Archipelago)

28 35 033 **Erithacus sibilans**
Rufous-tailed Robin
Siberia to China, Indochina; Taiwan; Hainan

28 35 034 **Erithacus luscinia**
Thrush Nightingale
Widespread Palearctic region; winters to central Africa

28 35 035 **Erithacus megarhynchos**
Common Nightingale
Widespread southern Palearctic region; winters to Africa

28 35 036 **Erithacus calliope**
Siberian Rubythroat
Widespread eastern Palearctic, Oriental regions

28 35 037 **Erithacus svecicus**
Bluethroat
Widespread Palearctic region, Oriental mainland; Alaska

28 35 038 **Erithacus pectoralis**
Himalayan Rubythroat
Himalayas of Turkestan to Siberia, Kamchatka, Burma

28 35 039 **Erithacus ruficeps**
Rufous-headed Robin
Tsinling Mountains of north-central China

28 35 040 **Erithacus obscurus**
Black-throated Robin
Dense thickets of north-central China

28 35 041 **Erithacus pectardens**
Firethroat
Mountains of southeast Tibet to southwest China

		Date	Location

28 35 042	**Erithacus brunneus** *Indian Blue Robin*	Himalayas of Kashmir to Burma; winters Sri Lanka
28 35 043	**Erithacus cyane** *Siberian Blue Robin*	Eastern Palearctic (Siberia to Indonesia, Malaysia)
28 35 044	**Erithacus cyanurus** *Orange-flanked Bush-Robin*	Eastern Palearctic, Oriental mainland and islands
28 35 045	**Erithacus chrysaeus** *Golden Bush-Robin*	Himalayas of Kashmir to Szechwan, Burma, Tonkin
28 35 046	**Erithacus indicus** *White-browed Bush-Robin*	Himalayas of Nepal to Szechwan, Tonkin; Taiwan
28 35 047	**Erithacus hyperythrus** *Rufous-breasted Bush-Robin*	Mountains of Nepal to Tibet, Assam, Burma (rare)
28 35 048	**Erithacus johnstoniae** *Collared Bush-Robin*	Confined to the Island of Taiwan
28 35 049	**Cossypha roberti** *White-bellied Akalat*	Cameroon to western Uganda
28 35 050	**Cossypha bocagei** *Rufous-cheeked Robin-Chat*	Angola to southeastern Zaire, northern Zambia
28 35 051	**Cossypha polioptera** **(insulana)** *Gray-winged Robin-Chat*	Dense forests of Angola to the Sudan, Kenya, Tanzania
28 35 052	**Cossypha archeri** *Archer's Robin-Chat*	Ruwenzori Mountains to western Uganda
28 35 053	**Cossypha isabellae** *Mountain Robin-Chat*	High mountain forests of Cameroon highlands
28 35 054 +	**Cossypha natalensis** *Red-capped Robin-Chat*	Widespread Africa south of the Sahara
28 35 055	**Cossypha dichroa** *Chorister Robin-Chat*	Natal to southern Cape Province
28 35 056	**Cossypha semirufa** *Ruppell's Robin-Chat*	Forests of Eritrea, Ethiopia to Tanzania
28 35 057	**Cossypha heuglini** *White-browed Robin-Chat*	Highlands of Ethiopia to South Africa
28 35 058	**Cossypha cyanocampter** *Blue-shouldered Robin-Chat*	Sierra Leone to southern Sudan, western Kenya
28 35 059	**Cossypha caffra** *Cape Robin*	Widespread Ethiopia to South Africa (mainly highlands)
28 35 060	**Cossypha anomala** *Olive-flanked Robin-Chat*	Tanzania to Malawi, Zambia

		Date	Location
28 35 061	**Cossypha humeralis** *White-throated Robin-Chat*		Riverside scrub of Rhodesia to Cape Province
28 35 062	**Cossypha ansorgei** *Angola Cave-Chat*		Open stalactite caves of Angola
28 35 063	**Cossypha niveicapilla** *Snowy-headed Robin-Chat*		Gambia to Ethiopia, Kenya, Tanzania, Angola
28 35 064	**Cossypha heinrichi** *Angolan Robin-Chat*		Savanna edges of northern Angola
28 35 065	**Cossypha albicapilla** *White-crowned Robin-Chat*		Densely wooded ravines of Senegal to Ethiopia
28 35 066	**Modulatrix stictigula** *Spot-throat*		Heavy forests of southern Tanzania and Malawi
28 35 067	**Cichladusa guttata** *Spotted Morning Warbler*		Southern Ethiopia and Sudan to Kenya, Uganda, Tanzania
28 35 068	**Cichladusa arquata** *Morning Warbler*		Eastern Zaire to Uganda, Kenya, Zambia, Malawi
28 35 069	**Cichladusa ruficauda** *Red-tailed Morning Warbler*		Palm biotope of Gabon to lower Congo, northern Angola
28 35 070	**Alethe diademata** *White-tailed Alethe*		Forests of Upper Guinea to Togo
28 35 071	**Alethe castanea** *Fire-crested Alethe*		Lowland forests of Nigeria to Zaire, Uganda
28 35 072	**Alethe poliophrys** *Red-throated Alethe*		Mountain forests of eastern Zaire and Uganda
28 35 073	**Alethe fülleborni** *White-chested Alethe*		Evergreen forests of southern Tanzania to Malawi, Zambia
28 35 074	**Alethe montana** *Usambara Alethe*		Known only from Usambara Mountains of northeast Tanzania
28 35 075	**Alethe lowei** *Iringa Alethe*		Known only from Iringa Province of southern Tanzania
28 35 076	**Alethe poliocephala** *Brown-chested Alethe*		Forests of Zaire to southern Sudan, Kenya, Tanzania
28 35 077	**Alethe choloensis** *Cholo Mountain Alethe*		Cholo Mountains of Malawi and Mozambique
28 35 078	**Copsychus saularis** *Magpie Robin*		Widespread Oriental region mainland and islands
28 35 079	**Copsychus sechellarum** *Seychelles Magpie Robin*		Seychelles (rare—30 birds on Frigate Island in 1974)

	Date	Location

28 35 080 **Copsychus albospecularis**
Madagascar Magpie Robin   Widespread Madagascar

28 35 081 **Copsychus malabaricus**
White-rumped (Common) Shama   Widespread Oriental mainland and islands

28 35 082 **Copsychus stricklandii (cebuensis)**
Black Shama   Philippines (endemic to Cebu Island—endangered)

28 35 083 **Copsychus luzoniensis**
White-browed Shama   Widespread throughout the Philippine Islands

28 35 084 **Copsychus niger**
Palawan Shama   Philippines (Balabac, Calamianes and Palawan Islands)

28 35 085 **Copsychus pyrropygus**
Rufous-tailed Shama   Malay Peninsula; Sumatra; Borneo

28 35 086 **Irania gutturalis**
White-throated Robin   Asia Minor; winters to Kenya and Tanzania

28 35 087 **Phoenicurus alaschanicus**
Alashan Redstart   Mountains of southwest China

28 35 088 **Phoenicurus erythronotus**
Eversmann's Redstart   Mountains of Kashmir to western China

28 35 089 **Phoenicurus caeruleocephalus**
Blue-headed Redstart   Mountains of Afghanistan to Nepal, Sikkim, Bhutan

28 35 090 **Phoenicurus ochruros**
Black Redstart   Widespread Palearctic region

28 35 091 **Phoenicurus phoenicurus**
Common Redstart   Widespread Palearctic region

28 35 092 **Phoenicurus hodgsoni**
Hodgson's Redstart   Mountains of Garhwal to Szechwan, Kansu, northeast Burma

28 35 093 **Phoenicurus frontalis**
Blue-fronted Redstart   Afghanistan to western China, Indochina, Tonkin

28 35 094 **Phoenicurus schisticeps**
White-throated Redstart   Himalayas of Nepal to western China, northeast Burma

28 35 095 **Phoenicurus auroreus**
Daurian Redstart   Siberia to Sikkim, Indochina; Hainan; Taiwan

28 35 096 **Phoenicurus moussieri**
Moussier's Redstart   Bare plateaus of Morocco, Algeria and Tunisia

	Date	Location
28 35 097 Phoenicurus erythrogaster *Guldenstadt's Redstart*		Mongolia to Afghanistan, Kashmir, Nepal, Sikkim
28 35 098 Rhyacornis bicolor *Philippine Water Redstart*		Philippines (endemic Luzon Island)
28 35 099 Rhyacornis fuliginosus *Plumbeous Redstart*		Pakistan to China, Indochina; Hainan; Taiwan
28 35 100 Hodgsonius phaenicuroides *White-bellied Redstart*		Himalayas of Kashmir to Yunnan, Burma, Laos, Tonkin
28 35 101 Cinclidium leucurum (cambodianum) *White-tailed Robin*		Nepal to Yunnan, Malaya, Indochina; Taiwan
28 35 102 Cinclidium diana *Sunda Blue Robin*		Mountains of Sumatra and Java
28 35 103 Cinclidium frontale *Blue-fronted Robin*		Nepal, Sikkim to Laos, Tonkin
28 35 104 Grandala coelicolor *Grandala*		Snowline of Kashmir to Kansu, northeast Burma
28 35 105 Sialia sialis *Eastern Bluebird*		Widespread southeast Canada to Honduras
28 35 106 Sialia mexicana *Western Bluebird*		Southwestern Canada to southern Mexico
28 35 107 Sialia currucoides *Mountain Bluebird*		Western North America (Alaska to central Mexico)
28 35 108 Enicurus scouleri *Little Forktail*		Himalayas of Kashmir to Sikiang, Burma, Tonkin; Taiwan
28 35 109 Enicurus velatus *Lesser Forktail*		Sumatra and Java
28 35 110 Enicurus ruficapillus *Chestnut-naped Forktail*		Rocky streams of Malay Peninsula, Sumatra, Borneo
28 35 111 Enicurus immaculatus *Black-backed Forktail*		Himalayas of Garhwal to Burma, northwest Thailand
28 35 112 Enicurus schistaceus *Slaty-backed Forktail*		Himalayas of Nepal to Yunnan, Malaya, Indochina
28 35 113 Enicurus leschenaulti (frontalis) *White-crowned Forktail*		Sikkim to southern China, Indochina; Hainan; Greater Sundas
28 35 114 Enicurus maculatus *Spotted Forktail*		Himalayas of Kashmir to Yunnan, Burma, Annam, Tonkin

	Date	Location
28 35 115 **Cochoa purpurea** *Purple Cochoa*		Himalayas of Nepal to Yunnan, Burma, Tonkin
28 35 116 **Cochoa viridis** *Green Cochoa*		Himalayas of Nepal to Yunnan, Burma, Annan, Tonkin, Laos
28 35 117 **Cochoa azurea** *Malaysian Cochoa*		Highlands of Sumatra, Java
28 35 118 **Myadestes townsendi** *Townsend's Solitaire*		Mountains of Alaska to northwest Mexico (Jalisco)
28 35 119 **Myadestes obscurus** *Brown-backed Solitaire*		Mountains of Mexico to Honduras; Tres Marias Islands
28 35 120 **Myadestes elisabeth** *Cuban Solitaire*		Cuba and Isle of Pines (endangered)
28 35 121 **Myadestes genibarbis** *Rufous-throated Solitaire*		Mountain forests of West Indies (endangered)
28 35 122 **Myadestes ralloides** *Andean Solitaire*		Mountains of Costa Rica to northern Bolivia, Venezuela
28 35 123 **Myadestes unicolor** *Slate-colored Solitaire*		Mountains of southeast Mexico to Nicaragua
28 35 124 **Myadestes leucogenys** *Rufous-brown Solitaire*		Ecuador to Guyana, coastal southeast Brazil, Peru
28 35 125 + **Entomodestes leucotis** *White-eared Solitaire*		Andes of Peru, Bolivia (La Paz, Cochabamba)
28 35 126 **Entomodestes coracinus** *Black Solitaire*		Andes of Colombia to northwest Ecuador
28 35 127 **Stizorhina fraseri** *Fraser's Rusty Flycatcher*		Zaire to the Sudan, Uganda
28 35 128 **Stizorhina finschii** *Finsch's Rusty Flycatcher*		Sierra Leone to Nigeria
28 35 129 **Neocossyphus rufus** *Red-tailed Thrush*		Cameroon to Tanzania; Zanzibar
28 35 130 **Neocossyphus poensis** *White-tailed Thrush*		Lowland forests of Senegal to Zaire, Uganda
28 35 131 **Cercomela sinuata** *Sickle-wing Chat*		Confined to the Cape Province of South Africa
28 35 132 **Cercomela familiaris** *Red-tailed (Familiar) Chat*		Widespread Africa south of the Sahara; Yemen
28 35 133 **Cercomela tractrac** *Layard's Chat*		Namibia to Cape Province of South Africa
28 35 134 **Cercomela schlegelii** *Karoo Chat*		Semi-deserts of southern Angola to South Africa

		Date	Location
28 35 135	**Cercomela fusca** *Brown Rock Chat*		Endemic to northern half of Indian Subcontinent
28 35 136	**Cercomela dubia** *Sombre Rock Chat*		Central Ethiopia to Somalia (rare)
28 35 137	**Cercomela melanura** *Black-tailed Rock Chat*		Eastern Sudan, Eritrea, Ethiopia, Somalia to Arabia
28 35 138	**Cercomela scotocerca** *Brown-tailed Rock Chat*		Red Sea environs to Somalia, Ethiopia, Kenya
28 35 139	**Cercomela sordida** *Hill Chat*		High altitude rocky moorlands of Ethiopia to Tanzania
28 35 140	**Saxicola rubetra** *Whinchat*		Widespread western Palearctic region
28 35 141	**Saxicola macrorhyncha** *Stoliczka's Bushchat*		Deserts of Afghanistan to Pakistan
28 35 142	**Saxicola insignis** *Hodgson's Bushchat*		Mountains of Mongolia to Tibet, western China
28 35 143	**Saxicola dacotiae** *Canary Islands Chat*		Confined to the Canary Islands
28 35 144	**Saxicola torquata** *Stonechat*		Widespread Palearctic, Oriental, Ethiopian regions
28 35 145	**Saxicola leucura** *White-tailed Bushchat*		Pakistan, India, Nepal to Burma
28 35 146	**Saxicola caprata** **(delacouri)** *Pied Bushchat*		Widespread Oriental mainland and islands; New Guinea
28 35 147	**Saxicola jerdoni** *Jerdon's Bushchat*		Eastern India to southwest China, Indochina
28 35 148	**Saxicola ferrea** *Gray Bushchat*		Himalayas of Afghanistan to Szechwan, Indochina; Taiwan
28 35 149	**Saxicola gutturalis** *Timor Bushchat*		Confined to Timor Island (Lesser Sundas)
28 35 150	**Myrmecocichla tholloni** *Congo Moorchat*		Open grasslands of Zaire to central Angola
28 35 151	**Myrmecocichla aethiops** *Anteater Chat*		Semiarid belt from Senegal to East Africa
28 35 152	**Myrmecocichla** **formicivora** *Southern Anteater Chat*		Open grasslands of Angola, Rhodesia to South Africa
28 35 153	**Myrmecocichla nigra** *Sooty Chat*		Widespread open country of Africa south of the Sahara

		Date	Location
28 35 154	**Myrmecocichla arnotti** *Arnott's Chat*		Open woodlands of Tanzania to South Africa
28 35 155	**Myrmecocichla albifrons** *White-fronted Black Chat*		Open woodlands of Gambia to Ethiopia
28 35 156	**Myrmecocichla melaena** *Rüppell's Chat*		High plateau of southern Eritrea and central Ethiopia
28 35 157	**Thamnolaea cinnamomeiventris** *Cliff Chat*		Boulder-strewn hillsides of Ethiopia to South Africa
28 35 158	**Thamnolaea coronata** *White-crowned Cliff Chat*		Rocky gorges of Nigeria to the Sudan
28 35 159	**Thamnolaea semirufa** *White-winged Cliff Chat*		Confined to highlands of Ethiopia and Eritrea
28 35 160	**Oenanthe bifasciata** *Buff-streaked Wheatear*		Confined to extreme southern tip of Africa
28 35 161	**Oenanthe isabellina** *Isabelline Wheatear*		Widespread Palearctic region; winters to Africa, India
28 35 162	**Oenanthe bottae (heuglini)** *Red-breasted Wheatear*		Ethiopia, Eritrea to Arabia
28 35 163	**Oenanthe xanthoprymna** *Red-rumped Wheatear*		Deserts of Egypt to Persia, Baluchistan
28 35 164	**Oenanthe oenanthe (phillipsi)** *Northern Wheatear*		Widespread Palearctic, Oriental, Ethiopian regions; Alaska
28 35 165	**Oenanthe deserti** *Desert Wheatear*		Widespread southern Palearctic region
28 35 166	**Oenanthe hispanica** *Black-eared Wheatear*		Arid southern Europe and North Africa
28 35 167	**Oenanthe finschii** *Finsch's (Arabian) Wheatear*		Arid North Africa to Asia Minor
28 35 168	**Oenanthe picata** *Variable Wheatear*		Stony semi-deserts of northern India to Iran, Baluchistan
28 35 169	**Oenanthe lugens (lugubris)** *Mourning Wheatear*		Sudan, Ethiopia to Iran, Baluchistan
28 35 170	**Oenanthe monacha** *Hooded Wheatear*		Sudan, Ethiopia to northwest India
28 35 171	**Oenanthe alboniger** *Hume's Wheatear*		Iran, Afghanistan to Iraq, Oman
28 35 172	**Oenanthe pleschanka** *Pied Wheatear*		Arid southern Europe and North Africa

		Date	Location
28 35 173	**Oenanthe leucopyga** *White-rumped Black Wheatear*		Coastal deserts of North Africa (Rio de Oro to Red Sea)
28 35 174	**Oenanthe leucura** *Black Wheatear*		Rocky deserts and mountains of Mediterranean basin
28 35 175	**Oenanthe monticola** *Mountain Chat*		Dry rocky areas of Angola to South Africa
18 35 176	**Oenanthe moesta** *Red-rumped Wheatear*		Arid coastal North Africa (Rio de Oro to Egypt)
28 35 177	**Oenanthe pileata** *Capped Wheatear*		Widespread barren areas of Angola to Kenya, South Africa
28 35 178	**Chaimarrornis leucocephalus** *River Chat*		Turkestan to China, Indochina; Hainan
28 35 179	**Saxicoloides fulicata** *Indian Robin*		Sri Lanka; India and southern Nepal
28 35 180	**Monticola imerinus** *Littoral Rock-Thrush*		Widespread Madagascar
28 35 181	**Monticola bensoni** *Benson's Rock-Thrush*		Widespread Madagascar
28 35 182	**Monticola sharpei** *Forest Rock-Thrush*		Forests of eastern Madagascar
28 35 183	**Monticola rupestris** *Cape Rock-Thrush*		Rocky mountainous areas of southern tip of Africa
28 35 184	**Monticola explorator** *Sentinel Rock-Thrush*		Rocky mountainous areas of southern tip of Africa
28 35 185	**Monticola brevipes** *Short-toed Rock-Thrush*		Wooded stony hills of Angola to South Africa
28 35 186	**Monticola rufocinerea** *Little Rock-Thrush*		Forest ravines of Ethiopia, Sudan to Uganda, Tanzania
28 35 187	**Monticola angolensis** *Angola Rock-Thrush*		Open bush of Angola to Tanzania, Mozambique
28 35 188	**Monticola saxatilis** *Rock-Thrush*		Open rocky regions of southern Europe to North Africa
28 35 189	**Monticola cinclorhynchus** *Blue-capped Rock-Thrush*		Himalayas of Afghanistan to Burma; winters India
28 35 190	**Monticola rufiventris** *Chestnut-bellied Rock-Thrush*		Pakistan to southern China, Burma, Indochina
28 35 191	**Monticola solitarius** *Blue Rock-Thrush*		Widespread Palearctic, Oriental regions

		Date	Location

28 35 192	**Monticola gularis** *White-throated Rock-* *Thrush*		Forests of northeast Asia to Burma, Malaya, Indochina
28 35 193	**Myiophoneus blighi** *Ceylon Whistling-Thrush*		Mountain streams of Sri Lanka
28 35 194	**Myiophoneus melanurus** *Shiny Whistling-Thrush*		Montane moss forests of Sumatra
28 35 195	**Myiophoneus glaucinus** *Sunda Whistling-Thrush*		Submontane forests of Sumatra, Java and Borneo
28 35 196	**Myiophoneus robinsoni** *Malayan Whistling-Thrush*		Endemic to Malay Peninsula (Selangor and Pahang)
28 35 197	**Myiophoneus horsfieldii** *Malabar Whistling-Thrush*		Endemic to Malabar Hills of peninsular India
28 35 198	**Myiophoneus insularis** *Taiwan Whistling-Thrush*		Endemic to forest streams of Taiwan
28 35 199	**Myiophoneus caeruleus** **(flavirostris)** *Blue Whistling-Thrush*		Turkestan to India, China, Indochina; Java; Sumatra
28 35 200	**Geomalia heinrichi** *Celebes Thrush*		Mountains of Celebes Islands
28 35 201	**Zoothera schistacea** *Tanimbar Thrush*		Confined to Tanimbar Island (southern Moluccas)
28 35 202	**Zoothera dumasi** *Moluccan Ground-Thrush*		High mountains of Ceram and Buru Islands (Moluccas)
28 35 203	**Zoothera interpres** *Chestnut-capped Thrush*		Malay Peninsula; Greater and Lesser Sundas; Philippines
28 35 204	**Zoothera erythronota** *Celebes Ground-Thrush*		Celebes and Lesser Sunda Islands
28 35 205	**Zoothera wardii** *Pied Thrush*		Himalayas of Garhwal to Sikkim; India; Sri Lanka
28 35 206	**Zoothera cinerea** *Ashy Ground-Thrush*		Philippines (endemic to Luzon and Mindoro— endangered)
28 35 207	**Zoothera peronii** *Timor Ground-Thrush*		Confined to Timor and Damar Islands (Lesser Sundas)
28 35 208	**Zoothera citrina** *Orange-headed Thrush*		Widespread Oriental region mainland and islands
28 35 209	**Zoothera everetti** *Everett's Ground-Thrush*		Mountains of Borneo (Kinabalu to Dulit—rare)
28 35 210	**Zoothera sibirica** *Siberian Thrush*		Northeast Asia to Malaya, Indochina; Greater Sundas

		Date	Location
28 35 211	**Zoothera naevia** *Varied Thrush*		Wet conifer forests of Alaska to northern Baja California
28 35 212	**Zoothera pinicola** *Aztec Thrush*		High mountains of Chihuahua to Veracruz, Oaxaca
28 35 213	**Zoothera piaggiae** *Abyssinian Ground-Thrush*		Highlands of Ethiopia to Tanzania
28 35 214	**Zoothera oberlaenderi** *Congo Ground-Thrush*		Lowland forests of eastern Zaire and western Uganda
28 35 215	**Zoothera gurneyi** *Orange Ground-Thrush*		Cameroon to Angola, Mozambique, South Africa
28 35 216	**Zoothera camaronensis** *Black-eared Ground-Thrush*		Lowland forests of Cameroon, adjacent Zaire (rare)
28 35 217	**Zoothera princei** *Gray Ground-Thrush*		Dense lowland forests of Liberia to northeast Zaire
28 35 218	**Zoothera crossleyi** *Crossley's Thrush*		High mountains of Cameroon to eastern Zaire
28 35 219	**Zoothera guttata** *Spotted Ground-Thrush*		Low evergreen forests of Mozambique to Cape Province
28 35 220	**Zoothera spiloptera** *Spot-winged Thrush*		Submontane forests of Sri Lanka
28 35 221	**Zoothera andromedae** *Sunda Ground-Thrush*		Philippines (Luzon, Mindanao, Mindoro Islands)
28 35 222	**Zoothera mollissima (griseiceps)** *Plain-backed Thrush*		Pakistan to Yunnan, Burma, Tonkin
28 35 223	**Zoothera dixoni** *Long-tailed Thrush*		Himalayas of Garhwal to western China, Burma, Tonkin
28 35 224	**Zoothera dauma** *Tiger (White's) Thrush*		Asia; Oriental mainland and islands to eastern Australia
28 35 225	**Zoothera talaseae** *New Britain Thrush*		Confined to New Britain Island
28 35 226	**Zoothera margaretae** *San Cristobal Thrush*		Confined to San Cristobal Island (eastern Solomons)
28 35 227	**Zoothera monticola** *Long-billed Thrush*		Himalayas of Garhwal to northern Burma, Tonkin
28 35 228	**Zoothera marginata** *Dark-sided Thrush*		Himalayas of Nepal to Yunnan, Thailand
28 35 229	**Zoothera terrestris** *Kittlitz' Thrush*		Extinct. Inhabited Bonin Island off China coast

	Date	Location
28 35 230 **Amalocichia sciateriana** *Greater New Guinea Thrush*		High mountains of Snow Mountains and southeast New Guinea
28 35 231 **Amalocichia incerta** *Lesser New Guinea Thrush*		Mountain forests of New Guinea
28 35 232 **Cataponera turdoides** *Celebes Mountain Thrush*		Mountain forests of Celebes Islands
28 35 233 **Nesocichia eremita** *Tristan Thrush*		Tristan de Cunha, Nightingale, Inaccessible Islands (endangered)
28 35 234 **Cichiherminia iherminieri** *Forest Thrush*		Forests of Lesser Antilles (endangered)
28 35 235 **Phaeornis obscurus** *Hawaiian Thrush*		Hawaiian Islands (except Maui—endangered)
28 35 236 **Phaeornis palmeri** *Small Kauai Thrush (Puaiohi)*		Confined to Kauai Island (Hawaii—endangered)
28 35 237 **Catharus gracilirostris** *Black-billed Nightingale-Thrush*		Mountains of Costa Rica and western Panama
28 35 238 **Catharus aurantilrostris** *Orange-billed Nightingale-Thrush*		Highlands of Mexico to Colombia, Venezuela; Trinidad
28 35 239 **Catharus fuscater** *Slaty-backed Nightingale-Thrush*		Mountain forests of Costa Rica to northern Bolivia
28 35 240 **Catharus occidentalis** *Russet Nightingale-Thrush*		High mountains of western Mexico (Sinaloa to Oaxaca)
28 35 241 **Catharus frantzii** *Ruddy-capped Nightingale-Thrush*		Cloud forests of southern Mexico to western Panama
28 35 242 **Catharus mexicanus** *Black-headed Nightingale-Thrush*		Humid highlands of northeast Mexico to western Panama
28 35 243 **Catharus dryas** *Spotted Nightingale-Thrush*		Highlands of southern Mexico to northwest Argentina
28 35 244 **Catharus fuscescens** *Veery*		Eastern North America; winters to Amazonia
28 35 245 **Catharus minimus** *Gray-cheeked Thrush*		Holarctic: eastern Siberia, Canada; winters to Peru, Brazil
28 35 246 **Catharus ustulatus** *Swainson's Thrush*		Widespread North America; winters Mexico to Argentina

		Date	Location
28 35 247	**Catharus guttatus** *Hermit Thrush*		Widespread Alaska to United States; winters to Guatemala
28 35 248	**Hylocichla mustelina** *Wood Thrush*		Eastern Canada, United States; winters to Panama
28 35 249	**Platycichla flavipes** *Yellow-legged Thrush*		Mainly highlands of Venezuela to northeast Argentina
28 35 250	**Platychichla leucops** *Pale-eyed Thrush*		Mountains of Guyana to northern Bolivia, adjacent Roraima (Brazil)
28 35 251	**Turdus bewsheri** *Comoro Thrush*		Confined to the Comoro Islands (Indian Ocean)
28 35 252	**Turdus olivaceofuscus** *Olivaceous Thrush*		São Thomé and Principé Islands (Gulf of Guinea)
28 35 253	**Turdus olivaceus (pelios)** *Olive Thrush*		Africa south of the Sahara
28 35 254	**Turdus abyssinicus** *African Mountain Thrush*		High mountains of eastern and central Africa
28 35 255	**Turdus helleri** *Taita Thrush*		Confined to Taita Hills of southeast Kenya (endangered)
28 35 256	**Turdus libonyanus** *Kurrichane Thrush*		Africa south of the Sahara
28 35 257	**Turdus tephronotus** *African Bare-eyed Thrush*		Central Ethiopia, Somalia to Tanzania
28 35 258	**Turdus menachensis** *Yemen Thrush*		Confined to southern Arabian Peninsula
28 35 259	**Turdus ludoviciae** *Somali Blackbird*		Known only from highlands of Somalia
28 35 260	**Turdus litsipsirupa** *Groundscraper Thrush*		Ethiopia to South Africa
28 35 261	**Turdus dissimilis** *Black-breasted Thrush*		Bangladesh to southern China, Burma, Thailand, Tonkin
28 35 262	**Turdus unicolor** *Tickell's Thrush*		Himalayas of Garhwal, Kashmir to Nepal, Sikkim
28 35 263	**Turdus cardis** *Japanese Thrush*		Northeast Asia to southeast China, Indochina; Hainan
28 35 264	**Turdus albocinctus** *White-collared Blackbird*		Himalayas of Garhwal to western China, northwest Burma
28 35 265	**Turdus torquatus** *Ring Ouzel*		Widespread western Palearctic region

		Date	Location
28 35 266	**Turdus boulboul** *Gray-winged Blackbird*		Pakistan to southern China, Indochina, Tonkin
28 35 267	**Turdus merula** *Common Blackbird*		Widespread Palearctic and Oriental mainlands
28 35 268	**Turdus hortulorum** *Gray-backed Thrush*		Northeast Asia to China, Indochina; Hainan; Taiwan
28 35 269	**Turdus poliocephalus** *Island Thrush*		Islands from Sumatra, Taiwan to Samoa, New Guinea
28 35 270	**Turdus chrysolaus** *Brown-headed Thrush*		Japan, northeast Asia; Philippines; Hainan; Taiwan
28 35 271	**Turdus celaenops** *Seven Islands Thrush*		Confined to the Japanese Islands
28 35 272	**Turdus rubrocanus** *Chestnut Thrush*		Pakistan to Sikkim, western China, Burma, Thailand
28 35 273	**Turdus kessleri** *Kessler's Thrush*		Kansu, Szechwan to Sikiang (accidental Sikkim)
28 35 274	**Turdus feae** *Gray-sided Thrush*		Northern China to eastern India, Indochina
28 35 275	**Turdus pallidus** *Pale Thrush*		Northeast Asia to China; Taiwan; Philippines
28 35 276	**Turdus obscurus** *Eye-browed Thrush*		Eastern Palearctic, Oriental region mainland and islands
28 35 277	**Turdus ruficollis** *Black-throated Thrush*		Widespread eastern Palearctic region
28 35 278	**Turdus naumanni** **(eunomus)** *Dusky Thrush*		Northeast Asia to the Himalayas, Indochina; Taiwan
28 35 279	**Turdus pilaris** *Fieldfare*		Widespread Palearctic region
28 35 280	**Turdus iliacus** **(musicus)** *Redwing*		Widespread Palearctic region
28 35 281	**Turdus philomeios** *Common Song Thrush*		Widespread Palearctic region; introduced Australia
28 35 282	**Turdus mupinensis** *Verreaux's Song Thrush*		Southwest China (Szechwan to Yunnan)
28 35 283	**Turdus viscivorus** *Mistle Thrush*		Widespread Palearctic region
28 35 284	**Turdus aurantius** *White-chinned Thrush*		Wooded hills and mountains of Jamaica
28 35 285	**Turdus ravidus** *Grand Cayman Thrush*		West Indies (Grand Cayman Island—probably extinct)

	Date	Location

28 35 286 **Turdus plumbeus**
Red-legged Thrush
Mountains and lowlands of West Indies

28 35 287 **Turdus chiguanco**
Chiguanco Thrush
Andes of southern Ecuador to Argentina (Córdoba)

28 35 288 **Turdus nigrescens**
Sooty Robin
High mountains of Costa Rica to western Panama

28 35 289 **Turdus fuscater**
Great Thrush
Andes of Venezuela to Boliva (La Paz, Cochabamba)

28 35 290 **Turdus serranus**
Glossy-black Thrush
Mountains of Venezuela to southeast Bolivia

28 35 291 **Turdus nigriceps**
Slaty Thrush
Mountains of Ecuador to Argentina, eastern Brazil

28 35 292 **Turdus reevei**
Plumbeous-backed Thrush
Arid littoral of southwest Ecuador to northwest Peru

28 35 293 **Turdus olivater**
Black-hooded Thrush
Mountains of Guyana to Colombia, adjacent Brazil (Roraima)

28 35 294 **Turdus maranonicus**
Marañon Thrush
Known only from upper Marañon Valley of northern Peru

28 35 295 **Turdus fulviventris**
Chestnut-bellied Thrush
Mountains of Venezuela to northern Peru (Cajamarca)

28 35 296 **Turdus rufiventris**
+
Rufous-bellied Thrush
Eastern Brazil to central Argentina (La Rioja, Buenos Aires)

28 35 297 **Turdus falcklandii**
+
Austral Thrush
Southern Chile and Argentina; Falklands; Juan Fernandez Island

28 35 298 **Turdus leucomelas**
Pale-breasted Thrush
Northern South America to northeast Argentina, Brazil

28 35 299 **Turdus amaurochalinus**
Creamy-bellied Thrush
Eastern Brazil to Peru, Argentina (Rio Negro)

28 35 300 **Turdus plebejus**
Mountain Robin
Mountains of southern Mexico (Chiapas) to western Panama

28 35 301 **Turdus ignobilis**
Black-billed Thrush
Northern South America to Bolivia, Amazonian Brazil

28 35 302 **Turdus lawrencii**
Lawrence's Thrush
Tropical forests of western Amazonian basin

28 35 303 **Turdus fumigatus**
Cocoa Thrush
Northern South America to Bolivia; Brazil; West Indies

28 35 304 **Turdus hauxwelli**
Hauxwell's Thrush
Western Amazon basin (possible race T. fumigatus)

		Date	Location
28 35 305	**Turdus obsoletus** *Pale-vented Thrush*		Costa Rica to Bolivia (possible race *T. fumigatus*)
28 35 306	**Turdus haplochrous** *Unicolored Thrush*		Bolivia (known from a single specimen from Santa Cruz)
28 35 307	**Turdus grayi** *Clay-colored Robin*		Tropical eastern Mexico to Caribbean Colombia
28 35 308	**Turdus nudigenis** *Bare-eyed Thrush*		Guianas to northwest Peru; Lesser Antilles
28 35 309	**Turdus jamaicensis** *White-eyed Thrush*		Mountain forests and wooded hills of Jamaica
28 35 310 +	**Turdus albicollis** *White-necked Robin*		Southern Mexico to northeast Argentina, Brazil
28 35 311	**Turdus rufopalliatus** *Rufous-backed Robin*		Western Mexico (Sonora to Oaxaca); Tres Marias Islands
28 35 312	**Turdus swalesi** *La Selle Thrush*		Hispaniola (high ridge of Morne La Selle east to Dominican Republic)
28 35 313	**Turdus rufitorques** *Rufous-collared Robin*		Highlands of Chiapas (Mexico) to El Salvador, Honduras
28 35 314	**Turdus infuscatus** *Black Robin*		Cloud forests of eastern Mexico to Honduras
28 35 315	**Turdus migratorius** **(confinis)** *American Robin*		Alaska to southern Mexico; Baja California; winters to Guatemala
28 35 316	**Turdus assimilis** *White-throated Robin*		Mainly highlands of Mexico to western Colombia, Ecuador

FAMILY: ORTHONYCHINIDAE (Logrunners)

28 36 001	**Orthonyx temminckii** *Spine-tailed Logrunner*		Southern Queensland, New South Wales; New Guinea
28 36 002	**Orthonyx spaldingii** *Black-headed Logrunner*		Tropical rainforests of northeast Queensland
28 36 003	**Androphobus viridis** *Green-backed Babbler*		Snow and Weyland Mountains of New Guinea
28 36 004	**Psophodes olivaceus** *Eastern Whipbird*		Coastal northeast Queensland to Victoria

		Date	Location

28 36 005 **Psophodes nigrogularis**
Western Whipbird — Western, South Australia; Kangaroo Island (endangered)

28 36 006 **Psophodes cristatus**
Chirruping Wedgebill — Australia (widespread throughout interior *mulga* zone)

28 36 007 **Psophodes occidentalis**
Chiming Wedgebill — Arid western Australia (north of *mulga-eucalypt* zone)

28 36 008 **Cinclosoma punctatum**
Spotted Quail-Thrush — Southern Queensland to Victoria; Tasmania

28 36 009 **Cinclosoma castanotum**
Chestnut Quail-Thrush — Western South Australia, adjacent Victoria, New South Wales

28 36 010 **Cinclosoma cinnamomeum (castaneothorax)**
Cinnamon Quail-Thrush — Western Australia to Queensland, Victoria

28 36 011 **Cinclosoma alisteri**
Nullarbor Quail-Thrush — Australia (*dongas* depressions on Nullarbor Plains)

28 36 012 **Cinclosoma ajax**
Ajax Scrub Robin — Lowland forests of New Guinea

28 36 013 **Eupetes leucostictus**
High Mountain Eupetes — High mountains of New Guinea

28 36 014 **Eupetes caerulescens**
Lowland Eupetes — Lowland forests of New Guinea

28 36 015 **Eupetes castanonotus**
Mid-mountain Eupetes — Lower mountain slopes of New Guinea

28 36 016 **Eupetes macrocerus**
Malaysian Rail-Babbler — Malay Peninsula; Sumatra; Borneo

28 36 017 **Melampitta lugubris**
Lesser Melampitta — Mountain forests of New Guinea

28 36 018 **Melampitta gigantea**
Greater Melampitta — Arfak and Nassau Mountains of New Guinea

28 36 019 **Ifrita kowaldi**
Blue-capped Babbler — Mountain forests of New Guinea

FAMILY: TIMALIIDAE (Babblers)

28 37 001 **Pellorneum ruficeps**
Puff-throated Babbler — Nepal, India to southwest China, Indochina

28 37 002 **Pellorneum palustre**
Marsh Babbler — Marshy lowlands of eastern India, Bangladesh

	Date	Location

28 37 003   **Pellorneum fuscocapillum**
Brown-capped Babbler   Jungle forests of Sri Lanka

28 37 004   **Pellorneum capistratum**
Black-capped Babbler   Malay Peninsula; Sumatra; Java; Borneo

28 37 005   **Pellorneum albiventre**
Spot-throated Babbler   Bhutan, Assam, India to Indochina

28 37 006   **Trichastoma tickelli**
Buff-breasted Babbler   Assam to southwest China, Indochina; Sumatra

28 37 007   **Trichastoma pyrrogenys**
Temminck's Jungle Babbler   Sumatra; Java; Borneo

28 37 008   **Trichastoma malaccense**
Short-tailed Babbler   Malay Peninsula; Sumatra; Borneo

28 37 009   **Trichastoma cinereiceps**
Ashy-headed Babbler   Philippine Islands (Balabac and Palawan)

28 37 010   **Trichastoma rostratum**
White-chested Babbler   Malay Peninsula; Sumatra; Borneo

28 37 011   **Trichastoma bicolor**
Ferruginous Babbler   Malay Peninsula; Sumatra; Borneo

28 37 012   **Trichastoma sepiarium**
Horsfield's Babbler   Malay Peninsula; Java; Sumatra; Borneo

28 37 013   **Trichastoma celebense**
Celebes Jungle Babbler   Confined to the Celebes Islands

28 37 014   **Trichastoma abbotti**
Abbot's Babbler   Nepal to Assam, Malaya, Indochina; Sumatra; Borneo

28 37 015   **Trichastoma perspicillatum**
Black-browed Jungle Babbler   Known only from southern Borneo (rare)

28 37 016   **Trichastoma vanderbilti**
Vanderbilt's Babbler   Known only from Sumatra (rare)

28 37 017 ✝   **Trichastoma pyrrhopterum**
Mountain Illadopsis   Dense forest undergrowth of Kenya, Tanzania, Zaire

28 37 018   **Trichastoma cleaveri**
Blackcap Akalat   Sierra Leone to Cameroon, Zaire

28 37 019 ✝   **Trichastoma albipectus**
Scaly-breasted Illadopsis   Zaire to Kenya, southern Sudan

28 37 020   **Trichastoma rufescens**
Rufous-winged Illadopsis   Forests of Sierra Leone to Ghana

28 37 021   **Trichastoma rufipennis**
Pale-breasted Illadopsis   Dense forest undergrowth of Cameroon to Kenya

		Date	Location

28 37 022 **Trichastoma fulvescens**
Brown Illadopsis
Southern Sudan, Uganda, western Kenya and Tanzania

28 27 023 **Trichastoma puveli**
Puvel's Illadopsis
Forests of Guinea, Sierra Leone and Lagos

28 37 024 **Trichastoma poliothorax**
Gray-chested Illadopsis
Mountain forests of Cameroon to Lake Tanganyika

28 37 025 **Leonardina woodi**
Bagobo Babbler
Philippines (endemic to Mindanao Island)

28 37 026 **Ptyrticus turdinus**
Thrush Babbler
Forest streams of northeast Zaire to southwest Sudan

28 37 027 **Malacopteron magnirostre**
Moustached Babbler
Malay Peninsula; Sumatra; Borneo

28 37 028 **Malacopteron affine**
Sooty-capped Babbler
Malay Peninsula; Sumatra; Borneo

28 37 029 **Malacopteron cinereum**
Scaly-crowned Babbler
Malaya, Indochina; Java; Sumatra; Borneo

28 37 030 **Malacopteron magnum**
Rufous-crowned Babbler
Malay Peninsula; Sumatra; Borneo; Palawan

28 37 031 **Malacopteron palawanense**
Red-headed Tree Babbler
Philippines (Balabac and Palawan Islands)

28 37 032 **Malacopteron albogulare**
Gray-breasted Babbler
Lowland forests of Malaya; Sumatra; Borneo

28 37 033 **Pomatorhinus hypoleucos**
Large Scimitar-Babbler
Bangladesh to southern China, Indochina; Hainan

28 37 034 **Pomatorhinus erythrogenys**
Rusty-cheeked Scimitar-Babbler
Himalayas of Kashmir to Burma, Thailand

28 37 035 **Pomatorhinus erythrocnemis**
Spot-breasted Scimitar-Babbler
Bangladesh, Assam to Indochina; Taiwan

28 37 036 **Pomatorhinus horsfieldii**
Indian Scimitar-Babbler
Widespread Sri Lanka; southern India

28 37 037 **Pomatorhinus schisticeps**
White-browed Scimitar-Babbler
Himalayas of Nepal, India to Indochina

28 37 038 **Pomatorhinus montanus**
Chestnut-backed Scimitar-Babbler
Malay Peninsula; Java; Sumatra; Borneo

		Date	Location

28 37 039	**Pomatorhinus ruficollis** *Rufous-necked Scimitar-Babbler*		Nepal to southern China, Indochina; Taiwan; Hainan
28 37 040	**Pomatorhinus ochraceiceps** *Red-billed Scimitar-Babbler*		Widespread Assam to southwest China, Indochina
28 37 041	**Pomatorhinus ferruginosus** *Coral-billed Scimitar-Babbler*		Himalyas of Nepal to Burma, Thailand, Laos, Tonkin
28 37 042	**Pomatostomus isidorei** *Rufous Babbler*		Lowland forests of New Guinea and Misol Island
28 37 043	**Pomatostomus temporalis (rubeculus)** *Gray-crowned Babbler*		Widespread Australia (except southwest); New Guinea
28 37 044	**Pomatostomus superciliosus** *White-browed Babbler*		Arid southern Australia
28 37 045	**Pomatostomus halli** *Hall's Babbler*		*Mulga* of southern Queensland (rare and local)
28 37 046	**Pomatostomus ruficeps** *Chestnut-crowned Babbler*		*Casuarina* saltbush country of southeast Australia
28 37 047	**Xiphirhynchus superciliaris** *Slender-billed Scimitar-Babbler*		Himalayas of Nepal, Sikkim to Yunnan
28 37 048	**Jabouilleia danjoui** *Short-tailed Scimitar-Babbler*		Evergreen forests of Annam (rare endemic)
28 37 049	**Rimator malacoptilus** *Long-billed Wren-Babbler*		Himalayas of Sikkim to Indochina, Tonkin; Sumatra
28 37 050	**Ptilocichla leucogrammica** *Bornean Wren-Babbler*		Spottily distributed lowlands of Borneo (rare)
28 37 051	**Ptilocichla mindanensis** *Streaked Wren-Babbler*		Widespread throughout Philippine Islands
28 37 052	**Ptilocichla falcata** *Falcated Wren-Babbler*		Philippines (Balabac and Palawan Islands)
28 37 053	**Kenopia striata** *Striped Wren-Babbler*		Malay Peninsula; Sumatra; Borneo
28 37 054	**Napothera rufipectus** *Sumatran Wren-Babbler*		Highlands of Sumatra

		Date	Location
28 37 055	**Napothera atrigularis** *Black-throated Wren-Babbler*		Sparsely distributed lowland forests of Borneo
28 37 056	**Napothera macrodactyla** *Large Wren-Babbler*		Malay Peninsula; Sumatra; Java
28 37 057	**Napothera marmorata** *Marbled Wren-Babbler*		Forests of central Malaya; western Sumatra
28 37 058	**Napothera crispifrons** *Limestone Wren-Babbler*		Limestone hills of Tenasserim, Thailand, Indochina
28 37 059	**Napothera brevicaudata** *Streaked Wren-Babbler*		Assam to southwest China, Malaya, Indochina; Hainan
28 37 060	**Napothera crassa** *Mountain Wren-Babbler*		High mountains of Borneo (Kinabalu to Tama Abo)
28 37 061	**Napothera rabori** *Luzon Wren-Babbler*		Philippines (known only from Luzon Island)
28 37 062	**Napothera epilepidota** *Eye-browed Wren-Babbler*		Assam to Malaya, Indochina; Greater Sundas
28 37 063	**Pnoepyga albiventer** *Scaly-breasted Wren-Babbler*		Himalayas of Nepal to Szechwan, Burma, Tonkin
28 37 064	**Pnoepyga pusilla** *Pygmy Wren-Babbler*		Widespread Oriental mainland and islands
28 37 065	**Spelaeornis caudatus** *Short-tailed Wren-Babbler*		Extreme eastern Nepal (Ilam District) to Bhutan
28 37 066	**Spelaeornis troglodytoides** *Bar-winged Wren-Babbler*		Himalayas of Bhutan to southwest China, Burma
28 37 067	**Spelaeornis badeigularis** *Mishmi Wren-Babbler*		India (known from one specimen from Mishmi Hills)
28 37 068	**Spelaeornis formosus** *Spotted Wren-Babbler*		Himalayas of Sikkim to Fukien, Burma (rare)
28 37 069	**Spelaeornis chocolatinus** *Long-tailed Wren-Babbler*		Assam to southwest China, Burma, Tonkin
28 37 070	**Spelaeornis longicaudatus** *Assam Wren-Babbler*		Confined to the mountains of Assam
28 37 071	**Sphenocichla humei** *Wedge-billed Wren-Babbler*		Forests of Assam, Sikkim to northern Burma (rare)
28 37 072	**Neomixis tenella** *Common Jery*		Widespread savannas and mangroves of Madagascar

	Date	Location
28 37 073 **Neomixis viridis** *Green Jery*		Highland interior forests of Madagascar
28 37 074 **Neomixis striatigula** *Stripe-throated Jery*		Lowland forests of southern Madagascar
28 37 075 **Neomixis flavoviridis** *Wedge-tailed Jery*		Widespread highland forests of Madagascar
28 37 076 **Stachyris rodolphei** *Deignan's Babbler*		Thailand (bamboo forests of Doi Chiang Dao)
28 37 077 **Stachyris rufifrons** *Rufous-fronted Babbler*		Sikkim to Malaya; Sumatra; Borneo
28 37 078 **Stachyris ambigua** *Buff-chested Babbler*		Sikkim to Assam, Burma, Indochina
28 37 079 **Stachyris ruficeps** *Rufous-capped Babbler*		Nepal to Yunnan, Indochina; Hainan; Taiwan
28 37 080 **Stachyris pyrrhops** *Black-chinned Babbler*		Himalyas of Kashmir, Garhwal, Nepal
28 37 081 **Stachyris chrysaea** *Golden Babbler*		Nepal to Yunnan, Malaya, Indochina; Sumatra
28 37 082 **Stachyris plateni** *Pygmy Tree-Babbler*		Philippines (endemic to Mindanao Island)
28 37 083 **Stachyris capitalis** *Black-crowned Tree-Babbler*		Widespread throughout the Philippine Islands
28 37 084 **Stachyris speciosa** *Rough-templed Tree-Babbler*		Philippines (endemic to Negros Island)
28 37 085 **Stachyris whiteheadi** *Whitehead's Tree-Babbler*		Philippines (endemic to Luzon Island)
28 37 086 **Stachyris striata** *Striped Tree-Babbler*		Philippines (endemic to Luzon Island)
28 37 087 **Stachyris nigrorum** *Negros Tree-Babbler*		Philippines (endemic to Negros Island)
28 37 088 **Stachyris hypogrammica** *Palawan Tree-Babbler*		Philippines (endemic to Palawan Island)
28 37 089 **Stachyris grammiceps** *White-breasted Tree-Babbler*		Known only from western Java
28 37 090 **Stachyris herberti** *Sooty Babbler*		Lowlands of central Laos (known from one specimen)
28 37 091 **Stachyris nigriceps** *Gray-throated Babbler*		Nepal to Malaya, Indochina; Borneo; Sumatra
28 37 092 **Stachyris poliocephala** *Gray-headed Babbler*		Malay Peninsula; Sumatra; Borneo

		Date	Location
28 37 093	**Stachyris striolata** *Spot-necked Babbler*		Southern China to Indochina; Hainan; Sumatra
28 37 094	**Stachyris oglei** *Snowy-throated Babbler*		Known only from Assam
28 37 095	**Stachyris maculata** *Chestnut-rumped Babbler*		Malay Peninsula; Sumatra; Borneo
28 37 096	**Stachyris leucotis** *White-necked Babbler*		Malay Peninsula; Sumatra; Borneo
28 37 097	**Stachyris nigricollis** *Black-throated Babbler*		Malay Peninsula; Sumatra; Borneo
28 37 098	**Stachyris thoracica** *White-collared Babbler*		Sumatra and Java
28 37 099	**Stachyris erythroptera** *Chestnut-winged Babbler*		Malay Peninsula; Sumatra; Borneo
28 37 100	**Stachyris melanothorax** *Pearly-cheeked Babbler*		Java and Bali
28 37 101	**Dumetia hyperythra** *White-throated Babbler*		Lowlands of Sri Lanka, India and Nepal
28 37 102	**Rhopocichla atriceps** *Black-headed Babbler*		Evergreen biotope of western India; Sri Lanka
28 37 103	**Macronous flavicollis** *Yellow-collared Tit-Babbler*		Known only from Java and Kangean Islands
28 37 104	**Macronous gularis** *Striped Tit-Babbler*		Nepal to Malaya, Indochina; Greater Sundas; Palawan
28 37 105	**Macronous kelleyi** *Gray-faced Tit-Babbler*		Forests of southern Laos, Annam
28 37 106	**Macronous striaticeps** *Brown Tit-Babbler*		Widespread Philippine islands and Sulu Archipelago
28 37 107	**Macronous ptilosus** *Fluffy-backed Tit-Babbler*		Malay Peninsula; Sumatra; Borneo
28 37 108	**Micromacronus leytensis** *Miniature Tit-Babbler*		Philippines (Leyte and Mindanao)
28 37 109	**Timalia pileata** *Chestnut-capped Babbler*		India to southern China, Indochina; Java
28 37 110	**Chrysomma sinense** *Yellow-eyed Babbler*		Pakistan to southern China, Indochina
28 37 111	**Moupinia altirostris** *Jerdon's Babbler*		Grassy areas of Pakistan to Assam, Burma
28 37 112	**Moupinia poecilotis** *Chestnut-tailed Babbler*		Mountains of Szechwan to Yunnan (China)

	Date	Location

28 37 113 **Turdoides nipalensis**
Spiny Babbler
Nepal (from Doti to Taplejung District)

28 37 114 **Turdoides altirostris**
Iraq Babbler
Reed beds of Tigris-Euphrates Valley

28 37 115 **Turdoides caudatus**
Common Babbler
Iraq to western Nepal, India

28 37 116 **Turdoides earlei**
Striated Babbler
Pakistan, northern India, Nepal to Assam, Burma

28 37 117 **Turdoides gularis**
White-throated Babbler
Dry plains of Burma (common endemic)

28 37 118 **Turdoides longirostris**
Slender-billed Babbler
Grassy plains of Nepal to Assam, western Burma

28 37 119 **Turdoides malcolmi**
Large Gray Babbler
Dry, scrubby lowlands of India

28 37 120 **Turdoides squamiceps**
Arabian Babbler
Aquaba and northern Sinai Peninsula

28 37 121 **Turdoides fulvus**
Fulvous Babbler
Sudan to Ethiopia, Eritrea

28 37 122 **Turdoides aylmeri**
Scaly Chatterer
Ethiopia to Tanzania

28 37 123 **Turdoides rubiginosus**
Rufous Chatterer
Widespread Africa south of the Sahara

28 37 124 **Turdoides subrufus**
Rufous Babbler
Lowland plains and foothills of southern India

28 37 125 **Turdoides striatus**
Jungle Babbler
Sri Lanka; Pakistan, southern Nepal to Bangladesh

28 37 126 **Turdoides rufescens**
Ceylon Rufous Babbler
Common throughout forests of Sri Lanka

28 37 127 **Turdoides affinis**
White-headed Babbler
Dry lowlands and foothills of India; Sri Lanka

28 37 128 **Turdoides melanops**
Black-lored Babbler
Tanzania to Angola, northern Namibia

28 37 129 **Turdoides tenebrosus**
Dusky Babbler
Western Ethiopia, southern Sudan to Zaire

28 37 130 **Turdoides reinwardtii**
Blackcap Babbler
Forest edges of Senegal to Central African Republic

28 37 131 **Turdoides plebejus**
Brown Babbler
Bushy savanna of Nigeria to Kenya

28 37 132 **Turdoides leucocephalus**
White-headed Babbler
Nile Valley south of Khartoum to Eritrean coast; Eritrea

28 37 133 **Turdoides jardineii**
Arrow-marked Babbler
Kenya, Uganda to South Africa

		Date	Location
28 37 134	**Turdoides squamulatus** *Squamulated Babbler*		Kenya to Ethiopia, Somalia
28 37 135	**Turdoides leucopygius** *White-rumped Babbler*		Swamps and reed beds of Ethiopia to South Africa
28 37 136	**Turdoides hindei** *Hinde's Pied Babbler*		Highlands of Kenya (Kikuyu and Ukamba Provinces—rare)
28 37 137	**Turdoides hypoleucus** *Northern Pied Babbler*		Woodland scrub of Kenya and Tanzania
28 37 138	**Turdoides bicolor** *Bicolored Babbler*		Confined to southern tip of Africa
28 37 139	**Turdoides gymnogenys** *Bare-cheeked Babbler*		Southern Angola and adjacent Namibia
28 37 140	**Babax lanceolatus** *Chinese Babax*		Thin scattered forests of Assam, southern China to Burma
28 37 141	**Babax waddelli** *Giant Babax*		Arid scrub of Sikkim to southeast Tibet
28 37 142	**Babax koslowi** *Kozlov's Babax*		Mekong Valley (Tsinghai and Hsikang)
28 37 143	**Garrulax cinereifrons** *Ashy-headed Laughingthrush*		Wet zone and adjacent mountains of Sri Lanka
28 37 144	**Garrulax palliatus** *Gray-and-brown Laughingthrush*		Primary mountain forests of Sumatra and Borneo
28 37 145	**Garrulax rufifrons** *Red-fronted Laughingthrush*		Confined to mountains of western Java
28 37 146	**Garrulax perspicillatus** *Masked Laughingthrush*		Mountains of southern China to Indochina
28 37 147	**Garrulax albogularis** *White-throated Laughingthrush*		Himalayas of Kashmir to western China, Tonkin
28 37 148	**Garrulax leucolophus** *White-crested Laughingthrush*		Himalayas of Garhwal to Yunnan, Indochina; Sumatra
28 37 149	**Garrulax monileger** *Lesser Necklaced Laughingthrush*		Nepal to Yunnan, Indochina; Hainan
28 37 150	**Garrulax pectoralis** *Greater Necklaced Laughingthrush*		Nepal to Yunnan, Indochina; Hainan
28 37 151	**Garrulax lugubris** *Black Laughingthrush*		Forests of Malay Peninsula; Sumatra; Borneo

		Date	Location
28 37 152	**Garrulax striatus** *Striated Laughingthrush*		Evergreen forests of Garhwal, Nepal to Szechwan, Burma
28 37 153	**Garrulax strepitans** *White-necked Laughingthrush*		Burma, Tenasserim to Indochina
28 37 154	**Garrulax milleti** *Black-hooded Laughingthrush*		Forests of Annam
28 37 155	**Garrulax maesi** *Gray Laughingthrush*		High mountains forests of southwest China to Tonkin, Laos
28 37 156	**Garrulax chinensis** *Black-throated Laughingthrush*		Southern China to Indochina; Hainan
28 37 157	**Garrulax nuchalis** *Chestnut-backed Laughingthrush*		Assam to Burma
28 37 158	**Garrulax vassali** *White-cheeked Laughingthrush*		Forests of Annam, Laos
28 37 159	**Garrulax galbanus** **(courtoisi)** *Austen's Laughingthrush*		Assam, southwest China to Chin Hills of Burma
28 37 160	**Garrulax delesserti** **(gularis)** *Rufous-vented Laughingthrush*		Southwest India to Bhutan, Assam, Indochina
28 37 161	**Garrulax variegatus** *Variegated Laughingthrush*		Himalayas of Kashmir, Garhwal, Nepal
28 37 162	**Garrulax davidi** *Père David's Laughingthrush*		Mongolia to northern China, Manchuria
28 37 163	**Garrulax sukatschewi** *Sukatchev's Laughingthrush*		China (mountain forests of southern Kansu)
28 37 164	**Garrulax cineraceus** *Moustached Laughingthrush*		Assam to southern China, Burma
28 37 165	**Garrulax rufogularis** *Rufous-chinned Laughingthrush*		Himalayas of Pakistan to Assam, Burma, Tonkin
28 37 166	**Garrulax lunulatus** *Barred Laughingthrush*		Mountains of northwest China
28 37 167	**Garrulax bieti** *Biet's Laughingthrush*		Mountains of western Szechwan to northern Yunnan

	Date	Location

| 28 37 168 | **Garrulax maximus** |
| | *Giant Laughingthrush* | Mountains of western China, southeast Tibet |

| 28 37 169 | **Garrulax ocellatus** |
| | *White-spotted Laughingthrush* | Himalayas of Garhwal, Nepal to Szechwan, Burma |

| 28 37 170 | **Garrulax caerulatus** |
| | *Gray-sided Laughingthrush* | Oak-rhododendron forests of Nepal to southwest China, Burma |

| 28 37 171 | **Garrulax poecilorhynchus** |
| | *Scaly-headed Laughingthrush* | Known only from Fukien and Szechwan (China) |

| 28 37 172 | **Garrulax mitratus** |
| | *Chestnut-capped Laughingthrush* | Malay Peninsula; Sumatra; Borneo |

| 28 37 173 | **Garrulax ruficollis** |
| | *Rufous-necked Laughingthrush* | Mixed forests of Nepal to southwest China, Burma |

| 28 37 174 | **Garrulax merulinus** |
| | *Spot-breasted Laughingthrush* | Assam to southwest China, Indochina |

| 28 37 175 | **Garrulax canorus** |
| | *Hwamei Laughingthrush* | Dense mountain scrub of southern China to Indochina |

| 28 37 176 | **Garrulax sannio** |
| | *White-browed Laughingthrush* | Assam to southern China, Indochina; Hainan |

| 28 37 177 | **Garrulax cachinnans** |
| | *Nilgiri Laughingthrush* | Nilgiri Hills of peninsular India |

| 28 37 178 | **Garrulax jerdoni** |
| | *White-breasted Laughingthrush* | Evergreen biotope of southwestern India |

| 28 37 179 | **Garrulax lineatus** |
| | *Streaked Laughingthrush* | Himalayas of Afghanistan to Nepal, Sikkim, Bhutan |

| 28 37 180 | **Garrulax virgatus** |
| | *Striped Laughingthrush* | Southeast Tibet to Assam, Burma |

| 28 37 181 | **Garrulax austeni** |
| | *Brown-capped Laughingthrush* | Evergreen forests of Assam to Burma |

| 28 37 182 | **Garrulax squamatus** |
| | *Blue-winged Laughingthrush* | Evergreen forests of Nepal to Yunnan, Burma, Tonkin |

| 28 37 183 | **Garrulax subunicolor** |
| | *Scaly Laughingthrush* | Nepal to Yunnan, Burma, Tonkin |

| 28 37 184 | **Garrulax elliotii** |
| | *Elliot's Laughingthrush* | High mountains of western China |

		Date	Location

28 37 185 **Garrulax henrici**
Prince Henry's Laughingthrush
High dry scrub of southeast Tibet

28 37 186 **Garrulax affinis**
Black-faced Laughingthrush
Nepal to Szechwan, Burma, Tonkin; Hainan

28 37 187 **Garrulax erythrocephalus**
Chestnut-crowned Laughingthrush
Himalayas of Pakistan to Burma, Malaya, Laos, Tonkin

28 37 188 **Garrulax yersini**
Collared Laughingthrush
Langbian Plateau of southern Annam

28 37 189 **Garrulax formosus**
Red-winged Laughingthrush
Southwest China (Szechwan, Yunnan) to Tonkin

28 37 190 **Garrulax milnei**
Red-tailed Laughingthrush
Southern China to Burma, Thailand, Laos, Tonkin

28 37 191 **Liocichla phoenicea (ripponi)**
Crimson-winged Laughingthrush
Himalayas of Nepal, Sikkim to Yunnan

28 37 192 **Liocichla steerii**
Steere's Babbler
Highlands of southern Taiwan

28 37 193 **Leiothrix argentauris**
Silver-eared Mesia
Himalayas of Pakistan to Burma, Malaya; Sumatra

28 37 194 **Leiothrix lutea**
Red-billed Leiothrix
Himalyas of Pakistan to Szechwan, Burma, Tonkin

28 37 195 **Cutia nipalensis**
Nepal Cutia
Himalayas of Nepal to Yunnan, Malaya, Indochina

28 37 196 **Pteruthius rufiventer**
Black-headed Shrike-Babbler
Nepal to Yunnan, Burma, Tonkin

28 37 197 **Pteruthius flaviscapis**
White-browed Shrike-Babbler
Himalayas of Pakistan to Malaya, Indochina; Greater Sundas

28 37 198 **Pteruthius xanthochlorus**
Green Shrike-Babbler
Himalayas of Pakistan to Szechwan, Burma

28 37 199 **Pteruthius melanotis**
Black-eared Shrike-Babbler
Himalayas of Nepal to Yunnan, Malaya, Indochina

28 37 200 **Pteruthius aenobarbus**
Chestnut-fronted Shrike-Babbler
Assam to southern China, Indochina

28 37 201 **Gampsorhynchus rufulus**
White-hooded Babbler
Bamboo jungles of Nepal to Malaya, Indochina

		Date	Location
28 37 202	**Actinodura egertoni** *Nepal Barwing*		Evergreen forests of Nepal to Burma
28 37 203	**Actinodura ramsayi** *Spectacled Barwing*		Southwest China to Burma, Thailand, Laos, Tonkin
28 37 204	**Actinodura nipalensis** *Hoary Barwing*		Oak-rhododendron forests of Nepal to Yunnan, Burma
28 37 205	**Actinodura waldeni** *Streak-throated Barwing*		Assam to western China, Burma
28 37 206	**Actinodura souliei** *Streaked Barwing*		Evergreen forests of southwest China, Tonkin
28 37 207	**Actinodura morrisoniana** *Taiwan Barwing*		Confined to evergreen forests of Taiwan
28 37 208	**Minla cyanouroptera** *Blue-winged Minla*		Himalayas of Nepal to Yunnan, Malaya, Indochina
28 37 209	**Minla strigula** *Chestnut-tailed Minla*		Himalayas of Kashmir to Yunnan, Malaya, Indochina
28 37 210	**Minla ignotincta** *Red-tailed Minla*		Himalayas of Nepal to Szechwan, Burma, Tonkin
28 37 211	**Alcippe chrysotis** *Golden-breasted Fulvetta*		Himalayas of Nepal to Yunnan, Burma, Tonkin
28 37 212	**Alcippe variegaticeps** *Yellow-fronted Fulvetta*		China (Kwangsi—known from one specimen)
28 37 213	**Alcippe cinerea** *Yellow-throated Fulvetta*		Himalayas of Nepal to Burma, Laos, Tonkin
28 37 214	**Alcippe castaneceps** *Rufous-winged Fulvetta*		Himalayas of Nepal to Yunnan, Malaya, Indochina
28 37 215	**Alcippe vinipectus** *White-browed Fulvetta*		Himalayas of Kashmir to Yunnan, Burma, Tonkin
28 37 216	**Alcippe striaticollis** *Stripe-necked Fulvetta*		Mountains of southern China
28 37 217	**Alcippe ruficapilla** *Spectacled Fulvetta*		Himalayas to southern China, Laos, Tonkin; Hainan
28 37 218	**Alcippe cinereiceps** *Streak-throated Fulvetta*		Himalayas to southern China, Laos, Tonkin; Hainan
28 37 219	**Alcippe rufogularis** *Rufous-throated Fulvetta*		Himalayas of Bhutan to southwest China, Indochina
28 37 220	**Alcippe brunnea** *Brown-eared Fulvetta*		Assam to southern China, Tonkin; Taiwan; Hainan
28 37 221	**Alcippe brunneicauda** *Brown Fulvetta*		Malay Peninsula; Sumatra; Borneo
28 37 222	**Alcippe poioicephala** *Brown-cheeked Fulvetta*		India to southwest China, Indochina

		Date	Location
28 37 223	**Alcippe pyrrhoptera** *Javanese Fulvetta*		Highlands of western and central Java
28 37 224	**Alcippe peracensis** *Mountain Fulvetta*		Evergreen forests of Malaya, Indochina
28 37 225	**Alcippe morrisonia** *Gray-cheeked Fulvetta*		Southern China to Burma, Indochina; Taiwan; Hainan
28 37 226	**Alcippe nipalensis** *Nepal Fulvetta*		Himalayas of Nepal to Yunnan, Assam, Burma
28 37 227	**Alcippe abyssinica** *Abyssinian Hill Babbler*		Rain forests of Ethiopia to Tanzania
28 37 228	**Alcippe atriceps** *Ruwenzori Fulvetta*		Mountain forests of Ruanda, Burundi to western Uganda
28 37 229	**Lioptilus nigricapillus** *Bush Blackcap*		Damp forest areas of extreme southeast Africa
28 37 230	**Lioptilus gilberti** *White-throated Mountain-Babbler*		Cameroon (confined to Mt. Kupé)
28 37 231	**Lioptilus rufocinctus** *Red-collared Mountain-Babbler*		Western Ruanda to eastern Zaire (Mt. Musokolo)
28 37 232	**Lioptilus chapini** *Schouteden's Mountain-Babbler*		Eastern Zaire (Lake Edward to Lake Albert)
28 37 233	**Parophasma galinieri** *Abyssinian Catbird*		Confined to the highlands of Ethiopia
28 37 234	**Phyllanthus atripennis** *Capuchin Babbler*		Dense secondary forests of Senegal to western Uganda
28 37 235	**Crocias langbianis** *Gray-crowned Crocias*		Annam (mountains of Langbian Plateau—rare endemic)
28 37 236	**Crocias albonotatus** *Spotted Sibia*		Confined to the highlands of Java
28 37 237	**Heterophasia annectens** *Rufous-backed Sibia*		Sikkim to Yunnan, Indochina, Tonkin
28 37 238	**Heterophasia capistrata** *Black-capped Sibia*		Himalayas of Pakistan to Nepal, Sikkim
28 37 239	**Heterophasia gracillis** *Gray Sibia*		Assam to southwest China, Burma
28 37 240	**Heterophasia melanoleuca** *Black-headed Sibia*		Southwest China to Burma, Annam, Tonkin, Laos
28 37 241	**Heterophasia auricularis** *White-eared Sibia*		Confined to Island of Taiwan

		Date	Location

28 37 242	**Heterophasia pulchella** *Beautiful Sibia*	Himalayas of Assam to southwest China, Burma
28 37 243	**Heterophasia picaoides** *Long-tailed Sibia*	Nepal to Yunnan, Indochina; Sumatra
28 37 244	**Yuhina castaniceps** *Striated Yuhina*	Sikkim to Yunnan, Thailand, Indochina; Borneo
28 37 245	**Yuhina bakeri** *White-naped Yuhina*	Himalayas of Kashmir to Nepal, Yunnan, northern Burma
28 37 246	**Yuhina flavicollis** *Yellow-naped Yuhina*	Himalayas of Kashmir to Yunnan, Indochina
28 37 247	**Yuhina gularis** *Stripe-throated Yuhina*	Himalayas of Kashmir, Garhwal to Yunnan, Laos
28 37 248	**Yuhina humilis** *Burmese Yuhina*	Evergreen forests of Burma, Tenasserim
28 37 249	**Yuhina diademata** *White-collared Yuhina*	Northeast Burma, northwest Tonkin, adjacent China
28 37 250	**Yuhina occipitalis** *Rufous-vented Yuhina*	Oak-rhododendron forests of Nepal to Yunnan, Burma
28 37 251	**Yuhina brunneiceps** *Formosan Yuhina*	Confined to Island of Taiwan
28 37 252	**Yuhina nigrimenta** *Black-chinned Yuhina*	Himalayas of Kashmir, Garhwal to Yunnan, Laos
28 37 253	**Yuhina zantholeuca** *White-bellied Yuhina*	Himalayas of Nepal to Malaya, Indochina; Sumatra
28 37 254	**Malia grata** *Celebes Malia*	Confined to mountains of Celebes Islands
28 37 255	**Myzornis pyrrhoura** *Fire-tailed Myzornis*	Nepal, Sikkim to Yunnan, northeast Burma
28 37 256	**Horizorhinus dohrni** *Dohrn's Thrush-Babbler*	Confined to Principé Island (Gulf of Guinea)
28 37 257	**Oxylabes madagascariensis** *White-throated Oxylabes*	Lowland and mid-mountain forests of eastern Madagascar
28 37 258	**Mystacornis crossleyi** *Crossley's Babbler*	Humid forests of eastern Madagascar

FAMILY: CHAMAEIDAE (Wrentit)

28 38 001	**Chamaea fasciata** *Wrentit*	Chaparral belt of Oregon to Baja California

		Date	Location

FAMILY: PANURIDAE (Parrotbills)

28 39 001	**Panurus biarmicus**		
	Bearded Tit		Spottily distributed reed beds of Palearctic region
28 39 002	**Conostoma oemodium**		
	Great Parrotbill		High *ringal* bamboo zone of Nepal to Szechwan, Burma
28 39 003	**Paradoxornis paradoxus**		
	Three-toed Parrotbill		Himalayas of southwest China
28 39 004	**Paradoxornis unicolor**		
	Brown Parrotbill		Himalayas of Nepal to southwest China, Burma
28 39 005	**Paradoxornis flavirostris**		
	Black-breasted Parrotbill		Himalayas of Nepal (?), Sikkim to Assam, Burma
28 39 006	**Paradoxornis guttaticollis**		
	Spot-breasted Parrotbill		Assam to southwest China, Indochina
28 39 007	**Paradoxornis conspicillatus**		
	Spectacled Parrotbill		Mountains of southwest China
28 39 008	**Paradoxornis ricketti**		
	Yunnan Parrotbill		Mountains of southwest China (Yunnan)
28 39 009	**Paradoxornis webbianus**		
	Vinous-throated Parrotbill		Manchuria to southern China, Burma; Korea; Taiwan
28 39 010	**Paradoxornis alphonsianus**		
	Ashy-throated Parrotbill		Mountains of southwest China, adjacent Tonkin
28 39 011	**Paradoxornis zappeyi**		
	Dusky Parrotbill		Southern China (endemic to Hsikang Province)
28 39 012	**Paradoxornis przewalskii**		
	Przewalski's Parrotbill		China (endemic to Kansu Province)
28 39 013	**Paradoxornis fulvifrons**		
	Fulvous Parrotbill		High bamboo zone of Nepal to Szechwan, northeast Burma
28 39 014	**Paradoxornis nipalensis (verreauxi)**		
	Black-throated Parrotbill		Mountains of Nepal to Yunnan, Indochina; Taiwan
28 39 015	**Paradoxornis davidianus**		
	Short-tailed Parrotbill		Southeast China to Burma, Thailand, Laos, Tonkin
28 39 016	**Paradoxornis atrosuperciliaris**		
	Black-browed Parrotbill		Himalayas of Sikkim to Yunnan, Thailand, Laos
28 39 017	**Paradoxornis ruficeps**		
	Red-headed Parrotbill		Himalayas of Sikkim to Yunnan, Burma, Laos, Tonkin
28 39 018	**Paradoxornis gularis**		
	Gray-headed Parrotbill		Sikkim to Szechwan, Indochina; Hainan

	Date	Location
28 39 019 **Paradoxornis heudei** *Yangtze Parrotbill*		Reed beds of Yangtze River (endangered)

FAMILY: PICATHARTIDAE (Rockfowl)

	Date	Location
28 40 001 **Picathartes gymnocephalus** *Yellow-headed Rockfowl*		Forests of Guinea to Ghana, Togo (endangered)
28 40 002 **Picathartes oreas** *Red-headed Rockfowl*		Forests of Cameroon and Gabon (endangered)

FAMILY: SYLVIIDAE (Old World Warblers)

	Date	Location
28 41 001 **Microbates collaris** *Collared Gnatwren*		Southeast Colombia to Surinam, Brazil north of the Amazon
28 41 002 **Microbates cinereiventris** *Half-collared Gnatwren*		Tropical southern Nicaragua to Peru (Puno)
28 41 003 **Ramphocaenus melanurus (rufiventris)** *Long-billed Gnatwren*		Humid southeast Mexico to Amazon basin
28 41 004 **Polioptila caerulea** *Blue-gray Gnatcatcher*		United States to Guatemala, Bahamas, Cuba; winters to Honduras
28 41 005 **Polioptila melanura** *Black-tailed Gnatcatcher*		Arid southwest United States to central Mexico
28 41 006 **Polioptila nigriceps** *Black-capped Gnatcatcher*		Arid western Mexico (Sorora to Colima)
28 41 007 **Polioptila lembeyei** *Cuban Gnatcatcher*		Semiarid scrub of southern Cuba
28 41 008 **Polioptila albiloris** *White-lored Gnatcatcher*		Arid southern Mexico to northwest Costa Rica
28 41 009 **Polioptila plumbea** *Tropical Gnatcatcher*		Yucatan Peninsula to Peru, eastern Brazil
28 41 010 **Polioptila lactea** *Cream-bellied Gnatcatcher*		Southeast Brazil (Espirito Santo) to northwest Argentina
29 41 011 **Polioptila guianensis** *Guianan Gnatcatcher*		Southern Venezuela to Surinam, adjacent Brazil
28 41 012 **Polioptila schistaceigula** *Slate-throated Gnatcatcher*		Tropical forests of eastern Panama to northwest Ecuador

	Date	Location
28 41 013 **Polioptila dumicola** *Masked Gnatcatcher*		Tableland of Brazil to Bolivia, central Argentina
28 41 014 **Tesia castaneocoronata** *Chestnut-headed Tesia*		Himalayas of Nepal to Yunnan, Burma, Thailand; Tonkin
28 41 015 **Tesia cyaniventer** *Gray-bellied Tesia*		Himalayas of Nepal to Yunnan, Indochina; Java; Sumatra
28 41 016 **Tesia olivea** *Slaty-bellied Tesia*		Sikkim to southwest China, Thailand, Laos, Tonkin
28 41 017 **Tesia superciliaris** *Javan Ground-Warbler*		Confined to montane forests on the Island of Java
28 41 018 **Tesia everetti** *Everett's Tesia*		Restricted to the Island of Hainan
28 41 019 **Psamathia annae** *Palau Warbler*		Secondary scrub and grasslands of Palau Island (Micronesia)
28 41 020 **Cettia subulata** *Timor Bush-Warbler*		Confined to Island of Timor (Lesser Sundas)
28 41 021 **Cettia whiteheadi** *Short-tailed Bush-Warbler*		Mountains of Borneo (Kinabalu to Mt. Liang Kubung)
28 41 022 **Cettia squameiceps** *Stub-tailed Bush-Warbler*		Northeast Asia to southeast Asia; Hainan; Taiwan
28 41 023 **Cettia pallidipes** *Pale-footed Bush-Warbler*		Himalayas of Nepal to Szechwan, Indochina; Andamans
28 41 024 **Cettia diphone** **(canturians)** *Manchurian Bush-Warbler*		Northeast Asia to southern China, Tonkin, Thailand; Philippines
28 41 025 **Cettia fortipes** **(montanus)** *Brownish-flanked Bush-* *Warbler*		Himalayas to southern China, Indochina; Greater Sundas; Taiwan
28 41 026 **Cettia major** *Large Bush-Warbler*		Himalayas of Garhwal to Szechwan, northwest Thailand
28 41 027 **Cettia flavolivaceus** *Aberrant Bush-Warbler*		Himalayas of Garhwal to Yunnan, Indochina
28 41 028 **Cettia acanthizoides** *Yellow-bellied Bush-* *Warbler*		Himalayas of Garhwal to Szechwan, Burma; Taiwan
28 41 029 **Cettia brunnifrons** *Gray-sided Bush-Warbler*		Himalayas of Kashmir to Yunnan, Burma

		Date	Location

28 41 030 **Cettia cetti**
Cetti's Warbler — Mediterranean basin environs

28 41 031 **Bradypterus baboecala**
Little Rush-Warbler — Ethiopia to South Africa

28 41 032 **Bradypterus graueri**
Grauer's Rush-Warbler — Papyrus swamps of Uganda and Zaire

28 41 033 **Bradypterus grandis**
Giant Swamp-Warbler — Known only from southern Cameroon and Gabon (rare)

28 41 034 **Bradypterus carpalis**
White-winged Warbler — Papyrus swamps of southwest Uganda

28 41 035 **Bradypterus cinnamomeus**
Cinnamon Bracken Warbler — Ethiopia to Tanzania, Malawi

28 41 036 **Bradypterus victorini**
Victorin's Bush-Warbler — Confined to mountains of Cape Province (South Africa)

28 41 037 **Bradypterus barratti**
Barratt's Scrub-Warbler — Dense ravines of Rhodesia, Mozambique, adjacent South Africa

28 41 038 **Bradypterus sylvaticus**
Knysna Scrub-Warbler — Coastal forest scrub of eastern Cape Province (South Africa)

28 41 039 **Bradypterus alfredi**
Bamboo Warbler — Highland bamboo forests of Zaire to Tanzania, Botswana

28 41 040 **Bradypterus thoracicus**
Spotted Bush-Warbler — Russia, Manchuria to Kashmir, China, Burma, Laos

28 41 041 **Bradypterus major**
Large-billed Bush-Warbler — Eastern Palearctic region, Oriental mainland

28 41 042 **Bradypterus tacsanowskius**
Chinese Bush-Warbler — Bhutan to central China, Burma, Thailand, Indochina

28 41 043 **Bradypterus luteoventris**
Brown Bush-Warbler — Himalayas of Nepal to Yunnan, Burma, Indochina; Taiwan

28 41 044 **Bradypterus seebohmi (montis)**
Russet Bush-Warbler — Southeast China to Annam; Philippines; Java; Timor; Taiwan

28 41 045 **Bradypterus caudatus**
Long-tailed Ground-Warbler — Philippines (Luzon and Mindanao Islands)

	Date	Location

28 41 046 Bradypterus accentor
Kinabalu Friendly Warbler — Known only from Mt. Kinabalu (north Borneo)

28 41 047 Bradypterus castaneus
Chestnut Grass-Warbler — Confined to the Moluccas Islands

28 41 048 Bradypterus palliseri
Palliser's Warbler — Dwarf bamboo montane forests of Sri Lanka

28 41 049 Locustella fasciolata
Gray's Grasshopper-Warbler — Siberia to the Philippines; Celebes; New Guinea

28 41 050 Locustella amnicola
Sakhalin Warbler — Sakhalin, Tonino-Anivsky Peninsula, Kurile Islands and Hokkaido

28 41 051 Locustella luscinioides
Savi's Warbler — Widespread Palearctic region

28 41 052 Locustella fluviatilis
River Warbler — Widespread Palearctic region

28 41 053 Locustella certhiola
Pallas' Warbler — Widespread Palearctic region, Oriental mainland and islands

28 41 054 Locustella ochotensis
Middendorf's Warbler — Sea of Okhutsk to Japan; Borneo; Philippines; Celebes

28 41 055 Locustella pleskei
Taczanowski's Warbler — Korea and Seven Islands of Izu; winters to southern China

28 41 056 Locustella naevia
Pale Grasshopper-Warbler — Widespread Palearctic region; winters to India

28 41 057 Locustella lanceolata
Lanceolated Warbler — Ural Mountains to Japan, China, Malaya, Indochina; Borneo

28 41 058 Lusciniola melanopogon
Eurasian Moustached Warbler — Mediterranean basin environs

28 41 059 Acrocephalus paludicola
Aquatic Warbler — Spottily distributed open marshes of Europe

28 41 060 Acrocephalus schoenobaenus
European Sedge Warbler — Widespread Palearctic region

28 41 061 Acrocephalus agricola
Paddyfield Warbler — Iran, India to China, Burma, Thailand

28 41 062 Acrocephalus concinens
Blunt-winged Warbler — Central Asia to southwest China, Indochina

28 41 063 Acrocephalus bistrigiceps
Black-browed Reed-Warbler — Siberia to India, Malaya, Indochina

		Date	Location
28 41 064	**Acrocephalus sorghophilus** *Speckled Reed-Warbler*		China and Manchuria to the Philippines
28 41 065	**Acrocephalus orinus** *Large-billed Reed-Warbler*		India (known from a single specimen from Sutlej Valley)
28 41 066	**Acrocephalus dumetorum** *Blyth's Reed-Warbler*		Russia, Siberia to Burma, India, northeast Africa
28 41 067	**Acrocephalus baeticatus** *African Reed-Warbler*		Sudan, Ethiopia to South Africa
28 41 068	**Acrocephalus scirpaceus** *European Reed-Warbler*		Widespread western Palearctic region
28 41 069	**Acrocephalus palustris** *European Marsh-Warbler*		Widespread western Palearctic region
28 41 070	**Acrocephalus stentoreus** *Clamorous Reed-Warbler*		Southern Palearctic, Oriental region to Australia
28 41 071	**Acrocephalus arundinaceus** *Great Reed-Warbler*		Widespread western Palearctic region
28 41 072	**Acrocephalus orientalis** *Oriental Reed-Warbler*		Widespread eastern Palearctic region, Oriental mainland
28 41 073	**Acrocephalus luscinia** *Nightingale Reed-Warbler*		Marianas Islands (endangered in southern part of range)
28 41 074	**Acrocephalus aedon** *Thick-billed Warbler*		Northern Asia to southeast Asia; Andamans; Nicobars
28 41 075	**Acrocephalus rehsei** *Finsch Reed-Warbler*		Confined to Nawodo Island (Marianas)
28 41 076	**Acrocephalus familiaris** *Laysan Millerbird*		Extinct since 1923. Inhabited Laysan and Nihoa Islands
28 41 077	**Acrocephalus kingi** *Nihoa Millerbird*		Hawaii (Nihoa Island—seriously endangered)
28 41 078	**Acrocephalus aequinoctialis** *Equinoctial Warbler*		Confined to the Polynesian Archipelago
28 41 079	**Acrocephalus caffra** *Tahitian Warbler*		Confined to islands ot Tahiti and Moorea
28 41 080	**Acrocephalus atypha** *Tuamotu Reed-Warbler*		Confined to the Tuamotu Archipelago (French Polynesia)

		Date	Location
28 41 081	**Acrocephalus mendenae** *Marquesas Reed-Warbler*		Distributed throughout islands in the Marquesas Archipelago
28 41 082	**Acrocephalus vaughanii** *Pitcairn Warbler*		Confined to Pitcairn Island (French Polynesia)
28 41 083	**Acrocephalus gracilirostris** *Lesser Swamp-Warbler*		Zaire, Uganda to Tanzania, Rhodesia
28 41 084	**Acrocephalus rufescens** *Greater Swamp-Warbler*		Comeroon to Kenya, Tanzania, Rhodesia
28 41 085	**Acrocephalus brevipennis** *Cape Verde Warbler*		Confined to the Cape Verde Islands
28 41 086	**Acrocephalus newtoni** *Madagascar Swamp-Warbler*		Plateau regions of Madagascar
28 41 087	**Bebrornis rodericanus** *Rodriguez Warbler*		Seychelles (confined to Rodriguez Island — endangered)
28 41 088	**Bebrornis sechellensis** *Seychelles Warbler*		Seychelles (50 birds on Cousin Island 1972— endangered)
28 41 089	**Nesillas typica** *Madagascar Brush-Warbler*		Widespread Madagascar
28 41 090	**Nesillas mariae** *Comoro Brush-Warbler*		Confined to the Comoro Islands (Indian ocean)
28 41 091	**Nesillas aldabranus** *Aldabra Brush-Warbler*		Comoros (confined to Middle Island—rare)
28 41 092	**Thamnornis chloropetoides** *Kiritika (Thamnornis)*		Semiarid regions of southern Madagascar
28 41 093	**Chloropeta natalensis (batesi)** *Natal Yellow Warbler*		Ethiopia to South Africa
28 41 094	**Chloropeta similis** *Mountain Yellow Warbler*		Highlands of eastern Zaire to Kenya, Tanzania, Malawi
28 41 095	**Chloropeta gracilirostris** *Yellow Swamp-Warbler*		Papyrus swamps of Uganda, Botswanna
28 41 096	**Hippolais icterina** *Icterine Warbler*		Western Palearctic region to central Africa
28 41 097	**Hippolais polyglotta** *Melodious Warbler*		Mediterranean basin environs

		Date	Location
28 41 098	**Hippolais olivetorum** *Olive Tree Warbler*		Balkan Peninsula, Asia Minor to southern Africa
28 41 099	**Hippolais languida** *Upcher's Warbler*		Palestine to Iran, Transcaspia, Afghanistan; winters to Africa
28 41 100	**Hippolais pallida** *Olivaceous Warbler*		Widespread western Palearctic region; winters to Africa
28 41 101	**Hippolais caligata** *Booted Warbler*		Russia, western Siberia to India
28 41 102	**Sylvia nisoria** *Barred Warbler*		Western Palearctic; winters to East Africa
28 41 103	**Sylvia hortensis** *Orphean Warbler*		Mediterranean basin environs
28 41 104	**Sylvia leucomelaena** *Red Sea Warbler*		Red Sea coastal area environs
28 41 105	**Sylvia borin** *Garden Warbler*		Widespread Paleartic region
28 41 106	**Sylvia atricapilla** *Black-cap Warbler*		Widespread Palearctic region
28 41 107	**Sylvia communis** *Greater Whitethroat*		Western Palearctic region to central Africa
28 41 108	**Sylvia curruca** *Lesser Whitethroat*		Western Palearctic region, Indian Subcontinent
28 41 109	**Sylvia minula** *Desert Lesser Whitethroat*		Iran, Transcaspia to deserts of central Asia
28 41 110	**Sylvia althaea** *Hume's Lesser Whitethroat*		Mountains of Iran, Afghanistan to the Himalayas
28 41 111	**Sylvia nana** *Desert Warbler*		Deserts of North Africa to Mongolia
28 41 112	**Sylvia rüppelli** *Rüppell's Warbler*		East Africa to Asia Minor
28 41 113	**Sylvia melanocephala** *Sardinian Warbler*		Mediterranean basin environs
28 41 114	**Sylvia melanothorax** *Cyprus Warbler*		Confined to the Island of Cyprus
28 41 115	**Sylvia mystacea** *Ménétries' Warbler*		Near East to Asia Minor
28 41 116	**Sylvia cantillans** *Subalpine Warbler*		Mediterranean basin environs
28 41 117	**Sylvia conspicillata** *Spectacled Warbler*		Mediterranean basin environs; Canary Islands

		Date	Location
28 41 118	**Sylvia deserticola** *Tristram's Warbler*		Mountains of Morocco, Algeria, Tunisia
28 41 119	**Sylvia ticehursti** *Moroccan Warbler*		Morocco (known from a single specimen collected in 1939)
28 41 120	**Sylvia undata** *Dartford Warbler*		Southern England to Mediterranean basin
28 41 121	**Sylvia sarda** *Marmora's Warbler*		Western Mediterranean Islands and coastal Tunisia
28 41 122	**Phylloscopus trochilus** *European Willow Warbler*		Widespread Palearctic region
28 41 123	**Phylloscopus collybita** *Chiffchaff*		Widespread Palearctic region
28 41 124	**Phylloscopus neglectus** *Plain Willow Warbler*		Iran, Transcaspia to India
28 41 125	**Phylloscopus bonelli** *Bonelli's Warbler*		Southwestern Palearctic region; winters to the Sudan
28 41 126	**Phylloscopus tytleri** *Tytler's Warbler*		Pine forests of Himalayas of Kashmir to Nepal
28 41 127	**Phylloscopus sibilatrix** *Wood Warbler*		Widespread Palearctic region
28 41 128	**Phylloscopus affinis** *Tickell's Leaf Warbler*		Himalayas of Kashmir to Tibet, Yunnan, Burma
28 41 129	**Phylloscopus subaffinis** *Buff-throated Warbler*		Nepal to China, Burma, Thailand, Annam, Laos, Tonkin
28 41 130	**Phylloscopus griseolus** *Olivaceous Willow Warbler*		Outer Mongolia to Nepal, Pakistan, Baluchistan
28 41 131	**Phylloscopus fuligiventer** *Smoky Leaf Warbler*		Grassy lowlands of Nepal, Sikkim, Bhutan, Assam
28 41 132	**Phylloscopus fuscatus** *Dusky Warbler*		Siberia to India, Indochina; Hainan; Taiwan; Andamans
28 41 133	**Phylloscopus armandii** *Yellow-streaked Warbler*		Northern China to Burma, Thailand, Laos
28 41 134	**Phylloscopus schwarzi** *Radde's Warbler*		Northeast Asia to southern China, Indochina
28 41 135	**Phylloscopus pulcher** *Orange-barred Warbler*		Himalayas of Kashmir to Szechwan, Burma, Indochina
28 41 136	**Phylloscopus inornatus** *Inornate Warbler*		Northern Asia to India, Indochina; Taiwan; Hainan

		Date	Location
28 41 137	**Phylloscopus subviridis**		
	Brooks' Willow Warbler		Afghanistan to Himalayas of Garhwal, India
28 41 138	**Phylloscopus proregulus**		
	Pallas' Warbler		Northern Asia to India, Indochina; Hainan
28 41 139	**Phylloscopus maculipennis**		
	Gray-faced Warbler		Himalayas of Kashmir to Yunnan, Indochina
28 41 140	**Phylloscopus borealis**		
	Arctic Warbler		Palearctic region; Oriental mainland and islands; Alaska
28 41 141	**Phylloscopus magnirostris**		
	Large-billed Leaf Warbler		Sri Lanka; India to Szechwan, Burma; Andamans
28 41 142	**Phylloscopus trochiloides**		
	Greenish Warbler		Europe to Manchuria, Indochina; Hainan; Andamans
28 41 143	**Phylloscopus nitidus**		
	Green Warbler		Caucasus Mountains to Afghanistan; winters to India
28 41 144	**Phylloscopus tenellipes**		
	Pale-legged Leaf Warbler		Northeast Asia to Malaya, Indochina; Hainan; Nicobars
28 41 145	**Phylloscopus occipitalis**		
	Crowned Willow Warbler		Himalayas of Kashmir to Manchuria, Japan
28 41 146	**Phylloscopus coronatus**		
	Eastern Crowned Warbler		Northeast Asia to Southeast Asia; Taiwan; Java; Sumatra
28 41 147	**Phylloscopus ijimae**		
	Ijima's Warbler		Japan (Seven Islands of Izu)
28 41 148	**Phylloscopus reguloides**		
	Blyth's Leaf Warbler		Himalayas of Kashmir to Yunnan, Burma, Indochina
28 41 149	**Phylloscopus davisoni**		
	White-tailed Leaf Warbler		Southern China to Burma, Tenasserim, Indochina
28 41 150	**Phylloscopus cantator**		
	Black-browed Warbler		Himalayas of Nepal to Burma, Thailand, Laos; Hainan
28 41 151	**Phylloscopus ricketti**		
	Sulphur-breasted Warbler		Southern China to Indochina; Hainan
28 41 152	**Phylloscopus trivirgatus**		
	Mountain Leaf Warbler		Malay Peninsula; Philippines to New Guinea, Solomons
28 41 153	**Phylloscopus amoenus**		
	Kulambangra Warbler		Mountain forests of Solomon Islands
28 41 154	**Phylloscopus olivaceus**		
	Philippine Leaf Warbler		Philippine Islands and the Sulu Archipelago

		Date	Location
28 41 155	**Phylloscopus cebuensis** *DuBois' Leaf Warbler*		Philippine Islands (Cebu, Negros, Luzon Islands)
28 41 156	**Phylloscopus ruficapillus** *Yellow-throated Warbler*		Evergreen forests of Tanzania to South Africa
28 41 157	**Phylloscopus laurae** *Mrs. Boulton's Warbler*		Upland forests of Angola, Botswanna and Zambia
28 41 158	**Phylloscopus laetus** *Red-faced Woodland Warbler*		Bamboo zone of western Uganda (Ruwenzoris to the Virungas)
28 41 159	**Phylloscopus budongoensis** *Uganda Woodland Warbler*		Heavy forests of eastern Zaire to Kenya
28 41 160	**Phylloscopus herberti** *Herbert's Warbler*		Mountain forests of Cameroon, Fernando Po
28 41 161	**Phylloscopus umbrovirens** *Brown Woodland Warbler*		Highlands of Ethiopia, Eritrea to Tanzania; Arabia
28 41 162	**Seicercus burkii** *Golden-spectacled Warbler*		Himalayas of Pakistan to Yunnan, Burma, Indochina
28 41 163	**Seicercus poliogenys** *Gray-cheeked Warbler*		Himalayas of Nepal, Sikkim to Yunnan, Burma, Indochina
28 41 164	**Seicercus affinis** *Allied Warbler*		Nepal to southern China, Burma, Annam, Laos
28 41 165	**Seicercus montis** *Yellow-breasted Warbler*		Malay peninsula; Sumatra; Borneo; Timor; Palawan
28 41 166	**Seicercus castaneiceps** *Chestnut-headed Warbler*		Nepal to China, Malaya, Indochina; Sumatra
28 41 167	**Seicercus xanthoschistos** *Gray-hooded Warbler*		Himalayas of Kashmir to southwest China, Burma
28 41 168	**Seicercus grammiceps** *Sunda Warbler*		Greater and Lesser Sunda Islands
28 41 169	**Abroscopus hodgsoni** *Broad-billed Warbler*		Nepal to southwest China, Burma, Laos, Tonkin
28 41 170	**Abroscopus albogularis** *White-throated Warbler*		Nepal to southern China, Indochina; Hainan; Taiwan
28 41 171	**Abroscopus superciliaris** *Yellow-bellied Warbler*		Himalayas of Nepal to Yunnan, Indochina; Greater Sundas
28 41 172	**Abroscopus schisticeps** *Black-faced Warbler*		Nepal to Szechwan, Indochina; Hainan; Taiwan

	Date	Location

28 41 173 Regulus calendula
Ruby-crowned Kinglet
North America and Mexico; Guadalupe Island; winters to Guatemala

28 41 174 Regulus regulus
Goldcrest
Widespread Palearctic region (except Africa)

28 41 175 Regulus ignicapillus
Firecrest
Widespread Palearctic region

28 41 176 Regulus goodfellowi
Taiwan Firecrest
Confined to the Island of Taiwan

28 41 177 Regulus satrapa
Golden-crowned Kinglet
Alaska through mountains of Mexico to Guatemala

28 41 178 Leptopoecile sophiae
Severtzov's Tit-Warbler
High semi-deserts of Turkestan to Sikkim

28 41 179 Leptopoecile elegans
Crested Tit-Warbler
Mountains of Kansu, Tsinghai, Tibet, Sikiang

28 41 180 Scotocerca inquieta
Streaked Scrub Warbler
Palearctic deserts of Morocco to India

28 41 181 Rhopophilus pekinensis
White-browed Chinese Warbler
Lowland forests of China, Tibet, Turkestan; rare Korea

28 41 182 Cisticola textrix
Cloud Cisticola
Grassy heaths of Angola to Zambia and South Africa

28 41 183 Cisticola brunnescens
Pectoral-patch Cisticola
Widespread grassy swamps of Ethiopia to South Africa

28 41 184 Cisticola ayresii
Wing-snapping Cisticola
Open grassy plains of Angola to Kenya and South Africa

28 41 185 Cisticola eximia
Black-backed Cisticola
Open grassy plains of Nigeria to Ethiopia, Eritrea

28 41 186 Cisticola dambo
Cloud-scraper Cisticola
Dry short grass of eastern Angola to Zaire, Zambia

28 41 187 Cisticola exilis
Golden-headed Cisticola
Widespread Oriental mainland and islands to Australia

28 41 188 Cisticola juncidis
Zitting (Fan-tailed) Cisticola
Widespread Palearctic, Oriental regions to Australia

28 41 189 Cisticola haesitata
Socotra Cisticola
Confined to Socotra Island (Indian Ocean off East Africa)

Date   Location

28 41 190	**Cisticola cherina** *Madagascar Cisticola*	Grassy plains of Madagascar and Seychelles Islands
28 41 191	**Cisticola aridula** *Desert Cisticola*	Dry short grass country of Senegal to the Sudan, Ethiopia
28 41 192	**Cisticola natalensis** *Croaking Cisticola*	Widespread grasslands of Africa south of the Sahara
28 41 193	**Cisticola robusta** *Stout Cisticola*	Rank grass of Ethiopia to Angola, Zambia
28 41 194	**Cisticola aberdare** *Aberdare Cisticola*	Known only from the Aberdare Mountains of Kenya
28 41 195	**Cisticola subruficapilla** *Gray-backed Cisticola*	Dry heath of extreme southern tip of Africa
28 41 196	**Cisticola lais** *Wailing Cisticola*	Dry uplands of Kenya to Angola and South Africa
28 41 197	**Cisticola rufilata** *Grey Cisticola*	Dry scrub of Angola to Botswanna and South Africa
28 41 198	**Cisticola cinereola** *Ashy Cisticola*	Acacia woodlands of Ethiopia, Somalia to Kenya
28 41 199	**Cisticola restricta** *Tana River Cisticola*	Tana River environs of Tanzania (known from 6 specimens)
28 41 200	**Cisticola chiniana** *Rattling Cisticola*	Widespread thorn bush of Africa south of the Sahara
28 41 201	**Cisticola bodessa** *Bodessa Cisticola*	Highlands of Ethiopia
28 41 202	**Cisticola njombe** *Churring Cisticola*	High plateau of Tanzania and Malawi
28 41 203	**Cisticola ruficeps** *Red-pate Cisticola*	Thornbush of Senegal to Ethiopia, Eritrea
28 41 204	**Cisticola nana** *Tiny Cisticola*	Acacia woodlands of Ethiopia to Tanzania
28 41 205	**Cisticola brachyptera** *Short-winged Cisticola*	Widespread and common Africa south of the Sahara
28 41 206	**Cisticola rufa** *Rufous Cisticola*	Savanna and semiarid thorn bush of Gambia to Cameroon
28 41 207	**Cisticola troglodytes** *Foxy Cisticola*	Nigeria and eastern Cameroon to the Nile Valley
28 41 208	**Cisticola fulvicapilla** *Piping Cisticola*	Light bushveldt of Angola, Tanzania to South Africa
28 41 209	**Cisticola angusticauda** *Tabora Cisticola*	Light woodlands of Kenya, Zaire to Zambia

		Date	Location

28 41 210 **Cisticola aberrans**
Lazy Cisticola
Thick scrub and grass of Rhodesia to South Africa

28 41 211 **Cisticola lateralis**
Whistling Cisticola
Savanna woodlands of Gambia to Angola, Uganda

28 41 212 **Cisticola woosnami**
Trilling Cisticola
Brachystegia woodlands of Zaire to Tanzania, Malawi, Zambia

28 41 213 **Cisticola anonyma**
Chattering cisticola
Grassy plains of Ghana to Angola

28 41 214 **Cisticola bulliens**
Bubbling Cisticola
Lower Congo River and southwestern Zaire to Angola

28 41 215 **Cisticola erythrops**
Red-faced Cisticola
Moist grasslands of Africa south of the Sahara

28 41 216 **Cisticola cantans**
Singing Cisticola
Ethiopia, the Sudan to Rhodesia, Malawi, Zambia

28 41 217 **Cisticola hunteri**
Hunter's Cisticola
High mountains of Kenya and Tanzania

28 41 218 **Cisticola chubbi**
Chubb's Cisticola
Wooded mountains of northeast Zaire, Kenya, Tanzania

28 41 219 **Cisticola galactotes**
Winding Cisticola
Widespread marshes of Africa south of the Sahara

28 41 220 **Cisticola carruthersi**
Carruther's Cisticola
Papyrus swamps of northern Zaire to Kenya

28 41 221 **Cisticola pipiens**
Chirping Cisticola
Papyrus swamps of eastern Angola, southern Zaire, Zambia

28 41 222 **Cisticola tinniens**
Tinkling Cisticola
Marshes of Zaire to Angola, South Africa

28 41 223 **Prinia subflava**
Tawny-flanked Prinia
Widespread grasslands of Africa south of Sahara

28 41 224 **Prinia flavicans**
Black-chested Prinia
Open thornbush of Angola to Zambia and South Africa

28 41 225 **Prinia maculosa**
Karoo Prinia
Karoo veld of southern Africa

28 41 226 **Prinia somalica**
Pale Prinia
Acacia zone of Ethiopia, Somalia to northern Kenya

28 41 227 **Prinia inornata**
Tawny-flanked Prinia
Pakistan to southern China, Indochina; Hainan; Taiwan; Java

28 41 228 **Prinia leucopogon**
White-chinned Prinia
Southern Nigeria, Cameroon to Zaire, Angola, Zambia

	Date	Location
28 41 229 **Prinia leontica** *Sierra Leone Prinia*		Dense ravines of Guinea and Sierra Leone
28 41 230 **Prinia robertsi** *Roberts' Prinia*		Highland forests of eastern Rhodesia
28 41 231 **Prinia substriata** *Namaqua Prinia*		Streamside scrub of Cape Province of South Africa (rare)
28 41 232 **Prinia molleri** *São Thomé Prinia*		Confined to São Thomé Island (Gulf of Guinea)
28 41 233 **Prinia bairdii** *Banded Prinia*		Cameroon to northern Angola, Zaire, Kenya
28 41 234 **Prinia pectoralis** *Rufous-eared Prinia*		Arid lowland scrub of Namibia to Cape Province
28 41 235 **Prinia gracilis** *Graceful Prinia*		Egypt and Somalia eastward through the Indian Subcontinent
28 41 236 **Prinia socialis** *Ashy Prinia*		Common throughout *sarpat* grass region of peninsular India
28 41 237 **Prinia rufescens** *Rufescent Prinia*		Nepal to Yunnan, Malaya, Indochina
28 41 238 **Prinia hodgsoni** *Gray-breasted Prinia*		India to southwest China, Malaya, peninsular Thailand
28 41 239 **Prinia flaviventris** *Yellow-Bellied Prinia*		Widespread Oriental mainland and islands
28 41 240 **Prinia familiaris** *Bar-winged Prinia*		Java, Sumatra and Bali
28 41 241 **Prinia polychroa** *Brown Prinia*		Southwest China to Indochina; Java
28 41 242 **Prinia criniger** *Striated Prinia*		Himalayas of Pakistan to Yunnan, Burma; Taiwan
28 41 243 **Prinia sylvatica** *Jungle Prinia*		Sri Lanka; India to Assam
28 41 244 **Prinia atrogularis** *Hill Prinia*		Himalayas of Nepal to Yunnan, Malaya, Indochina; Sumatra
28 41 245 **Prinia burnesii** *Western Long-tailed Prinia*		Elephant grass plains of Pakistan (Indus River basin)
28 41 246 **Prinia cinerascens** *Eastern Long-tailed Prinia*		Elephant grass plains of Bangladesh River basins
28 41 247 **Prinia buchanani** *Rufous-fronted Prinia*		Widespread thornscrub of Indian Subcontinent

		Date	Location

28 41 248 **Prinia cinereocapilla**
Hodgson's Prinia — Himalayan foothills of northern India and Nepal

28 41 249 **Apalis flavida**
Yellow-breasted Apalis — Widespread Africa south of the Sahara

28 41 250 **Apalis binotata**
Masked Apalis — Highland forests of Cameroon and Zaire

28 41 251 **Apalis ruddi**
Rudd's Apalis — Coastal evergreen woodlands of Mozambique

28 41 252 **Apalis jacksoni**
Black-throated Apalis — Tropical southeast Sudan, Uganda to Kenya, Angola

28 41 253 **Apalis chariessa**
White-winged Apalis — Mountain plateaus of eastern Kenya to Malawi

28 41 254 **Apalis nigriceps**
Black-capped Apalis — Forests of Sierra Leone to northeast Zaire, Uganda

28 41 255 **Apalis thoracica (murina)**
Bar-throated Apalis — Forests and woodlands of Tanzania to South Africa

28 41 256 **Apalis cinerea**
Gray Apalis — Forests of Angola to Kenya, Tanzania, Zaire

28 41 257 **Apalis alticola**
Brown-headed Apalis — Forests of southeast Zaire to Tanzania and Zambia

28 41 258 **Apalis karamojae**
Karamoja Apalis — Uganda (known from one specimen from Mt. Kamalinga)

28 41 259 **Apalis rufogularis**
Buff-throated Apalis — Nigeria to northern Angola, Kenya, Zambia

28 41 260 **Apalis argentea**
Kungwe Apalis — Kungwe-Mahare and Ubende areas of western Tanzania

28 41 261 **Apalis porphyrolaema**
Chestnut-throated Apalis — High altitude bamboo zone of Ruwenzori and Rwanda Mountains

28 41 262 **Apalis sharpii (bamendae)**
Bamenda Apalis — Highlands of Sierra Leone to Cameroon

28 41 263 **Apalis melanocephala**
Black-headed Apalis — Forests of Kenya, Tanzania to Malawi, Mozambique

28 41 264 **Apalis chirindensis**
Chirinda Apalis — Highlands of Mozambique and eastern Rhodesia

28 41 265 **Apalis pulchra**
Black-collared Apalis — Cameroon highlands to the Sudan and Kenya

28 41 266 **Apalis ruwenzori**
Collared Apalis — Eastern Zaire to the Ruwenzori Mountains

		Date	Location

28 41 267	**Apalis moreaui** *Long-billed Apalis*	Tanzania (Amani forests of Usambara Mountains)
28 41 268	**Apalis melanura** *Angola Slender-tailed Apalis*	Angola and southern Zaire to Zambia
28 41 269	**Graminicola bengalensis** *Large Grass-Warbler*	Nepal to southern China, Thailand, Tenasserim; Hainan
28 41 270	**Melocichla mentalis** *African Moustached Warbler*	Angola to the Sudan, Kenya, Malawi, Zambia
28 41 271	**Sphenoeacus afer** *Cape Grass Bird*	Moist grasslands of southern Rhodesia to Cape Province
28 41 272	**Achaetops pycnopygius** *Damara Rock-jumper*	Mountains of southern Angola and northern Namibia
28 41 273	**Dromaeocercus brunneus** *Brown Emu-tail*	Highland forests of eastern Madagascar
28 41 274	**Dromaeocercus seebohmi** *Gray Emu-tail*	High plateaus of eastern Madagascar (rare)
28 41 275	**Incana incana** *Socotra Warbler*	Confined to Socotra Island (Indian Ocean off east Africa)
28 41 276	**Spiloptila clamans** *Cricket Warbler*	Desert edges of Mali to Eritrea
28 41 277	**Spiloptila rufifrons** *Red-faced Apalis*	Scrub of the Sudan, Ethiopia, Somalia to Tanzania
28 41 278	**Urolais epichlora** *Green Longtail*	Cameroon mountain, Banso, Manenguba highlands, Obudu Plateau
28 41 279	**Heliolais erythroptera** *Red-wing Warbler*	Grassy woodlands of Guinea to Kenya, Mozambique
28 41 280	**Poliolais lopezi** *Lopez's Warbler*	Mountain forests of Fernando Po, Cameroon, Manenguba, Kupe
28 41 281	**Phyllolais pulchella** *Buff-bellied Warbler*	Acacia thornbush of Senegal to Eritrea and the Sudan
28 47 282	**Drymocichla incana** *Red-winged Gray Warbler*	Woodlands of Cameroon to the Sudan and Uganda
28 47 283	**Orthotomus sutorius** (**longicaudus**) *Common Tailorbird*	Sri Lanka; India to China, Malaya, Indochina; Java

	Date	Location
28 47 284 Orthotomus atrogularis *Dark-necked Tailorbird*		Sikkim to southwest China, Indochina; Philippines; Sumatra; Borneo
28 41 285 Orthotomus derbianus *Luzon Tailorbird*		Philippines (endemic Luzon and Catanduanes Islands)
28 41 286 Orthotomus ruficeps (sepium) *Ashy Tailorbird*		Malay Peninsula; Java; Sumatra; Borneo; Palawan
28 41 287 Orthotomus sericeus *Red-headed Tailorbird*		Malay Peninsula; Java; Sumatra; Borneo; Philippines
28 41 288 Orthotomus cucullatus *Mountain Tailorbird*		Sikkim to southern China, Indochina; Greater Sundas; Philippines
28 41 289 Orthotomus cinereiceps *White-eared Tailorbird*		Philippines (endemic Basilan and Mindanao Islands)
28 41 290 Orthotomus samarensis *Samar Tailorbird*		Philippines (Bohol, Leyte and Samar Islands)
28 41 291 Orthotomus nigriceps *Black-headed Tailorbird*		Philippines (endemic to Mindanao Island)
28 41 292 Orthotomus metopias *Red-capped Tailorbird*		Dense forest undergrowth of Tanzania to Mozambique
28 41 293 Bathmocercus † **cerviniventris (rufus)** *Black-faced Rufous Warbler*		Marshes of Sierra Leone to Zaire, Sudan, Kenya
28 41 294 Bathmocercus winifredae *Mrs. Moreau's Warbler*		Evergreen forests of Ulugure Mountains of eastern Tanzania
28 41 295 Camaroptera brachyura *Green-backed Camaroptera*		Dense bush of Kenya to South Africa
28 41 296 Camaroptera † **brevicaudata (harterti)** *Gray-backed Camaroptera*		Widespread Africa south of the Sahara
28 41 297 Camaroptera fasciolata *Barred Camaroptera*		Scrub of Angola, Namibia, Zambia to South Africa
28 41 298 Camaroptera stierlingi *Stierling's Camaroptera*		Tanzania to Rhodesia, Mozambique, Zambia
28 41 299 Camaroptera simplex *Gray Camaroptera*		Lowlands of Ethiopia to Angola, Zambia

		Date	Location

28 41 300	**Camaroptera superciliaris** *Yellow-browed Camaroptera*	Forests of Sierra Leone to northern Angola, Uganda
28 41 301	**Camaroptera chloronota** *Olive-green Camaroptera*	Secondary forests of Senegal to Zaire, Kenya
28 41 302	**Euryptila subcinnamomea** *Cinnamon-breasted Gray Warbler*	Desert scrub of western Namibia to Cape Province
28 41 303	**Hypergerus atriceps** *Oriole Warbler (Moho)*	Senegal to Cameroon, Central African Republic
28 41 304	**Eminia lepida** *Gray-capped Warbler*	Uganda to central Kenya, northeast Tanzania
28 41 305	**Eremomela icteropygialis** *Yellow-bellied Eremomela*	Open bush of Africa south of the Sahara
28 41 306	**Eremomela salvadorii** *Salvadori's Eremomela*	Open bush of Angola to Zaire, Zambia,
28 41 307	**Eremomela flavicrissalis** *Yellow-vented Eremomela*	Arid thornbush of Ethiopia, Somalia and Kenya
28 41 308	**Eremomela scotops** *Greencap Eremomela*	Savanna of Kenya to Angola, Zambia, Malawi
28 41 309	**Eremomela canescens** *Green-backed Eremomela*	Acacia of Ethiopia to southern Chad and Cameroon
28 41 310	**Eremomela pusilla** *Smaller Green-backed Eremomela*	Widespread Senegal to Uganda and Kenya
28 41 311	**Eremomela gregalis** *Yellow-rumped Eremomela*	*Karoo* scrub of southern Namibia to Cape Province
28 41 312	**Eremomela badiceps** *Brown-crowned Eremomela*	Sierra Leone to Angola, the Sudan, Kenya
28 41 313	**Eremomela turneri** *Turner's Eremomela*	Cultivated areas of eastern Zaire to western Kenya
28 41 314	**Eremomela artricollis** *Black-necked Eremomela*	Open woodlands of southern Angola, Zaire, Zambia
28 41 315	**Eremomela usticollis** *Burnt-necked Eremomela*	Acacia thornveld of southern Africa
28 41 316	**Sylvietta ruficapilla** *Red-capped Crombec*	Zaire to Angola, Rhodesia, Zambia
28 41 317	**Sylvietta leucophrys (chapini)** *White-browed Crombec*	Mountain forests of eastern Zaire, Kenya, Uganda, Tanzania

		Date	Location
28 41 318	**Sylvietta virens** Green Crombec		Senegal to Angola and Uganda
28 41 319	**Sylvietta denti** Lemon-bellied Crombec		Secondary forests of Sierra Leone to Zaire
28 41 320	**Sylvietta whytii** Red-faced Crombec		Bush of Ethiopia to Mozambique, Malawi, Rhodesia
28 41 321	**Sylvietta brachyura** African Crombec		Dry bush of Africa south of the Sahara
28 41 322	**Sylvietta philippae** Short-billed Crombec		Acacia steppes of interior of Somalia
28 41 323	**Sylvietta rufescens** Long-billed Crombec		Woodlands of Zaire to South Africa
28 41 324	**Sylvietta isabellina** Somali Crombec		Dry acacia steppes of Ethiopia to Somalia, Kenya
29 41 325	**Hemitesia neumanni** Neumann's Bush-Warbler		Mountain forests of eastern Zaire to Lake Tanganyika
28 41 326	**Graueria vittata** Grauer's Warbler		Dense mountain forests of eastern Zaire border
28 41 327	**Parisoma subcaeruleum** Cape Tit-Warbler		Acacia of Angola, Zambia to South Africa
28 41 328	**Parisoma layardi** Layard's Tit-Warbler		Dry desert scrub of Namibia to South Africa
28 41 329	**Parisoma lugens** Brown Tit-Warbler		Woodlands of Ethiopia to Malawi, Zambia
28 41 330	**Parisoma boehmi** Banded Tit-Warbler		Acacia of Ethiopia to Somalia, Kenya, Tanzania
28 41 331	**Parisoma buryi** Arabian Tit-Warbler		Southwest Arabia (known from five specimens)
28 41 332	**Macrosphenus concolor** Gray Longbill		Dense forests of Sierra Leone to Zaire
28 41 333	**Macrosphenus pulitzeri** Pulitzer's Longbill		Angola (known from two specimens from Benguella)
28 41 334	**Macrosphenus kretschmeri** Kretschmer's Longbill		Coastal and inland scrub of Tanzania to Mozambique
28 41 335	**Macrosphenus flavicans** Yellow Longbill		Dense forests of Fernando Po, Cameroon to Angola, Uganda
28 41 336	**Macrosphenus kempi** Kemp's Longbill		Dense forests of Sierra Leone to Nigeria
28 41 337	**Randia pseudozosterops** Rand's Warbler		Highland forests of eastern Madagascar (rare)
28 41 338	**Amaurocichla bocagei** Bocage's Longbill		Confined to São Thomé Island (Gulf of Guinea)

		Date	Location
28 41 339	**Chaetornis striatus** *Bristled Grass-Warbler*		Coarse grasslands of Indian Subcontinent
28 41 340	**Schoenicola platyura** **(brevirostris)** *African Fan-tailed Warbler*		High grasslands of Africa south of the Sahara
28 41 341	**Megalurus pryeri** *Japanese Marsh Warbler*		China (Yangtze and Hopeh Valleys); Japan (Hondo)
28 41 342	**Megalurus timoriensis** *Tawny Marshbird*		Australia to New Guinea, Timor, the Philippines
28 41 343	**Megalurus albolimbatus** *Fly River Grass Warbler*		Fly River area of southern New Guinea
28 41 344	**Megalurus palustris** *Striated Marsh Warbler*		India to Malaya, Indochina; Java; Philippines
28 41 345	**Megalurus gramineus** *Little Grassbird*		*Typha* and *lignum* swamps of Australia and Tasmania
28 41 346	**Bowdleria punctata** *Fernbird*		Widespread swamp and fern lowlands of New Zealand
28 41 347	**Cinclorhamphus mathewsi** *Rufous Songlark*		Widespread savanna of Australia (except Tasmania)
28 41 348	**Cinclorhamphus cruralis** *Brown Songlark*		Australia (except Cape York Peninsula); Tasmania
28 41 349	**Eremiornis carteri** *Spinifex Bird*		*Spinifex* grass zone of northern Australia
28 41 350	**Megalurulus mariei** *New Caledonian Grass Warbler*		Grasslands and open heathlands of New Caledonia
28 41 351	**Cichlornis whitneyi** *Thicket Warbler*		New Hebrides (highland primeval forests of Espiritu Santo)
28 41 352	**Cichlornis grosvenori** *Whitman's Thicket Warbler*		Confined to New Britain Island
28 41 353	**Ortygocichla rubiginosa** *Rufous-faced Thicket Warbler*		Confined to New Britain Island
28 41 354	**Trichocichla rufa** *Long-legged Warbler*		Fiji Islands (Viti Levu only—possibly extinct)
28 41 355	**Buettikoferella bivittata** *Timor Thicket Warbler*		Timor Island (Lesser Sundas)
28 41 356	**Vitia parens** *Shade Warbler*		Solomons (mountain forests of San Cristobal Island)

	Date	Location

28 41 357 Vitia ruficapilla
Fiji Warbler — Fiji (mountains of Kandavu, Viti Levu, Vanua Levu, Taviuni)

28 41 358 Stenostira scita
Fairy Warbler — River banks of arid South Africa

28 41 359 Hyliota flavigaster
African Yellow-bellied Warbler — Widespread Africa south of the Sahara

28 41 360 Hyliota australis
Southern Yellow-bellied Warbler — Zaire to Tanzania, Zambia, Malawi, Mozambique

28 41 361 Hyliota violacea (nehrkorni)
Violet-backed Warbler — Liberia to Zaire

28 41 362 Hylia prasina
Green Hylia — Senegal to Zaire, Kenya, northern Angola

28 41 363 Clytomyias insignis
Rufous Wren-Warbler — High mountain forests of New Guinea

28 41 364 Chenorhamphus grayi
Broad-billed Wren-Warbler — Lowlands of northern New Guinea and adjacent islands (rare)

28 41 365 Todopsis wallacii
Wallace's Wren-Warbler — Lowlands of New Guinea, Misol, Japen, Aru Islands

28 41 366 Todopsis cyanocephala
Blue Wren-Warbler — Lowlands of New Guinea, Salawati, Biak, Aru Islands

28 41 367 Malurus cyaneus
Blue Wren — Queensland to Victoria; Tasmania

28 41 368 Malurus melanotus
Black-backed Wren — Queensland to Victoria, South Australia

28 41 369 Malurus callainus
Turquoise Wren — Western Australia to central Australia

28 41 370 Malurus splendens
Banded Blue Wren — Endemic to southwestern Australia

28 41 371 Malurus leucopterus (cyanotus)
White-winged Wren — Widespread arid interior of Australia

28 41 372 Malurus lamberti
Variegated Wren — Coastal Queensland to New South Wales

28 41 373 Malurus assimilis
Purple-backed Wren — Widespread Australia

28 41 374 Malurus leuconotus
White-backed Wren — Interior of South Australia (possible race *M. leucopterus*)

	Date	Location

28 41 375 **Malurus elegans**
           Red-winged Wren   Swampy undergrowth of coastal southwestern
                                      Australia

28 41 376 **Malurus amabilis**
           Lovely Wren   Tropical undergrowth of Cape York Peninsula

28 41 377 **Malurus dulcis**
           Lavender-flanked Wren   Arnhem Land and northern Western Australia

28 41 378 **Malurus pulcherrimus**
           Blue-breasted Wren   Confined to southwestern Australia

28 41 379 **Malurus melanocephalus**
           Red-backed Wren   Coastal northern and eastern Australia

28 41 380 **Malurus coronatus**
           Lilac-crowned Wren   Coastal northern Australia

28 41 381 **Malurus alboscapulatus**
           Black-and-white Wren-   Lowland and mid-mountain grasslands of New Guinea
           Warbler

28 41 382 **Amytornis textilis**
           Western Grasswren   Saltbush flats of southern Australia

28 41 383 **Amytornis prunelli**
           Dusky Grasswren   Porcupine grass zone of central Australia

28 41 384 **Amytornis modestus**
           Thick-billed Grasswren   New South Wales, southern and central Australia

28 41 385 **Amytornis goyderi**
           Eyrean Grasswren   Dense canegrass of lower Macumba River (South
                                      Australia—rare)

28 41 386 **Amytornis striatus**
           (whitei)
           Striped Grasswren   Eastern and central Australia

28 41 387 **Amytornis barbatus**
           Gray Grasswren   Dwarf lignum plains of New South Wales

28 41 388 **Amytornis dorotheae**
           Red-winged Grasswren   Lower McArthur River of Northern Territory of
                                      Australia (rare)

28 41 389 **Amytornis woodwardi**
           White-throated Grasswren Restricted to Northern Territory of Australia (rare)

28 41 390 **Amytornis housei**
           Black Grasswren   Kimberly Divide of Northwestern Australia (rare)

28 41 391 **Stipiturus malachurus**
           Southern Emu-Wren   Southwestern Australia; southeastern Australia;
                                      Tasmania

28 41 392 **Stipiturus mallee**
           Mallee Emu-Wren   Confined to *mallee* zone of Victoria and South
                                      Australia

		Date	Location

28 41 393   **Stipiturus ruficeps**
Rufous-crowned Emu-Wren   Arid western and central Australia

28 41 394   **Dasyornis brachypterus**
Eastern Bristlebird   Coastal southern Queensland to Victoria (rare)

28 41 395   **Dasyornis longirostris**
Western Bristlebird   Coastal corner of Southwest Australia (rare)

28 41 396   **Dasyornis broadbenti**
Rufous Bristlebird   Victoria, South and Western Australia

28 41 397   **Gerygone olivacea**
White-throated Gerygone   Southeast New Guinea and coastal northeast Australia

28 41 398   **Gerygone hypoxantha**
Salvadori's Gerygone   New Guinea (Biak Island—probable race *G. magnirostris*)

28 41 399   **Gerygone mouki (richmondi)**
Northern Gerygone   Mountains of eastern Australia

28 41 400   **Gerygone palpebrosa**
Black-throated Gerygone   New Guinea, Arus, Cape York peninsula

28 41 401   **Gerygone flavida**
Fairy Gerygone   Australia (rain forests and mangroves of coastal eastern Queensland)

28 41 402   **Gerygone magnirostris**
Large-billed Gerygone   Coastal northern Australia; New Guinea and adjacent islands

28 41 403   **Gerygone tenebrosa**
Dusky Gerygone   Coastal northwestern Australia

28 41 404   **Gerygone chloronota**
Green-backed Gerygone   Coastal northwest Australia to New Guinea, Waigeu Islands

28 41 405   **Gerygone levigaster**
Buff-breasted Gerygone   Widespread Australia

28 41 406   **Gerygone cantator**
Mangrove Gerygone   Coastal eastern Australia (possible race *G. levigaster*)

28 41 407   **Gerygone fusca**
White-tailed Gerygone   Coastal northern Australia

28 41 408   **Gerygone cinerea**
Gray Gerygone   Arfak, Snow Mountains to southeast New Guinea

28 41 409   **Gerygone chrysogaster**
Yellow-bellied Gerygone   New Guinea and adjacent islands

28 41 410   **Gerygone ruficollis**
Treefern Gerygone   High mountains of New Guinea

		Date	Location

28 41 411	**Gerygone flavolateralis** *Fantail Gerygone*		New Caledonia and New Hebrides Islands
28 41 412	**Gerygone igata** *New Zealand Gerygone*		Widespread forests of New Zealand
28 41 413	**Gerygone albofrontata** *Chatham Island Gerygone*		Confined to Chatham Island (off New Zealand)
28 41 414	**Gerygone inornata** *Timor Gerygone*		Confined to Timor Island (Lesser Sundas)
28 41 415	**Gerygone sulphurea** *Flyeater*		Widespread Malay Peninsula, Indochina to New Guinea
28 41 416	**Smicrornis brevirostris (flavescens)** *Weebill*		Widespread dry forests of Australia
28 41 417	**Aphelocephala leucopsis** *Southern Whiteface*		Arid scrub of southern Australia
28 41 418	**Aphelocephala pectoralis** *Chestnut-breasted Whiteface*		Arid deserts of South Australia
28 41 419	**Aphelocephala nigricincta** *Banded Whiteface*		Arid interior of central Australia
28 41 420	**Acanthiza nana** *Little Thornbill*		Dry forests and woodlands of eastern Australia
28 41 421	**Acanthiza lineata** *Striated Thornbill*		Dry forests and woodlands of southeast Australia
28 41 422	**Acanthiza pusilla** *Brown Thornbill*		Queensland to Victoria; Tasmania
28 41 423	**Acanthiza apicalis** *Broad-tailed Thornbill*		Low scrub of southern Australia
28 41 424	**Acanthiza katherina** *Mountain Thornbill*		Mountain forests of Queensland
28 41 425	**Acanthiza murina** *DeVis Tree Warbler*		High mountains of New Guinea
28 41 426	**Acanthiza ewingi** *Tasmanian Thornbill*		Tasmania, King and Flinders Islands
28 41 427	**Acanthiza robustirostris** *Slate-backed Thornbill*		*Mulga* zone of central Australia
28 41 428	**Acanthiza inornata** *Western Thornbill*		Dry forests of southwestern Australia
28 41 429	**Acanthiza iredalei** *Samphire Thornbill*		*Samphire* zone of southwestern Australia

		Date	Location

28 41 430 Acanthiza reguloides
Buff-tailed Thornbill
Open woodlands of Queensland to Victoria

28 41 431 Acanthiza chrysorrhoa
Yellow-tailed Thornbill
Savanna of Australia south of Tropic of Capricorn

28 41 432 Acanthiza uropygialis
Chestnut-tailed Thornbill
Dry savanna of southern half of Australia

28 41 433 Acanthornis magnus
Scrub-Tit
Dense forest undergrowth of Tasmania

28 41 434 Sericornis spilodera
Pale-billed Sericornis
Lowlands of New Guinea, Japen, Waigeu and Aru Islands

28 41 435 Sericornis beccarii
Beccari's Sericornis
Cape York Peninsula; lowlands of New Guinea

28 41 436 Sericornis virgatus
Perplexing Sericornis
Arfak, Japen Island, Sepik Mountains of New Guinea

28 41 437 Sericornis nouhuysi
Large Mountain Sericornis
Mountains of central and eastern New Guinea

28 41 438 Sericornis frontalis
White-browed Sericornis
Australia (coastal Queensland to Victoria)

28 41 439 Sericornis maculatus
Spotted Sericornis
Coastal southwestern Australia (possible race *S. frontalis*)

28 41 440 Sericornis humilis
Brown Sericornis
Tasmania, islands of Bass Strait (possible race *S. frontalis*)

28 41 441 Sericornis perspicillatus
Buff-faced Sericornis
Mountain forests of New Guinea

28 41 442 Sericornis magnirostris
Large-billed Sericornis
Australia (coastal Queensland to Victoria)

28 41 443 Sericornis rufescens
Rufous Sericornis
Arfak Mountains of New Guinea

28 41 444 Sericornis nigroviridis
Black-and-green Sericornis
New Guinea (known from one specimen from Watut River)

28 41 445 Sericornis papuensis
Papuan Sericornis
Mid-mountain forests of eastern New Guinea

28 41 446 Sericornis arfakianus
Gray-green Sericornis
Submontane forests of New Guinea

28 41 447 Sericornis lathami
Yellow-throated Sericornis
Australia (coastal Queensland to Victoria)

28 41 448 Sericornis keri
Atherton Sericornis
Mountain rain forests of northeast Queensland

28 41 449 Oreoscopus gutturalis
Fern Wren
Mountain rain forests of northeast Queensland

	Date	Location
28 41 450 **Crateroscelis murina** *Lowland Mouse-Babbler*		Lowland forests of New Guinea and adjacent islands
28 41 451 **Crateroscelis nigrorufa** *Mid-mountain Mouse-Babbler*		Mid-mountains of southeast New Guinea to Snow, Weyland Mountains
28 41 452 **Crateroscelis robusta** *Mountain Mouse-Babbler*		High mountain forests of New Guinea
28 41 453 **Calamanthus fuliginosus** *Field Wren*		Open country of southern Australia; Tasmania
28 41 454 **Calamanthus campestris** *Rufous Field Wren*		Open country of southern Australia (possible race *C. fuliginosus*)
28 41 455 **Hylacola pyrrhopygia** *Chestnut-tailed Heath-Wren*		New South Wales, Victoria, South Australia
28 41 456 **Hylacola cauta** *Shy Heath-Wren*		New South Wales, South and Western Australia
28 41 457 **Pyrrholaemus brunneus** *Redthroat*		Semiarid southern half of Australia
28 41 458 **Chthonicola sagittata** *Australian Speckled Warbler*		Australia (southern Queensland to Victoria)
28 41 459 **Origma solitaria** *Rock Warbler*		Australia (Hawkesbury sandstone area of New South Wales
28 41 460 **Pycnoptilus floccosus** *Pilotbird*		Australia (confined to eastern Victoria and New South Wales)
28 41 461 **Mohoua albicilla** *Whitehead*		New Zealand (North, Great, Little Barrier, Kaati Island)
28 41 462 **Mohoua ochrocephala** *Yellowhead*		New Zealand (forests of Stewart and South Island)
28 41 463 **Finschia novaeseelandiae** *New Zealand Brown Creeper*		New Zealand (forests of Stewart and South Island)
28 41 464 **Epthianura albifrons** *White-fronted Chat*		Savanna of southern Australia; Tasmania
28 41 465 **Epthianura tricolor** *Crimson Chat*		Widespread grassy plains, savanna throughout Australia
28 41 466 **Epthianura aurifrons** *Orange Chat*		Widespread *samphire*, saltbush areas throughout Australia

		Date	Location
28 41 467	**Epthianura crocea** *Yellow Chat*		Spottily distributed saltbush lagoons of northern Australia
28 41 468	**Ashbyia lovensis** *Desert (Gibber) Chat*		Arid stony plains of south-central Australia
28 41 469	**Lamprolia victoriae** *Silktail*		Fiji (mountain forests of Taviuni and Vanua Levu Islands)

FAMILY: MUSCICAPIDAE (Old World Flycatchers)

28 42 001	**Bradornis microrhynchus (pumilus)** *Large Gray Flycatcher*		Widespread Ethiopia to Tanzania, Malawi
28 42 002	**Bradornis mariquensis** *Mariqua Flycatcher*		Arid thornbush of Namibia to South Africa
28 42 003	**Bradornis pallidus** *Pale Flycatcher*		Widespread Africa south of the Sahara
28 42 004	**Bradornis infuscatus** *Chat Flycatcher*		Arid scrub of southern Angola to South Africa
28 42 005	**Empidornis semipartitus** *Silverbird*		Acacia woodland of Ethiopia to Kenya, Uganda
28 42 006	**Melaenornis chocolatina** *Slaty Flycatcher*		Highlands of Ethiopia to Angola, Tanzania
28 42 007	**Melaenornis ardesiaca** *Yellow-eyed Black Flycatcher*		Dense forests of eastern Zaire, adjacent Uganda
28 42 008	**Melaenornis annamarulae** *Liberian Flycatcher*		Liberia (primary forests of Mt. Nimba)
28 42 009	**Melaenornis edolioides** *Northern Black Flycatcher*		Senegal to Kenya, Ethiopia
28 42 010	**Melaenornis pammelaina** *Southern Black Flycatcher*		Widespread Kenya to Angola, South Africa
28 42 011	**Melanenornis silens** *Fiscal Flycatcher*		Southern Mozambique to Cape Province
28 42 012	**Fraseria ocreata** *Forest Flycatcher*		Woodlands of Sierra Leone to Zaire, Uganda
28 42 013	**Fraseria cinerascens** *White-browed Forest Flycatcher*		Forest streams of Liberia to Zaire (rare)
28 42 014	**Rhinomyias addita** *Buru Jungle Flycatcher*		Confined to Buru Island (Moluccas)

		Date	Location
28 42 015	**Rhinomyias oscillans** *Flores Jungle Flycatcher*		Confined to Flores Island (Lesser Sundas)
28 42 016	**Rhinomyias olivacea** *Olive-backed Jungle* *Flycatcher*		Malay Peninsula; Java; Sumatra; Borneo
28 42 017	**Rhinomyias brunneata** *Brown-chested Flycatcher*		Southeast China to Malaya; Nicobar Islands
28 42 018	**Rhinomyias umbratilis** *Gray-chested Jungle* *Flycatcher*		Malay Peninsula, Sumatra, Borneo
28 42 019	**Rhinomyias ruficauda** *Rufous-tailed Jungle* *Flycatcher*		Philippine Islands; Borneo
28 42 020	**Rhinomyias colonus** *Celebes Jungle Flycatcher*		Confined to Celebes Islands
28 42 021	**Rhinomyias gularis** *White-throated Jungle* *Flycatcher*		Philippine Islands; Borneo
28 42 022	**Rhinomyias insignis** *Luzon Jungle Flycatcher*		Philippines (endemic northern Luzon Island)
28 42 023	**Rhinomyias goodfellowi** *Goodfellow's Jungle* *Flycatcher*		Philippines (endemic Mindanao Island)
28 42 024	**Ficedula hypoleuca** *Pied Flycatcher*		Widespread mixed forests of western Palearctic region
28 42 025	**Ficedula albicollis** *Collared Flycatcher*		Mixed forests of southern Palearctic region
28 42 026	**Ficedula zanthopygia** *Yellow-rumped Flycatcher*		Eastern Palearctic, Oriental mainland and islands
28 42 027	**Ficedula narcissina** *Narcissus Flycatcher*		East to southeast Asia; Borneo; Philippines; Hainan; Taiwan
28 42 028	**Ficedula mugimaki** *Mugimaki Flycatcher*		Northeast Asia to southeast Asia; Greater Sundas
28 42 029	**Ficedula parva** *Red-throated Flycatcher*		Palearctic, Oriental region mainland; Borneo
28 42 030	**Ficedula strophiata** *Rufous-gorgeted* *Flycatcher*		Kashmir to Szechwan, Burma, Tonkin, Laos
28 42 031	**Ficedula monileger** *White-gorgeted Flycatcher*		Himalayas of Nepal to Burma, Annam, Tonkin, Laos
28 42 032	**Ficedula solitaria** *Rufous-browed Flycatcher*		Malay Peninsula, Indochina; Sumatra

		Date	Location
28 42 033	**Ficedula hyperythra** *Snowy-browed Flycatcher*		Widespread Oriental region mainland and islands
28 42 034	**Ficedula rufigula** *Celebes Red-throated Flycatcher*		Celebes Islands
28 42 035	**Ficedula dumetoria** *Rufous-chested Flycatcher*		Malay Peninsula; Java; Sumatra; Borneo
28 42 036	**Ficedula basilanica** *Little Slaty Flycatcher*		Philippines (Basilan, Mindanao, Leyte, Samar Islands)
28 42 037	**Fidecula buruensis** *Buru Flycatcher*		Confined to Buru Island (Moluccas)
28 42 038	**Ficedula henrici** *Damar Flycatcher*		Moluccas (known only from Damar Island)
28 42 039	**Ficedula hodgsonii (amabilis)** *Slaty-backed Flycatcher*		Nepal to Kansu, Burma, Thailand, Laos
28 42 040	**Ficedula platenae** *Palawan Flycatcher*		Philippines (confined to Palawan Island)
28 42 041	**Ficedula crypta** *Vaurie's Flycatcher*		Philippines (known only from Mindanao Island)
28 42 042	**Ficedula bonthaina** *Celebes Blue Flycatcher*		Confined to the Celebes Islands
28 42 043	**Ficedula harterti** *Sumba Blue Flycatcher*		Confined to Sumba Island (Lesser Sundas)
28 42 044	**Ficedula nigrorufa** *Black-and-orange Flycatcher*		Highland evergreen *sholas* of peninsular India
28 42 045	**Ficedula timorensis** *Timor Blue Flycatcher*		Confined to Timor Island (Lesser Sundas)
28 42 046	**Ficedula westermanni** *Little Pied Flycatcher*		Widespread Oriental mainland and islands
28 42 047	**Ficedula superciliaris** *Ultramarine Flycatcher*		Pakistan, Garhwal to Yunnan, Burma; winters to Australia
28 42 048	**Ficedula tricolor (leucomelanura)** *Slaty-blue Flycatcher*		Himalayas of Kashmir to southwest China, Burma, Laos, Tonkin
28 42 049	**Ficedula sapphira** *Sapphire Flycatcher*		Nepal to Yunnan, Burma, Thailand, Laos
28 42 050	**Cyanoptila cyanomelana** *Blue-and-white Flycatcher*		Eastern Palearctic, Oriental mainland and islands

		Date	Location

28 42 051 **Niltava grandis**
Large Niltava
Nepal to Yunnan, Malaya, Indochina; Sumatra

28 42 052 **Niltava macgrigoriae**
Small Niltava
Himalayas of Pakistan to Yunnan, Burma, Tonkin

28 42 053 **Niltava davidi**
Fukien Niltava
Southern China, adjacent Annam, Tonkin, Laos

28 42 054 **Niltava sundara**
Rufous-bellied Niltava
Himalayas of Pakistan to Yunnan, Burma, Thailand, Laos

28 42 055 **Niltava vivida**
Vivid Niltava
Assam to southwest China, Indochina; Taiwan

28 42 056 **Niltava sumatrana**
Rufous-vented Niltava
Forest undergrowth of Malay Peninsula; Sumatra

28 42 057 **Niltava lemprieri**
Philippine Hill Niltava
Philippines (Balabac, Calamianes, Palawan Islands)

28 42 058 **Niltava hyacinthina**
Hyacinthine Niltava
Timor and Sumba Islands (Lesser Sundas)

28 42 059 **Niltava hoevelli**
Hoevell's Niltava
Celebes Islands

28 42 060 **Niltava sanfordi**
Sandford's Niltava
Celebes Islands

28 42 061 **Niltava concreta**
White-tailed Niltava
Malay Peninsula; Sumatra; Borneo

28 42 062 **Niltava ruecki**
Rueck's Niltava
Sumatra (known from two specimens)

28 42 063 **Niltava herioti**
Blue-breasted Niltava
Philippines (endemic to Luzon Island)

28 42 064 **Niltava hainana**
Hainan Niltava
Southern China to Indochina; Hainan

28 42 065 **Niltava pallipes**
White-bellied Niltava
Evergreen *sholas* of peninsular India

28 42 066 **Niltava poliogenys**
Pale-chinned Niltava
Nepal to Assam, southwest China, Burma

28 42 067 **Niltava unicolor**
Pale Blue Niltava
Himalayas of India to Yunnan, Indochina; Greater Sundas

28 42 068 **Niltava rubeculoides**
Blue-throated Niltava
Himalayas of Pakistan to Yunnan, Malaya, Indochina

28 42 069 **Niltava banyumas (whitei)**
Hill Niltava
Nepal to Yunnan, Indochina; Java; Borneo

28 42 070 **Niltava superba (venusta)**
Bornean Niltava
Submontane resident throughout Borneo

	Date	Location
28 42 071	**Niltava caerulata** *Large-billed Niltava*	Lowland forests of Sumatra and Borneo
28 42 072	**Niltava turcosa** *Malaysian Niltava*	Forests of Malaya, Sumatra, Borneo
28 42 073	**Niltava tickelliae** *Tickell's Niltava*	Sri Lanka; India to Indochina; winters to Celebes
28 42 074	**Niltava rufigastra** *Mangrove Niltava*	Malaya; Greater Sundas; Celebes; Philippines
28 42 075	**Muscicapella hodgsoni** *Pygmy Blue Flycatcher*	Himalayas of Nepal to Malaya; Sumatra; Borneo
28 42 076	**Muscicapa striata** *Spotted Flycatcher*	Widespread Africa, Europe to central Asia
28 42 077	**Muscicapa sibirica** *Siberian Flycatcher*	Widespread Lake Baikal to southeast Asia
28 42 078	**Muscicapa griseisticta** *Gray-streaked Flycatcher*	Eastern Palearctic, Oriental region; New Guinea
28 42 079	**Muscicapa latirostris** *Asian Brown Flycatcher*	Manchuria to southeast Asia; Greater Sundas; Andamans
28 42 080	**Muscicapa williamsoni** *Brown-streaked Flycatcher*	Sumatra (rare Malay Peninsula and Indochina)
28 42 081	**Muscicapa segregata** *Sumba Flycatcher*	Sumba Island (Lesser Sundas)
28 42 082	**Muscicapa muttui** *Brown-breasted Flycatcher*	Sri Lanka; India to Assam, Sikkim
28 42 083	**Muscicapa ruficauda** *Rufous-tailed Flycatcher*	Afghanistan, Kashmir, Nepal to Assam
28 42 084	**Muscicapa ferruginea (rufilata)** *Ferruginous Flycatcher*	India to Malaya, Indochina; Taiwan; Hainan
28 42 085	**Muscicapa gambagae** *Gambagae Dusky Flycatcher*	Light woodlands of Ghana to Ethiopia, Somalia
28 42 086	**Muscicapa adusta** *African Dusky Flycatcher*	Widespread Africa south of the Sahara
28 42 087	**Muscicapa aquatica** *Swamp Flycatcher*	Swamps of southern Sudan to Zambia
28 42 088	**Muscicapa olivascens** *Olivaceous Flycatcher*	Forests of Gold Coast to eastern Zaire (rare)
28 42 089	**Muscicapa lendu** *Chapin's Flycatcher*	Eastern Zaire (known from one specimen from Djugu)

	Date	Location

28 42 090	**Muscicapa cassini** *Cassin's Flycatcher*	Forests of Sierra Leone to Zambia
28 42 091	**Muscicapa epulata** *Little Gray Flycatcher*	Forests of Liberia to Zaire
28 42 092	**Muscicapa sethsmithii** *Yellow-footed Flycatcher*	Primary forests of Cameroon to Uganda, Zaire
28 42 093	**Muscicapa caerulescens** *Little Blue Flycatcher*	Widespread Africa south of the Sahara
28 42 094	**Muscicapa comitata** *Dusky Blue Flycatcher*	Forests of eastern Zaire to Uganda, the Sudan
28 42 095	**Muscicapa tessmanni** *Tessman's Flycatcher*	West Africa (Gold Coast to Guinea)
28 42 096	**Muscicapa infuscata** **(fuliginosa)** *African Sooty Flycatcher*	Cameroon to Zaire, the Sudan, Uganda
28 42 097	**Muscicapa ussheri** *Ussher's Flycatcher*	Sierra Leone to the Gold Coast
28 42 098	**Muscicapa boehmi** *Boehm's Flycatcher*	Tanzania to Angola, Malawi
28 42 099	**Muscicapa sordida** *Ceylon Blue Flycatcher*	Widespread forested uplands of Sri Lanka
28 42 100	**Muscicapa thalassina** *Verditer Flycatcher*	Nepal, India to Yunnan, Malaya; Sumatra; Borneo
28 42 101	**Muscicapa panayensis** *Panay Flycatcher*	Philippines (Negros, Panay, Luzon, Mindoro, Mindanao)
28 42 102	**Muscicapa albicaudata** *Nilgiri Flycatcher*	Widespread and common throughout southwest India
28 42 103	**Muscicapa indigo** *Indigo Flycatcher*	High mountains of Sumatra, Java and Borneo
28 42 104	**Myioparus plumbeus** *Gray Tit-Flycatcher*	Senegal to Ethiopia, South Africa
28 42 105	**Myioparus griseigularis** *Gray-throated Flycatcher*	Eastern Zaire and adjacent Uganda
28 42 106	**Humblotia flavirostris** *Humblot's Flycatcher*	Comoro Islands (Indian Ocean)
28 42 107	**Newtonia amphichroa** *Dark Newtonia*	Humid forests of eastern Madagascar
28 42 108	**Newtonia brunneicauda** *Common Newtonia*	Widespread wooded areas of Madagascar
28 42 109	**Newtonia archboldi** *Archbold's Newtonia*	Semiarid regions of southwest Madagascar
28 42 110	**Newtonia fanovanae** *Fanovana Newtonia*	Madagascar (known from one specimen)

	Date	Location
28 42 111 **Microoca leucophaea** *Jacky-winter*		Australia, Port Moresby area of New Guinea
28 42 112 **Microoca brunneicauda** *Brown-tailed Flycatcher*		Australia (doubtful species . . . known from a single specimen)
28 42 113 **Microoca flavigaster** *Lemon-breasted Flycatcher*		Coastal northern Australia; New Guinea
28 42 114 **Microoca hemixantha** *Tanimbar Microoca*		Confined to Island of Tanimbar (southern Moluccas)
28 42 115 **Microoca griseoceps** *Little Yellow Microoca*		Southern New Guinea; Cape York Peninsula of Australia
28 42 116 **Microoca flavovirescens** *Olive Microoca*		New Guinea, Arus and adjacent islands
28 42 117 **Microoca papuana** *Papuan Microoca*		Mountains of New Guinea (Vogelkop to southeast New Guinea)
28 42 118 **Culicicapa ceylonesis** *Gray-headed Flycatcher*		Widespread Oriental region mainland and islands
28 42 119 **Culicicapa helianthea** *Canary Flycatcher*		Widespread throughout the Philippine Islands
28 42 120 **Peltops montanus** *Mountain Peltops Flycatcher*		Mountains of New Guinea
28 42 121 **Peltops blainvillii** *Lowland Peltops Flycatcher*		New Guinea lowlands and adjacent islands
28 42 122 **Monachella muelleriana** *River Flycatcher*		New Guinea and New Britain Islands
28 42 123 **Eugerygone rubra** *Red-backed Gerygone*		Mountain forests of New Guinea
28 42 124 **Petroica multicolor** *Scarlet Robin*		Southern Australia, Tasmania, islands of Bass Strait
28 42 125 **Petroica goodenovii** *Red-capped Robin*		Widespread interior of Australia
28 42 126 **Petroica phoenicea** *Flame Robin*		Tasmania; adjacent Australian mainland
28 42 127 **Petroica archboldi** *Rock Robin Flycatcher*		New Guinea (known only from Mt. Wilhelmina)
28 42 128 **Petroica rodinogaster** *Pink Robin*		Victoria; Tasmania; islands of Bass Strait
28 42 129 **Petroica rosea** *Rose Robin*		Coastal central Queensland to Victoria

		Date	Location
28 42 130	**Petroica bivittata** *Forest Robin Flycatcher*		High mountains of New Guinea
28 42 131	**Petroica cucullata** *Hooded Robin*		Widespread open forests and savanna of Australia
28 42 132	**Petroica macrocephala** *Tomtit*		New Zealand, Stewart, Snares and Chatham Islands
28 42 133	**Petroica vittata** *Dusky Robin*		Tasmania and islands of Bass Strait
28 42 134	**Petroica australis** *New Zealand Robin*		New Zealand and adjacent islands
28 42 135	**Petroica traversi** *Chatham Island Robin*		Chathams (Little Mangare Island—endangered)
28 42 136	**Eopsaltria leucops** *White-faced Robin*		New Guinea and Cape York Peninsula of Australia
28 42 137	**Eopsaltria capito** *Pale Yellow Robin*		Coastal Queensland to New South Wales
28 42 138	**Eopsaltria australis** *Yellow Robin*		Dry forests of southeast Australia
28 42 139	**Eopsaltria griseogularis** *Western Yellow Robin*		*Casuarina* zone of southwestern Australia
28 42 140	**Eopsaltria chrysorrhoa** *Northern Yellow Robin*		Coastal rain forests of Queensland to New South Wales
28 42 141	**Eopsaltria georgiana** *White-breasted Robin*		Coastal acacia scrub of southwestern Australia
28 42 142	**Eopsaltria flaviventris** *Yellow-bellied Robin*		Confined to New Caledonia Island
28 42 143	**Peneoenanthe pulverulenta** *Mangrove Robin*		Australia to New Guinea and the Aru Islands
28 42 144	**Philentoma pyrhopterum** *Rufous-winged Flycatcher*		Evergreen forests of Malaya; Sumatra; Borneo
28 42 145	**Philentoma velatum** *Maroon-breasted Flycatcher*		Evergreen forests of Malaya; Java; Sumatra; Borneo
28 42 146	**Poecilodryas brachyura** *White-breasted Flycatcher*		Submontane forests of northwest and northern New Guinea
28 42 147	**Poecilodryas hypoleuca** *Black-and-white Flycatcher*		Lowlands of New Guinea and western Papuan Islands
28 42 148	**Poecilodryas superciliosa** *White-browed Robin*		Australia (wet forests of coastal northern Queensland)

	Date	Location

28 42 149	**Poecilodryas placens** *Olive-yellow Flycatcher*	Lowland forests of New Guinea (rare)
28 42 150	**Poecilodryas albonotata** *Black-throated Flycatcher*	Mid-mountain forests of New Guinea
28 42 151	**Poecilodryas cerviniventris** *Buff-sided Robin*	Coastal northwest Australia to northwest Queensland
28 42 152	**Peneothello sigillatus** *White-winged Thicket- Flycatcher*	High mountains of New Guinea
28 42 153	**Peneothello cryptoleucus** *Gray Thicket-Flycatcher*	Arfak and Weyland Mountains of New Guinea
28 42 154	**Peneothello cyanus** *Slaty Thicket-Flycatcher*	Mid-mountain forests of New Guinea
28 42 155	**Peneothello bimaculatus** *White-rumped Thicket- Flycatcher*	Uncommon mid-mountain forests of New Guinea
28 42 156	**Heteromyias albispecularis** *Ground Thicket-Flycatcher*	Mountains of New Guinea
28 42 157	**Heteromyias cinereifrons** *Gray-headed Robin*	Australia (rain forests of Cape York Peninsula)
28 42 158	**Pachycephalopsis hattamensis** *Green Thicket-Flycatcher*	Snow Mountains to Vogelkop range of New Guinea
28 42 159	**Pachycephalopsis poliosoma** *White-throated Thicket- Flycatcher*	Weyland and Snow Mountains to southeast New Guinea
28 42 160	**Megabyas flammulatus** *Shrike Flycatcher*	Secondary forests of Sierra Leone to Uganda, Zaire, Angola
28 42 161	**Bias musicus** *Black-and-white Flycatcher*	Tropical Africa south of the Sahara
28 42 162	**Pseudobias wardi** *Ward's Flycatcher*	Dense forests of eastern Madagascar
28 42 163	**Batis capensis** *Cape Puffback*	Forests of Kenya to South Africa
28 42 164	**Batis mixta** *East African Puffback*	Coastal Kenya (Sokoke Forest) to southern Malawi
28 42 165	**Batis margaritae** *Boulton's Puffback*	Evergreen forests of southern Angola and Zambia

		Date	Location

28 42 166	**Batis diops**	
	Ruwenzori Puffback	Mountains of eastern Zaire border and western Uganda
28 42 167	**Batis fratrum**	
	Zululand Puffback	Coastal scrub of Mozambique to Zululand (South Africa)
28 42 168	**Batis molitor**	
	Chin-spot Puffback	Acacia belt of southern Sudan, Kenya to South Africa
28 42 169	**Batis soror**	
	Mozambique Puffback	Coastal scrub of Kenya to Mozambique
28 42 170	**Batis pririt**	
	Pririt Puffback	Acacia belt of southern Angola to South Africa
28 42 171	**Batis senegalensis**	
	Senegal Puffback	Semiarid Senegal to Cameroon
28 42 172	**Batis orientalis**	
	Gray-headed Puffback	Thorn scrub of Ethiopia, Eritrea to southern Niger River
28 42 173	**Batis perkeo**	
	Pygmy Puffback	Acacia and thorn scrub of Ethiopia and Somalia
28 42 174	**Batis minor**	
	Black-headed Puffback	Semiarid Ethiopia, Somalia to Angola, Tanzania
28 42 175	**Batis minulla**	
	Angola Puffback	Cameroon to Angola and western Zaire (rare)
28 42 176	**Batis minima**	
	Forest Puffback	Heavy forests of Gabon and northeast Zaire (rare)
28 42 177	**Batis ituriensis**	
	Ituri Puffback	Zaire (Ituri forest—possible race *B. minima*)
28 42 178	**Batis poensis**	
	Fernando Po Puffback	Liberia to Cameroon, Fernando Po (rare)
28 42 179 +	**Platysteira cyanea** *Common Wattle-eye*	Forests of Kenya, Uganda, Tanzania, Ethiopia
28 42 180	**Platysteira albifrons**	
	White-fronted Wattle-eye	Southwestern Zaire and northern Angola (rare)
28 42 181 +	**Platysteira peltata** **(laticincta)** *Black-throated Wattle-eye*	Uganda, Kenya, Tanzania to Malawi, Zambia, Angola
28 42 182 +	**Platysteira concreta** **(ansorgei)** *Yellow-bellied Wattle-eye*	Forests of eastern Zaire to Uganda, Kenya (rare)
28 42 183 +	**Platysteira blissetti** **(chalybea)** *Red-cheeked Wattle-eye*	Dense forests of Sierra Leone to Kenya, Uganda, Zaire
28 42 184	**Platysteira castanea**	
	Chestnut Wattle-eye	Sierra Leone to Angola, Sudan, Kenya, Tanzania

	Date	Location

28 42 185	**Platysteira tonsa** *White-spotted Wattle-eye*	Forests of Nigeria to Semliki Valley; Fernando Po
28 42 186	**Erythrocercus holochlorus** *Little Yellow Flycatcher*	Highlands of Kenya, southern Somalia to Tanzania
28 42 187	**Erythrocercus mccallii** *Chestnut-capped Flycatcher*	Dense forests of Nigeria to Zaire, Uganda
28 42 188	**Erythrocercus livingstonei** *Livingstone's Flycatcher*	Woodland and scrub of Malawi, Rhodesia, Mozambique
28 42 189	**Erannornis longicauda** *Blue Flycatcher*	Woodlands of Sierra Leone to southern Sudan, Uganda, Kenya
28 42 190	**Erannornis albicauda** *White-tailed Blue Flycatcher*	Woodlands of southern Zaire to Angola, Malawi, Zambia
28 42 191	**Trochocercus albonotatus** *White-tailed Crested Flycatcher*	Highland forests of Kenya, Uganda, Tanzania to Malawi
28 42 192	**Trochocercus albiventris** *White-bellied Crested Flycatcher*	Fernando Po; Cameroon highlands to Uganda, Zaire
28 42 193	**Trochocercus nigromitratus** *Dusky Crested Flycatcher*	Forests of Liberia and Gabon to central Zaire
28 42 194	**Trochocercus cyanomelas** *African Crested Flycatcher*	Forests of Uganda, western Tanzania, southern Zaire, Zambia
28 42 195	**Trochocercus nitens** *Blue-headed Crested Flycatcher*	Forests of Sierra Leone to Angola, Uganda, Zaire
28 42 196	**Terpsiphone viridis** *African Paradise Flycatcher*	Widespread Africa south of the Sahara
28 42 197	**Terpsiphone rufocinerea** *Rufous-vented Paradise Flycatcher*	Forests of Cameroon to western Zaire, northern Angola
28 42 198	**Terpsiphone atrochalybeia** *São Thomé Paradise Flycatcher*	Confined to Island of São Thomé (Gulf of Guinea)
28 42 199	**Terpsiphone mutata** *Madagascar Paradise Flycatcher*	Wooded areas of Madagascar

		Date	Location
28 42 200	**Terpsiphone corvina** *Seychelles Paradise Flycatcher*		Seychelles (confined to La Digne Island—endangered)
28 42 201	**Terpsiphone bourbonnensis** *Coq de Bois*		Confined to Mascarene Islands (Indian Ocean)
28 42 202	**Terpsiphone paradisi** *Asian Paradise Flycatcher*		Widespread Oriental region mainland and islands
28 42 203	**Terpsiphone atrocaudata** *Black Paradise Flycatcher*		East Asia; Japan; Philippines; Hainan; Taiwan; Sumatra
28 42 204	**Terpsiphone rufiventer (nigriceps)** *Red-bellied Paradise Flycatcher*		Senegal to Angola, the Semliki Valley
28 42 205	**Terpsiphone unirufa** *Rufous Paradise Flycatcher*		Widespread Philippine Islands
28 42 206	**Terpsiphone cinnamomea** *Cinnamon Paradise Flycatcher*		Philippine Islands and Sulu Archipelago
28 42 207	**Terpsiphone cyanescens** *Blue Paradise Flycatcher*		Philippines (Calamaines and Palawan Islands)
28 42 208	**Eutrichomyias rowleyi** *Rowley's Flycatcher*		Celebes Islands (known from a single specimen)
28 42 209	**Hypothymis helenae (personata)** *Short-crested Blue Monarch*		Philippines (Camiguin North, Luzon, Polillo, Samar Islands)
28 42 210	**Hypothymis coelestis** *Celestial Blue Monarch*		Widespread throughout the Philippine Islands
28 42 211	**Hypothymis azurea** *Black-naped Monarch*		Widespread Oriental region mainland and islands
28 42 212	**Hypothymis puella** *Moluccan Monarch*		Confined to Moluccas Islands
28 42 213	**Seisura inquieta** *Restless Flycatcher*		Widespread Australia to New Guinea
28 42 214	**Machaerirhynchus flaviventer** *Yellow-breasted Flatbill*		Rain forests of Queensland; New Guinea and adjacent islands
28 42 215	**Machaerirhynchus nigripectus** *Black-breasted Flatbill*		Mid-mountains of New Guinea

		Date	Location
28 42 216	**Chasiempis sandwichensis** *Elapaio*		Hawaiian Islands (Kauai, Oahu, Hawaii)
28 42 217	**Pomarea dimidiata** *Cook Island Flycatcher*		Confined to Rarotonga and Cook Islands
28 42 218	**Pomarea nigra** *Tahiti Flycatcher*		Tahiti and Maupiti Islands (endangered)
28 42 219	**Pomarea mendozae** *Marquesas Flycatcher*		Confined to the northern Marquesas Islands
28 42 220	**Pomarea iphis** *Ua Huka Flycatcher*		Marquesas (Ua Huka Island—possible race *P. mendozae*)
28 42 221	**Pomarea whitneyi** *Fatuhiva Flycatcher*		Marquesas (confined to Fatu Hiva Island)
28 42 222	**Mayrornis schistaceus** *Vanikoro Flycatcher*		Santa Cruz Archipelago (confined to Vanikoro Island)
28 42 223	**Mayrornis versicolor** *Versicolor Flycatcher*		Fiji Islands (known only from Ongea Levu Island)
28 42 224	**Mayrornis lessoni** *Fiji Slaty Flycatcher*		Lowlands and mountain forests of major Fiji Islands
28 42 225	**Neolalage banksiana** *New Hebrides Flycatcher*		Confined to the New Hebrides Islands
28 42 226	**Clythorhynchus pachycephaloides** *Southern Shrikebill*		Confined to New Caledonia Island
28 42 227	**Clytorhynchus vitiensis** *Fiji Shrikebill*		Widespread central Polynesian Islands
28 42 228	**Clytorhynchus nigrogularis** *Black-faced Shrikebill*		Mountain forests of large Fiji Islands
28 42 229	**Clytorhynchus hamlini** *Rennell Shrikebill*		Solomon Islands (confined to Rennell Island)
28 42 230	**Metabolus rugensis** *Truk Monarch*		Caroline Islands (confined to Truk Island)
28 42 231	**Monarcha axillaris** *Black Monarch*		Mountains of New Guinea and Goodenough Island
28 42 232	**Monarcha rubiensis** *Rufous Monarch*		Lowlands of New Guinea
28 42 233	**Monarcha alecto** *Shining Monarch*		Widespread mangroves of Australia to New Guinea
28 42 234	**Monarcha hebetior** *Dull Monarch*		Confined to New Britain Island
28 42 235	**Monarcha cinerascens** *Gray-headed Monarch*		Timor, New Guinea, Solomons and Moluccas

		Date	Location

28 42 236 Monarcha melanopsis
Black-faced Monarch — Coastal Queensland to Victoria; eastern New Guinea

28 42 237 Monarcha frater (canescens)
Pearly Monarch — Mountains of New Guinea; Cape York Peninsula

28 42 238 Monarcha erythrostica
Bougainville Monarch — Lowland and mountain rain forests of Shortland Islands, Bougainville

28 42 239 Monarcha castaneiventris
Chestnut-bellied Monarch — Confined to the Solomon Islands

28 42 240 Monarcha richardsii
Richard's Monarch — Confined to the Celebes Islands

28 42 241 Monarcha leucotis
White-eared Monarch — Coastal Cape York Peninsula to New South Wales

28 42 242 Monarcha guttula
Spot-winged Monarch — New Guinea, Arus and adjacent islands

28 42 243 Monarcha julianae
Kofiau Monarch — New Guinea (known from a single specimen from Kofiau Island)

28 42 244 Monarcha mundus
Tanimbar Monarch — Moluccas (confined to Tanimbar Island)

28 42 245 Monarcha trivirgata
Spectacled Monarch — Eastern Australia, New Guinea, Moluccas, Timor

28 42 246 Monarcha sacerdotum
Mee's Monarch — Confined to Flores Island (Lesser Sundas)

28 42 247 Monarcha leucurus
Kai Monarch — Moluccas (confined to Kai Island)

28 42 248 Monarcha barbata
Pied Monarch — Confined to the Solomon Islands

28 42 249 Monarcha infelix
Admirality Island Monarch — Confined to Admiralty Island

28 42 250 Monarcha menckei
Menke's Monarch — Confined to the northern Melanesian Islands

28 42 251 Monarcha vidua
San Cristobal Monarch — Solomon Islands (confined to San Cristobal Island)

28 42 252 Monarcha browni
Kulambangra Monarch — Solomons (Kulambangra, New Georgia, Vangunu, Gatukai Islands)

28 42 253 Monarcha verticalis
New Britain Pied Monarch — Confined to New Britain Island

28 42 254 Monarcha ateralba
Bismarck Monarch — Confined to islands of the Bismarck Archipelago

	Date	Location

28 42 255 **Monarcha godeffroyi**
Yap Monarch — Caroline Islands (confined to Yap Island)

28 42 256 **Monarcha brehmii**
Biak Monarch — New Guinea (confined to Biak Island)

28 42 257 **Monarcha manadensis**
Black-and-white Monarch — Lowland forests throughout New Guinea

28 42 258 **Monarcha chrysomela**
Black-and-yellow Monarch — New Guinea and Bismarck Archipelago

28 42 259 **Monarcha takatsukasae**
Tinian Monarch — Mariannas (confined to Tinian Island)

28 42 260 **Monarcha sericeus**
New Hebrides Monarch — Confined to the New Hebrides Islands

28 42 261 **Monarcha pileatus**
Tufted Monarch — Confined to the Moluccas Islands

28 42 262 **Arses kaupi**
Australian Pied Flycatcher — Australia (rain forests of Cape York Peninsula)

28 42 263 **Arses telescophthalmus**
(lorealis)
Frill-necked Flycatcher — New Guinea, Cape York Peninsula, adjacent western Islands

28 42 264 **Myiagra pluto**
Ponape Broadbill — Caroline Islands (confined to Ponape Island)

28 42 265 **Myiagra oceanica**
Micronesian Broadbill — Caroline Islands (confined to Truk Island)

28 42 266 **Myiagra freycineti**
Guam Broadbill — Confined to Guam Island

28 42 267 **Myiagra erythrops**
Palau Broadbill — Confined to Palau Island (Philippine Sea)

28 42 268 **Myiagra galeata**
Helmeted Broadbill — Confined to the Moluccas Islands

28 42 269 **Myiagra rubecula**
Leaden Flycatcher — Coastal eastern and northern Australia; New Guinea

28 42 270 **Myiagra atra**
Black Myiagra — Numfor and Biak Islands (off New Guinea)

28 42 271 **Myiagra ferrocyanea**
Solomon Broadbill — Confined to the Solomon Islands

28 42 272 **Myiagra caledonica**
Melanesian Broadbill — New Hebrides and New Caledonia Islands

28 42 273 **Myiagra vanikorensis**
Vanikoro Broadbill — New Hebrides and Fiji Islands

28 42 274 **Myiagra albiventris**
Samoan Broadbill — Samoa (forests of Savii and Upolu Islands)

		Date	Location
28 42 275	**Myiagra cyanoleuca** *Satin Flycatcher*		Coastal eastern Australia; Tasmania; New Guinea; New Britain
28 42 276	**Myiagra ruficollis** *Broad-billed Myiagra*		Coastal northern Australia; New Guinea; Arus; Timor
28 42 277	**Myiagra azureocapilla** *Blue-crested Broadbill*		Montane forests of Fiji (Viti Levu, Vanua Levu, Taviuni)
28 42 278	**Rhipidura hypoxantha** *Yellow-bellied Fantail*		Himalayas of India to southwest China, Indochina
28 42 279	**Rhipidura threnothorax** *Sooty Thicket Fantail*		Lowlands of New Guinea, Arus, Waigeu, Salawati, Japen Islands
28 42 280	**Rhipidura maculipectus** *Black Thicket Fantail*		Lowlands of New Guinea, Arus and western Papuan Islands
28 42 281	**Rhipidura leucothorax** *White-breasted Thicket Fantail*		Widespread lowlands of New Guinea
28 42 282	**Rhipidura superciliaris** *Blue Fantail*		Philippines (Basilan, Mindanao, Bohol. Leyte, Samar)
28 42 283	**Rhipidura cyaniceps** *Blue-headed Fantail*		Mountain forests of Philippine Islands
28 42 284	**Rhipidura phoenicura** *Red-tailed Fantail*		Montane forests of Island of Java
28 42 285	**Rhipidura nigrocinnamomea** *Black-and-Cinnamon Fantail*		Philippines (mountain forests of Mindanao Island)
28 42 286	**Rhipidura opistherythra** *Red-backed Fantail*		Moluccas (confined to Tanimbar Island)
28 42 287	**Rhipidura lepida** *Palau Fantail*		Confined to Palau Island (Philippine Sea—endangered)
28 42 288	**Rhipidura dedemi** *Tanimbar Fantail*		Moluccas (confined to Tanimbar Island)
28 42 289	**Rhipidura superflua** *Moluccan Fantail*		Confined to the Moluccas Islands
28 42 290	**Rhipidura sulaensis** *Sula Fantail*		Confined to the Sula Archipelago
28 42 291	**Rhipidura teysmanni** *Celebes Fantail*		Confined to the Celebes Islands
28 42 292	**Rhipidura rufifrons** *Rufous-fronted Fantail*		Rain forests of Australia; Tasmania; New Guinea

		Date	Location

28 42 293	**Rhipidura dahli** *New Britain Fantail*	Confined to New Britain Island
28 42 294	**Rhipidura matthiae** *St. Matthias Fantail*	St. Matthias Islands (north of Bismarck Archipelago)
28 42 295	**Rhipidura personata** *Kandavu Fantail*	Fiji Islands (endemic to Kandavu Island)
28 42 296	**Rhipidura rufidorsa** *Gray-breasted Rufous Fantail*	Lowlands of New Guinea, Misol and Japen Islands
28 42 297	**Rhipidura brachyrhyncha** *Dimorphic Fantail*	High mountain forests of New Guinea
28 42 298	**Rhipidura spilodera** *Spotted Fantail*	New Caledonia, New Hebrides and Fiji Islands
28 42 299	**Rhipidura rennelliana** *Rennel Fantail*	Solomon Islands (confined to Rennell Island)
28 42 300	**Rhipidura drownei** *Mountain Fantail*	Mountain forests of the Solomon Islands
28 42 301	**Rhipidura tenebrosa** *Dusky Fantail*	Solomon Islands (confined to San Cristobal Island)
28 42 302	**Rhipidura fuliginosa** *Gray Fantail*	Australia, Tasmania, New Zealand to the Solomons
28 42 303	**Rhipidura nebulosa** *Samoan Fantail*	Forests of Samoa (Savii and Upolu Islands)
28 42 304	**Rhipidura malaitae** *Malaita Fantail*	Solomon Islands (mountain forests of Malaita Island)
28 42 305	**Rhipidura atra** *Black Fantail*	Mountains of New Guinea and Waigeu Island
28 42 306	**Rhipidura hyperythra** *Chestnut-bellied Fantail*	Lowlands of New Guinea, Japen and Aru Islands
28 42 307	**Rhipidura euryura** *White-bellied Fantail*	Montane forests of Island of Java
28 42 308	**Rhipidura albolimbata** *Friendly Fantail*	Mountains of New Guinea
28 42 309	**Rhipidura albicollis** *White-throated Fantail*	Himalayas of Kashmir to southern China, Indochina; Sundas
28 42 310	**Rhipidura albogularis** *White-spotted Fantail*	Common and widespread peninsular India
28 42 311	**Rhipidura aureola** *White-browed Fantail*	Pakistan to southwest China, Burma, Indochina
28 42 312	**Rhipidura javanica** *Pied Fantail*	Malaya, Indochina; Philippines; Greater Sundas

		Date	Location
28 42 313	**Rhipidura rufiventris (setosa)** *Northern Fantail*		Australia to the Solomons, Moluccas, Lesser Sundas
28 42 314	**Rhipidura perlata** *Perlated Fantail*		Malay Peninsula; Java; Sumatra; Borneo
28 42 315	**Rhipidura cockerelli** *Cockerell's Fantail*		Confined to the Solomon Islands
28 42 316	**Rhipidura leucophrys** *Willie Wagtail*		Australia to New Guinea, Solomons, Moluccas, Lesser Sundas
28 42 317	**Eulacestoma nigropectus** *Wattled Shriketit*		Mountains of New Guinea
28 42 318	**Falcunculus frontatus** *Australian Shrikeitit*		Widespread dry forests and woodlands of Australia
28 42 319	**Oreoica gutturalis** *Crested Bellbird*		Dry woodlands throughout Australia
28 42 320	**Pachycare flavogrisea** *Golden-faced Pachycare*		Mid-mountain forests of New Guinea
28 42 321	**Rhagologus leucostigma** *Mottled Whistler*		Mid-mountain forests of New Guinea
28 42 322	**Hylocitrea bonensis** *Celebes Whistler*		Mountains of Celebes Islands
28 42 323	**Pachycephala raveni** *Rano Rano Whistler*		Mountains of central Celebes Islands
28 42 324	**Pachycephala rufinucha** *Rufous-naped Whistler*		Mountain forests of New Guinea
28 42 325	**Pachycephala tenebrosa** *Sooty Whistler*		Weyland, Snow, Hindenburg, Snow Mountains of New Guinea (rare)
28 42 326	**Pachycephala olivacea** *Olive Whistler*		Coastal New South Wales, Victoria; Tasmania
28 42 327	**Pachycephala rufogularis** *Red-lored Whistler*		*Malee* of eastern Victoria, adjacent South Australia
28 42 328	**Pachycephala inornata** *Gilbert Whistler*		Dry woodlands of southern Australia
28 42 329	**Pachycephala hypoxantha** *Bornean Mountain Whistler*		Mid-mountain forests of Borneo
28 42 330	**Pachycephala cinerea** *Mangrove Whistler*		Southeast India to Indochina; Greater Sundas; Andamans

		Date	Location

28 42 331 **Pachycephala phaionota**
Island Whistler
Moluccas to the Arus, adjacent islands

28 42 332 **Pachycelphala
hyperythra**
Rufous-breasted Whistler
Submontane forests of New Guinea

28 42 333 **Pachycelphala modesta**
Brown-backed Whistler
High mountains of New Guinea

28 42 334 **Pachycephala
philippinensis**
Yellow-bellied Whistler
Widespread throughout the Philippine Islands

28 42 335 **Pachycephala
sulfuriventer**
Celebes Mountain Whistler
Mountain forests of Celebes Islands

28 42 336 **Pachycephala meyeri**
Vogolkop Whistler
Endemic to Vogelkop Mountains of New Guinea
(rare)

28 42 337 **Pachycephala soror**
Sclater's Whistler
Mid-mountain forests of New Guinea and
Goodenough Island

28 42 338 **Pachycephala simplex
(griseiceps)**
Brown Whistler
Mangroves and wet forests of northern Australia to
New Guinea

28 42 339 **Pachycelpala orpheus**
Timor Whistler
Lesser Sundas (confined to Timor and Wetar
Islands)

28 42 340 **Pachycephala pectoralis**
Golden Whistler
Australia to New Guinea, New Caledonia, Java

28 42 341 **Pachycephala flavifrons**
Samoan Whistler
Samoa (forest sub-stage of Savaii and Upolu
Islands)

28 42 342 **Pachycephala
caledonica**
New Caledonia Whistler
Confined to mountain forests of New Caledonia

28 42 343 **Pachycephala implicata**
Mountain Whistler
Mountain forests of Solomon Islands

28 42 344 **Pachycephala nudigula**
Sunda Whistler
Confined to the Lesser Sundas Islands

28 42 345 **Pachycephala lorentzi**
Lorentz's Whistler
Snow and Telefomin Mountains of New Guinea

28 42 346 **Pachycephala schlegelii**
Schlegel's Whistler
Common montane forests of New Guinea

28 42 347 **Pachycephala aurea**
Yellow-backed Whistler
Foothills of Snow and Weyland Mountains of New
Guinea (rare)

	Date	Location
28 42 348 **Pachycephala rufiventris** (**monacha**) *Rufous Whistler*		Australia to New Guinea, New Caldeonia, Moluccas
28 42 349 **Pachycephala lanioides** *White-breasted Whistler*		Mangroves of coastal northern Australia
28 42 350 **Colluricincla megarhyncha** *Rufous Shrike-Thrush*		Coastal Queensland; New Guinea; Celebes (Sangihe Island)
28 42 351 **Colluricincla parvula** *Little Shrike-Thrush*		Coastal northwestern Australia, Northern Territory
28 42 352 **Colluricincia boweri** *Stripe-breasted Shrike-Thrush*		Australia (mountain rain forests of Cape York Peninsula
28 42 353 **Colluricincla harmonica** (**rufiventris**) *Gray Shrike-Thrush*		Widespread Australia; Tasmania; New Guinea
28 42 254 **Colluricincla woodwardi** *Sandstone Thrush*		Coastal sandstone cliffs of north-central Australia
28 42 355 **Pitohui kirhocephalus** *Variable Pitohui*		New Guinea, Arus and western Papuan Islands
28 42 356 **Pitohui dichrous** *Black-headed Pitohui*		Arfak Mountains to southeast New Guinea; Japen Island
28 42 357 **Pitohui incertus** *Mottle-breasted Pitohui*		Lowland forests of southern New Guinea (rare)
28 42 358 **Pitohui ferrugineus** *Rusty Pitohui*		Widespread lowlands of New Guinea; Arus, western Papuan Islands
28 42 359 **Pitohui cristatus** *Crested Pitohui*		Lowlands and mid-mountains of New Guinea
28 42 360 **Pitohui nigrescens** *Black Pitohui*		Mid-mountain forests of New Guinea (rare)
28 42 361 **Pitohui tenebrosus** *Palau Pitohui (Morning Bird)*		Confined to Palau Island (Philippine Sea)
28 42 362 **Turnagra capensis** *New Zealand Thrush*		New Zealand (forests of North and South Island—endangered)

FAMILY: AEGITHALIDAE (Bushtits)

| 28 43 001 **Aegithalos caudatus** *Long-tailed Tit* | | Widespread Palearctic region |

		Date	Location

28 43 002 **Aegithalos leucogenys**
Kashmir Tit
Mountains of Kashmir, Afghanistan, Baluchistan

28 43 003 **Aegithalos concinnus**
Black-throated Tit
Himalayas of Kashmir to Yunnan, Indochina; Taiwan

28 43 004 **Aegithalos iouschistos**
Himalayan Tit
Himalayas of Nepal to Szechwan, northern Burma

28 43 005 **Aegithalos fuliginosus**
Sooty Tit
Mountains of western and central China

28 43 006 **Aegithalos niveogularis**
White-throated Tit
Birch and pine forests of Kashmir, Garhwal, Nepal

28 43 007 **Psaltria exilis**
Pygmy Tit
Mountains of western and central Java

28 43 008 **Psaltriparus minimus (melanotis)**
Common Bushtit
Southwest Canada to highlands of Guatemala; Baja California

FAMILY: REMIZIDAE (Penduline Tits)

28 44 001 **Remiz pendulinus**
Penduline Tit
Widespread Palearctic region

28 44 002 **Anthoscopus punctifrons**
Sennar Penduline Tit
Southern edge of Sahara Desert of North Africa

28 44 003 **Anthoscopus parvulus**
Yellow Penduline Tit
Lake Chad to the southern Sudan

28 44 004 **Anthoscopus musculus**
Mouse-colored Tit
Southern Sudan to Somalia, Uganda, Kenya, Tanzania

28 44 005 **Anthoscopus flavifrons**
Yellow-fronted Penduline Tit
Forests of Nigeria to Zaire

28 44 006 **Anthoscopus caroli (sylviella)**
African Penduline Tit
Widespread Angola to Kenya, Tanzania, South Africa

28 44 007 **Anthoscopus sylviella**
Hagenia Penduline Tit
Highlands of Kenya to South Africa

28 44 008 **Anthoscopus minutus**
Cape Penduline Tit
Southern Angola to South Africa

28 44 009 **Auriparus flaviceps**
Verdin
Deserts of southwest United States to central Mexico

28 44 010 **Cephalopyrus flammiceps**
Fire-capped Tit
Himalayas of Afghanistan, Kashmir to Yunnan

	Date	Location

FAMILY: PARIDAE (Chickadees and Titmice)

28 45 001	**Parus palustris** *Marsh Tit*	Discontinuously Palearctic (Eurasia, China, Burma)
28 45 002	**Parus lugubris** *Sombre Tit*	Lowlands and mountain slopes of Balkan Peninsula
28 45 003	**Parus montanus** *Willow Tit*	Widespread western Palearctic region
28 45 004	**Parus atricapillus** *Black-capped Chicakadee*	Alaska, Canada to southern United States
28 45 005	**Parus carolinensis** *Carolina Chickadee*	New Jersey, Ohio south to peninsular Florida
28 45 006	**Parus sclateri** *Mexican Chickadee*	Mountains of southwest United States to southern Mexico
28 45 007	**Parus gambeli** *Mountain Chickadee*	Mountains of southwest Canada to Baja California
28 45 008	**Parus superciliosus** *White-browed Tit*	Mountains of western China
28 45 009	**Parus davidi** *Père David's Tit*	Mountains of western China
28 45 010	**Parus cinctus** *Gray-headed Chickadee*	Northern Palearctic region; Alaska
28 45 011	**Parus hudsonicus** *Boreal Chickadee*	Alaska, Canada to northern United States
28 45 012	**Parus rufescens** *Chestnut-backed Chickadee*	Western North America (Alaska to central California)
28 45 013	**Parus wollweberi** *Bridled Titmouse*	Mountains of southwest United States to southern Mexico
28 45 014	**Parus rubidiventris** *Rufous-vented Tit*	Himalayas of Garhwal to Shensi
28 45 015	**Parus rufonuchalis** *Simia Black Tit*	Oak-rhododendron forests of Afghanistan to Nepal
28 45 016	**Parus melanolophus** *Spot-winged Black Tit*	Himalayas of Afghanistan to Nepal
28 45 017	**Parus ater** *Coal Tit*	Widespread conifer forests of Palearctic region
28 45 018	**Parus venustulus** *Yellow-bellied Tit*	China (Kwantung to Szechwan)
28 45 019	**Parus elegans** *Elegant Tit*	Widespread throughout the Philippine Islands
28 45 020	**Parus amabilis** *Palawan Tit*	Philippines (Balabac and Palawan Islands)

		Date	Location
28 45 021	**Parus cristatus** *Crested Tit*		Widespread pine forests of Palearctic region
28 45 022	**Parus dichrous** *Gray-crested Tit*		Himalayas of Kashmir to western China, Burma
28 45 023	**Parus afer** *African Gray Tit*		Kenya, Angola to South Africa
28 45 024	**Parus griseiventris** *Northern Gray Tit*		Zaire, Tanzania to South Africa
28 45 025	**Parus niger** *Southern Black Tit*		Lowland forests of Zambia to South Africa
28 45 026	**Parus leucomelas** *Black Tit*		Woodlands and forests of Africa south of the Sahara
28 45 027	**Parus albiventris** *White-breasted Tit*		Acacia steppes, coastal scrub of Cameroon to Tanzania
28 45 028	**Parus leuconotus** *White-backed Black Tit*		Wooded mountain gorges of Ethiopia
28 45 029	**Parus funereus** *Dusky Tit*		Forests of Cameroon to western Kenya, Uganda, Sudan
28 45 030	**Parus fasciiventer** *Stripe-breasted Tit*		High mountains of eastern Zaire to Uganda
28 45 031	**Parus fringillinus** *Red-throated Tit*		Masailand steppes of southern Kenya to Tanzania
28 45 032	**Parus rufiventris** *Cinnamon-breasted Tit*		Upland forests of Tanzania to Rhodesia
28 45 033	**Parus major** *Great Tit*		Pine forests of Palearctic and Oriental regions
28 45 034	**Parus bokharensis** *Turkestan Tit*		Highlands of Turkestan to Afghanistan
28 45 035	**Parus monticolus** *Green-backed Tit*		Pakistan Himalayas to Yunnan, Indochina; Taiwan
28 45 036	**Parus nuchalis** *White-winged Black Tit*		Discontinuous semiarid northwest India; southern India
28 45 037	**Parus xanthogenys** *Black-lored Tit*		Himalayas of Garhwal to Yunnan, Indochina
28 45 038	**Parus spilonotus** *Yellow-cheeked Tit*		Himalayas of Nepal to southern China, Thailand
28 45 039	**Parus holsti** *Yellow Tit*		Confined to the mountains of Taiwan
28 45 040	**Parus caeruleus** *Blue Tit*		Widespread western Palearctic region

		Date	Location
28 45 041	**Parus cyanus** *Azure Tit*		Russia to central Europe
28 45 042	**Parus varius** *Varied Tit*		Manchuria; Korea; Japan to Taiwan
28 45 043	**Parus semilarvatus** *White-fronted Tit*		Philippine Islands (Luzon and Mindanao)
28 45 044	**Parus inornatus** *Plain Titmouse*		Western United States to Baja California, extreme northeast Sonora
28 45 045	**Parus atricristatus** *Black-crested Titmouse*		Oklahoma, Texas to southeast Mexico (Veracruz)
28 45 046	**Parus bicolor** *Tufted Titmouse*		Widespread eastern United States
28 45 047	**Melanochlora sultanea** *Sultan Tit*		Himalayas of Nepal to Indochina; Sumatra; Hainan
28 45 048	**Sylviparus modestus** *Yellow-browed Tit*		Evergreen Himalayan forests of Kashmir to Fukien

FAMILY: SITTIDAE (Nuthatches)

		Location
28 46 001	**Sitta europaea** *Eurasian Nuthatch*	Oak, spruce, pine forests of Palearctic region
28 46 002	**Sitta nagaensis** *Chestnut-vented Nuthatch*	Mountains of Tibet to Fukein, Burma, Annam
28 46 003	**Sitta castanea** *Chestnut-bellied Nuthatch*	Mountains of Baluchistan to Indochina
28 46 004	**Sitta himalayensis** *White-tailed Nuthatch*	Himalayas of Garhwal to Yunnan, Burma, Tonkin
28 46 005	**Sitta victoriae** *White-browed Nuthatch*	Burma (endemic to alpine forests of Mt. Victoria)
28 46 006	**Sitta pygmaea** *Pygmy Nuthatch*	Pine forests of southwest Canada to southern Mexico
28 46 007	**Sitta pusilla** *Brown-headed Nuthatch*	Southeast United States; Grand Bahama Island
28 46 008	**Sitta whiteheadi** *Corsican Nuthatch*	Confined to mountain forests of Corsica
28 46 009	**Sitta ledanti** *Kabylian Nuthatch*	Algeria (discovered in 1976 in Atlas Mountains)
28 46 010	**Sitta yunnanensis** *Yunnan Nuthatch*	Pine forests of western China
28 46 011	**Sitta canadensis** *Red-breasted Nuthatch*	Alaska to southern United States; vagrant northern Mexico

		Date	Location
28 46 012	**Sitta villosa** *Chinese Nuthatch*		Montane forests of China; rare in winter in Korea
28 46 013	**Sitta leucopsis** *White-cheeked Nuthatch*		Mountains of Afghanistan, Kashmir to western China
28 46 014	**Sitta carolinensis** *White-breasted Nuthatch*		Southern Canada to southern Mexico; Baja California
28 46 015	**Sitta krueperi** *Krueper's Nuthatch*		Asia Minor to Transcaspia and Caucasus Mountains
28 46 016	**Sitta neumayer** *Rock Nuthatch*		Balkan Peninsula to the Black Sea
28 46 017	**Sitta tephronota** *Persian Nuthatch*		Pine forests of Iran, Afghanistan, Baluchistan
28 46 018	**Sitta frontalis** *Velvet-fronted Nuthatch*		Widespread Oriental mainland and islands
28 46 019	**Sitta solangiae** *Yellow-billed Nuthatch*		High alpine forests of Tonkin, Annam
28 46 020	**Sitta azurea** *Blue Nuthatch*		Forests of Malaya; Sumatra; Java
28 46 021	**Sitta magna** *Giant Nuthatch*		Forests of southwest China, Burma, Thailand
28 46 022	**Sitta formosa** *Beautiful Nuthatch*		Forests of Sikkim to northern Burma, Laos, Tonkin
28 46 023	**Tichodroma muraria** *Wall Creeper*		Mountain cliffs of Palearctic region

FAMILY: NEOSITTIDAE (Australian Nuthatches)

28 47 001	**Neositta chrysoptera** *Orange-winged Sittella*		Open forests of southeast Queensland to Victoria
28 47 002	**Neositta papuensis** *Papuan Sittella*		Mountain forests of New Guinea
28 47 003	**Neositta pileata** *Black-capped Sittella*		Mainly confined to *mulga* zone of Australia
28 47 004	**Neositta striata** *Striated Sittella*		Open forests of Cape York Peninsula (Australia)
28 47 005	**Neositta leucocephala** *White-headed Sittella*		Coastal southeast Queensland to New South Wales
28 47 006	**Neositta leucoptera** *White-winged Sittella*		Northern Australia (except Cape York Peninsula)
28 47 007	**Daphoenositta miranda** *Pink-faced Nuthatch*		Mountain forests of New Guinea

Date   Location

FAMILY: CERTHIIDAE (Creepers)

28 48 001 **Certhia familiaris**
Brown (Common)   Holarctic forests of northern hemisphere
Creeper

28 48 002 **Certhia brachydactyla**
Short-toed Creeper   Widespread western Palearctic region

28 48 003 **Certhia himalayana**
Himalayan Creeper   Mountains of Nepal, Afghanistan to China, Burma

28 48 004 **Certhia nipalensis**
Nepalese Creeper   Himalayas of Nepal to Assam, Burma

28 48 005 **Certhia discolor**
Sikkim Creeper   Himalayas of Nepal to Yunnan, Indochina, Tonkin

28 48 006 **Salpornis spilonotus**
Spotted Creeper   Africa to Asia south of the Himalayas

FAMILY: RHABDORNITHIDAE (Philippine Creepers)

28 49 001 **Rhabdornis mysticalis**
Stripe-headed Creeper   Widespread throughout Philippine Islands

28 49 002 **Rhabdornis inornatus**
Plain-headed Creeper   Philippines (Samar, Negros, Luzon, Mindanao)

FAMILY: CLIMACTERIDAE (Treecreepers)

28 50 001 **Climacteris erythrops**
Red-browed Treecreeper   Extreme southeast Queensland to Victoria

28 50 002 **Climacteris affinis**
White-browed Treecreeper   *Mulga* and *mallee* zone of southern Australia

28 50 003 **Climacteris picumnus
(melanota)**
Brown Treecreeper   Queensland to Victoria; Tasmania

28 50 004 **Climacteris rufa**
Rufous Treecreeper   Forests, open woodlands of southwestern Australia

28 50 005 **Climacteris melanura
(wellsi)**
Black-tailed Treecreeper   Open forests and woodlands of northern Australia

28 50 006 **Climacteris leucophaea
(placens)**
White-throated   Queensland to Victoria; Tasmania; New Guinea
Treecreeper

	Date	Location

FAMILY: DICAEIDAE (Flowerpeckers)

28 51 001	**Melanocharis arfakiana** *Obscure Berrypecker*	Mountains of New Guinea (known from two specimens)
28 51 002	**Melanocharis nigra** *Black Berrypecker*	New Guinea, Arus and western Papuan Islands
28 51 003	**Melanocharis longicauda** *Mid-mountain Berrypecker*	Mountains of New Guinea
28 51 004	**Melanocharis versteri** *Fan-tailed Berrypecker*	Mountains of New Guinea
28 51 005	**Melanocharis striativentris** *Streaked Berrypecker*	Mountains of New Guinea (except Vogelkop)
28 51 006	**Rhamphocharis crassirostris** *Spotted Berrypecker*	Mountains of New Guinea
28 51 007	**Prionochilus olivaceus** *Olive-backed Flowerpecker*	Widespread throughout the Philippine Islands
28 51 008	**Prionochilus maculatus** *Yellow-breasted Flowerpecker*	Malaya; Sumatra; Borneo
28 51 009	**Prionochilus percussus** *Crimson-breasted Flowerpecker*	Malaya; Java; Sumatra; Borneo
28 51 010	**Prionochilus plateni** *Palawan Flowerpecker*	Balabac, Culion and Palawan Islands
28 51 011	**Prionochilus xanthopygius** *Yellow-rumped Flowerpecker*	Borneo and North Natunas Islands
28 51 012	**Prionochilus thoracicus** *Scarlet-breasted Flowerpecker*	Malay Peninsula; Borneo
28 51 013	**Dicaeum annae** *Flores Flowerpecker*	Confined to Flores Island (Lesser Sundas)
28 51 014	**Dicaeum agile (modestum)** *Thick-billed Flowerpecker*	Widespread Oriental region mainland and islands
28 51 015	**Dicaeum everetti** *Brown-backed Flowerpecker*	Malaya; Borneo; Rhio Archipelago
28 51 016	**Dicaeum aeruginosum** *Striped Flowerpecker*	Widespread Philippine Islands and Palawan Island

		Date	Location
28 51 017	**Dicaeum proprium** *Gray-breasted* *Flowerpecker*		Philippines (known from a single specimen from Mindanao)
28 51 018	**Dicaeum chrysorrheum** *Yellow-vented* *Flowerpecker*		Widespread Oriental region mainland and islands
28 51 019	**Dicaeum melanoxanthum** *Yellow-bellied* *Flowerpecker*		Himalayas of Nepal, Sikkim to Burma, Thailand, Laos
28 51 020	**Dicaeum vincens** *Legge's Flowerpecker*		Rain forests of southwestern Sri Lanka (rare)
28 51 021	**Dicaeum aureolimbatum** *Minahassa Flowerpecker*		Confined to the Celebes Islands
28 51 022	**Dicaeum nigrilore** *Olive-capped* *Flowerpecker*		Philippines (mountains of Mindanao Island)
28 51 023	**Dicaeum anthonyi** *Yellow-crowned* *Flowerpecker*		Philippines (Luzon and Mindanao Islands)
28 51 024	**Dicaeum bicolor** *Bicolored Flowerpecker*		Widespread throughout the Philippine Islands
28 51 025	**Dicaeum quadricolor** *Four-colored* *Flowerpecker*		Presumed extinct: occurred on Cebu Island (Philippines)
28 51 026	**Dicaeum australe** *Philippine Flowerpecker*		Widespread throughout the Philippine Islands
28 51 027	**Dicaeum retrocinctum** *Mindoro Flowerpecker*		Philippines (endemic Mindoro Island)
28 51 028	**Dicaeum trigonostigma** *Orange-bellied* *Flowerpecker*		Widespread Oriental region mainland and islands
28 51 029	**Dicaeum hypoleucum** *White-bellied* *Flowerpecker*		Widespread throughout the Philippine Islands
28 51 030	**Dicaeum erythrorhynchos** *Pale-billed Flowerpecker*		Sri Lanka; India to Burma, Tenasserim
28 51 031	**Dicaeum concolor (minullum)** *Plain Flowerpecker*		Widespread Oriental region mainland and islands
28 51 032	**Dicaeum pygmaeum** *Pygmy Flowerpecker*		Philippines (Luzon, Mindanao, Balabac, Calamianes, Palawan)
28 51 033	**Dicaeum nehrkorni** *Nehrkorn's Flowerpecker*		Mountains of the Celebes Islands

		Date	Location
28 51 034	**Dicaeum vulneratum** *Moluccan Flowerpecker*		Confined to the Moluccas Islands
28 51 035	**Dicaeum erythrothorax** *Buru Flowerpecker*		Moluccas (confined to Buru Island)
28 51 036	**Dicaeum pectorale** *Olive-crowned Flowerpecker*		New Guinea (Vogelkop and western Papuan Islands)
28 51 037	**Dicaeum eximium** *Bismarck Flowerpecker*		Confined to islands of the Bismarck Archipelago
28 51 038	**Dicaeum aeneum** *Midget Flowerpecker*		Confined to the Solomon Islands
28 51 039	**Dicaeum tristrami** *San Cristobal Flowerpecker*		Solomon Islands (confined to San Cristobal Island)
28 51 040	**Dicaeum igniferum** *Fire-tailed Flowerpecker*		Confined to the Lesser Sunda Islands
28 51 041	**Dicaeum maugei** *Timor Flowerpecker*		Lesser Sundas (confined to Timor Island)
28 51 042	**Dicaeum sanguinolentum** *Javan Fire-breasted Flowerpecker*		Confined to the Island of Java
28 51 043	**Dicaeum hirundinaceum** *Mistletoe Flowerpecker*		Mistletoe zone of Australia; Aru Islands
28 51 044	**Dicaeum celebicum** *Black-sided Flowerpecker*		Mountains of Borneo and Celebes Islands
28 51 045	**Dicaeum monticolum** *Fire-breasted Flowerpecker*		Mountains of Borneo
28 51 046	**Dicaeum ignipectus** *Buff-bellied Flowerpecker*		Widespread Oriental region mainland and islands
28 51 047	**Dicaeum cruentatum** *Scarlet-backed Flowerpecker*		Widespread Oriental region mainland and islands
28 51 048	**Dicaeum trochileum** *Scarlet-headed Flowerpecker*		Borneo; Java; Bali; Kangean; Lombok Islands
28 51 049	**Dicaeum geelvinkianum** *Red-capped Flowerpecker*		New Guinea, islands of Geelvink Bay, D'Entrecastreaux Archipelago
28 51 050	**Oreocharis arfaki** *Tit Berrypecker*		Mountains of New Guinea
28 51 051	**Paramythia montium** *Crested Berrypecker*		High mountains of New Guinea

		Date	Location

28 51 052	**Pardalotus quadragintus** *Forty-spotted Pardalote*	Eucalypt forests of Tansmania and King Island
28 51 053	**Pardalotus punctatus** *Spotted Pardalote*	Forests and woodlands of Australia, Tasmania
28 51 054	**Pardalotus xanthopygus** *Yellow-tailed Pardalote*	*Mallee* of western Australia to New South Wales, Victoria
28 51 055	**Pardalotus rubricatus** *Red-browed Pardalote*	Widespread savanna of Australia
28 51 056	**Pardalotus striatus** *Yellow-tipped Pardalote*	Southeast Queensland to Victoria; Tasmania
28 51 057	**Pardalotus ornatus** *Red-tipped Pardalote*	Southeast Queensland to Victoria
28 51 058	**Pardalotus substriatus** *Striated Pardalote*	Arid Australia (south of the Tropic of Capricorn)
28 51 059	**Pardalotus melanocephalus** *Black-headed Pardalote*	Savanna of northern and eastern Australia

FAMILY: NECTARINIIDAE (Sunbirds)

28 52 001	**Anthreptes gabonicus** *Mouse-brown Sunbird*	Coastal mangroves of Gambia to mouth of the Congo River
28 52 002	**Anthreptes fraseri** **(axillaris)** *Scarlet-tufted Sunbird*	Sierra Leone to Angola, Uganda, Zaire
28 52 003	**Anthreptes reichenowi** *Plain-backed Sunbird*	Lowland evergreen forests of Kenya to Mozambique
28 52 004	**Anthreptes anchietae** *Anchieta's Sunbird*	Angola to Tanzania, Mozambique, Malawi, Zambia
28 52 005	**Anthreptes simplex** *Plain Sunbird*	Malay Peninsula; Sumatra; Borneo
28 52 006	**Anthreptes malacensis** *Brown-throated Sunbird*	Malaya, Indochina; Sundas; Philippines; Celebes
28 52 007	**Anthreptes rhodolaema** *Red-throated Sunbird*	Malay Peninsula; Sumatra; Borneo; Palawan
28 52 008	**Anthreptes singalensis** *Ruby-cheeked Sunbird*	Nepal to Malaya, Indochina; Greater Sundas
28 52 009	**Anthreptes longuemarei** *Violet-backed Sunbird*	Widespread savanna of Africa south of the Sahara
28 52 010	**Anthreptes orientalis** *Eastern Violet-backed Sunbird*	Ethiopian Plateau (possible race *A. longuemarei*))

		Date	Location
28 52 011	**Anthreptes neglectus** *Uluguru Violet-backed Sunbird*		Coastal evergreen forests of Tanzania to Mozambique
28 52 012	**Anthreptes aurantium** *Violet-tailed Sunbird*		Riverine forests of southern Nigeria to lower Congo River
28 52 013	**Anthreptes pallidigaster** *Amani Sunbird*		Lowland forests of eastern Kenya to Tanzania
28 52 014	**Anthreptes pujoli** *Berlioz' Sunbird*		Guinea (known from a single specimen collected 1958)
28 52 015	**Anthreptes rectirostris** *Gray-chinned Sunbird*		Senegal to Angola, western Kenya
28 52 016	**Anthreptes collaris** *Collared Sunbird*		Widespread and common throughout Ethiopian region
28 52 017	**Anthreptes platurus (metallicus)** *Pygmy Sunbird*		Widespread *acacia* belt of Senegal to Arabia
28 52 018	**Hypogramma hypogrammicum (macularia)** *Purple-naped Sunbird*		Southwest China to Malaya, Indochina; Sumatra; Borneo
28 52 019	**Nectarinia seimundi** *Little Green Sunbird*		Sierra Leone to northern Angola, eastern Zaire
28 52 020	**Nectarinia batesi** *Bates' Sunbird*		Widespread Ivory Coast to Zambia
28 52 021	**Nectarinia olivacea** *Olive Sunbird*		Highlands of Africa south of the Sahara
28 52 022	**Nectarinia ursulae** *Ursula's Sunbird*		Cameroon highlands, Obudu and Bamenda Plateaus
28 52 023	**Nectarinia veroxii** *Mouse-colored Sunbird*		Low coastal bush of Somalia to South Africa
28 52 024	**Nectarinia balfouri** *Socotra Sunbird*		Confined to Socotra Island (Indian Ocean)
28 52 025	**Nectarinia reichenbachii** *Reichenbach's Sunbird*		Ghana to northeast Zaire
28 52 026	**Nectarinia hartlaubii** *Principé Island Sunbird*		Common lowlands of Principé Island (Gulf of Guinea)
28 52 027	**Nectarinia newtonii** *Yellow-breasted Sunbird*		Widespread São Thomé Island (Gulf of Guinea)
28 52 028	**Nectarinia thomensis** *São Thomé Giant Sunbird*		São Thomé Island (Gulf of Guinea—rare)
28 52 029	**Nectarinia oritis** *Cameroon Sunbird*		Montane forests of Cameroon and Obudu Plateaus

		Date	Location
28 52 030	**Nectarinia alinae** *Blue-headed Sunbird*		Montane forests of Ruwenzori Mountains and Kivu area
28 52 031	**Nectarinia bannermani** *Bannerman's Sunbird*		Angola to Zambia
28 52 032	**Nectarinia verticalis** *Green-headed Sunbird*		Widespread savanna of Africa south of the Sahara
28 52 033	**Nectarinia cyanolaema** *Blue-throated Sunbird*		Forests of Sierra Leone to Uganda, Angola
28 52 034	**Nectarinia fuliginosa** *Carmelite Sunbird*		Open country of coastal Liberia to Angola
28 52 035	**Nectarinia rubescens** *Green-throated Sunbird*		Forests of Cameroon to Angola, Kenya, Zambia
28 52 036	**Nectarinia amethystina** *Amethyst Sunbird*		Open woodlands of Ethiopia to South Africa
28 52 037	**Nectarinia senegalensis** **(cruentata)** *Scarlet-chested Sunbird*		Common and widespread throughout Africa
28 52 038	**Nectarinia hunteri** *Hunter's Sunbird*		Arid thorn savanna of Somalia, Ethiopia to northeast Tanzania
28 52 039	**Nectarinia adelberti** *Buff-throated Sunbird*		Sierra Leone to the Gold Coast
28 52 040	**Nectarinia zeylonica** *Purple-rumped Sunbird*		India to western Burma
28 52 041	**Nectarinia minima** *Small Sunbird*		Common resident coastal western peninsular India
28 52 042	**Nectarinia sperata** **(brasiliana)** *Purple-throated Sunbird*		Widespread Oriental mainland and islands
28 52 043	**Nectarinia sericea** *Black Sunbird*		Celebes, Moluccas to New Guinea and Bismarck Archipelago
28 52 044	**Nectarinia calcostetha** *Copper-throated Sunbird*		Malaya, Indochina; Greater Sundas; Celebes; Palawan
28 52 045	**Nectarinia dussumieri** *Seychelles Sunbird*		Common throughout the Seychelles Islands
28 52 046	**Nectarinia lotenia** *Loten's Sunbird*		Widespread and endemic to Sri Lanka
28 52 047	**Nectarinia jugularis** *Olive-backed Sunbird*		Southeast Asia to Australasia; Philippines; Sundas
28 52 048	**Nectarinia buettikoferi** *Sumba Sunbird*		Lesser Sunda Islands

		Date	Location

28 52 049	**Nectarinia solaris** *Timor Sunbird*	Lesser Sunda Islands
28 52 050	**Nectarinia asiatica** *Purple Sunbird*	Iran to India, Burma, Thailand, Indochina
28 52 051	**Nectarinia souimanga** *Souimanga Sunbird*	Widespread throughout Madagascar, Aldabra Island
28 52 052	**Nectarinia humbloti** *Humblot's Sunbird*	Confined to the Comoro Islands (Indian Ocean)
28 52 053	**Nectarinia comorensis** *Anjouan Sunbird*	Comoro and Anjouan Islands (Indian Ocean)
28 52 054	**Nectarinia coquerellii** *Mayotte Sunbird*	Comoro Islands (confined to Mayotte Island)
28 52 055	**Nectarinia venusta** *Variable Sunbird*	Common and widespread Africa south of the Sahara
28 52 056	**Nectarinia talatala** *White-bellied Sunbird*	Dry acacia veld of Angola, Mozambique to South Africa
28 52 057	**Nectarinia oustaleti** *Angola Sunbird*	*Brachystegia* woodlands of Angola to Malawi, Tanzania
28 52 058	**Nectarinia fusca** *Dusky Sunbird*	Arid thornbush of southern Angola, Namibia to South Africa
28 52 059	**Nectarinia chalybea** **(gertrudis)** *Southern Double-collared Sunbird*	*Brachystegia* highlands of southern Africa
28 52 060	**Nectarinia afra** *Greater Double-collared Sunbird*	Highlands of Zaire, Uganda to South Africa
28 52 061	**Nectarinia mediocris** **(moreaui)** *Eastern Double-collared Sunbird*	Alpine forests and scrub of Kenya to Rhodesia
28 52 062	**Nectarinia preussi** *Northern Double-collared Sunbird*	Sudan to Uganda, Kenya, Zaire
28 52 063	**Nectarinia neergaardi** *Neergaard's Sunbird*	Coastal bush of Mozambique to Zululand
28 52 064	**Nectarinia chloropygia** *Olive-bellied Sunbird*	Sierra Leone to Angola, Tanzania, the Sudan
28 52 065	**Nectarinia minulla** *Tiny Sunbird*	Ivory Coast to the Semliki Forests of East Africa
28 52 066	**Nectarinia regia** *Regal Sunbird*	Eastern Zaire, Uganda to western Tanzania

		Date	Location
28 52 067	**Nectarinia loveridgei** *Loveridge's Sunbird*		Uluguru Mountain rain forests of Tanzania
28 52 068	**Nectarinia rockefelleri** *Rockefeller's Sunbird*		High mountains of eastern Zaire (west of Lake Kivu)
28 52 069	**Nectarinia violacea** *Orange-breasted Sunbird*		Montane heathlands of Cape Province of South Africa
28 52 070	**Nectarinia habessinica** *Shining Sunbird*		Ethiopia to the Sudan, northern Kenya; Arabia
28 52 071	**Nectarinia bouvieri** *Orange-tufted Sunbird*		Highlands of Cameroon to Zaire, Uganda, Kenya
28 52 072	**Nectarinia osea** *Northern Orange-tufted Sunbird*		Lake Chad to the Sudan, Arabia
28 52 073	**Nectarinia cuprea** *Copper Sunbird*		Open woodlands of Africa south of the Sahara
28 52 074	**Nectarinia tacazze** *Tacazze Sunbird*		Mountains of Ethiopian Plateau to northern Tanzania
28 52 075	**Nectarinia bocagii** *Bocage's Sunbird*		Lowland marshes of central Angola to southern Zaire
28 52 076	**Nectarinia purpureiventris** *Purple-breasted Sunbird*		*Symphonia* zone of Ruwenzori Mountains to eastern Zaire
28 52 077	**Nectarinia shelleyi** *Shelley's Sunbird*		*Brachystegia* woodlands of Malawi and Tanzania
28 52 078	**Nectarinia mariquensis** *Mariqua Sunbird*		Acacia zone of Ethiopia to South Africa
28 52 079	**Nectarinia bifasciata (tsavoensis)** *Purple-banded Sunbird*		Gabon, Angola, Kenya to South Africa
28 52 080	**Nectarinia pembae** *Pemba Sunbird*		Lamu District of eastern Kenya; Pemba Island
28 52 081	**Nectarinia chalcomela** *Violet-breasted Sunbird*		Coastal Somalia to Kenya (rare)
28 52 082	**Nectarinia coccinigaster** *Splendid Sunbird*		Savanna of Senegal to Gabon and the Sudan
28 52 083	**Nectarinia erythrocerca** *Red-chested Sunbird*		Eastern Zaire to the Sudan, Kenya, Uganda, Tanzania
28 52 084	**Nectarinia congensis** *Congo Black-bellied Sunbird*		Forested banks of upper Congo and Ubangi Rivers
28 52 085	**Nectarinia pulchella** *Beautiful Sunbird*		Widespread Senegal to Somalia, Kenya, Tanzania

		Date	Location

28 52 086 Nectarinia nectarinioides
Smaller Black-bellied Sunbird
Ethiopia to Somalia, Tanzania, Uganda, Zaire

28 52 087 Nectarinia famosa
Malachite Sunbird
Highland bamboo zone of Ethiopia to South Africa

28 52 088 Nectarinia johnstoni
Scarlet-tufted Malachite Sunbird
High mountains of eastern Zaire and western Uganda

28 52 089 Nectarinia notata
Madagascar Sunbird
Lowland forests of Madagascar (rare in south); Comoros

28 52 090 Nectarinia johannae
Johanna's Sunbird
Forest edges of Sierra Leone to central Zaire

28 52 091 Nectarinia superba
Superb Sunbird
Forests of Sierra Leone to Angola, Zaire, Uganda

28 52 092 Nectarinia kilimensis
Bronzy Sunbird
Highlands of northeast Zaire, Kenya, Uganda, Tanzania

28 52 093 Nectarinia reichenowi
Golden-winged Sunbird
Highlands of Kenya, Uganda, Tanzania, eastern Zaire

28 52 094 Aethopyga primigenius
Hachisuka's Sunbird
Philippines (endemic to mountains of Mindanao)

28 52 095 Aethopyga boltoni
Apo Sunbird
Philippines (endemic to mountains of Mindanao)

28 52 096 Aethopyga flagrans
Flaming Sunbird
Philippines (Catanduanes, Luzon, Guimaras, Panay, Negros)

28 52 097 Aethopyga pulcherrima
Mountain Sunbird
Mountains of major Philippine Islands

28 52 098 Aethopyga duyvenbodei
Sanghir Sunbird
Confined to Sanghir Islands (north of Celebes)

28 52 099 Aethopyga shelleyi
Lovely Sunbird
Widespread Philippine Islands, Sulu Archipelago

28 52 100 Aethopyga gouldiae
Gould's Sunbird
Himalayas of Kashmir to Sikiang, Burma, Indochina

28 52 101 Aethopyga nipalensis
Nepal Sunbird
Himalayas of Kashmir to Burma, Thailand, Annam, Laos

28 52 102 Aethopyga eximia
Kuhl's Sunbird
Mountains of Island of Java

28 52 103 Aethopyga christinae
Fork-tailed Sunbird
Southeast China to Indochina; Hainan

		Date	Location

28 52 104 Aethopyga saturata
Black-throated Sunbird   Himalayas of Kashmir to Yunnan, Indochina

28 52 105 Aethopyga siparaja
Yellow-backed Sunbird   Widespread Oriental region mainland and islands

28 52 106 Aethopyga mystacalis
Scarlet Sunbird   Malay Peninsula; Java; Sumatra; Borneo

28 52 107 Aethopyga ignicauda
Fire-tailed Sunbird   Himalayas of Kashmir to Yunnan, northeast Burma

**28 52 108 Arachnothera
longirostra**
Little Spiderhunter   Widespread Oriental region mainland and islands

**28 52 109 Arachnothera
crassirostris**
Thick-billed Spiderhunter   Malay Peninsula; Sumatra; Borneo

28 52 110 Arachnothera robusta
Long-billed Spiderhunter   Malay Peninsula; Java; Sumatra; Borneo

28 52 111 Arachnothera flavigaster
Spectacled Spiderhunter   Malay Peninsula; Sumatra; Borneo

**28 52 112 Arachnothera
chrysogenys**
Yellow-eared Spiderhunter   Malay Peninsula; Java; Sumatra; Borneo

**28 52 113 Arachnothera clarae
(philippensis)**
Naked-faced Spiderhunter   Philippines (Luzon, Leyte, Samar, Mindanao)

28 52 114 Arachnothera affinis
*Gray-breasted
Spiderhunter*   Malay Peninsula; Java; Sumatra; Borneo

28 52 115 Arachnothera magna
Streaked Spiderhunter   Himalayas of India to Yunnan, Malaya, Indochina

28 52 116 Arachnothera everetti
Kinabalu Spiderhunter   Confined to mountains of north Borneo

28 52 117 Arachnothera juliae
Whitehead's Spiderhunter   Confined to mountains of Borneo

FAMILY: ZOSTEROPIDAE (White-eyes)

28 53 001 Zosterops erythropleura
*Chestnut-flanked White-
eye*   East Asia to Southeast Asia

**28 53 002 Zosterops japonica
(simplex)**
Japanese White-eye   East Asia to southeast Asia; Philippines; Hainan,
Taiwan

		Date	Location
28 53 003	**Zosterops palpebrosa** *Oriental White-eye*		Widespread Oriental region mainland and islands
28 53 004	**Zosterops ceylonensis** *Ceylon Hill White-eye*		Common and endemic to mountain forests of Sri Lanka
28 53 005	**Zosterops conspicillata** *Bridled White-eye*		Common throughout islands of Micronesia
28 53 006	**Zosterops salvadorii** *Engano White-eye*		Confined to Engano Island (off Sumatra)
28 53 007	**Zosterops atricapilla** *Black-capped White-eye*		Mountains of Malaya, Sumatra and Borneo
28 53 008	**Zosterops everetti** *Everett's White-eye*		Submontane forests of Malaya; Borneo; Philippines
28 53 009	**Zosterops nigrorum** *Philippine Yellow White-eye*		Widespread throughout the Philippine Islands
28 53 010	**Zosterops montana** *Mountain White-eye*		Mountains of Philippine Islands and Palawan
28 53 011	**Zosterops wallacei** *Wallace's White-eye*		Confined to the Lesser Sunda Islands
28 53 012	**Zosterops flava** *Javan White-eye*		Confined to Island of Java; accidental Borneo
28 53 013	**Zosterops chloris** **(citrinella)** *Pale Silver-eye*		Moluccas to the Arus, islands in Torres Strait
28 53 014	**Zosterops consobrinorum** *Peninsular White-eye*		Southeast Peninsula of the Celebes Islands
28 53 015	**Zosterops grayi** *Great Kai White-eye*		Southern Moluccas (confined to Great Kai Island)
28 53 016	**Zosterops uropygialis** *Little Kai White-eye*		Southern Moluccas (confined to LIttle Kai Island)
28 53 017	**Zosterops anomala** *Celebes White-eye*		Confined to the Celebes Islands
28 53 018	**Zosterops atriceps** *Moluccan White-eye*		Moluccas (Halmahera, Batjan, Morotai Islands)
28 53 019	**Zosterops atrifrons** **(minor)** *Black-fronted White-eye*		Mountains of New Guinea and the Moluccas
28 53 020	**Zosterops mysorensis** *Biak White-eye*		Confined to Biak Island (off New Guinea)
28 53 021	**Zosterops fuscicapilla** *Yellow-bellied Mountain White-eye*		Mountains of western New Guinea

		Date	Location
28 53 022	**Zosterops buruensis** *Buru White-eye*		Moluccas (confined to Buru Island)
28 53 023	**Zosterops kuehni** *Amboina White-eye*		Moluccas (confined to Amboina Island)
28 53 024	**Zosterops novaeguineae** *New Guinea Mountain White-eye*		Mountains of New Guinea and the Aru Islands
28 53 025	**Zosterops metcalfii** *Yellow-throated White-eye*		Solomons (Shortlands, Choiseul, Ysabel, Florida Islands)
28 53 026	**Zosterops natalis** *Christmas Island White-eye*		Confined to Christmas Island (southwest Pacific)
28 53 027	**Zosterops lutea** *Mangrove White-eye*		Mangroves of coastal northern Australia
28 53 028	**Zosterops griseotincta** *Louisiades White-eye*		Small islands east of New Guinea and Solomon Islands
28 53 029	**Zosterops rennelliana** *Rennell White-eye*		Solomon Islands (confined to Rennell Island)
28 53 030	**Zosterops vellalavella** *Vella Lavella White-eye*		Vella Lavella Island (New Georgia group of the Solomons)
28 53 031	**Zosterops luteirostris** *Ganonga White-eye*		Ganonga Island (New Georgia group of the Solomons)
28 53 032	**Zosterops rendovae** *Central Solomons White-eye*		Central Solomon Islands (except Kulambangra)
28 53 033	**Zosterops meyeni** *Philippine White-eye*		Common throughout the Philippine Islands
28 53 034	**Zosterops murphyi** *Kulambangra White-eye*		Solomon Islands (mountains of Kulambangra Island)
28 53 035	**Zosterops ugiensis** *Gray-throated White-eye*		Solomons (mountains of Bougainville, Guadalcanal, San Cristobal)
28 53 036	**Zosterops stresemanni** *Malaita White-eye*		Solomon Islands (widespread Malaita Island)
28 53 037	**Zosterops sanctaecrucis** *Santa Cruz White-eye*		Solomon Islands (common and widespread Santa Cruz Island)
28 53 038	**Zosterops samoensis** *Samoan White-eye*		Samoa (confined to mountains of Savaii Island)
28 53 039	**Zosterops explorator** *Layard's White-eye*		Hill forests of larger Fiji Islands

	Date	Location
28 53 040 **Zosterops flavifrons** *Yellow-fronted White-eye*		Widespread New Hebrides and Banks Islands
28 53 041 **Zosterops minuta** *Small Lifu White-eye*		New Caledonia (confined to Lifu Island)
28 53 042 **Zosterops xanthochroa** *Green-backed White-eye*		Mountains of New Caledonia and Maré Island
28 53 043 **Zosterops lateralis** *Gray-backed White-eye*		Fiji Islands to Australia, New Zealand
28 53 044 **Zosterops strenua** *Lord Howe White-eye*		Extinct since about 1928. Inhabited Lord Howe Island
28 53 045 **Zosterops tenuirostris** *Slender-billed White-eye*		Norfolk Island (north of New Zealand)
28 53 046 **Zosterops albogularis** *Norfolk Island White-eye*		Norfolk Island (north of New Zealand)
28 53 047 **Zosterops inornata** *Large Lifu White-eye*		Forests of New Caledonia
28 53 048 **Zosterops cinerea** *Gray-brown White-eye*		Caroline Islands (Ponape, Kusaie, Palau Islands)
28 53 049 **Zosterops abyssinica** *White-breasted White-eye*		Red Sea environs
28 53 050 **Zosterops pallida** *Pale White-eye*		Widespread Ethiopia to South Africa
28 53 051 **Zosterops senegalensis** *Yellow White-eye*		Africa south of the Sahara
28 53 052 **Zosterops virens** *Green White-eye*		Widespread Africa south of the Sahara
28 53 053 **Zosterops borbonica** *Mascarene White-eye*		Mauritius and Bourbon Islands (Indian Ocean)
28 53 054 **Zosterops ficedulina** *Principe Island White-eye*		Principé and São Thomé Islands (Gulf of Guinea)
28 53 055 **Zosterops griseovirescens** *Annobon White-eye*		Confined to Annobon Island (Gulf of Guinea)
28 53 056 **Zosterops maderaspatana** *Madagascar White-eye*		Madagascar and Aldabra Islands
28 53 057 **Zosterops mayottensis** *Mayotte White-eye*		Comoro Islands (Indian Ocean)
28 53 058 **Zosterops modesta** *Seychelles White-eye*		Seychelles (confined to Mahe Island—endangered)
28 53 059 **Zosterops mouroniensis** *Comoro White-eye*		Comoro Islands (Indian Ocean)
28 53 060 **Zosterops olivacea** *Mauritius White-eye*		Known only from Mauritius Island (Indian Ocean)

		Date	Location
28 53 061	**Zosterops chloronothus** _Reunion White-eye_		Reunion Island (possible race _Z. olivacea_)
28 53 062	**Zosterops vaughani** _Pemba White-eye_		Confined to Pemba Island (off Tanzania)
28 53 063	**Speirops brunnea** _Fernando Po Speirops_		Fernando Po Island (Gulf of Guinea—endangered)
28 53 064	**Speirops leucophaea** _Principé Island Speirops_		Principé Island (Gulf of Guinea)
28 53 065	**Speirops lugubris** _Black-capped Speirops_		Cameroon Mountain; São Thomé Island (Gulf of Guinea)
28 53 066	**Woodfordia superciliosa** _Woodford's White-eye_		Solomon Islands (confined to Rennell Island)
28 53 067	**Woodfordia lacertosa** _Sanford's White-eye_		Confined to Santa Cruz Island (southwest Pacific)
28 53 068	**Rukia palauensis** _Palau White-eye_		Micronesia (confined to Palau Island)
28 53 069	**Rukia oleaginea** _Large Yap White-eye_		Micronesia (confined to Yap Island)
28 53 070	**Rukia ruki** _Large Truk White-eye_		Micronesia (confined to Truk Island—endangered)
28 53 071	**Rukia longirostra (sanfordi)** _Large Ponape White-eye_		Micronesia (confined to Ponape Island—endangered)
28 53 072	**Tephrozosterops stalkeri** _Stalker's White-eye_		Moluccas (confined to mountains of Ceram Island)
28 53 073	**Madanga ruficollis** _Buru Mountain White-eye_		Southern Moluccas (mountains of Buru Island)
28 53 074	**Lophozosterops pinaiae** _Ceram White-eye_		Moluccas (mountains of Ceram Island)
28 53 075	**Lophozosterops goodfellowi** _Goodfellow's White-eye_		Philippines (confined to Mindanao Island)
28 53 076	**Lophozosterops squamiceps** _Celebes Gray-throated White-eye_		Mountains of the Celebes Islands
28 53 077	**Lophozosterops javanica** _Javan Gray-throated White-eye_		Mountains of Java and Bali

	Date	Location

28 53 078 Lophozosterops superciliaris
Sunda White-eye — Lesser Sundas (mountains of Flores and Sumbawa Islands)

28 53 079 Lophozosterops dohertyi
Doherty's White-eye — Lesser Sundas (mountains of Flores and Sumbawa Islands)

28 53 080 Oculocincta squamifrons
Pygmy White-eye — Montane moss forests of Borneo

28 53 081 Heleia muelleri
Timor White-eye — Lesser Sundas (lowlands of western Timor Island)

28 53 082 Heleia crassirostris
Sunda Mountain White-eye — Lesser Sundas (mountains of Flores and Sumbawa Islands)

28 53 083 Chlorocharis emiliae
Mountain Black-eye — High montane resident of Borneo

28 53 084 Hypocryptadius cinnamomeus
Cinnamon White-eye — Philippines (confined to Mindanao Island)

FAMILY: MELIPHAGIDAE (Honeyeaters)

28 54 001 Timeliopsis fulvigula
Mountain Straight-billed Honeyeater — Mid-mountains of New Guinea

28 54 002 Timeliopsis griseigula
Lowland Straight-billed Honeyeater — Lowland forests of southeast and northwest New Guinea

28 54 003 Melilestes megarhynchus
Long-billed Honeyeater — New Guinea and adjacent islands

28 54 004 Melilestes bougainvillei
Bougainville Honeyeater — Solomon Islands (mountains of Bougainville Island)

28 54 005 Toxohamphus novaeguineae
Yellow-bellied Longbill — New Guinea, Arus, Japen and western Papuan Islands

28 54 006 Toxorhamphus poliopterus
Slaty-chinned Longbill — Mountains of New Guinea (except for the Voeglkop)

28 54 007 Oedistoma iliolophum
Gray-bellied Longbill — New Guinea, western Papuan Islands, d'Entrecasteaux Archipelago

		Date	Location
28 54 008	**Oedistoma pygmaeum** *Pygmy Longbill*		New Guinea and adjacent islands
28 54 009	**Glycichaera fallax (claudi)** *Green-backed Honeyeater*		Northeast Australia, New Guinea, western Papuan Islands
28 54 010	**Lichmera lombokia** *Lombok Honeyeater*		Lesser Sundas (confined to Lombok Island)
28 54 011	**Lichmera argentauris** *Olive Honeyeater*		Moluccas and islands of western New Guinea region
28 54 012	**Lichmera indistincta** *Brown Honeyeater*		Australia, New Guinea, Arus, Lesser Sundas
28 54 013	**Lichmera incana** *Silver-eared Honeyeater*		New Caledonia, New Hebrides, Loyalty Islands
28 54 014	**Lichmera alboauricularis** *White-eared Honeyeater*		Northern and southeast New Guinea
28 54 015	**Lichmera squamata** *Scaled Honeyeater*		Moluccas (confined to Tanimbar Island)
28 54 016	**Lichmera deningeri** *Buru Honeyeater*		Moluccas (Mountains of Buru Island)
28 54 017	**Lichmera monticola** *Ceram Honeyeater*		Moluccas (mountains of Ceram Island)
28 54 018	**Lichmera flavicans** *Timor Honeyeater*		Lesser Sundas (confined to Timor Island)
28 54 019	**Lichmera notabilis** *Wetar Honeyeater*		Lesser Sundas (confined to Wetar Island)
28 54 020	**Lichmera cockerelli** *White-streaked Honeyeater*		Tea-tree swamps of Cape York Peninsula of Australia
28 54 021	**Myzomela blasii** *Amboina Honeyeater*		Moluccas (Ceram and Amboina Islands)
28 54 022	**Myzomela albigula** *White-chinned Myzomela*		Islands off extreme southeast New Guinea
28 54 023	**Myzomela cineracea** *Bismarck Honeyeater*		Confined to New Britain Island (Bismarck Archipelago)
28 54 024	**Myzomela eques** *Red-spot Myzomela*		New Guinea, New Britain and Rook Islands
28 54 025	**Myzomela obscura** *Dusky Honeyeater*		Northern Australia, New Guinea, Arus, Moluccas
28 54 026	**Myzomela cruentata** *Red Myzomela*		Mid-mountain forests of Bismarck Archipelago, New Guinea

		Date	Location
28 54 027	**Myzomela nigrita** *Black Honeyeater*		New Guinea, Bismarck Archipelago, Solomon Islands
28 54 028	**Myzomela pulchella** *New Ireland Honeyeater*		Confined to New Ireland Island (Bismarck Archipelago)
28 54 029	**Myzomela kuehni** *Wetar Myzomela*		Lesser Sundas (confined to Wetar Island)
28 54 030	**Myzomela erythrocephala** *Red-headed Myzomela*		Mangroves of northern Australia, New Guinea, Sumba Islands
28 54 031	**Myzomela adolphinae** *Mountain Myzomela*		Mid-mountains of New Guinea
28 54 032	**Myzomela sanguinolenta** *Scarlet Myzomela*		Queensland to Victoria; Celebes to New Caledonia
28 54 033	**Myzomela cardinalis** *Cardinal Honeyeater*		Samoa to New Hebrides, Loyalty, Solomons
28 54 034	**Myzomela chermesina** *Rotuma Honeyeater*		Celebes (confined to Rotuma Island)
28 54 035	**Myzomela sclateri** *Sclater's Honeyeater*		Small islands off New Guinea and New Britain
28 54 036	**Myzomela lafargei** *Scarlet-naped Honeyeater*		Widespread throughout the Solomon Islands
28 54 037	**Myzomela melanocephala** *Black-headed Myzomela*		Solomon Islands (Florida, Savo, Guadalcanal)
28 54 038	**Myzomela eichhorni** *Eichhorn's Myzomela*		Widespread throughout the major Solomon Islands
28 54 039	**Myzomela malaitae** *Malaita Myzomela*		Solomon islands (confined to Malaita Island)
28 54 040	**Myzomela tristrami** *Tristram's Myzomela*		Solomons (Ugi, San Cristobal and Santa Ana Islands)
28 54 041	**Myzomela jugularis** *Orange-breasted Myzomela*		Common throughout the Fiji Islands
28 54 042	**Myzomela erythromelas** *New Britain Myzomela*		Confined to New Britain Island (Bismarck Archipelago)
28 54 043	**Myzomela vulnerata** *Timor Myzomela*		Lesser Sundas (confined to Timor Island)
28 54 044	**Myzomela rosenbergii** *Black-and-red Myzomela*		Mountains of New Guinea and Goodenough Island

		Date	Location
28 54 045	**Certhionyx niger** *Black Honeyeater*		Arid savanna throughout Australia
28 54 046	**Certhionyx variegatus** *Pied Honeyeater*		Arid savanna throughout Australia
28 54 047	**Meliphaga mimikae** *Large Spot-breasted Meliphaga*		Central and eastern New Guinea
28 54 048	**Meliphaga montana** *White-eared Mountain Meliphaga*		Widespread mountains of New Guinea
28 54 049	**Meliphaga orientalis** *Small Spot-breasted Meliphaga*		Waigeu Island and mid-mountains of New Guinea
28 54 050	**Meliphaga albonotata** *White-marked Meliphaga*		Lowland forests of New Guinea
28 54 051	**Meliphaga aruensis** *Puff-backed Meliphaga*		Forests of New Guinea and adjacent islands
28 54 052	**Meliphaga analoga** *Mimic Meliphaga*		New Guinea, Arus and western Papuan Islands
28 54 053	**Meliphaga vicina** *Louisiades Meliphaga*		Lowlands of Tagula Island (Louisiade Archipelago)
28 54 054	**Meliphaga gracillis** *Slender-billed Honeyeater*		Open forests of Queensland, New Guinea, Aru Islands
28 54 055	**Meliphaga notata** *Lesser Lewin Honeyeater*		Lowland rain forests of Cape York Peninsula of Australia
28 54 056	**Meliphaga flavirictus** *Yellow-gaped Meliphaga*		Lowlands and submontane forests of New Guinea
28 54 057	**Meliphaga lewinii** *Lewin Honeyeater*		Australia (rain forests of Queensland to Victoria)
28 54 058	**Meliphaga flava** *Yellow Honeyeater*		Australia (open forests of northern Queensland)
28 54 059	**Meliphaga albilineata** *White-lined Honeyeater*		Australia (confined to Arnhem Land, Northern Territory)
28 54 060	**Meliphaga virescens** *Singing Honeyeater*		Australia, lowlands of New Guinea and adjacent islands
28 54 061	**Meliphaga versicolor** *Varied Honeyeater*		Mangroves of Queensland, New Guinea and adjacent islands
28 54 062	**Meliphaga fasciogularis** *Mangrove Honeyeater*		Australia (mangroves of Queensland and New South Wales)

		Date	Location
28 54 063	**Meliphaga inexpectata** *Guadalcanal Honeyeater*		Solomon Islands (confined to Guadalcanal)
28 54 064	**Meliphaga fusca** *Fuscous Honeyeater*		Australia (open forests of Queensland to Victoria)
28 54 065	**Meliphaga flavescens** *Yellow-tinted Honeyeater*		Northern Australia; southeast New Guinea
28 54 066	**Meliphaga plumula** *Yellow-fronted Honeyeater*		Dry woodlands throughout Australia
28 54 067	**Meliphaga chrysops** *Yellow-faced Honeyeater*		Queensland to Victoria; adjacent South Australia
28 54 068	**Meliphaga cratitia** *Purple-gaped Honeyeater*		*Mallee* of southern Australia
28 54 069	**Meliphaga keartlandi** *Gray-headed Honeyeater*		Arid savanna of northern Australia
28 54 070	**Meliphaga penicillata** *White-plumed Honeyeater*		Riverine woodlands throughout Australia
28 54 071	**Meliphaga ornata** *Yellow-plumed Honeyeater*		*Mallee* woodlands of southern Australia
28 54 072	**Meliphaga reticulata** *Reticulated Honeyeater*		Lesser Sundas (confined to Timor Island)
28 54 073	**Meliphaga leucotis** *White-eared Honeyeater*		Queensland to Victoria; southwestern Australia
28 54 074	**Meliphaga flavicollis** *Yellow-throated* *Honeyeater*		Tasmania and islands of Bass Strait
28 54 075	**Meliphaga melanops** *Yellow-tufted Honeyeater*		Open forests of woodlands of Queensland to Victoria
28 54 076	**Meliphaga cassidix** *Helmeted Honeyeater*		Southern Victoria (Australia—rare and endangered)
28 54 077	**Meliphaga unicolor** *White-gaped Honeyeater*		Mangroves and riverine forests of northern Australia
28 54 078	**Meliphaga flaviventer** **(chrysotis)** *Tawny-breasted* *Honeyeater*		Mangroves of Australia, New Guinea, Aru Islands
28 54 079	**Meliphaga polygramma** *Spotted Honeyeater*		New Guinea and adjacent islands
28 54 080	**Meliphaga macleayana** *Macleay's Honeyeater*		Australia (rain forests of Cape York Peninsula)
28 54 081	**Meliphaga frenata** *Bridled Honeyeater*		Australia (rain forests of Cape York Peninsula)
28 54 082	**Meliphaga subfrenata** *Black-fronted Honeyeater*		Vogelkop, Huon Mountains to southeast New Guinea

		Date	Location
28 54 083	**Meliphaga obscura** *Obscure Honeyeater*		Vogelkop Mountains to southeast New Guinea
28 54 084	**Oreornis chrysogenys** *Orange-cheeked Honeyeater*		Timberline of Snow Mountains of New Guinea
28 54 085	**Foulehaio carunculata** *Wattled Honeyeater*		Samoa, Fiji Islands and Lau Archipelago
28 54 086	**Foulehaio provocator** *Kandavu Honeyeater*		Fiji Islands (endemic to Kandavu Island)
28 54 087	**Cleptornis marchei** *Golden Honeyeater*		Marianas (endemic to Saipan Island)
28 54 088	**Apalopteron familiare** *Bonin Island Honeyeater*		Endemic to Bonin Island (off Chinese coast)
28 54 089	**Melithreptus brevirostris** *Brown-headed Honeyeater*		Southeast Queensland to Victoria, western Australia
28 54 090	**Melithreptus lunatus** *White-naped Honeyeater*		Queensland to Victoria; southwestern Australia
28 54 091	**Melithreptus albogularis** *White-throated Honeyeater*		Northern tropical Australia; southern New Guinea
28 54 092	**Melithreptus affinis** *Black-headed Honeyeater*		Open forests of Tasmania, islands of Bass Strait
28 54 093	**Melithreptus gularis** *Black-chinned Honeyeater*		Queensland to Victoria; adjacent South Australia
28 54 094	**Melithreptus laetior** *Golden-backed Honeyeater*		Open forests and woodlands of northern Australia
28 54 095	**Melithreptus validirostris** *Strong-billed Honeyeater*		Tasmania and islands of Bass Strait
28 54 096	**Entomyzon cyanotis** *Blue-faced Honeyeater*		Eastern and northern Australia; southeast New Guinea
28 54 097	**Notiomystis cincta** *Stitchbird*		New Zealand (Little Barrier Island—endangered)
28 54 098	**Pycnopygius ixoides** *Olive-brown Honeyeater*		Widespread lowland forests of New Guinea
28 54 099	**Pycnopygius cinereus** *Gray Honeyeater*		Mid-mountains of New Guinea
28 54 100	**Pycnopygius stictocephalus** *Streak-capped Honeyeater*		Lowlands of New Guinea, Salawati and Aru Islands
28 54 101	**Philemon meyeri** *Meyer's Friarbird*		Lowlands of eastern New Guinea
28 54 102	**Philemon brassi** *Brass's Friarbird*		New Guinea (lowlands of Idenburg River)

		Date	Location
28 54 103	**Philemon citreogularis** *Little Friarbird*		Northeast Australia, southern New Guinea, adjacent islands
28 54 104	**Philemon inornatus** *Timor Friarbird*		Lesser Sundas (confined to Timor Island)
28 54 105	**Philemon gilolensis** *Gilolo Friarbird*		Moluccas (Batjan, Halmahera, Morotai Islands)
28 54 106	**Philemon fuscicapillus** *Morotai Friarbird*		Moluccas (confined to Morotai Island)
28 54 107	**Philemon subcorniculatus** *Ceram Friarbird*		Moluccas (confined to Ceram Island)
28 54 108	**Philemon moluccensis** *Moluccan Friarbird*		Moluccas (Buru, Kai, Tanimber Islands)
28 54 109	**Philemon buceroides (gordoni)** *Sandstone Friarbird*		Coastal northern Australia (Arnhem Land) to Timor Island
28 54 110	**Philemon novaeguineae (yorki)** *Helmeted Friarbird*		Cape York Peninsula; New Guinea and adjacent islands
28 54 111	**Philemon cockerelli** *Bismarck Friarbird*		Confined to New Britain Island (Bismarck Archipelago)
28 54 112	**Philemon eichhorni** *Eichhorn's Honeyeater*		Confined to New Ireland Island (Bismarck Archipelago)
28 54 113	**Philemon albitorques** *Admiralty Island Honeyeater*		Confined to the Admiralty Islands
28 54 114	**Philemon argenticeps** *Silver-crowned Friarbird*		Open forest and woodlands of tropical northern Australia
28 54 115	**Philemon corniculatus** *Noisy (Bald) Friarbird*		Queensland to Victoria; southeast New Guinea
28 54 116	**Philemon diemenensis** *New Caledonia Friarbird*		Forests of New Caledonia, Maré and Lifu Islands
28 54 117	**Ptiloprora plumbea** *Leaden Honeyeater*		Mid-mountain forests of New Guinea (rare)
28 54 118	**Ptiloprora meekiana** *Meek's Streaked Honeyeater*		Mid-mountains of New Guinea
28 54 119	**Ptiloprora erythropleura** *Red-sided Streaked Honeyeater*		Mid-mountain forests of western New Guinea

		Date	Location
28 54 120	**Ptiloprora guisei** *Red-backed Honeyeater*		Mid-mountains of central and western New Guinea
28 54 121	**Ptiloprora perstriata** *Black-backed Streaked Honeyeater*		Central mountains of New Guinea (except Vogelkop)
28 54 122	**Melidectes fuscus** *Sooty Honeyeater*		High mountains of New Guinea (except Vogelkop, Huon)
28 54 123	**Melidectes princeps** *Long-bearded Honeyeater*		High mountains of central highlands of New Guinea
28 54 124	**Melidectes nouhuysi** *Short-bearded Honeyeater*		Timberline of Snow Mountains of New Guinea
28 54 125	**Melidectes ochromelas** *Mid-mountain Melidectes*		Mid-mountains of New Guinea
28 54 126	**Melidectes leucostephes** *White-fronted Melidectes*		Vogelkop Mountains of New Guinea
28 54 127	**Melidectes belfordi (foersteri)** *Belford's Melidectes*		Widespread mountains of New Guinea
28 54 128	**Melidectes torquatus** *Cinnamon-breasted Melidectes*		Mid-mountains of New Guinea
28 54 129	**Melipotes gymnops** *Arfak Melipotes*		Vogelkop and Wondiwol Mountains of New Guinea
28 54 130	**Melipotes fumigatus** *Common Melipotes*		Widespread mountains of New Guinea
28 54 131	**Melipotes ater** *Huon Melipotes*		Mountain forests of Huon Peninsula of New Guinea
28 54 132	**Vosea whitemanensis** *New Britain Honeyeater*		Whiteman Mountains of New Britain Island
28 54 133	**Myza celebensis** *Celebes Honeyeater*		Mountains of the Celebes Islands
28 54 134	**Myza sarasinorum** *Mengkoka Honeyeater*		Mountains of the Celebes Islands
28 54 135	**Meliarchus sclateri** *San Cristobal Honeyeater*		Solomons (mountains of San Cristobal Island)
28 54 136	**Gymnomyza viridis** *Giant Forest Honeyeater*		Fiji Islands (Viti Levu, Vanua Levu, Taviuni)
28 54 137	**Gymnomyza samoensis** *Mao Honeyeater*		Samoan Islands (Savii, Upolu, Tutuila)
28 54 138	**Gymnomyza aubryana** *Crow Honeyeater*		Mountain forests of New Caledonia

		Date	Location
28 54 139	**Moho braccatus** *Kauai Oo*		Hawaii (Alakai Swamp of Kauai—endangered)
28 54 140	**Moho bishopi** *Molokai Oo*		Hawaii (Molokai Island—presumed extinct since 1904)
28 54 141	**Moho apicalis** *Oahu Oo*		Extinct since about 1837. Inhabited Oahu, Hawaiian Islands
28 54 142	**Moho nobilis** *Hawaii Oo*		Big Island of Hawaii (presumed extinct since turn of the century)
28 54 143	**Chaetoptila augustipluma** *Kioea*		Extinct since about 1859. Inhabited big Island of Hawaii
28 54 144	**Phylidonyris pyrrhoptera** *Crescent Honeyeater*		Coastal southeast Australia, Tasmania, Bass Strait islands
28 54 145	**Phylidonyris novaehollandiae** *Yellow-winged Honeyeater*		Coastal New South Wales to Western Australia; Tasmania
28 54 146	**Phylidonyris nigra** *White-cheeked Honeyeater*		Coastal heathlands of west, south, and eastern Australia
28 54 147	**Phylidonyris albifrons** *White-fronted Honeyeater*		Arid woodlands of western and southern Australia
28 54 148	**Phylidonyris melanops** *Tawny-crowned Honeyeater*		Coastal southern Australia; Tasmania
28 54 149	**Phylidonyris undulata** *Barred Honeyeater*		Confined to New Caledonia Island
28 54 150	**Phylidonyris notabilis** *White-bellied Honeyeater*		New Hebrides and Banks Islands
28 54 151	**Ramsayornis fasciatus** *Bar-breasted Honeyeater*		Australia (Fitzroy River to Queensland)
28 54 152	**Ramsayornis modestus** *Modest Honeyeater*		Mangroves of Queensland, New Guinea, adjacent islands
28 54 153	**Plectorhyncha lanceolata** *Striped Honeyeater*		Queensland to New South Wales; adjacent South Australia
28 54 154	**Conopophila whitei** *Gray Honeyeater*		Arid scrub of western Australia

		Date	Location
28 54 155	**Conopophila albogularis** *Rufous-banded* *Honeyeater*		Arnhem Land, Cape York Peninsula to New Guinea, Arus
28 54 156	**Conopophila rufogularis** *Red-throated Honeyeater*		Riverine forests and woodlands of northern Australia
28 54 157	**Conopophila picta** *Painted Honeyeater*		Open forests of Northern Territory to Victoria
28 54 158	**Zanthomyza phrygia** *Regent Honeyeater*		Queensland to Victoria; adjacent South Australia
28 54 159	**Cissomela pectoralis** *Banded Honeyeater*		Forests and woodlands of coastal northern Australia
28 54 160	**Acanthorhynchus** **tenuirostris** *Eastern Spinebill*		Queensland to Victoria; Tasmania; islands of Bass Strait
28 54 161	**Acanthorhynchus** **superciliosus** *Western Spinebill*		Extreme coastal southwestern Australia
28 54 162	**Manorina melanophrys** *Bell Miner*		Coastal southeast Queensland to Victoria
28 54 163	**Manorina** **melanocephala** *Noisy Miner*		Queensland to Victoria; Tasmania; islands of Bass Strait
28 54 164	**Manorina flavigula** *White-rumped Miner*		*Mallee*, heath regions throughout Australia
28 54 165	**Manorina melanotis** **(obscura)** *Dusky Miner*		Victoria to South Australia
28 54 166	**Anthornis melanura** *New Zealand Bellbird*		Forests throughout New Zealand and adjacent islands
28 54 167	**Anthochaera rufogularis** *Spine-cheeked* *Honeyeater*		Woodlands and desert scrub throughout Australia
28 54 168	**Anthochaera** **chrysoptera** *Little Wattlebird*		Queensland to Victoria; Tasmania; southwest Australia
28 54 169	**Anthochaera** **carunculata** *Red Wattlebird*		New South Wales to Western Australia
28 54 170	**Anthochaera paradoxa** *Yellow Wattlebird*		Eucalypt forests of Tasmania, islands of Bass Strait

		Date	Location

28 54 171 **Prosthemadera novaeseelandiae**
Tui
Forests of New Zealand, Auckland, Kermadec, Chatham Islands

28 54 172 **Promerops cafer**
Cape Sugarbird
Mountains of Cape Province of South Africa

28 54 173 **Promerops gurneyi**
Gurney's Sugarbird
Rhodesia to Cape Province of South Africa

FAMILY: EMBERIZIDAE (Buntings, Sparrows and Allies)

28 55 001 **Melophus lathami**
Crested Bunting
Pakistan to southern China, Indochina; Taiwan

28 55 002 **Latoucheornis siemsseni**
Chinese Bunting
Mountains of Kansu to Szechwan (rare)

28 55 003 **Emberiza calandra**
Corn Bunting
Widespread Palearctic region

28 55 004 **Emberiza citrinella**
Yellowhammer
Widespread Palearctic region

28 55 005 **Emberiza leucocephala**
Pine Bunting
Widespread eastern Palearctic region

28 55 006 **Emberiza cia**
Rock Bunting
Widespread Palearctic, Oriental region mainland

28 55 007 **Emberiza cioides**
Meadow Bunting
Widespread eastern Palearctic region

28 55 008 **Emberiza jankowskii**
Jankowski's Bunting
Ussuriland to Manchuria; Korea

28 55 009 **Emberiza buchanani**
Gray-necked Bunting
Armenia, Transcaspia to Mongolia

28 55 010 **Emberiza stewarti**
White-capped Bunting
Iran to Kashmir, Garhwal, Nepal

28 55 011 **Emberiza cineracea**
Cinereous Bunting
Arid rocky slopes of Red Sea environs

28 55 012 **Emberiza hortulana**
Ortolan Bunting
Western Palearctic region; winters North Africa

28 55 013 **Emberiza caesia**
Cretzchmar's Bunting
Southern Europe to Asia Minor; winters North Africa

28 55 014 **Emberiza cirlus**
Cirl Bunting
Western Europe and Mediterranean basin environs

28 55 015 **Emberiza striolata**
Striped Bunting
Sahara oases to Red Sea, Arabia and India

		Date	Location
28 55 016	**Emberiza impetuani** Pale Rock Bunting		Semiarid Zaire, Angola to South Africa
28 55 017	**Emberiza tahapisi** Cinnamon-breasted Bunting		Widespread and common Ethiopian region
28 55 018	**Emberiza socotrana** Socotra Mountain Bunting		Highlands of Socotra Island (Indian Ocean)
28 55 019	**Emberiza capensis** Cape Bunting		Rocky mountain slopes of South Africa
28 55 020	**Emberiza yessoensis** Japanese Reed Bunting		Siberia, Manchuria, China; Japan
28 55 021	**Emberiza tristrami** Tristram's Bunting		Siberia to southern China, Laos, Burma
28 55 022	**Emberiza fucata** Gray-hooded Bunting		East Asia to Southeast Asia; Hainan; Taiwan
28 55 023	**Emberiza pusilla** Little Bunting		Widespread Palearctic and Oriental region mainland
28 55 024	**Emberiza chrysophrys** Yellow-browed Bunting		Siberia to southern China
28 55 025	**Emberiza rustica** Rustic Bunting		Widespread northern Palearctic region
28 55 026	**Emberiza elegans** Yellow-throated Bunting		East Asia, China to Burma; Taiwan
28 55 027	**Emberiza aureola** Yellow-breasted Bunting		Widespread Palearctic, Oriental mainland and islands
28 55 028	**Emberiza poliopleura** Somali Golden-breasted Bunting		Sudan, Ethiopia, Somalia to Tanzania
28 55 029	**Emberiza flaviventris** Golden-breasted Bunting		Widespread and common Africa south of the Sahara
28 55 030	**Emberiza affinis (forbesi)** Brown-rumped Bunting		Semiarid Senegal to Ethiopia
28 55 031	**Emberiza cabanisi (orientalis)** Cabanis' Bunting		Open woodlands of Sierra Leone to Mozambique
28 55 032	**Emberiza rutila** Chestnut Bunting		East Asia, Oriental mainland; Taiwan
28 55 033	**Emberiza koslowi** Koslov's Bunting		Junction of borders of Tibet, Tsinghai, Szechwan
28 55 034	**Emberiza melanocephala** Black-headed Bunting		Widespread Palearctic region; occasional India, China

		Date	Location
28 55 035	**Emberiza bruniceps** *Red-headed Bunting*		Afghanistan to Caspian region; winters to India
28 55 036	**Emberiza sulphurata** *Japanese Yellow Bunting*		China; Korea; Japan; Taiwan; Philippines
28 55 037	**Emberiza spodocephala** *Black-faced Bunting*		Eastern Palearctic, Oriental region mainland
28 55 038	**Emberiza variabilis** *Gray Bunting*		Coasts of Kamchatka, Sakhalin, Japan
28 55 039	**Emberiza pallasi** *Pallas' Reed Bunting*		Siberia, Mongolia, Manchuria and China
28 55 040	**Emberiza schoeniclus** *Common Reed Bunting*		Reed-beds, swamps of northern Palearctic region
28 55 041	**Calcarius mccownii** *McCown's Longspur*		Plains of southwest Canada to northwest Mexico (Durango)
28 55 042	**Calcarius lapponicus** *Lapland Longspur* *Lapland Bunting (Br.)*		Holarctic circumpolar; winters to southern United States, Eurasia
28 55 043	**Calcarius pictus** *Smith's Longspur*		Alaska, Canada; winters to southern United States
28 55 044	**Calcarius ornatus** *Chestnut-collared Longspur*		Prairies of southern Canada; winters to northern Mexico
28 55 045	**Plectrophenax nivalis (hyperboreus)** *Snow Bunting*		Holarctic circumpolar
28 55 046	**Calamospiza melanocorys** *Lark Bunting*		Western Canada and United States; winters to Mexico
28 55 047	**Zonotrichia illiaca** *Fox Sparrow*		Western North America; winters to Baja California
28 55 048	**Zonotrichia melodia** *Song Sparrow*		Widespread North America; winters to central Mexico
28 55 049	**Zonotrichia lincolnii** *Lincoln's Sparrow*		Western North America; winters to El Salvador
28 55 050	**Zonotrichia georgiana** *Swamp Sparrow*		Eastern Canada, United States; winters to Mexico
28 55 051	**Zonotrichia capensis** *Rufous-collared (Andean) Sparrow*		Widespread highlands of southeast Mexico to Tierra del Fuego
28 55 052	**Zonotrichia querula** *Harris' Sparrow*		North-central Canada; winters to south-central United States

		Date	Location
28 55 053	**Zonotrichia leucophrys** *White-crowned Sparrow*		Western North America; winters to central Mexico
28 55 054	**Zonotrichia albicollis** *White-throated Sparrow*		Alaska, northeast United States; winters to southern U.S.
28 55 055	**Zonotrichia atricapilla** *Golden-crowned Sparrow*		Alaska, western Canada; winters to northwest Mexico
28 55 056	**Junco vulcani** *Volcano Junco*		Volcanic summits of Costa Rica and western Panama
28 55 057	**Junco hyemalis (oreganus) (insularis)** *Northern (Dark-eyed) Junco*		Widespread Alaska, United States; winters to northern Mexico
28 55 058	**Junco phaeonotus (bairdi)** *Mexican Junco*		Mountains of southwest United States to Guatemala
28 55 059	**Junco caniceps** *Gray-headed Junco*		Mountains of western United States; winters to northwest Mexico
28 55 060	**Ammodramus sandwichensis (princeps)** *Savannah Sparrow*		Alaska to Guatemala; winters to Honduras, West Indies
28 55 061	**Ammodramus maritimus** *Seaside Sparrow*		Coastal eastern United States to Gulf Coast of Texas
28 55 062	**Ammodramus caudacutus** *Sharp-tailed Sparrow*		Prairies of Canada, eastern United States
28 55 063	**Ammodramus leconteii** *Leconte's Sparrow*		Prairies of central north America; winters to Gulf states
28 55 064	**Ammodramus bairdii** *Baird's Sparrow*		Great Plains of North America; winters to Mexico
28 55 065	**Ammodramus baileyi** *Sierra Madre Sparrow*		Pine forests of southwest Mexico (Durango, Jalisco, Morelos)
28 55 066	**Ammodramus henslowii** *Henslow's Sparrow*		Central and northeast United States
28 55 067	**Ammodramus savannarum** *Grasshopper Sparrow*		Southern Canada to Ecuador; West Indies
28 55 068	**Ammodramus humeralis** *Grassland Sparrow*		Widespread tropical, subtropical South America

		Date	Location
28 55 069	**Ammodramus aurifrons** *Yellow-browed Sparrow*		Tropical Venezuela to eastern Bolivia, Amazonian Brazil
28 55 070	**Spizella arborea** *Tree Sparrow*		Alaska, northern Canada; winters to central United States
28 55 071	**Spizella passerina** *Chipping Sparrow*		Widespread Canada to Nicaragua; migrant in north
28 55 072	**Spizella pusilla** *Field Sparrow*		Canada, United States east of Rockies; winters to Mexico
28 55 073	**Spizella wortheni** *Worthen's Sparrow*		Arid northeast Mexico (possible race *S. pusilla*)
28 55 074	**Spizella atrogularis** *Black-chinned Sparrow*		Arid southwest United States to southern Mexico
28 55 075	**Spizella pallida** *Clay-colored Sparrow*		Western Canada, United States; winters to Guatemala
28 55 076	**Spizella breweri** *Brewer's Sparrow*		Western Canada, United States; winters to northern Mexico
28 55 077	**Pooecetes gramineus** *Vesper Sparrow*		Canada to southern United States; winters to Guatemala
28 55 078	**Chondestes grammacus** *Lark Sparrow*		Southern Canada to northern Mexico; winters to El Salvador
28 55 079	**Amphispiza bilineata** *Black-throated Sparrow*		Deserts of southwest United States to central Mexico
28 55 080	**Amphispiza belli** *Sage Sparrow*		Arid western United States, Baja California, Sonora, Chihuahua
28 55 081	**Aimophila mystacalis** *Bridled Sparrow*		Arid Mexican central plateau (Verazruz to Oaxaca)
28 55 082	**Aimophilia humeralis** *Black-chested Sparrow*		Highlands of southwest Mexico (Jalisco to Puebla)
28 55 083	**Aimophila ruficauda** *Stripe-headed Sparrow*		Arid southwest Mexico (Durango) to Costa Rica
28 55 084	**Almophila sumichrasti** *Sumichrast's Sparrow*		Arid southern Mexico (Pacific slope of southern Oaxaca)
28 55 085 +	**Aimophila stolzmanni** *Tumbes Sparrow*		Arid littoral of southwest Ecuador to northwest Peru

		Date	Location

28 55 086 **Aimophila strigiceps**
Stripe-capped Sparrow — Grasslands of northern Argentina

28 55 087 **Aimophila aestivalis**
Bachman's Sparrow — Open pine-oak woods of southeast United States

28 55 088 **Aimophila botterii**
(petenica)
Botteri's Sparrow — Arid open country of Arizona, Texas to southern Mexico

28 55 089 **Aimophila cassinii**
Cassin's Sparrow — Arid southwest United States, northern Mexico

28 55 090 **Aimophila quinquestriata**
Five-striped Sparrow — Arid Arizona-Mexico border south locally to Jalisco

28 55 091 **Aimophila carpalis**
Rufous-winged Sparrow — Arid southern Arizona to northwest Mexico (Sinaloa)

28 55 092 **Aimophila ruficeps**
Rufous-crowned Sparrow — Highlands of southwest United States to southern Mexico

28 55 093 **Aimophila notosticta**
Oaxaca Sparrow — Mexico (arid highlands of central Oaxica—rare)

28 55 094 **Aimophila rufescens**
Rusty Sparrow — Arid northern Mexico to northwest Costa Rica

28 55 095 **Torreornis inexpectata**
Zapata Sparrow — Arid coastal southeast Cuba, Zapata Swamp (endangered)

28 55 096 **Oriturus superciliosus**
Striped Sparrow — Mountains of the Mexican Tableland

28 55 097 **Phrygilus atriceps**
+ *Black-hooded Sierra-Finch* — Highlands of southwest Peru to northern Chile, Argentina

28 55 098 **Phrygilus gayi**
+ *Gray-hooded Sierra-Finch* — Highlands of Peru to Straits of Magellan

28 55 099 **Phrygilus patagonicus**
+ *Patagonian Sierra-Finch* — Central Argentina and Chile to Cape Horn Archipelago

28 55 100 **Phrygilus fruticeti**
+ *Mourning Sierra-Finch* — Highlands of Peru to southern Chile, Argentina

28 55 101 **Phrygilus unicolor**
Plumbeous Sierra-Finch — Páramo of northwest Venezuela to Tierra del Fuego

28 55 102 **Phrygilus dorsalis**
Red-backed Sierra-Finch — Puna of Bolivia to northern Chile and Argentina

28 55 103 **Phrygilus erythronotus**
White-throated Sierra-Finch — Puna grasslands of Peru and Bolivia

		Date	Location

28 55 104 **Phrygilus plebejus**
Ash-breasted Sierra-Finch
Andes of Ecuador to central Chile and Argentina

28 55 105 **Phrygilus carbonarius**
Carbonated Sierra-Finch
Bushy ravines and pastures of central Argentina

28 55 106 **Phrygilus alaudinus**
Band-tailed Sierra-Finch
Andes of Ecuador to Chile, Argentina (Córdoba)

28 55 107 **Melanodera melanodera**
Black-throated Finch
Southern Argentina, Chile (Santa Cruz to Tierra del Fuego); Falkland Islands

28 55 108 **Melanodera xanthogramma**
Yellow-bridled Finch
Southern Argentina and Chile to Cape Horn Archipelago

2855 109 **Haplospiza rustica**
Slaty Finch
Highlands of southern Mexico to Bolivia (Cochabamba)

28 55 110 **Haplospiza unicolor**
Uniform Finch
Southeast Brazil (Minas Gerais) to Argentina (Misiones)

28 55 111 **Acanthidops bairdi**
Peg-billed Finch
Mountains of Costa Rica

28 55 112 **Lophospingus pusillus**
Black-crested Finch
Eastern Bolivia, Paraguay to western Argentina (San Luis)

28 55 113 **Lophospingus griseocristatus**
Gray-crested Finch
Andes of Bolivia to northwest Argentina (Salta)

28 55 114 **Donacospiza albifrons**
Long-tailed Reed-Finch
Southeast Brazil (Minas Gerais) to northeast Argentina

28 55 115 **Rowettia goughensis**
Gough Island Finch
Endemic to Gough Island (South Atlantic Ocean)

28 55 116 **Nesospiza acunhae**
Tristan Finch
Nightingale and Tristan de Cunha Islands (endangered)

28 55 117 **Nesospiza wilkinsi**
Big-billed Bunting
Inaccessible and Nightingale Islands (endangered)

28 55 118 **Diuca speculifera**
White-winged Diuca-Finch
Andes of Peru (Ancash) to northern Chile (Arica)

28 55 119 **Diuca diuca**
Common Diuca-Finch
Southeast Brazil (Rio Grande do Sul) to central Chile

28 55 120 **Idiopsar brachyurus**
Short-tailed Finch
Puna of southeast Peru to northwest Argentina

		Date	Location
28 55 121	**Piezorhina cinerea** *Cinereous Finch*		Arid coastal northwest Peru (south to Libertad)
28 55 122	**Xenospingus concolor** *Slender-billed Finch*		Coastal western Peruvian Andes to northern Chile
28 55 123	**Incaspiza pulchra** *Great Inca-Finch*		Western Andes of Peru (Ancash to Lima)
28 55 124	**Incaspiza personata** *Rufous-backed Inca-Finch*		Subtropical, temperate Andes of Peru
28 55 125	**Incaspiza ortizi** *Gray-winged Inca-Finch*		Andes of northern Peru (mainly Marañon Valley)
28 55 126	**Incaspiza laeta** *Buff-bridled Inca-Finch*		Andes of northern Peru (upper Marañon Valley)
28 55 127	**Incaspiza watkinsi** *Little Inca-Finch*		Arid northern Peru (upper Marañon Valley)
28 55 128	**Poospiza thoracica** *Bay-chested Warbling-Finch*		Southeast Brazil (Espirito Santo to Rio Grande do Sul)
28 55 129	**Poospiza boliviana** *Bolivian Warbling-Finch*		Andes of Bolivia (Cochabamba to Tarija)
28 55 130	**Poospiza alticola** *Plain-tailed Warbling-Finch*		Andes of northern Peru (Libertad, Ancash)
28 55 131	**Poospiza hypochondria** *Rufous-sided Warbling-Finch*		Temperate Andes of Bolivia to northwest Argentina
28 55 132	**Poospiza erythrophrys** *Rusty-browed Warbling-Finch*		Andes of Bolivia to Argentina (Catamarca)
28 55 133	**Poospiza ornata** *Cinnamon Warbling-Finch*		Argentina (La Rioja to Salta)
28 55 134	**Poospiza nigrorufa** *Black-and-rufous Warbling-Finch*		Extreme southeast Brazil to Bolivia, Argentina
28 55 135	**Poospiza lateralis** *Red-rumped Warbling-Finch*		Southeast Brazil (Minas Gerais) to northeast Argentina
28 55 136	**Poospiza rubecula** *Rufous-breasted Warbling-Finch*		Temperate Andes of Peru (Libertad to Lima)
28 55 137	**Poospiza garleppi** *Cochabamba Mountain-Finch*		*Polylepis* woodlands of Bolivia (Cochabamba—endangered)
28 55 138	**Poospiza baeri** *Tucumán Mountain-Finch*		Temperate northwest Argentina (Tucumán—endangered)

		Date	Location

28 55 139 Poospiza caesar
Chestnut-breasted Warbling-Finch

Andes of southeast Peru (Cuzco and Puno)

28 55 140 Poospiza hispaniolensis
Collared Warbling-Finch

Arid littoral of southwest Ecuador to Peru (Ica)

28 55 141 Poospiza torquata
Ringed Warbling-Finch

Subtropical Bolivia. Paraguay to central Argentina

28 55 142 Poospiza melanoleuca (cinerea)
Black-capped Warbling-Finch

Brazilian Matto Grosso to Bolivia, northern Argentina

28 55 143 Sicalis citrina
Stripe-tailed Yellow-Finch

Northern South America to northwest Argentina, Brazil

28 55 144 Sicalis lutea
Puna Yellow-Finch

Andes of southern Peru to northwest Argentina

28 55 145 Sicalis uropygialis
Bright-rumped Yellow-Finch

Andes of Peru to northwest Argentina, Chile

28 55 146 Sicalis luteocephala
Citron-headed Yellow-Finch

Highlands of Bolivia (Cochabamba to Chuquisaca)

28 55 147 Sicalis auriventris
Greater Yellow-Finch

High Andes of Chile, Argentina (Mendoza, Neuquén)

28 55 148 Sicalis olivascens
+
Greenish Yellow-Finch

Andes of Peru to Chile, Argentina (Mendoza)

28 55 149 Sicalis columbiana
Orange-fronted Yellow-Finch

Amazonian Brazil, adjacent Venezuela to Peru

28 55 150 Sicalis flaveola
+
Saffron Finch

Widespread tropical South America

28 55 151 Sicalis luteola
+
Grassland Yellow-Finch

Southern Mexico through South America east of the Andes

28 55 152 Sicalis raimondii
Raimondi's Yellow-Finch

Western Andes of Peru (Cajamarca to Arequipa)

28 55 153 Sicalis taczanowskii
Sulphur-throated Finch

Arid littoral of southwest Ecuador to Peru (Liberatad)

28 55 154 Sicalis lebruni
Patagonian Yellow-Finch

Southern Argentina, Chile (possible race S. olivascens)

28 55 155 Emberizoides herbicola
Wedge-tailed Grass-Finch

Southwest Costa Rica to northeast Argentina

		Date	Location
28 55 156	**Emberizoides duidae** *Duida Grass-Finch*		Venezuela (Cerro Duida—possible race *E. herbicola*)
28 55 157	**Emberizoides ypiranganus** *Lesser Grass-Finch*		Southeast Brazil (São Paulo) to northeast Argentina
28 55 158	**Embernagra platensis** *Great Pampa-Finch*		Eastern Brazil to eastern Bolivia and Argentina
28 55 159	**Embernagra longicauda** *Buff-throated Pampa-Finch*		Brazil (known only from Morro de Chapeu, Bahia)
28 55 160	**Volatinia jacarina** *Blue-black Grassquit*		Tropical Mexico to northern Argentina, Chile
28 55 161	**Sporophila frontalis** *Buffy-fronted Seedeater*		Southeast Brazil (Espirito Santo) to Argentina (Misiones)
28 55 162	**Sporophila falcirostris** *Temminck's Seedeater*		Coastal southeast Brazil (Bahia to São Paulo)
28 55 163	**Sporophila schistacea** *Slate-colored Seedeater*		Southern Mexico to northern Bolivia, northeast Brazil
28 55 164	**Sporophila intermedia** *Gray Seedeater*		*Llanos* of Colombia to Guyana
28 55 165	**Sporophila plumbea** *Plumbeous Seedeater*		Tropical South America to northeast Argentina, Brazil
28 55 166	**Sporophila americana (aurita)** *Variable Seedeater*		Gulf slope of Mexico to Amazonia
28 55 167	**Sporophila torqueola** *White-collared Seedeater*		Southern Texas to western Panama
28 55 168	**Sporophila collaris** *Rusty-collared Seedeater*		Eastern Brazil (Goiás) to northern Argentina
28 55 169	**Sporophila lineola (bouvronides)** *Lined Seedeater*		Tropical South America to northern Argentina, Brazil
28 55 170	**Sporophila luctuosa** *Black-and-white Seedeater*		Andes of northwest Venezuela to northern Bolivia
28 55 171	**Sporophila nigricollis** *Yellow-bellied Seedeater*		Costa Rica to northeast Argentina, Brazil; Trinidad
28 55 172	**Sporophila ardesiaca** *Dubois' Seedeater*		Eastern Brazil (Minas Gerais, Espirito Santo)
28 55 173	**Sporophila melanops** *Hooded Seedeater*		Brazil (known from one specimen collected in Goiás in 1870)
28 55 174	**Sporophila obscura** *Dull-colored Seedeater*		Northwest Venezuela to northwest Argentina

		Date	Location
28 55 175	**Sporophila caerulescens** *Double-collared Seedeater*		Eastern and central Brazil to northern Argentina
28 55 176	**Sporophila albogularis** *White-throated Seedeater*		Eastern Brazil (Piaui to Espirito Santo)
28 55 177	**Sporophila leucoptera** *White-bellied Seedeater*		Eastern Brazil to northern Argentina, Bolivia
28 55 178	**Sporophila peruviana** *Parrot-billed Seedeater*		Arid littoral of southwest Ecuador to Peru (Ica)
28 55 179	**Sporophila simplex** *Drab Seedeater*		Pacific slopes of upper Marañon Valley of Peru
28 55 180	**Sporophila nigrorufa** *Black-and-tawny Seedeater*		Campos of eastern Bolivia, adjacent Matto Grosso of Brazil
28 55 181	**Sporophila bouvreuil** *Capped Seedeater*		Surinam, eastern Brazil to northeast Argentina
28 55 182	**Sporophila insulata** *Tumaco Seedeater*		Colombia (Tumaco Island—not recorded since 1912—probably extinct)
28 55 183	**Sporophila minuta** *Ruddy-breasted Seedeater*		Arid Pacific lowlands of Mexico (Nayarit) to Argentina
28 55 184	**Sporophila hypoxantha** *Tawny-bellied Seedeater*		Southern Brazil, Bolivia, Paraguay and Argentina
28 55 185	**Sporophila hypochroma** *Rufous-rumped Seedeater*		Southeast Bolivia to northeast Argentina (Corrientes)
28 55 186	**Sporophila ruficollis** *Dark-throated Seedeater*		Southern Brazil (Goiás) to central Argentina, Bolivia
28 55 187	**Sporophila palustris** *Marsh Seedeater*		Southeast Brazil to central Argentina (Entre Rios)
28 55 188	**Sporophila castaneiventris** *Chestnut-bellied Seedeater*		Tropical South America to Bolivia, Amazonian Brazil
28 55 189	**Sporophila cinnamomea** *Chestnut Seedeater*		Eastern Brazil (Rio Araguia) to Paraguay (rare)
28 55 190	**Sporophila melanogaster** *Black-bellied Seedeater*		Southeast Brazil (Minas Gerais to Rio Grande do Sul)
28 55 191	**Sporophila telasco** *Chestnut-throated Seedeater*		Coastal southwest Colombia to northern Chile (Arica)
28 55 192	**Oryzoborus crassirostris (maximiliani)** *Large-billed Seed-Finch*		Widespread tropical zone of South America

	Date	Location

28 55 193 **Oryzoborus angolensis**
+ **(funereus)**
Lesser Seed-Finch — Widespread Gulf lowlands of Mexico to northern Argentina

28 55 194 **Amaurospiza concolor (relicta)**
Blue Seedeater — Mountains of southern Mexico to western Ecuador (rare)

28 55 195 **Amaurospiza moesta**
Blackish-blue Seedeater — Eastern Brazil (Maranhão) to northeast Argentina (Misiones)

28 55 196 **Melopyrrha nigra**
Cuban Bullfinch — Cuba, Isle of Pines and Grand Cayman Island

28 55 197 **Dolospingus fringilloides**
White-naped Seedeater — Southern Venezuela (Amazonas), adjacent northern Brazil

28 55 198 **Catamenia analis**
Band-tailed Seedeater — Mountains of Colombia to Chile, Argentina

28 155 199 **Catamenia inornata**
Plain-colored Seedeater — Mountains of northwest Venezuela to Argentina

28 55 200 **Catamenia homochroa**
+ *Paramo Seedeater* — Andes of Venezuela to Bolivia, adjacent Brazil

28 55 201 **Catamenia oreophila**
Santa Maria Seedeater — Santa Marta Mountains of Colombia (possible race *C. homochroa*)

28 55 202 **Tiaris canora**
Melodious (Cuban) Grassquit — Cuba; introduced Bahamas

28 55 203 **Tiaris olivacea**
Yellow-faced Grassquit — Gulf slope of Mexico to Venezuela; Greater Antilles

28 55 204 **Tiaris bicolor**
Black-faced Grassquit — Coastal Venezuela, Colombia; West Indies

28 55 205 **Tiaris fuliginosa**
Sooty Grassquit — Eastern Colombia to Guyana, southeast Brazil; Trinidad

28 55 206 **Loxipasser anoxanthus**
Yellow-shouldered Grassquit — Hills and mountains of Jamaica

28 55 207 **Loxigilla portoricensis**
Puerto Rican Bullfinch — Woodlands of Puerto Rico (endangered)

28 55 208 **Loxigilla violacea**
Greater Antillean Bullfinch — Bahamas, Hispaniola and Jamaica

28 55 209 **Loxigilla noctis**
Lesser Antillean Bullfinch — Shrubbery and forest undergrowth of Lesser Antilles

		Date	Location
28 55 210	**Melanospiza richardsoni** *St. Lucia Black Finch*		West Indies (mountains of St. Lucia Island)
28 55 211	**Geospiza magnirostris** *Large Ground-Finch*		Galapagos Islands
28 55 212	**Geospiza fortis** *Medium Ground-Finch*		Galapagos Islands
28 55 213	**Geospiza fuliginosa** *Small Ground-Finch*		Galapagos Islands
28 55 214	**Geospiza difficilis** *Sharp-beaked Ground-Finch*		Galapagos Islands
28 55 215	**Geospiza scandens** *Cactus Finch*		*Opuntia* cactus forests of Galapagos Islands
28 55 216	**Geospiza conirostris** *Large Cactus Finch*		*Opuntia* cactus forests of Galapagos Islands
28 55 217	**Camarhynchus crassirostris** *Vegetarian Tree-Finch*		Galapagos Islands
28 55 218	**Camarhynchus psittacula** *Large Tree-Finch*		Galapagos Islands
28 55 219	**Camarhynchus pauper** *Medium Tree-Finch*		Galapagos (highlands of Floreana Island)
28 55 220	**Camarhynchus parvulus** *Small Tree-Finch*		Galapagos Islands
28 55 221	**Camarhynchus pallidus** *Woodpecker Finch*		Galapagos Islands
28 55 222	**Camarhynchus heliobates** *Mangrove Finch*		Galapagos (mangroves of Fernandina and Isabela Islands)
28 55 223	**Certhidea olivacea** *Warbler Finch*		Common throughout the Galapagos Islands
28 55 224	**Pinaroloxias inornata** *Cocos Island Finch*		Cocos Island (off Costa Rica—endangered)
28 55 225	**Pipilo chlorurus** *Green-tailed Towhee*		Western United States; winters to central Mexico
28 55 226	**Pipilo ocai** *Collared Towhee*		Conifer forests of southwest Mexico (Jalisco to Oaxaca)
28 55 227	**Pipilo erythrophthalmus** *Rufous-sided Towhee*		Widespread southern Canada to Guatemala
28 55 228	**Pipilo socorroensis** *Socorro Towhee*		Confined to Socorro Island (off west coast of Mexico)

		Date	Location
28 55 229	**Pipilo fuscus** *Brown Towhee*		Semiarid western United States to southern Mexico
28 55 230	**Pipilo aberti** *Abert's Towhee*		Arid southwest United States, adjacent northwest Mexico
28 55 231	**Pipilo albicollis** *White-throated Towhee*		Mountains of southern Mexico (Guerrero to Oaxaca)
28 55 232	**Melozone kieneri** *Rusty-crowned Ground-Sparrow*		Pacific slope of Mexico (Sonora to Oaxaca)
28 55 233	**Melozone biarcuatum** *White-faced Ground-Sparrow*		Pacific slope of Chiapas (Mexico) to Costa Rica
28 55 234	**Melozone leucotis** *White-eared Ground-Sparrow*		Highlands of Chiapas (Mexico) to Costa Rica
28 55 235 +	**Arremon taciturnus** *Pectoral Sparrow*		Widespread tropical South America
28 55 236	**Arremon flavirostris** *Saffron-billed Sparrow*		Interior of eastern Brazil to Bolivia, northern Argentina
28 55 237	**Arremon aurantiirostris** *Orange-billed Sparrow*		Humid lowlands of southeast Mexico to northeast Peru
28 55 238	**Arremon schlegeli** *Golden-winged Sparrow*		Tropical northern Venezuela to Colombia (Santander)
28 55 239 +	**Arremon abeillei** *Black-capped Sparrow*		Arid littoral of southwest Ecuador to Peru
28 55 240	**Arremonops rufivirgatus** *Olive Sparrow*		Southern Texas to northwest Costa Rica
28 55 241	**Arremonops tocuyensis** *Tocuyo Sparrow*		Arid tropical Colombia and Venezuela
28 55 242	**Arremonops chloronotus** *Green-backed Sparrow*		Lowlands of southeast Mexico to Guatemala, Honduras
28 55 243	**Arremonops conirostris** *Black-striped Sparrow*		Tropical Honduras to Venezuela, Ecuador, adjacent Brazil
28 55 244	**Atlapetes gutturalis** *Yellow-throated Brush-Finch*		Subtropical highlands of Chiapas (Mexico) to Colombia
28 55 245	**Atlapetes albinucha** *White-naped Brush-Finch*		Highlands of southern Mexico (Veracruz to Chiapas)

		Date	Location

28 55 246 **Atlapetes melanocephalus**
Santa Marta Brush-Finch — Santa Marta Mountains of Colombia

28 55 247 **Atlapetes albofrenatus**
Moustached Brush-Finch — Subtropical Andes of Venezuela, eastern Colombia

28 55 248 **Atlapetes pallidinucha**
Pale-naped Brush-Finch — Andes of Venezuela to Ecuador

28 55 249 **Atlapetes rufinucha**
Rufous-naped Brush-Finch — Andes of Venezuela to Bolivia (Santa Cruz)

28 55 150 **Atlapetes fuscoolivaceus**
Dusky-headed Brush-Finch — Subtropical upper Magdalena Valley of Colombia

28 55 251 **Atlapetes flaviceps**
Olive-headed Brush-Finch — Colombia (known from two specimens collected in Tolima in 1911)

28 55 252 **Atlapetes tricolor**
✛ *Tricolored Brush-Finch* — Pacific Colombia to Peru (Libertad, Junin)

28 55 253 **Atlapetes semirufus**
Ochre-breasted Brush-Finch — Mountains of Venezuela (Táchira) to Colombia (Boyacá)

28 55 254 **Atlapetes fulviceps**
Fulvous-headed Brush-Finch — Andes of Bolivia to northwest Argentina (Jujuy)

28 55 255 **Atlapetes personatus**
Tepui Brush-Finch — Subtropical Venezuela, adjacent Brazil (Amazonas)

28 55 256 **Atlapetes citrinellus**
Yellow-striped Brush-Finch — Subtropical Andes of northwest Argentina, Paraguay

28 55 257 **Atlapetes rufigenis**
Rufous-eared Brush-Finch — Andes of central Peru (upper Marañon Valley)

28 55 258 **Atlapetes leucopterus**
✛ *White-winged Brush-Finch* — Andes of western Ecuador to western Peru

28 55 259 **Atlapetes schistaceus**
✛ *Slaty Brush-Finch* — Andes of northwest Venezuela to Peru (Junin)

28 55 260 **Atlapetes seebohmi**
Bay-crowned Brush-Finch — Subtropical southwest Ecuador, western Peru

28 55 261 **Atlapetes nationi**
Rusty-bellied Brush-Finch — Arid subtropical western Andes of Peru

28 55 262 **Atlapetes albiceps**
✛ *White-headed Brush-Finch* — Arid southwest Ecuador to western Peru (Cajamarca)

28 55 263 **Atlapetes pallidiceps**
Pale-headed Brush-Finch — Arid scrub of southwest Ecuador (Azuay)

		Date	Location

28 55 264 **Atlapetes brunneinucha**
+   **(apertus)**
         Chestnut-capped Brush-   Highlands of Mexico to Andes of Peru
         Finch

28 55 265 **Atlapetes**
-+   **torquatus(virenticeps)**
         Striped Brush-Finch   Mountains of southern Mexico to northwest Argentina

28 55 266 **Atlapetes atricapillus**
         Black-headed Brush-Finch   Upper tropical Costa Rica to northern Colombia

28 55 267 **Atlapetes leucopis**
         White-rimmed Brush-Finch   Subtropical Colombia to eastern Ecuador

28 55 268 **Atlapetes pileatus**
         Rufous-capped Brush-   Oak-pine forests of Mexico (Chihuahua to Oaxaca)
         Finch

28 55 269 **Pezopetes capitalis**
         Large-footed Finch   Mountains of Costa Rica to western Panama
                                        (Chiriqui)

28 55 270 **Oreothraupis**
         arremonops
         Tanager-Finch   Subtropical Pacific Colombia to northwest Ecuador

28 55 271 **Pselliophorus tibialis**
         Yellow-thighed Finch   Highlands of Costa Rica to western Panama
                                        (Chiriqui)

28 55 272 **Pselliophorus**
         luteoviridis
         Yellow-green Finch   Highlands of western Panama (Cerro Flores,
                                        Chiriqui)

28 55 273 **Lysurus castaneiceps**
+   *Olive Finch*   Highlands of Colombia to southeast Peru (Cuzco)

28 55 274 **Lysurus crassirostris**
         Sooty-faced Finch   Highlands of Costa Rica and western Panama

28 55 275 **Urothraupis stolzmanni**
         Black-backed Bush-   Central Andes of Colombia to eastern Ecuador
         Tanager

28 55 276 **Charitospiza eucosma**
         Coal-crested Finch   *Cerrado, campos* of Brazil to Argentina (Misiones)

28 55 277 **Coryphaspiza melanotis**
         Black-masked Finch   Eastern Brazil (Minas Gerais) to northeast Argentina

28 55 278 **Saltatricula multicolor**
+   *Many-colored Chaco-Finch*   Southern Bolivia to Uruguay, central Argentina

28 55 279 **Gubernatrix cristata**
         Yellow Cardinal   Extreme southeast Brazil to Argentina (Rio Negro)

28 55 280 **Coryphospingus pileatus**
         Pileated Finch   Arid tropical Venezuela, Colombia, Brazil

		Date	Location
28 55 281	**Coyphospingus cucullatus**		
	Red-crested Finch		Tropical Guianas to Argentina, Brazil
28 55 282	**Rhodospingus cruentus**		
	Crimson Finch		Arid littoral of western Ecuador to Peru (Piura)
28 55 283	**Paroaria coronata**		
	Red-crested Cardinal		Southeast Brazil to northern Argentina, southeast Bolivia
28 55 284	**Paroaria dominicana**		
	Red-cowled Cardinal		Eastern Brazil (Maranhão to Minas Gerais)
28 55 285	**Paroaria gularis**		
	Red-capped Cardinal		Eastern South America to Bolivia, Amazonian Brazil
28 55 286	**Paroaria baeri**		
	Crimson-fronted Cardinal		Central Brazil (Goiás, Matto Grosso—endangered)
28 55 287	**Paroaria capitata**		
	Yellow-billed Cardinal		Southeast Bolivia, southern Brazil to northern Argentina
28 55 288	**Spiza americana**		
	Dickcissel		United States east of Rockies; winters to northern South America
28 55 289	**Pheucticus chrysopeplus**		
	Yellow Grosbeak		Pacific slope of Mexico (Sonora) to Guatemala
28 55 290	**Pheucticus tibialis**		
	Black-thighed Grosbeak		Mountains of Costa Rica and western Panama
28 55 291	**Pheucticus chrysogaster**		
	Golden-bellied Grosbeak		Mountains of Colombia to southern Peru
28 55 292	**Pheucticus aureoventris**		
	Black-backed Grosbeak		Andes of Venezuela to Bolivia, Paraguay, Argentina
28 55 293	**Pheucticus ludovicianus**		
	Rose-breasted Grosbeak		Eastern Canada, United States; winters to Peru, West Indies
28 55 294	**Pheucticus melanocephalus**		
	Black-headed Grosbeak		Mountains of southwest Canada to southern Mexico
28 55 295	**Cardinalis cardinalis**		
	Common (Red) Cardinal		Widespread Canada to Honduras
28 55 296	**Cardinalis phoeniceus**		
	Vermilion Cardinal		Arid littoral of Venezuela to northeast Colombia
28 55 297	**Cardinalis sinuatus**		
	Pyrrhuloxia		Arid southwest United States to central Mexico; Baja California
28 55 298	**Caryothraustes canadensis**		
	Yellow-green Grosbeak		Eastern Panama to southeast Colombia, Amazonian Brazil

		Date	Location
28 55 299	**Caryothraustes humeralis** *Yellow-shouldered Grosbeak*		Eastern Colombia to southeast Peru. southwest Brazil
28 55 300	**Caryothraustes poliogaster** *Black-faced Grosbeak*		Gulf lowlands of Mexico to western Panama
28 55 301	**Rhodothraupis celaeno** *Crimson-collared Grosbeak*		Eastern Mexico only (Nuevo Leon to Veracruz and Puebla)
28 55 302	**Periporphyrus erythromelas** *Red-and-black Grosbeak*		Southeast Venezuela to Surinam, adjacent Brazil
28 55 303 ✝	**Pitylus grossus (fuliginosus)** *Slate-colored Gosbeak*		Nicaragua to southeast Brazil, northeast Argentina
28 55 304	**Saltator atriceps** *Black-headed Saltator*		Tropical coastal Mexico (Tamaulipas, Guerro) to central Panama
28 55 305	**Saltator maximus** *Buff-throated Saltator*		Tropical Mexico (Veracruz) to Bolivia, Amazonian Brazil
28 55 306	**Saltator atripennis** *Black-winged Saltator*		Andes of Colombia, western Ecuador
28 55 307	**Saltator similis** *Green-winged Saltator*		Southeast Brazil to northeast Argentina and Bolivia
28 55 308 ✝	**Saltator coerulescens** *Grayish Saltator*		Semiarid Mexico to Argentina (widespread west of Andes)
28 55 309	**Saltator orenocensis** *Orinocan Saltator*		Arid tropical scrub of Venezuela, northeast Colombia
28 55 310	**Saltator maxillosus** *Thick-billed Saltator*		Eastern Brazil (Espirito Santo) to western Argentina
28 55 311	**Saltator aurantiirostris (nigriceps)** *Golden-billed Saltator*		Andes of Ecuador to northern Argentina, southern Brazil
28 55 312	**Saltator cinctus** *Masked Saltator*		Eastern Ecuador to Andes of central Peru
28 55 313	**Saltator atricollis** *Black-throated Saltator*		Campos of eastern Brazil, Paraguay, northeast Bolivia
28 55 314	**Saltator rufiventris** *Rufous-bellied Saltator*		Andes of Bolivia and northwest Argentina
28 55 315	**Saltator albicollis** *Streaked Saltator*		Costa Rica to western Peru; West Indies

		Date	Location

28 55 316 **Passerina glaucocaerulea**
Indigo Grosbeak
Southern Brazil (São Paulo) to northeast Argentina

28 55 317 **Passerina cyanoides**
+
Blue-black Grosbeak
Gulf lowlands of Mexico to Amazonia

28 55 318 **Passerina brissonii**
Ultramarine Grosbeak
Northern Venezuela to Argentina, Brazil

28 55 319 **Passerina parellina**
Blue Bunting
Tropical Mexico to Nicaragua

28 55 320 **Passerina caerulea**
Blue Grosbeak
United States to Costa Rica; winters to Panama

28 55 321 **Passerina cyanea**
Indigo Bunting
Eastern Canada to Gulf states; winters to Panama, West Indies

28 55 322 **Passerina amoena**
Lazuli Bunting
Western North America (British Columbia to southern Mexico)

28 55 323 **Passerina versicolor**
Varied Bunting
Semiarid southwest United States to Guatemala

28 55 324 **Passerina ciris**
Painted Bunting
Southern United States, Mexico; winters to Panama, Cuba

28 55 325 **Passerina rositae**
Rose-bellied Bunting
Tropical Pacific slope of southern Mexico (Oaxaca, Chiapas)

28 55 326 **Passerina leclancherii**
Orange-breasted Bunting
Pacific slope of southwest Mexico (Jalisco to Chiapas)

28 55 327 **Passerina caerulescens**
Blue Finch
Campos of interior of Brazil, eastern Bolivia

FAMILY: CATAMBLYRHYNCHIDAE (Plush-capped Finch)

28 56 001 **Catamblyrhynchus diadema**
+
Plush-capped Finch
Mountains of Venezuela to northwest Argentina

FAMILY: THRAUPIDAE (Tanagers)

28 57 001 **Orchesticus abeillei**
Brown Tanager
Southeast Brazil (Bahia to Paraná)

28 57 002 **Schistochlamys ruficapillus**
Cinnamon Tanager
Drier regions of east and central Brazil

		Date	Location
28 57 003	**Schistochlamys melanopis** *Black-faced Tanager*		Northern South America to northern Bolivia, Brazil
28 57 004	**Neothraupis fasciata** *White-banded Tanager*		Campos of Brazil to Bolivia (Santa Cruz)
28 57 005	**Cypsnagra hirundinacea** *White-rumped Tanager*		Campos of Brazil to northern Paraguay and Bolivia
28 57 006	**Conothraupis speculigera** *Black-and-white Tanager*		Southwest Ecuador to northern Peru
28 57 007	**Conothraupis mesoleuca** *Cone-billed Tanager*		Known only from Matto Grosso of Brazil (Cuyabá)
28 57 008	**Lamprospiza melanoleuca** *Red-billed Pied Tanager*		Amazonian Brazil, adjacent Peru (Puno), the Guianas
28 57 009	**Cissopis leveriana** *Magpie Tanager*		Northern South America to northeast Argentina, Brazil
28 57 010 +	**Chlorornis riefferii** *Grass-green Tanager*		Andes of Colombia to Bolivia (Cochabamba)
28 57 011	**Sericossypha loricata** *Scarlet-throated Tanager*		Arid interior of eastern Brazil
28 57 012	**Sericossypha albocristata** *White-capped Tanager*		Andes of northwest Venezuela to central Peru (Junin)
28 57 013	**Nesospingus speculiferus** *Puerto Rican Tanager*		Mountain and upland forests of Puerto Rico
28 57 014 +	**Chlorospingus ophthalmicus** *Common Bush-Tanager*		Mountains of central Mexico to northwest Argentina
28 57 015	**Chlorospingus tacarcunae** *Tacarcuna Bush-Tanager*		Known only from eastern Panama (Serrania del Darién)
28 57 016	**Chlorospingus inornatus** *Mount Pirri Bush-Tanager*		Highlands of eastern Panama (Darién)
28 57 017	**Chlorospingus punctulatus** *Dotted Bush-Tanager*		Highlands of central Panama (Veraguas and Coclé)
28 57 018	**Chlorospingus semifuscus** *Dusky-bellied Bush-Tanager*		Western Andes of Colombia to western Ecuador

		Date	Location

28 57 019 Chlorospingus zeledoni
Volcano Bush-Tanager

Mountains of Costa Rica (possible color phase C. pileatus)

28 57 020 Chlorospingus pileatus
Sooty-capped Bush-Tanager

Mountains of Costa Rica and western Panama

28 57 021 Chlorospingus parvirostris
Short-billed Bush-Tanager

Andes of Colombia to northwest Bolivia

28 57 022 Chlorospingus flavigularis
Yellow-throated Bush-Tanager

Mountains of western Panama to northwest Bolivia

28 57 023 Chlorospingus flavovirens
Yellow-green Bush-Tanager

Western Andes of Colombia and northwest Ecuador

28 57 024 Chlorospingus canigularis
Ashy-throated Bush-Tanager

Mountains of Costa Rica to Peru (Cajamarca)

28 57 025 Cnemoscopus rubrirostris
Gray-hooded Hemispingus

Andes of northwest Venezuela to Peru (Junin)

28 57 026 Hemispingus atropileus
Black-capped Hemispingus

Andes of northwest Venezuela to northwest Bolivia (La Paz)

28 57 027 Hemispingus calophrys
Yellow-throated Hemispingus

Andes of Ecuador to Peru

28 57 028 Hemispingus parodii
Parodi's Hemispingus

Andes of southeast Peru (Cuzco)

28 57 029 Hemispingus superciliaris
Superciliared Hemispingus

Andes of northwest Venezuela to northwest Bolivia

28 57 030 Hemispingus reyi
Gray-capped Hemispingus

Andes of northwest Venezuela

28 57 031 Hemispingus frontalis
Oleaginous Hemispingus

Mountains of northwest Venezuela to Peru (Cuzco)

28 57 032 Hemispingus melanotis
Black-eared Hemispingus

Mountains of northwest Venezuela to northwest Bolivia

28 57 033 Hemispingus goeringi
Slaty-backed Hemispingus

Andes of northwest Venezuela (Mérida and Táchira)

		Date	Location

28 57 034 **Hemispingus rufosuperciliaris**
Rufous-browed Hemispingus — Andes of central Peru (Huánuco)

28 57 035 **Hemispingus verticalis**
Black-headed Hemispingus — Temperate and páramo zone of Venezuela and Colombia

28 57 036 **Hemispingus xanthophthalmus**
Drab Hemispingus — Andes of central Peru (Amazonas to Cuzco)

28 57 037 **Hemispingus trifasciatus**
Three-striped Hemispingus — Andes of Peru (Junin) to Bolivia (La Paz, Cochabamba)

28 57 038 **Pyrrhocoma ruficeps**
Chestnut-headed Tanager — Southeast Brazil (Espirito Santo) to northeast Argentina

28 57 039 **Thlypopsis fulviceps**
Fulvous-headed Tanager — Eastern Andes of Colombia to northern Venezuela

28 57 040 **Thlypopsis ornata**
Rufous-chested Tanager — Andes of southern Colombia to Peru (Lima, Cuzco)

28 57 041 **Thlypopsis pectoralis**
Brown-flanked Tanager — Andes of central Peru (Huánuco, Junin)

28 57 042 **Thlypopsis sordida**
Orange-headed Tanager — Tropical South America to northern Argentina, Brazil

28 57 043 **Thlypopsis inornata**
Buff-bellied Tanager — Subtropical Andes of northern Peru (west of the Marañon)

28 57 044 **Thlypopsis ruficeps**
Rust-and-yellow Tanager — Andes of southern Peru to northwest Argentina

28 57 045 **Hemithraupis guira**
Guira Tanager — Tropical South America to northern Argentina, Brazil

28 57 046 **Hemithraupis ruficapilla**
Rufous-headed Tanager — Southeast Brazil (Bahia to Santa Catarina)

28 57 047 **Hemithraupis flavicollis**
Yellow-backed Tanager — Eastern Panama to northern Bolivia, eastern Brazil

28 57 048 **Chrysothlypis chrysomelas**
Black-and-yellow Tanager — Highlands of Costa Rica and Panama

28 57 049 **Chrysothlypis salmoni**
Scarlet-and-white Tanager — Pacific slope of Colombia to northwest Ecuador

28 57 050 **Nemosia pileata**
Hooded Tanager — Tropical South America to northwest Argentina, Brazil

28 57 051 **Nemosia rourei**
Cherry-throated Tanager — Brazil (known from one specimen collected in 1870 in Rio de Janeiro)

		Date	Location
28 57 052	**Phaenicophilus palmarum** *Black-crowned Palm-Tanager*		Lowlands of Hispaniola and Saona Islands
28 57 053	**Phaenicophilus poliocephalus** *Gray-crowned Palm-Tanager*		Lowlands of Hispaniola and Gonâve Islands
28 57 054	**Calyptophilus frugivorus** *Chat-Tanager*		Hispaniola and Gonâve Islands
28 57 055	**Nephelornis oneilli** *Pardusco Tanager*		Eastern Andes of central Peru (Huánuco)
28 57 056	**Rhodinocichla rosea** *Rose-breasted Thrush-Tanager*		Western Mexico (Sinaloa) to northern Colombia, Venezuela
28 57 057	**Mitrospingus cassinii** *Dusky-faced Tanager*		Costa Rica to Pacific Colombia, northwest Ecuador
28 57 058	**Mitrospingus oleagineus** *Olive-backed Tanager*		Eastern Venezuela, Guyana, adjacent Brazil (Roraima)
28 57 059	**Chlorothraupis carmioli** *Carmiol's Tanager*		Tropical forests of Nicaragua to Bolivia (Cochabamba)
28 57 060	**Chlorothraupis olivacea** *Lemon-browed Tanager*		Tropical eastern Panama to northwest Ecuador
28 57 061	**Chlorothraupis stolzmanni** *Ochre-breasted Tanager*		Tropical western Colombia to western Ecuador (Chimbo)
28 57 062	**Orthogonys chloricterus** *Olive-green Tanager*		Southeast Brazil (Espirito Santo to Santa Catarina)
28 57 063	**Eucometis penicillata** *Gray-headed Tanager*		Southern Mexico to northeast Argentina, southern Brazil
28 57 064	**Lanio fulvus** *Fulvous Shrike-Tanager*		Tropical Guianas to Peru, Brazil north of the Amazon
28 57 065	**Lanio versicolor** *White-winged Shrike-Tanager*		Amazonian Brazil, adjacent eastern Peru and Bolivia
28 57 066	**Lanio aurantius** *Black-throated Shrike-Tanager*		Gulf lowlands of southeast Mexico to Honduras
28 57 067	**Lanio leucothorax** *White-throated Shrike-Tanager*		Nicaragua, Costa Rica and western Panama

		Date	Location
28 57 068	**Creurgops verticalis** *Rufous-crested Tanager*		Andes of northwest Venezuela to southeast Peru
28 57 069	**Creurgops dentata** *SlatyTanager*		Andes of southeast Peru to northern Bolivia
28 57 070	**Heterospingus xanthopygius** *Scarlet-browed Tanager*		Eastern Panama (Darién) to northwest Ecuador
28 57 071	**Heterospingus rubrifrons** *Sulphur-rumped Tanager*		Costa Rica and northwest Panama
28 57 072	**Tachyphonus cristatus** *Flame-crested Tanager*		Tropical South America to northern Bolivia, Brazil
28 57 073	**Tachyphonus rufiventer** *Yellow-crested Tanager*		Eastern Peru, adjacent western Brazil, Bolivia (La Paz)
28 57 074	**Tachyphonus surinamus** *Fulvous-crested Tanager*		Tropical South America to eastern Peru, Amazonian Brazil
28 57 075	**Tachyphonus nattereri** *Natterer's Tanager*		Brazil (known from two specimens collected in 1870 in Matto Grosso)
28 57 076	**Tachyphonus luctuosus** *White-shouldered Tanager*		Tropical Honduras to northern Bolivia, Amazonian Brazil
28 57 077	**Tachyphonus delatrii** *Tawny-crested Tanager*		Tropical Nicaragua to northwest Ecuador
28 57 078 +	**Tachyphonus coronatus** *Ruby-crowned Tanager*		Southeast Brazil (Minas Gerais) to Argentina (Misiones)
28 57 079	**Tachyphonus rufus** *White-lined Tanager*		Costa Rica to Argentina, Brazil; Trinidad
28 57 080	**Tachyphonus phoenicius** *Red-shouldered Tanager*		Tropical South America to northeast Peru, Amazonian Brazil
28 57 081	**Trichothraupis melanops** *Black-goggled Tanager*		Eastern Peru to northeast Argentina, eastern Brazil
28 57 082	**Habia rubica** *Red-crowned Ant-Tanager*		Tropical Mexico to northeast Argentina, Brazil
28 57 083	**Habia fuscicauda** *Red-throated Ant-Tanager*		Tropical Mexico to Caribbean Colombia
28 57 084	**Habia atrimaxillaris** *Black-cheeked Ant-Tanager*		Pacific Coast of Costa Rica (Osa Peninsula)

		Date	Location
28 57 085	**Habia gutturalis** *Sooty Ant-Tanger*		Tropical middle Magdalena Valley of Colombia
28 57 086	**Habia cristata** *Crested Ant-Tanager*		Western Andes of Colombia (Antioquia to Cauca)
28 57 087	**Piranga bidentata** *Flame-colored Tanager*		Cloud forests of Mexico to western Panama
28 57 088	**Piranga flava** *Hepatic Tanager*		Widespread southwest United States to northern Argentina
28 57 089	**Piranga rubra** *Summer Tanager*		United States to Mexico; winters to Amazonia, West Indies
28 57 090	**Piranga roseogularis** *Rose-throated Tanager*		Yucatán Peninsula, Peten of Guatemala; Cozumel Island
28 57 091	**Piranga olivacea** *Scarlet Tanager*		Eastern Canada, United States; winters to Amazonia
28 57 092	**Piranga ludoviciana** *Western Tanager*		Widespread western North America; winters to Costa Rica
28 57 093	**Piranga leucoptera** *White-winged Tanager*		Mountains of eastern Mexico to northwest Bolivia
28 57 094	**Piranga erythrocephala** *Red-headed Tanager*		Sierra Madre Mountains of Sonora to Oaxaca (Mexico)
28 57 095	**Piranga rubriceps** *Red-hooded Tanager*		Mountains of Colombia to Peru (San Martin)
28 57 096	**Calochaetes coccineus** *Vermilion Tanager*		Tropical southeast Colombia (Caqueta) to Peru (Junin)
28 57 097	**Ramphocelus sanguinolentus** *Crimson-collared Tanager*		Humid southeast Mexico to northwest Panama
28 57 098	**Ramphocelus nigrogularis** *Masked Crimson Tanager*		Tropical southeast Colombia to Peru, west Amazonian Brazil
28 57 099	**Ramphocelus dimidiatus** *Crimson-backed Tanager*		Tropical Panama to Colombia, northwest Venezuela
28 57 100	**Ramphocelus melanogaster** *Black-bellied Tanager*		Eastern Peru (Hullaga River Valley)
28 57 101	**Ramphocelus carbo** *Silver-beaked Tanager*		Tropical South America to Bolivia, Paraguay, Brazil

	Date	Location
28 57 102 Ramphocelus bresilius *Brazilian Tanager*		*Capoeira* of eastern Brazil (Paraiba to Santa Catarina)
28 57 103 Ramphocelus passerinii *Scarlet-rumped Tanager*		Tropical southeast Mexico to western Panama
28 57 104 Ramphocelus flammigerus *Flame-rumped Tanager*		Western Colombia (Cauca Valley to Nariño)
28 57 105 Ramphocelus icteronotus *Yellow-rumped Tanager*		Tropical, subtropical Panama to northwest Ecuador
28 57 106 Spindalis zena *Stripe-headed Tanager*		Bahamas, Greater Antilles and Cozumel Island
28 57 107 Thraupis episcopus (virens) *Blue-gray Tanager*		Widespread southeast Mexico to Amazonia; Trinidad; Tobago
28 57 108 Thraupis sayaca *Sayaca Tanager*		Tropical South America to northeast Argentina, Brazil
28 57 109 Thraupis cyanoptera *Azure-shouldered Tanager*		Southeast Brazil (Espirito Santo) to eastern Paraguay
28 57 110 Thraupis ornata *Golden-chevroned Tanager*		*Capoeira* of southeast Brazil (Bahia to Santa Catarina)
28 57 111 Thraupis abbas *Yellow-winged Tanager*		Humid forests of eastern Mexico to Nicaragua
28 57 112 Thraupis palmarum *Palm Tanager*		Nicaragua to Bolivia, Paraguay, Brazil; Trinidad
28 57 113 Thraupis cyanocephala *Blue-capped Tanager*		Temperate mountains of Venezuela to Bolivia (Cochabamba)
28 57 114 Thraupis bonariensis *Blue-and-yellow Tanager*		Temperate Andes of Ecuador to northern Chile, Argentina
28 57 115 Cyanicterus cyanicterus *Blue-backed Tanager*		Eastern Venezuela, the Guianas and northern Brazil
28 57 116 Buthraupis arcaei *Blue-and-gold Tanager*		Foothills of Caribbean Costa Rica to western Panama
28 57 117 Buthraupis melanochlamys *Black-and-gold Tanager*		Central and western Andes of Colombia
28 57 118 Buthraupis rothschildi *Golden-chested Tanager*		Tropical Pacific Colombia (Chocó) to northwest Ecuador

		Date	Location
28 57 119	**Buthraupis edwardsi**		
	Moss-backed Tanager		Pacific Colombia to northwest Ecuador
28 57 120	**Buthraupis aureocincta**		
	Gold-ringed Tanager		Subtropical Colombia (Rio San Juan, Chocó)
28 57 121	**Buthraupis montana**		
	Hooded Mountain-Tanager		Mountains of Venezuela to Bolivia (Cochabamba)
28 57 122	**Buthraupis eximia**		
	Black-chested Mountain-Tanager		Mountains of northwest Venezuela to Ecuador
28 57 123	**Buthraupis aureodorsalis**		
	Golden-backed Mountain-Tanager		Humid temperate zone of central Peru
28 57 124	**Buthraupis wetmorei**		
	Masked Mountain-Tanager		Temperate central Andes of Colombia to Ecuador
28 57 125	**Wetmorethraupis sterrhopteron**		
	Orange-throated Tanager		Tropical upper Marañon Valley of northern Peru
28 57 126	**Anisognathus lacrymosus**		
	Lacrimose Mountain-Tanager		Mountains of Venezuela to Peru (Junin)
28 57 127	**Anisognathus igniventris**		
	Scarlet-bellied Mountain-Tanager		Mountains of Venezuela to Bolivia (Cochabamba)
28 57 128	**Anisognathus flavinuchus**		
	Blue-winged Mountain-Tanager		Mountains of Venezuela to Bolivia (Cochabamba)
28 57 129	**Anisognathus notabilis**		
	Black-chinned Mountain-Tanager		Pacific Colombia to northwest Ecuador
28 57 130	**Anisognathus melanogenys**		
	Black-cheeked Mountain-Tanager		Subtropical, temperate Santa Marta Mountains of Colombia
28 57 131	**Stephanophorus diadematus**		
	Diademed Tanager		Southeast Brazil (Minas Gerais) to northeast Argentina
28 57 132	**Iridosornis porphyrocephala**		
	Purplish-mantled Tanager		Central Andes of Colombia to Ecuador (Loja)
28 57 133	**Iridosornis analis**		
	Yellow-throated Tanager		Southeast Ecuador to Peru (Puno)
28 57 134	**Iridosornis jelskii**		
	Golden-collared Tanager		Temperate Peru (Huánuco) to Bolivia (La Paz)

		Date	Location
28 57 135	**Iridosornia rufivertex** *Golden-crowned Tanager*		Temperate forests of Venezuela to Ecuador
28 57 136 ✛	**Iridosornis reinhardti** *Yellow-scarfed Tanager*		Eastern Peru (San Martin to Junin)
28 57 137	**Dubusia taeniata** *Buff-breasted Mountain-Tanager*		Andes of Venezuela to central Peru, Bolivia
28 57 138	**Dubusia castaneoventris** *Chestnut-bellied Mountain-Tanager*		Temperate Andes of Peru to Bolivia
28 57 139	**Pipraeidea melanonota** *Fawn-breasted Tanager*		Mountains of Colombia to northern Argentina, Brazil
28 57 140	**Euphonia jamaica** *Jamaican Euphonia*		Widespread open country of Jamaica
28 57 141	**Euphonia plumbea** *Plumbeous Euphonia*		Tropical Venezuela to Surinam, northern Amazonian Brazil
28 57 142	**Euphonia affinis** *Scrub Euphonia*		Semiarid regions of Mexico to Costa Rica
28 57 143	**Euphonia luteicapilla** *Yellow-crowned Euphonia*		Eastern Nicaragua, Costa Rica and Panama
28 57 144	**Euphonia chlorotica** *Purple-throated Euphonia*		Widespread Colombia to Argentina east of the Andes
28 57 145	**Euphonia trinitatis** *Trinidad Euphonia*		Tropical northern Venezuela and Colombia; Trinidad
28 57 146	**Euphonia concinna** *Velvet-fronted Euphonia*		Tropical Magdalena Valley of Colombia
28 57 147	**Euphonia saturata** *Orange-crowned Euphonia*		Upper tropical Colombia to northwest Peru
28 57 148	**Euphonia finschi** *Finsch's Euphonia*		Guianas, Venezuela, adjacent Brazil (Roraima)
28 57 149	**Euphonia violacea** *Violaceous Euphonia*		Tropical South America to northeast Argentina; Brazil
28 57 150	**Euphonia laniirostris** *Thick-billed Euphonia*		Costa Rica to Bolivia, Brazil
28 57 151	**Euphonia hirundinacea (lauta)** *Yellow-throated Euphonia*		Gulf lowlands of eastern Mexico to Panama (Chiriqui)
28 57 152	**Euphonia chalybea** *Green-throated Euphonia*		Southeast Brazil (Espirito Santo) to northeast Argentina
28 57 153	**Euphonia musica** *Antillean Euphonia*		Hispaniola, Gonâve, Puerto Rico, Lesser Antilles

		Date	Location
28 57 154	**Euphonia elegantissima** *Blue-hooded Euphonia*		Highlands of Mexico to Argentina; West Indies
28 57 155	**Euphonia cyanocephala** *Golden-rumped Euphonia*		Eastern Brazil (Ceará) to northeast Argentina (Misiones)
28 57 156	**Euphonia fulvicrissa** *Fulvous-vented Euphonia*		Tropical Costa Rica, Panama to northwest Ecuador
28 57 157	**Euphonia imitans** *Spot-crowned Euphonia*		Southern Costa Rica to western Panama (Chiriqui)
28 57 158	**Euphonia gouldi** *Olive-backed Euphonia*		Gulf slope of southeast Mexico to northwest Panama
28 57 159	**Euphonia chrysopasta** *Golden-bellied Euphonia*		Tropical South America to Bolivia, Amazonian Brazil
28 57 160	**Euphonia mesochrysa** *Bronze-green Euphonia*		Subtropical Colombia to Bolivia (La Paz, Cochabamba)
28 57 161	**Euphonia minuta** *White-vented Euphonia*		Tropical Mexico (Chiapas) to Amazonian Brazil
28 57 162	**Euphonia anneae** *Tawny-capped Euphonia*		Highlands of Costa Rica to Colombia (Chocó)
28 57 163	**Euphonia xanthogaster** *Orange-bellied Euphonia*		Eastern Panama to Bolivia (La Paz, Cochabamba)
28 57 164	**Euphonia rufiventris** *Rufous-bellied Euphonia*		Southern Venezuela to Bolivia, Amazonian Brazil
28 57 165	**Euphonia pectoralis** *Chestnut-bellied Euphonia*		Southeast Brazil (Goiás) to northeast Argentina
28 57 166	**Euphonia cayennensis** *Golden-sided Euphonia*		Guianas, Venezuela, east Amazonian Brazil
28 57 167	**Chlorophonia flavirostris** *Yellow-collared Chlorophonia*		Tropical southeast Colombia, northwest Ecuador
28 57 168	**Chlorophonia cyanea** *Blue-naped Chlorophonia*		Northern South America to northeast Argentina, Brazil
28 57 169	**Chlorophonia pyrrhophrys** *Chestnut-breasted Chlorophonia*		Andes of northwest Venezuela to eastern Ecuador
28 57 170	**Chlorophonia callophrys** *Golden-browed Chlorophonia*		Mountains of Costa Rica to western Panama
28 57 171	**Chlorophonia occipitalis** *Blue-crowned Chlorophonia*		Mountains of southeast Mexico to Nicaragua

	Date	Location
28 57 172 Chlorochrysa phoenicotis *Glistening-green Tanager*		Highlands of Pacific Colombia to northwest Ecuador
28 57 173 Chlorochrysa calliparaea *Orange-eared Tanager*		Subtropical Andes of Colombia to Bolivia
28 57 174 Chlorochrysa nitidissima *Multicolored Tanager*		Central and western Andes of Colombia
28 57 175 Tangara inornata *Plain-colored Tanager*		Tropical southeast Costa Rica to northern Colombia
28 57 176 Tangara cabanisi *Azure-rumped Tanager*		Cloud forests of Chiapas and southwest Guatemala (rare)
28 57 177 Tangara palmeri *Gray-and-gold Tanager*		Eastern Panama, Pacific Colombia to northwest Ecuador
28 57 178 Tangara mexicana *Turquoise Tanager*		South America east of Andes to Bolivia, Brazil; Trinidad
28 57 179 Tangara chilensis *Paradise Tanager*		Northern South America to Bolivia, Amazonian Brazil
28 57 180 Tangara fastuosa *Seven-colored Tanager*		*Capoeira* of eastern Brazil (Pernambuco and Alagoas)
28 57 181 Tangara seledon + *Green-headed Tanager*		Southeast Brazil (Bahia) to Argentina (Misiones)
28 57 182 Tangara cyanocephala *Red-necked Tanager*		Eastern Brazil (Ceará) to northeast Argentina (Misiones)
28 57 183 Tangara desmaresti + *Brassy-breasted Tanager*		Coastal southeast Brazil (Rio de Janeiro to Paraná)
28 57 184 Tangara cyanoventris *Gilt-edged Tanager*		Southeast Brazil (Bahia to São Paulo)
28 57 185 Tangara johannae *Blue-whiskered Tanager*		Pacific Colombia to western Ecuador (Los Ríos)
28 57 186 Tangara schrankii + *Green-and-gold Tanager*		West Amazonian Brazil, adjacent Colombia to Bolivia
28 57 187 Tangara florida *Emerald Tanager*		Costa Rica, Panama and Pacific Colombia
28 57 188 Tangara arthus *Golden Tanager*		Mountains of northern Venezuela to northern Bolivia
28 57 189 Tangara icterocephala *Silver-throated Tanager*		Highlands of Costa Rica to northwest Ecuador
28 57 190 Tangara xanthocephala *Saffron-crowned Tanager*		Mountains of Venezuela to northern Bolivia

		Date	Location

28 57 191	**Tangara chrysotis** *Golden-eared Tanager*		Andes of Colombia to northern Bolivia
28 57 192	**Tangara parzudakii** *Flame-faced Tanager*		Mountains of Venezuela to Peru (Cuzco)
28 57 193	**Tangara xanthogastra** *Yellow-bellied Tanager*		Tropical Venezuela to northwest Bolivia, Brazil
28 57 194	**Tangara punctata** *Spotted Tanager*		Northern South America to Bolivia, Amazonian Brazil
28 57 195	**Tangara guttata** **(chrysophrys)** *Speckled Tanager*		Costa Rica to Venezuela, Colombia, Brazil (Roraima)
28 57 196	**Tangara varia** *Dotted Tanager*		Tropical Venezuela to Surinam, adjacent Brazil
28 57 197	**Tangara rufigula** *Rufous-throated Tanager*		Pacific Colombia to western Ecuador (El Oro)
28 57 198	**Tangara gyrola** *Bay-headed Tanager*		Costa Rica to northern Bolivia, Amazonian Brazil
28 57 199	**Tangara lavinia** *Rufous-winged Tanager*		Pacific lowlands of Guatemala to northwest Ecuador
28 57 200	**Tangara cayana** *Burnished-buff Tanager*		Tropical South America to Bolivia, Paraguay, Brazil
28 57 201	**Tangara cucullata** *Hooded Tanager*		West Indies (St. Vincent and Grenada Islands)
28 57 202	**Tangara peruviana** *Black-cheeked Tanager*		Southeast Brazil (Espirito Santo to Santa Catarina)
28 57 203	**Tangara preciosa** *Chestnut-backed Tanager*		Southeast Brazil (São Paulo) to northeast Argentina
28 57 204	**Tangara vitriolina** *Scrub Tanager*		Dry highlands of Colombia to northwest Ecuador
28 57 205	**Tangara rufigenis** *Rufous-cheeked Tanager*		Coastal mountain forests of Venezuela
28 57 206	**Tangara ruficervix** *Golden-naped Tanager*		Andes of Colombia to northwest Bolivia
28 57 207	**Tangara labradorides** *Metallic-green Tanager*		Andes of Colombia to northern Peru (San Martin)
28 57 208	**Tangara cyanotis** *Blue-browed Tanager*		Andes of Colombia to northwest Bolivia (Cochabamba)
28 57 209	**Tangara cyanicollis** *Blue-necked Tanager*		Mountains of Venezuela to Bolivia, Brazil
28 57 210	**Tangara larvata** *Golden-masked Tanager*		Gulf lowlands of southeast Mexico to western Ecuador

Date   Location

28 57 211   **Tangara nigrocincta**
             Masked Tanager   Widespread northern South America east of the
                                      Andes

000   Tanagers; Honeycreepers   **000**

Date   Location

28 57 217   **Tangara argyrofenges**
             Green-throated Tanager   Subtropical eastern Peru, Bolivia (La Paz,
                                         Cochabamba)

28 57 218   **Tangara cyanoptera**
             Black-headed Tanager   Colombia to Guyana, adjacent Brazil

28 57 219   **Tangara pulcherrima**
             Golden-collared   Andes of Colombia to Peru (Cuzco)
             Honeycreeper

28 57 220   **Tangara velia**
             Opal-rumped Tanager   Tropical South America to Peru, Brazil

28 57 221   **Tangara callophrys**
             Opal-crowned Tanager   West Amazonian Brazil, adjacent Colombia to Peru

28 57 222   **Tangara fucosa**
             Green-naped Tanager   Darién highlands of eastern Panama (rare)

28 57 223   **Tangara arnaulti**
             Arnault's Tanager   Unique (probable hybrid *T. preciosa* × *T. cayana*)

FAMILY: COEREBIDAE (Honeycreepers)

28 58 001   **Dacnis albiventris**
             White-bellied Dacnis   Tropical Colombia to northeast Peru, Brazil (Pará)

28 58 002   **Dacnis lineata**
             Black-faced Dacnis   Tropical South America to Bolivia, Amazonian Brazil

28 58 003   **Dacnis flaviventer**
             Yellow-bellied Dacnis   Venezuela to northern Bolivia, west Amazonia Brazil

28 58 004   **Dacnis hartlaubi**
             Turquoise Dacnis-Tanager Western Andes of Colombia (endangered)

28 58 005   **Dacnis nigripes**
             Black-legged Dacnis   Southeast Brazil (Minas Gerais to Santa Catarina)

		Date	Location
28 58 006	**Dacnis venusta** *Scarlet-thighed Dacnis*		Tropical Costa Rica to northwest Ecuador
28 58 007	**Dacnis cayana** *Blue Dacnis*		Tropical Nicaragua to northeast Argentina, Brazil
28 58 008	**Dacnis viguieri** *Viridian Dacnis*		Eastern Panama (Darién) to northwest Colombia
28 58 009	**Dacnis berlepschi** *Scarlet-breasted Dacnis*		Tropical southwest Colombia, northwest Ecuador
28 58 010	**Chlorophanes spiza** *Green Honeycreeper*		Humid lowlands of southern Mexico to Amazonian Brazil
28 58 011	**Cyanerpes nitidus** *Short-billed Honeycreeper*		Venezuela to Peru, western Amazonian Brazil
28 58 012	**Cyanerpes lucidus** *Shining Honeycreeper*		Humid lowlands of Chiapas to northwest Colombia
28 58 013	**Cyanerpes caeruleus** *Purple Honeycreeper*		Tropical South America to Amazonian Brazil, Bolivia
28 58 014	**Cyanerpes cyaneus** *Red-legged (Blue) Honeycreeper*		Gulf lowlands of southern Mexico to Amazonian Brazil; Cuba
28 58 015	**Xenodacnis parina** *Tit-like Dacnis*		*Polylepis* woodlands of Andes of Peru
28 58 016	**Oreomanes fraseri** *Giant Conebill*		Andes of extreme southern Colombia to Bolivia
28 58 017	**Diglossa baritula (sittiodes)** *Cinnamon Flower-piercer*		Highlands of Mexico (Jalisco) to northwest Argentina
28 58 018	**Diglossa lafresnayii** *Glossy Flower-piercer*		Andes of Venezuela to northwest Bolivia
28 58 019	**Diglossa carbonaria (humeralis)** *Carbonated Flower-piercer*		Andes of Venezuela to northwest Bolivia
28 58 020	**Diglossa venezuelensis** *Venezuelan Flower-piercer*		Mountains of northeast Venezuela (Monagas, Sucre)
28 58 021	**Diglossa albilatera** *White-sided Flower-piercer*		Mountains of Venezuela to northern Peru
28 58 022	**Diglossa duidae** *Scaled Flower-piercer*		Mountains of eastern Venezuela, adjacent Brazil (Roraima)
28 58 023	**Diglossa major** *Greater Flower-piercer*		Mountains of eastern Venezuela, adjacent Brazil (Roraima)
28 58 024	**Diglossa indigotica** *Indigo Flower-piercer*		Pacific slope of Colombia and Ecuador

		Date	Location
28 58 025 +	**Diglossa glauca** *Deep-blue Flower-piercer*		Andes of eastern Colombia to northwest Bolivia
28 58 026	**Diglossa caerulescens** *Bluish Flower-piercer*		Temperate Andes of Colombia to northwest Bolivia
28 58 027 +	**Diglossa cyanea** *Masked Flower-piercer*		Andes of Venezuela to Bolivia
28 58 028	**Diglossa plumbea** *Slaty Flower-piercer*		Highlands of Costa Rica and western Panama
28 58 029	**Euneornis campestris** *Orangequit*		Open wooded highlands of Jamaica
28 58 030	**Conirostrum speciosum** *Chestnut-vented Conebill*		Widespread tropical South America east of the Andes
28 58 031	**Conirostrum leucogenys** *White-eared Conebill*		Tropical Panama (Darién), Colombia, Venezuela
28 58 032	**Conirostrum bicolor** *Bicolored Conebill*		Tropical South America to Peru, Amazonian Brazil
28 58 033	**Conirostrum margaritae** *Pearly-breasted Conebill*		Western Amazonian Brazil, adjacent northeast Peru
28 58 034	**Conirostrum cinereum** *Cinereous Conebill*		Temperate Andes of Colombia to northern Chile
28 58 035 +	**Conirostrum tamarugensis** *Tamarugo Conebill*		Andes of southwest Peru (Arequipa) to northern Chile
28 58 036	**Conirostrum ferrugineiventre** *White-browed Conebill*		Andes of central Peru to northwest Bolivia
28 58 037	**Conirostrum rufum** *Rufous-browed Conebill*		Upper subtropical to temperate mountains of Colombia
28 58 038 +	**Conirostrum sitticolor** *Blue-backed Conebill*		Andes of northwest Venezuela to northern Bolivia
28 58 039 +	**Conirostrum albifrons** *Capped Conebill*		Mountains of northern Venezuela to northern Bolivia
28 58 040 +	**Coereba flaveola** *Bananaquit*		Southern Mexico to northeast Argentina; West Indies

FAMILY: TERSINIDAE (Swallow-Tanager)

28 59 001	**Tersina viridis** *Swallow-Tanager*		Eastern Panama to northeast Argentina

Date   Location

FAMILY: PARULIDAE (American Wood Warblers)

28 60 001 **Mniotilta varia**
Black-and-white Warbler   Canada to Gulf states; winters to West Indies,
Ecuador

28 60 002 **Vermivora bachmanii**
Bachman's Warbler   Eastern United States; winters Cuba, Bahamas
(endangered)

28 60 003 **Vermivora chrysoptera**
Golden-winged Warbler   Eastern North America; winters Guatemala to
Colombia, Venezuela

28 60 004 **Vermivora pinus**
Blue-winged Warbler   Eastern United States; winters southern Mexico to
Panama

28 60 005 **Vermivora peregrina**
Tennessee Warbler   Breeds Canada, adjacent states; winters to
Colombia, West Indies

28 60 006 **Vermivora celata**
Orange-crowned Warbler   Western North America; winters to Guatemala

28 60 007 **Vermivora ruficapilla**
Nashville Warbler   Northern North America; winters to Guatemala

28 60 008 **Vermivora virginiae**
Virginia's Warbler   Mountains of western United States; winters to
southern Mexico

28 60 009 **Vermivora crissalis**
Colima Warbler   Chisos Mountains of Texas to central Mexico (rare)

28 60 010 **Vermivora luciae**
Lucy's Warbler   Arid southwest United States to central Mexico
(Guerrero)

28 60 011 **Vermivora gutturalis**
Flame-throated Warbler   Mountains of Costa Rica and western Panama

28 60 012 **Vermivora superciliosa**
Crescent-chested Warbler   Oak-pine and cloud forests of Mexico to Nicaragua

28 60 013 **Parula americana**
Northern Parula Warbler   Eastern North America; winters to Nicaragua, West
Indies

28 60 014 **Parula pitiayumi**
Tropical Parula Warbler   Tropical woodlands of southern Texas to northern
Argentina

28 60 015 **Dendroica petechia**
(erithachorides)
Yellow Warbler   Alaska to Brazil, Peru; Galapagos Islands; West
Indies

28 60 016 **Dendroica pensylvanica**
Chestnut-sided Warbler   Eastern North America; winters Guatemala to
Colombia

		<u>Date</u>	<u>Location</u>
28 60 017	**Dendroica cerulea** *Cerulean Warbler*		Eastern North America; winters Colombia to Bolivia
28 60 018	**Dendroica caerulescens** *Black-throated Blue Warbler*		Eastern North America; winters to Colombia, West Indies
28 60 019	**Dendroica plumbea** *Plumbeous Warbler*		Rain forests, woodland scrub of Lesser Antilles
28 60 020	**Dendroica pharetra** *Arrow-headed Warbler*		Mountain forests and wooded hills of Jamaica
28 60 021	**Dendroica angelae** *Elfin Woods Warbler*		Restricted to high mountain ridges of Puerto Rico
28 60 022	**Dendroica pinus** *Pine Warbler*		Eastern North America, West Indies; winters to Mexico
28 60 023	**Dendroica graciae** *Grace's Warbler*		Mountains of southwest United States to Nicaragua
28 60 024	**Dendroica adelaidae** *Adelaide's Warbler*		Puerto Rico, Vieques, Barbuda and St. Lucia Islands
28 60 025	**Dendroica pityophila** *Olive-capped Warbler*		Cuba, Grand Bahama and Abaco Islands
28 60 026	**Dendroica dominica** *Yellow-throated Warbler*		Eastern United States; winters to Costa Rica, West Indies
28 60 027	**Dendroica nigrescens** *Black-throated Gray Warbler*		Mountains of western North America; winters to Guatemala
28 60 028	**Dendroica townsendi** *Townsend's Warbler*		Mountains of western North America; winters to Nicaragua
28 60 029	**Dendroica occidentalis** *Hermit Warbler*		Mountains of western United States; winters to Nicaragua
28 60 030	**Dendroica chrysoparia** *Golden-cheeked Warbler*		Breeds in Texas (Edwards Plateau); winters to Nicaragua
28 60 031	**Dendroica virens** *Black-throated Green Warbler*		Eastern North America; winters to Mexico, West Indies
28 60 032	**Dendroica discolor** *Prairie Warbler*		Eastern North America; winters to Nicaragua, West Indies
28 60 033	**Dendroica vitellina** *Vitelline Warbler*		West Indies (Cayman and Swan Islands)
28 60 034	**Dendroica tigrina** *Cape May Warbler*		Eastern North America; winters West Indies, rarely Panama

	Date	Location

28 60 035 **Dendroica fusca**
+ *Blackburnian Warbler* — Eastern North America; winters Costa Rica to Peru

28 60 036 **Dendroica magnolia**
Magnolia Warbler — Eastern North America; winters to Colombia, West Indies

28 60 037 **Dendroica coronata (auduboni)**
Yellow-rumped Warbler — Widespread North America; winters to Colombia, West Indies

28 60 038 **Dendroica palmarum**
Palm Warbler — Northeast North America; winters to Honduras, Greater Antilles

28 60 039 **Dendroica kirtlandii**
Kirtland's Warbler — Breeds in Michigan; winters Bahamas (endangered)

28 60 040 **Dendroica striata (breviunguis)**
Blackpoll Warbler — Northern North America; winters Colombia to Brazil

28 60 041 **Dendroica castanea**
Bay-breasted Warbler — Northeast North America; winters to Colombia, Venezuela

28 60 042 **Catharopeza bishopi**
Whistling Warbler — Lesser Antilles (mountain forests of St. Vincent Island—rare)

28 60 043 **Setophaga ruticilla**
American Redstart — Breeds North America; winters to Ecuador, West Indies

28 60 044 **Seiurus aurocapillus**
Ovenbird — Eastern North America; winters to Colombia, West Indies

28 60 045 **Seiurus noveboracensis**
Northern Waterthrush — Northern North America; winters to Peru, West Indies

28 60 046 **Seiurus motacilla**
Louisiana Waterthrush — Eastern United States; winters to Colombia, West Indies

28 60 047 **Limnothlypis swainsonii**
Swainson's Warbler — Southeast United States; winters to Honduras, West Indies

28 60 048 **Helmitheros vermivorus**
Worm-eating Warbler — Eastern United States; winters to Panama, West Indies

28 60 049 **Protonotaria citrea**
Prothonotary Warbler — Eastern United States; winters to Colombia, Venezuela, West Indies

28 60 050 **Geothlypis trichas (chapalensis)**
Common Yellowthroat — Widespread North America, Mexico; winters to Colombia, West Indies

	Date	Location

28 60 051 **Geothlypis beldingi**
Peninsular (Belding's) Yellowthroat
Southern half of Baja California (to about 28° south)

28 60 052 **Geothlypis flavovelata**
Yellow-crowned Yellowthroat
Mexico (coastal marshes of Tamaulipas and Veracruz)

28 60 053 **Geothlypis rostrata**
Bahaman Yellowthroat
Shrubbery and bracken of the Bahamas

28 60 054 **Geothlypis semiflava**
Olive-crowned Yellowthroat
Pacific lowlands of Honduras to Ecuador

28 60 055 **Geothlypis speciosa**
Black-polled Yellowthroat
Highland marshes of south-central Mexico

28 60 056 **Geothlypis nelsoni**
Hooded Yellowthroat
Mexico (mountains of Coahuila to Oaxaca)

28 60 057 **Geothlypis chiriquensis**
Chiriqui Yellowthroat
Chiriqui volcano area of southwest Costa Rica to Pacific western Panama

28 60 058 **Geothlypis aequinoctialis**
Masked Yellowthroat
Tropical southwest Costa Rica to northern Argentina

28 60 059 **Geothlypis poliocephalia**
Gray-crowned Yellowthroat
Lowlands of southern Texas to Pacific western Panama

28 60 060 **Oporornis formosus**
Kentucky Warbler
Eastern United States; winters to Venezuela, Colombia

28 60 061 **Oporornis agilis**
Connecticut Warbler
Breeds northern North America; winters to Brazil

28 60 062 **Oporornis philadelphia**
Mourning Warbler
Southeast Canada, adjacent United States; winters to Ecuador

28 60 063 **Oporornis tolmiei**
MacGillivray's Warbler
Western North America; winters Mexico to Panama

28 60 064 **Microligea palustris**
Ground Warbler
Mainly highlands of Hispaniola and Beata Islands

28 60065 **Teretistris fernandinae**
Yellow-headed Warbler
Forest undergrowth of western Cuba and Isle of Pines

28 60 066 **Teretistris fornsi**
Oriente Warbler
Eastern Cuba to Matanzas Province

28 60 067 **Leucopeza semperi**
Semper's Warbler
Mountain forests of St. Lucia Island (endangered)

28 60 068 **Wilsonia citrina**
Hooded Warbler
Eastern United States; winters Mexico to Panama

	Date	Location

28 60 069 **Wilsonia pusilla**
Wilson's Warbler
Northern and western North America; winters to Panama

28 60 070 **Wilsonia canadensis**
Canada Warbler
Eastern North America; winters to Peru, Brazil

28 60 071 **Cardellina rubrifrons**
Red-faced Warbler
Mountains of southwest United States to Guatemala

28 60 072 **Ergaticus ruber**
Red Warbler
Mountain pine forests of Mexico (Sinaloa to Oaxaca)

28 60 073 **Ergaticus versicolor**
Pink-headed Warbler
Mountains of southern Mexico (Chiapas) and Guatemala

28 60 074 **Myioborus pictus**
Painted Redstart
Mountains of southwest United States to Nicaragua

28 60 075 **Myioborus miniatus**
Slate-throated Redstart
Mexico to Bolivia, Guyana, adjacent Brazil

28 60 076 **Myioborus brunniceps**
Brown-capped Redstart
Northern South America to western Argentina

28 60 077 **Myioborus pariae**
Yellow-faced Redstart
Subtropical Paria Peninsula of Venezuela

28 60 078 **Myioborus cardonai**
Saffron-breasted Redstart
Venezuela (subtropical Cerro Guaiquinima, Bolivar)

28 60 079 **Myioborus torquatus**
Collared Redstart
Mountains of Costa Rica and western Panama

28 60 080 **Myioborus ornatus**
Golden-fronted Redstart
Tropical Andes of northwest Venezuela, Colombia

28 60 081 **Myioborus melanocephalus**
Spectacled Redstart
Andes of Colombia to Bolivia (Cochabamba)

28 60 082 **Myioborus albifrons**
White-fronted Redstart
Andes of Venezuela (Trujillo, Táchira, Mérida)

28 60 083 **Myioborus flavivertex**
Yellow-crowned Redstart
Santa Marta Mountains of Colombia

28 60 084 **Myioborus albifacies**
White-faced Redstart
Amazonas Mountains of Colombia

28 60 085 **Euthlypis lachrymosa**
Fan-tailed Warbler
Western Mexico (Sonora) to northwest Nicaragua

28 60 086 **Basileuterus fraseri**
Gray-and-gold Warbler
Arid littoral of southwest Ecuador to Peru (Tumbes)

28 60 087 **Basileuterus bivittatus**
Two-banded Warbler
Northern South America to northwest Argentina

28 60 088 **Basileuterus chrysogaster**
Golden-bellied Warbler
Tropical Colombia to southern Peru (Junin, Puno)

		Date	Location
28 60 089	**Basileuterus flaveolus** *Flavescent (Baird's)* *Warbler*		Northern Venezuela to eastern Brazil, Paraguay
28 60 090 ✢	**Basileuterus luteoviridis** *Citrine Warbler*		Andes of western Venezuela to Bolivia (Cochabamba)
28 60 091 ✢	**Basileuterus signatus** *Pale-legged Warbler*		Andes of Colombia to northwest Argentina (Jujuy)
28 60 092	**Basileuterus nigrocristatus** *Black-crested Warbler*		Andes of northern Venezuela to Peru (Ancash)
28 60 093	**Basileuterus griseiceps** *Gray-headed Warbler*		Subtropical coastal mountains of Venezuela
28 60 094	**Basileuterus basilicus** *Santa Marta Warbler*		Temperate Santa Marta Mountains of Colombia
28 60 095	**Basileuterus cinereicollis** *Gray-throated Warbler*		Highlands of northwest Venezuela, Colombia
28 60 096	**Basileuterus conspicillatus** *White-lored Warbler*		Santa Marta Mountains of Colombia
28 60 097 ✢	**Basileuterus coronatus** *Russet-crowned Warbler*		Andes of Venezuela to Bolivia (Cochabamba)
28 60 098	**Basileuterus culicivorus** *Golden-crowned Warbler*		Mexico to northern Argentina, eastern Brazil
28 60 099	**Basileuterus rufifrons (delatrii)** *Rufous-capped Warbler*		Highlands of Mexico to Colombia, Venezuela
28 60 100	**Basileuterus belli** *Golden-browed (Bell's)* *Warbler*		Cloud forests of Mexico to Honduras
28 60 101	**Basileuterus melanogenys (ignotus)** *Black-cheeked Warbler*		Mountains of Costa Rica and western Panama
28 60 102 ✢	**Basileuterus tristriatus** *Three-striped Warbler*		Highlands of Costa Rica to northern Venezuela and Bolivia
28 60 103	**Basileuterus trifasciatus** *Three-banded Warbler*		Subtropical southwest Ecuador to Peru (Libertad)
28 60 104	**Basileuterus hypoleucus** *White-bellied Warbler*		Brazil (Goiás, Minas Gerais) to Paraguay
28 60 105	**Basileuterus leucoblepharus** *White-browed Warbler*		Coastal southeast Brazil to northeast Argentina

		Date	Location
28 60 106	**Basileuterus leucophrys** *White-striped Warbler*		Central Brazil (São Paulo, Matto Grosso)
28 60 107	**Phaeothlypis fulvicauda** *Buff-rumped Warbler*		Lowlands of Honduras to Peru, western Brazil
28 60 108	**Phaeothlypis rivularus** *River Warbler*		Honduras to northeast Argentina, Brazil
28 60 109	**Peucedramus taeniatus** *Olive Warbler*		Mountains of southwest United States to Nicaragua
28 60 110	**Xenoligea montana** *White-winged Warbler*		Mountains of Hispaniola
28 60 111	**Granatellus venustus** **(francescae)** *Red-breasted Chat*		Western Mexico (Sinaloa to Chiapas)
28 60 112	**Granatellus sallaei** *Gray-throated Chat*		Eastern Mexico (Veracruz) to Guatemala
28 60 113	**Granatellus pelzelni** *Rose-breasted Chat*		Tropical South America to Bolivia, Amazonian Brazil
28 60 114	**Icteria virens** *Yellow-breasted Chat*		Southern Canada to Mexico; winters to central Panama

FAMILY: ZELEDONIIDAE (Wren-Thrush)

28 61 001	**Zeledonia coronata** *Wren-Thrush*		Humid mountain forests of Costa Rica and western Panama

FAMILY: DREPANIDIDAE (Hawaiian Honeycreepers)

28 62 001	**Loxops virens** *Amakihi*		Rain forests of main islands of Hawaii
28 62 002	**Loxops parva** *Lesser Amakihi*		Hawaii (rain forests of Kauai)
28 62 003	**Loxops sagittirostris** *Greater Amakihi*		Hawaii (probably extinct—no records since about 1900)
28 62 004	**Loxops maculata** *Hawaiian Creeper*		Main islands of Hawaii
28 62005	**Loxops coccinea** *Akepa*		Hawaiian Islands (Hawaii, Kauai, Maui—endangered)

		Date	Location
28 62 006	**Hemignathus obscurus** *Akialoa*		Hawaii (presumed extinct since early 1900s)
28 62 007	**Hemignathus procerus** *Kauai Akialoa*		Alakai Swamp of Kauai Island (endangered)
28 62 008	**Hemignathus lucidus** *Nukupuu*		Hawaii (Maui and Kauai Islands—endangered)
28 62 009	**Hemignathus wilsoni** *Akiapolaau*		Confined to Island of Hawaii (endangered)
28 62 010	**Pseudonestor xanthophrys** *Maui Parrotbill*		Confined to *ohia* forests of Maui (endangered)
28 62 011	**Melamprosops phaeosoma** *Black-faced Honeycreeper*		Northeast slope of Haleakala crater (Maui Island)
28 62 012	**Psittirostra psittacea** *Ou*		Confined to Islands of Hawaii and Kauai (endangered)
28 62 013	**Psittirostra cantans** *Laysan Finch*		Hawaii (confined to Laysan and Nihoa Islands—endangered)
28 62 014	**Psittirostra bailleui** *Palila*		Hawaii (southern and western flanks of Mauna Kea—endangered)
28 62 015	**Psittirostra palmeri** *Greater Koa Finch*		Extinct since about 1896. Inhabited Island of Hawaii
28 62 016	**Psittirostra flaviceps** *Lesser Koa Finch*		Extinct since about 1891. Inhabited Island of Hawaii
28 62 017	**Psittirostra kona** *Grosbeak Finch*		Extinct since about 1896. Inhabited Island of Hawaii
28 62 018	**Himatione sanguinea** *Apapane*		Wet *ohia* forests of Hawaiian islands
28 62 019	**Palmeria dolei** *Crested Honeycreeper*		*Ohia* forests of island of Maui
28 62 020	**Ciridops anna** *Ula-Ai-Hawane*		Extinct since early 1890s. Inhabited Island of Hawaii
28 62 021	**Vestiaria coccinea** *Iiwi*		Highlands of main Hawaiian Islands
28 62 022	**Drepanis pacifica** *Mamo*		Extinct since 1880s. Inhabited big Island of Hawaii
28 62 023	**Drepanis funerea** *Black Mamo*		Extinct since 1907. Inhabited Molokai Island

Date Location

FAMILY: CYCLARHIDAE (Peppershrikes)

28 63 001 **Cyclarhis gujanensis**
Rufous-browed Northeast Mexico to Brazil, northern Argentina
Peppershrike

28 63 002 **Cyclarhis nigrirostris**
Black-billed Peppershrike Highlands of western Colombia and Ecuador

FAMILY: VIREOLANIIDAE (Shrike-Vireos)

28 64 001 **Vireolanius melitophrys**
Chestnut-sided Shrike- Oak forests of southern Mexico (Jalisco) to
Vireo Guatemala

28 64 002 **Smaragdolanius
pulchellus (eximius)**
Green Shrike-Vireo Gulf lowlands of southeast Mexico to Colombia,
Venezuela

28 64 003 **Smaragdolanius leucotis**
Slaty-capped Shrike-Vireo Northern South America to Amazonian Brazil, Bolivia

FAMILY: VIREONIDAE (Vireos)

28 65 001 **Neochloe brevipennis**
Slaty Vireo Oak-pine forests of southern Mexico (rare and local)

28 65 002 **Vireo huttoni**
Hutton's Vireo Western North America (British Columbia to
Guatemala)

28 65 003 **Vireo atricapillus**
Black-capped Vireo South-central United States, Coahuila; winters to
central Mexico

28 65 004 **Vireo griseus
(perquisitor)**
White-eyed Vireo Eastern United States, Mexico; winters to Nicaragua,
Cuba

28 65 005 **Vireo pallens**
Mangrove Vireo Mexico, Yucatán Peninsula to Costa Rica, Nicaragua

28 65 006 **Vireo caribaeus**
St. Andrew Vireo Widespread St. Andrew Island (West Indies)

28 65 007 **Vireo bairdi**
Cozumel Vireo Deciduous forests of Cozumel Island (off Yucatan
Peninsula)

28 65 008 **Vireo gundlachii**
Cuban Vireo Humid to semiarid Cuba and Isle of Pines

		Date	Location
28 65 009	**Vireo crassirostris** *Thick-billed Vireo*		Widespread throughout the Greater Antilles
28 65 010	**Vireo bellii** *Bell's Vireo*		Arid western United States, northern Mexico; winters to Nicaragua
28 65 011	**Vireo vicinior** *Gray Vireo*		Southwest United States, Baja California; winters to Durango
28 65 012	**Vireo nelsoni** *Dwarf Vireo*		Mountains of southwest Mexico (Michoacan to Oaxaca—rare)
28 65 013	**Vireo hypochryseus** *Golden Vireo*		Pacific slope of Mexico (Sonora to Oaxaca); Tres Marias Islands
28 65 014	**Vireo modestus** *Jamaican Vireo*		Widespread Island of Jamaica
28 65 015	**Vireo nanus** *Flat-billed Vireo*		Semiarid scrub of Hispaniola and Gonâve Island
28 65 016	**Vireo latimeri** *Puerto Rican Vireo*		Mainly confined to limestone hills of Puerto Rico
28 65 017	**Vireo osburni** *Blue Mountain Vireo*		Mainly confined to mountain rain forests of Jamaica
28 65 018	**Vireo carmioli** *Yellow-winged Vireo*		Mountains of Costa Rica and western Panama
28 65 019	**Vireo solitarius** *Solitary Vireo*		Canada to El Salvador; winters to Nicaragua, Cuba, Jamaica
28 65 020	**Vireo flavifrons** *Yellow-throated Vireo*		Canada to Gulf states; winters to Colombia, West Indies
28 65 021	**Vireo philadelphicus** *Philadelphia Vireo*		Eastern North America; winters to Panama, rarely Colombia
28 65 022	**Vireo olivaceus** *Red-eyed Vireo*		Widespread Canada to Argentina; West Indies
28 65 023	**Vireo flavoviridis** *Yellow-green Vireo*		Southern Texas to Panama; winters to Brazil
28 64 024	**Vireo magister** *Yucatán Vireo*		Yucatán Peninsula and adjacent islands to Honduras
28 65 025	**Vireo altiloquus** *Black-whiskered Vireo*		Florida, West Indies; winters to Brazil, Peru
28 65 026	**Vireo gilvus (leucophrys)** *Warbling Vireo*		Open woodlands of Canada to northwest Bolivia

		Date	Location
28 65 027	**Hylophilus poicilotis** *Rufous-crowned Greenlet*		Eastern Brazil to northern Bolivia, northeast Argentina
28 65 028	**Hylophilus thoracicus** *Lemon-chested Greenlet*		Tropical northern South America to Bolivia, Brazil
28 65 029	**Hylophilus semicinereus** *Gray-chested Greenlet*		Tropical Amazonian Brazil, French Guiana, Venezuela
28 65 030	**Hylophilus pectoralis** *Ashy-headed Greenlet*		Tropical Guianas, Amazonian Brazil, northeast Bolivia
28 65 031	**Hylophilus sclateri** *Tepui Greenlet*		Mountains of Guyana, Venezuela, adjacent Brazil (Roraima)
28 65 032	**Hylophilus muscicapinus** *Buff-cheeked Greenlet*		Tropical Guianas, Venezuela, Amazonian Brazil
28 65 033	**Hylophilus brunneiceps** *Brown-headed Greenlet*		Southeast Colombia, Venezuela, northeast Brazil
28 65 034	**Hylophilus semibrunneus** *Rufous-naped Greenlet*		Subtropical mountains of Venezuela to Ecuador
28 65 035	**Hylophilus aurantiifrons** *Golden-fronted Greenlet*		Central Panama to northern Colombia and Venezuela
28 65 036	**Hylophilus hypoxanthus** *Dusky-capped Greenlet*		Tropical Venezuela to northern Bolivia, Amazonian Brazil
28 65 037	**Hylophilus flavipes** (**viridiflavus**) *Scrub Greenlet*		Costa Rica to northern Colombia, Venezuela
28 65 038	**Hylophilus ochraceiceps** *Tawny-crowned Greenlet*		Gulf lowlands of southern Mexico to western Amazon basin
28 65 039	**Hylophilus decurtatus** (**minor**) *Gray-headed Greenlet*		Rain forests of southeast Mexico to western Ecuador
28 65 040	**Hylophilus olivaceus** *Olivaceous Greenlet*		Subtropical mountains of eastern Ecuador to central Peru

FAMILY: ICTERIDAE (Troupials and Allies)

28 66 001 +	**Psarocolius oseryi** *Casqued Oropendola*		Tropical eastern Ecuador to Peru (Puno)
28 66 002	**Psarocolius latirostris** *Band-tailed Oropendola*		Tropical western Brazil, adjacent Peru, Ecuador

		Date	Location
28 66 003	**Psarocolius decumanus** *Crested Oropendola*		Panama to northern Argentina; Trinidad; Tobago
28 66 044	**Psarocolius viridis** *Green Oropendola*		Tropical northern South America to Amazonian Brazil, Peru
28 66 005	**Psarocolius atrovirens** *Dusky-green Oropendola*		Subtropical southeast Peru to northern Bolivia
28 66 006	**Psarocolius angustifrons** *Russet-backed Oropendola*		Northern South America to Bolivia, west Amazonian Brazil
28 66 007	**Psarocolius wagieri** *Chestnut-headed Oropendola*		Gulf lowlands of southern Mexico to northwest Ecuador
28 66 008	**Gymnostinops montezuma** *Montezuma Oropendola*		Gulf lowlands of southern Mexico to central Panama
28 66 009	**Gymnostinops cassini** *Chestnut-mantled Oropendola*		Tropical northwest Colombia (lower Atrato Valley)
28 66 010	**Gymnostinops bifasciatus** *Para Oropendola*		Brazil (forests of Rio Tocantins to lower Amazonia)
28 66 011	**Gymnostinops guatimozinus** *Black Oropendola*		Tropical eastern Panama to northwest Colombia
28 66 012	**Gymnostinops yuracares** *Olive Oropendola*		Widespread tropical western Amazon basin
28 66 013 †	**Cacicus cela (vitellinus)** *Yellow-rumped Cacique*		Tropical Panama to northern Bolivia, eastern Brazil
28 66 014 ⊥	**Cacicus haemorrhous** *Red-rumped Cacique*		Tropical South America to northeast Argentina, Brazil
28 66 015	**Cacicus uropygialis** *Scarlet-rumped Cacique*		Lowland forests of Nicaragua to northern Peru
28 66 016	**Cacicus chrysopterus** *Golden-winged Cacique*		Forests of southeast Brazil to northern Argentina
28 66 017	**Cacicus koepckeae** *Selva Cacique*		Eastern Peru (known from two specimens from Loreto)
28 66 018	**Cacicus leucorhamphus** *Mountain Cacique*		Mountains of Venezuela to Bolivia (La Paz, Cochabamba)
28 66 019	**Cacicus chrysonotus** *Bolivian Cacique*		Southeast Peru and Bolivia (probable race *C. leucorhamphus*)

		Date	Location
28 66 020	**Cacicus sclateri** *Ecuadorean Cacique*		Tropical forests of eastern Ecuador
28 66 021	**Cacicus solitarius** *Solitary Cacique*		Widespread tropical zone of South America
28 66 022	**Cacicus melanicterus** *Mexican Cacique*		Pacific lowlands of Mexico (Sonora to Chiapas)
28 66 023	**Amblycercus holosericeus** *Yellow-billed Cacique*		Lowland forests of eastern Mexico to Bolivia (Cochambamba)
28 66 024	**Icterus cayanensis** *Epaulet Oriole*		Widespread tropical open woodlands of South America
28 66 025	**Icterus chrysocephalus** *Moriche Oriole*		Tropical Guianas to Peru, northern Brazil
28 66 026	**Icterus chrysater** *Yellow-backed Oriole*		Highlands of Mexico (Veracruz) to Colombia, Venezuela
28 66 027	**Icterus nigrogularis** *Yellow Oriole*		Tropical Colombia to the Guianas; Trinidad; Margarita Island
28 66 028	**Icterus leucopteryx** *Jamaican Oriole*		Jamaica; St. Andrews; Grand Cayman Island (endangered)
28 66 029	**Icterus auratus** *Orange Oriole*		Confined to Yucatán Peninsula of Mexico
28 66 030	**Icterus mesomelas** *Yellow-tailed Oriole*		Tropical southern Mexico to Peru (Libertad)
28 66 031	**Icterus auricapillus** *Orange-crowned Oriole*		Tropical eastern Panama to Colombia, Venezuela
28 66 032	**Icterus graceannae** *White-edged Oriole*		Desert scrub of western Ecuador to Peru (Libertad)
28 66 033	**Icterus xantholemus** *Yellow-throated Oriole*		Ecuador (unique—possible immature *I. mesomelas*)
28 66 034	**Icterus pectoralis** *Spot-breasted Oriole*		Arid lowlands of southwest Mexico (Colima) to Costa Rica
28 66 035	**Icterus gularis** *Lichtenstein's (Altamira) Oriole*		Southern Texas to Nicaragua, Costa Rica
28 66 036	**Icterus pustulatus (sclateri)** *Streaked-back Oriole*		Arid Pacific slope of Mexico to Costa Rica; Tres Marias Islands

		Date	Location

28 66 037 **Icterus cucullatus**
Hooded Oriole
Southwest United States to Honduras; Baja California

28 66 038 **Icterus icterus**
Troupial
Tropical northern South America to Brazil, Bolivia

28 66 039 **Icterus galbula**
(bullockii) (abeillei)
Northern Oriole
Canada to Mexico; winters to Colombia and
Venezuela

28 66 040 **Icterus spurius**
(fuertesi)
Orchard Oriole
Southeast Canada to Mexico; winters to Colombia,
Venezuela

28 66 041 **Icterus dominicensis**
(prosthemelas)
Black-cowled Oriole
Gulf lowlands of Mexico to Panama; West Indies

28 66 042 **Icterus wagleri**
Black-vented (Wagler's)
Oriole
Widespread Mexico to Nicaragua

28 66 043 **Icterus laudabilis**
St. Lucia Oriole
Lesser Antilles (confined to St. Lucia Island)

28 66 044 **Icterus bonana**
Martinique Oriole
Lesser Antilles (confined to Martinique Island)

28 66 045 **Icterus oberi**
Montserrat Oriole
Lesser Antilles (confined to Montserrat Island)

28 66 046 **Icterus graduacauda**
Black-headed Oriole
Southern Texas, Mexico to northwest Guatemala

28 66 047 **Icterus maculialatus**
Bar-winged Oriole
Mexico (Chiapas), Guatemala and El Salvador

28 66 048 **Icterus parisorum**
Scott's Oriole
Arid southwest United States to southern Mexico
(Oaxaca)

28 66 049 **Nesopsar nigerrimus**
Jamaican Blackbird
Humid mountain forests of Jamaica

28 66 050 **Xanthopsar flavus**
Saffron-cowled Blackbird
Southeast Brazil (Rio Grande do Sul) to northeast
Argentina

28 66 051 **Gymnomystax**
mexicanus
Oriole Blackbird
Tropical northern South America to Amazonian Brazil,
Peru

28 66 052 **Xanthocephalus**
xanthocephalus
Yellow-headed Blackbird
Widespread southern Canada to southern Mexico

	Date	Location

28 66 053
✛   **Agelaius xanthophthalmus**
Pale-eyed Blackbird   Upper tropical Peru (Huánuco)

28 66 054
✛   **Agelaius thilius**
Yellow-winged Blackbird   Temperate southeast Brazil to Bolivia, Chile, Argentina

28 66 055   **Agelaius phoeniceus**
Red-winged Blackbird   Widespread Canada to Costa Rica; West Indies

28 66 056   **Agelaius tricolor**
Tricolored Blackbird   Pacific United States (Oregon) to Baja California

28 66 057   **Agelaius icterocephalus**
Yellow-hooded Blackbird   Northern South America to Peru, Amazonian Brazil

28 66 058   **Agelaius humeralis**
Tawny-shouldered Blackbird   Widespread lowlands of Cuba and Haiti

28 66 059   **Agelaius xanthomus**
Yellow-shouldered Blackbird   Lowlands of Puerto Rico and Mona Island

28 66 060
✛   **Agelaius cyanopus**
Unicolored Blackbird   Northeast Brazil to northeast Argentina

28 66 061   **Agelaius ruficapillus**
Chestnut-capped Blackbird   French Guiana to southern Brazil, Argentina

28 66 062
✛   **Sturnella supercillaris**
White-browed Blackbird   Brazil (Ceará) to eastern Argentina and Bolivia

28 66 063   **Sturnella militaris**
Red-breasted Blackbird   Tropical Panama to the Guianas, Colombia, Argentina

28 66 064
✛   **Sturnella bellicosa**
Peuvian Red-breasted Meadowlark   Southwest Ecuador to western Peru, northern Chile

28 66 065   **Sturnella defilippi**
Lesser Red-breasted Meadowlark   Southeast Brazil (Paraná) to central Argentina

28 66 066
✛   **Sturnella loyca**
Long-tailed Meadowlark   Northwest Argentina, Chile to Tierra del Fuego; Falkland Islands

28 66 067   **Sturnella magna**
Eastern Meadowlark   Southeast Canada to northern Brazil; Cuba

28 66 068   **Sturnella neglecta**
Western Meadowlark   Southwest Canada to southern Mexico; Baja California

28 66 069   **Pseudoleistes guirahuro**
Yellow-rumped Marshbird   Eastern Brazil (Goiás) to northeast Argentina

		Date	Location

28 66 070 **Pseudoleistes virescens**
+ *Brown-and-yellow* Southeast Brazil (Rio Grande do Sul) to central
Marshbird Argentina

28 66 071 **Amblyramphus**
+ **holosericeus**
Scarlet-headed Blackbird Southeast Brazil to northern Bolivia, northeast
Argentina

28 66 072 **Hypopyrrhus**
pyrohypogaster
Red-bellied Grackle Subtropical Colombia east of the Andes

28 66 073 **Curaeus curaeus**
Austral Blackbird Central Argentina, Chile to Cape Horn Archipelago

28 66 074 **Curaeus forbesi**
Forbes' Blackbird Eastern Brazil (Pernambuco, Minas Gerais)

28 66 075 **Gnorimopsar chopi**
Chopi Blackbird Eastern Brazil to eastern Bolivia, northern Argentina

28 66 076 **Oreopsar bolivianus**
Bolivian Blackbird Highlands of Bolivia (Cochabamba, Chuquisaca,
Potosi)

28 66 077 **Lampropsar tanagrinus**
Velvet-fronted Grackle Tropical South America to Amazonian Brazil, Bolivia

28 66 078 **Macroagelaius subalaris**
Mountain Grackle Western slope of eastern Andes of Colombia

28 66 079 **Macroagelaius imthurni**
Golden-tufted Grackle Montane forests of Guyana, immediately adjacent
Brazil, Venezuela

28 66 080 **Dives atroviolaceus**
Cuban Blackbird Widespread Cuba; rare Isle of Pines

28 66 081 **Dives dives**
Melodious Blackbird Gulf slope of eastern Mexico to Nicaragua

28 66 082 **Dives warszewiczi**
Scrub Blackbird Semiarid coastal scrub of southwest Ecuador to Peru

28 66 083 **Cassidix mexicanus**
Great-tailed Grackle Lowlands of southwest United States to southwest
Peru

28 66 084 **Cassidix major**
Boat-tailed Grackle Atlantic and Gulf coasts of New Jersey to Texas

28 66 085 **Cassidix palustris**
Slender-billed Grackle Extinct. Inhabited headwaters of Rio Lerma, Mexico
City

28 66 086 **Cassidix nicaraguensis**
Nicaraguan Grackle Confined to Lakes Nicaragua and Managua
(endangered)

28 66 087 **Quiscalus quiscula**
Common Grackle Southern Canada to Gulf states (east of Rockies)

	Date	Location

28 66 088 Quiscalus niger
Greater Antillean Grackle — Greater and Lesser Antilles (West Indies)

28 66 089 Quiscalus lugubris
Carib Grackle — Tropical Colombia to northeast Brazil; West Indies

28 66 090 Euphagus carolinus
Rusty Blackbird — Alaska, Canada to Gulf states

28 66 091 Euphagus cyanocephalus
Brewer's Blackbird — Western Canada and United States; winters to Isthmus of Tehuantepec

28 66 092 Molothrus badius
+
Bay-winged Cowbird — Eastern Brazil (Piaui) to central Argentina

28 66 093 Molothrus armenti
Bronze-brown Cowbird — Colombia (Leticia—known from two specimens collected 1851)

28 66 094 Molothrus rufoaxillaris
Screaming Cowbird — Southeast Brazil to Bolivia, central Argentina

28 66 095 Molothrus bonariensis
+
Shiny (Glossy) Cowbird — Eastern Panama (rare) to Argentina, Chile; Lesser Antilles

28 66 096 Molothrus aeneus
Bronzed (Red-eyed) Cowbird — Lowlands of southwest United States to Panama

28 66 097 Molothrus ater
Brown-headed Cowbird — Southern Canada to Isthmus of Tehuantepec; Cozumel Island

28 66 098 Scaphidura oryzivora
Giant Cowbird — Southern Mexico to Brazil, Argentina; Trinidad; Tobago

28 66 099 Dolichonyx oryzivorus
Bobolink — Canada to Argentina; West Indies; Galapagos Islands

FAMILY: FRINGILLIDAE (Canaries, Siskins and Allies)

28 67 001 Fringilla coelebs
Chaffinch — Widespread Palearctic region

28 67 002 Fringilla teydea
Canary Islands Chaffinch — Canary Islands (Tenerife and Gran Canaria Islands)

28 67 003 Fringilla montifringilla
Brambling — Widespread Palearctic region

28 67 004 Serinus pusillus
Gold-fronted Serin — Caucasus mountains to Kashmir, Garhwal, Nepal

28 67 005 Serinus serinus
Common Serin — Widespread Palearctic region

		Date	Location
28 67 006	**Serinus syriacus** *Syrian (Tristram's) Serin*		Asia Minor (Syria and Lebanon)
28 67 007	**Serinus canaria** *Common Canary*		Canary islands; Azores; Madeira Island
28 67 008	**Serinus citrinella** *Citril Finch*		Montane conifer forests of southern Europe
28 67 009	**Serinus thibetanus** *Tibetan Serin*		Nepal, Sikkim to Tibet, Yunnan, northeast Burma
28 67 010	**Serinus canicollis** **(flavivertex)** *Yellow-crowned Canary*		Highlands of Ethiopia to South Africa
28 67 011	**Serinus nigriceps** *Black-headed Serin*		Endemic to highlands of Ethiopia
28 67 012	**Serinus ankoberensis** *Ankober Serin*		Highlands of Ethiopia (new species discovered 1978)
28 67 013	**Serinus frontalis** *Yellow-fronted Citril*		Ruanda to Zaire, Tanzania, Zambia
28 67 014	**Serinus citrinelloides** *African Citril*		Submontane forests of Eritrea, Ethiopia to Rhodesia
28 67 015	**Serinus capistratus** *Black-faced Canary*		Woodlands of Angola to Kenya, Rhodesia
28 67 016	**Serinus kiliensis** *Van Someren's Canary*		Papyrus swamps of western Kenya, adjacent Uganda
28 67 017	**Serinus scotops** *Forest Canary*		Forests of southern tip of Africa
28 67 018	**Serinus leucopygius** *White-rumped Seedeater*		Senegal to the Sudan, Ethiopia
28 67 019	**Serinus atrogularis** *Yellow-rumped Seedeater*		Widespread lowlands of Ethiopia to South Africa
28 67 020	**Serinus citrinipectus** *Lemon-breasted Canary*		Known only from southern Mozambique (rare)
28 67 021	**Serinus mozambicus** *Yellow-fronted Canary*		Widespread Africa south of the Sahara
28 67 022	**Serinus donaldsoni** *Grosbeak Canary*		Ethiopia, Somalia to Kenya, Tanzania
28 67 023	**Serinus flaviventris** *Yellow Canary*		Coastal scrub of Namibia to South Africa
28 67 024	**Serinus sulphuratus** *Brimstone Canary*		Highlands of eastern Zaire, Kenya to South Africa
28 67 025	**Serinus albogularis** *White-throated Seedeater*		Riverine scrub of Angola to South Africa

		Date	Location
28 67 026	**Serinus flavigula** *Yellow-throated Seedeater*		Ethiopia (probable hybrid—known from one specimen collected 1888)
28 67 027	**Serinus dorsostriatus** *White-bellied Canary*		Highlands of Ethiopia to Tanzania
28 67 028	**Serinus gularis** **(reichardi)** *Streaky-headed Seedeater*		Woodlands of Ethiopia to South Africa
28 67 029	**Serinus mennelli** *Black-eared Seedeater*		Highlands of Angola, Zaire to Mozambique
28 67 030	**Serinus tristriatus** *Brown-rumped Seedeater*		Eritrea, Ethiopia and Somalia
28 67 031	**Serinus menachensis** *Yemen Seedeater*		Bushy hills of Yemen to Amiri, Arabia
28 67 032	**Serinus striolatus** *Streaky Seedeater*		Montane forests of Ethiopia to Rhodesia
28 67 033	**Serinus burtoni** *Thick-billed Seedeater*		Cameroon highlands to Zaire, Kenya, Tanzania
28 67 034	**Serinus rufobrunneus** *Principé Seedeater*		São Thomé and Principé Islands (Gulf of Guinea)
28 67 035	**Serinus leucopterus** *White-winged Seedeater*		Mountains of southwest Cape Province (rare)
28 67 036	**Serinus totta** *Cape Siskin*		Mountains of Cape Province of South Africa
28 67 037	**Serinus alario** **(leucolaema)** *Black-headed Canary*		Arid Namibia to South Africa
28 67 038	**Serinus estherae** *Malay Goldfinch*		Malaya; Philippines (Mindanao only)
28 67 039	**Neospiza concolor** *São Thomé Goldfinch*		Endemic to São Thomé Island (probably extinct)
28 67 040	**Linurgus olivaceus** *Oriole Finch*		Fernando Po; highlands of Cameroon to Kenya, Tanzania
28 67 041	**Rhynchostruthus socotranus** *Golden-winged Grosbeak*		Socotra Island; Somalia to Arabia
28 67 042	**Carduelis chloris** *European Greenfinch*		Widespread western Palearctic region
28 67 043	**Carduelis sinica** *Gray-capped Greenfinch*		Kamchatka to southern China; Taiwan
28 67 044	**Carduelis spinoides** *Yellow-breasted Greenfinch*		Himalayas of Pakistan to Szechwan, Burma, Annam

		Date	Location
28 67 045	**Carduelis ambigua** *Black-headed Greenfinch*		Tibet to southwest China, Burma, Tonkin, Laos
28 67 046	**Carduelis spinus** *Eurasian Siskin*		Palearctic region, eastern China; Taiwan; Philippines
28 67 047	**Carduelis pinus** *Pine Siskin*		Mountains of Alaska to southern Mexico
28 67 048	**Carduelis atriceps** *Black-capped Siskin*		Mountains of southern Mexico (Chiapas) and Guatemala
28 67 049	**Carduelis spinescens** *Andean Siskin*		Mountains of northwest Venezuela to Colombia
28 67 050	**Carduelis yarrellii** *Yellow-faced Siskin*		Tropical northern Venezuela to eastern Brazil
28 67 051	**Carduelis cucullata** *Red Siskin*		Tropical Venezuela, Colombia (nearing extinction)
28 67 052	**Carduelis crassirostris** *Thick-billed Siskin*		High Andes of Peru to Argentina, Chile
28 67 053	**Carduelis magellanica (santaecrucis)** *Hooded Siskin*		Widespread tropical to temperate South America
28 67 054	**Carduelis dominicensis** *Antillean Siskin*		Mountain pine forests of Hispaniola
28 67 055	**Carduelis siemiradzkii** *Saffron Siskin*		Arid littoral of tropical western Ecuador
28 67 056	**Carduelis olivacea** *Olivaceous Siskin*		Subtropical eastern Ecuador to northern Bolivia
28 67 057	**Carduelis notata** *Black-headed Siskin*		Mountains of western and southern Mexico to Nicaragua
28 67 058	**Carduelis xanthogaster** *Yellow-bellied Siskin*		Mountains of Costa Rica to northern Bolivia
28 67 059	**Carduelis atrata** *Black Siskin*		Puna of Peru to Chile, Argentina (Mendoza)
28 67 060	**Carduelis uropygialis** *Yellow-rumped Siskin*		Temperate Andes of Peru to Chile, Argentina (Mendoza)
28 67 061	**Carduelis barbata** *Black-chinned Siskin*		Central Chile, Argentina to Cape Horn Archipelago
28 67 062	**Carduelis tristis** *American Goldfinch*		Widespread and common Canada to southern Mexico; Baja California
28 67 063	**Carduelis psaltria** *Lesser Goldfinch*		Widespread western United States to northern Peru

		Date	Location
28 67 064	**Carduelis lawrencei** _Lawrence's Goldfinch_		Southwest United States and northern Mexico; Baja California
28 67 065	**Carduelis carduelis** _European Goldfinch_		Widespread Palearctic region
28 67 066	**Acanthis flammea** _Common Redpoll_		Holarctic circumpolar
28 67 067	**Acanthis hornemanni** _Hoary Redpoll_ _Artic Redpoll (Br.)_		Holarctic circumpolar
28 67 068	**Acanthis flavirostris** _Twite_		Widespread Palearctic region
28 67 069	**Acanthis cannabina** _Eurasian Linnet_		Widespread Palearctic region
28 67 070	**Acanthis yemenensis** _Yemen Linnet_		Mountains of Hejaz, Asir, Yemen
28 67 071	**Acanthis johannis** _Warsangli Linnet_		Somalia (known from one specimen collected 1919)
28 67 072	**Leucosticte nemoricola** _Hodgson's Rosy Finch_		Himalayas of Afghanistan to Kansu, northeast Burma
28 67 073	**Leucosticte brandti** _Brandt's Rosy Finch_		Mountains of Monogolia to Kashmir, Nepal, Sikkim
28 67 074	**Leucosticte arctoa** _Arctic Rosy Finch_		Northeast Asia, northwest North America
28 67 075	**Leucosticte tephrocotis** _Gray-crowned Rosy Finch_		Alaska to highlands of southwest United States
28 67 076	**Leucosticte atrata** _Black Rosy Finch_		Mountains of western United States
28 67 077	**Leucosticte australis** _Brown-capped Rosy Finch_		Mountains of Wyoming, New Mexico
28 67 078	**Callacanthis burtoni** _Himalayan Red-browed Finch_		Himalayas of Kashmir to Nepal and Sikkim
28 67 079	**Rhodopechys sanguinea** _Crimson-winged Finch_		Mountains of Morocco, Algeria to Turkey
28 67 080	**Rhodopechys githaginea** _Trumpeter Finch_		Canaries, Mediterranean basin to Arabia
28 67 081	**Rhodopechys mongolica** _Mongolian Finch_		Iran, Afghanistan to Monogolia
28 67 082	**Rhodopechys obsoleta** _Desert Finch_		Palestine to Russian and Chinese Turkestan
28 67 083	**Uragus sibiricus** _Long-tailed Rosefinch_		Eastern Palearctic; Japan

		Date	Location
28 67 084	**Urocynchramus pylzowi** *Przewalski's Rosefinch*		Himalayas of Nepal to Assam, Yunnan
28 67 085	**Carpodacus rubescens** *Blanford's Rosefinch*		Himalayas of Nepal to Assam, Yunnan, Kansu
28 67 086	**Carpodacus nipalensis** *Dark-breasted Rosefinch*		Himalayas of Kashmir to Yunnan, Burma, Tonkin
28 67 087	**Carpodacus erythrinus** *Common Rosefinch*		Widespread Palearctic, Oriental region mainland
28 67 088	**Carpodacus purpureus** *Purple Finch*		Highlands of Canada, United States to northwest Mexico; Baja California
28 67 089	**Carpodacus cassinii** *Cassin's Finch*		Mountains of southwest Canada to central Mexico
28 67 090	**Carpodacus mexicanus** *House Finch (Linnet)*		British Columbia to southern Mexico; introduced Hawaii
28 67 091	**Carpodacus pulcherrimus** *Beautiful Rosefinch*		Himalayas of Garhwal, Nepal to Szechwan and Mongolia
28 67 092	**Carpodacus eos** *Pink-rumped Rosefinch*		Mountains of Tsinghai, Szechwan, Sikiang
28 67 093	**Carpodacus rhodochrous** *Pink-browed Rosefinch*		High Himalayas of Kashmir to Nepal and Sikkim
28 67 094	**Carpodacus vinaceus** *Vinaceous Rosefinch*		Mountains of Nepal to Szechwan, Burma; Taiwan
28 67 095	**Carpodacus edwardsii** *Dark-rumped Rosefinch*		Himalayas of Nepal to Kansu, Sikiang, Burma
28 67 096	**Carpodacus synoicus** *Sinai Rosefinch*		Sinai Peninsula to Afghanistan
28 67 097	**Carpodacus roseus** *Pallas' Rosefinch*		Eastern Palearctic region
28 67 098	**Carpodacus trifasciatus** *Three-banded Rosefinch*		Coniferous forests of western China
28 67 099	**Carpodacus rhodopeplus** *Spot-winged Rosefinch*		Himalayas of Nepal, Sikkim to Szechwan, Burma
28 67 100	**Carpodacus thura** *White-browed Rosefinch*		Himalayas of Afghanistan, Garhwal to Szechwan
28 67 101	**Carpodacus rhodochlamys** *Red-mantled Rosefinch*		Alpine zone of mountains of central Asia
28 67 102	**Carpodacus rubicilloides** *Streaked Great Rosefinch*		Mountains of Kashmir, Nepal to Yunnan

	Date	Location

28 67 103 **Carpodacus rubicilla**
Great Rosefinch — Mountains of Asia Minor to Nepal, Sikkim, Mongolia

28 67 104 **Carpodacus puniceus**
Red-breasted Rosefinch — Himalayas of Kashmir, Nepal to Szechwan

28 67 105 **Carpodacus roborowskii**
Roborovski's Rosefinch — High mountains of Tsinghai (China)

28 67 106 **Chaunoproctus ferreorostris**
Bonin Islands Grosbeak — Extinct. Inhabited Bonin Islands off coast of China

28 67 107 **Pinicola enucleator**
Pine Grosbeak — Holarctic circumpolar coniferous forests

28 67 108 **Pinicola subhimachala**
Crimson-browed Finch — Himalayas of Nepal to Sikiang, Burma

28 67 109 **Haematospiza sipahi**
Scarlet Finch — Himalayas of Garhwal to Yunnan, Burma, Laos, Tonkin

28 67 110 **Loxia pytyopsittacus**
Parrot Crossbill — Coniferous forests of Scandinavian Peninsula

28 67 111 **Loxia curvirostra**
Red Crossbill — Holarctic circumpolar coniferous forests

28 67 112 **Loxia leucoptera**
White-winged Crossbill — Holarctic circumpolar larch forests; Hispaniola

28 67 113 **Pyrrhula nipalensis**
Brown Bullfinch — Himalayas of India to Sikiang, Malaya; Taiwan

28 67 114 **Pyrrhula leucogenys**
Philippine Bullfinch — Philippines (endemic to Mindanao and Luzon)

28 67 115 **Pyrrhula aurantiaca**
Orange Bullfinch — Northwest Himalayas (Chitral east to Vale of Kashmir)

28 67 116 **Pyrrhula erythrocephala**
Red-headed Bullfinch — Himalayas of Kashmir to Tibet, Bhutan

28 67 117 **Pyrrhula erythaca**
Beavan's Bullfinch — Himalayas of Sikkim to Szechwan, Burma; Taiwan

28 67 118 **Pyrrhula pyrrhula**
Common Bullfinch — Widespread Palearctic region

28 67 119 **Coccothraustes coccothraustes**
Hawfinch — Widespread Palearctic region

28 67 120 **Coccothraustes migratorius (melanura)**
Yellow-billed Grosbeak — China, Burma, Indochina; Taiwan; Hongkong

28 67 121 **Coccothraustes personatus**
Japanese Grosbeak — Eastern Palearctic region

		Date	Location
28 67 122	**Coccothraustes icterioides** *Black-and-yellow Grosbeak*		Western Himalayas (Utter Pradesh to Afghanistan)
28 67 123	**Coccothraustes affinis** *Collared Grosbeak*		Mountains of Kashmir to Tibet, Yunnan, Burma
28 67 124	**Coccothraustes melanozanthos** *Spot-winged Grosbeak*		Himalayas of Kashmir to Yunnan, Burma, Laos
28 67 125	**Coccothraustes carnipes** *White-winged Grosbeak*		Mountains of Iran to Szechwan, Burma
28 67 126	**Coccothraustes vespertinus** *Evening Grosbeak*		Mountains of Canada to Mexico
28 67 127	**Coccothraustes abeillei** *Hooded Grosbeak*		Sierra Madre Mountains of Mexico to Guatemala
28 67 128	**Pyrrhoplectes epauletta** *Gold-naped Finch*		Himalayas of Garhwal to Sikiang, Burma

FAMILY: ESTRILDIDAE (Waxbills and Allies)

28 68 001	**Parmoptila woodhousei (rubrifrons)** *Flowerpecker Weaver-Finch*		Forests of Nigeria to northern Angola, Zaire
28 68 002	**Nigrita fusconota** *White-breasted Negro-Finch*		Fernando Po; Guinea to Angola, Kenya
28 68 003	**Nigrita bicolor** *Chestnut-breasted Negro-Finch*		Senegal to Uganda, northern Angola; Principé Island
28 68 004	**Nigrita luteifrons** *Pale-fronted Negro-Finch*		Secondary forests of Nigeria to Angola, Uganda
28 68 005	**Nigrita canicapilla** *Gray-headed Negro-Finch*		Tropical Guinea to Uganda, Zaire; Fernando Po
28 68 006	**Nesocharis shelleyi** *Fernando Po Olive-back*		Highlands of Cameroon mountain; Fernando Po Island
28 68 007	**Nesocharis ansorgei** *White-collared Olive-back*		Highland marshes of eastern Zaire, adjacent Uganda
28 68 008	**Nesocharis capistrata** *Gray-headed Olive-back*		Gambia to the Sudan, Uganda, northeast Zaire

		Date	Location
28 68 009	**Pytilia phoenicoptera** *Red-winged Pytilia*		Grasslands of Senegal to the Sudan, Ethiopia
28 68 010	**Pytilia hypogrammica** *Yellow-winged Pytilia*		Sierra Leone to the northern Zaire border
28 68 011	**Pytilia afra** *Orange-winged Pytilia*		Sudan and Ethiopia to Angola, Mozambique
28 68 012	**Pytilia melba** *Green-winged Pytilia*		Widespread Africa south of the Sahara
28 68 013	**Mandingoa nitidula** *Green-backed Twin-spot*		Sierra Leone to Angola, Ethiopia, Uganda
28 68 014	**Cryptospiza reichenovii** *Red-faced Crimson-wing*		Bamboo forests of Senegal to Somalia, Mozambique
28 68 015	**Cryptospiza salvadorii** *Ethiopian Crimson-wing*		Mountains of Ethiopia to Zaire, Uganda
28 68 016	**Cryptospiza jacksoni** *Dusky Crimson-wing*		Dense montane forests of eastern Zaire and Uganda
28 68 017	**Cryptospiza shelleyi** *Shelley's Crimson-wing*		Montane forests of eastern Zaire (Ruwenzori, Kivu)
28 68 018	**Pyrenestes sanguineus** *Crimson Seedcracker*		Lowland swamps of Sierra Leone to Gabon
28 68 019	**Pyrenestes ostrinus** *Black-bellied Seedcracker*		Ghana to Uganda, Angola, Tanzania, Mozambique
28 68 020	**Pyrenestes minor** *Lesser Seedcracker*		Riverine forests of Tanzania, Mozambique and Malawi
28 68 021	**Spermophaga poliogenys** *Grant's Blue-bill*		Heavy primary forests of eastern Zaire to Uganda
28 68 022	**Spermophaga haematina** *Blue-bill*		Swampy thickets of Gambia to Zaire (rare)
28 68 023	**Spermophaga ruficapilla** *Red-headed Blue-bill*		Angola to eastern Zaire, western Tanzania
28 68 024	**Clytospiza monteiri** *Brown Twin-spot*		Grasslands of Cameroon to the Sudan, Angola, Uganda
28 68 025	**Hypargos margaritatus** *Pink-throated Twin-spot*		Coastal scrub of Mozambique and northeast Zululand
28 68 026	**Hypargos niveoguttatus** *Peter's Twin-spot*		Kenya to Mozambique, Rhodesia, eastern Angola
28 68 027	**Euschistospiza dybowskii** *Dusky Twin-spot*		Montane grasslands of Sierra Leone to the Sudan, Angola

		Date	Location

28 68 028 **Euschistospiza cinereovinacea**
Dusky Fire-Finch — Grasslands west and north of Lake Tanganyika

28 68 029 **Lagonosticta rara**
Black-bellied Waxbill — Senegal to Ethiopia, the Sudan, Uganda

28 68 030 **Lagonosticta rufopicta**
Bar-breasted Waxbill — Senegal to Angola, Tanzania, Zaire, the Sudan

28 68 031 **Lagonosticta nitidula**
Brown Waxbill — Wet grasslands of Angola to Zaire, Zambia

28 68 032 **Lagonosticta senegala**
Red-billed Waxbill — Widespread Africa south of the Sahara

28 68 033 **Lagonosticta rubricata**
African Waxbill — Widespread Africa south of the Sahara

28 68 034 **Lagonosticta landanae**
Pale-billed Waxbill — Savanna of Angola and Cabinda

28 68 035 **Lagonosticta rhodopareia (jamesoni)**
Jameson's Waxbill — Arid Africa south of the Sahara

28 68 036 **Lagonosticta larvata (vinacea)**
Vinaceous Waxbill — Senegal to Ethiopia, the Sudan, Uganda

28 68 037 **Uraeginthus angolensis**
Cordon-bleu — Angola to Tanzania, South Africa

28 68 038 **Uraeginthus bengalus**
Red-cheeked Cordon-bleu — Widespread Ethiopian region

28 68 039 **Uraeginthus cyanocephala**
Blue-capped Cordon-bleu — Deserts of Somalia to Kenya, Tanzania

28 68 040 **Uraeginthus granatina**
Violet-eared Waxbill — Thornscrub of southern Africa

28 68 041 **Uraeginthus ianthinogaster**
Purple Grenadier — Ethiopia, Somalia to Tanzania

28 68 042 **Estrilda caerulescens**
Lavender Fire-Finch — Senegal to the Central African Republic

28 68 043 **Estrilda perreini**
Lavender Waxbill — Angola to Tanzania, Zambia, South Africa

28 68 044 **Estrilda thomensis (cinderella)**
Neumann's Waxbill — Angola; São Thomé Island (known from two specimens circa 1888)

28 68 045 **Estrilda melanotis**
Yellow-bellied Waxbill — Widespread eastern Ethiopian region

	Date	Location
28 68 046	**Estrilda paludicola** *Fawn-breasted Waxbill*	Angola to Ethiopia, Tanzania, Zambia
28 68 047	**Estrilda melpoda** *Orange-cheeked Waxbill*	Grasslands of Gambia to Angola, Zambia
28 68 048	**Estrilda rhodopyga** *Crimson-rumped Waxbill*	Grasslands of Ethiopia to the Sudan, south to Malawi
28 68 049	**Estrilda rufibarba** *Arabian Waxbill*	Confined to southwest Arabia (Kunfuda to Aden)
28 68 050	**Estrilda troglodytes** *Black-rumped Waxbill*	Semiarid Senegal to Ethiopia, the Sudan, Uganda
28 68 051	**Estrilda astrild** *Common Waxbill*	Widespread Africa south of the Sahara
28 68 052	**Estrilda nigriloris** *Kiabo Waxbill*	Southern Zaire (Lake Upemba and Lualaba River— rare)
28 68 053	**Estrilda nonnula** *Black-crowned Waxbill*	Cameroun to Kenya, Tanzania, the Sudan, Zaire
28 68 054	**Estrilda atricapilla** *Black-headed Waxbill*	Lowlands of Cameroon to Uganda, Kenya, Zaire
28 68 055	**Estrilda erythronotos** *Black-faced Waxbill*	Thorn scrub of Ethiopia to South Africa
28 68 056	**Estrilda charmosyna** *Black-cheeked Waxbill*	Somalia to Ethiopia, Kenya
28 68 057	**Amandava amandava** *Red Avadavat*	Widespread Oriental region mainland and islands
28 68 058	**Amandava formosa** *Green Avadavat*	Widespread northern half of peninsular India
28 68 059	**Amandava subflava** *Zebra Waxbill*	Widespread Africa south of the Sahara
28 68 060	**Ortygospiza atricollis** *Common Quail-Finch*	Widespread swamps of Africa south of the Sahara
28 68 061	**Ortygospiza gabonensis** *Black-chinned Quail-Finch*	Widespread grassy swamps of Ethiopian region
28 68 062	**Ortygospiza locustella** *Locust Finch*	Wet grasslands of Tanzania to Malawi, Zaire
28 68 063	**Aegintha temporalis** *Australian Red-browed Finch*	Cape York Peninsula to Victoria, South Australia
28 68 064	**Emblema picta** *Painted Finch*	Widespread porcupine grass zone of Australia
28 68 065	**Emblema bella** *Firetail Finch*	Heath and woodlands of southeast Australia, Tasmania

		Date	Location
28 68 066	**Emblema oculata** *Red-eared Finch*		Coastal southwest Australia
28 68 067	**Emblema guttata** *Diamond Firetail Finch*		Queensland to Victoria, adjacent South Australia
28 68 068	**Oreostruthus fuliginosus** *Crimson-sided Mountain Finch*		High mountains of New Guinea
28 68 069	**Neochmia phaeton** **(albiventer)** *Crimson Finch*		Tropical northern Australia; southern New Guinea
28 68 070	**Neochmia ruficauda** *Star Finch*		Grassy river and swamp margins of northern Australia
28 68 071 +	**Poephila guttata** *Zebra Finch*		Dry open woodlands throughout Australia
28 68 072	**Poephila bichenovii** *Double-barred Finch*		Savanna of northern Australia to New South Wales
28 68 073	**Poephila personata** *Masked Finch*		Savanna, grassy plains of tropical northern Australia
28 68 074	**Poephila acuticauda** *Long-tailed Finch*		Northwest Australia to western Queensland
28 68 075	**Poephila cincta** *Black-throated Finch*		Woodlands of Cape York Peninsula to New South Wales
28 68 076	**Erythrura hyperythra** *Tawny-breasted Parrot-Finch*		Widespread islands of the Oriental region
28 68 077	**Erythrura prasina** *Pin-tailed Parrot-Finch*		Malay Peninsula, Thailand, Laos; Greater Sundas
28 68 078	**Erythrura viridifacies** *Green-faced Parrot-Finch*		Philippines (endemic Luzon and Negros Islands)
28 68 079	**Erythrura tricolor** *Timor Parrot-Finch*		Moluccas and Lesser Sundas Islands
28 68 080	**Erythrura trichroa** *Blue-faced Parrot-Finch*		Queensland to New Guinea, Solomons, Celebes, New Hebrides
28 68 081	**Erythrura papuana** *Papuan Parrot-Finch*		Mountains of New Guinea
28 68 082	**Erythrura coloria** *Mindanao Parrot-Finch*		Philippines (confined to Mindanao Island)
28 68 083	**Erythrura psittacea** *Red-throated Parrot-Finch*		Confined to New Caledonia Island
28 68 084	**Erythrura pealii** *Peale's Parrot-Finch*		Widespread major islands of Fiji Archipelago

		Date	Location
28 68 085	**Erythrura cyanovirens** *Red-headed Parrot-Finch*		Samoa to the New Hebrides Islands
28 68 086	**Erythrura kleinschmidti** *Pink-billed Parrot-Finch*		Fiji (endemic to Viti Levu—rare and endangered)
28 68 087	**Chloebia gouldiae** *Gouldian Finch*		Savanna of tropical northern Australia
28 68 088	**Aidemosyne modesta** *Plum-headed Finch*		Wooded savanna of Queensland to New South Wales
28 68 089	**Lonchura malabarica** *White-throated Munia*		Senegal to the Sudan; India; Sri Lanka
28 68 090 ✝	**Lonchura griseicapilla (caniceps)** *Gray-headed Silverbill*		Ethiopia to Kenya, Uganda, Tanzania
28 68 091	**Lonchura nana** *Madagascar Mannikin*		Widespread Madagascar
28 68 092	**Lonchura cucullata** *Bronze Mannikin*		Widespread Africa south of the Sahara
28 68 093	**Lonchura bicolor (poensis)** *Black-and-white Mannikin*		Widespread Ethiopian region
28 68 094	**Lonchura fringilloides** *Magpie (Pied) Mannikin*		Widespread Africa south of the Sahara
28 68 095	**Lonchura striata** *White-rumped Munia*		Widespread Indian Subcontinent to Sumatra
28 68 096	**Lonchura leucogastroides** *Javan Munia*		Sumatra; Java; Bali; Lombok Islands
28 68 097	**Lonchura fuscans** *Dusky Munia*		Borneo and Cagayan Sulu Archipelago
28 68 098	**Lonchura molucca** *Moluccan Mannikin*		Confined to the Moluccas Islands
28 68 099	**Lonchura punctulata** *Spotted Munia*		Widespread Oriental mainland and islands
28 68 100	**Lonchura kelaarti** *Black-throated Mannikin*		Common southwest India; Sri Lanka
28 68 101	**Lonchura leucogaster (leucogastra)** *White-bellied Munia*		Malay Peninsula; Sumatra; Borneo; Philippines
28 68 102	**Lonchura tristissima** *Streak-headed Mannikin*		Western and central New Guinea mountain streams
28 68 103	**Lonchura leucosticta** *White-spotted Mannikin*		Lowlands of southern New Guinea

		Date	Location

28 68 104 **Lonchura quinticolor**
Five-colored Mannikin   Confined to the Lesser Sunda Islands

28 68 105 **Lonchura malacca
(atricapilla)**
Chestnut Munia   Widespread Oriental region mainland and islands

28 68 106 **Lonchura maja**
White-headed Munia   Malay Peninsula; Sumatra; Java

28 68 107 **Lonchura pallida**
Celebes Munia   Confined to the Celebes Islands

28 68 108 **Lonchura grandis**
Great-billed Mannikin   Lowlands of eastern New Guinea

28 68 109 **Lonchura vana**
Arfak Mannikin   Grasslands of Arfak Mountains of New Guinea

28 68 110 **Lonchura caniceps**
Gray-headed Mannikin   Savannas and marshes of eastern New Guinea

28 68 111 **Lonchura nevermanni**
White-crowned Mannikin   Lowlands of southern New Guinea

28 68 112 **Lonchura spectabilis**
New Britain Mannikin   Northern New Guinea to New Britain Island

28 68 113 **Lonchura forbesi**
New Ireland Mannikin   Confined to New Ireland Island

28 68 114 **Lonchura hunsteini**
Black-breasted Mannikin   Micronesia (New Hanover and Ponape Islands)

28 68 115 **Lonchura flaviprymna**
Yellow-rumped Finch   Northwest Australia and Northern Territory

28 68 116 **Lonchura
castaneothorax**
Chestnut-breasted Finch   Coastal northern Australia; eastern New Guinea

28 68 117 **Lonchura stygia**
Black Mannikin   Lowlands of southern New Guinea

28 68 118 **Lonchura teerinki**
Grand Valley Mannikin   Grasslands of Snow Mountains of New Guinea

28 68 119 **Lonchura monticola**
Alpine Mannikin   Alpine grasslands of southeast New Guinea

28 68 120 **Lonchura montana**
Snow Mountain Mannikin   Snow Mountains of New Guinea

28 68 121 **Lonchura melaena**
New Britain Munia   Confined to New Britain Island

28 68 122 **Lonchura nigerrima**
*Black-breasted Weaver-
Finch*   Caroline Islands (Ponape and Truk (?)—rare)

28 68 123 **Lonchura pectoralis**
Pictorella Finch   Northwest Australia to Cape York Peninsula

		Date	Location

			Date	Location
28 68 124	**Padda fuscata**			
	Timor Sparrow			Lesser Sundas (Timor and Samau Islands)
28 68 125	**Padda oryzivora**			
	Java Sparrow			Java; Bali: introduced Oriental mainland and islands
28 68 126	**Amadina fasciata**			
	Cut-throat			Thornbush of Africa south of the Sahara
28 68 127	**Amadina erythrocephala**			
	Red-headed Finch			Thornbush of Angola to South Africa
28 68 128	**Pholidornis rushiae**			
	Tit-Hylia			Sierra Leone to southern Nigeria, Angola, Uganda

FAMILY: PLOCEIDAE (Weavers and Allies)

28 69 001	**Bubalornis albirostris (niger)**		
	Buffalo Weaver		Widespread Africa south of the Sahara
28 69 002	**Dinemellia dinemelli**		
	White-headed Buffalo Weaver		Northern Sudan and Ethiopia to Kenya, Uganda
28 69 003	**Plocepasser mahali**		
	White-browed Sparrow-Weaver		Arid bush of Ethiopia to South Africa
28 69 004	**Plocepasser superciliosus**		
	Chestnut-crowned Sparrow-Weaver		Senegal to Ethiopia, Zaire
28 69 005	**Plocepasser donaldsoni**		
	Donaldson-Smith's Sparrow-Weaver		Rocky deserts of southwest Ethiopia, northern Kenya
28 69 006	**Plocepasser rufoscapulatus**		
	Rufous-backed Sparrow-Weaver		*Brachystegia* highlands of Angola, Zambia, Malawi, Zambia
28 69 007	**Histurgops ruficauda**		
	Rufous-tailed Weaver		Mwanza to Arusha, Tabora, Mkalama region of Tanzania
28 69 008	**Pseudonigrita arnaudi**		
	Gray-headed Social Weaver		Thornbush of the Sudan, Ethiopia to Tanzania
28 69 009	**Pseudonigrita cabanisi**		
	Black-capped Social Weaver		Dry thornbush of Ethiopia to Tanzania
28 69 010	**Philetairus socius**		
	Social Weaver		Thornbush of Namibia to Zambia, South Africa

		Date	Location

28 69 011	**Passer ammodendri** *Saxaul Sparrow*	Turkestan to Mongolia, western China
28 69 012	**Passer domesticus** *House Sparrow*	Southern Palearctic; introduced worldwide
28 69 013	**Passer hispaniolensis** *Spanish Sparrow*	Southern Palearctic; winters to India, Nile Valley
28 69 014	**Passer pyrrhonotus** *Jungle Sparrow*	Iran, Baluchistan to Pakistan
28 69 015	**Passer castanopterus** *Somali Sparrow*	Widespread and common Somalia to Ethiopia, Kenya
28 69 016	**Passer rutilans** *Cinnamon Sparrow*	Himalayas of Afghanistan to Szechwan, Korea, Japan; Taiwan
28 69 017	**Passer flaveolus** *Plain-backed Sparrow*	Burma, Malaya, Thailand to Indochina
28 69 018	**Passer moabiticus** *Dead Sea Sparrow*	Dead Sea region of Iraq and Iran
28 69 019	**Passer iagoensis (motitensis)** *Great Sparrow*	Widespread acacia veld of Africa, Canaries, Socotra Island
28 69 020	**Passer melanurus** *Cape Sparrow (Mossie)*	Namibia to Zambia, South Africa
28 69 021	**Passer griseus** *Gray-headed Sparrow*	Common and widespread Africa south of the Sahara
28 69 022	**Passer simplex** *Desert Sparrow*	Deserts of North Africa to Iran, Transcaspia
28 69 023	**Passer montanus** *Eurasian Tree Sparrow*	Widespread Palearctic, Oriental mainland and islands
28 69 024	**Passer luteus (euchiorus)** *Golden Sparrow*	Semiarid Mali to Ethiopia, Somalia, Arabia
28 69 025	**Passer eminibey** *Chestnut Sparrow*	Papyrus swamps of the Sudan, Ethiopia to Tanzania
28 69 026	**Carpospiza brachydactyla** *Pale Rock Sparrow*	Asia Minor; winters to the Sudan and Eritrea
28 69 027	**Petronia xanthocollis** *Chestnut-shouldered Sparrow*	Southern Iraq to India, Nepal; Sri Lanka
2869 028	**Petronia petronia** *Rock Sparrow*	Canaries; Mediterranean basin to central Asia
28 69 029	**Petronia superciliaris** *Yellow-throated Sparrow*	Open woodlands of southern half of Africa

		Date	Location
28 69 030	**Petronia dentata** *Bush Petronia*		Senegal to Eritrea, southwest Arabia
28 69 031	**Montifringilla nivalis** *Eurasian Snow Finch*		The Alps, Carpathians, Caucusus, Himalayas
28 69 032	**Montifringilla adamsi** *Tibetan Snow Finch*		Desert steppes of Kashmir, Nepal, Sikkim
28 69 033	**Montifringilla taczanowskii** *White-rumped Snow Finch*		Tibet to Sikkim, Sikiang, Tsinghai
28 69 034	**Montifringilla davidiana** *Père David's Snow Finch*		Mountains of Siberia to Mongolia, Tibet, Sikkim
28 69 035	**Montifringilla ruficollis** *Red-necked Snow Finch*		Northwest China to Tibet, Sikkim
28 69 036	**Montifringilla blanfordi** *Blandord's Snow Finch*		Mountains of northwest China to Sikkim
28 69 037	**Montifringilla theresae** *Theresa's Snow Finch*		Known only from the mountains of Afghanistan
28 69 038	**Sporopipes squamifrons** *Scaly Weaver*		Thornbush of Angola to Zambia, South Africa
28 69 039	**Sporopipes frontalis** *Speckle-fronted Weaver*		Semiarid Senegal to the Red Sea environs
28 69 040	**Amblyospiza albifrons** *Grosbeak Weaver*		Swampy lowlands of Africa south of the Sahara
28 69 041	**Ploceus baglafecht (stuhlmanni)** *Baglafecht Weaver*		Grasslands of Ethiopia, Sudan to Cameroon, Zaire
28 69 042	**Ploceus bannermani** *Bannerman's Weaver*		Mountain forests of western Cameroon (rare)
28 69 043	**Ploceus batesi** *Bates' Weaver*		Southern Cameroon forests (rare)
28 69 044	**Ploceus nigrimentum** *Black-chinned Weaver*		Angola and western Zaire (rare)
28 69 045	**Ploceus bertrandi** *Bertrand's Weaver*		Highlands of Tanzania to Mozambique and Malawi
28 69 046	**Ploceus pelzeini** *Slender-billed Weaver*		Ghana to Kenya, Tanzania, Zambia
28 69 047	**Ploceus subpersonatus** *Loango Slender-billed Weaver*		Gabon coast to mouth of the Congo River (rare)
28 69 048	**Ploceus luteolus** *Little Weaver*		Thornscrub of Senegal to Somalia, Tanzania
28 69 049	**Ploceus ocularis** *Spectacled Weaver*		Widespread Ethiopian region

		Date	Location

28 69 050   **Ploceus nigricollis**
           Black-necked Weaver   Widespread damp lowlands of Ethiopian region

28 69 051   **Ploceus alienus**
           Strange Weaver   Mountain forests of Ruwenzori Mountains (rare)

28 69 052   **Ploceus melanogaster**
           Black-billed Weaver   Fernando Po; Cameroon highlands to Kenya

28 69 053   **Ploceus capensis
(temporalis)**
           Cape Weaver   Angola to Zambia, South Africa

28 69 054   **Ploceus subaureus**
           African Golden Weaver   Lowlands of Kenya to South Africa

28 69 055   **Ploceus xanthops**
           Holub's Golden Weaver   Angola to Kenya, South Africa

28 69 056   **Ploceus aurantius**
           Orange Weaver   Reed-beds of Senegal to Kenya, Tanzania

28 69 057   **Ploceus heuglini
(atrogularis)**
           *Heughlin's Masked
Weaver*   Senegal to the Sudan, Uganda, Kenya

28 69 058   **Ploceus bojeri**
+   *Golden Palm Weaver*   Somalia to northeast Tanzania; Manda Island

28 69 059   **Ploceus castaneiceps**
           Taveta Golden Weaver   Riverine scrub of southeast Kenya to eastern
Tanzania

28 69 060   **Ploceus princeps**
           Principé Golden Weaver   Common and widespread Principé Island (Gulf of
Guinea)

28 69 061   **Ploceus xanthopterus**
           *Brown-throated Golden
Weaver*   Rivers and swamps of Mozambique, Malawi to Natal

28 69 062   **Ploceus castanops**
           *Northern Brown-throated
Weaver*   Eastern Zaire border to Lake Kivu environs

28 69 063   **Ploceus galbula**
           Ruppell's Weaver   The Sudan, Ethiopia to Arabia

28 69 064   **Ploceus taeniopterus
(reichardi)**
           Northern Masked Weaver   The Sudan, Ethiopia to Uganda, Zaire, Tanzania

28 69 065   **Ploceus intermedius**
           Masked Weaver   Widespread Ethiopia to South Africa

28 69 066   **Ploceus velatus
(vitellinus)**
           Vitelline Masked Weaver   Widespread Ethiopian region

28 69 067   **Ploceus spekei**
+   *Speke's Weaver*   Thornbush of Ethiopia to Kenya, Tanzania

	Date	Location
28 69 068 **Ploceus spekeoides** *Fox's Weaver*		Moist woodlands of northwest to central Uganda
28 69 069 **Ploceus cucullatus** **(nigriceps)** *Black-headed Weaver*		Widespread Africa south of the Sahara
28 69 070 **Ploceus grandis** *Giant Weaver*		Endemic to São Thomé Island (Gulf of Guinea)
28 69 071 **Ploceus nigerrimus** **(castaneofuscus)** *Viellot's Weaver*		Tropical Sierra Leone to Angola, Kenya, Tanzania
28 69 072 **Ploceus weynsi** *Weyn's Weaver*		Forests of northern Zaire to Uganda (rare)
28 69 073 **Ploceus golandi** *Clarke's Weaver*		Kenya (known from a small population in Sokoke Forest-endangered)
28 69 074 **Ploceus dicrocephalus** *Jubaland Weaver*		Southern Ethiopia, Somalia to northeast Kenya
28 69 075 **Ploceus melanocephalus** **(capitalis)** *Yellow-backed Weaver*		Senegal to Ethiopia, Tanzania, Zambia
28 69 076 **Ploceus jacksoni** *Jackson's Weaver*		Riverine swamps of southeast Sudan, Zaire, Tanzania
28 69 077 **Ploceus badius** *Cinnamon Weaver*		Blue Nile Valley and the southern Sudan
28 69 078 **Ploceus rubiginosus** *Chestnut Weaver*		Widespread acacia veld of Ethiopia to Nambia
28 69 079 **Ploceus aureonucha** *Golden-naped Weaver*		Forests of northeast Zaire (Ituri District—rare)
28 69 080 **Ploceus tricolor** *Yellow-mantled Weaver*		Forests of Sierra Leone to Angola, Uganda (rare)
28 69 081 **Ploceus albinucha** *White-naped Black Weaver*		Forests of Fernando Po; Cameroon to Uganda, Zaire
28 69 082 **Ploceus nelicourvi** *Nelicourvi Weaver*		Wooded regions of eastern Madagascar
28 69 083 **Ploceus sakalava** *Sakalava Weaver*		Locally common throughout Madagascar
28 69 084 **Ploceus hypoxanthus** **(chrysaea)** *Asian Golden Weaver*		Burma to Indochina; Sumatra; Java
28 69 085 **Ploceus superciliosus** *Compact Weaver*		Sierra Leone to Ethiopia, Kenya, Angola
28 69 086 **Ploceus benghalensis** *Bengal Weaver*		Reed swamps and grassy plains of Pakistan to Assam

		Date	Location
28 69 087	**Ploceus manyar** *Streaked Weaver*		Pakistan, India to Indochina; Java; Bali
28 69 088	**Ploceus philippinus** *Baya Weaver*		India to southwest China, Indochina; Sumatra; Java
28 69 089	**Ploceus megarhynchus** *Himalayan Weaver*		Himalayan foothills from Bhutan to Assam
28 69 090	**Ploceus bicolor** *Forest Weaver*		Widespread forested areas of Ethiopian region
28 69 091	**Ploceus flavipes** *Yellow-legged Weaver*		Rain forests of northeast Zaire (rare)
28 69 092	**Ploceus preussi** *Golden-backed Weaver*		Sierra Leone to Cameroon, Zaire
28 69 093	**Ploceus dorsomaculatus** *Yellow-capped Weaver*		Forests of Cameroon to northeast Zaire
28 69 094	**Ploceus olivaceiceps (nicolli)** *Olive-headed Golden Weaver*		*Brachystegia* woodlands of Tanzania, Malawi, Mozambique
28 69 095	**Ploceus insignus** *Brown-capped Weaver*		Montane forests of Cameroon to Kenya, Tanzania
28 69 096	**Ploceus angolensis** *Bar-winged Weaver*		*Brachystegia* woodlands of Angola to Zaire, Zambia
28 69 097	**Ploceus sanctaethomae** *São Thomé Weaver*		Highlands of São Thomé Island (Gulf of Guinea)
28 69 098	**Malimbus coronatus** *Red-crowned Malimbe*		Forests of southern Cameroon to the Semliki Valley
28 69 099	**Malimbus cassini** *Cassin's Malimbe*		Swamps of southern Nigeria to northern Zaire
28 69 100	**Malimbus scutatus** *Red-vented Malimbe*		Coastal forests of Sierra Leone to Gabon
28 69 101	**Malimbus racheliae** *Rachel's Malimbe*		Coastal forests of Nigeria to Gabon
28 69 102	**Malimbus ibadanensis** *Ibadan Malimbe*		Known only from Ibadan, eastern Nigeria (rare)
28 69 103	**Malimbus nitens** *Gray's Malimbe*		Moist woodlands of Sierra Leone to Uganda, Zaire
28 69 104	**Malimbus rubricollis** *Red-headed Weaver*		Forests of Senegal to Kenya, Angola
28 69 105	**Malimbus erythrogaster** *Red-bellied Malimbe*		High bush of southern Nigeria to the Semliki Valley
28 69 106	**Malimbus malimbicus** *Crested Malimbe*		Rain forests of Senegal to Uganda, Zaire

		Date	Location

28 69 107 **Malimbus rubriceps (melanotis)**
Red-headed Malimbe

Widespread bush of Africa south of the Sahara

28 69 108 **Malimbus ballmanni**
Ballmann's Weaver

Southwest Ivory Coast (known from one specimen collected 1974)

28 69 109 **Quelea cardinalis**
Cardinal Quelea

Grasslands of the Sudan, Ethiopia to Zambia

28 69 110 **Quelea erythrops**
Red-headed Quelea

Grasslands of Africa south of the Sahara

28 69 111 **Quelea quelea**
Red-billed Quelea

Widespread grasslands of Africa south of the Sahara

28 69 112 **Foudia madagascariensis**
Madagascar Fody

Madagascar; Seychelles; Amirante Islands

28 69 113 **Foudia eminentissima**
Red-headed Fody

Madagascar; Aldabra; the Comoro Islands

28 69 114 **Foudia rubra**
Mauritius Fody

Confined to Mauritius Island (Indian Ocean—endangered)

28 69 115 **Foudia bruante**
Reunion Fody

Existence doubtful. If it once existed, inhabited Reunion Island

23 69 116 **Foudia sechellarum**
Seychelles Fody

Seychelles Islands (Cousin, Cousine, Frigate—endangered)

28 69 117 **Foudia flavicans**
Rodriquez Fody

Confined to Rodriquez Island (Indian Ocean)

28 69 118 **Foudia omissa**
Red Forest Fody

Central plateau and forests of eastern Madagascar

28 69 119 **Euplectes anomalus**
Bob-tailed Weaver

Banks of the Congo River system and southeast Cameroon

28 69 120 **Euplectes afer**
Yellow-crowned Bishop

Tropical swampy grasslands of Ethiopian region

28 69 121 **Euplectes diadematus**
Fire-fronted Bishop

Coastal eastern Kenya to Tanzania

28 69 122 **Euplectes gierowii**
Black Bishop

Grasslands of Ethiopia to Zaire, northern Angola

28 69 123 **Euplectes nigroventris**
Black-vented Bishop

Somalia to Tanzania; Zanzibar; Pemba

28 69 124 **Euplectes hordeaceus**
Black-winged Red Bishop

Grasslands of Africa south of the Sahara

		Date	Location
28 69 125	**Euplectes orix** *Red Bishop*		Grasslands of Africa south of the Sahara
28 69 126	**Euplectes aureus** *Golden-backed Bishop*		Coastal Gabon to Angola; São Thomé Island
28 69 127	**Euplectes capensis** *Yellow Bishop*		Grasslands of the Sudan, Ethiopia to South Africa
28 69 128	**Euplectes axillaris** *Fan-tailed Whydah*		Grasslands of the eastern half of Africa
28 69 129	**Euplectes macrourus** **(macrocercus)** *Yellow-mantled Whydah*		Grasslands of Africa south of the Sahara
28 69 130	**Euplectes hartlaubi** *Marsh Whydah*		Swampy lowlands of Cameroon to Kenya, Tanzania, Malawi
28 69 131	**Euplectes albonotatus** *White-winged Whydah*		Grasslands of Africa south of the Sahara
28 69 132	**Euplectes ardens** *Red-collared Whydah*		Grasslands of Africa south of the Sahara
28 69 133	**Euplectes progne** *Long-tailed Whydah*		Highlands of Kenya, Angola to South Africa
28 69 134	**Euplectes jacksoni** *Jackson's Whydah*		Highlands of Kenya and Tanzania
28 69 135	**Anomalospiza imberbis** *Parasitic (Cuckoo)* *Weaver*		Widespread grasslands of Ethiopian region
28 69 136	**Vidua chalybeata** **(wilsoni)** *Green Indigo-Bird*		Widespread Ethiopian region
28 69 137	**Vidua wilsoni** *Purple Indigo-Bird*		Senegal to the southern Sudan, northwest Kenya
28 69 138	**Vidua funerea** *Dusky Indigo-Bird*		Widespread Africa south of the Sahara
28 69 139	**Vidua purpurascens** *Black Indigo-Bird*		Angola to Tanzania, Zambia
28 69 140	**Vidua hypocherina** *Steel-blue Whydah*		Widespread Ethiopian region
28 69 141	**Vidua fischeri** *Straw-tailed Whydah*		Thornbrush and desert scrub of Ethiopia to Tanzania
28 69 142	**Vidua regia** *Shaft-tailed Whydah*		Dry thornbush of Angola to South Africa
28 69 143	**Vidua macroura** *Pin-tailed Whydah*		Widespread Africa south of the Sahara
28 69 144	**Vidua paradisaea** *Paradise Whydah*		Widespread Africa south of the Sahara

	Date	Location

28 69 145 Vidua orientalis
Broad-tailed Whydah   Widespread Africa south of the Sahara

FAMILY: STURNIDAE (Starlings)

28 70 001 Aplonis zelandicus
Rusty-winged Starling   Lowland forests of New Hebrides and Banks Islands

27 70 002 Aplonis santovestris
Mountain Starling   New Hebrides (mountains of Espiritu Santo Island)

28 70 003 Aplonis pelzelni
Ponape Mountain Starling   Mountain forests of Ponape Island (endangered)

28 70 004 Aplonis atrifuscus
Samoan Starling   Forests of main Samoan Islands

28 70 005 Aplonis corvinus
Kusaie Mountain Starling   Kusaie Island (Micronesia—probably extinct)

28 70 006 Aplonis mavornata
Raiatia Starling   Extinct. Inhabited Raiatia, Society Islands

28 70 007 Aplonis cinerascens
Rarotonga Starling   Rarotonga and Cook Islands

28 70 008 Aplonis tabuensis
Polynesian Starling   Fiji, Samoa to the New Hebrides Islands

28 70 009 Aplonis striatus
Striated Starling   Confined to forests of New Caledonia and Loyalty Islands

28 70 010 Aplonis fuscus
Norfolk Island Starling   Lord Howe and Norfolk Islands (endangered)

28 70 011 Aplonis opacus
Micronesian Starling   Islands of Micronesia (Marianas to Carolines)

28 70 012 Aplonis cantoroides
Singing Starling   Solomon Islands to New Guinea, Bismarck Archipelago

28 70 013 Aplonis crassa
Tanimbar Starling   Lesser Sundas (Tanimbar Island—possible race *A. cantoroides*)

28 70 014 Aplonis feadensis
Atoll Starling   Coral islands and atolls of the Solomon Islands

28 70 015 Aplonis insularis
Rennell Starling   Solomon Islands (Rennell Island—possible race *A. feadensis*)

28 70 016 Aplonis dichroa
San Cristobal Starling   Solomon Islands (confined to San Cristobal Island)

28 70 017 Aplonis grandis
Brown-winged Starling   Forests of Solomon Islands

		Date	Location
28 70 018	**Aplonis mysolensis** *Moluccan Starling*		Moluccas to western Papuan Islands
28 70 019	**Aplonis magnus** *Long-tailed Starling*		New Guinea (lowlands of Biak and Numfor Islands)
28 70 020	**Aplonis minor** *Lesser Glossy Starling*		Philippines (endemic to Mindanao Island)
28 70 021	**Aplonis panayensis** *Philippine Glossy Starling*		Widespread Oriental region mainland and islands
28 70 022	**Aplonis metallicus** *Metallic Starling*		Moluccas, Solomons, New Guinea to Cape York Peninsula
28 70 023	**Aplonis mystaceus** *Grant's Starling*		Lowlands of southern New Guinea
28 70 024	**Aplonis brunneicapillus** *White-eyed Starling*		Solomons (lowlands of Bougainville and Rendova Islands)
28 70 025	**Poeoptera kenricki** *Kenrick's Starling*		Kilamanjaro, Meru, Usambara Mountains of Tanzania
28 70 026	**Poeoptera stuhlmanni** *Stuhlmann's Starling*		Forests of Zaire to Uganda, Kenya, Ethiopia
28 70 027	**Poeoptera lugubris** *Narrow-tailed Starling*		Forests of Sierra Leone to Angola and western Uganda
28 70 028	**Grafisia torquata** *White-collared Starling*		Cameroon to Zaire
28 70 029	**Onychognathus walleri** *Waller's Starling*		Forests of Kenya to Tanzania, Malawi
28 70 030	**Onychognathus nabouroup** *Pale-winged Starling*		Deserts of Angola, Namibia to South Africa
28 70 031	**Onychognathus morio** *Red-winged Starling*		Widespread Ethiopian region
28 70 032	**Onychognathus blythii** *Somali Starling*		Eritrea, eastern Ethiopia to Somalia; Socotra Island
28 70 033	**Onychognathus frater** *Socotra Starling*		Confined to Socotra Island (Indian Ocean off East Africa)
28 70 034	**Onychognathus tristramii** *Tristram's Starling*		Confined to the Sinai Peninsula, Aqaba
28 70 035	**Onychognathus fulgidus** *Chestnut-winged Starling*		Forests of Sierra Leone to Angola and the Sudan
28 70 036	**Onychognathus tenuirostris** *Slender-billed Starling*		Eritrea to Zaire, Malawi, Rhodesia

		Date	Location

28 70 037 **Onychognathus albirostris**
White-billed Starling — Blue Nile gorge of Somalia, Ethiopia and Kenya

28 70 038 **Onychognathus salvadorii**
Bristle-crowned Starling — Rocky gorges of Somalia, Ethiopia to Kenya

28 70 039 **Lamprotornis iris**
Emerald Starling — Open savanna of Guinea to the Ivory Coast

28 70 040 **Lamprotornis cupreocauda**
Coppery-tailed Starling — Upper Guinea forests of Sierra Leone to Ghana

28 70 041 **Lamprotornis purpureiceps**
Purple-headed Starling — Forests of Nigeria to southwest Zaire, Uganda

28 70 042 **Lamprotornis corruscus**
Black-breasted Starling — Coastal bush of Kenya to South Africa; Zanzibar

28 70 043 **Lamprotornis purpureus**
Purple Glossy Starling — Senegal to the Sudan, Uganda, Kenya

28 70 044 **Lamprotornis nitens**
Red-shouldered Glossy Starling — Acacia steppes of southern Africa

28 70 045 **Lamprotornis chalcurus**
Short-tailed Glossy Starling — Widespread Senegal to Kenya

28 70 046 **Lamprotornis chalybaeus**
Blue-eared Glossy Starling — Widespread Ethiopian region

28 70 047 **Lamprotornis chloropterus**
Lesser Blue-eared Starling — Widespread Ethiopian region

28 70 048 **Lamprotornis acuticaudus**
Sharp-tailed Glossy Starling — Angola, northern Zaire, Zambia

28 70 049 **Lamprotornis splendidus**
Splendid Glossy Starling — Widespread Ethiopian region

28 70 050 **Lamprotornis ornatus**
Principé Glossy Starling — Confined to Principé Island (Gulf of Guinea)

28 70 051 **Lamprotornis australis**
Burchell's Glossy Starling — Bush country of southern Africa

28 70 052 **Lamprotornis mevesii**
Meve's Glossy Starling — Woodlands of southern Africa

28 70 053 **Lamprotornis purpuropterus**
Ruppell's Long-tailed Starling — Ethiopia to Kenya, Uganda, Tanzania

		Date	Location
28 70 054	**Lamprotornis caudatus** *Long-tailed Glossy Starling*		Senegal to the Sudan
28 70 055	**Cinnyricinclus femoralis** *Abbott's Starling*		Forests of southern Kenya to northeast Tanzania
28 70 056	**Cinnyricinclus sharpii** *Sharpe's Starling*		Mountain forests of Kenya, Uganda, Tanzania
28 70 057	**Cinnyricinclus leucogaster** *Violet-backed Starling*		Forests and woodlands of Ethiopian region; Arabia
28 70 058	**Speculipastor bicolor** *Magpie Starling*		Erratic wanderer southern Ethiopia, Kenya and Somalia
28 70 059	**Neocichla gutturalis** *White-winged Babbling Starling*		Savanna of Angola to Tanzania, Malawi, Zambia
28 70 060	**Spreo fischeri** *Fischer's Starling*		Dry acacia country of Ethiopia to Tanzania
28 70 061	**Spreo bicolor** *African Pied Starling*		Open woodlands of South Africa
28 70 062	**Spreo albicapillus** *White-crowned Starling*		Acacia belt of Ethiopia to Somalia
28 70 063	**Spreo superbus** *Superb Starling*		Ethiopia to Somalia, southern Sudan, Tanzania
28 70 064	**Spreo shelleyi** *Shelley's Starling*		Thornbush of Somalia, Ethiopia, Kenya
28 70 065	**Spreo pulcher** *Chestnut-bellied Starling*		Senegal to the Sudan, Ethiopia, Eritrea
28 70 066	**Spreo hildebrandti** *Hildebrandt's Starling*		Thornbush of southern Kenya to northern Tanzania
28 70 067	**Cosmopsarus regius** *Golden-breasted (Regal) Starling*		Dry bush country of Ethiopia, Somalia to Tanzania
28 70 068	**Cosmopsarus unicolor** *Ashy Starling*		Semiarid bush country of Tanzania
28 70 069	**Saroglossa aurata** *Madagascar Starling*		Wooded areas of eastern and western Madagascar
28 70 070	**Saroglossa spiloptera** *Spot-winged Starling*		Lowlands of India to Burma, Thailand
28 70 071	**Creatophora cinerea** *Wattled Starling*		Africa south of the Sahara
28 70 072	**Necropsar leguati** *Rodriguez Starling*		Extinct. Inhabited Met Island, south of Rodriguez
28 70 073	**Fregilupus varius** *Reunion Starling*		Extinct. Inhabited Reunion Island, Indian Ocean

	Date	Location
28 70 074 **Sturnus senex** *Ceylon Starling*		Mountain forests of wet zone of Sri Lanka (rare)
28 70 075 **Sturnus malabaricus** *Chestnut-tailed Starling*		India to southern China, Burma, Thailand, Indochina
28 70 076 **Sturnus erythropygius** *White-headed Myna*		Andaman and Nicobari Islands (Indian Ocean)
28 70 077 **Sturnus pagodarum** *Brahminy Myna*		Afghanistan, India to Assam; Sri Lanka
28 70 078 **Sturnus sericeus** *Silky Starling*		China, Annam, Tonkin; Hainan; Calayan Island (Philippines)
28 70 079 **Sturnus philippensis** *Violet-backed Starling*		Oriental region mainland and islands
28 70 080 **Sturnus sturninus** *Daurian Starling*		East Asia, Oriental region mainland and islands
28 70 081 **Sturnus roseus** *Rose-colored Starling*		Eastern Europe to western Asia, India; Sri Lanka
28 70 082 **Sturnus vulgaris** *Common Starling*		Southern Palearctic; introduced and widespread worldwide
28 70 083 **Sturnus unicolor** *Spotless Starling*		Portugal, Spain, Corsica, Sardinia and Sicily
28 70 084 **Sturnus cineraceus** *White-cheeked Starling*		East Asia, China, Indochina; Philippines; Hainan; Taiwan
28 70 085 **Sturnus contra** *Asian Pied Starling*		India to southwest China, Indochina; Java; Sumatra
28 70 086 **Sturnus nigricollis** *Black-collared Starling*		Southern China to Malaya, Burma, peninsular Thailand
28 70 087 **Sturnus burmannicus** *Jerdon's Starling*		Burma, Thailand, Cochinchina, Annam, Laos
28 70 088 **Sturnus melanopterus** *Black-winged Starling*		Lowlands of Java, Bali, Lombok Islands
28 70 089 **Sturnus sinensis** *White-shouldered Starling*		Widespread Oriental region mainland and islands
28 70 090 **Leucopsar rothschildi** *Rothschild's Myna*		Confined to Bubunan District of north coast of Bali (endangered)
28 70 091 **Acridotheres tristis** *Common Myna*		Oriental mainland (introduced widely worldwide)
28 70 092 **Acridotheres ginginianus** *Bank Myna*		Lowlands of India and *terai* of southern Nepal

		Date	Location
28 70 093	**Acridotheres fuscus (mahrattensis)** *Jungle Myna*		India to China, Burma, Thailand, Malaya; Sumatra
28 70 094	**Acridotheres grandis (javanicus)** *White-vented Myna*		Widespread Oriental mainland and islands
28 70 095	**Acridotheres albocinctus** *Collared Myna*		Assam to southwest China, Burma
28 70 096	**Acridotheres cristatellus** *Crested Myna*		Southern China to Indochina; Hainan; Taiwan
28 70 097	**Ampeliceps coronatus** *Golden-crested Myna*		Assam, southern China to Malaya, Indochina
28 70 098	**Mino anais** *Golden-breasted Myna*		Lowlands of New Guinea, Salawati and Japen Islands
28 70 099	**Mino dumontii** *Yellow-faced Myna*		New Guinea to the Solomon Islands
28 70 100	**Basilornis celebensis** *Celebes Myna*		Confined to the Celebes Islands
28 70 101	**Basilornis galeatus** *Sula Myna*		Banggai and Sula Islands (Molucca Sea)
28 70 102	**Basilornis corythaix** *Seram Myna*		Moluccas (confined to Ceram Island)
28 70 103	**Basilornis miranda** *Mount Apo Myna*		Philippines (endemic to Mt. Apo, Mindanao Island)
28 70 104	**Streptocitta albicollis (torquata)** *Buton Starling*		New Caledonia and Celebes Islands
28 70 105	**Streptocitta albertinae** *Sula Starling*		Confined to the Sula Islands (Molucca Sea)
28 70 106	**Sarcops calvus** *Coleto*		Widespread Philippine Islands to Sulu Archipelago
28 70 107	**Gracula ptilogenys** *Ceylon Myna*		Widespread and endemic to Sri Lanka
28 70 108	**Gracula religiosa** *Hill Myna*		Widespread Oriental region mainland and islands
28 70 109	**Enodes erythrophris** *Celebes Myna*		Confined to the Celebes Islands
28 70 110	**Scissirostrum dubium** *Grosbeak Starling*		Celebes, Togian and Peling Islands
28 70 111	**Buphagus africanus** *Yellow-billed Oxpecker*		Widespread Ethiopian region
28 70 112	**Buphagus erythrorhynchus** *Red-billed Oxpecker*		Widespread Ethiopia to South Africa

	Date	Location

FAMILY: ORIOLIDAE (Orioles)

28 71 001   **Oriolus szalayi**
Brown Oriole   New Guinea and western Papuan Islands

28 71 002   **Oriolus phaeochromus**
Halmahera Oriole   Moluccas (confined to Halmahera Island)

28 71 003   **Oriolus forsteni**
Seram Oriole   Moluccas (confined to Ceram Island)

28 71 004   **Oriolus bouroensis**
Tanimbar Oriole   Moluccas (confined to Tanimbar and Buru Islands)

28 71 005   **Oriolus viridifuscus**
Timor Oriole   Lesser Sundas (Timor and Wetar Islands)

28 71 006   **Oriolus sagittatus**
Olive-backed Oriole   Northern, eastern Australia to southeast New Guinea

28 71 007   **Oriolus flavocinctus**
Yellow Oriole   Tropical northern Australia; southern New Guinea;
Arus

28 71 008   **Oriolus xanthonotus**
Dark-throated Oriole   Malay Peninsula; Greater Sundas; Philippines;
Palawan

28 71 009   **Oriolus albiloris**
White-lored Oriole   Philippines (Luzon—possible race *O. xanthonotus*)

28 71 010   **Oriolus isabellae**
Isabella Oriole   Philippines (Bataan Peninsula and northern Luzon)

28 71 011   **Oriolus oriolus**
Eurasian Golden Oriole   Widespread southern Palearctic region

28 71 012   **Oriolus auratus**
African Golden Oriole   Tropical Africa (Senegal to Kenya)

28 71 013   **Oriolus chinensis**
Black-naped Oriole   Widespread Oriental mainland and islands

28 71 014   **Oriolus tenuirostris**
Slender-billed Oriole   Nepal to southwest China, Indochina

28 71 015   **Oriolus chlorocephalus**
Green-headed Oriole   Mountains of Tanzania to Mozambique

28 71 016   **Oriolus crassirostris**
St. Thomas Oriole   Confined to São Thomé Island (Gulf of Guinea)

28 71 017   **Oriolus brachyrhynchus**
*Western Black-headed
Oriole*   Forests of southern Nigeria to Angola, Uganda

28 71 018   **Oriolus monacha**
*Black-headed Forest
Oriole*   Mountain forests of Ethiopia and Eritrea

28 71 019   **Oriolus larvatus**
*African Black-headed
Oriole*   Africa south of the Sahara

	Date	Location

28 71 020 Oriolus nigripennis
Black-winged Oriole   Sierra Leone to southern Sudan, Tanzania, Angola

28 71 021 Oriolus xanthornus
Black-hooded Oriole   Sri Lanka; India to Malaya; Sumatra; Borneo;
                                       Andamans

28 71 022 Oriolus hosii
Black Oriole   Mountains of Borneo (except Kinabalu)

28 71 023 Oriolus cruentus
Black-and-Crimson Oriole   Malay Peninsula; Java; Sumatra; Borneo

28 71 024 Oriolus traillii
Maroon Oriole   Himalayas of Nepal to Indochina; Hainan; Taiwan

28 71 025 Oriolus mellianus
Silver Oriole   China (mountains of Kwantung, Kwangsi, Szechwan)

28 71 026 Sphecotheres vieilloti
Southern Figbird   Queensland to New South Wales; southeast New
                                       Guinea

**28 71 027 Sphecotheres
flaviventris**
Yellow Figbird   Tropical northern Australia; Kai Island (southern
                                       Moluccas)

28 71 028 Sphecotheres viridis
Timor Figbird   Lesser Sundas (confined to Timor Island)

**28 71 029 Sphecotheres
hypoleucus**
Wetar Figbird   Lesser Sundas (confined to Wetar Island)

FAMILY: DICRURIDAE (Drongos)

**28 72 001 Chaetorhynchus
papuensis**
Papuan Drongo   Mountain forests of New Guinea

**28 72 002 Dicrurus ludwigii
(sharpei)**
Square-tailed Drongo   Forests of Senegal to Kenya, Rhodesia

28 72 003 Dicrurus atripennis
Shining Drongo   Sierra Leone to Gabon

28 72 004 Dicrurus adsimilis
Fork-tailed Drongo   Africa to India

28 72 005 Dicrurus fuscipennis
Comoro Drongo   Grand Comoro Island (Indian Ocean)

28 72 006 Dicrurus aldabranus
Aldabra Drongo   Aldabra Island (Indian Ocean)

28 72 007 Dicrurus forficatus
*Madagascar Crested
Drongo*   Woodlands of Madagascar and Anjouan Islands

		Date	Location

28 72 008	**Dicrurus waldenii**		
	Mayotte Drongo		Comoro Archipelago (confined to Mayotte Island)
28 72 009	**Dicrurus macrocercus**		
	Black Drongo		Iran to India, China; Hainan; Taiwan; Java
28 72 010	**Dicrurus leucophaeus**		
	Ashy Drongo		Afghanistan to China, Malaya; Andamans; Greater Sundas
28 72 011	**Dicrurus caerulescens**		
	White-bellied Drongo		Sri Lanka; India and Nepal
28 72 012	**Dicrurus annectans**		
	Crow-billed Drongo		Himalayas to southern China, Indochina; Greater Sundas
28 72 013	**Dicrurus aeneus**		
	Bronzed Drongo		India to Malaya; Sumatra; Borneo; Hainan; Taiwan
28 72 014	**Dicrurus remifer**		
	Lesser Racket-tailed Drongo		India to Indochina; Sumatra; Java
28 72 015	**Dicrurus balicassius**		
	Balicassiao		Widespread throughout the Philippine Islands
28 72 016	**Dicrurus hottentottus (bracteatus)**		
	Spangled Drongo		India to China; Solomons; Philippines; New Guinea; Australia
28 72 017	**Dicrurus megarhynchus**		
	Ribbon-tailed Drongo		Confined to New Ireland Island
28 72 018	**Dicrurus montanus**		
	Celebes Mountain Drongo		Confined to the mountains of Celebes Islands
28 72 019	**Dicrurus andamanensis**		
	Andaman Drongo		Confined to Andaman Islands (Indian Ocean)
28 72 020	**Dicrurus paradiseus**		
	Greater Racket-tailed Drongo		India to Indochina; Andamans; Nicobars; Greater Sundas

FAMILY: CALLAEIDAE (Wattlebirds)

28 73 001	**Callaeas cinerea**		
	Kokako		New Zealand and adjacent islands (endangered)
28 73 002	**Creadion carunculatus**		
	Saddleback		Hen and South Cape Islands (New Zealand— endangered)
28 73 003	**Heteralocha acutirostris**		
	Huia (New Zealand Wattlebird)		Extinct since 1907. Inhabited Northern Island of New Zealand

	Date	Location

FAMILY: GRALLINIDAE (Mudnest Builders)

28 74 001	**Grallina cyanoleuca** *Magpie-Lark (Mudlark)*	Open woodlands throughout Australia; rare Tasmania
28 74 002	**Grallina bruijni** *Torrentlark*	Mountain streams of New Guinea
28 74 003	**Corcorax melanorhamphos** *White-winged Chough*	Queensland to Victoria; adjacent South Australia
28 74 004	**Struthidea cinerea** *Apostlebird*	Queensland to Victoria; isolated population Northern Territory

FAMILY: ARTAMIDAE (Wood Swallows)

28 75 001	**Artamus fuscus** *Ashy Wood Swallow*	Sri Lanka; India to Yunnan, Indochina; Hainan
28 75 002	**Artamus leucorhynchus** *White-breasted Wood Swallow*	Australia to Moluccas, New Guinea, Borneo, Philippines, Fiji
28 75 003	**Artamus monachus** *Celebes Wood Swallow*	Celebes and Sula Islands
28 75 004	**Artamus maximus** *Greater Wood Swallow*	Mid-mountains of New Guinea
28 75 005	**Artamus insignis** *Bismarck Wood Swallow*	New Britain and New Ireland Islands (Bismarck Archipelago)
28 75 006	**Artamus personatus** *Masked Wood Swallow*	Widespread Australia (except Tasmania and Cape York Peninsula)
28 75 007	**Artamus superciliosus** *White-browed Wood Swallow*	Queensland to Victoria; Tasmania
28 75 008	**Artamus cinereus** *Black-faced Wood Swallow*	Widespread Australia (except Tasmania); Timor Island
28 75 009	**Artamus cyanopterus** *Dusky Wood Swallow*	Eastern, southwest Australia; Tasmania; Bass Strait islands
28 75 010	**Artamus minor** *Little Wood Swallow*	Widespread Australia (except southern coastal area)

　Date　　　　　　Location

FAMILY: CRACTICIDAE (Bellmagpies)

28 76 001　**Cracticus mentalis**
　　　　　　Black-backed Butcherbird　　Cape York Peninsula; southeast New Guinea

28 76 002　**Cracticus torquatus
　　　　　　(argenteus)**
　　　　　　Gray Butcherbird　　Timbered areas of Australia; Tasmania

28 76 003　**Cracticus nigrogularis**
　　　　　　Pied Butcherbird　　Desert areas of Australia

28 76 004　**Cracticus quoyi**
　　　　　　Black Butcherbird　　Northern Territory,Queensland; New Guinea; Arus

28 76 005　**Cracticus cassicus**
　　　　　　Black-headed Butcherbird　　Lowlands of New Guinea and adjacent islands

28 76 006　**Cracticus louisiadensis**
　　　　　　Louisiade Butcherbird　　Confined to Tagula Island (Louisiade Archipelago)

28 76 007　**Gymnorhina tibicen**
　　　　　　Black-backed Magpie　　Australia; New Guinea (introduced New Zealand)

28 76 008　**Gymnorhina dorsalis**
　　　　　　Western Magpie　　Eucalypt forests of western Australia

28 76 009　**Gymnorhina hypoleuca**
　　　　　　White-backed Magpie　　Victoria, South Australia; Tasmania

28 76 010　**Strepera graculina**
　　　　　　Pied Currawong　　Queensland to Victoria; Tasmania

28 76 011　**Strepera fuliginosa**
　　　　　　Black Currawong　　Tasmania; Flinders and King Islands

28 76 012　**Strepera versicolor
　　　　　　(arguta)**
　　　　　　Gray Currawong　　Southwest Australia to New South Wales; Tasmania

FAMILY: PTILONORHYNCHIDAE (Bowerbirds)

28 77 001　**Ailuroedus buccoides**
　　　　　　White-eared Catbird　　New Guinea and western Papuan Islands

28 77 002　**Ailuroedus crassirostris**
　　　　　　Green Catbird　　Queensland to New South Wales; New Guinea; Arus

28 77 003　**Ailuroedus melanotis**
　　　　　　Spotted Catbird　　Cape York Peninsula; New Guinea; Arus

28 77 004　**Scenopoeetes
　　　　　　dentirostris**
　　　　　　Tooth-billed Bowerbird　　Mountain rain forests of northeast Queensland

28 77 005　**Archboldia papuensis**
　　　　　　Archbold's Bowerbird　　Snow Mountains and central highlands of New Guinea

		Date	Location
28 77 006	**Amblyornis inoratus** *Gardener Bowerbird*		Vogelkop and Wandammen Mountains of New Guinea
28 77 007	**Amblyornis macgregoriae** *MacGregor's Bowerbird*		Upper mountain forests of New Guinea
28 77 008	**Amblyornis subalaris** *Striped Bowerbird*		Mountains of southeast New Guinea
28 77 009	**Amblyornis flavifrons** *Yellow-fronted Bowerbird*		Western New Guinea (known from 4 skins)
28 77 010	**Prionodura newtoniana** *Golden Bowerbird*		Mountain rain forests of northeast Queensland
28 77011	**Sericulus aureus** *Golden Regent Bowerbird*		Foothills and lower mountains of New Guinea
28 77 012	**Sericulus bakeri** *Adelbert Regent Bowerbird*		Known only from Adelbert Mountains of New Guinea
28 77 013	**Sericulus chrysocephalus** *Australian Regent Bowerbird*		Coastal rain forests of Queensland to New South Wales
28 77 014	**Ptilonorhynchus violaceus** *Satin Bowerbird*		Discontinuous rain forests of Queensland to Victoria
28 77 015	**Chlamydera maculata** *Spotted Bowerbird*		Woodland, arid savanna throughout Australia
28 77 016	**Chlamydera guttata** *Western Bowerbird*		Dry interior of Australia (possible race *C. maculata*)
28 77 017	**Chlamydera nuchalis** *Great Gray Bowerbird*		Woodland, open forests of tropical northern Australis
28 77 018	**Chlamydera lauterbachi** *Lauterbach's Bowerbird*		Mid-mountain grasslands of New Guinea
28 77 019	**Chlamydera cerviniventris** *Fawn-breasted Bowerbird*		Cape York Peninsula; eastern New Guinea

FAMILY: PARADISAEIDAE (Birds of Paradise)

28 78 001	**Loria loriae** *Loria's Bird of Paradise*		High mountains of New Guinea (except Vogelkop and Huon)
28 78 002	**Loboparadisea sericea** *Wattle-billed Bird of Paradise*		Mountains of the trunk of New Guinea

		Date	Location
28 78 003	**Cnemophilus macgregorii** *Sickle-crested Bird of Paradise*		High mountains of eastern and southeast New Guinea
28 78 004	**Macgregoria pulchra** *Macgregor's Bird of Paradise*		High mountains of west and southeast New Guinea
28 78 005	**Lycocorax pyrrhopterus** *Paradise (Silky) Crow*		Muluccan Archipelago
28 78 006	**Manucodia ater** *Glossy-mantled Manucode*		New Guinea and adjacent islands
28 78 007	**Manucodia jobiensis** *Jobi Manucode*		New Guinea and Japen Island
28 78 008	**Manucodia chalybatus** *Crinkle-collared Manucode*		New Guinea and Misol Island
28 78 009	**Manucodia comrii** *Curl-crested Manucode*		Eastern Papuan Islands; d'Entrecasteaux Archipelago
28 78 010	**Phonygammus keraudrenii** *Trumpetbird*		New Guinea; d'Entrecasteux Archipelago; Cape York Peninsula
28 78 011	**Ptiloris paradiseus** *Paradise Riflebird*		Rain forests of Queensland and New South Wales
28 78 012	**Ptiloris victoriae** *Queen Victoria Riflebird*		Rain forests of northeast Queensland (Cairns District)
28 78 013	**Ptiloris magnificus** *Magnificent Riflebird*		Widespread New Guinea and northeast Australia
28 78 014	**Semioptera wallacei** *Wallace's Standardwing*		Moluccas (Halmahera and Batjan Islands)
28 78 015	**Seleucidis melanoleuca** *Twelve-wired Bird of Paradise*		Lowland forests of New Guinea and Salawati Island
28 78 016	**Paradigallia carunculata** *Long-tailed Paradigalla*		Arfak and western Snow Mountains of New Guinea
28 78 017	**Paradigalla brevicauda** *Short-tailed Paradigalla*		Midmountains of trunk of New Guinea
28 78 018	**Drepanornis albertisi** *Black-billed Sicklebill*		Widespread mountains of New Guinea
28 78 019	**Drepanornis bruijnii** *White-billed Sicklebill*		Lowland forests of northwest New Guinea
28 78 020	**Epimachus fastuosus** *Black Sicklebill*		Midmountains of Vogelkop and trunk of New Guinea

		Date	Location
28 78 021	**Epimachus meyeri** *Brown Sicklebill*		Weyland and Snow Mountains to southeast New Guinea
28 78 021	**Astrapia nigra** *Arfak Astrapia*		Known only from Arfak Mountains of New Guinea
28 78 023	**Astrapia splendidissima** *Splendid Astrapia*		Midmountains of trunk of New Guinea
28 78 024	**Astrapia mayeri** *Ribbon-tailed Bird of Paradise*		Central highlands of New Guinea
28 78 025	**Astrapia stephaniae** *Princess Stephanie Bird of Paradise*		Mountains of southeast New Guinea
28 78 026	**Astrapia rothchildi** *Huon Astrapia*		New Guinea (Rawlinson and Saruwaged Mountains)
28 78 027	**Lophorina superba** *Superb Bird of Paradise*		Midmountain forests throughout New Guinea
28 78 028	**Parotia sefilata** *Six-plumed Parotia*		Mountains of New Guinea
28 78 029	**Parotia carolae** *Queen Carola's Parotia*		Midmountains of the trunk of New Guinea
28 78 030	**Parotia lawesii** *Lawes' Parotia*		Midmountains of eastern New Guinea
28 78 031	**Parotia wahnesi** *Wahnes' Parotia*		Known only from the midmountains of the Huon Peninsula
28 78 032	**Pteridophora alberti** *King of Saxony Bird of Paradise*		Midmountains of the trunk of New Guinea
28 78 033	**Cicinnurus regius** *King Bird of Paradise*		New Guinea; Arus and adjacent western islands
28 78 034	**Diphyllodes magnificus** *Magnificent Bird of Paradise*		New Guinea, Japen, western Papuan Islands
28 78 035	**Diphyllodes respublica** *Wilson's Bird of Paradise*		Western Papuan Islands (Waigeu and Batanta)
28 78 036	**Paradisaea apoda** *Greater Bird of Paradise*		Lowlands of Aru Island and south New Guinea
28 78 037	**Paradisaea raggiana** *Count Raggi's Bird of Paradise*		Low mountain forests of eastern New Guinea
28 78 038	**Paradisaea minor** *Lesser Bird of Paradise*		New Guinea, Japen, western Papuan Islands

	Date	Location

28 78 039 Paradisaea decora
Goldie's Bird of Paradise   Mountains of d'Entrecasteaux Archipelago

28 78 040 Paradisaea rubra
Red Bird of Paradise   Lowland forests of western Papuan Islands

28 78 041 Paradisaea guilielmi
Emperor of Germany Bird   New Guinea (midmountains of Huon Peninsula)
of Paradise

28 78 042 Paradisaea rudolphi
Blue Bird of Paradise   Midmountains of eastern New Guinea

FAMILY: CORVIDAE (Crows anu Jays)

28 79001 Platylophus galericulatus
Malay (Crested) Jay   Tropical forests of Malay Peninsula; Greater Sundas

28 79 002 Platysmurus leucopterus
Black Magpie   Forests of Malay Peninsula; Sumatra; Borneo

28 79 003 Gymnorhinus cyanocephala
Pinyon Jay   Arid pine highlands of Alaska to Baja California; casual Chihuahua

28 79 004 Cyanocitta cristata
Blue Jay   Eastern Canada and eastern United States

28 79 005 Cyanocitta stelleri
Steller's Jay   Highlands of southern Alaska to Nicaragua

28 79 006 Aphelocoma coerulescens
Scrub Jay   Western United States to southern Mexico

28 78 007 Aphelocoma ultramarina
Mexican Jay   Mountains of southwest United States to southern Mexico

28 79 008 Aphelocoma unicolor
Unicolored Jay   Mountains of southern Mexico to Honduras

28 79 009 Cyanolyca viridicyana (armillata)
White-collared Jay   Montane forests of Venezuela to western Bolivia

28 79 010 Cyanolyca pulchra
Beautiful Jay   Western Andes of southwest Colombia and northwest Ecuador

28 79 011 Cyanolyca cucullata
Azure-hooded Jay   Humid mountain forests of southeast Mexico to Panama

		Date	Location
28 79 012	**Cyanolyca pumilo** *Black-throated Jay*		Mountain forests of Chiapas (Mexico) to El Salvador
28 79 013	**Cyanolyca nana** *Dwarf Jay*		Pine-oak forests of Mexico (Veracruz, Oaxaca—rare)
28 79 014	**Cyanolyca mirabilis** *White-throated Jay*		Pine-oak forests of southwest Mexico (Guerrero, Oaxaca—rare)
28 79 015	**Cyanolyca argentigula** *Silver-throated Jay*		Mountains of Costa Rica to western Panama
28 79 016	**Cyanolyca turcosa** *Turquoise Jay*		Andes of southern Colombia to northwest Peru
28 79 017	**Cissilopha melanocyanea** *Bushy-crested Jay*		Mainly highlands of Guatemala to Nicaragua
28 79 018	**Cissilopha sanblasiana** *San Blas Jay*		Western Mexico (Pacific slope of Nayarit to Guerrero)
28 79 019	**Cissilopha yucatanica** *Yucatán Jay*		Tabasco, Yucatán Peninsula, Petén of Guatemala, Belize
28 79 020	**Cissilopha beecheil** *Purplish-backed Jay*		Western Mexico (Pacific slope of Sonora to Nayarit)
28 79 021	**Cyanocorax caeruleus** *Azure Jay*		Southeast Brazil (São Paulo) to northeast Argentina
28 79 022 +	**Cyanocorax cyanomelas** *Purplish Jay*		Southeast Peru to northeast Argentina, southwest Brazil
28 79 023	**Cyanocorax violaceus** *Violaceous Jay*		Guianas to western Brazil, eastern Peru
28 79 024	**Cyanocorax cristatellus** *Curl-crested Jay*		*Cerrado* of tableland of eastern Brazil
28 79 025	**Cyanocorax heilprini** *Azure-naped Jay*		Colombia, western Venezuela, adjacent Brazil
28 79 026	**Cyanocorax cayanus** *Cayenne Jay*		Guianas, Venezuela, adjacent Brazil, Colombia
28 79 027	**Cyanocorax affinis** *Black-chested Jay*		Costa Rica to Colombia, northwest Venezuela
28 79 028 +	**Cyanocorax chrysops** *Plush-crested Jay*		Brazil south of Amazon to Bolivia, northern Argentina
28 79 029	**Cyanocorax cyanopogon** *White-naped Jay*		Eastern Brazil (Pará to Paraná, Paraiba)

Date	Location

28 79 030 **Cyanocorax mystacalis**
           White-tailed Jay   Arid littoral of western Ecuador to northwest Peru

28 79 031 **Cyanocorax dickeyi**
           Tufted Jay   Mountains of western Mexico (Sinaloa, Durango, Nayarit)

28 79 032 **Cyanocorax yncas**
           Green Jay   Southeast Texas to Bolivia (La Paz)

28 79 033 **Psilorhinus morio (mexicanus)**
           Brown Jay   Southern Texas, Caribbean slope to northwest Panama

28 79 034 **Calocitta formosa**
           Magpie Jay   Pacific slope of Mexico to northwest Costa Rica

28 79 035 **Garrulus glandarius**
           Eurasian Jay   Temperate forests of Palearctic, Oriental mainland

28 79 036 **Garrulus lanceolatus**
           Lanceolated Jay   Himalayan oak forests of Afghanistan to Nepal

28 79 037 **Garrulus lidthi**
           Lidth's (Ryukyu) Jay   Japan (Amami Oshima and Tokinoshima Islands)

28 79 038 **Perisoreus canadensis**
           Gray Jay   Alaska to mountains of southwest United States

28 79 039 **Perisoreus infaustus**
           Siberian Jay   Coniferous forests of Scandinavia to northern Asia

28 79 040 **Perisoreus internigrans**
           Szechwan Jay   Subalpine coniferous forests of Szechwan to Sikiang

28 79 041 **Urocissa ornata**
           Ceylon Magpie   Jungle hill forests of Sri Lanka

28 79 042 **Urocissa caerulea**
           Taiwan Magpie   Confined to mountain forests of Taiwan

28 79 043 **Urocissa flavirostris**
           Golden-billed Magpie   Himalayas of Nepal to Yunnan, Burma, Tonkin

28 79 044 **Urocissa erythorhyncha**
           Blue Magpie   Himalayas to Malaya, Indochina; Hainan

28 79 045 **Urocissa whiteheadi**
           White-winged Magpie   Mountains of southern China to Indochina; Hainan

28 79 046 **Cissa chinensis**
           Green Magpie   Garhwal Himalayas to Indochina; Sumatra; Borneo

28 79 047 **Cissa thalassina**
           Short-tailed Magpie   Java; mountains of north Borneo

28 79 048 **Cyanopica cyana**
           Azure-winged Magpie   Discontinuously distributed Iberian Peninsula to east Asia

		Date	Location
28 79 049	**Dendrocitta vagabunda (rufa)** *Rufous Treepie*		Widespread India to Indochina; Hainan; Taiwan
28 79 050	**Dendrocitta occipitalis** *Sumatran Treepie*		Wooded mountains of Sumatra and Borneo
28 79 051	**Dendrocitta formosae** *Gray Treepie*		India to Indochina; Hainan; Taiwan
28 79 052	**Dendrocitta leucogastra** *Southern Treepie*		Lowland rain forests of southern India
28 79 053	**Dendrocitta frontalis** *Collared Treepie*		Himalayas of India to Assam, Burma, southwest China; Tonkin
28 79 054	**Dendrocitta baileyi** *Andaman Treepie*		Wooded country of Andaman Islands
28 79 055	**Crypsirina temia** *Racket-tailed Treepie*		Malay Peninsula, Indochina; Greater Sundas
28 79 056	**Crypsirina cucullata** *Hooded Treepie*		Lowland forests of Burma
28 79 057	**Temnurus temnurus** *Rachet-tailed Treepie*		Forests of Annam, Tonkin, Laos; Hainan
28 79 058	**Pica pica** *Black-billed Magpie*		Widespread Holarctic circumpolar regions
28 79 059	**Pica nuttalli** *Yellow-billed Magpie*		Inland California Valleys west of Sierra Nevada
28 79 060	**Zavattariornis stresemanni** *Streseman's Bush Crow*		Boran district of southern Ethiopia
28 79 061	**Podoces hendersoni** *Henderson's Ground Jay*		Mongolia, Tibet and adjacent China
28 79 062	**Podoces biddulphi** *Biddulph's Ground Jay*		Central Asia (deserts of Sinkiang)
28 79 063	**Podoces panderi** *Pander's Ground Jay*		Deserts of Turkestan to Aral Sea
28 79 064	**Podoces pleskei** *Plesky's Ground Jay*		Desert steppes of Iran, Baluchistan
28 79 065	**Pseudopodoces humilis** *Hume's Ground Jay*		Desert biotope of Nepal, Sikkim, Tibet, southeast China
28 79 066	**Nucifraga columbiana** *Clark's Nutcracker*		Mountains of Alaska to Baja California; casual Sonora
28 79 067	**Nucifraga caryocatactes** *Eurasian Nutcracker*		Alpine zone of Palearctic region

		Date	Location

28 79 068 **Pyrrhocorax pyrrhocorax**
Red-billed Chough — High mountains of southern Palearctic region

28 79 069 **Pyrrhocorax graculus**
Yellow-billed Chough — High mountains of southern Europe, Morocco to Asia

28 79 070 **Ptilostomus afer**
Piapiac — *Borassus* palm zone of Senegal to Uganda

28 79 071 **Corvus monedula**
Common Jackdaw — Widespread Palearctic region

28 79 072 **Corvus dauuricus**
Daurian Jackdaw — Widespread eastern Asia

28 79 073 **Corvus splendens**
House Crow — Iran, India to China, Burma, Thailand

28 79 074 **Corvus moneduloides**
New Caledonian Crow — Forests of New Caledonia and Loyalty Islands

28 79 075 **Corvus enca**
Slender-billed Crow — Malaya; Greater Sundas, Celebes; Philippines

28 79 076 **Corvus typicus**
Celebes Pied Crow — Central and southern Celebes and Butung Islands

28 79 077 **Corvus unicolor**
Banggai Crow — Celebes (confined to Banggai Island—possible race *C. typicus*)

28 79 078 **Corvus florensis**
Flores Crow — Confined to Flores Island (Lesser Sundas—rare)

28 79 079 **Corvus kubaryi**
Guam Crow — Mariannas (forests of Guam and Rota Islands)

28 79 080 **Corvus validus**
Moluccan Crow — Occurs on all main Moluccan Islands

28 79 081 **Corvus woodfordi (meeki)**
White-billed Crow — Forests of Solomon Islands

28 79 082 **Corvus fuscicapillus**
Brown-headed Crow — Arus and western Papuan Islands (Waigeu, Geimen)

28 79 083 **Corvus tristis**
Bare-faced Crow — Widespread New Guinea and adjacent islands

28 79 084 **Corvus capensis**
Cape Rook — Somalia, Ethiopia, the Sudan to South Africa

28 79 085 **Corvus frugilegus**
Rook — Widespread Palearctic region

28 79 086 **Corvus brachyrhynchos**
American (Common) Crow — Widespread Canada and United States to northwest Mexico

28 79 087 **Corvus caurinus**
Northwestern Crow — Coastal Alaska to northwestern United States

	Date	Location

28 79 088 Corvus imparatus
Mexican Crow

East coast of Mexico (Nuevo León to Veracruz)

28 79 089 Corvus sinaloae
Sinaloa Crow

Pacific slope of Mexico (Sonora to Colima)

28 79 090 Corvus ossifragus
Fish Crow

Eastern United States (Rhode Island to Texas)

28 79 091 Corvus palmarum
Palm Crow

Lowlands and mountains of Cuba and Hispaniola

28 79 092 Corvus jamaicensis
Jamaican Crow

Woodlands and parks of Jamaica

28 79 093 Corvus nasicus
Cuban Crow

Cuba; Isle of Pines; Grand Caicos Island

28 79 094 Corvus leucognaphalus
White-necked Crow

Hispaniola; rare in Puerto Rico, Gonâve, Saona
Islands

28 79 095 Corvus corone (cornix)
Carrion Crow

Widespread Palearctic region

28 79 096 Corvus macrorhynchos
Large-billed Crow

Widespread Oriental region mainland and islands

28 79 097 Corvus orru (cecilae)
Papuan Crow

Moluccas to New Guinea; Australia

28 79 098 Corvus bennetti
Little Crow

Mulga, dry scrub throughout Australia

28 79 099 Corvus coronoides
Australian Raven

Woodlands and coastal dunes of Australia; Tasmania

28 79 100 Corvus mellori
Little Raven

Scrub and woodland of South Australia, Victoria, New
South Wales

28 79 101 Corvus tasmanicus
Forest Raven

Tasmania; adjacent Otway Range of Victoria

28 79 102 Corvus torquatus
Collared Crow

Eastern China to Indochina; Hainan; Taiwan

28 79 103 Corvus albus
Pied Crow

Africa south of the Sahara; Madagascar; Aldabra

28 79 104 Corvus tropicus
Hawaiian Crow

Montane forests of Island of Hawaii—endangered

28 79 105 Corvus cryptoleucus
White-necked Raven

Arid southwest United States to central Mexico

28 79 106 Corvus ruficollis
Brown-necked Raven

Deserts of North Africa to Afghanistan

28 79 107 Corvus corax
Northern Raven

Widespread Palearctic, Nearctic regions

		Date	Location
28 79 108	**Corvus rhipidurus** *Fan-tailed Raven*		Arid Red Sea environs to East Africa
28 79 109	**Corvus albicollis** *White-naped Raven*		Uganda, Kenya to South Africa
28 79 110	**Corvus crassirostris** *Thick-billed Raven*		Mountains and high plateaus of Eritrea, Ethiopia

Bibliography

Ali, S., BIRDS OF SIKKIM, Oxford University Press, London, 1962

Ali, S., BIRDS OF KERALA, Oxford University Press, London, 1969

Ali, S., HANDBOOK OF THE BIRDS OF INDIA AND PAKISTAN, Oxford University Press, London, 1970 (10 volumes)

Alexander, W. B., BIRDS OF THE OCEAN, Putnam, New York, 1963

American Birding Association, CHECKLIST: BIRDS OF CONTINENTAL UNITED STATES AND CANADA, 1975

American Ornithologists Union, CHECKLIST OF NORTH AMERICAN BIRDS, Fifth Edition, Baltimore, 1957

Austin, O., THE BIRDS OF KOREA, Bulletin Museum of Comparative Zoology, 1948

Baker, R., AVIFAUNA OF MICRONESIA, University of Kansas, 1951

Bannerman, D. A., THE BIRDS OF WEST AND EQUATORIAL AFRICA, Oliver and Boyd, Edinburgh, 1971

Bannerman, D. and M., HANDBOOK OF THE BIRDS OF CYPRUS, Oliver and Boyd, Edinburgh, 1971

Benson, S. V., BIRDS OF LEBANON AND JORDAN, International Committee for Preservation of Birds, 1970

Benson, Brooke, Dowsett and Irwin, BIRDS OF ZAMBIA, Collins, London, 1973

Berger, A. J., HAWAIIAN BIRDLIFE, University of Hawaii Press, Honolulu, 1972

Blake, E. R., BIRDS OF MEXICO, University of Chicago Press, 1953

Blake, E. R., MANUAL OF NEOTROPICAL BIRDS (Volume I), University of Chicago Press, 1977

Bond, J., BIRDS OF THE WEST INDIES, Collins, London, 1974

Brown, L., AFRICAN BIRDS OF PREY, Collins, London, 1970

Brown and Amadon, EAGLES, HAWKS AND FALCONS OF THE WORLD, McGraw-Hill, New York, 1968 (2 volumes)

Brudenell-Bruce, P. G. C., BIRDS OF THE BAHAMAS, Taplinger, New York, 1975

Bruner, P. L., BIRDS OF FRENCH POLYNESIA, Pacific Scientific Information Center, Honolulu, 1972

Bryan, E. H., LIFE IN THE MARSHALL ISLANDS, Pacific Scientific Information Center, Honolulu, 1972

Burton, J. A., OWLS OF THE WORLD, Dutton, New York, 1975

Cooper and Forshaw, BIRDS OF PARADISE AND BOWER BIRDS, Collins, Sydney, 1977

Cramp and Simmons, BIRDS OF THE WESTERN PALEARCTIC, Oxford University Press, London, 1977

Delacour and Amadon, CURASSOWS AND RELATED BIRDS, American Museum of Natural History, New York, 1973

Delacour, J., THE PHEASANTS OF THE WORLD, Spur Publications, Surrey, England, 1977

Delacour, J., BIRDS OF MALAYSIA, Macmillan, New York, 1947

De Schauensee, R. M., THE SPECIES OF BIRDS OF SOUTH AMERICA, Livingston, Narbeth, Pa., 1966

De Schauensee, R. M., THE BIRDS OF COLOMBIA, Livingston, Narbeth, Pa., 1964

De Schauensee and Phelps, BIRDS OF VENEZUELA, Princeton University Press, 1978

DuPont, J. E., PHILIPPINE BIRDS, Delaware Museum of Natural History, Greenville, Delaware, 1971

Eisenmann, E., THE SPECIES OF MIDDLE AMERICAN BIRDS, Linnaean Society, New York, 1955

Etchécopar and Hüe, THE BIRDS OF NORTH AFRICA, Oliver and Boyd, Edinburgh, 1967

Etchécopar and Hüe, LES OISEAUX DE CHINE, Centre National de la Recherche Scientifique, Papeete, Tahiti, 1978 (Non-Passerines)

Falla, Sibson and Turbott, THE NEW GUIDE TO THE BIRDS OF NEW ZEALAND, Collins, Auckland, 1978

ffrench, R., GUIDE TO THE BIRDS OF TRINIDAD AND TOBAGO, Livingston, Wynnewood, Pa., 1973

Fisher and Peterson, THE WORLD OF BIRDS, Doubleday, New York, 1964

Fleming, Fleming and Bangdel, BIRDS OF NEPAL, Vakils House, Bombay, 1976

Forshaw, J. M., PARROTS OF THE WORLD, Doubleday, New York, 1973

Gallagher and Woodcock, THE BIRDS OF OMAN, Quartet Books, London, 1980

Garrido, O. H., CATALOGO DE LAS AVES DE CUBA, Academia de Ciencias de Cuba, Havana, 1975

Gilliard, E. T., BIRDS OF PARADISE AND BOWER BIRDS, Natural History Press, New York, 1969

Glenister, A. G., BIRDS OF THE MALAY PENINSULA, Oxford University Press, London, 1971

Goodwin, D., PIGEONS AND DOVES OF THE WORLD, British Museum of Natural History, London, 1967

Goodwin, D., CROWS OF THE WORLD, Cornell University Press, Ithaca, New York, 1976

Gore and Won Pyong-Oh, BIRDS OF KOREA, Tawon Publishing Co., Seoul, 1971

Greenway, J. C., EXTINCT AND VANISHING BIRDS OF THE WORLD, American Committee for International Wildlife Protection, New York, 1958

Hall and Moreau, AN ATLAS OF SPECIATION IN AFRICAN PASSERINE BIRDS, British Museum of Natural History, London, 1970

Hancock and Elliot, HERONS OF THE WORLD, Harper & Row, New York, 1978
Harper and Kinsky, SOUTHERN ALBATROSSES AND PETRELS: AN IDENTIFICA-
    TION GUIDE, Price Milburn, Wellington, 1978
Harris, M., BIRDS OF THE GALAPAGOS, Taplinger, New York, 1974
Haverschmidt, F., BIRDS OF SURINAM, Oliver and Boyd, Edinburgh, 1971
Henry, G. M., A GUIDE TO THE BIRDS OF CEYLON, Oxford University Press, Lon-
    don, 1971
Herklots, G. A. C., HONG KONG BIRDS, South China Morning Post, Hong Kong,
    1967
Hill, R., AUSTRALIAN BIRDS, Thomas Nelson, Sydney, 1967
Humphrey, Bridge, Reynolds and Peterson, BIRDS OF ISLA GRANDE (TIERRA DEL
    FUEGO), University of Kansas, 1970
Johnsgard, P., HANDBOOK OF WATERFOWL BEHAVIOR, Cornell University
    Press, Ithaca, New York, 1965
Johnson, A. W., BIRDS OF CHILE, Platt Establecimientos Gráficos, Buenos Aires,
    1965
King and Dickenson, A FIELD GUIDE TO THE BIRDS OF SOUTHEAST ASIA,
    Houghton Mifflin, Boston, 1975
Kobayashi, Keisuke, BIRDS OF JAPAN, Hoikusha Publishing Co., Osaka, 1965
Koepke, M., BIRDS OF THE DEPARTMENT OF LIMA, PERU, Livingston Press,
    Wynnwood, Pa., 1970
Lack, D., DARWIN'S FINCHES, Peter Smith, Gloucester, Mass., 1968
Land, H. C., BIRDS OF GUATEMALA, International Committee for Bird Preserva-
    tion, 1970
Lekagul, B., BIRD GUIDE OF THAILAND, Association for Conservation of Wildlife,
    Bangkok, 1965
Lippens and Wille, LES OISEAUX DU ZAÏRE, Lannoo Tielt, Brussels, 1976
Macdonald, J. D., BIRDS OF AUSTRALIA, Reed, Sydney, 1973
Mackworth-Praed and Grant, AFRICAN HANDBOOK OF BIRDS, Longmans, Lon-
    don, 1960–1973 (6 volumes)
Mayr, E., BIRDS OF THE SOUTHWEST PACIFIC, Macmillan, New York, 1945
McGill, A., AUSTRALIAN WARBLERS, Bird Observers Club, Melbourne, 1970
McLachlan and Liversidge, ROBERTS' BIRDS OF SOUTH AFRICA, Central News
    Agency, Cape Town, 1971
Mercer, R. A., A FIELD GUIDE TO FIJI BIRDS, Fiji Museum Special Publications,
    1967
Milon, Petter and Randrianasolo, FAUNE DE MADAGASCAR, Malagasy Govern-
    ment Printing Office, Tananarive, 1973
Moffett and Wilder, CHINESE BIRDS, Peking Society of Natural History, Peiping,
    1948
Morony, Bock and Farrand, REFERENCE LIST OF THE BIRDS OF THE WORLD,
    American Museum of Natural History, New York, 1975
Olrog, C., LAS AVES SUDAMERICANAS, Universidad Nacional de Tucuman, Argen-
    tina, 1968
Ornithological Society of Turkey, CHECKLIST OF THE BIRDS OF TURKEY,
    Ankarra, 1971

Penny, M., BIRDS OF THE SEYCHELLES, Taplinger, New York, 1974

Peters, James, CHECK-LIST OF BIRDS OF THE WORLD, Harvard University Press, 1931–1979 (14 of 15 volumes)

Peterson, R. T., FIELD GUIDE TO BIRDS EAST OF THE ROCKIES, Houghton Mifflin, Boston, 1980

Peterson, R. T., FIELD GUIDE TO WESTERN BIRDS, Houghton Mifflin, Boston, 1967

Peterson, Mountfort and Hollom, FIELD GUIDE TO THE BIRDS OF BRITAIN AND EUROPE, Houghton Mifflin, Boston, 1967

Peterson and Chalif, FIELD GUIDE TO MEXICAN BIRDS, Houghton Mifflin, Boston, 1973

Pizzey, G., FIELD GUIDE TO THE BIRDS OF AUSTRALIA, Princeton University Press, 1980

Prozesky, O. P. M., A FIELD GUIDE TO THE BIRDS OF SOUTHERN AFRICA, Collins, London, 1970

Rand, A. L., DISTRIBUTION AND HABITS OF MADAGASCAR BIRDS, Bulletin of American Museum of Natural History, New York, 1936 (volume lxxii)

Rand and Gilliard, HANDBOOK OF NEW GUINEA BIRDS, Natural History Press, New York, 1968

Rand McNally, THE INTERNATIONAL ATLAS, Rand McNally, Chicago, 1974

Ratti, J. T., THE CLASSIFICATION OF AVIAN SPECIES AND SUBSPECIES, American Birds, New York, November 1980

Ridgely, R., A GUIDE TO THE BIRDS OF PANAMA, Princeton University Press, 1976

Ripley, S. D., RAILS OF THE WORLD, David Godine, Boston, 1977

Rountree, Guerin, Pelte and Vinson, CATALOGUE OF THE BIRDS OF MAURITIUS, The Mauritius Institute, Bulletin 3, Volume 3

Rutgers, A., BIRDS OF ASIA, Tatlinger, New York, 1968

Serle, Morel and Hartwig, GUIDE TO THE BIRDS OF ZAMBIA, Collins, London, 1973

Serle, Morel and Hartwig, A FIELD GUIDE TO THE BIRDS OF WEST AFRICA, Collins, London, 1977

Severinghaus, S. R., A NEW GUIDE TO THE BIRDS OF TAIWAN, Mei Ya Publications, Taipei, 1976

Slater, P., FIELD GUIDE TO AUSTRALIAN BIRDS, Livingston, Wynnwood, Pa., 1970–1974 (2 volumes)

Slud, P., THE BIRDS OF COSTA RICA, Bulletin of the American Museum of Natural History, Volume 128, New York, 1964

Smythies, B. E., THE BIRDS OF BORNEO, Oliver and Boyd, London, 1960

Snyder, D. E., BIRDS OF GUYANA, Peabody Museum, Salem, Mass., 1966

Sparks and Soper, PENGUINS, David and Charles, Newton Abbot Devon, 1968

Staub, F., BIRDS OF THE MASCARENES AND SAINT BRANDON, Organisation Normale des Enterprises, Port Louis, Mauritius, 1976

Stresemann, E., DIE VOGEL VON CELEBES, Journal of Ornithology, 1939–1941 (87:299–425; 88:1–135, 389–487; 89:1–102)

Thornton, Ian, DARWIN'S ISLANDS, Natural History Press, New York, 1971

Todd, F., WATERFOWL: DUCKS, GEESE AND SWANS OF THE WORLD, Sea World Press, San Diego, 1979

Tuck and Heinzel, A FIELD GUIDE TO THE SEABIRDS OF BRITAIN AND THE WORLD, Collins, London, 1978

Urban and Brown, CHECKLIST OF THE BIRDS OF ETHIOPIA, Haile Sellassie University, Addis Ababa, 1971

Van Bemmel, A. C. V., BIRDS OF THE MOLUCCAN ISLANDS, Treubia 19:323–402, 1948

Van Tyne and Berger, FUNDAMENTALS OF ORNITHOLOGY, John Wiley and Sons, New York, 1959

Vaurie, C., BIRDS OF THE PALEARCTIC FAUNA, Witherby, London, 1964 (2 volumes)

Vaurie, C., TIBET AND ITS BIRDS, Witherby, London, 1972

Walkinshaw, L., CRANES OF THE WORLD, Winchester, New York, 1973

Watson, G. E., BIRDS OF THE ANTARCTIC AND SUB-ANTARCTIC, American Geophysical Union, Washington, D.C., 1975

White, C. M. N., A REVISED CHECKLIST OF AFRICAN NON-PASSERINE BIRDS, Government Printing Office, Lusaka, 1965

Wildash, P., BIRDS OF SOUTH VIETNAM, Charles Tuttle, Rutland, Vermont, 1968

Williams, J. G., FIELD GUIDE TO THE BIRDS OF EAST AFRICA, Collins, London, 1980

Wilson, E., BIRDS OF THE ANTARCTIC, Humanities Press, New York, 1968

Woods, R. W., BIRDS OF THE FALKLAND ISLANDS, Oswestry, Shropshire, 1975

Yamashina, Y., BIRDS IN JAPAN: A FIELD GUIDE, Tokyo News Service, Tokyo, 1961

Index of Scientific Names

Index of Common Names